Windows NT File System Internals

Windows NT File System Internals
A Developer's Guide

Rajeev Nagar

O'REILLY™

Cambridge · Köln · Paris · Sebastopol · Tokyo

Windows NT File System Internals: A Developer's Guide
by Rajeev Nagar

Copyright © 1997 O'Reilly & Associates, Inc. All rights reserved.
Printed in the United States of America.

Published by O'Reilly & Associates, Inc., 101 Morris Street, Sebastopol, CA 95472.

Editor: Robert Denn

Production Editor: Mary Anne Weeks Mayo

Printing History:

September 1997:   First Edition.

This book is printed on acid-free paper with 85% recycled content, 15% post-consumer waste. O'Reilly & Associates is committed to using paper with the highest recycled content available consistent with high quality.

ISBN: 1-56592-249-2   [12/97]

This book is dedicated to:

My parents, Maya and Yogesh

My wife and best friend, Priya

Our beautiful daughters, Sana and Ria

For it is their faith, support, and encouragement

that inspires me to keep striving

Table of Contents

Preface

Over the past three years, Windows NT has come to be regarded as a serious, stable, viable, and highly competitive alternative to most other commercially available operating systems. It is also one of the very few *new* commercially released operating systems that has been developed more or less from scratch in the last 15 years, and can claim to have achieved a significant amount of success. However, Microsoft has not yet documented, in any substantial manner, the guts of this increasingly important platform. This has resulted in a dearth of reliable information available on the internals of the Windows NT operating system.

This book focuses on explaining the internals of the Windows NT I/O subsystem, the Windows NT Cache Manager, and the Windows NT Virtual Memory Manager. In particular, it focuses on file system driver and filter driver implementation for the Windows NT platform, which often requires detailed information about the above-mentioned components.

Intended Audience

This book is intended for those who have a need *today* for understanding a significant portion of the Windows NT operating system, and also for those among us who simply are curious about what makes Windows NT tick.

Typically, the book should be interesting and useful to you if you design or implement kernel-mode software, such as file system or device drivers. It should also be interesting to those of you who are studying or teaching operating system design and wish to understand the Windows NT operating system a little bit better. Finally, if you are a system administrator who *really* wants to know what it is that you have just spent the vast majority of your annual budget on (operating system licenses, additional third-party driver licenses for virus-checking software, and so on), this book should help satisfy your curiosity.

The approach taken in writing this book is that the information provided should give you *more* than what you can get from any other documentation that is currently available. Therefore, I expend a lot of effort discussing the whys and hows that underlie the design and implementation of the Windows NT I/O subsystem, Virtual Memory Manager, and Cache Manager. For those of you who need to implement a file system or filter driver module right this minute, there is a substantial amount of code included that should get you well along on your way.

Above all, this book is intended as a guide and reference to assist you in understanding a major portion of the Windows NT operating system better than you do today. I hope it will help to make you more informed about the operating system itself, which in turn should help you exploit the operating-system-provided functionality in an optimal manner.

Windows NT File System Internals was written with certain assumptions in mind: I assume that you understand the fundamentals of operating systems and therefore, do not need me to explain what an operating system is; at the same time, I do not assume that you understand file system technology (especially on the Windows NT platform) in any great detail, although such understanding will undoubtedly help you if and when you decide to design and implement a file system yourself. I further assume that you know how to develop programs using a high-level language such as C. Finally, I assume that you have some interest in the subject matter of this book; otherwise, I find it hard to imagine why anyone would want to subject themselves to more than 700 pages of excruciatingly detailed information about the I/O subsystem and associated components.

Book Contents and Organization

In order to design and develop complex software such as file system drivers or other kernel-mode drivers, it becomes necessary to first understand the operating system environment thoroughly. At the same time, I always find it useful to have sample code to play with that can assist me when I start designing and developing my own software modules. Therefore, I have organized this book along the following lines.

Part 1: Overview

This part of the book provides you with the required background material that is essential to successfully designing and developing Windows NT kernel-mode drivers. This portion of the book should be of particular interest to those of you who intend to actually develop kernel-mode software for the Windows NT platform.

Chapter 1, Windows NT System Components

This chapter provides an introduction to the various components that together constitute the kernel-mode portion of the Windows NT operating system. The overall architecture of the operating system is discussed, followed by a brief discussion on the Windows NT Kernel and the Windows NT Executive components.

Chapter 2, File System Driver Development

This chapter provides an introduction to file system and filter drivers. Some common driver development issues that arise when designing for the Windows NT platform are also discussed here, including a discussion on allocating and freeing kernel memory, working efficiently with linked lists of structures, and using Unicode strings in your driver. Finally, discussions on the Windows NT object name space and the MUP and MPR components, which are of interest to developers who wish to design network redirectors, are presented in this chapter.

Chapter 3, Structured Driver Development

Designing well-behaved kernel-mode software is the focus of this chapter. Exception dispatching support provided by the operating system is discussed here; the section on structured exception handling discusses how you can develop robust kernel-mode software. There is also a detailed discussion of the various synchronization primitives that are available to kernel-mode developers, and which are essential to writing correct system software. The synchronization primitives discussed here include spin locks, dispatcher objects, and read-write locks.

Part 2: The Managers

Part 2 of this book describes the Windows NT I/O Manager, the Windows NT Virtual Memory Manager, and the Windows NT Cache Manager in considerable detail from the perspective of a developer who wishes to design and implement file system drivers. Regardless of whether or not you eventually choose to design and implement kernel-mode software for the Windows NT platform, these chapters should be useful to you and will provide you with a detailed understanding of some important and complex Windows NT operating system software modules.

Chapter 4, The NT I/O Manager

This chapter takes a detailed look at the Windows NT I/O Manager. The components of the I/O subsystem, as well as the design principles that guided the development of the I/O Manager and I/O subsystem components, are discussed here; so is the concept of *thread-context*, which is extremely important for kernel-mode driver developers. This chapter also provides a description of some of the more important system data structures and of handling synchronous and asynchronous I/O requests. Finally, a high-level overview of the operating system boot sequence is included.

Chapter 5, The NT Virtual Memory Manager

Topics discussed in this chapter include the functionality provided by the VMM, process address space layout, physical memory management and virtual address space manipulation support provided by the Virtual Memory Manager, and memory-mapped file support. This chapter provides an overview on how page fault handling is provided by the VMM, on the workings of the modified page writer, and finally, on the interactions of the Virtual Memory Manager with file system drivers.

Chapter 6, The NT Cache Manager I

This chapter provides an introduction to the Windows NT Cache Manager. The functionality provided by the Cache Manager is discussed here, followed by a discussion on how cached read and write I/O requests are jointly handled by the I/O Manager, file system drivers, and the Cache Manager. The various Cache Manager interfaces are introduced, followed by a discussion on the clients that typically request services from the Windows NT Cache Manager. Some important data structures required for successful interaction with the Cache Manager are also described. Finally, there is a discussion on how file size manipulation can be successfully performed for cached files.

Chapter 7, The NT Cache Manager II

This chapter provides an overview of how the Windows NT Cache Manager uses internal data structures to provide caching services to the rest of the system. File system drivers must be cognizant of certain requirements that they must fulfill to interact successfully with the Cache Manager; these requirements are discussed here. This chapter also has details of each of the various interfaces (function calls) that are available to Cache Manager clients.

Chapter 8, The NT Cache Manager III

Topics discussed in this chapter include flushing the system cache, terminating caching for a file, descriptions of certain miscellaneous Cache-Manager-provided function calls, and the interactions of the Cache Manager with the I/O Manager, and the Virtual Memory Manager. Finally, read-ahead and delayed-write functionality, provided by the Windows NT Cache Manager, is discussed.

Part 3: The Drivers

Part 3 describes how to use the information provided in Parts 1 and 2 of this book. This portion of the book focuses exclusively on actual design and development of two types of kernel-mode drivers. It could also be used as a reference in understanding how the various Windows NT file systems process user requests for file I/O and as an aid to understanding what is actually going on in the system when you debug any lower-level kernel-mode driver that you may have developed.

Chapter 9, Writing a File System Driver I

This chapter provides an introduction to file system design and also describes how to configure (via Registry entries) your file system driver implementation on a Windows NT system. A comprehensive description of the important data structures that you should implement in order to develop a Windows NT file system driver is also provided. Details on how you can implement the create/ open, read, and write dispatch routines in your file system driver are included.

Chapter 10, Writing A File System Driver II

This chapter contains discussions of some important concepts that you should understand when trying to design a Windows NT file system driver; these include the concept of the top-level component for an IRP and how to implement support for asynchronous I/O requests in your file system driver. A description of how to implement support for processing the directory control, cleanup, and close requests is also provided.

Chapter 11, Writing a File System Driver III

Topics discussed in this chapter include the fast I/O method for data access, implementing callback routines in your FSD for use by the Windows NT Cache Manager and Virtual Memory Manager, dispatch routines including flushing file buffers, getting and setting volume information, implementing byte-range lock support, supporting opportunistic locking, and implementing support for file system control and device I/O control requests (including a detailed discussion on handling mounting and verification requests for logical volumes). Finally, there is a detailed discussion of how to implement a mini-file system recognizer driver for your file system driver product.

Chapter 12, Filter Drivers

A description of the functionality that can be provided by a filter driver is followed by some examples of customer requirements where filter driver development can be useful. Topics discussed here include getting a pointer to the appropriate target device, attaching to the target device object, the consequences of executing an attach operation, and the various I/O-Manager-provided support functions available for use by a filter driver.

Appendixes

Appendix A, Windows NT System Services

This appendix contains a detailed listing of the major Windows NT I/O Manager-provided *native* system calls.

Appendix B, MPR Support

This appendix describes functions that network redirectors should implement to provide MPR support.

Appendix C, Building Kernel-Mode Drivers

This appendix provides an overview of the build process used to create kernel-mode drivers.

Appendix D, Debugging Support

An introduction to the Microsoft *WinDbg* source-level debugger is provided.

Appendix E, Recommended Readings and References

A list of recommended readings is provided for your benefit if you wish to delve further into or get more detailed information on some of the topics discussed in this book.

Appendix F, Additional Sources for Help

This appendix lists some online sources and other resources that you can explore for more information on kernel-mode development for Windows NT.

I would suggest that the chapters be read in the sequence in which they are organized. However, advanced readers who understand the basic kernel-mode environment on the Windows NT platform may wish to skip directly to Part 2 of this book. Throughout this book, an effort has been made to avoid forward references to undefined terms; however, such references are flagged whenever they cannot be avoided.

Accompanying Diskette

A diskette accompanies this book and is often referred to in various chapters of the book. This diskette contains source code for the following:*

A file system driver template

Note carefully that this is simply a skeleton driver that does not provide for most of the functionality typically implemented by file system drivers. The code has been compiled for the Intel x86 platform. The code has not been tested, however, and should never be used as is without major enhancement and testing efforts on your part.

---

* Many of the file system dispatch routines are also documented and discussed in the text.

This driver source is provided as a framework for you to use to design and implement a real file system driver for the Windows NT environment.

A filter driver implementation

The filter driver for which source has been provided intercepts all I/O requests targeted to a specified mounted logical volume. You can extend this filter driver source code to implement any value-added functionality you wish to provide to your customers.

If you intend to develop kernel-mode software for the Windows NT platform, I strongly recommend that you obtain at least a *Professional Level Subscription* to the Microsoft Developer's Network (MSDN). This subscription will provide you with access to the Windows NT Device Driver's Kit (DDK), associated documentation, and a reasonable number of additional benefits. Contact the Microsoft Developer's Network at *http://www.microsoft.com/msdn* for additional details.

Note that the source code provided on the accompanying disk has only been compiled using the Microsoft Visual C++ compiler (Version 4.2). This compiler can be purchased directly from Microsoft. They can be reached on the World Wide Web at *http://www.microsoft.com/visualc.*

Finally, you should note that successful compilation of the file system driver source requires a header file (`ntifs.h`) that is currently only available from Microsoft by purchasing a Windows NT IFS kit. This kit was released in April 1997 and is sold as a separate product by Microsoft from the MSDN subscription. You can obtain more information about this product at *http://www.microsoft.com/ hwdev/ntifskit.* Although many of the structure, constant, and type definitions contained in the header file have been provided in this book, they are subject to frequent·change, and I would encourage you to carefully evaluate your requirements and try to purchase this product if at all possible.

Conventions Used in This Book

This book uses the following font conventions:

Italic

is used for World Wide Web URL addresses, to display email addresses, to display Usenet newsgroup addresses, and to highlight special terms the first time they are defined.

`Constant Width`

is used to display command names, filenames, field names, constant definitions, type (structure) definitions, and in code examples.

Acknowledgments

I consider myself extremely fortunate to have known, studied under, and worked with some of the most exceptional minds in the field of computer science. I would like to especially thank the following individuals: for introducing me to synchronization primitives and serving as an advisor to a much-harried and perennially late-to-complete-thesis graduate student, Dr. Sheau-Dong Lang at the University of Central Florida. Also, Dr. Ronald Dutton of the University of Central Florida for teaching me the fundamentals of algorithm design and analysis, and supporting me through one of the most difficult periods in my academic life. I would like to acknowledge the trust, support, and friendship of Robert Smith, whom I consider a mentor and friend and who entrusted me, a rookie engineer, to write his first commercial file system driver. I would also like to thank my colleagues at each of the companies I have worked at, namely, Micro Design International, Inc., Transarc Inc., and Hewlett-Packard Inc., for their support and advice. My grateful thanks to our technical reviewers: Mike Kazar, Derrel Blain, and David J. Van Maren who took time from their busy schedules to review this book.

Many thanks to the people at O'Reilly and Associates who have contributed to this effort: Mary Anne Weeks Mayo was the production project manager and quality was assured by Ellie Fountain Maden, John Files, Nicole Gipson Arigo, and Sheryl Avruch. Seth Maislin wrote the index. Madeline Newell and Colleen Miceli lent critical freelance support. Mike Sierra contributed his FrameMaker tool-tweaking prowess. Chris Reilley and Robert Romano were responsible for the crisp illustrations you see in the book. The book's interior was designed by Nancy Priest, Edie Freedman designed the front cover, and Hanna Dyer designed the back cover.

Finally, many thanks to Robert Denn for his editorial support over the past year and, most importantly, for his patience and trust that I would eventually complete this effort. It has been a pleasure working with him.

I

Overview

Part I introduces the Windows NT Operating System and some of the issues of file system driver development.

- Chapter 1, *Windows NT System Components*
- Chapter 2, *File System Driver Development*
- Chapter 3, *Structured Driver Development*

1

Windows NT System Components

The focus of this book is the Windows NT *file system* and the interaction of the file system with the other core operating system components. If you are interested in providing value-added software for the Windows NT platform, the topics on *filter driver* design and development should provide you with a good understanding of some of the mechanics involved in designing such software.

File systems and filter drivers don't exist in a vacuum, but interact heavily with the rest of the operating system. This chapter provides an overview of the main components of the Windows NT operating system.

The Basics

Operating systems deal with issues that users prefer to forget, including initializing processor states, coordinating multiple CPUs, maintaining CPU cache coherency, managing the local bus, managing physical memory, providing virtual memory support, dealing with external devices, defining and scheduling user processes/threads, managing user data stored on external devices, and providing the foundation for an easily manageable and user-friendly computing system. Above all, the operating system must be perceived as reliable and efficient, since any perceived lack of these qualities will almost certainly result in the universal rejection and thereby in the quick death of the operating system.

Contrary to what you may have heard, Windows NT is not a state-of-the-art operating system by any means. It employs concepts and principles that have been known for years and have actually been implemented in many other commercial operating systems. You can envision the Windows NT platform as the result of a confluence of ideas, principles, and practices obtained from a wide variety of sources, from both commercial products and research projects conducted by universities.

Design principles and methodologies from the venerable UNIX and OpenVMS operating system platforms, as well as the MACH operating system developed at CMU, are obvious in Windows NT. You can also see the influence of less sophisticated systems, such as MS-DOS and OS/2. However, do not be misled into thinking that Windows NT can be dismissed as just another conglomeration of rehashed design principles and ideas. The fact that the designers of Windows NT were willing to learn from their own experiences in designing other operating systems and the experiences of others has led to the development of a fairly stable and serious computing platform.

The Core Architecture

Certain philosophies derived from the MACH operating system are visible in the design of Windows NT. These include an effort to minimize the size of the kernel and to implement parts of the operating system using the client-server model, with a message-passing method to transfer information between modules. Furthermore, the designers have tried to implement a layered operating system, where each component interacts with other layers via a well-defined interface.

The operating system was designed specifically to run in both single-processor and symmetric multiprocessor environments.

Finally, one of the primary goals was to make the operating system easily portable across many different hardware architectures. The designers tried to achieve this goal by using an object-based model to design operating system components and by abstracting out those small pieces of the operating system that are hardware-dependent and therefore need to be reimplemented for each supported platform; the more portable components can, theoretically, simply be recompiled for the different architectures.

Figure 1-1 illustrates how the Windows NT operating system is structured. The figure shows that Windows NT can be broadly divided into two main components: user mode and kernel mode.

User mode

The operating system provides support for protected subsystems. Each protected subsystem resides in its own process with its memory protected from other subsystems. Memory protection support is provided by the Windows NT Virtual Memory Manager.

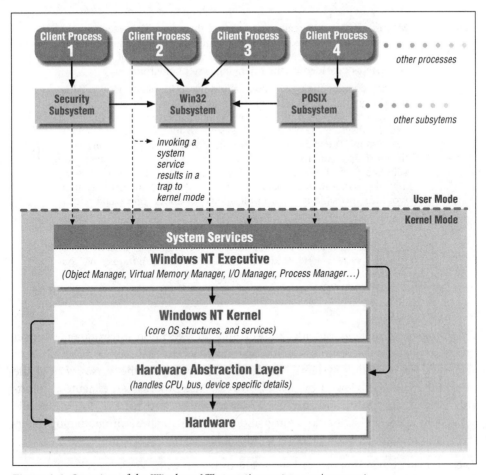

Inside the figure:

Client Process 1 **Client Process 2** **Client Process 3** **Client Process 4**   • • • • • • •
other processes

Security Subsystem **Win32 Subsystem** **POSIX Subsystem**   • • • • • • •
other subsytems

invoking a system service results in a trap to kernel mode

User Mode
Kernel Mode

System Services

Windows NT Executive
(Object Manager, Virtual Memory Manager, I/O Manager, Process Manager...)

Windows NT Kernel
(core OS structures, and services)

Hardware Abstraction Layer
(handles CPU, bus, device specific details)

Hardware

Figure 1-1. Overview of the Windows NT operating system environment

The subsystems provide well-defined Application Programming Interfaces (APIs) that can be used by user-mode processes to obtain desired functionality. The subsystems then communicate with the kernel-mode portion of the operating system using well-defined system service calls.

NOTE	Microsoft has never really documented the operating-system-provided system-service calls. They instead encourage application developers for the Windows NT platform to use the services of one of the subsystems provided by the operating system environment.

By not documenting the native Windows NT system service APIs, the designers have tried to maintain an abstract view of the operating system. Therefore, applications only interact with their preferred native subsystem, leaving the subsystem to interact with the operating system. The benefit to Microsoft of using this philosophy is to tie most applications to the easily portable Win32 subsystem (the subsystem of choice and, sometimes, the subsystem of necessity), and also to allow the operating system to evolve more easily than would be possible if major applications depended on certain specific native Windows NT system services.

However, it is sometimes more efficient (or necessary) for Windows NT applications and kernel-mode driver developers to be able to access the system services directly. In Appendix A, *Windows NT System Services*, you'll find a list of the system services provided by the Windows NT I/O Manager to perform file I/O operations.

Environment subsystems provide an API and an execution environment to user processes that emulates some specific operating system (e.g., an OS/2 or UNIX or Windows 3.x operating system). Think of a subsystem as the *personality* of the operating system as viewed by a user process. The process can execute comfortably within the safe and nurturing environment provided by the specific subsystem without having to worry about the capabilities, programming interfaces, and requirements of the core Windows NT operating system.

The following environment subsystems are provided with Windows NT:

Win32

The native execution environment for Windows NT. Microsoft actively encourages application developers to use the Win32 API in their software to obtain operating system services.

This subsystem is also more privileged than the others.* It is solely responsible for managing the devices used to interact with users; the monitor, keyboard, and mouse are all controlled by the Win32 subsystem. It is also the

---

* In reality, this is the only subsystem that is actively encouraged by Microsoft for use by third-party application program designers. The other subsystems work (more often than not) but seem to exist only as checklist items. If, for example, you decided to develop an application using the POSIX subsystem instead, you will undoubtedly encounter limitations and frustrations due to the very visible lack of commitment on behalf of Microsoft in making the subsystem fully functional and full featured.

sole Window Manager for the system and defines the policies that control the appearance of graphical user interfaces.

POSIX

This exists to provide support to applications conforming to the POSIX 1003.1 source-code standard. If you have applications that were developed to use the APIs defined in that standard, you should theoretically be able to compile, link, and execute them on a Windows NT platform.

There are severe restrictions on functionality provided by the POSIX subsystem that your applications must be prepared to accept. For example, no networking support is provided by the POSIX subsystem.

OS/2

Provides API support for 16-bit OS/2 applications on the Intel x86 hardware platform.

WOW (Windows on Windows)

This provides support for 16-bit Windows 3.x applications. Note, however, that 16-bit applications that try to control or access hardware directly will not execute on Windows NT platforms.

VDM (Virtual DOS Machine)

Provided to support execution of 16-bit DOS applications. As in the case of 16-bit Windows 3.x applications, any process attempting to directly control or access system hardware will not execute on Windows NT.

Integral subsystems extend the operating system into user space and provide important system functionality. These include the user-space components of the Security subsystem (e.g., the Local Service Authority); the user-space components of the Windows NT LAN Manager Networking software; and the Service Control Manager responsible for loading, unloading, and managing kernel-mode drivers and system services, among others.

Kernel mode

The difference between executing code in kernel mode and in user mode is the hardware privilege level at which the CPU is executing the code.

Most CPU architectures provide at least two hardware privilege levels, and many provide multiple levels. The hardware privilege level of the CPU determines the possible set of instructions that code can execute. For example, when executing in user mode, processes cannot directly modify or access CPU registers or page-tables used for virtual memory management. Allowing all user processes access to such privileges would quickly result in chaos and would preclude any serious tasks from being performed on the CPU.

Windows NT uses a simplified hardware privilege model that has two privilege levels: *kernel mode*, which allows code to do anything necessary on the processor;* and *user mode*, where the process is tightly constrained in the range of allowed operations.

If you're familiar with the Intel x86 architecture set, kernel mode is equivalent to the *Ring 0* privilege level for processors in the set and user mode to *Ring 3*.

The terms kernel mode and user mode, although often used to describe code (functions), are actually privilege levels associated with the processor. Therefore, the term *kernel-mode code* simply means that the CPU will always be in kernel-mode privilege level when it executes that particular code, and the term *user-mode code* means that the CPU will execute the code at user-mode privilege level.

Typically, as a third-party developer, you cannot execute Windows NT programs while the CPU is at kernel-mode privilege level unless you design and develop Windows NT kernel-mode drivers.

The kernel-mode portion of Windows NT is composed of the following:

The Hardware Abstraction Layer (HAL)
> The Windows NT operating system was designed to be portable across multiple architectures. In fact, you can run Windows NT on Intel x86 platforms, DEC Alpha platforms, and also the MIPS-based platforms (although support for this architecture has recently been discontinued by Microsoft). Furthermore, there are many kinds of external buses that you could use with Windows NT, including (but not limited to) ISA, EISA, VL-Bus, and PCI bus architectures. The Windows NT developers created the HAL to isolate hardware-specific code. The HAL is a relatively thin layer of software that interfaces directly with the CPU and other hardware system components and is responsible for providing appropriate abstractions to the rest of the system.

> The rest of the Windows NT Kernel sees an idealized view of the hardware, as presented by the HAL. All differences across multiple hardware architectures are managed internally by the HAL. The set of functions exported by the HAL are invoked by both the core operating system components (e.g., the Windows NT Kernel component), and device drivers added to the operating system.

> The HAL exports functions that allow access to system timers, I/O buses, DMA and Interrupt controllers, device registers, and so on.

---

* Code that executes in kernel mode can do virtually anything with the system. This includes crashing the system or corrupting user data. Therefore, with the flexibility of kernel-mode privileges comes a lot of responsibility that kernel-mode designers must be aware of.

The Windows NT Kernel

The Windows NT Kernel provides the fundamental operating system functionality that is used by the rest of the operating system. Think of the kernel as the module responsible for providing the building blocks that can subsequently be used by the Windows NT Executive to provide all of the powerful functionality offered by the operating system. The kernel is responsible for providing process and thread scheduling support, support for multiprocessor synchronization via spin lock structures, interrupt handling and dispatching, and other such functionality.

The Windows NT Kernel is described further in the next section.

The Windows NT Executive

The Executive comprises the largest portion of Windows NT. It uses the services of the kernel and the HAL, and is therefore highly portable across architectures and hardware platforms. It provides a rich set of system services to the various subsystems, allowing them to access the operating system functionality.

The major components of the Windows NT Executive include the Object Manager, the Virtual Memory Manager, the Process Manager, the I/O Manager, the Security Reference Monitor, the Local Procedure Call facility, the Configuration Manager, and the Cache Manager.

File systems, device drivers, and intermediate drivers form a part of the I/O subsystem that is managed by the I/O Manager and are part of the Windows NT Executive.

The Windows NT Kernel

The Windows NT Kernel has been described as the heart of the operating system, although it is quite small compared to the Windows NT Executive. The kernel is responsible for providing the following basic functionality:

- Support for kernel objects
- Thread dispatching
- Multiprocessor synchronization
- Hardware exception handling
- Interrupt handling and dispatching
- Trap handling
- Other hardware specific functionality

The Windows NT Kernel code executes at the highest privilege level on the processor.* It is designed to execute concurrently on multiple processors in a symmetric multiprocessing environment.

The kernel cannot take page faults; therefore, all of the code and data for the kernel is always resident in system memory. Furthermore, the kernel code cannot be preempted; therefore, context switches are not allowed when a processor executes code belonging to the kernel. However, all code executing on any processor can always be interrupted, provided the interrupt level is higher than the level at which the code is executing.

IRQ Levels

The Windows NT Kernel defines and uses Interrupt Request Levels (IRQLs) to prioritize execution of kernel-mode components. The particular IRQL at which a piece of kernel-mode code executes determines its *hardware priority*. All interrupts with an IRQL that is less than or equal to the IRQL of the currently executing kernel-mode code are masked off (i.e., disabled) by the Windows NT Kernel. However, the currently executing code on a processor can be interrupted by any software or hardware interrupt with an IRQL greater than that of the executing code. IRQLs are hierarchically ordered and are defined as follows (in increasing order of priority):

PASSIVE_LEVEL

Normal thread execution interrupt levels. Most file system drivers are asked to provide functionality by a thread executing at IRQL PASSIVE_LEVEL, though this is not guaranteed. Most lower-level drivers, such as device drivers, are invoked at a higher IRQL than PASSIVE_LEVEL.

This IRQL is also known as LOW_LEVEL.

APC_LEVEL

Asynchronous Procedure Call (APC) interrupt level. Asynchronous Procedure Calls are invoked by a software interrupt, and affect the control flow for a target thread. The thread to which an APC is directed will be interrupted, and the procedure specified when creating the APC will be executed in the context of the interrupted thread at APC_LEVEL IRQL.

DISPATCH_LEVEL

Thread dispatch (scheduling) and Deferred Procedure Call (DPC) interrupt level. DPCs are defined in Chapter 3, *Structured Driver Development*. Once a

---

* The highest privilege level is defined as the level at which the operating system software has complete and unrestricted access to all capabilities provided by the underlying CPU architecture.

thread IRQL has been raised to DPC level or greater, thread scheduling is automatically suspended.

Device Interrupt Levels (DIRQLs)

Platform-specific number and values of the device IRQ levels.

`PROFILE_LEVEL`

Timer used for profiling.

`CLOCK1_LEVEL`

Interval timer clock 1.

`CLOCK2_LEVEL`

Interval timer clock 2.

`IPI_LEVEL`

Interprocessor interrupt level used only on multiprocessor systems.

`POWER_LEVEL`

Power failure interrupt.

`HIGHEST_LEVEL`

Typically used for machine check and bus errors.

`APC_LEVEL` and `DISPATCH_LEVEL` interrupts are software interrupts. They are requested by the kernel-mode code and are lower in priority than any of the hardware interrupt levels. The interrupts in the range `CLOCK1_LEVEL` to `HIGH_LEVEL` are the most time-critical interrupts, and they are therefore the highest priority levels for thread execution.

Support for Kernel Objects

The Windows NT Kernel also tries to maintain an object-based environment. It provides a core set of objects that can be used by the Windows NT Executive and also provides functions to access and manipulate such objects. Note that the Windows NT Kernel does not depend upon the Object Manager (which forms part of the Executive) to manage the kernel-defined object types.

The Windows NT Executive uses objects exported by the kernel to construct even more complex objects made available to users.

Kernel objects are of the following two types:

Dispatcher objects

These objects control the synchronization and dispatching of system threads. Dispatcher objects include thread, event, timer, mutex, and semaphore object types. You will find a description of most of these object types in Chapter 3.

Control objects

> These objects affect the operation of kernel-mode code but do not affect dispatching or synchronization. Control objects include APC objects, DPC objects, interrupt objects, process objects, and device queue objects.

The Windows NT Kernel also maintains the following data structures:

Interrupt Dispatcher Table

> This is a table maintained by the kernel to associate interrupt sources with appropriate Interrupt Service Routines.

Processor Control Blocks (PRCBs)

> There is one PRCB for each processor on the system. This structure contains all sorts of processor-specific information, including pointers to the thread currently scheduled for execution, the next thread to be scheduled, and the idle thread.

NOTE   Each processor has an idle thread that executes whenever no other thread is available. The idle thread has a priority below that of all other threads on the system. The idle thread continuously loops looking for work such as processing the DPC queue and initiating a context switch whenever another thread becomes ready to execute on the processor.

Processor Control Region

> This is a hardware architecture-specific kernel structure that contains pointers to the PRCB structure, the Global Descriptor Table (GDT), the Interrupt Descriptor Table (IDT), and other information.

DPC queue

> This global queue contains a list of procedures to be invoked whenever the IRQL on a processor falls below IRQL `DISPATCH_LEVEL`.

Timer queue

> A global timer queue is also maintained by the NT Kernel. This queue contains the list of timers that are scheduled to expire at some future time.

Dispatcher database

> The thread dispatcher module maintains a database containing the execution state of all processors and threads on the system. This database is used by the dispatcher module to schedule thread execution.

In addition to the object types mentioned above, the Windows NT Kernel maintains device queues, power notification queues, processor requester queues, and other such data structures required for the correct functioning of the kernel itself.

Processes and Threads

A *process* is an object* that represents an instance of an executing program. In Windows NT, each process must have at least one *thread* of execution. The process abstraction is composed of the process-private virtual address space for the process, the code and data that is private to the process and contained within the virtual address space, and system resources that have been allocated to the process during the course of execution.

Note that process objects are not schedulable entities in themselves. Therefore you cannot actually schedule a process to execute. However, each process contains one or more schedulable threads of execution.

Each thread object executes program code for the process and is therefore scheduled for execution by the Windows NT Kernel. As noted above, more than one thread can be associated with any process, and each thread is scheduled for execution individually.

The context of a thread object consists of user- and kernel-stack pointers for the thread, a program counter for the thread indicating the current instruction being executed, system registers (including integer and floating-point registers) containing state information, and other processor status maintained while the thread is executing.

Each thread has a scheduling state associated with it. The possible states are *initialized, ready-to-run, standby, running, waiting,* and *terminated.* Only one thread can be in the *running* state on any processor at any given instant, though multiple threads can be in this state on multiprocessor systems (one per processor).

Threads have execution priority levels associated with them; higher priority threads are always given preference during scheduling decisions and always preempt the execution of lower priority threads. Priority levels are categorized into the *real-time* priority class and the *variable* priority class.

---

* The Windows NT Kernel defines the fundamental thread and process objects. The Windows NT Executive uses the core structures defined by the kernel to define Executive thread and process object abstractions.

NOTE   It is possible to encounter situations of *priority-inversion* on Windows NT systems, where a lower-priority thread may be holding a critical resource required by a higher-priority thread (even a thread executing with real-time priority). Any thread that is of higher-priority than the one holding the critical resource would then get the opportunity to execute even if it has a priority lower than that of the thread waiting for the resource.*

The scenario described above violates the assumption that higher priority threads will always preempt and execute before any lower priority threads are allowed to execute. This could lead to incorrect behavior, especially in situations where thread priorities *must* be maintained (e.g., for real-time processes). Kernel-mode designers must anticipate and understand that these situations can occur unless they ensure that resource acquisition hierarchies are correctly defined and maintained.

Windows NT does not provide support for features such as *priority inheritance* that could automatically help avoid the priority inversion problem.

Most kernel-provided routines for programmatically manipulating or accessing thread or process structures are not exposed to third-party driver developers.

Thread Context and Traps

A *trap* is the processor-provided mechanism for capturing the context of an executing thread when certain events occur. Events that cause a trap include interrupts, exception conditions (described in Chapter 3), or a system service call causing a change in processor mode from user mode to kernel mode of execution.

When a trap condition occurs, the operating system *trap handler* is invoked.† The Windows NT trap handler code saves the information for an executing thread in the form of a *call frame* before invoking an appropriate routine to process the trap condition. Here are two components of a call frame:

A trap frame
    This contains the volatile register state.

* Priority inversion requires three threads to be running concurrently: the *high-priority* thread that requires the critical resource, the *low-priority* thread that has the resource acquired, and the *intermediate-priority* thread that does not want or need the resource and therefore gets the opportunity to preempt the low-priority thread (because it has a higher relative priority) but also (in the process) prevents the high-priority thread from executing even though it has a relatively lower priority.

† The trap handler is written in assembly, is highly processor- and architecture-specific, and is a core piece of functionality provided by the Windows NT Kernel.

An exception frame
> When exception conditions occur that cause the trap handler to be invoked, the nonvolatile register state is also saved.

In addition, the trap handler also saves the previous machine state and any information that will allow the thread to resume execution after the trap condition has been processed appropriately.

The Windows NT Executive

The Windows NT Executive is composed of distinct modules, or subsystems, each of which assumes responsibility for a primary piece of functionality. Typically, references to Windows NT kernel-mode code actually refer to modules in the Executive.

The Executive provides a rich set of system service calls (an API) for subsystems to access its services. In addition, the Executive also provides comprehensive support to developers who wish to extend the existing functionality. Development is usually in the form of third-party device drivers, installable file system drivers, and other intermediate and filter drivers used to provide value-added services.

The various components that comprise the Windows NT Executive maintain more or less strict boundaries around themselves. Once again, the object-based nature of the operating system manifests itself in the prolific use of abstract data types and methods. Modules do not directly access the internal data structures of other modules; note that, although the designers have managed to stick to well-defined interfaces internally, modules still make many assumptions when they invoke each other. The assumptions are often in the form of *expectations* of what processing the called module will perform and how error conditions will be handled and/or reported. Finally, as you will observe later in this book, the synchronization hierarchy employed by the Executive components when they recursively invoke each other is more than just a little complicated.

The Windows NT Object Manager

All components of the Windows NT Executive that export data types for use by other kernel-mode modules use the services of the Object Manager to define, create, and manage the data types, as well as instances of the data types.

The NT Object Manager manages objects. An object is defined as an opaque data structure implemented and manipulated by a specific kernel-mode (Executive) component. Each object may have a set of operations defined for it; these include operations to create an instance of the object, delete an instance of the object, wait for the object to be signaled, and signal the object.

The Object Manager provides the capabilities to do the following:

- Add new object types to the system dynamically (note that the Object Manager does not concern itself with the internal data structure of the object).

- Allow modules to specify security and protection for instances of the object type.

- Provide methods to create and delete object instances.

- Allow the module defining an object type to provide its own methods (such as methods for create, close, and delete operations) to manipulate instances of object types.

- Provide a consistent methodology to maintain references of instances of the object type.

- Provide a global naming hierarchy based upon the more commonly used file system hierarchy *inverted-tree* format.

The Object Manager maintains a global name space for Windows NT. All named objects in the system can be accessed via this name space. The object name space is modeled on normal filenaming conventions. Therefore, there is a global root directory named "\" created by the Object Manager during system initialization. Executive components can create directories and subdirectories under the root directory and then create instances of defined object types under any such directory. Whenever an object is created or inserted (even for file-system-defined objects such as files and directories), parsing of the object name begins at the root of the Object-Manager-maintained name space. If an object type has a *parse method* defined for it (as for example, file objects representing open file system files and directories), the Object Manager invokes the parse method for the object. Chapter 2, *File System Driver Development*, provides additional information on how the Object Manager handles requests to open or create on-disk file or directory objects.

The object type structure maintained by the NT Object Manager contains information such as the type of memory pool from which instances of the object type should be allocated, the valid access types for the object, pointers to procedures associated with the object (these are optional and could include pointers to create, open, close, delete, and other such procedures), and some synchronization structure maintained by the Object Manager for all object instances of the particular type.

Each object instance has a standard object header and an object-type-specific object body associated with it. The standard object header contains information such as pointers to the name of the object (if any), a security descriptor associated with the object (if any), the access mode for the object, reference counts for the object, a pointer to the object type (to which the object instance belongs), and other attributes associated with the object.

Whenever a thread successfully opens an instance of a particular object type, the NT Object Manager returns to the requesting thread an opaque *handle* to the object instance. Note that there can be more than one handle to any object instance at any given point in time. For example, object handles can potentially be inherited.

The Object Manager maintains information associated with each object handle, including a pointer to the object instance, the access information for the open operation, and other attributes for the handle. Note that there is no direct relationship between the handle and the pointer to the open instance of the object type. The handle is typically an index into an object table, which is composed of an array of object table entries.

WARNING   Handles are specific to a process. Therefore, if a thread successfully performs a create and open operation and obtains a handle in return, all threads for the particular process can use that handle.

However, if the same handle is used in the context of a thread associated with any other process, you will receive an error code indicating that the handle is invalid.[*]

Other Windows NT Executive Components

As mentioned earlier, the other major components of the Windows NT Executive are as follows:

The Process Manager

This component is responsible for the creation and deletion of processes and threads. It uses the services provided by the Windows NT Kernel to perform tasks such as suspending an executing process, resuming execution of a process, providing process information, and so on.

---

[*] Although this may not make sense to you yet, this error is a leading cause of frustration to driver developers who open a resource in their `DriverEntry()` routine and then try to use the returned handle in some other dispatch routine, which is typically executed in the context of another thread (and process).

The Local Procedure Call (LPC) facility

This facility is the mechanism by which messages can be passed between two processes on the same node.* The client process typically passes parameters to a server process and requests some services. In return, it may receive some processed data back from the server process.

The client's call to the server is intercepted by a stub in the client process that packages the parameters being sent to the server procedure. Then the LPC facility provides the mechanism for the client process to transmit the data to the server and then wait for a response back from the server. This is done using a *Port* object, defined and created by the LPC facility.

The LPC facility is modeled on the Remote Procedure Call mechanism used to implement the client-server model across machines connected by a local or wide area network. The LPC facility is better optimized for communication within a node where all processes have access to the same physical memory.

Security Reference Monitor

This module is responsible for enforcing security policy on the local node. It also provides object auditing facilities.

Virtual Memory Manager

The Windows NT Virtual Memory Manager (VMM) manages all available physical memory on the local node. It is also responsible for providing virtual memory management functionality to the rest of the operating system, as well as to all applications that execute on the node.

Almost all kernel-mode and user-mode modules must interact with the Virtual Memory Manager component. Most modules are clients of the Virtual Memory Manager and therefore depend on the VMM to provide memory management services. File systems, however, are special, because they must often provide services to the VMM (e.g., for reading or writing page files). File system designers must understand thoroughly the interactions of file system drivers with the VMM module. The VMM is discussed in greater detail in Chapter 5, *The NT Virtual Memory Manager*.

Cache Manager

The Windows NT Executive contains a dedicated caching module to provide virtual block caching functionality (in system memory) for file data stored on secondary storage media. The Cache Manager uses the services of the Windows NT Virtual Memory Manager to provide caching functionality. All of the native NT file system driver implementations use the services of the Cache

---

* A single node can be defined as a computer containing either a single processor or multiple processors. Multiple nodes can potentially be networked together to create a Windows NT cluster.

Manager. The Windows NT Cache Manager is discussed in detail in Chapters 6–8.

I/O Manager

The Windows NT I/O Manager defines and manages the framework within which all kernel-mode drivers (including file system, network, disk, intermediate, and filter drivers) can reside. The I/O Manager is described in detail in Chapter 4, *The NT I/O Manager.*

2

File System Driver Development

In this chapter:
- *What Are File System Drivers?*
- *What Are Filter Drivers?*
- *Common Driver Development Issues*
- *Windows NT Object Name Space*
- *Filename Handling for Network Redirectors*

The focus of this book is on kernel-mode file system driver and filter driver development for the Windows NT operating system. However, before beginning a discussion on how to design and implement a kernel-mode file system or filter driver, you need a good understanding of just what the file system and filter drivers do. Knowing what these drivers can and cannot do will help you decide whether it is worth all the trouble to design one.

In this chapter, I will briefly discuss the various types of file system drivers and filter drivers to give you some idea of the functionality that is traditionally expected from them. I will also discuss some common concepts used during the design and implementation of kernel-mode drivers in Windows NT. Topics discussed here include how to make portions of your kernel-mode driver pageable, how to allocate and free kernel memory required during execution, how to use some of the system-defined structures and functions to create linked lists, and how to troubleshoot and debug your driver. It may be best for you to skim through this material initially, then refer back to it once you have read some of the succeeding chapters and have begun the process of designing and developing your kernel-mode file system or filter driver.

One of the challenges I faced when trying to design a file system driver for Windows NT was understanding how user-specified filenames are treated. I will discuss this as part of a larger discussion on the name space, which is managed by the Windows NT Object Manager. I will also discuss the roles played by the Multiple Provider Router (MPR) component and the Multiple UNC Provider (MUP) in supporting network file system drivers, which must be integrated with the name space on the local node. Chapters following this one examine some of the topics presented here in considerable depth.

What Are File System Drivers?

A *file system driver* is a component of the storage management subsystem. It provides the means for users to store information to and retrieve it from nonvolatile media such as disks or tapes.

Functionality Provided by a File System Driver

A file system driver implementation typically provides the following functionality to the user:*

- Ability to create, modify, and delete *files*†

- Ability to share files and transfer information between them easily, though in a secure and controlled manner

- Ability to structure the contents of a file in a manner appropriate to the application

- Ability to identify stored files by their symbolic/logical names, instead of specifying the physical device name

- Ability to view the data logically, rather than dealing with a more detailed physical view

The above functionality is provided by all commercially available local (disk based) file system driver implementations. In addition to this functionality, remote file systems, both networked and distributed, provide the following functionality, to some degree or another, depending upon the sophistication of the file system used:

- Network transparency

- Location transparency

- Location independence

- User mobility

- File mobility

Not all of the functionality listed here provided by all remote file system implementations. However, as file system technology evolves, more and more sophisticated network file systems meet or exceed many of these goals.

---

* See the book *An Introduction To Operating Systems* by Harvey Deitel. Consult Appendix E, *Recommended Readings and References*, for more information.

† A *file* is a named collection of user data stored on secondary storage devices (e.g., disk drives).

Types of File System Drivers

There are different kinds of file system driver implementations that you can design, implement, and install. They include local file systems, network filesystems, and distributed file systems.

Disk (local) file system drivers

Local file systems manage data stored on disks connected directly to a host computer.

The file system driver receives requests to open, create, read, write, and close files stored on such disks. These requests typically originate in user processes and are dispatched to the file system via the I/O subsystem manager. Figure 2-1 illustrates how a local file system driver provides services to a user thread.

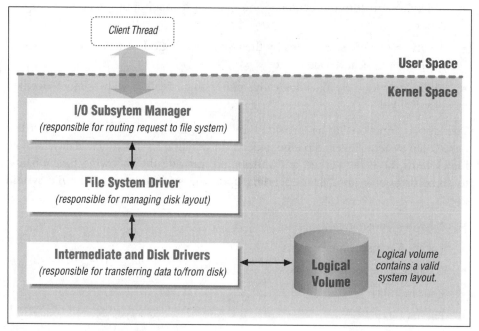

Figure 2-1. Local file system

In the figure, the disk driver transfers data to and from a *logical disk* connected to the system. The logical disk is simply a storage abstraction; from the perspective of the file system, it is a linear sequence of fixed-size, randomly accessible blocks of storage. In reality, a logical disk could be a portion of a physical disk (commonly known as a *partition*), or it could be an entire physical disk, or it could even be some combination of partitions residing across multiple physical disks (known as a *logical volume*). Software modules called *logical volume managers* allow the file system driver to see a contiguous sequence of available disk space and hide all of the details of mapping logical blocks to the correct physical blocks.

Logical volume management software often provides features such as software mirroring of data, striping across multiple physical disks, as well as capabilities to resize logical volumes dynamically. Therefore, you will often see such software advertised as fault-tolerant software.

To be managed by a local file system driver, each logical volume must have a valid file system layout. The file system layout includes appropriate file system metadata information, specific to the type of file system driver used. For example, the FASTFAT file system driver requires a completely different on-disk layout than the NTFS file system driver. It uses structures very different from those used by NTFS to store user data.

On Windows NT systems, whenever you use the `format` utility on a logical volume, you are actually creating the file system metadata (management) structures that will later be used by the file system driver to provide functionality such as allocating space for user data storage, associating stored user data with the user-specified filename, and creating catalogs (directory structures) used in retrieving user files.

Before a user can begin accessing data stored on logical volumes, the logical volume must be mounted on the system. When a logical volume is mounted, a file system driver verifies the metadata and begins managing the volume, using the metadata stored on the volume and setting up appropriate in-memory data structures based on the metadata.

Local file systems provide a single name space for each mounted logical volume. Most commercially available, modern file system implementations provide a hierarchical, tree-structured layout. This tree structure consists of directories (container objects), and files (named user data objects) contained within directories. Each directory, as well as each file contained within a directory, has a unique filename associated with it. The valid character set that can be used to construct a filename is dependent upon the specific file system implementation. For example, the native NTFS file system allows some characters that the FASTFAT file system typically disallows. Most file systems and the I/O subsystem explicitly disallow certain characters. For example, the "\" character is used on Windows NT-based systems as a path separator and cannot be part of a valid filename.

Figure 2-2 shows a hierarchical file system name space as presented by a local file system driver. Each object in this file system can be uniquely identified by a name, starting with the root of the file system. The important thing to note is that each mounted logical volume has its own hierarchical tree structure with a unique root directory serving as the top-level container object for that logical volume.

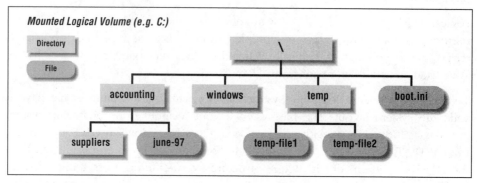

Figure 2-2. Hierarchical name space for directories and files

The user of a mounted logical volume is always aware of the particular mounted logical volume that she is accessing. If she wishes to access a file that does not reside on the currently mounted logical volume, she has to ensure that the logical volume on which the file resides is both accessible and mounted. Then she can specify the complete file pathname identifying the file, beginning at the root of the logical volume on which the file resides, to access the contents of the file.

Network file systems

As the name suggests, network file systems allow users to share locally connected disks with other users over a local or wide area network. For example, say you have a physical disk *C:* connected to your machine. Now you may want to allow me direct access to the files and directories stored under the *accounting* subdirectory on your *C:* local drive. To do this, both you and I would have to use the services of a network file system. This network file system would allow me to access the shared files on your disk, just as if I were accessing my own local disk.

There are two components to each network file system implementation:

The client-side redirector
> There must be a software component, executing on my node, that will take my requests for accessing files stored in your *C:\accounting* directory and transfer them across the network to be processed on your machine. Furthermore, this software component must be capable of receiving data from your machine and handing it back to me.

The server on the node where the disk is being shared
> Once the redirector on the client sends a request across the network, a software component on the server system must respond to this request.

The server component then has two major tasks to perform; the first is to interface with the remote client using a well-defined protocol, and the second is to interface with the local file systems to obtain data on behalf of the client node.

Figure 2-3 shows the client and server components of the network file system implementation.

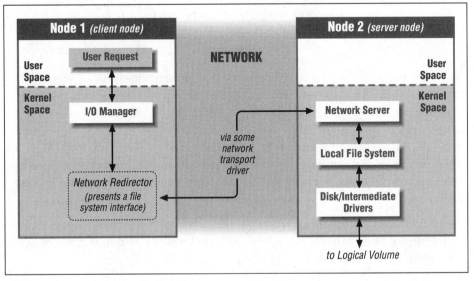

Figure 2-3. Remote (network) file system

The most common example of a remote file system to NT users is the LAN Manager Network, which supports the sharing of directories, logical volumes, printers, and other remote resources. The LAN Manager Network consists of the LAN Manager Redirector component executing in the kernel on client nodes and the LAN Manager Server software executing in the kernel on server nodes exporting local file systems or other resources such as printers and the SMB (Server Message Block) network protocol used by the two components to transfer data across the network.

NOTE   In 1996, Microsoft submitted a networking protocol specification called the Common Internet File System (CIFS) 1.0 to the Internet Engineering Task Force as an Internet-Draft document. Microsoft has since been working with other parties to get CIFS published as an Informational RFC. CIFS is the latest incarnation of the SMB protocol specification and is expected to be a part of future updates to Windows NT 4.x and Windows 95. Throughout this book, I use the term SMB to refer to the networking protocol implementation used by the Microsoft LAN Manager Redirector and Server components; however, you can easily substitute the term CIFS for SMB.

Note that the redirector is the component that presents itself as a file system on the client node. This allows users to request access to remote data just as they would request data from her local file system. The redirector handles all of the mechanics of getting the data for users from across the network. Although networks are inherently unreliable (especially wide area networks), it is the responsibility of the redirector to try to reestablish lost connections transparently, or to return appropriate errors so that the application can retry the request if required.

The server does not need to present a file-system-like interface, because clients on the server node can use the services of the local file system directly to access data stored on the disk drives local to the server.

Both the redirector and the server use a transport protocol to transfer data and commands across the network. There are many transport protocols, such as the TCP/IP protocol, the UDP/IP, and Microsoft-specific protocols such as NetBIOS. The transport protocols may be connection-oriented (e.g., TCP/IP, NetBIOS), so that they provide a virtual circuit to the redirector and server software, or connectionless (e.g., UDP/IP).

Figure 2-4 illustrates how a server node can share a particular directory with clients across the network. To the client node, the shared directory forms the root of a distinct logical volume. Requests from the client node to the networked volume are handled by the redirector, which is responsible for transmitting the request across the network to the server node. The network server software on the server node processes the request, utilizing the local file system on the server node to access and manipulate the shared volume. Finally, the server returns the results of the operation to the remote client.

In the case of network file systems, the client is aware of the fact that the user is accessing data residing on the server node. Therefore, although all of the mechanics of data transfer are hidden from the user of the file system, the user is

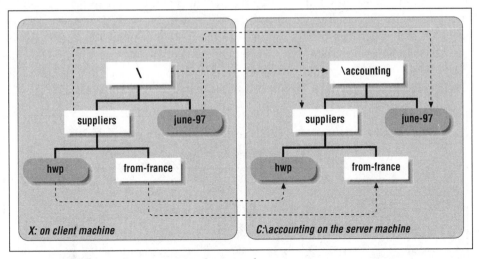

Figure 2-4. Sharing a directory across the network

always aware of which data is stored locally and which is obtained from a remote server node.

Finally, you should note that applications on the server node use local file system services to access file data residing on the shared logical volumes. In certain cases, this may lead to data consistency problems if file data from shared logical volumes is also cached on client nodes. Local (disk-based) file system drivers are often expected to cooperate with network server software to help avoid such data consistency problems whenever possible.

Distributed file systems

Distributed file systems have evolved from standard network file systems. They present a single name space to the user and completely hide the actual physical location of the data from the user of the file system.

This means that a user supplies a single pathname to identify the required file, regardless of the physical location of the file. Therefore, a user can access resources residing on a remote server machine without even realizing it.

Architecturally, distributed file systems look very much like network file systems, since they also have client software executing on client nodes and server software executing on remote nodes to make their resources available across the network. The primary difference, however, is the single name space provided by distributed file systems over and above what is offered by simpler network file systems. Note that both client and server software could be concurrently executing on any node that participates in the implementation of the distributed file system.

Figure 2-5 illustrates how a distributed file system presents a single name space to the user of the file system. A client of the file system on *node 1* can access all of the files and directories that constitute the file system without regard for where they physically reside. There is a single (virtual) global root directory for the file system tree. Although not illustrated in the figure, any point in the global name space could in actuality be a *mount point* for a remotely exported subtree.

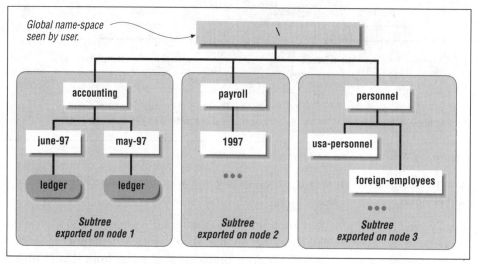

Figure 2-5. Global name space presented by distributed file systems

NOTE   A *mount point* is simply a named directory in the file system name space to which a remotely exported subtree can be grafted. In Figure 2-5 above, you can see that the *accounting, payroll,* and *personnel* directories are mount points for the distributed file system. The *accounting* directory has a subtree from *node 1* grafted on, the *payroll* directory allows access to data stored on *node 2*, while the *personnel* directory allows access to data stored on *node 3*. Any user of this file system can now transparently access a file or a directory without regard for where the data actually resides. The user simply sees a single name space for the entire distributed file system.

When a user tries to access anything below a mount point, the client software on the node must forward the request to the remote server that is actually exporting the contents below the accessed mount point, allowing the server to process the user request.

Many distributed file systems use another approach to access data stored remotely. The client software often transfers data from the remote server on behalf of the requesting process and caches it locally. This obviates the need to contact a remote server every time a user asks for previously requested data stored there. However, sophisticated client-server cache consistency processes are required to maintain data coherency across the entire network.

Sometimes, distributed file systems provide global data consistency guarantees exceeding those provided by the network file system implementations. For example, a distributed file system could guarantee that all users of the file system would always see the same view of a file's contents even if they were concurrently accessing and modifying the file on multiple (geographically distributed) client nodes.

Special (pseudo) file systems

Often, you will encounter kernel-mode software that presents a file-system-like interface to the user but actually does something completely different when the interface calls are exercised. For example, the */proc* file system on UNIX systems actually allows a user to access and potentially modify the address space of a running process.

Basically, any kernel-mode driver that presents a file-system-like interface but performs special functionality (different from the traditional task of managing data stored on physical devices) can be considered a special file system implementation.

Other examples of special file system implementations include kernel-mode drivers that provide hierarchical storage management (HSM) functionality, or drivers that present virtual file systems (e.g., some commercially available source code control systems).

Windows NT and File System Drivers

File system drivers are a component of the I/O subsystem on the Windows NT platform and therefore must conform to the interface defined by the NT I/O Manager.

The Windows NT I/O Manager has defined a standard interface to which all kernel-mode drivers must conform. This interface applies equally to local file system drivers, network and distributed file system redirector software, intermediate drivers, filter drivers, and device drivers. File system drivers can be loaded dynamically under Windows NT and can theoretically also be unloaded dynamically.[*]

The Windows NT/ I/O Manager provides a comprehensive set of support routines for file system driver designers to use. These routines allow the new file system to utilize common services and behave consistently (just as the native file systems

---

[*] In practice, it is very difficult to implement a file system that can be dynamically unloaded. It is possible, though, with a lot of foresight and care in the design and implementation of the file system driver. Most people, however, do not find the result worth all of the effort required.

do) on Windows NT machines. Furthermore, there is a well-defined, although poorly documented,* set of interfaces that the file system driver designer must conform to, in order to interact successfully with the Windows NT Virtual Memory Manager and the Windows NT Cache Manager.

Using a File System

There are two ways in which a user can take advantage of the services provided by a file system driver:

Invoke standard system service calls

This is by far the most commonly used method of requesting access to files and directories. The user process simply invokes standard system service calls to request operations such as opening or creating a file, reading or writing file data, and closing the file.

Use I/O control requests sent to a file system driver

Sometimes, applications need to request specific services that cannot be requested using one of the canned system service calls. In these situations, as long as a file system can do the desired operation, a user can send the request and data directly to the file system driver via the *File System Control* (FSCTL) interface.

A typical example of using standard system services to request access to a file is when a process must read the contents of file *C:\payroll\june-97.* The sequence of operations executed by a typical application process using the Win32 subsystem is as follows:

1. Open the file.

   The requesting process will typically invoke the Win32 `CreateFile()` service routines, specifying the name of the file to be opened, the access mode desired for the open file, and other related arguments. Internally, the Win32 subsystem invokes the `NtCreateFile()` system service call to request the open operation on behalf of the caller.†

   At this point, the CPU switches to kernel-mode privilege level. The code implementing the system call `NtCreateFile()` is implemented by the I/O Manager, which is a component of the Windows NT Executive, and the kernel-mode privilege level is required to run functions implemented by the I/O Manager. The open/create request meanders around the NT Executive,

---

* Until this book was written.

† Any user-space process can directly invoke the `NtCreateFile()` system service routine. Unfortunately, these system service routines have not been well documented by Microsoft. Appendix A, *Windows NT System Services,* has a comprehensive list of the available system services.

dispatched first to the I/O Manager via the `NtCreateFile()` invocation, then to the NT Object Manager to parse the user-supplied name, and finally back into the I/O Manager to identify the file system driver managing the mounted logical volume *C:*. Once the file system driver has been identified, the I/O Manager invokes the file system driver create/open dispatch entry point to process the user request.

Finally, the file system driver performs appropriate processing and returns the results of the create/open operation to the I/O Manager, which in turn returns the results to the Win32 subsystem (the privilege level switches back to user-mode), and the Win32 subsystem eventually returns the results to the requesting process.

2. Read the file data.

   If the open operation succeeds, a handle is returned back to the requesting process. The requesting process now asks to read data in the file, specifying the starting offset and the number of bytes to be read. Typically, the `Read-File()` function call provided by the Win32 subsystem invokes the `NtReadFile()` system service routine on behalf of the requesting process.

   The `NtReadFile()` routine is also implemented by the NT I/O Manager. Because the requesting process must supply a valid file handle, obtained from a previous successful create operation, to request a read, the I/O Manager can easily identify an internal data structure corresponding to the open operation performed earlier. This internal data structure, called a *file object*, will be comprehensively described later in this book. From the file object structure, the I/O Manager can determine the logical volume that contains the open file and will then forward the read request to the file system driver for further processing.

   The file system driver will return as much of the user-requested data as it can and will return the results of the operation back to the I/O Manager. Eventually, the results of the read request will be returned back to the requesting process via the Win32 subsystem.

3. Close the file.

   Once the requesting process has finished processing the contents of the file, it performs a close operation for the file handle received from the previously executed open request. The close handle operation informs the system that the process no longer needs to access the file data.

   The close file process invokes the Win32 `CloseHandle()` function to close the open file handle. The Win32 subsystem in turn invokes the `NtClose()` system service routine.

The file system is notified by the I/O Manager that the user process has closed the file handle, and the file system is free to dispose of any state information it may have maintained for the open file.

There are many file operations that can be requested by a user in addition to the three described here. However, the basic methodology is the same: a process or thread opens or creates a file, performs some operations on the file, and finally closes the open file handle. Note that the NT system services are available to all threads executing on a Windows NT system, including user-mode threads and kernel-mode threads. Furthermore, the NT system services are available regardless of the subsystem (Win32, POSIX, OS/2) used by a requesting process.

NOTE   The system service routines provided by the NT I/O Manager are generic and very comprehensive. They have to be generic because, as mentioned earlier, the services must be capable of supporting requests generated by a user from any one of the supported Windows NT subsystems, which are quite diverse in themselves.

As a matter of fact some of the most powerful functionality provided by the I/O Manager and the file system drivers is often not available (or provided) by the Windows NT subsystems and the *only* way to request the desired functionality is to invoke the system services directly. Therefore, it is more of a pity that Microsoft does not do a better job documenting the available Windows NT system service calls.

Support provided for file system control requests by file system drivers is described in detail later in this book.

The File System Driver Interface

A well-defined interface between the file system driver code and the rest of the operating system must exist, if the operating system is to support multiple file system drivers, including those developed by third-party companies. This interface should clearly document the various interactions between the components involved in satisfying a user request to access file data; the description must also provide for suitable abstractions so that the many varied types of file systems can be successfully integrated into the rest of the operating system.

The goal should be to create modularized components that can be easily substituted and extended without requiring extensive, complicated, and expensive redesign of the entire system. It seems as though the designers of the I/O subsystem started out trying to meet exactly these goals. Therefore, there are well-defined methods for a file system to install, load, and register itself with the rest of the operating system. The I/O Manager also sends very well defined I/O request packets describing user requests to a file system driver for further processing. Last, but not least, there is a fairly comprehensive list of supporting routines that a file system designer can use to make life easier and to better integrate the new file system with the rest of the system.

Unfortunately, things tend to become more than a little messy when you consider the different ways the file system and the operating system interact. Sometimes, as a result of these complex interactions, the abstractions that system designers try to maintain start to break down. The situation is made much worse when the operating system and the file system are jointly responsible to provide support for cached data, and also for supporting memory-mapped files. In Windows NT, for example, the Virtual Memory Manager depends on the file system to provide support for page files used to implement virtual memory support. However, the file system, in turn, depends upon the Virtual Memory Manager for allocation of memory required to process file system requests. This recursive relationship tends to make life even more complicated.

Although the designers at Microsoft who developed the Windows NT operating system seem to have made a strong effort to maintain a clean demarcation between the file system and the rest of the operating system, it seems as though, over time, the lines have gotten more than a little blurred and that more and more implicit behaviors and functionality have become ingrained in the system. This leads to more complicated design and code, and requires extensive documentation from Microsoft for third-party file system designers to develop a successful and robust file system driver.

The sort of documentation that third-party developers would like to have access to was not available when this book went to press. This book will help you understand the system better and give you a starting point to achieve your desired goals.

What Are Filter Drivers?

A filter driver is an intermediate driver that intercepts requests targeted to some existing software module (e.g., the file system or a disk driver). By intercepting the request before it reaches its intended target, the filter driver has the opportunity to either extend, or simply replace, the functionality provided by the original recipient of the request.

NOTE   It isn't required that the filter driver always supplant the existing driver; that would simply become a case of unnecessarily reinventing the wheel. The filter driver can instead focus on providing whatever specialized functionality it needs to implement, while still allowing the existing code to perform what it does best, provide the original functionality.

For example, consider the existing file systems shipped with the Windows NT operating system. They consist of the FASTFAT (the legacy FAT file system support) file system, the NTFS (log-based) file system, the CDFS file system for CD-ROM media, the LAN Manager Redirector to access remote shared drives, and so on. None of the file systems, however, currently provides support for online encryption and decryption of stored data.

Now suppose that you are a security expert who knows how to design and implement an incredibly secure encryption algorithm. You wish to develop and sell software that would encrypt user data before it ever got stored on disk, and automatically decrypt it before giving it back to an authorized user. So how would you go about designing your software?

You certainly do not want to write a completely new file system driver, because that would be too time consuming, and it would not really provide any added value to the end user. What you really want to do is design a filter driver that intercepts requests in either of the following places:

Above the file system

    To allow your code to intercept the user request before the file system driver ever gets the opportunity to see it.

Below the file system

    To allow your driver to perform any required processing after the file system has finished its tasks. However, your driver can do whatever you need before the request is received by a disk driver, or by a network driver that is asked by the file system to obtain data from secondary storage devices or from across the network.

    In this scenario, you can perform your magic somewhere along the way before the data either is written to the disk or returned to the user.

Figure 2-6 illustrates two different places where you can insert your filter driver software.

Once you have inserted your filter driver at an appropriate place in the driver hierarchy, you can intercept I/O requests from the user, perform your magic, and then forward the request to the existing module (either the file system or the disk

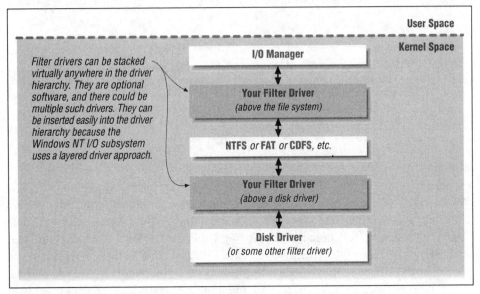

Figure 2-6. Filter drivers in the driver hierarchy

driver) so that they can continue to provide functionality, such as managing the mounted logical volume or transferring data to or from the physical disks.

So if you insert your filter driver so that it intercepts I/O requests dispatched to a file system driver, you can encrypt the data before it is passed into the file system for transfer to secondary storage, and you can decrypt it after the file system has retrieved the encrypted data from secondary storage, before it sends the data back to the user.

If, however, you decide to intercept requests below the file system, then you would follow the same methodology, except that now you would get a chance to modify the buffer only after it had passed through the file system and either before it is written out to disk (or across the network), or immediately after it has been retrieved from disk (or from across the network), but before it is returned to the file system.

It is relatively easy to insert a filter driver into the existing driver hierarchy in either of these two places, without having to redesign all other existing Windows NT file system, disk, and other intermediate drivers, because all drivers in the I/O subsystem must conform to a well-defined, layered driver interface.

This means, for example, that all drivers must respond to a standard set of requests that the I/O Manager could issue. Furthermore, there is a standard method by which a kernel-mode driver (or the I/O Manager itself) requests the services provided by another driver in the calling hierarchy. Every driver in the

hierarchy must also respond to an I/O request in the expected manner, regardless
of the caller.

NOTE   The I/O subsystem does not mandate that all drivers implement
                their dispatch routines in exactly the same way; the only condition
                is that the drivers are aware of their own response to standard I/O
                Manager requests and are therefore aware of the impact they have
                by inserting themselves into the driver hierarchy.

Although everything seems to be just perfect for you to immediately begin
designing your incredibly secure encryption/decryption algorithm for the
Windows NT platform, there are some details that you will unfortunately have to
consider. Ideally, the Windows NT I/O subsystem would be so modular that
implementing your functionality should be a piece of cake. In reality, you must
understand some subtle interactions that manifest themselves, depending on
where in the driver hierarchy you decide to insert your filter driver. Chapter 12,
Filter Drivers, focuses exclusively on the issues involved in designing a filter
driver for the Windows NT platform.

Common Driver Development Issues

This book discusses many issues that kernel-mode file system and filter driver
designers should understand thoroughly. There are some common development
issues, however, that I would like to briefly discuss in this section. These include
how to allocate and free memory in your kernel-mode driver, and how to implement some rudimentary debugging support in your driver.

Consult the Microsoft Driver Development Kit (DDK) documentation for additional details on some of the functions described here. Some of the material in
this section uses terms that will be defined later in the book. Therefore, skim
through the material during your first reading of this book and then come back to
reread it after you have read through at least Chapter 4, *The NT I/O Manager*.

Working with Kernel Memory

In Chapter 5, *The NT Virtual Memory Manager*, you will read about the NT VMM
in considerable detail. However, there are some fairly common issues involved
with driver development and the need for kernel memory that I will describe
here. The code fragments presented later in this book assume that you have a
good understanding of how to allocate and free kernel memory.

You must answer the following questions as you begin designing a kernel-mode driver:

- Does my driver occupy paged or nonpaged memory?

- Can I page out driver code?

- How do I allocate kernel memory on demand?

- How do I free previously allocated memory?

- Are there any issues I must be aware of when attempting to acquire or free kernel memory?

Pageable kernel-mode drivers

By default, the kernel loader will load all driver executables and any global data that you may have defined in your driver into nonpaged memory. Therefore, if you want your driver to reside in nonpaged memory, there is nothing further you need to do besides compiling, linking, and loading the driver.

Furthermore, the kernel loads the entire driver executable (and any associated dynamic link libraries) all at once, before invoking any driver initialization routines. Although it may not make much sense to you at this time, after loading the executable into memory, the kernel loader closes the executable file, allowing a user to delete even the currently executing driver image.

It is possible to specify to the loader the portions of your driver that you wish to make pageable. This can be done by using the following compiler directive in your driver code:[*]

```
#ifdef ALLOC_PRAGMA
#pragma         alloc_text(PAGE, function_name1)
#pragma         alloc_text(PAGE, function_name2)
// You can list additional functions at this point just as the two
// functions are listed above …
#endif // ALLOC_PRAGMA
```

Be careful, though, that you never allow any routine that could possibly be invoked at a high IRQL to be paged out. File system drivers can never allow any code or data to be paged out that might be required to satisfy page fault requests from the NT Virtual Memory Manager.

It is also possible for a kernel-mode driver to determine at run-time whether certain sections of driver code and/or data should be paged out or locked into memory. To do this, the driver must perform the following actions:

---

[*] The functions referenced in a `pragma` statement must be defined in the same compilation unit as the `pragma`.

- To make a code section pageable, use the following compiler directive in your code,

```
#ifdef ALLOC_PRAGMA
#pragma alloc_text(PAGExxxx, function_name1)
#pragma alloc_text(PAGExxxx, function_name2)
...
#endif
```

  where **xxxx** is an optional, four-character, unique identifier for the driver's pageable section.

- To make a data section pageable, use the following compiler directive in your code:

```
#ifdef ALLOC_PRAGMA
#pragma data_seg(PAGE)...
// Define your pageable data section module here.
#pragma data_seg() // Ends the pageable data section.
```

- Invoke `MmLockPagableCodeSection()` and `MmLockPagableCodeSec-tionByHandle()` to lock code sections that were marked as pageable in memory.

- Invoke `MmLockPagableDataSection()` and `MmLockPagableDataSec-tionByHandle()` to lock data sections that were marked as pageable.

- Invoke `MmUnlockPagableImageSection()` to unlock any code or data section that may have been locked using the functions listed above.

There are two additional routines provided by the VMM that you should be aware of (and look up in the DDK documentation) if you wish to page out the entire driver or reset paging attributes back to their original settings:

`MmPageEntireDriver()`

This routine will make the entire driver pageable, overriding any section page attributes that were declared earlier using compiler directives.

`MmResetDriverPaging()`

This function will reset the paging attributes back to the initially declared attributes.

Finally, to automatically have the Memory Manager discard sections of code that you won't need once the driver has been initialized, use the following compiler directives:

```
#ifdef ALLOC_PRAGMA
#pragma alloc_text(INIT, DriverEntry)
#pragma alloc_text(INIT, function1_called_by_driver_entry)
...
#endif // ALLOC_PRAGMA
```

Be careful to specify only those functions that can be safely discarded and will never again be required once the driver initialization has been completed.

Allocating kernel memory

Every kernel-mode driver requires memory to store private data. Typically, your driver will request memory from the NT Virtual Memory Manager. Whenever your driver requests memory, it must determine whether it needs paged or nonpaged memory. If your driver can afford to incur page faults during execution when accessing allocated memory, try to use paged memory whenever possible.

NOTE   Most lower-level disk and network drivers typically can't use pageable data because their code often executes at high IRQ levels that do not allow page faults.* However, file systems (which are often considerably larger and more resource intensive than disk drivers) do sometimes have the opportunity to allocate certain memory from the paged pool. If you can use pageable memory in your driver, always take the extra effort to identify the memory that could be pageable and specify the paged pool type when requesting memory from the Virtual Memory Manager.

Nonpaged memory is a limited resource available to the entire system. Though the amount of memory reserved for nonpaged pool depends upon the type of system used (and the amount of physical memory available on the system), it is definitely something to be conservatively used.†

The following support routines are provided by the Windows NT Executive to kernel-mode drivers for allocating memory:

- `ExAllocatePool()`
- `ExAllocatePoolWithQuota()`
- `ExAllocatePoolWithTag()`
- `ExAllocatePoolWithQuotaTag()`

---

* See Chapter 5 for a detailed discussion on page fault handling performed by the Windows NT Virtual Memory Manager. This chapter also further explains why kernel-mode drivers must not incur page faults at high IRQ levels.

† The NT Virtual Memory Manager uses a private algorithm to determine the total amount of nonpaged pool reserved on a node. This algorithm uses the total amount of physical memory on the system as the determining factor to compute the amount of nonpaged pool. The Virtual Memory Manager also attempts to increase the amount of nonpaged pool (if required) up to a precomputed maximum value. Finally, although the initially allocated nonpaged pool is contiguous, it tends to get fragmented, and the Virtual Memory Manager makes no attempts to ensure that the pool stays contiguous when expanding it.

Note that all of the pool allocation support routines are nonblocking in Windows NT. In other words, the memory allocation function invoked will return memory if it is currently available; otherwise, the functions will return NULL (indicating that memory could not be allocated). On many other operating system platforms (e.g., many UNIX derivatives), kernel-mode components are allowed to specify whether the memory allocation function should block (wait) for memory to become available, or return failure immediately.

Whenever your driver invokes one of these functions to request memory, it must specify the type of memory required:

NonPagedPool

> The pool allocation package will return either a pointer to nonpageable memory or NULL.

PagedPool

> Always specify this type if your application can handle a page fault when accessing the allocated memory. Never allocate paged memory if you have any synchronization structures (described in the next chapter) contained within the allocated memory.

NonPagedPoolMustSucceed

> If all else fails and you simply must get memory immediately, use this pool type. Note that the memory reserved for this type is an extremely scarce resource. It may be as low as 16KB on a system, though the amount is variable. If you request pool of this type (and only do that if you failed to get memory any other way), and if the Virtual Memory Manager cannot provide you with the requested memory, it will bugcheck the system (described later in this chapter) with an error code of MUST_SUCCEED_POOL_EMPTY.

NonPagedPoolCacheAligned

> This allocates nonpaged memory that is aligned on a CPU-specific boundary, determined by the data cache line size. Note that this option defaults to the NonPagedPool allocation type on Intel platforms.

PagedPoolCacheAligned

> A request to allocate pageable memory aligned along the CPU data cache line size.

NonPagedPoolCacheAlignedMustSucceed

> Once again, use this option to request nonpaged memory only as a last resort.

The pool allocation package initializes several lists, each containing blocks of a certain fixed size. Whenever you request memory using one of the ExAllocate-Pool() functions listed above, the support routine will try to allocate a fixed-size block that is closest in size (greater than or equal to) the requested amount.

If your request exceeds a page, however, or if the requested amount exceeds the size of the largest-size block in the various lists, or if there is no available block of the appropriate size in the preallocated lists, the Virtual Memory Manager will allocate the requested amount from any available system memory of the appropriate type.

NOTE   When the lists of preallocated blocks are empty, the Virtual Memory Manager will allocate at least one page of memory, split it up, and put any remaining amount (after returning the requested amount of memory to the caller) on the appropriate block list.

Unfortunately, however, for requests for nonpaged pool where the requested amount is greater than `PAGE_SIZE`, the pool allocation support routine will not attempt to split up any unused amount. This wastes precious nonpaged memory, another reason why you should be extremely conservative in your requests for this type of memory.

If there is simply no memory available of the requested type, the Virtual Memory Manager will return NULL to the caller or bugcheck* if you request memory from the must-succeed pool.

It is also possible for your driver to use one of `MmAllocateNonCached-Memory()` or `MmAllocateContiguousMemory()`† to request nonpaged, or physically contiguous, memory, respectively. These routines are not typically used by file system or filter drivers, which use either the Executive pool routines or other constructs, such as zones or lookaside lists (described below), for memory management.

Using zones

Kernel-mode drivers can fragment the physical memory available to the system if they repeatedly allocate and free small amounts of memory (less than 1 `PAGE_SIZE`). This can cause all sorts of problems for the rest of the system, including degradation of system performance.

---

* To bugcheck the system is to bring down (halt) the system in a controlled manner. Typically, the `Ke-BugCheck()` function is used, which will bring down the system while displaying the bugcheck code and possibly more information on the reason for the bugcheck operation. You should bugcheck a system only when your driver discovers an unrecoverable inconsistency that will corrupt the system.

† The contiguous memory is allocated from the list of nonpaged memory pages reserved at system initialization time. Note that there is no way to ensure that the system will have the amount of contiguous memory requested, because the nonpaged pool tends to become fragmented due to expansion and usage. The only advice typically given to kernel-mode driver designers that develop drivers requiring contiguous nonpaged memory is to load the memory early in the system boot cycle and to retain the contiguous memory given to the driver by the Virtual Memory Manager.

One way you can avoid this situation of fragmenting system memory is by preallocating a reasonably sized chunk of memory and then doing some of your own
memory management, allocating and freeing smaller-sized blocks from this preallocated chunk as necessary. This method avoids system fragmentation, because
the Virtual Memory Manager is usually out of the picture once you have preallocated your fixed-sized chunk. You only need to go back to the Virtual Memory
Manager when you run out of memory in your chunk and need to expand its size.

To help you incorporate this method of memory management into your driver,
the Windows NT Executive provides a set of support utilities. These functions
work on a *zone*, for which your driver must have preallocated memory. Another
requirement is that the size of each block that can be allocated from the zone is
fixed at the time of zone initialization. Therefore, if you have a fixed-size data
structure that is smaller than the size of one page, and if you know that you will
be repeatedly allocating and freeing memory for structures of this type, you
should seriously consider using the zone method (or the lookaside list discussed
later) to perform the memory allocation and deallocation.

Note that the method used here requires your driver to retain a preallocated piece
of memory. The trade-off is a possible waste of kernel memory, since you would
typically allocate the chunk at driver-initialization time (especially when your
driver does not require the memory for a long time), against the possibility of fragmenting the kernel pool of available pages.

Here is the sequence of operations you must follow to use the zones method:

1. Determine the size of the memory chunk you are likely to need.

   Be careful not to allocate either too much or too little memory for the zone.
   Allocating too much memory is simply being wasteful, and allocating too little
   will result in having to allocate more, leading to memory fragmentation, something you wish to avoid.

TIP   Determining the optimal amount of memory that should be prealло-
               cated for a zone is often an iterative task. However, as a general
               rule, you should be conservative with the amount of memory re-
               served for a zone. If you allocate too little memory, under most cir-
               cumstances the worst-case scenario will be that your driver has to
               go back to the VMM for more memory at run-time. If you allocate
               too much memory (more than you will ever use), you will have ef-
               fectively denied access to the excess memory to all components in
               the system and could thereby even cause some components to fail.

---

2. Allocate the zone using one of the `ExAllocatePool()` routines listed
   previously.

You have a choice of allocating from nonpaged or paged pool. Note that the base address of your piece of memory must be aligned on a 8-byte boundary (i.e., the base address should be a multiple of 8).

3. Allocate and initialize a spin lock or use some other synchronization mechanism to protect modifications to the list.

   Synchronization structures, including Executive spin locks, are discussed extensively in the next chapter.

4. Define a structure of type `ZONE_HEADER` somewhere in global memory (or in a driver object extension).

   Driver object extensions are discussed in Chapter 4. The `ZONE_HEADER` structure serves as a control structure for the zone, used by the zone management support routines to allocate and free entries from the zone.

5. Invoke `ExInitializeZone()` to initialize the zone header.

   You will also have to pass in (as arguments to the routine) a pointer to the zone you allocated in Step 2 and the size of the structures that you expect to allocate from the zone. The size of the structures you expect to allocate must be aligned on a 8-byte boundary.

   Also note that a `ZONE_SEGMENT_HEADER`-sized block of memory from the chunk of memory you supply will be used by the zone manipulation routines to maintain some additional control information. The rest of the preallocated memory will be carved out into the fixed-size blocks (of the size specified by you) for use by your driver.

Now the zone is ready for use by your driver. Whenever you need a new structure from the zone, use either the `ExAllocateFromZone()` or the `ExInterlockedAllocateFromZone()` functions. The only difference between these two functions is that the interlocked version accepts a pointer to the Executive spin lock structure that you previously initialized, and will automatically guarantee list consistency by using the spin lock to provide synchronization. If you decide to use the noninterlocked version instead, you are responsible for ensuring that the list does not get corrupted due to concurrent access and modification by multiple threads. Therefore, you must use some appropriate synchronization method in your driver.

To return a previously allocated structure to a zone, use either the `ExFreeToZone()` or the `ExInterlockedFreeToZone()` support routines provided.

Do not use the zone manipulation routines at an IRQL greater than `DISPATCH_LEVEL`, because you will not be able to use the synchronization structures (spin locks or another) at a higher IRQL.

In the event that you do need to extend the size of a zone, you must use the `ExExtendZone()` function provided. Once again, you must pass a newly allocated chunk of memory that will be used to extend the zone. Remember that the base address of this memory must also be aligned along a 8-byte boundary.

Unfortunately, there is no routine provided that decreases the size of a previously extended zone. Therefore, any chunk allocated and used when you initialize or extend the zone will be unavailable to the rest of the system until the machine is rebooted. This places the responsibility on your driver to ensure that you are fairly accurate in your estimates of how much memory should be reserved for the zone.

The file system example code provided in Part 3 uses zones for memory management. Examine the source code for the sample file system driver on the accompanying diskette for examples of using this method in your driver.

Using lookaside lists

Although using zones helps to reduce fragmentation of system memory, there are some disadvantages you must be aware of when you use zones.

- Your driver must preallocate the memory for the zone, usually at driver initialization time, even though this memory may not be used until much later.

- You must be fairly accurate about your memory requirements; you cannot release any excess memory that you may have allocated during peak driver utilization.

  When you design and use your driver, you will see that there are periods when your driver is simply overwhelmed with requests. At such times, naturally, your memory requirements will increase. If you use zones, there is a distinct probability that your zone will get depleted at such times. Then, you must either allocate memory directly from the system or extend the zone.

  Extending the zone means that the newly allocated memory cannot be released until a system reboot—not a very appealing prospect. Allocating directly from the system means that you have to maintain some sort of flag in your allocated structure indicating where the memory came from so that you could release it appropriately (either back to the zone if it came from the zone, or back to the system if you allocated using a direct invocation to an `ExAllocatePool()` routine).

- You must use either some private synchronization mechanism or, more typically, a spin lock to synchronize access to the zone.

The lookaside list is a new structure defined in Windows NT 4.0, and with the associated support routines, it addresses the limitations of the zone method.

When you invoke the `ExInitializeNPagedLookasideList()` or the `ExInitializePagedlookasideList()` functions to initialize the list, no memory is preallocated. Instead, entries are allocated on an as-needed basis when you actually require the memory. Although your driver is free to supply pointers to your driver-specific *allocate* and *free* functions when initializing the list header, this is optional and the Windows NT Executive pool management package will use the `ExAllocatePoolWithTag()` function (and the corresponding free routine) by default.

Second, you are required to specify a *list depth* at initialization time. This depth specifies the maximum number of entries of the desired size that will be queued on the list. Note that the list becomes populated with available entries as you allocate and then subsequently free the memory.

Therefore, when you start requiring memory and the package begins allocating some on your behalf, any freed entries will not be given back to the system but will instead be queued onto the list head until the *depth* number of entries have been queued. Any entries allocated and released beyond this value will automatically be returned to the system.

This allows your driver to increase your memory consumption during peak usage periods without having either to retain the memory until the next boot cycle or maintain the state information (using flags) in your allocated structures to determine where to return the memory when you release it.

Finally, on architectures that provide Windows NT with the appropriate instruction support, the `ExAllocateFromNPagedLookasideList()` (or the `ExAllocateFromPagedLookasideList()`) function and the corresponding release functions will use an atomic 8-byte compare-exchange operation to synchronize access to the list instead of using the `FAST_MUTEX` or `KSPIN_LOCK` (described in the next chapter) associated with the list. This is a considerably more efficient method of synchronization.

Remember to always allocate the `NPAGED_LOOKASIDE_LIST` list header or the `PAGED_LOOKASIDE_LIST` list header from nonpaged memory.

Available kernel stack

Each thread executing on the Windows NT platform has both a user stack, used when the thread is executing in user mode, and a kernel stack, used only when the thread is executing in kernel mode.

Whenever a thread requests system services causing a switch to kernel mode, the *trap* mechanism always switches stacks and replaces the user-space stack with the kernel-space stack allocated for the thread. This kernel stack is of fixed size and is therefore a limited resource. On Windows NT 3.51 and earlier, the kernel stack was limited to two pages of memory; therefore, on Intel architectures, each thread was restricted to an 8KB kernel stack. Beginning with Windows NT 4.0, the kernel stack size has been increased to 12KB. However, this is not sufficient in itself for your driver to be extravagant in its use of available stack space.

There is a lot of recursive behavior exhibited by the higher level drivers in Windows NT, especially with the file system drivers, the NT Virtual Memory Manager, and the NT Cache Manager. This can lead to situations where the kernel stack gets depleted rather rapidly. Furthermore, the highly layered model of drivers within the I/O subsystem can cause the kernel stack to be depleted if the driver hierarchy becomes too deep and if one or more drivers in the hierarchy are not careful about their stack usage.

Be warned that the kernel stack cannot be increased dynamically. Therefore, always be prudent in your usage of local variables that reside on the stack. If you develop a filter driver that inserts itself into a driver hierarchy, be extremely frugal with your usage of the stack space, because you may inadvertently push the stack consumption beyond the limit and bring down the system unexpectedly.

Working with Unicode Strings

All character strings are represented internally by the Windows NT operating system as Unicode (16-bit wide) characters (also called *wide characters*). This allows the system to more easily accommodate and work with languages not based on the Latin alphabet.

When you design your driver, be prepared to receive strings in Unicode and to be able to manipulate such strings. Each Unicode string is represented using the UNICODE_STRING structure defined by the system. This structure consists of the following fields:

Length
> This is the length of the string in bytes (not characters). It does not include the terminating NULL character if the string is null-terminated.

MaximumLength
> This is the actual length of the buffer in bytes. Note that it is possible to have a maximum length that is much greater than the Length field.

Buffer
> The is a pointer to the actual wide-character string constant. Wide-character strings do not necessarily have to be null terminated since the Length field above describes the number of valid bytes contained in the string.
>
> Any string you wish to store in the associated Buffer must have a length (in bytes) that is less than or equal to the MaximumLength.

NOTE   To use a null-terminated wide-character string in a UNICODE_STRING structure, initialize the Length field to the number of bytes contained in the wide-character string constant, excluding the UNICODE_NULL character; initialize the MaximumLength field to the size of the string constant (this should include the entire buffer including the space allocated for the UNICODE_NULL character).

There are a variety of support routines provided to facilitate manipulation of Unicode strings. The DDK header files contain the function declarations:

RtlInitUnicodeString

This function initializes a counted Unicode string. You can either pass in an optional wide-character null-terminated source string or NULL. The target Unicode string Buffer will either be initialized to point to the Buffer field in the null-terminated source string (if supplied) or will be initialized to NULL. The Length and MaximumLength fields will be appropriately initialized.*

RtlAnsiStringToUnicodeString

Given a source ANSI string, this routine will convert the string to Unicode and initialize the contents of the target string to contain the converted character string. You can either request the routine to allocate memory for the target wide-character string or supply the memory yourself by initializing Maximum-Length in the target Unicode string structure to the length of your passed-in buffer. If you do request that the routine allocate memory for you, then remember to free the memory by invoking the RtlFreeUnicodeString() function (see below).

RtlUnicodeStringToAnsiString

This routine converts a source Unicode string to a target ANSI string.

RtlCompareUnicodeString

A case-sensitive or case-insensitive comparison of two Unicode strings is performed. This function returns 0 if the strings are equal, a value less than 0 if the first Unicode string is less than the second one, and a value greater than 0 if the first Unicode string is greater than the second.

RtlEqualUnicodeString

This function performs either a case-sensitive or a case-insensitive comparison of two Unicode strings. TRUE is returned if the strings are equal and FALSE otherwise.

---

* If a source wide-character string constant is supplied, the Length of the target string will be set to the number of non-null characters in the source string multiplied by sizeof(WCHAR). The Maximum-Length field will be initialized to the value contained in the Length field + sizeof(UNICODE_NULL).

RtlPrefixUnicodeString

This function is defined as follows:

```
BOOLEAN
RtlPrefixUnicodeString(
    IN PUNICODE_STRING      String1,
    IN PUNICODE_STRING      String2,
    IN BOOLEAN              CaseInSensitive
)
```

This function will return TRUE if `String1` is a prefix of the counted string `String2`. If both strings are equal, this function will return TRUE.

RtlUpcaseUnicodeString

This function converts a copy of the source string into upper case Unicode characters and writes out the resulting string into the target string argument. It will also allocate memory for the target string if you request it to; otherwise you must pass in a target string with memory already allocated.

Use the `RtlFreeUnicodeString()` function to free the memory allocated for you by this function.

RtlDowncaseUnicodeString

This routine performs the converse of the `RtlUpcaseUnicodeString()` function above.

RtlCopyUnicodeString

A copy of the source Unicode string is put into the target string. As many Unicode characters as possible will be copied, given the `MaximumLength` field of the target string. The caller is always responsible for preallocating memory for the target of the copy operation.

RtlAppendUnicodeStringToString

This function will concatenate two Unicode strings. If the contents of the `Length` field in the target plus the `Length` of the source is greater than the value contained in the `MaximumLength` field in the target, the function will return STATUS_BUFFER_TOO_SMALL.

RtlAppendUnicodeToString

This is similar to the `RtlAppendUnicodeStringToString()` function except that the source Unicode string is simply a wide-character string instead of a buffered Unicode string.

RtlFreeUnicodeString

Any memory allocated by a previous invocation to `RtlAnsiStringToUnicodeString()` or `RtlUpcaseUnicodeString()` is released.

Declaring a wide-character (16-bit character set) string constant is a simple matter of appending an L before the string constant. For example, the ANSI string constant `"This is a string"` could easily be declared as a wide-character string as L"This is a string". The size of each character comprising a wide-character string is computed as sizeof(WCHAR). The wide-character string constant can then be used to create a UNICODE_STRING structure by initializing the Buffer field to point to the wide-character string constant and initializing the Length and MaximumLength fields appropriately.

Be careful not to treat Unicode characters as if they were simple ANSI. For example, you cannot assume that there is any kind of relationship between upper- and lowercase Unicode characters. Therefore, some of your assumptions (including allocating a fixed-sized table to contain the character set) will no longer be valid with respect to Unicode strings.

Linked-List Manipulation

Most drivers need to link together internal data structures, or create driver-specific queues. Typically, you will use linked lists to perform such functionality. The Windows NT Executive provides system-defined data structures and support functions for manipulating linked lists.

There are three types of linked list support functions and structures defined by the Windows NT DDK:

Singly linked lists

> The DDK provides a predefined structure to use to create your own singly linked lists. The structure is defined as follows:

```
typedef struct _SINGLE_LIST_ENTRY {
    struct _SINGLE_LIST_ENTRY    *Next;
} SINGLE_LIST_ENTRY, *PSINGLE_LIST_ENTRY;
```

> You should declare a variable of this type to serve as the list anchor. Initialize the Next field to NULL in the list anchor before attempting to use it. For example, you can have a field either in your driver extension structure or in global memory associated with the driver that is declared as follows:

```
SINGLE_LIST_ENTRY       PrivateListHead;
```

> Each structure that you wish to link together using this list entry type should also contain a field of type SINGLE_LIST_ENTRY. For example, if you wish to queue structures of type SFsdPrivateDataStructure, you would define the data structure as follows:

```
typedef SFsdPrivateDataStructure {
    // Define all sorts of fields...
    SINGLE_LIST_ENTRY       NextPrivateStructure;
    // All sorts of other fields...
}
```

Now, whenever you wish to queue an instance of the **SFsdPrivateData-Structure** onto a linked list, use either of the following routines:

— **PushEntryList()**

This function takes two arguments: a pointer to the list anchor for the linked list and a pointer to the field of type **SINGLE_LIST_ENTRY** in your data structure that you wish to queue. Therefore, if you have a variable called **SFsdAPrivateStructure** of type **SFsdPrivateData-Structure**, you can invoke this routine as follows:

```
PushEntryList(&PrivateListHead,
             &(SFsdAPrivateStructure.NextPrivateStructure));
```

You must ensure that this invocation is protected by some sort of internal synchronization mechanism that your driver uses.

— **ExInterlockedPushEntryList()**

The only difference between this function call and the **PushEntry-List()** function is that you must supply a pointer to an initialized variable of type **KSPIN_LOCK** when you invoke this function. Synchronization is automatically provided by the **ExInterlockedPushEntryList()** function via the spin lock that you provide.

Note that you must ensure that all of the list entry structures you pass in to the **ExInterlockedPushEntryList()** have been allocated from nonpaged pool, because the system cannot take a page fault once a spin lock has been acquired.

Corresponding routines that unlink the first entry from the list are the **PopEntryList()** and the **ExInterlockedPopEntryList()** functions.

Doubly linked lists

The following structure type is predefined by the Windows NT operating system for supporting doubly linked lists:

```
typedef struct _LIST_ENTRY {
    struct _LIST_ENTRY * volatile Flink;
    struct _LIST_ENTRY * volatile Blink;
} LIST_ENTRY, *PLIST_ENTRY, *RESTRICTED_POINTER PRLIST_ENTRY;
```

Just as in the case of singly linked lists, you must define a variable of type **LIST_ENTRY** to serve as your list anchor. You should use the **Initialize-ListHead(&SFsdListAnchorOfTypeListEntry)** macro to initialize the forward and backward pointers in the list anchor variable. Note that the forward and backward pointers are initialized to point to the list anchor; therefore, never expect to get a NULL list entry pointer when you traverse the list (the doubly linked list is organized as a circular list).

If you wish to link together structures of a particular type, ensure that a field of type `LIST_ENTRY` is associated with (typically contained in) the structure definition. For example, you can define a structure called `SFsdPrivate-DataStructure` as follows:

```
typedef SFsdPrivateDataStructure {
    // Define all sorts of fields...
    LIST_ENTRY        NextPrivateStructure;
    // All sorts of other fields...
}
```

To queue an instance of a structure of type `SFsdPrivateDataStructure`, you can now use the following macros/functions:

— `InsertHeadList()`

  This macro takes as arguments a pointer to the list anchor (which must have been initialized using `InitializeListHead()` described above) and a pointer to the field of type `LIST_ENTRY` in the structure to be queued, and inserts the entry at the head of the list.

  For example, you can invoke this macro, as shown here, to queue an instance called `SFsdAPrivateStructure` of the `SFsdPrivateData-Structure` structure type:

```
InsertHeadList(&SFsdListAnchorOfTypeListEntry,
           &(SFsdAPrivateStructure.NextPrivateStructure));
```

— `InsertTailList()`

  Similar to the `InsertHeadList` described above except that it inserts the entry at the tail of the list.

— `RemoveHeadList()` or `RemoveTailList()`

  These macros simply require a pointer to the list anchor. The former will return a pointer to the entry removed from the head of the list and the latter will return a pointer to the entry removed from the tail of the list.

— `RemoveEntryList()`

  This macro takes as an argument a pointer to the `LIST_ENTRY` field in the structure to be removed.

There are interlocked versions (written as functions) of the macros described above. These functions take as an additional argument a pointer to an initialized variable of type `KSPIN_LOCK`, which is used to synchronize access to the list. The list entries must always be allocated from non-paged pool if you wish to use the interlocked functions to manipulate the linked list.

You should use the `IsListEmpty()` macro to determine whether a doubly linked list is empty. This macro returns TRUE if the `Flink` and `Blink` fields in the list anchor structure both point to the list anchor. Otherwise, the macro returns FALSE.

S-Lists

This is a new structure introduced in Windows NT 4.0 to support interlocked, singly linked lists efficiently. To use this structure, you should define a list anchor of the following type:

```
typedef union _SLIST_HEADER {
    ULONGLONG Alignment;
    struct {
        SINGLE_LIST_ENTRY  Next;
        USHORT             Depth;
        USHORT             Sequence;
    };
} SLIST_HEADER, *PSLIST_HEADER;
```

The `ExInitializeSListHead()` function can be used to initialize a S-List linked list anchor. Your driver must supply a pointer to the list anchor structure when invoking this function. Ensure that the list anchor is allocated from nonpaged pool. Furthermore, you should allocate and initialize a spin lock to be used when you add or remove entries from the list.

The `ExInterlockedPushEntrySList()` and the `ExInterlockedPop-EntrySList()` functions that are provided to add and remove list entries may not use the spin lock but may instead try to use an 8-byte atomic compare-exchange instruction on those architectures that support it.

All entries for the S-List linked list must be allocated from nonpaged pool.

You can also use the `ExQueryDepthSListHead()` to determine the number of entries currently on the list. This is convenient, since you no longer have to maintain a separate count of the number of entries (as you might have to if you use an anchor of type `SINGLE_LIST_ENTRY` structure instead).

Using the CONTAINING_RECORD macro

The Windows NT DDK provides the following macro, which is very useful to all kernel-mode driver developers:

```
#define CONTAINING_RECORD(address, type, field)     \
    ((type*)((PCHAR)(address) - (PCHAR)(&((type *)0)->field)))
```

This macro can be used to get the base address of any in-memory structure, as long as you know the address of the field contained in the structure. The macro definition is quite simple: your driver supplies the address to a field in the structure, the structure type, and the field name; the macro will compute the *field offset* (in bytes) for the supplied field in the structure and subtract the computed offset number of bytes from the supplied field pointer address to get the base address of the structure itself.

The CONTAINING_RECORD macro allows you the flexibility to place fields of type LIST_ENTRY and SINGLE_LIST_ENTRY anywhere in the containing data structure. You can use this macro whenever you need to determine the address of an in-memory data structure, if you know the address of a field contained in the structure.

As an example of how the CONTAINING_RECORD macro can be used by your driver, consider the following structure defined by a kernel-mode file system driver:

```
typedef struct _SFsdFileControlBlock {
    // Some fields that will be expanded upon later in this book.
    ...
    // To be able to access all open file(s) for a volume, we will
    // link all FCB structures for a logical volume together
    LIST_ENTRY                      NextFCB;
    ...
} SFsdFCB, *PtrSFsdFCB;

LIST_ENTRY              SFsdAllLinkedFCBs;
```

The interesting field in the SFsdFCB structure is the NextFCB field. This field is of type LIST_ENTRY and will presumably be used to insert FCB structures onto a doubly linked list. The global variable SFsdAllLinkedFCBs is used to serve as the list anchor.

The interesting point to note is that the NextFCB field is *not* the first field in the SFsdFCB structure.[*] Rather, it is somewhere in the middle of the structure definition. However, given the address of the NextFCB field, the CONTAINING_ RECORD macro is used to determine the address of the FCB structure itself. The following code fragment traverses and processes all FCB structures that are linked to the SFsdAllLinkedFCBs global variable:[†]

```
LIST_ENTRY         TmpListEntryPtr = NULL;
PtrSFsdFCB         PtrFCB = NULL;

TmpListEntryPtr = SFsdAllLinkedFCBs.Flink;
while (TmpListEntryPtr != &SFsdAllLinkedFCBs) {
    PtrFCB = CONTAINING_RECORD(TmpListEntryPtr, SFsdFCB, NextFCB);
    // Process the FCB now.
    ...;
    // Get a pointer to the next list entry.
```

---

[*] A common method of manipulating linked lists of structures is to place link pointers at the head of the structure and to cast the link pointer to the structure type when following pointers in the linked list.

[†] I have deliberately omitted any synchronization code to simply illustrate the use of the CONTAINING_ RECORD macro.

```
        TmpListEntryPtr = TmpListEntryPtr->Flink;
}
```

Therefore, note once again that your driver is not required to place fields of type
LIST_ENTRY and SINGLE_LIST_ENTRY at the head of the containing data
structures, as long as you use the CONTAINING_RECORD (or some equivalent)
macro to get a pointer to the base structure.

Preparing to Debug the Driver

Here are some simple points to keep in mind when designing your kernel-mode
driver:

Insert debug breakpoints

Appendix D, *Debugging Support*, describes debugging the kernel-mode driver
in greater detail. Note for now that if you have a debugger attached to your
target machine, you can insert the DbgBreakPoint() function call in your
code to break into the debugger when certain conditions occur.

Be careful to place appropriate #ifdef statements around your debug breakpoint statements so you can easily disable the break statements in a
nondebug build of the driver. Here's a method I've used:

```
#if DBG
#define    SFsdBreakPoint()         DbgBreakPoint()
#else
#define    SFsdBreakPoint()
#endif
```

The DBG variable has a value of 1 when you compile your driver using a
checked build environment. In this case, any SFsdBreakPoint() statements in your driver will be activated. The expectation is that you will only
execute the debug version of your driver during the development and test
phase and that you will always have a debug host node connected to the
target machine executing your driver. However, if you compile the driver
using the *free* (nondebug) build environment, the SFsdBreakPoint() statement will be rendered harmless.

· The Windows NT DDK also provides a KdBreakPoint() function that is
defined exactly as the SFsdBreakPoint() function described here. Therefore, you may choose to simply use KdBreakPoint() in your code and be
assured that the breakpoint will be automatically rendered harmless in a nondebug build.

Insert debug print statements

You can use the KdPrint() macro that is defined to DbgPrint() in a
debug version of the driver code. You can supply a formatted string to this
function just as you would do with a printf() function call.

The `KdPrint()` macro automatically becomes non-operational in the nondebug version of the driver executable.

Insert bugcheck (panic) calls in your driver

Never bring down the system unless you absolutely have to. And there are very few reasons indeed to bring down a live production system executing your code.* Instead, explore every alternative available if you detect inconsistencies in your code. Try to disable your driver if you can, stop processing requests, shut down the offending module, anything to avoid halting the system.

But there still might be situations (especially during development) when you may wish to bugcheck the system. There are two alternative function calls that you can invoke to bring down the system immediately in a controlled manner:

— `KeBugCheck()`

This function takes a single **unsigned long** argument (the **BugCheck-Code**), which can be the reason that you have decided to terminate system execution. Internally, `KeBugCheck()` simply invokes `KeBugCheckEx()` described below.

— `KeBugCheckEx()`

This function takes a maximum of five possible arguments. The first is the **BugCheckCode**, the remaining four are optional arguments (each of type **unsigned long**) you may supply that provide more information to the user of the system and can possibly assist in postmortem analysis of the cause for the bugcheck.

There are no restrictions mandated by the system as to what the values of these four optional arguments should be.

If there is no debugger connected to the system, the system will do the following:

— Disable all interrupts on the node.

— Ask all other nodes (in a multiprocessor system) to stop execution.

— Use `HalDisplayString()` to print a message.

The user will see the infamous blue screen of death (BSOD) on their monitor. The message

```
STOP: 0x%1X (0x%1X, 0x%1X, 0x%1X, 0x%1X)
```

---

* Some exceptions that immediately come to mind are if continuing system execution could cause system security to be compromised or would lead to user data corruption. In such situations, it is preferable to bugcheck the system rather than to continue running.

will be displayed, with the bugcheck code displayed first, followed by each of the optional arguments supplied to `KeBugCheckEx()`.

— If a message can be associated with the bugcheck code, invoke `HalDisplayString()` to print the descriptive message.

— The `KeBugCheckEx()` function will then attempt to dump the machine state.

If any of the bugcheck arguments is a valid code address, the system will try to print the name of the image file that contains the code address.

The routine prints the version of the operating system executing on the node and then attempts to display the list of the node's loaded modules. The number of loaded module names displayed depends upon the number of lines of text that can be displayed on your monitor. Finally, the function will try to dump out some of the current stack frame. The system will then stop execution.

If, however, a debugger is connected to the system, the `KeBugCheckEx()` function will display the message

```
Fatal System Error: 0x%1X (0x%1X, 0x%1X, 0x%1X, 0x%1X)
```

on your debug host node, using the `DbgPrint()` function call. Then, the system will break into the debugger using the `DbgBreakPoint()` function call. You now have the opportunity to examine the system state to determine the cause of the error. If you ask the system to continue, the code sequence described above is executed.

Windows NT Object Name Space

As described in Chapter 1, *Windows NT System Components*, the designers of Windows NT have tried hard to make it an object-based system. There is a comprehensive set of object types that are defined by the system, and each object type has appropriate methods (or functions) associated with it to allow kernel-mode components to access and modify objects of the type.

Windows NT object types include adapter objects, controller objects, process objects, thread objects, driver objects, device objects, file objects, timer objects, and so on. One such special object type is the directory object. This object is simply a container object that, in turn, contains objects of other types.

The Object Manager allows each object to have an optional name associated with it. This facilitates the sharing of objects across processes, since more than one process can potentially open the same named object of a particular type. The Object Manager therefore manages a single, global name space for a node running the Windows NT operating system.

Following in the footsteps of most modern-day commercial file system implementations, the NT Object Manager presents a hierarchical name space to the rest of the system. There is a root directory object called \ for this global name space. All named objects can be located by specifying an absolute pathname for the object starting at the root of the object name space. Note that the Object Manager allows the creation of named object directories contained within directory objects, thereby providing a multilevel tree hierarchy.

The Object Manager also supports a special object type called the symbolic link object type. A symbolic link is simply an alias for another named object.

Figure 2-7 shows a typical name space presented by the NT Object Manager:

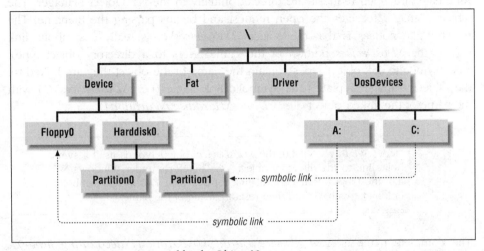

Figure 2-7. Name space presented by the Object Manager

The NT Object Manager defines object types when requested by other NT components. Certain object types are predefined by the Windows NT Object Manager. Whenever a Windows NT Executive component requests a new type to be defined by the NT Object Manager, the component has the option of providing pointers to the parse, close, and delete callback functions to be associated with all object instances of that particular type. The Object Manager remembers these function pointers and invokes the callback functions whenever a parse, close, or cleanup operation is being performed on an object instance of the particular type.

Whenever a user process or an application tries to open an object, it must supply an absolute pathname to the NT Object Manager. The Object Manager begins parsing the name, one token at a time. Whenever the Object Manager encounters an object that has a parsing callback function associated with it, the Object Manager suspends its own parsing of the name, and invokes the parsing function supplied for the object, passing it the remainder of the user-supplied pathname (the portion that has not yet been parsed).

So how is all of this relevant to file system drivers or network redirectors?

Consider what happens when a user process tries to open the file *C:\accounting\june-97.*

The user's open request is submitted to the Win32 subsystem, which translates the *C:* portion of the name to the string *\DosDevices\C:* before forwarding the request to the Windows NT Executive for further processing.* The complete name sent to the Windows NT kernel is *\DosDevices\C:\accounting\june-97.*

All create and open requests are directed initially to the NT Object Manager. The Object Manager receives the open request and begins parsing the filename. The first thing it notices is that the object *\DosDevices\C:* is really a symbolic link object (the *\DosDevices* portion of the name refers to a directory object type). Since symbolic link object types contain the name of the object they are linked to, the Object Manager replaces the symbolic link name (i.e., *\DosDevices\C:*) with the name of the linked object (i.e., *\Device\Harddisk0\Partition1*).

NOTE   Under Windows NT 4.0, the *\DosDevices* object type is itself a symbolic link to the directory object *\??*. Therefore, under Windows NT 4.0, the Object Manager will first replace the *\DosDevices* symbolic link name with *\??* and then restart parsing of the name.

The complete name is now *\Device\Harddisk0\Partition1\accounting\june-97.* Once the Object Manager has performed the name replacement, it begins the parsing of the pathname once again, beginning at the root of the object name, space. The object name space, including the portion managed by the file system is illustrated in Figure 2-8.

Now, the Object Manager traverses the global object name space until it encounters the *Partition1* device object. This is a device object type defined by the Windows NT I/O Manager. The I/O Manager also supplies a parsing routine when creating this object type. Therefore, the Object Manager stops any further parsing of the pathname and instead forwards the open request to the Windows

---

* Note that the *C:* drive letter name is simply a shortcut provided by the Win32 subsystem to the *\DosDevices\C:* symbolic link object type in the Windows NT object name space. Therefore, the Win32 subsystem is responsible for expanding the name before forwarding the request to the Windows NT Executive. This is also the reason why you cannot use the *C:\. . .* pathname if you try to open or create a filename from within the NT Executive (for example, from within your driver). You must instead use the Windows NT Object Manager recognizable pathname, beginning at the root of the Object Manager name space.

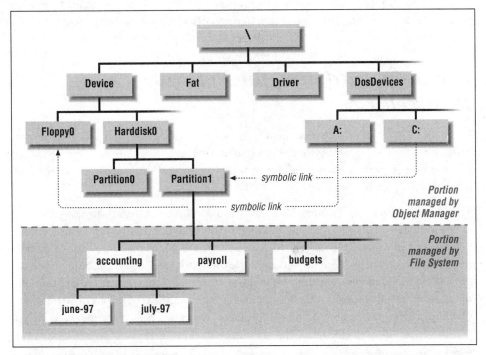

Figure 2-8. Object name space

NT I/O Manager's parsing routine. The string passed to the Windows NT I/O Manager is that portion of the pathname that has not yet been parsed by the Object Manager, namely *\accounting\june-97*. When invoking the parsing routine, the Object Manager also passes a pointer to the *Partition1* device object to the NT I/O Manager.

The Windows NT I/O Manager now executes a reasonably complicated sequence of instructions to perform the open operation on behalf of the caller. This sequence is described in considerable detail in subsequent chapters. For now, you should note that the I/O Manager will typically identify the file system driver that is currently managing the mounted logical volume for the physical disk represented by *Partition1*, the named device object. Once it has identified the appropriate file system driver, the I/O Manager will simply forward the open request to the file system driver's create/open dispatch routine.

Now, it is the responsibility of the file system driver to process the user request. Note that the filename passed to the file system driver is the portion that was not parsed by the NT Object Manager: *\accounting\june-97*.

This is how user open/create requests end up in a file system driver. Understanding the sequence of operations that lead to the invoking of the file system create/open dispatch entry point will be quite valuable when we begin to explore the implementation of the file system create/open dispatch entry point and the file system mount logical volume implementation in greater detail.

Filename Handling for Network Redirectors

Earlier in this chapter, we saw how a network redirector is a kernel-mode software module that presents a file system interface to local users, but in reality communicates with server modules on remote nodes to obtain data from the remote shared logical volumes.

The Multiple Provider Router (MPR) and the Multiple Universal Naming Convention Provider (MUP) modules interact with the network redirector to present the appearance of a local file system to the user on the client machine. These components, in conjunction with a kernel-mode network redirector module, have the responsibility of integrating the name space of the remote (shared) logical volume file system into the local name space on the client node. Therefore, to design and develop a network redirector module for the Windows NT operating system, you will have to understand both of these components fairly well.

Multiple Provider Router (MPR)

The MPR module is a user-mode DLL executing on client nodes. It serves as a buffer between the common application utilities that are network-aware and the multiple network providers that may execute on the client node.

NOTE   A network provider is a software module designed to work in close cooperation with the network redirector. The network provider serves as a sort of interface to the rest of the system, allowing network-aware applications to request some common functionality from the network redirector in a standard fashion, without having to develop code specific to each type of redirector that may be installed on the client node.

You may be wondering how there can be multiple network redirectors on a single client node. Having multiple redirectors installed and running on a client node is not really an unusual condition if you stop to think about it. The Windows NT operating system ships with the LAN Manager Redirector that is supplied with the operating system itself. In addition, there are commercially available implementations of the Network File System (NFS) protocol as well as the

Distributed File System (DFS) protocol that are also implemented as network redirectors. Then, think about all of the third-party developers like yourself who design and implement a network file system, and you could easily end up with a situation where a client node will have more than one network redirector installed.

So what exactly does the MPR do? Consider the **net** command that is available on your Windows NT client node. This command allows the user to create a new connection to a shared, remote network drive. Furthermore, it allows the user to obtain information about the connection to the remote node, browse shared network resources on remote nodes, delete the connection when it's no longer needed, and perform other similar tasks. As the user of the network or as an application developer who wishes to interact with the multiple network redirectors that may be installed on the machine, you would prefer to interact with the network redirectors in some standard manner, without dealing with the peculiarities of any particular network.

This is exactly what the MPR attempts to facilitate. The MPR has defined two sets of routines, each belonging to a distinct, well-defined interface. There is a set of network-independent APIs that are supported by the MPR DLL and are available to all Win32 application developers who wish to request services from a network redirector/provider. Similarly, there is another set of provider APIs that are invoked by the MPR DLL and must be implemented by the various network redirectors.

Therefore, a Win32 application trying to create a new network connection (for example) would invoke a standard Win32 API routine called `WNetAddConnection()` or `WNetAddConnection2()`. These functions are implemented within the MPR DLL. Upon receiving this request, the MPR DLL will invoke the `NPAddConnection()` or an equivalent routine that must be provided by each network provider DLL that has registered itself with the MPR. Once such a request is received by the network provider DLL, the network provider can determine whether it will process the request, returning the results of the operation back to the MPR for subsequent forwarding onto the original requesting process, or whether it will allow the MPR to do the work. Note that in order to process requests, the network provider DLL will often invoke the kernel-mode network redirector software using file system control requests. Chapter 11, *Writing a File System Driver III*, explains how file system control requests are processed by the file system driver (redirector).

NOTE   To register a network provider DLL with the MPR, the Registry on
           the client node must be modified. If you design and implement a
           network redirector and also decide to ship a network provider DLL
           with it, your installation program will probably perform all the ap-
           propriate modifications for you.

           Appendix B, *MPR Support*, describes the modifications that must be
           made to the Registry in order to install your network provider DLL.

The order in which the various network provider DLLs are invoked is dependent
upon the order in which the providers are listed in the Registry on the client node.

In the case of the `NPAddConnection()` request issued by the MPR to the
network provider DLL, the DLL most likely submits the request to the kernel-
mode redirector. The redirector attempts to contact the remote node specified in
the arguments to the request, tries to locate the shared resource on the remote
node, and also tries to make the connection on behalf of the requesting process.

If the request succeeds, and if the requesting process had specified it, the
network provider DLL may also try to create a symbolic link as a drive letter (e.g.,
X:) to represent the newly created connection to the remote shared resource
object. The symbolic link may refer either to a new device object created by the
kernel-mode redirector, representing the new connection, or to the common redirector device object itself.* In either case, whenever the user's process attempts to
access the name space below the *X:* drive letter, the request will be redirected by
the I/O Manager to the network redirector in the kernel for further processing.

Consult Appendix B for a description of the functions that your network provider
must implement in order to support the common Windows NT network-aware
applications. If you implement a network provider DLL that supports the functions described, your network redirector will be able to take advantage of system-
supplied utilities, such as the `net` command to add/delete/query connections to
remote (shared) resources.

Multiple UNC Provider

The Windows NT platform also allows users to access remote (shared) resources
using the Universal Naming Convention (UNC). This convention is pretty simple

---

* The network-provided DLL typically uses the Win32 function `DefineDosDevices()` to create the
drive letter (symbolic link object type). Also note that most file systems and network redirectors create a
named device object representing the file system device or the redirector device. Often, drive letters (symbolic links) for remote shared network drives refer to the network redirector device object.

in its design: each shared remote resource can be uniquely identified by the name `\\server_name\shared_resource_name`.

There are very few restrictions on the characters that can be used in either the server name and the shared resource name. You cannot use the "\" character as part of either the server name or the shared resource name, but most other common characters are allowed. The other restriction that you must be aware of is that the total length of the UNC name (including the name of the remote server and the name of the shared resource) cannot exceed 255 characters.

So when a user tries to access a remote shared resource by using a UNC name, how does the name get resolved?

Since UNC is Win32-specific, the Win32 subsystem is always looking for UNC names specified by a user process. Upon encountering such a name, the Win32 subsystem replaces the "\\" characters with the name `\Device\UNC` and then submits the request to the Windows NT Executive.

The `\Device\UNC` object type is really a symbolic link to the object `\Device\Mup`. The MUP driver is an extremely simple kernel-mode driver module (unlike the MPR module discussed above, which resides in user space) that has been described as a resource locator and is typically loaded automatically at system boot time. It creates a device object of type `FILE_DEVICE_MULTI_UNC_PROVIDER` during the driver initialization.[*] It also implements a create/open dispatch routine that is invoked whenever a create/open request targeted to the MUP driver is received, as in the case described above.

After the open request is received by the MUP driver, the MUP sends a special input/output control (IOCTL) to each network redirector that has registered itself with the MUP, asking the redirector whether it recognizes (and is willing to claim) some subset of the caller supplied name (i.e., `\server_name\shared_resource_name\...`).

Any redirector (or even more than one) can claim a portion of the remote resource name. The redirector recognizing the name must inform the MUP about the number of characters in the name string that it recognizes as a unique, valid, remote resource identifier. The first redirector that registers itself with the MUP has a higher priority than the next one to do so, and this ordering determines which redirector gets to process the user request, if more than one redirector recognizes the remote shared resource name.

---

[*] You will read in much greater detail about creating device objects and about device objects in general later in this book.

When any one redirector recognizes the name, the MUP prepends the name of the device object for the network redirector to the pathname string, replaces the name in the file object, and returns STATUS_REPARSE to the Object Manager. This time around, the request is directed to the network redirector that claimed the name for further processing. Now the MUP is completely out of the picture and will no longer be invoked for any operations pertaining to that particular create/open request.

The only other optimization performed by the MUP is to cache the portion of the name recognized by the redirector. The next time an open request is received beginning with the same string, the MUP checks its cache to see if the name is present, and if so, directly reroutes the request to the target network redirector device object without performing the tedious polling that it had done the first time around. Names are automatically discarded from the cache after some period of inactivity (typically if 15 minutes have elapsed since the name was last used in an open operation).

To work in conjunction with the MUP, your network redirector must do two things:

- Register itself with the MUP, using a system-supplied support routine called FsRtlRegisterUncProvider(). This typically is done by your driver at initialization.

- Respond to the special device control request issued by the MUP, asking your driver to check whether it recognizes a name.

Example code fragments are provided later in this book.

The next chapter discusses how you can incorporate structured exception handling and the various synchronization primitives available under Windows NT in your driver.

3

Structured Driver Development

Writing a kernel-mode driver is not easy. Unfortunately, installing a new kernel-mode driver on your production system is sometimes even worse. Drivers that execute as part of the NT Executive could potentially crash your system and do so in a way that makes it extremely hard to identify the responsible module. Furthermore, system crashes could occur with a certain regularity, or they might occur only occasionally (typically, it seems, when you are praying hard that they do not occur because you are doing something extremely important). Worse, a kernel-mode driver could corrupt your data, and do so in such a way that by the time you discover the corruption is taking place, it is too late to recover your data.

Therefore, if you are installing a new kernel-mode driver, there are certain expectations that you would have from such a driver, such as:

- The driver should not cause data corruption. This is a fundamental responsibility for kernel-mode driver designers and developers, and unfortunately, it is the hardest characteristic to evaluate objectively.*

- The driver should not cause system crashes. The objective is to ensure that even under adverse circumstances, when externally connected devices (such as disk drives or network cards) are not functioning correctly, the drivers must manage such errors gracefully. Note that the definition of handling an error gracefully is slightly nebulous: it might mean that the driver should be able to work around the situation if possible, or it might mean that the driver should (at the very least) be able to shut itself down (i.e., not provide the

---

* Therefore, it's rare that good system administrators take new drivers and install them in production environments immediately. A wise alternative would be to try out the driver on noncritical machines and evaluate its behavior over a reasonably long period of time. Unfortunately, the trial environment will probably not be an exact duplicate of the environment on the production machines, and the system administrator still can't be certain that the driver won't corrupt data in high-load, production environments.

associated functionality), but still allow the rest of the system to continue functioning normally.

- Expanding on the preceding point, software errors present in the driver code (which inevitably occur even when exceptional care is taken by developers) should not cause the system to crash. This might seem paradoxical since *bugs*, by definition, are unexpected and hence difficult to predict and manage. However, in many cases it is possible for kernel-mode driver developers to prepare for the eventuality that software errors might creep into the code and might not all be discovered during in-house testing. If the resulting driver is implemented correctly, it is indeed possible to ensure that, in most cases, such bugs do not result in system crashes.

- The driver should be able to provide adequate status reports to the system administrator. For example, if an error condition occurs, a clear, concise description of the problem should be conveyed by the driver to the administrator, allowing the administrator to try to rectify the problem if possible, or to be aware that certain loss of functionality has either already occurred or might occur shortly. Even when the driver and its devices are functioning correctly, there might be situations in which clear, concise status reports should be provided to system administrators. Data provided by drivers during error conditions could include information on recovered errors, certain performance-related statistics, or the values of automatically tuned driver parameters. This would allow administrators to understand the behavior and limitations of the system and might also afford them the opportunity to modify the work load or to further fine-tune driver parameters based on expected usage patterns.

The responsibility of achieving the expectations of the user falls squarely upon the kernel-mode driver designers and developers. The good news, however, is that it is possible to develop software for the Windows NT platform that meets the expectations listed here; indeed, the operating system provides ample support for developers to allow them to incorporate such desired features into their drivers.

Exception Dispatching Support

An exception is an atypical event that occurs due to the execution of some instruction by a thread. Exceptions are processed synchronously in the context of the thread that caused the exception condition. Since exception conditions are synchronous events that occur as a direct result of the execution of an instruction, they can be reproduced, provided that exactly the same conditions can be regenerated and the instruction is retried. The Windows NT Kernel provides support for exception dispatching when an exception is encountered.

The following events are representative of the kinds of exception conditions that can occur when executing code:[*]

- Integer divide-by-zero
- Memory access violations
- Integer overflow
- Floating-point overflow/underflow
- Floating-point divide-by-zero
- Floating-point reserved operand
- Debugger breakpoint
- Data-type misalignment
- Illegal instruction
- Privileged instruction
- Debugger single step
- Guard page violation
- Page read error
- Paging file quota exceeded

How the OS Responds to an Exception Condition

When an *exception* occurs, the processor switches to kernel mode and transfers control to a specific trap handler (at a fixed location in the kernel) for further processing. The trap handler module is subsequently responsible for invoking an appropriate function that can handle the condition which resulted in the trap. Examples of conditions that generate traps are software or hardware interrupts, exceptions, and invocations of system service calls.

Before transferring control to an interrupt/exception handler, the trap handler module records the execution state of the interrupted thread in a structure called the *trap frame*. Any information that might be lost while processing the trap condition is recorded within the trap frame; this allows the kernel to potentially resume execution at the same instruction that caused the trap condition, once the condition has been successfully processed.

The trap handler module in the Windows NT Kernel performs the following actions:

---

[*] See *Inside Windows NT,* by Helen Custer (Microsoft Press, 1993).

1. Creates a trap frame for the thread. This trap frame contains the contents of all the volatile registers, i.e., registers with contents that might get overwritten as a result of processing the exception condition.

2. Optionally creates an exception frame, which contains the contents of other nonvolatile registers. The trap handler module always creates an exception frame when processing an exception condition.

3. Creates an exception record structure, which contains the exception code describing the exception that occurred, the exception flags, the address in the code at which the exception occurred, and any other parameters that might be associated with the specific exception condition. The only value that is currently legal for the exception flags field is EXCEPTION_NONCONTINU-ABLE, indicating that this is a fatal exception and further processing should be terminated.

   Some exceptions may have additional parameters that are supplied by the trap handler to provide more information about the exception condition. The only such exception condition that has additional parameters supplied is EXCEPTION_ACCESS_VIOLATION, which provides two associated arguments, one indicating whether it was a read or a write operation that caused the access violation, and the other is the virtual address that was inaccessible.

4. Transfers control to the Windows NT kernel exception dispatcher module.* The exception dispatcher module in the Windows NT Kernel is called KiDispatchException().

Possible Outcomes from Processing an Exception

The exception dispatcher module in the kernel determines the processor mode in which the exception condition occurred. User-mode exceptions and kernel-mode exceptions are handled slightly differently, but the basic philosophy is the same. Before we go through the steps that the exception handler undertakes in processing the exception condition, we will first discuss briefly the possible outcomes from processing an exception condition.

Each exception condition can be processed by the exception handler module in one of three ways:

• The exception handler changes one or more of the conditions that caused the problem and then directs the exception dispatcher to retry the instruction.

---

* Some exception conditions are automatically handled by the trap handler and do not require transfer of control to the exception dispatcher module. For example, debugger breakpoints are handled directly by invoking the debugger.

For example, consider an exception that indicates a page fault occurred. The exception handler will invoke the page fault handler to bring the contents of the page into system memory from some secondary storage device or from across a network. The memory access is then retried and should now succeed.

Another example is when a code segment tries to allocate some memory and subsequently tries to access it. If the original memory allocation failed, accessing a pointer to that memory block results in a memory access violation. The following example illustrates such a condition:

```
int    *SomePtr = NULL;

// allocate 4K bytes
SomePtr = ExAllocatePool(PagedPool, 4096);

// Normally, the memory allocation request will succeed and SomePtr
// will contain a valid pointer address. However, it is possible that
// the request may occasionally fail. For the sake of discussion,
// assume that in the particular instance described below, the
// memory allocation request does fail and therefore ExAllocatePool()
// returns NULL.

// Although I personally recommend always checking the value of the
// returned pointer value above, many other designers might argue
// that structured exception handling allows for more readable
// code by avoiding unnecessary, multiple, if (...) {}, kind of
// statements.

RtlZeroMemory(SomePtr, 4096);
// If SomePtr was NULL, we'll get an exception in the statement above.
```

Invoking `RtlZeroMemory()` with a NULL pointer results in the `EXCEPTION_ACCESS_VIOLATION` exception being raised. In this case, the exception handler can set the value of `SomePtr` to point to some preallocated memory and retry the instruction.

WARNING   Retrying the assembly code that corresponds to `RtlZeroMemory()` (in this case) could lead to unexpected error conditions. Unless the compiled assembly code is closely examined, you can't be sure the modification of `SomePtr` in the exception handler results in the expected behavior, e.g., the compiler might have initialized a register with the initial value of `SomePtr`, which was NULL. Now, the value contained in the register will always be reused because the instruction that was retried might be a *move memory* instruction following the one that initialized the register. This means the reinitialization of `SomePtr` in the exception handler won't take effect, and the exception condition simply reoccurs in an infinite loop. Therefore, retrying of instructions that have led to an exception condition is a tricky proposition at best.

If desired, exception handlers can return a specific return code, indicating that the instruction resulting in the exception condition should be retried. Note that the constant value is actually unimportant but the fact that such a value is returned is noteworthy.

- The exception handler decides that the exception condition is one it does not wish to process.

  If this happens, an appropriate value is returned indicating that the exception should be propagated. Therefore, the exception dispatcher will continue searching for other handlers that might wish to process this exception.

  For example, imagine that a particular exception handler can process only one type of exception condition, say EXCEPTION_ACCESS_VIOLATION. If an exception indicating data misalignment is encountered, this particular exception handler will return a value indicating that it could not process the specific exception condition and that the dispatcher should continue traversing the call frames, looking for an exception handler that is prepared to process this specific exception.

- The exception handler executes a specific block of code, which processes the exception condition and then indicates to the caller that execution should resume following the exception handler code.

  In this case, the exception handler does not retry the instruction that caused the original exception condition, but instead tries to resume execution at the instruction immediately following the exception handler code.

  This method of processing the exception condition is substantially different from simply modifying some condition and retrying the instruction as described previously. Here, the exception handler performs some processing and then wants the instruction execution to resume immediately following the exception handler code. In the case where some condition causing the exception was modified (described earlier), the exception handler wanted execution to commence at the same instruction that caused the exception condition in the first place.

It is not necessary that the exception handler reside in the same function or procedure in which the exception condition occurred. It could have been in any of the routines that comprised the calling hierarchy.

For example, consider a situation in which *procedure_A* invokes *procedure_B*, which in turn invokes *procedure_C*. Further, imagine that an exception condition (say EXCEPTION_ACCESS_VIOLATION) was encountered at an instruction in *procedure_C*. It is quite possible that neither *procedure_B* nor *procedure_C* have an exception handler that is prepared to process the exception condition.

If an exception handler resides in *procedure_A*, and if the exception handler in *procedure_A* handles the exception condition, execution flow will resume in *procedure_A* at the instruction immediately following the exception handler code. The stack frames for *procedure_C* and *procedure_B* will be automatically unwound in order to resume execution in *procedure_A*. Figure 3-1 illustrates this.

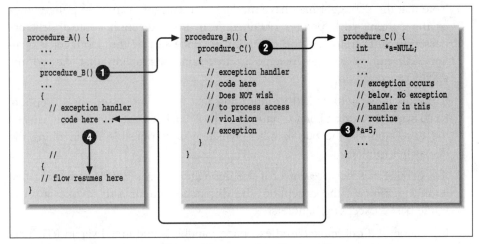

Figure 3-1. Flow of execution when an exception handler handles an exception

As you see, there are three different ways in which an exception handler might respond if called upon to process a particular exception condition.

As will be discussed later, part of unwinding the stack frames for *procedure_C* and *procedure_B* will cause any appropriate *termination handlers* to be invoked. This allows for systematic unwinding in those procedures and thereby prevents nasty side-effects such as deadlock conditions which might otherwise occur due to this unexpected transfer of flow of control from *procedure_C* to *procedure_A*.

Dispatching Kernel-Mode Exceptions

Given these different ways in which an exception handler might process an exception condition, it is useful to understand what the exception dispatcher code in the NT kernel, `KiDispatchException()`, actually does to process the exception condition. The following sequence of steps listed is executed by `KiDispatchException()` when it's invoked for an exception condition caused by a thread executing kernel-mode code:

1. First, the exception dispatcher checks to see if a debugger is active, and if so, it transfers control to the debugger.

   The debugger will indicate either that the exception has been processed by returning TRUE, or that the exception was not processed and the search for another handler should proceed.

   Note that the debugger may have modified the current instruction pointer and/ or the current stack pointer obtained from the execution context structure passed to it. Therefore, if the exception is processed by the debugger, execution will not necessarily resume at the same instruction that caused the exception condition.

   If the debugger returns TRUE, indicating that it has processed the exception, `KiDispatchException()` returns control back to the thread that caused the exception via the trap handler, which was responsible for invoking the dispatcher routine.

2. If a debugger is not present or if the debugger returns FALSE, indicating that it did not process the exception, the dispatcher attempts to invoke any call frame-based exception handlers.

   Invocation of a call frame-based exception handler is performed via an RTL function call, `RtlDispatchException()`. This routine is not typically exposed to third-party driver developers.

   The `RtlDispatchException()` function searches backward through the stack-based call frames looking for an exception handler prepared to process the exception. This search continues until either some exception handler returns a code indicating that the instruction that caused the exception condition should be retried, or the entire call hierarchy has been examined for possible appropriate exception handlers and none were found.

   Compilers for the Windows NT platform that support structured exception handling register exception handlers with the RTL, on behalf of executing threads. Unfortunately, the functions used to register and deregister exception handlers are not ordinarily exposed to third-party developers. The good news, however, is that it would be rare for a kernel-mode driver to need to access these routines directly, since the compiler typically provides structured handling support and performs the dirty work for you.

   The RTL package also provides an interface for compiler developers to register termination handlers on behalf of executing threads. Termination handlers are described later in this chapter.

3. In Step 2, a call frame-based exception handler may or may not be found.

   Even if one or more exception handlers were identified, these exception handlers might not be prepared to process the specific exception condition.

As described later in this section, structured exception handling allows you to check the type of exception condition and determine whether you wish to handle the exception in your exception handler or whether you wish to propagate the exception condition to the next possible exception handler.

If the return code from `RtlDispatchException()` is FALSE, indicating that the exception has not been processed, the exception dispatcher once again attempts to invoke any debugger that may be executing. This is called *second chance* processing and the actions undertaken at this time are the same as would be taken had a recursive exception been encountered.

If a debugger is connected, it has a final opportunity to keep the system alive. However, if no debugger is connected or if the debugger once again returns FALSE, the exception dispatcher will invoke `KeBugCheck()` and halt the entire system, resulting in the dreaded blue screen of death.

The reason for the system crash will be given as `KMODE_EXCEPTION_NOT_`
`HANDLED`. This indicates that no exception handler was found that would process the exception that occurred during kernel-mode execution. Unless extreme measures are called for, your code (if you happen to write a kernel-mode driver) should never, ever, cause such a blue screen.

Exception dispatching support, as well as support for registering call frame-based exception handlers, is provided by the Windows NT operating system and is not a function of (or dependent upon) any specific compiler. That said, you might note that unless you use a compiler that supports and uses the Windows NT exception handling model, you cannot develop code that can take advantage of the exception handling features provided by the operating system. The Microsoft C/C++ compiler provides structured exception handling support to both user-mode and kernel-mode code.

The Exception Dispatcher: User Mode Exceptions

The direct invocation of `RtlDispatchException()` by `KiDispatchException()` is done only for exceptions that occur while code is executing in kernel mode. If the exception occurs in user mode, `KiDispatchException()` performs slightly different processing.

A message is sent to the process's debug port using LPC (the local procedure call interface). If the port processes the exception, there is no further work for `KiDispatchException()`.

Consider the case, however, where the debug port for the process fails to handle the exception. Attempting to execute user-mode exception handlers in the kernel would not be a wise thing to do. At the very least, it would introduce a large security hole in the operating system. Therefore, the `KiDispatchException()`

function prepares to transfer control to a corresponding user-space exception dispatcher module.

The dispatcher function pushes the trap frame, the exception frame, and the exception record on the user space stack. Then, `KiDispatchExecution()` modifies the exception record such that, once control is returned from the exception dispatcher and the trap handler, a special user-space routine will be invoked that will further process the exception condition by invoking any user-mode exception handlers. Note that the modification performed here involves changing the instruction pointer value in the exception record to point to the user-space exception dispatcher function.

Treatment of user-mode exception handlers is similar in that the calling hierarchy is examined to see if any exception handler can be found that is prepared to process the exception. If none of the user-mode exception handlers process the exception condition, the process containing the thread that caused the exception condition is typically terminated. Termination of the user-space thread is generally done by the default exception handler, which is usually installed by the Win32 (and other) subsystems.

Now that you understand the sequence of actions that take place when an exception condition occurs, the next logical question to ask is: How do I write code that would be able to process unexpected events, such as exception conditions? Good question, and the next section provides you with one answer.

Structured Exception Handling (SEH)

The Windows NT Executive makes extensive use of structured exception handling. Each of the NT kernel-mode components tries to prepare for the eventuality that unexpected error situations might occur as a result of executing code, and these modules work hard to ensure that any unexpected error conditions do not bring down the entire system. It is extremely good practice for independent driver developers to also implement structured exception handling in their driver implementations. This results in more robust kernel-mode drivers, leading to a more stable Windows NT system, which in turn results in happier customers.

TIP As a kernel-mode driver designer, you can choose to avoid using structured exception handling in your driver. Many kernel-mode drivers do this and get away with it. However, if you develop file system drivers, I strongly urge you to use SEH in your driver, not only because it's the right thing to do, but also because some of the Windows NT Cache Manager support routines and some of the Virtual Memory Manager functions will raise exceptions, instead of returning errors under certain conditions that aren't catastrophic and shouldn't result in a system panic. The expectation is that the file system driver will handle such exceptions and treat them as regular error conditions.

If your driver uses structured exception handling, you can handle such exceptions gracefully; failure to use structured exception handling will result in an otherwise avoidable bugcheck condition.

Before we discuss what structured exception handling (SEH) is and the benefits that SEH can provide, let me tell you what structured exception handling cannot provide.

Structured exception handling is not a panacea for bad driver design or shoddy implementation. If you do not take care during driver design and development, no amount of structured exception handling is going to rectify the situation. Similarly, SEH cannot ensure that system crashes can be completely avoided; trying to access paged memory within code that executes at an IRQ level greater than or equal to IRQL `DISPATCH_LEVEL` will result in a guaranteed system crash, despite the presence of exception handlers.

Finally, SEH should become pervasive throughout the driver implementation in order to have substantial benefits from its usage. If exception handling is not implemented systematically throughout the driver code base, the implementation will still be vulnerable to unexpected error conditions in the portions of the code that are not protected by exception handlers.

Structured exception handling is a methodology by which a developer or designer can provide exception handlers that can process exception conditions, avoiding the default processing performed by `KiDispatchException()`, namely, the call to `KeBugCheck()`.

NOTE No default handler exists to catch all kernel-mode exception conditions. Therefore, if your file system or filter driver causes an exception to occur but does not provide any exception handler to process such exceptions, you will bring down the system.

Furthermore, structured exception handling allows the designer to provide a systematic method for unwinding from within a specific block of code. This systematic unwinding can help ensure that exception conditions do not result in deadlocks or hangs or other similar nasty conditions because the thread cannot perform adequate cleanup processing when trying to recover from an unexpected error condition.

SEH requires compiler support; on Windows NT, a compiler that provides support for SEH is the Microsoft C/C++ compiler.

As I mentioned earlier in this chapter, an exception condition results in control being transferred to the kernel trap handler. The trap handler might resolve certain obvious exception conditions or it may in turn transfer control to `KiDis-patchException()`, the exception dispatcher code within the NT kernel. `KiDispatchException()` in turn invokes `RtlDispatchException()` to invoke any exception handlers that the developer might have provided. Your exception handler must be registered with the run-time library for it to be invoked. This registration is performed transparently by the Microsoft C/C++ compiler, which generates appropriate code to achieve this whenever it encounters the `try-except` construct (described below) in your code. Similarly, automatic unwinding of your stack-based call frame is performed whenever an exception condition occurs and you have used the `try-finally` construct in your code. The C/C++ compiler, cooperating with the run-time library, generates appropriate code for unwinding the call frame.

Here are the two primary constructs of structured exception handling:

- The `try-except` construct allows you to create code that can handle unexpected events or exception conditions cleanly, and is defined as follows:

```
try {
    ...
    // Execute any code here.
    ...
} except ( /* call an exception filter here. */ ) {
    ...
    // Code executed only if the exception filter returns
    // a code of EXCEPTION_EXECUTE_HANDLER.
    // This code is called the exception handler code.
    // Once this code is executed, control is transferred to
    // the next instruction following the try-except construct.
    ...
}
```

  This construct consists of three parts: the `try` construct that allows you to define a block of code that is protected by your exception handler; the *exception filter* allows you to specify whether you wish to handle a specific exception condition; and the *exception handler* performs any exception condition-related processing.

- The `try-finally` construct allows you to specify a termination handler for a specific block of code. By doing so, you can ensure that correct cleanup-related processing is always performed, regardless of the method chosen to exit from the specific block of code. This construct is defined as follows:

```
try {
    ...
    // Execute any code here.
    ...
} finally {
    // Perform any cleanup here. The code within the finally
    // construct (also called the termination handler) will be
    // executed irrespective of the method chosen to exit from
    // the block of code protected by the try construct above.
}
```

The `try-finally` construct consists of two parts: the `try` construct that allows you to define a block of code that is protected by the termination handler, and the `finally` construct, which contains the code comprising the termination handler itself.

The try-except Construct

The `try-except` construct allows you to protect a block of code such that, if an exception occurs within the protected block of code, control is transferred (by the `RtlDispatchException()` routine) to your exception handler. In order for this transfer of control to take place, the compiler and the Windows NT Kernel have to cooperate.

The compiler, upon encountering a `try-except` construct, automatically inserts additional code that registers an exception handler for that particular block of code (called a frame) with the NT Kernel. As described earlier in this chapter, the kernel is then responsible for assuming control when an exception condition occurs, and subsequently, the kernel allows your exception handler to take a crack at handling the exception.

Every exception that occurs as a direct result of executing code within the frame protected by the exception handler results in an eventual transfer of control to the exception handler code, unless the exception is handled by the attached debugger. However, you may not want your exception handler to handle all possible exception conditions; therefore, you can utilize an *exception filter* to determine whether your code should handle the exception or not.

The exception filter is the portion of code that is bracketed following the **except** keyword. Note that the exception filter can be fairly complex and you can actually invoke a function called the *exception filter function* to perform any processing that is part of your exception filter. The exception filter can return one of three values:

- EXCEPTION_EXECUTE_HANDLER

- EXCEPTION_CONTINUE_SEARCH

- EXCEPTION_CONTINUE_EXECUTION

The EXCEPTION_EXECUTE_HANDLER return code value causes the exception handler to be executed. After the exception handler has completed its processing, execution flow resumes at the first instruction immediately following the exception handler. To understand this better, consider these sample routines:

```
NTSTATUS MyProcedure_A (
int             *SomeVariable)
{
    char        *APtrThatWasNotInitialized = NULL;
    int         AnotherInaneVariable = 0;
    NTSTATUS    RC = STATUS_SUCCESS;

    try {

        *SomeVariable = MyProcedure_B(APtrThatWasNotInitialized);

        // The following line is not executed if an exception occurred
        // in the procedure call.
        AnotherInaneVariable = 5;

    } except (EXCEPTION_EXECUTE_HANDLER) {
        RC = GetExceptionCode();
        DbgPrint("Exception encountered with value = 0x%x\n", RC);
    }

    // Execution flow resumes here once the exception has been handled.
    AnotherInaneVariable = 10;

    return(RC);
}

int MyProcedure_B (
char        *IHopeThisPtrWasInitialized)
{
    char        ACharThatIWillTryToReturn = 'A';

    // Exception occurs in the following line if "IHopeThisPtrWasInitialized"
    // is invalid.
    *IHopeThisPtrWasInitialized = ACharThatIWillTryToReturn;

    // The following code is never executed if an exception occurred above.
    ACharThatIWillTryToReturn = 'B';

    return(0);
}
```

As you can see in the code fragment, an exception condition will occur when `MyProcedure_B` attempts to copy a character using the input argument character pointer. Since `MyProcedure_B` does not have an exception handler, the handler in the calling function (`MyProcedure_A`) will be invoked. The exception filter in `MyProcedure_A` is trivial, it immediately returns `EXCEPTION_EXECUTE_HANDLER`. This results in the exception handler being invoked, which simply obtains the exception code (`STATUS_ACCESS_VIOLATION`) and issues a debug print call.

The interesting point to note is that execution flow (after the exception handler code has executed) resumes at the statement `AnotherInaneVariable = 10` in `MyProcedure_A`. All statements following the one that caused the exception in `MyProcedure_B` are skipped and so are any statements that follow the invocation of `MyProcedure_B` within the function `MyProcedure_A`. This resumption of execution at the instruction immediately after the exception handler code is achieved by unwinding of the stack-based call frames.

Although the exception filter was extremely trivial in the preceding example, it can potentially be quite complex. You can invoke a separate filter function to determine what you wish to do with the exception condition, but remember that the filter function must return one of the three status codes listed above. As an argument to the filter function, you can pass the exception code using the `GetExceptionCode()` intrinsic function call or you can use the `GetExceptionInformation()` intrinsic function call to pass even more information, such as the thread context represented by the contents of the processors' registers.

The `GetExceptionCode()` intrinsic function returns the exception code value;[*] this function can be invoked either within the exception filter or within the exception handler, while the `GetExceptionInformation()` intrinsic function can only be invoked within the exception filter.

Typically, your exception filter (or any filter function that you use) will not require the additional information contained in the `EXCEPTION_POINTERS` structure, returned by the `GetExceptionInformation()` function. Although it is theoretically possible to modify the contents of individual registers contained within this structure, doing so results in extremely nonportable, and probably nonmaintainable, code; I would highly discourage it.

Note that neither the `GetExceptionCode()` function call nor the `GetExceptionInformation()` call can be invoked from the exception filter function.

---

[*] It actually returns the same value that you could obtain from the `ExceptionCode` field in the `EXCEPTION_RECORD` structure defined later.

The following code fragment demonstrates the use of the exception filter function:

```
NTSTATUS MyProcedure_A (
int             *SomeVariable)
{
    char            *APtrThatWasNotInitialized = NULL;
    int             AnotherInaneVariable = 0;
    NTSTATUS        RC = STATUS_SUCCESS;

    try {

        *SomeVariable = MyProcedure_B(APtrThatWasNotInitialized);

        // The following line is not executed if an exception occurs
        // in the procedure call.
        AnotherInaneVariable = 5;

    } except (MyExceptionFilter(GetExceptionCode(),
                    GetExceptionInformation())) {
        RC = GetExceptionCode();
        DbgPrint("Exception with value = 0x%x\n", RC);
    }

    // Execution flow resumes here once the exception has been handled.
    AnotherInaneVariable = 10;

    return(RC);
}


int MyProcedure_B (
char        *IHopeThisPtrWasInitialized)
{
    char        ACharThatIWillTryToReturn = 'A';

    // Exception occurs in the next statement if the value of
    // IHopeThisPtrWasInitialized is invalid.
    *IHopeThisPtrWasInitialized = ACharThatIWillTryToReturn;

    // The following code is never executed if an exception occurred above.
    ACharThatIWillTryToReturn = 'B';

    return(0);
}


unsigned int MyExceptionFilter(
unsigned int            ExceptionCode,
PEXCEPTION_POINTERS     ExceptionPointers)
{
    // Assume we cannot handle this exception.
    unsigned int        RC = EXCEPTION_CONTINUE_SEARCH;

    //      This function is my exception filter function. It must return
    //      one of three values viz. EXCEPTION_EXECUTE_HANDLER,
    //      EXCEPTION_CONTINUE_SEARCH, or    EXCEPTION_CONTINUE_EXECUTION.
    //      In our example here, we decide to handle access violations only.
```

```
switch (ExceptionCode) {
    case STATUS_ACCESS_VIOLATION:
        RC = EXCEPTION_EXECUTE_HANDLER;
        break;
    default:
        break;
}

//    If you wish, you could further analyze the exception condition by
// examining the ExceptionPointers structure.

ASSERT((RC == EXCEPTION_EXECUTE_HANDLER) ||
        (RC == EXCEPTION_CONTINUE_SEARCH) ||
        (RC == EXCEPTION_CONTINUE_EXECUTION));

return(RC);
}
```

Exception handlers can be nested, either across procedure calls or even within the same function. Note that certain exception conditions are fatal errors (e.g., accessing paged memory that causes a page fault at an IRQL greater than or equal to `DISPATCH_LEVEL`) and will result in a system panic,* regardless of the fact that you had inserted exception handlers in your code. Therefore, as mentioned earlier in this chapter, do not assume that using exception handlers will guarantee that all error conditions can be effectively trapped.

The try-finally Construct

The `try-finally` construct represents a *termination handler* and is used to ensure consistent unwinding from within a block of code, even when exception conditions cause abrupt transfer of control to some other call frame. The concept here is very simple: consider a block of code protected within a `try-finally` construct. Before control is transferred to any instruction outside of the `try-finally` construct, statements enclosed within the `finally` portion of the construct are executed.

This simple example illustrates the point:

```
NTSTATUS MyProcedure_A (
int             *SomeVariable,
int             AnotherVariable)
{
    char            *APtrThatWasNotInitialized = NULL;
    int              AnotherInaneVariable = 0;
    int              AnotherInaneVariable2 = 0;
    NTSTATUS         RC = STATUS_SUCCESS;
```

---

* The VMM will bugcheck the system when it notices that the page fault was incurred at high IRQL.

```
    try {

        if (!AnotherVariable) {
            AnotherInaneVariable = 7;
        }

        *SomeVariable = MyProcedure_B(APtrThatWasNotInitialized,
                                            &AnotherInaneVariable);

        // The following line is not executed if an exception occurs
        // in the procedure call above.
        AnotherInaneVariable2 = 5;

    } except (MyExceptionFilter(GetExceptionCode(),
        GetExceptionInformation())) {
        // Even if an exception condition got us here, the value of
        // AnotherInaneVariable MUST be 15 since the statements within
        // the finally portion in MyProcedure_B get executed before we
        // start executing any code within the exception handler.
        ASSERT(AnotherInaneVariable == 15);
        RC = GetExceptionCode();
        DbgPrint("Exception with value = 0x%x\n", RC);
    }

    // I will assert that AnotherInaneVariable is set to 15 because the
    // assignment is within the "finally" construct in MyProcedure_B and hence
    // the assignment operation MUST have been performed.
    ASSERT(AnotherInaneVariable == 15);

    // Execution flow resumes here once the exception has been handled.
    AnotherInaneVariable = 10;

    return(RC);
}

int MyProcedure_B (
char            *IHopeThisPtrWasInitialized,
int              *AnotherInaneVariable)
{
    char        ACharThatIWillTryToReturn = 'A';

    try {

        if (*AnotherInaneVariable == 7) {
            // This is a BAD thing to do if you value system performance.
            // However, I am executing a return here to illustrate that the
            // code within the "finally" below will get executed even though
            // I am abruptly returning from this function call.
            return(1);
        }

        // Exception occurs here if IHopeThisPtrWasInitialized is invalid.
        *IHopeThisPtrWasInitialized = ACharThatIWillTryToReturn;
```

```
        // The following code is never executed if an exception occurs
        // above.
        ACharThatIWillTryToReturn = 'B';

    } finally {
        // Whatever happens above, i.e., whether a return statement was executed
        // or whether an exception condition occurred, the following code will
        // get executed. Note that if an exception did occur, the following
        // code will get executed BEFORE the code within the exception
        // handler in MyProcedure_A gets executed.
        *AnotherInaneVariable = 15;
    }

    return(0);
}
```

Code for the exception filter function **MyExceptionFilter()** was presented earlier while discussing the **try-except** construct.

There are three different ways that flow of control can be transferred out of **MyProcedure_B**:

- It is possible that the return statement within the **try-finally** construct does not get executed and no exception condition occurs.

  This would happen if, for example, **AnotherVariable** is initialized to a valid value.

  In this case, all of the statements between the **try** and the **finally** keywords will get executed; then the code within the **finally** construct that comprises the termination handler will execute and then return control to **MyProcedure_A** via the **return(0)** statement.

- Consider the case where **AnotherVariable** is set to 0. Now, the **return(1)** statement within **MyProcedure_B** will return control back to **MyProcedure_A**. However, due to the presence of the **try-finally** construct, the code within the **finally** portion will get executed before the **return(1)** statement is processed. Therefore, the value of ***Another-InaneVariable** will be set to 15.

- Now, consider the case where **AnotherVariable** is not set to 0, and **APtrThatWasNotInitialized** is set to NULL. We know that this will result in an exception condition (**STATUS_ACCESS_VIOLATION**) in **MyProcedure_B**. You are also aware that **MyProcedure_A** has an exception handler that will process this exception since the exception filter used by **MyProcedure_A** is willing to handle exceptions of this type.

  However, before the exception handler gets executed in **MyProcedure_A**, the kernel unwinds the stack-based call frames. Part of this unwinding involves execution of any statements within the termination handlers[*] that protect any of the frames comprising the calling hierarchy between `MyProcedure_A` and `MyProcedure_B`.

In our example, `MyProcedure_A` directly invokes `MyProcedure_B` and so there is only one frame to unwind from and one corresponding termination handler.

Since the affected block of code (in which the exception occurred) is protected by a termination handler, the statements within the `finally` portion will be executed before statements comprising the exception handler in `MyProcedure_A` are executed. Therefore, the value of `*AnotherInane-Variable` will be set to 15 and we have an `ASSERT` in the exception handler in `MyProcedure_A` to check for this fact.

Typically, termination handlers are not used to perform the kind of simple initialization shown in the example. Rather, termination handlers are used to ensure that any necessary cleanup is performed before transferring control to some other module. For example, if memory had been allocated for some temporary purpose, freeing of this memory can be done within the termination handler (some `BOOLEAN` variable can be checked to see if memory had indeed been allocated or the value of the pointer itself can be checked if the pointer is always guaranteed to have been initialized to NULL).

Similarly, if any locks had been acquired (e.g., some `ERESOURCE` type of resource or some `MUTEX` had been acquired), the lock can be released from within the termination handler. Therefore, the termination handler is a powerful tool that can ensure that all required cleanup is performed in a consistent fashion and is guaranteed to be done, regardless of the method used to exit from the protected module.

A word of caution

In the preceding example, I placed a `return(1)` statement in the middle of `MyProcedure_B` in a block of code protected by a termination handler. The purpose of using this `return` statement was to demonstrate that even if such statements are used to exit the protected frame, the termination handler will still be automatically executed due to the stack-based call frame unwinding that takes place. This concept applies to other C statements, such as `break` and `continue`, which cause a transfer of control to some other statement. If this transfer of

---

* It is possible to prevent call frame unwinding in certain cases by inserting a `return` statement within the termination handler. However, this could result in completely indecipherable and unmaintainable code, and I strongly urge you not to even consider such esoteric usage and implementation of termination handlers.

control is to an instruction outside of the protected frame, the termination handler will always get executed before such a transfer of control takes place.

However, if you care about the performance exhibited by your driver, you should try never to use such statements in any frame that is protected by a termination handler. The reason for this is simple: call frame unwinding is an expensive operation in terms of execution time. In fact, on some processor architectures, unwinding can result in the execution of literally hundreds of extra assembly instructions. Therefore, you should try to avoid such unwinding, unless it happens because of some exception condition.

NOTE   Exception conditions are, by definition, atypical events. Therefore, the prime consideration in dealing with an exception condition is to recover as gracefully as possible; performance considerations are secondary.

You might be concerned that avoiding the **return** statement in code that is protected by a termination handler could be very limiting. I would agree with that analysis; therefore, I will recommend that you use the following method to work around this limitation:

```
// Who says gotos are always bad ????
// Define the following macro in some global header file.
#define      try_return(S)         { (S); goto try_exit; }

NTSTATUS AnotherProcedureThatUsesATerminationHandler (void)
{
    NTSTATUS        RC = STATUS_SUCCESS;
    ...

    try {
        ...
        if (!NT_SUCCESS(RC)) {
            // Assume for example that some memory allocation failed above
            // and that normal execution cannot continue.
            // Use the try_return MACRO here instead of a simple return
            // statement.
            //  Note that any legitimate C statement can be executed as part of
            // the macro itself.
            try_return(RC);
        }
        ...

    try_exit:    NOTHING;

    } finally {
        ...
    }
    return(RC);
}
```

The `try_return` macro simply performs a jump to the end of the function (actually, it should cause a jump to the block of code just before the termination handler as illustrated in the code fragment). Additionally, it allows you to execute any legitimate C statement before the jump is performed. By using `try_return` instead of directly using a `return` statement, you can avoid the overhead of having the compiler perform call frame unwinding (to ensure that the termination handler code is executed) on your behalf.

By consistently utilizing the `try_return` macro in your code and also using termination handlers systematically, you can take complete advantage of the powerful functionality that termination handlers provide (especially with regard to consistent clean-up after error conditions that cause a premature exit from the frame) and yet not suffer from the performance degradation associated with call-frame unwinding.

Using both exception handlers and termination handlers together

Using both types of handlers together is the right way to both protect your code from unexpected exception conditions and also to ensure consistent clean-up within the frame. Typically, the following method can be employed:

```
NTSTATUS AProcedureForDemonstrationPurposes(void)
{
    NTSTATUS        RC = STATUS_SUCCESS;
    ....

    // The outer exception handler ensures that all exceptions will first
    // be directed to us.
    try {
        //    The inner termination handler is our guarantee that we will always
        //    get an opportunity to clean-up after ourselves.
        try {
            ....

            try_exit:    NOTHING;
        } finally {
            // Clean-up code goes here.
        }
    } except (/* the exception filter goes here */) {
        // My exception handler goes here.
    }
    return(RC);
}
```

Event Logging

Often, kernel-mode drivers need to convey information to the system administrator or to the user of the host machine. This information could include error messages possibly caused by software or malfunctioning of attached hardware peripherals, warning messages that might indicate recovered errors or the possibility of an impending error, and informational (or status) messages indicating that some important activity had transpired.

The Windows NT Event Log serves as a central repository for messages sent by various software modules on that machine. The event log is a database containing event records that have a fixed, defined format. A user can either use the system-supplied event log viewer to extract information from the event log database or use the API supplied by the Win32 subsystem environment to obtain such data.

NOTE   Although it might be possible to decipher the actual record structure of an event log entry in the file, if you wish to develop your own event log viewer, you might be better off simply using the Win32-based supplied API to access the event log file. This API includes calls to open the file, obtain individual records, and close the file.

The concept underlying the usage of the event logging facility in Windows NT is fairly simple. The kernel-mode driver logs an event indicating that something significant has occurred. Each event, which must be defined in a message file, has a unique event identifier associated with it. The event identifier has the same format as other **NTSTATUS** type of status codes (the format is described later). The logged event contains information such as the event identifier, the name of the component logging the event, or any strings or other binary data that should be associated with the event. The event log also allows the kernel module to include other pertinent information for events indicating an error condition, such as the number of times the operation has been retried (prior to logging the event), an offset in the device where the error occurred, the status that was returned by the driver to the I/O Manager in the I/O Request Packet (IRP), and other similar information.

Event identifiers have replacement strings associated with them. For example, the system-defined error **IO_ERR_PARITY** has the following replacement string associated with it (this string is typically read from the file *%SystemRoot%\system32\iologmsg.dll*):[*]

```
A parity error was detected on %1.
```[†]

---

[*] Note that *%SystemRoot%* is replaced by the location of the Windows NT installation of the host machine.

[†] This message also demonstrates the use of *insertion strings*. An insertion string is a string supplied by the driver when it records an event record. The first insertion string is represented as *%1*, the second as *%2*, and so on. The driver supplied insertion strings are automatically inserted into the text message by the event log viewer (which obtains the insertion strings from the event record).

The format of status codes returned by the system and of event identifiers created by independent drivers follows the figure below.

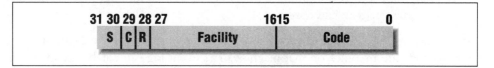

- S = Severity Code (2 bits). This can assume the following values:
  — 00 = Success
  — 01 = Informational
  — 10 = Warning
  — 11 = Error
- C = Customer Code Flag (1 bit). This bit should be set to 1 for status codes/ event identifiers defined by third-party drivers (which means that it should be set to 1 for any privately defined status codes in your driver).
- R = Reserved Bit (1 bit). Microsoft recommends that this bit be set to 0.
- Facility (12 bits). This indicates a group to which the error/status code belongs and can have one of the following values:
  — FACILITY_NONE (defined as 0x0)
  — FACILITY_RPC_RUNTIME (defined as 0x2)
  — FACILITY_RPC_STUBS (defined as 0x3)
  — FACILITY_IO_ERROR_CODE (defined as 0x4)

If you develop file system or filter drivers or other such kernel-mode drivers, you will typically set the value of Facility to 0x0 or to 0x4 for any status codes defined by you.

- The Code (16 bits). This can be set to any unique value for each status code defined in your driver. A typical error code your driver might define follows:

```
#define    MYDRIVER_ERROR_CODE_IO_FAILED        (0xE0047801)
```

If we expand the error code, we get the binary value 1110 0000 0000 0100 0111 1000 0000 0001.

This corresponds to the fact that this is an error condition (bit positions 30 and 31 are set to 1), this is a customer defined error (bit position 29 is set to 1), the reserved bit is set to 0, the facility that this error belongs to is FACILITY_IO_ERROR_CODE (since *Facility* is set to 0x4—bit positions 16 through 27), and the privately defined error code is 0x7801 (bit positions 0 through 15). Note that the privately defined error code can be any 16-bit value, as long as all such error codes defined by your driver are unique within your driver.*

So that the event viewer application (or any application that interprets the error log) can associate a textual description with your event identifier, your driver will have to supply a message file that contains the text associated with each particular event ID. For example, a typical text message that might be identified with our error defined previously could be as follows:

```
The driver tried to perform an I/O operation on the device. This I/O
operation failed due to a time-out condition (device did not respond
within the specified time-out period).
```

As you can see, providing the user with a clear explanation of the probable cause of failure is quite helpful. The system administrator might be able to use the error message supplied by you as a starting point to diagnose and rectify the cause for the failure. An appropriate message file can be created using the resource compiler used by your driver. Consult the documentation supplied with your resource compiler to determine how to create the message file.† Here is an example message file:

```
;Sample Message File.
;
;Filename: myeventfile.mc
;Module Name:    mydriver_event.h
;
;#ifndef    _MYDRIVER_EVENT_H_
;#define    _MYDRIVER_EVENT_H_
;Notes:
; This file is generated by the MC tool from the mydriver_event.mc file.

;Used from kernel mode. Do NOT use %1 for insertion strings since
;the I/O Manager automatically inserts the driver/device name as the
;first string.

MessageIdTypedef=ULONG

SeverityNames=(Success=0x0:STATUS_SEVERITY_SUCCESS
            Informational=0x1:STATUS_SEVERITY_INFORMATIONAL
            Warning=0x2:STATUS_SEVERITY_WARNING
            Error=0x3:STATUS_SEVERITY_ERROR)
```

---

* Although the error code defined by your driver might also be (coincidentally) defined by some other driver in the system, event identifiers are uniquely identified as a tuple consisting of (source, event ID). Therefore, as long as all identifiers within your driver are unique, you should not be concerned about providing unique values with respect to all other drivers in the system.

† Note that your resource compiler, while processing your input file, can create both the output message file as well as a header file that you can use with your driver. Therefore, you should have to define the event identifiers (and the associated text) in only one place, the input file to your resource compiler. This will help prevent discrepancies between any header files that your driver might use and the message file that eventually ships with your driver.

```
FacilityNames=(IO=0x004)

MessageId=0x7800 Facility=IO Severity=Informational
SymbolicName=MYDRIVER_INFO_DEBUG_SUPPORT
Language=English
This message and accompanying data is for DEBUG support only.
.


MessageId=0x7801 Facility=IO Severity=Error
SymbolicName=MYDRIVER_ERROR_CODE_IO_FAILED
Language=English
The driver tried to perform an I/O operation on the device. This I/O
operation failed due to a time-out condition (device did not respond
within the specified time-out period).
.


;
;Use the above entries as a template in creating your own message file.
;

;#endif // _MYDRIVER_EVENT_H_
```

It is possible to have insertion strings within text messages associated with event identifiers. Placeholders are denoted as %1, %2, etc. If you specify placeholders in your message, the driver can supply the strings to be inserted when writing the event log entry.However, note that the I/O Manager always inserts the device/ driver name as the first insertion string with every recorded event record. Even if the driver supplies insertion strings, they are placed after the device/driver name. The net result is that using %1 as a placeholder for an insertion string in your text (associated with an event identifier) will always result in the device/driver name being placed there, instead of the first driver-supplied insertion string. To obtain the first driver-supplied insertion string, use %2 as the placeholder; to get the second driver supplied insertion string, use %3, and so on.

How the Event Log Viewer Finds a Message File

For the event log viewer to be able to find your message file, your driver (or more likely, the application that installs your driver) will have to modify the Registry on the target machine. Typically, users will use the Win32 subsystem as their native subsystem. In this case, a unique subkey should be created by the installation utility under the Registry path: *CurrentControlSet\Services\EventLog\System.**

---

* Note that there are three possible locations under the **EventLog** key where your subkey could potentially be located: *Application* (for applications or user-mode drivers), *Security*, and *System* (for system-supplied and kernel-mode drivers). As kernel-mode driver developers, the logical and correct choice for your entry is under the *System* key.

This unique subkey should have the same name as the driver executable. For example, the subkey for the system-supplied AT disk driver is *atdisk*, which is the same as the name of the driver executable file (*atdisk.sys*). Within this subkey, at least two value entries must be created:

EventMessageFile
> This value is of type *REG_EXPAND_SZ* and contains the complete path and filename for the message file that contains the text messages corresponding to each event identifier. An example of a complete pathname and filename might be *%SystemRoot%\MyDriverDirectory\message.dll*.

TypesSupported
> This value is of type *REG_DWORD* and should be set to 0x7 for your driver, indicating that your driver supports events of type *EVENTLOG_ERROR_TYPE* (defined as 0x1), *EVENTLOG_WARNING_TYPE* (defined as 0x2), and *EVENTLOG_INFORMATION_TYPE* (defined as 0x4).

Once you have created the appropriate Registry entries and your installation program has copied the appropriate message file (in our example: *message.dll*) to the correct directory, the event log viewer application should be able to find and use the contents of your message file.

Recording Event Log Entries

Now that you have defined the appropriate event identifiers specific to your driver, you can use these event identifiers to record event log entries using support routines provided by the I/O Manager. Logging an event is performed in two steps:

1. An event/error log entry is allocated with `IoAllocateErrorLogEntry()`.

2. After the error log entry has been initialized, the event can be logged with `IoWriteErrorLogEntry()`.

The routine used to allocate an event log entry, so it can subsequently be recorded, is defined as follows:

```
PVOID
IoAllocateErrorLogEntry(
    IN PVOID        IoObject,
    IN UCHAR        EntrySize
);
```

Parameters:

`IoObject`

> This must point either to the device object* representing the device for which the error/event is being logged or to a driver object representing the driver controlling a device for which the event is being logged.

`EntrySize`

> The size of the object to be allocated. Since you as the developer can log binary data with the event log record, and you can also supply insertion strings that augment your message, the size of the entry should be calculated as follows,

```
sizeof(IO_ERROR_LOG_PACKET) + (n * sizeof(ULONG) +
        sizeof(InsertionStrings))
```

> where n = number of words of data to be dumped with the event record.

Functionality Provided:

The `IoAllocateErrorLogEntry()` will allocate an entry for your use. You can then initialize this entry and invoke `IoWriteErrorLogEntry()` to write to the event log. This routine returns a NULL pointer if it cannot allocate an entry for your use. In this case, you should not write the event at this time and wait for the next occurrence of the error, then you can retry this operation.

One note of caution: this routine references the device/driver object passed in as the `IoObject` argument. Therefore, once you invoke this routine, you must invoke the `IoWriteErrorLogEntry()` routine, which will dereference the object and release the memory allocated for the error log entry.

Initialization of the error log entry is quite simple and is well documented in the device driver reference supplied by Microsoft.

Once an event log entry has been obtained, you must invoke the `IoWriteErrorLogEntry()` routine to write the record to the event log. This routine is defined as follows:

```
VOID
IoWriteErrorLogEntry(
    IN PVOID          ElEntry
);
```

Parameters:

`ElEntry`

> The initialized event log entry to be recorded.

---

* See Chapter 4, *The NT I/O Manager*, for a discussion on device object and driver object structures.

Functionality Provided:

The `IoWriteErrorLogEntry()` queues the initialized event log entry to be written out. The actual write operation will be performed asynchronously by a system worker thread. Note that since this routine returns immediately after queuing the entry, the device/driver object will not yet have been dereferenced. The dereference will only occur after the entry has been asynchronously written to the event log.

NOTE   The way that the entry is asynchronously written to the event log file is also interesting. The system worker thread dequeues the event log record, inserts the device/driver name strings and then uses LPC (a local procedure call) to write the record to a special port where another user space thread writes the entry to the event log file. The system worker thread continues writing out all records until it encounters an error condition or until all the pending event log records have been sent to the port handler.

Driver Synchronization Mechanisms

One of the primary functions of a driver is to prevent data corruption. A principal cause of data corruption is a lack of synchronization between two or more concurrent threads of execution that manipulate the same data structures. Since Windows NT can execute on both uniprocessor as well as on symmetric multiprocessor machines, it becomes especially important for kernel-mode drivers to use synchronization primitives carefully. If you develop device drivers, take care when manipulating data structures shared by Interrupt Service Routines (ISRs) and threads that execute at normal IRQ level.

As discussed in Chapter 1, *Windows NT System Components*, the Windows NT kernel-mode environment contains the Executive as well as the Windows NT Kernel. The Executive is preemptible and parts of it are also pageable. The Kernel, however, is neither preemptible nor pageable. Although not preemptible, on multiprocessor machines, the kernel can execute concurrently on each processor.

In this section, we'll see the various synchronization primitives available to drivers forming part of the NT Executive. These synchronization primitives are either exported by the NT Kernel itself or by the NT Executive; the Executive uses the basic primitives supplied by the Kernel to construct more complex synchronization primitives. My intent is to provide an introduction to the different primitives available and to explain where each can be used. The sample code in the remainder of this book, especially file system and filter driver code, will make extensive use of some of these synchronization primitives. For further information on the syntax for calling the supporting routines mentioned in this section, consult the Microsoft Device Drivers Kit (DDK) documentation.

Spin Locks

The kernel spin lock structure is fundamental to providing synchronization across processors in a multiprocessor environment. Spin locks are used to provide mutual exclusion, i.e., a spin lock is used to ensure that only one thread executing on one processor can access the shared data protected by the spin lock. The sequence of instructions executed after acquiring the spin lock is also known as a *critical region*. The critical region ends when the spin lock is released.

When a thread on a processor acquires a spin lock, context switching (preemption of the thread) is disabled until the thread releases the spin lock. Similarly, any other thread, executing on another processor, will continuously try to gain access to the spin lock, making no progress until it succeeds. This method of busy-waiting (i.e., continuously attempting to check to see if the spin lock has become available) is also called *spinning* for the lock, hence leading to the name spin lock.*

The exact method used by the kernel to implement a spin lock is processor dependent; typically, however, an atomic *test-and-set* assembly instruction is used to implement the spin lock. The software tests the state of the lock variable and if it's free, sets it to the busy state. If the lock state is busy, the software keeps repeating execution of the test-and-set instruction.

NOTE   Often, to reduce bus contention, the test-and-set operation is not used continuously in the implementation of the spin lock. Rather, the operating system uses the test-and-set instruction once, and if it finds the lock state set to busy, then ordinary polling instructions are used until the lock state is found to be free. At this time, the test-and-set instruction is retried to obtain the lock.

Spin locks must be acquired by the thread executing on a processor at the highest IRQL at which all other attempts to acquire the same spin lock will be made.

Follow these few, simple rules to ensure correct behavior of your spin locks:

---

* The thread that is spinning for the lock cannot be preempted (just as the thread that has acquired the lock). However, these threads can be interrupted by an interrupt at a higher IRQL than the one at which they execute.

- Never refer to any pageable data once your code acquires a spin lock. Similarly, all code that executes once a spin lock is acquired must be nonpageable code.

  The reason for this restriction is that the system cannot service any page faults at an IRQL greater than or equal to the DISPATCH_LEVEL. Therefore, when a page fault occurs at a high IRQL, the system checks for pageable code and issues a KeBugCheck(), assuming that the condition is a direct result of a programming/design error.

- Try not to call other functions once you have acquired a spin lock. If you do need to call another function, be sure that none of the functions called refer to any pageable code or data.

- Because spin locks must be shared by all processors on a node, keep the spin lock for the minimum amount of time possible, then release it to allow another processor to acquire it.

It is possible to design and implement code in which a sequence of spin locks are acquired, i.e., you acquire spin lock #1 followed by a call to acquire spin lock #2, and so on. Or else, you might implement code in which you acquire a spin lock and then follow this up with one or more calls to acquire other synchronization primitives (e.g., mutexes). This could cause a deadlock condition. There is no deadlock checking performed when a processor acquires multiple spin locks and since dispatching or preemption is disabled once any spin lock is acquired, it is quite possible to create a system deadlock.

There are two types of spin locks that exist on Windows NT platforms:

Interrupt spin locks

These spin locks synchronize access to device driver data structures. They are acquired and released at the IRQL associated with the particular device managed by the device driver. The device driver usually does not allocate memory for spin locks itself, neither does it explicitly acquire or release interrupt spin lock structures. As a matter of fact, the kernel automatically acquires the spin lock associated with the interrupt before invoking the Interrupt Service Routine (ISR) for the interrupt, and releases it after the ISR execution has been completed.

The KeSynchronizeExecution() function, documented in the DDK, can be used to synchronize the execution of a device driver routine with the execution of an ISR for a specific interrupt. This function acquires the interrupt spin lock associated with the interrupt pointer, supplied as an argument to the routine after raising the IRQL for the thread to the DIRQL for the interrupt. KeSynchronizeExecution() then invokes the specified routine whose execution has to be synchronized with that of the ISR and finally releases the spin lock before returning to the caller.

Interrupt spin locks must always be used whenever a lower level driver wishes to synchronize the execution of a module with the ISR for the driver. Attempting to use an Executive spin lock will undoubtedly lead to data corruption and/or system deadlock situations.

Executive spin locks

Executive spin locks can only be acquired from threads executing at IRQL `PASSIVE_LEVEL`, `APC_LEVEL`, or `DISPATCH_LEVEL`. Therefore, they are typically used by higher level drivers such as file system drivers to synchronize access in multiprocessor environments. They can certainly be used by device driver developers, as long as they are not used to synchronize execution with the ISR for the drive driver.

The rest of this discussion assumes that you are using Executive spin locks to synchronize data access.

For the remainder of this book, we will focus on the usage of Executive spin locks.

To use Executive spin locks, you must first allocate enough storage for a spin lock structure. The storage for a spin lock must be allocated from nonpaged pool. Typically, your driver should either embed the spin lock definition in the driver extension, which is always allocated from nonpaged memory, or use a global definition, since all global variables within a kernel-mode driver are typically not pageable; or use an allocation function (e.g., `ExAllocatePool(NonPaged-Pool, sizeof(struct KSPIN_LOCK))`).

WARNING   If you happen to allocate a dispatcher object from paged pool instead of nonpaged pool, you will see some unexpected system bugchecks occur. Your driver might be working fine, but occasionally the system will bugcheck with an exception indicating that paged memory was accessed at high IRQL. The stack trace that you might obtain will not even point to your driver. This is because the kernel stores all threads waiting for active dispatcher objects on global linked lists. Each of these linked lists is protected by a spin lock. When the kernel traverses such a linked list with the spin lock acquired, and the object on the list happens to be paged out, you will encounter a system bugcheck. Note that the object might not always be paged out of memory, so your system might work fine, sometimes, though not always.

The following kernel support routines are available to you for manipulating an Executive spin lock:

`KeInitializeSpinlock()`

This routine accepts a pointer to the allocated spin lock structure. It will initialize the spin lock, and must be invoked before trying to acquire the spin lock for the first time.

`KeAcquireSpinLock() /KeAcquireSpinLockAtDpcLevel()`

These routines will spin trying to acquire the spin lock. A pointer to the spin lock to be acquired must be passed in as an argument. When either of these routines returns, the spin lock will have been acquired. The only difference between the two routines is that the `KeAcquireSpinLock()` routine will first raise the IRQL for the processor to `DISPATCH_LEVEL` and therefore return the old IRQL to the caller, to be used in releasing the spin lock, while `KeAcquireSpinLockAtDpcLevel()` assumes that the current IRQL is already at `DISPATCH_LEVEL`.

NOTE   On uniprocessor systems, the `KeAcquireSpinLockAtDpcLev-el()` doesn't do anything, i.e., it immediately returns control to the caller. Therefore, invoking this function (if appropriate) will result in a slight performance gain for your driver on uniprocessor systems.

`KeReleaseSpinLock() /KeReleaseSpinLockFromDpcLevel()`

These routines allow you to release a previously acquired spin lock. `KeReleaseSpinLock()` expects an additional parameter: the old IRQL returned from the previous call to `KeAcquireSpinLock()`. The processor is returned to the old IRQL, once the spin lock is released.

A spin lock should be used whenever synchronization is required across multiple processors, in arbitrary thread contexts, when processing interrupts, and when context switching has to be prevented. Furthermore, all the rules mentioned earlier should be followed whenever spin locks are used. If, however, you wish to provide synchronization across multiple processors in the context of some thread and you do not mind context switching occurring, then other Executive dispatcher objects (described in the next section) can be used.

Note the words *in arbitrary thread contexts* in the preceding paragraph. Spin locks can be used even by device drivers, whose entry points (such as read/write) are typically executed in the context of some arbitrary thread. It is even probable that such entry points for device drivers might be executed at high IRQL. Spin locks can be used freely by such drivers, while other dispatcher objects (such as mutexes or event objects) can only be used in a nonarbitrary thread context, i.e., the other dispatcher objects are used by file system drivers or filter drivers that sit above the file system.

NOTE   File system driver dispatch routines (e.g., read/write routines) are
               typically executed in the context of a system worker thread for asyn-
               chronous operations or in the context of the user thread initiated by
               an I/O request (e.g., a user application invoked the `ReadFile()`
               call). Since this is a nonarbitrary thread context, file systems are free
               to wait for dispatcher objects to be set to the signaled state.

               Device drivers, on the other hand, have IRPs (I/O Request Packets)
               queued. Each I/O Request Packet for a driver dispatch routine is
               subsequently dequeued (and the request initiated), in the context of
               whichever thread happens to be currently executing on that proces-
               sor. Therefore, since the dispatch routine for the device driver exe-
               cutes in the context of an arbitrary, unknown thread, waiting for
               dispatcher objects to be signaled is not allowed. Thread context is
               discussed in detail later in this book.

Dispatcher Objects

Kernel dispatcher objects are a set of abstractions, provided by the kernel to the
Executive, to support synchronization. These objects control dispatching and
synchronization of system operations. Dispatcher objects can be in one of two
states:

- *Signaled* state, in which no thread is currently accessing the shared data protected by the dispatcher objects or no other thread is currently within the critical section of the code.

- *Not-signaled* state, indicating that a thread is accessing shared data protected
  by the dispatcher objects and/or executing the critical region of the code.

Since your driver forms part of the NT Executive, you can use these dispatcher
objects to provide synchronization within your driver implementation. Note that
dispatcher objects provided by the kernel must be treated as opaque data structures. The kernel provides all functions that you might need to initialize, query
the state, set the state, and clear the state for these objects. You must provide the
storage needed to contain these objects. This storage must be provided from
nonpaged pool (similar to that provided for spin locks) and can be provided from
the driver extension structure, as a global variable, or as memory that is allocated
dynamically.

The method used to synchronize access to shared data or to control execution
within a critical region of code follows:

1. A thread needs to access a shared data resource (i.e., access some shared data or execute code within a critical region, so it invokes a Kernel Wait Routine).

   The wait routines that the thread can invoke are:

   — `KeWaitForSingleObject()`

   — `KeWaitForMultipleObjects()` or

   — `KeWaitForMutexObject()`

   If the objects being waited for are in the signaled state, the wait will be satisfied and control will return to the waiting thread. Note that before the wait is satisfied, the objects that were being waited for will be set to the not-signaled state, preventing any other thread, which might concurrently invoke a wait routine, from simultaneously getting access to the shared data resource.

2. Any other thread invoking a wait routine for one of the objects set to the not-signaled state in Step 1 will be suspended.

3. When the first thread completes processing the shared data resource, it will invoke an appropriate routine, depending upon the object used to achieve synchronization, `KeReleaseMutex()` or `KeSetEvent()`, to release the dispatcher objects and set the state of the dispatcher object to Signaled.

4. Now that the first thread has released the dispatcher objects, one of the threads waiting for the dispatcher objects, to gain access to the shared data resource, will be awakened.

   This thread will now be permitted access to the shared data resource.

NOTE   In the case of some synchronization objects, multiple threads will be awakened concurrently. However, only one of them will subsequently be able to acquire the synchronization object.

---

5. Steps 1 to 4 are repeated every time a thread wishes to access the shared data resource.

If a thread cannot gain access to the shared data resource (i.e., if the dispatcher object is in the not-signaled state because another thread is actively accessing the shared data or executing code within the critical region), the thread will be suspended or blocked, awaiting the release of the dispatcher object. This allows other threads in the system to continue executing and is very different from a spin lock, where the thread will be in a busy-wait state until it gains access. Dispatcher objects are therefore more conducive to better system performance.

As mentioned earlier in the discussion on spin locks, driver dispatch routines that execute in an arbitrary thread context cannot wait for dispatcher objects to be signaled. Also, it is considered a fatal error to wait for a nonzero time interval on a dispatcher object at IRQL that is greater than `PASSIVE_LEVEL`. Therefore, most device driver designers will not use dispatcher objects for mutual exclusion, but file system developers or developers of filter drivers that sit above the file system in the calling hierarchy can potentially use dispatcher objects.

Finally, note that when a thread invokes the kernel routine to wait for a dispatcher object (e.g., `KeWaitForSingleObject()`), the thread can specify a `TimeOut` interval. If the dispatcher object does not get signaled within the specified `TimeOut` interval, the thread will be awakened with a special status code of `STATUS_TIMEOUT`. This allows the thread to ensure that the wait will be a bounded one. If a `TimeOut` interval of 0 is supplied, the thread will never be put to sleep; the state of the object will be checked and if not-signaled, control will immediately be returned to the thread with the status of `STATUS_TIMEOUT`.

The following dispatcher objects are available to designers and developers of kernel-mode drivers:

- Event objects
- Timer objects
- Mutual exclusion objects
- Semaphore objects

In addition to the dispatcher objects listed here, threads can also wait for process, thread, and file object structures.

Event objects

Event objects are used to synchronize execution between multiple threads. They record the occurrence of an event that determines execution flow. Consider a producer-consumer relationship between two threads: producer thread A creates data to be processed while consumer thread B processes data whenever it becomes available. Since thread B does not know when data will become available, it has two options:

- Keep inquiring from thread A whether data is available for processing. This is not conducive to good system performance, since valuable processor cycles get consumed in this kind of busy-wait mode.
- Wait for thread A to inform it whenever data is made available.

Since the second option is clearly superior, it is most often used in such situations.

To implement this notification, an event object can be used.*

---

* Note that a counting semaphore (discussed later) could be used equally well for this purpose.

The event object must be initialized before it can be used. Initially, the event object would be set to the not-signaled state. Thread B would then invoke a wait call on this event object and would be suspended from execution until the wait can be satisfied. When thread A has data available for processing, it could invoke the `KeSetEvent()` call to signal the event object. This would result in thread B being inserted into the queue of threads that can be scheduled for execution. At some point, the system scheduler schedules thread B for execution, and thread B processes the data. This method can be repeated as often as required.

There are two types of event objects:

Notification event objects

> In this type of event object, every thread that is waiting for the event object is scheduled for execution once the event object is signaled. Also, the state of the event object, when signaled, is not automatically reset to the not-signaled state. Therefore, an explicit call to `KeResetEvent()` will have to be made by some thread to set the state of the event object to the not-signaled state.

> This type of event object is typically used when a single occurrence of an event, resulting in the event object being set to the signaled state, triggers execution by any other thread waiting for that event to occur. For example, consider the analogy of a car race: when the start signal is given, all cars in the competition take off, each trying to get to the finish line.

Synchronization event objects

> This type of event object is our producer-consumer example. Here, when the event object is set to the signaled state, only one waiting thread will be scheduled for execution and the event object is then automatically reset to the not-signaled state. This type of object ensures that only one thread accesses the shared data resource at any point in time.

The following kernel-mode support routines are available for interacting with event objects:

`KeInitializeEvent()`

> Your driver must allocate storage for the event object from nonpaged pool. Once you have allocated the storage, you must invoke this routine to initialize the event object before any thread attempts to wait for, signal, or reset it. When this routine is invoked, you can specify whether the event object should be a notification type object or a synchronization type object. You can also specify the initial state of the event object, signaled or not-signaled.

`IoCreateSynchronizationEvent()`

> Note that this is not strictly a kernel support routine, but one provided by the I/O Manager. This routine is only available in the Windows NT 4.0 and later

releases and allows your driver to request that a named synchronization event object be created or opened. Since this event object has a name, multiple drivers can now use the same event object to synchronize access to a shared data resource.*

This routine will either create a named event object, if no such event object exists (and also initialize the event object to the signaled state), or open a previously created event object. It returns two values, a pointer to and a handle for the event object. All the calls to manipulate event objects, listed below, can be used on the returned event object pointer. When your driver no longer needs to use this object, it should invoke the `ZwClose()` routine to close the returned handle.

KeSetEvent()

This routine allows you to set the state of the event object to the signaled state. One or more threads that are waiting for the object to be signaled will get scheduled for execution.

Consider the following pseudocode fragment:

```
thread_A {
    while (TRUE) {
        create new data;
        signal event object 1;
        wait for event object 2 to be signaled;
    }
}

thread_B {
    while (TRUE) {
        wait for event object 1 to be signaled;
        process data;
        signal event object 2;
    }
}
```

This code describes a typical producer-consumer relationship. Here we see that each thread performs a wait operation immediately after signaling an event object.

Signaling an event object is one point when the system scheduler might perform a context switch. However, since our threads will voluntarily put themselves to sleep following the signal operation, it seems redundant for them to be scheduled out, only to be rescheduled some time later and immediately put to sleep. It would be more efficient, instead, if they were allowed

---

* The event objects that you otherwise allocate storage for from within your driver are only accessible to your driver unless you implement some horrendous method of passing pointers between drivers, using a private IOCTL. Therefore, it was quite difficult for two or more drivers in Windows NT Version 3.51 and earlier versions to synchronize access to a shared data resource using event objects.

to continue executing after the signal operation so that they could put themselves to sleep and avoid the extra overhead of one unnecessary context switch. This can be achieved by specifying the `Wait` argument to `KeSetEvent()` as TRUE.

NOTE   Implementation of POSIX threads-style condition variables requires the capability to atomically release a mutex object and then put the thread that released the mutex to sleep. This can be achieved easily by specifying the `Wait` argument in `KeSetEvent()` as TRUE.

KeResetEvent()/KeClearEvent()

Both routines allows you to set the state of the object to the not-signaled state. `KeResetEvent()` also returns the previous state of the event object.

KeReadStateEvent()

This routine gives you the current value of the event object (signaled or not-signaled).

Timer objects

Timer objects are used to record the passage of time. If a thread wishes to perform a task after some time has elapsed or at a specified time value, it should use a timer object. The timer object has a state associated with it, either signaled or not-signaled. When the desired time interval passes, the timer object is set to the signaled state and all threads waiting for the timer object will have their wait satisfied and will be scheduled for execution.

Just as with other dispatcher objects, storage for the timer object must be provided in nonpaged memory by the driver. The timer object must be initialized to the not-signaled state.

There are two ways your driver can use a timer object:

- A thread in your driver might initialize a timer object and then invoke a wait routine (e.g., `KeWaitForSingleObject()`) to suspend execution until the timer object is set to the signaled state (after the specified time interval has elapsed).

- Alternatively, when setting the timer object to expire after the time period has elapsed, a Deferred Procedure Call (DPC) might be specified. When the time period expires, the DPC routine will be scheduled for execution, and any required processing could be performed within that DPC routine.

NOTE   Deferred Procedure Calls are another way of influencing the opera-
                tion of the kernel. The DPC provides the capability of breaking into
                the execution of the currently running thread (via a software inter-
                rupt), and executing a specified procedure at IRQL `DISPATCH_`
                `LEVEL`. No system services can be invoked when executing the
                DPC procedure and page faults are not tolerated. Furthermore,
                DPCs are not targeted to a specific thread like Asynchronous Proce-
                dure Calls. Whenever the current IRQL falls below `DISPATCH_LEV-`
                `EL`, a software interrupt will happen and the DPC dispatcher
                invoked. Typically, DPCs are used by device drivers to complete in-
                terrupt-handling-related processing.

                On any single processor, only one DPC can be executing at any giv-
                en instant in time. However, on multiprocessor systems, there could
                potentially be a DPC executing on each processor concurrently.
                Thread scheduling on the processor is suspended while the DPC is
                executing at IRQL `DISPATCH_LEVEL`

With the release of Windows NT 4.0, two types of timer objects are available:[*]

Notification timer object

> When this type of timer object is signaled, all threads that were waiting for
> this object have their waits satisfied. These threads will all get scheduled for
> execution.

Synchronization timer object

> When this type of timer object is signaled, only one thread waiting for the
> timer object will have its wait satisfied. The timer object will automatically be
> reset to the not-signaled state.

One further enhancement made in Windows NT 4.0 to timer objects is that you
can now specify periodic (recurring) timer objects. These timer objects will automatically be reinserted into the active timer list, as many times as specified in the
`Period` argument when setting the timer object.

The following kernel-mode support routines are available for interacting with
timer objects:

`KeInitializeTimer()/KeInitializeTimeEx()`

> The latter version is only available on the Windows NT 4.0 and subsequent
> releases. This routine expects a pointer to a timer object allocated in
> nonpaged memory. It will initialize the value of the timer object to the not-
> signaled state. With the `KeInitializeTimeEx()` routine, you can specify
> the type of the timer object (Synchronization type or Notification type).

---

[*] Windows NT 3.51 and earlier versions only supported the notification type of timer object.

KeSetTimer()/KeSetTimerEx()

This routine allows you to set a timer object. The time value is specified in system time units (100-nanosecond intervals). You have two choices: if you supply a negative time unit value, the value will be interpreted relative to the current time when the routine was invoked. If a positive value is supplied, it is interpreted as an absolute value; the time that the system was booted is taken as time unit 0.

The `KeSetTimerEx()` routine became available with the release of Windows NT 4.0 and it allows you to specify the number of times you wish the timer to be reactivated.

Note that you can specify a DPC routine to be invoked once the timer is set to the signaled state.

KeReadStateTimer()

This routine returns the current state of the timer (signaled or not-signaled).

KeCancelTimer()

This routine cancels a previously set timer if it has not yet expired. If there is an associated DPC routine, it is canceled too.

Two points should be noted here. First, canceling a timer does not set the state of the timer to the signaled state. Second, if the timer had previously expired and the associated DPC routine is in the queue, that DPC routine will not get canceled. Only if the timer had not previously expired will the associated DPC routine not get queued.

Mutex objects (mutual exclusion)

Mutex objects are similar to spin locks in that they allow only one thread to access a shared data resource at any given instant in time. Any other thread that attempts to acquire the same mutex object will be suspended until the first thread releases the mutex object. The fact that a thread will be suspended awaiting the mutex object to be signaled is the distinguishing feature between spin locks and mutex objects.

Storage for mutex objects must be provided by the driver from nonpaged pool. Also, the driver must ensure that any code executed once a mutex is acquired is not pageable. Mutex objects come in two varieties:

Fast mutex objects

A fast mutex is simply a wrapped-up event dispatcher object. It provides mutual exclusion semantics by allowing only one thread to acquire the mutex at any instant. When the mutex object is released (i.e., its corresponding event is signaled), only one other thread from those waiting for the mutex object will be scheduled for execution. Therefore, the concepts underlying the fast mutex data structure are the same as those for synchronization type event object structures.

Fast mutex objects do not provide any form of deadlock prevention support. Also, fast mutex objects cannot be recursively acquired. Therefore, if you implement code in which one thread tries to acquire fast mutex #1 followed by fast mutex #2 while another thread does so in the reverse order, you will get a deadlock situation. Similarly, any thread that tries to recursively obtain a fast mutex will deadlock with itself.

Support for fast mutex objects is provided by the NT Executive, because fast mutex objects are not among the primitive synchronization mechanisms exported by the Windows NT Kernel. Using fast mutexes is faster (hence the name) than using the normal mutex structures supported by the kernel. The routines to manipulate fast mutex objects follow:

`ExInitializeFastMutex()`

> Initializes the passed-in fast mutex structure. This is actually a macro that simply initializes the event object that comprises the fast mutex structure.

`ExAcquireFastMutex()/ExAcquireFastMutexUnsafe()`

> If the fast mutex is not currently acquired by another thread, this thread will be allowed to acquire the fast mutex. Any other thread that subsequently attempts to acquire this mutex will be suspended until the mutex is released.

> If the mutex had already been acquired by some other thread, the current thread will be blocked until the fast mutex becomes available.

> The difference between the two invocations is simple: if **ExAcquire-FastMutex()** is used, the Executive disables delivery of Asynchronous Procedure Calls (APCs) to the thread that has acquired the fast mutex. If **ExAcquireFastMutexUnsafe()** is used instead, the Executive assumes that the call is protected within a critical region* and hence does not bother to disable APCs.

---

* Highest level drivers such as file system drivers can invoke `KeEnterCriticalRegion()` and `KeLeaveCriticalRegion()` to note that the current thread is entering or leaving a critical region. Invoking `KeEnterCriticalRegion()` disables kernel-mode APCs. `KeLeaveCriticalRegion()` reenables delivery of kernel-mode APCs to the calling thread. The `KeEnterCriticalRegion()` macro should be invoked whenever your driver would find it awkward to be interrupted from its processing to receive a kernel-mode APC.

NOTE   Asynchronous Procedure Calls are a method by which control flow for a thread can be affected. An APC must be targeted toward a specific thread. This is in contrast to a DPC, which executes in the context of any arbitrary thread currently executing on the processor.

The thread to which an APC is directed will be interrupted (via a software interrupt), and the procedure specified when creating the APC will be executed in the context of the interrupted thread at a special IRQL, `APC_LEVEL`.

APCs can be delivered both in user mode and in kernel mode. Kernel-mode APCs come in two flavors: *normal* and *special*. Normal APCs can be disabled by a kernel-mode driver by invoking `KeEnterCriticalregion()`. However, special APCs cannot be disabled. Consult the DDK for more information on Asynchronous Procedure Calls.

ExReleaseFastMutex() /ExReleaseFastMutexUnsafe()

These calls release a previously acquired fast mutex. Note that the appropriate call to be used depends on which call was invoked to acquire the fast mutex, `ExAcquireFastMutex()` or `ExAcquireFastMutexUnsafe()`.

ExTryToAcquireFastMutex()

This routine will attempt to acquire the fast mutex. If it is successful, it will return TRUE (and will have blocked kernel-mode APCs). If it could not acquire the fast mutex, it will return FALSE. The caller then has the option of retrying immediately (polling) or retrying after some period of time.

Mutex objects

Mutex objects are similar to their fast mutex counterparts. However, mutex objects are supported by the NT Kernel, and they have the following additional features missing in the fast mutex implementations:

— Your driver can associate a level with each mutex object that it initializes.*

The kernel checks the level of the mutex being acquired to ensure that all previously acquired mutexes are at a level strictly less than the level of the current mutex (unless the same mutex is being acquired recursively).

— Mutex objects can be acquired recursively.

---

* The level associated with a mutex object should correspond to your locking hierarchy. For example, if your locking hierarchy dictates that mutex #1 is always acquired before mutex #2, then you should associate a lower level (lower nonzero numerical value) with mutex #1 and a higher level (higher nonzero numerical value) with mutex #2.

Therefore, a thread in your driver can safely reacquire the same mutex object multiple times. The only restriction is that the mutex should be released exactly the same number of times that it was acquired.

— When a thread in your driver has a wait on a mutex object satisfied, the priority of the thread is boosted to the lowest real-time priority in the system.

This priority will subsequently automatically be lowered when the mutex object is released.

— The owning process (for the thread that acquires the mutex) will not be paged out to secondary storage.

The following routines are provided by the NT Kernel to support mutex objects:

`KeInitializeMutex()`

Your driver must specify a valid nonzero `Level` argument if it needs to acquire multiple mutex objects concurrently (if you specify 0 as the value for `Level` for each mutex that you initialize, trying to acquire multiple mutex objects concurrently will result in a system bugcheck).

`KeReadStateMutex()`

This routine returns the current state of the mutex (signaled or not signaled).

`KeReleaseMutex()`

This routine is used to release a previously acquired mutex. If the thread releasing the mutex expects to immediately execute a call to a kernel wait routine (e.g., `KeWaitForSingleObject()`), it should supply the `Wait` argument as TRUE. This will avoid an unnecessary context switch.

Semaphore objects

Semaphore objects (counting semaphores) allow one or a specific number of threads to concurrently access a shared data resource. They can be used to provide mutual exclusion (similar to mutex objects) by specifying that only one thread should be allowed access to the shared object at any point in time. By allowing the flexibility of specifying the exact number of threads that can concurrently access shared data, they are ideal in situations where the amount of parallelism needs to be tightly controlled. Semaphores should be viewed as gates. As long as the gate is open, concurrent access to the shared data resource is allowed. Once the gate is shut, no more threads will be allowed access to the shared data resource.

Although similar to mutex objects, semaphores do not provide the deadlock checking facility provided by mutex objects. Acquisition of a semaphore does not result in disabling kernel-mode APCs. Note that storage for semaphore objects must be provided by your driver and should always be allocated from non-paged memory.

Here's how semaphores work. Each semaphore has an associated `Count` value. If the `Count` associated with the semaphore object is zero, any thread that waits for the semaphore object will be suspended. Whenever a thread that acquired the semaphore object releases the semaphore, the `Count` gets incremented by a specified amount (the `Adjustment` argument specified when releasing the semaphore). If incrementing the `Count` results in a transition from 0 to a nonzero value, then a certain number of waiting threads will have their wait satisfied.

Each time a wait is satisfied the `Count` gets decremented by 1; therefore, the number of waits that will get satisfied on a transition from 0 to a nonzero value will be equal to the value of the nonzero `Count`. The net result is that a fixed number of threads (bounded by the `Limit` value specified when initializing the semaphore) can concurrently acquire the semaphore and thereby concurrently access the shared resource.

The following routines are provided by the NT Kernel to support counting semaphore objects:

`KeInitializeSemaphore()`

> You can specify the initial value of the `Count` associated with the semaphore. If the `Count` is nonzero, the semaphore will be set to the signaled state. You must also specify the maximum count that will be allowed for the semaphore. This `Limit` argument bounds the number of concurrent accesses to the shared data resource protected by the semaphore.

`KeReleaseSemaphore()`

> When releasing a semaphore, your driver can specify the `Argument`, which is the amount by which the `Count` associated with the semaphore should be incremented. This might result in satisfying one or more waiting threads. Note that if incrementing the count by the supplied `Argument` value results in exceeding the original `Limit` value (specified when initializing the semaphore), or if you specify a negative value for the `Argument` variable, the thread performing the release will encounter an exception of `STATUS_SEMAPHORE_LIMIT_EXCEEDED`.

`KeReadStateSemaphore()`

> This routine returns the current value of the `Count` associated with the semaphore. This value should be interpreted as the number of waits that will be immediately satisfied for the semaphore object.

ERESOURCE Objects (Read/Write Locks)

The Windows NT Executive provides an important additional synchronization mechanism extensively used by file system drivers. The **ERESOURCE** structure is a primitive that provides single writer (exclusive access), multiple reader (shared access) semantics. Therefore, each thread has the flexibility of determining the type of access to request from the resource structure.

When a thread needs to modify the shared data protected by the resource, it must request the read/write lock exclusively. However, if the thread just needs to read the contents of the shared data protected by the resource, it will typically acquire the resource shared, allowing other threads to concurrently read the same shared data. If any thread acquires the resource exclusively, of course, no other thread can acquire it.

Storage for these read/write locks must be provided by the driver from nonpaged pool.

The **ERESOURCE** structure has the concept of an *owning thread* for the resource (multiple reader threads could concurrently own the same resource shared). Additionally, these read/write locks provide recursive acquisition functionality. However, the thread must release the lock as many times as it was acquired.

A note of caution: none of the dispatcher synchronization primitives discussed in this chapter needs to be uninitialized when a driver determines that the primitive is no longer needed and deallocates the memory reserved for the synchronization primitive. However, **ERESOURCE** structures must be uninitialized (or deleted from the global linked list of resources) before memory allocated for these structures can be deallocated.

Finally, all the resource manipulation routines require that the IRQL of the processor be less than or equal to **DISPATCH_LEVEL**.

NOTE   The **ERESOURCE** structure uses an Executive spin lock to protect internal fields within the resource structure. When acquiring this spin lock, the Executive raises the IRQL for the processor to **DISPATCH_ LEVEL**. Therefore, invoking any of the routines at an IRQL greater than **DISPATCH_LEVEL** could lead to a deadlock condition.

The following routines are provided by the NT Executive to support **ERESOURCE** structures:

ExInitializeResourceLite()

This simple routine initializes the resource structure allocated by the driver. The resource is added to a global linked list of resource structures, and therefore, it is important that the driver uninitialize the resource before freeing memory allocated to it.

ExDeleteResourceLite()

This routine unlinks the resource from the global linked list of resources. The memory reserved for this resource structure can subsequently be released.

ExAcquireResourceExclusiveLite()

This routine will attempt to acquire the resource structure exclusively (for write access). The thread requesting exclusive access can specify whether it wishes to wait (block) for the resource to become available. If the thread is not prepared to block, and if some other thread has the resource acquired shared or exclusively, this routine will return FALSE, indicating that the request to acquire the resource was unsuccessful.

ExTryToAcquireResourceExclusiveLite()

This routine is functionally equivalent to invoking `ExAcquireResourceExclusiveLite()` with the `Wait` argument set to FALSE. However, Microsoft literature claims that this call is more efficient.

ExAcquireResourceSharedLite()

This routine will attempt to acquire the resource structure shared (for read access). The thread requesting exclusive access can specify whether it wishes to wait (block) for the resource to become available. If the thread is not prepared to block and if some other thread has the resource acquired exclusively, this routine will return FALSE, indicating that the request to acquire the resource was unsuccessful. If other threads have this resource acquired shared, the current request for shared access will be successful and will return TRUE.

ExReleaseResourceForThreadLite()

Invoke this function to release a previously acquired resource. The thread ID (identifying the thread that is performing this operation) must be passed in as an argument to this routine. This thread ID can be obtained by a call to `ExGetCurrentResourceThread()`.

ExAcquireSharedStarveExclusive()

Typically, requests for resource acquisition are managed so that threads requesting exclusive access are not starved out. Starvation can occur under the following scenario:

A thread has the resource acquired shared. Subsequently, a request for exclusive acquisition arrives with the `Wait` argument set to TRUE. This request is therefore queued. Before the thread that has the resource shared releases the resource, another shared acquisition request is also received. If the NT Executive keeps satisfying the requests for shared acquisition while making the request for exclusive access wait, it is possible that the request for exclusive activation will get starved (i.e., will never be completed).

Therefore, the NT Executive will typically not satisfy a new request for shared access if a previous request for exclusive access is already queued.*

By using this call however, a thread deliberately requests that its request for shared access be given preference over any preexisting queued requests for exclusive access.

ExAcquireSharedWaitForExclusive()

This routine is the inverse of the previous one. Here, a shared access requester explicitly states that preference should be given to exclusive access requests even if such requests arrive after the current one. Therefore, the current request will only be satisfied if there are no pending exclusive requests for the resource (unless this is a recursive acquisition request).

Supporting Routines (RTLs)

The Windows NT Executive provides a substantial amount of support to kernel-mode driver developers via the run-time library and the filesystem run-time library.† These libraries should be explored thoroughly if you wish to develop kernel-mode drivers.

The run-time library consists of sets of routines that do the following:

- Manipulate doubly linked lists

- Query the Windows NT Registry and write information to the Registry

- Execute type conversion routines (character to string, etc.)

- Execute string manipulation routines for ASCII and Unicode strings (including conversion from ASCII to Unicode and vice versa)

- Copy, zero, move, fill, and compare memory blocks

- Perform 32-bit integer arithmetic and 64-bit large integer and long arithmetic (including conversion between types)

---

* Note that if a requesting thread already owns the resource exclusively and asks for shared access to the resource (recursively), the request is always granted.

† The file system run-time library (FSRTL) functions and structure headers are not declared in the DDK (although some of the RTL functions are exposed). However, throughout the course of this book, I will present important routines and structures defined in the file system run-time library. Microsoft released a Windows NT Installable File Systems (IFS) Developers Kit in April 1997. From all available information at the time of writing this book, the header files for structure definitions and function declarations contained within the FSRTL are only available as part of the Installable File Systems (IFS) kit from Microsoft for a sum of money in addition to the amount paid for the Device Driver's Kit (DDK).

- Perform time conversion and manipulation routines

- Create and manipulate security descriptors

Although routines contained in these two libraries are not discussed in detail here (see Chapter 2, *File System Driver Development*, for a discussion of some of them), example code throughout this book will use one or more of the functions, structure definitions, and macros contained within these libraries.

Run-time library functions can be easily identified by the prefix `Rtl` prepended to all function declarations. Similarly filesystem run-time library routines can be identified by the `FsRtl` prefix prepended to function declarations.

I highly recommend you familiarize yourself with the functionality provided by these two libraries, and that you use these routines in your driver whenever the need arises. You should use run-time library routines when you would have otherwise used standard C library routines, e.g., instead of using the `memcpy()` library call, try to use the `RtlCopyMemory()` supporting routine. This will ensure correct behavior of your driver on all platforms.

Although header files for both of these libraries must be purchased from Microsoft as part of an IFS kit, this book will provide descriptions and sample usage of important structure definitions and function declarations provided by each of these libraries.

II

The Managers

Part II provides a detailed description of the Windows NT Components vital to file I/O.

4

The NT I/O Manager

Successfully interfacing with external devices is essential for any computing system. A general-purpose commercial operating system like Windows NT must also interact with a variety of peripherals, the common ones most of us use each day, as well as the more uncommon external devices that might be useful in some specific settings. For example, we expect the NT operating system to provide us with built-in support for our hard disks, keyboard, mouse, and video monitor. If, however, I wish to attach a programmable toaster device to my system (my new invention), and I would like to control this device using my computer, which is running Windows NT, I suspect that I will have to develop a driver to control the device. Furthermore, if I expect to be successful in developing this driver, I will obviously have to look to the operating system to provide an appropriate environment and support structure that makes developing, installing, testing, and using this driver a task that might be difficult but not insurmountable.

Although some might argue that such expectations of support from an operating system are unreasonable, the Windows NT operating system does provide such a framework, so that mere mortals like you and me can develop necessary drivers to control such esoteric devices as a programmable toaster. In fact, the NT operating system provides a consistent, well-defined I/O subsystem within which all code required to interface with external devices can reside. The I/O subsystem is extensive, encompassing file system drivers, intermediate drivers, device drivers, and services to support and interface with such drivers. It is also consistent in its treatment of external devices.

In this chapter, I will present an introduction to the NT I/O Manager, the component responsible for creating, maintaining, and managing the NT I/O subsystem. To develop any kind of driver for the Windows NT operating system, an understanding of the framework provided by the I/O Manager is extremely important. First, I will describe some of the services provided by the I/O Manager. Next, I will present an overview of the components comprising the I/O subsystem, including a discussion of the various types of drivers that can exist within the I/O subsystem. I will then describe some common data structures that kernel-mode developers should be familiar with. Following this is a discussion on some common issues involving I/O requests sent to kernel-mode drivers. Finally, I will present a description of the system boot sequence, with emphasis on the activities of the I/O Manager and the drivers within the kernel.

The NT I/O Subsystem

The NT I/O subsystem is the framework within which all kernel-mode drivers controlling and interfacing with peripheral devices reside. This subsystem is composed of the following components (see Figure 4-1):

- The NT I/O Manager, which defines and manages the entire framework.

- File system drivers that are responsible for local, disk-based file systems.

- Network redirectors that accept I/O requests and issue them over the network to a file server. The redirectors are implemented similarly to other file system drivers.

- Network file servers that accept requests sent to them by redirectors on other nodes, and reissue these requests to local file system drivers. Although file servers do not need to be implemented as kernel-mode drivers, typically they are implemented as such for performance reasons.

- Intermediate drivers, such as SCSI class drivers. These drivers provide generic functionality that is common to a set of devices. Intermediate drivers also include drivers that provide added functionality, such as software mirroring or fault tolerance, by using the services of device drivers.

- Device drivers that interface directly with hardware, such as controller cards, network interface cards, and disk drives. These are typically the lowest-level kernel-mode drivers.

- Filter drivers that insert themselves into the driver hierarchy to perform functionality that is not directly available using the existing set of drivers. For example, a filter driver can layer itself above a file system driver, intercepting all requests that are issued to the file system driver. A filter driver could just as well layer itself below the file system driver, but above a device driver, intercepting all requests targeted to the device driver. Note that conceptually, the only tangible difference between filter drivers and other intermediate drivers is that filter drivers typically intercept requests targeted to some existing

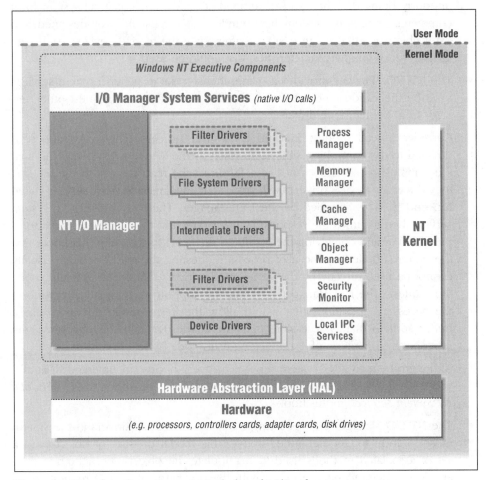

Figure 4-1. Kernel-mode components, including the I/O subsystem

device and then provide their own functionality, either in lieu of or in addition to the functionality provided by the driver that was the original recipient of the request.

Functionality Provided by the NT I/O Manager

The NT I/O Manager oversees the NT I/O subsystem. The following is a list of some of the functionality provided by the I/O Manager:

- The I/O Manager defines and supports a framework that allows the operating system to use peripherals connected to the system.

  The type and number of peripherals that can potentially be used with a Windows NT system is not limited, since new types of peripheral devices are continuously being designed and developed. Therefore, the I/O subsystem for a commercial operating system like Windows NT must be well-designed and extensible, such that it can easily accommodate the myriad devices, each with its own set of unique characteristics, that could be used.

- The NT I/O Manager provides a comprehensive set of generic system services used by the various subsystems to actually perform I/O or request other services from kernel-mode drivers.

  Consider a read request initiated by a user process. This read request is directed to the controlling subsystem, such as the Win32 subsystem. Note that the Win32 subsystem does not actually direct the read request to the file system driver or device driver itself; instead it invokes a system service called `NtReadFile()`, supplied by the I/O Manager. The `NtReadFile()` system service then assumes the responsibility for directing the request to the appropriate driver and conveying the results to the Win32 subsystem. Also note that the buffer supplied by the user process requesting the read operation usually cannot be used directly by the kernel-mode drivers that will eventually satisfy the request. The I/O Manager provides the support to automatically perform the necessary operations that would allow the kernel-mode drivers to use a buffer address that is accessible in kernel-mode. Later in this chapter, I will describe this operation of manipulating user-mode buffers in further detail.

  Although the native NT system services are very poorly documented (if at all), you can find a detailed description of these services in Appendix A, *Windows NT System Services,* in this book.

- The NT I/O Manager defines a single I/O model that all drivers in the system must conform to. As mentioned above, this model consists of objects and a set of associated methods used to manipulate the objects. Kernel-mode drivers do not need to be concerned with the originator of an I/O request, since they respond to all I/O requests in the same manner.

  This results in a consistent interface provided to users of the I/O subsystem, such as the Win32 or POSIX subsystem, and also protects the kernel-mode drivers from having to worry about the vagaries associated with the particular subsystem that issued the I/O request.

  Furthermore, since every kernel-mode driver must conform to this single I/O model, kernel-mode drivers can use services provided by each other, since a kernel-mode driver does not really care whether the I/O request originates in kernel-mode or user-mode. That said, if you do invoke the services of another kernel-mode driver from your kernel-mode driver, there are certain considerations that you must be aware of. These will be described later in this chapter.

Finally, the single I/O model allows for the implementation of layered kernel-mode drivers, which are supported by the NT I/O Manager. Each kernel-mode driver in a layered hierarchy can utilize the services of the underlying driver to complete a specific operation. In turn, the underlying driver can satisfy the issued request without concerning itself with whether the request came to it directly from some user process or from a driver that resides above it in the hierarchy of layered drivers.

- The I/O Manager supports installable file system implementations that use the peripheral devices connected to the system.

  The NT operating system includes support for the CD-ROM file system, the NTFS log-based file system, the legacy FAT file system, the LAN Manager File System Redirector, as well as the HPFS file system. In addition to supporting such native local- and network-based file systems, the I/O Manager provides the infrastructure for development of external, installable file systems, i.e., file system implementations from third-party vendors. You can purchase commercial implementations of NFS (the Network File System), DFS (the Distributed File System), and other file system and network redirector implementations.

- The NT I/O Manager supports dynamically loadable kernel-mode drivers.

- The I/O Manager provides support for device-independent services that can be utilized by other components of the NT operating system, as well as by kernel-mode drivers that are implemented by third-party vendors.

  If a kernel-mode driver needs to invoke the dispatch routine for another kernel-mode driver, it can use the `IoCallDriver()` service provided by the I/O Manager. Similarly, if a kernel-mode driver has to allocate a Memory Descriptor List (MDL) structure, the `IoAllocateMdl()` routine, can be used. There are other such services that are commonly used by kernel-mode components (including kernel-mode drivers), provided by the NT I/O Manager. The list of services is available in the Windows NT Device Drivers Kit (DDK).

- The NT I/O Manager interacts with the NT Cache Manager to support virtual block caching of file data.

  Later in this book, you will learn more about the functionality provided by the NT Cache Manager.

- The NT I/O Manager interacts with the NT Virtual Memory Manager and file system implementations to support memory-mapped files.

  In the next chapter, you will read in detail about memory-mapped files. Support for memory-mapped files is provided jointly by the NT I/O Manager, the NT Virtual Memory Manager, and the appropriate file system driver.

If you wish to develop kernel-mode drivers for Windows NT, your driver must conform to the specifications provided by the NT I/O Manager. This includes creating and maintaining some data structures defined by the I/O Manager and also supplying the methods that manipulate such objects. Furthermore, your driver must respond appropriately to requests issued by the NT I/O Manager, and your driver must return results of each operation back to the I/O Manager. It is extremely unlikely that you can successfully develop a kernel-mode driver that does not use any of the services provided by the NT I/O Manager. Therefore, you will need to understand well the framework provided by the NT I/O Manager. The remainder of this chapter addresses some of these issues in further detail.

Concepts in I/O Manager Design

The design of the NT I/O subsystem exhibits a number of characteristics described in the following sections.

Packet-based I/O

The I/O subsystem is *packet-based*; i.e., all I/O requests are submitted using I/O Request Packets (IRPs). IRPs are typically constructed by the I/O Manager in response to user requests and sent to the targeted kernel-mode driver. However, any kernel-mode component can create an IRP and issue it to a kernel-mode driver using the `IoAllocateIrp()` and `IoCallDriver()` I/O Manager routines described in the DDK.

The I/O Request Packet is the only method you can use to request services from an I/O subsystem driver. By strictly conforming to this packet-based I/O model, the NT I/O Manager ensures consistency across the I/O subsystem and enables the layered driver model, described later in this section.

Each IRP sent to a kernel-mode driver represents a pending I/O request to that driver. An IRP will continue to be outstanding until the recipient of the IRP invokes the `IoCompleteRequest()` service routine for that particular IRP. Invoking `IoCompleteRequest()` results in that I/O operation being marked as completed, and the I/O Manager then triggers any post-completion processing that was awaiting completion of the I/O request. A particular IRP can be completed only once; i.e., only one kernel-mode driver can invoke `IoComple-teRequest()` for any outstanding IRP in the system.

You should be aware that, although packet-based I/O is the rule in Windows NT, the NT I/O Manager, NT Cache Manager, and the various NT file system implementations collaborate to implement functionality called the *fast I/O path*, which is an exception to this rule. The fast I/O method of I/O operations is only valid for file system drivers. These operations are implemented using direct function calls into the file system drivers and the NT Cache Manager instead of using the normal IRP method. The fast I/O path is described in detail later in this book.

NT object model

The I/O Manager conforms to the NT Object Model defined and implemented by the Object Manager component of the NT Executive.

Kernel-mode drivers, peripheral devices, controller cards, adapter cards, interrupts, and instances of open files are all represented in memory as *objects* that can be manipulated. These objects also have a set of *methods*, a set of operations that can be performed on the object, associated with them. For example, each controller card in the system is represented by a *controller object*, while each instance of an open file is represented by the *file object* data structure. The controller object can only be accessed using one of the methods associated with the object. This same restriction also applies to the file object structure, as well as to all other object types defined by the I/O Manager.

Note that kernel-mode drivers developed for Windows NT have to conform to this object-based model along with the rest of the I/O subsystem. All drivers must initialize a driver object structure representing the loaded instance of the device driver itself. In addition, if the driver manages devices or peripherals attached to the system, it must create and initialize one or more device object structures.

Since the I/O Manager uses the NT object model, it can also use the services of the Security Subsystem to control access to objects. The I/O Manager supports named object structures. For example, file objects have a name associated with them indicating the on-disk file that they represent. You can also create other named objects, such as device objects, that can then be opened by other processes or kernel-mode drivers.

Layered drivers

The I/O Manager supports layered kernel-mode drivers. Each driver in the hierarchy accepts an *I/O Request Packet*, processes it, and then invokes the next driver in the hierarchy.

Drivers lower in the hierarchy are closer to the actual hardware. However, only the lowest drivers typically interact directly with hardware devices or cards. The layered driver model is a boon to designers who wish to provide value-added functionality not supplied with the base operating system. This feature enables intermediate and filter drivers to be inserted into the driver hierarchy whenever required, and therefore allows new functionality to be easily added to the system. Furthermore, since each driver in the hierarchy interacts with drivers above and below it in a consistent fashion, development, debugging, and maintenance of kernel-mode drivers is a lot easier than on most other operating system implementations.

Asynchronous I/O

The NT I/O Manager supports *asynchronous I/O,* allowing a thread to request I/O operations and continue performing other computational tasks until the previously requested I/O operations have been completed. This makes for greater parallelism in completing computational tasks as opposed to the purely sequential model in which a thread must wait for an I/O operation to proceed before it proceeds with other activity.

Figure 4-2 graphically illustrates the sequence of activities that occur when performing synchronous and asynchronous I/O operations. As you can see from the illustration, the thread using asynchronous I/O can continue performing computational activity in parallel with the servicing of the I/O request that it has initiated. This results in higher performance and higher net throughput for the system. Note that the default I/O mechanism is the synchronous model.

Preemptible and interruptible

The I/O subsystem is preemptible and interruptible. It is extremely important for all kernel-mode driver developers to understand these two concepts.

Every thread executing in kernel mode executes at a certain system-defined Interrupt Request Level (IRQL). Each IRQL has an interrupt vector assigned to it by the system, and there are a total of 32 different IRQLs defined by Windows NT. Any thread can have its execution interrupted due to an interrupt at a higher IRQL than the IRQL at which that thread is executing. When such an interrupt occurs, the Interrupt Service Routines (ISRs) associated with that particular interrupt are executed in the context of the currently executing thread. This results in a suspension of the current flow of execution so that thread can execute the ISR code.†

IRQ levels range from `PASSIVE_LEVEL` (defined as numeric value 0), which is the default level at which all user threads and system worker threads execute, to IRQL `HIGH_LEVEL` (defined as numeric value 31), which is the highest possible hardware IRQL in the system. Most file system dispatch routines are executed at IRQL `PASSIVE_LEVEL`. However, most lower-level device driver routines (for example, SCSI class driver read/write dispatch entry points) are executed at higher IRQ levels—typically at IRQL `DISPATCH_LEVEL` (defined as numeric value 2).

---

* The term *overlapped I/O* used by the Win32 subsystem refers to the same concept as that of asynchronous I/O supported by the NT I/O Manager.

† ISR execution can be interrupted as well if another, even higher-level interrupt occurs.

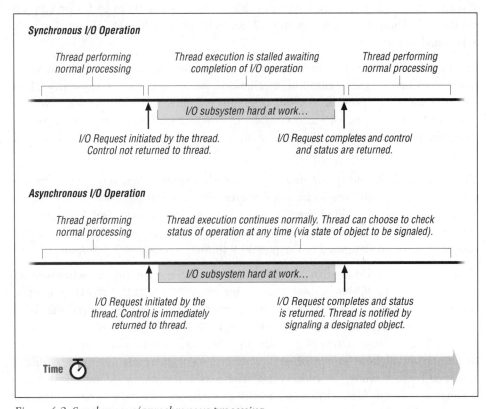

Figure 4-2. Synchronous/asynchronous processing

Since all code in the I/O subsystem is interruptible, drivers developed for the NT operating system must use appropriate synchronization and protection mechanisms to prevent data corruption for data accessed at different IRQ levels. For example, if your kernel-mode driver accesses a data structure at IRQL PASSIVE_ LEVEL in the context of a system worker thread, and if this driver also needs to access this same data structure at IRQL DISPATCH_LEVEL when servicing an interrupt request, the driver will have to use a spin lock that is always acquired at IRQL DISPATCH_LEVEL, which is the highest-level IRQL at which the spin lock could possibly be acquired, to provide mutually exclusive access to the data structure.*

Threads executing I/O subsystem code in the kernel are also *preemptible*. The Windows NT operating system associates execution priorities with threads. These priorities are typically variable, and most user-level threads and system worker

---

* Chapter 3, *Structured Driver Development,* provides a description of the available locking and synchronization primitives in the Windows NT kernel environment.

threads execute at relatively lower priorities, which allow them to be preempted by the NT scheduling code (in the NT Kernel) when a higher-priority thread is scheduled to run.

The fact that such threads could be preempted while executing kernel-mode code also necessitates synchronization mechanisms to ensure data consistency. This requirement is not present in other operating systems, such as the Windows 3.1 operating environment, or some versions of UNIX (e.g., HPUX, or SunOS), which currently do not allow preemption of threads or processes executing in kernel mode.

Kernel-mode driver designers must be extremely careful when acquiring common resources (e.g., read/write locks, semaphores) from within the context of different threads, because the Windows NT Kernel does not provide any built-in safeguards against programming errors resulting in situations like the priority inversion scenario described in Chapter 1, *Windows NT System Components.*

If you develop a driver that needs to acquire more than one synchronization resource at an IRQL that is less than or equal to `DISPATCH_LEVEL`, you must also be careful to define a strict locking hierarchy. For example, assume that your kernel-mode driver has to lock two `FAST_MUTEX` objects, *fast_mutex_1* and *fast_mutex_2*. You must define the order in which all threads in your driver can acquire both of these mutex objects. This order could be "acquire *fast_mutex_1* followed by *fast_mutex_2* or vice-versa. The reason for strictly defining and maintaining a locking hierarchy is to avoid a situation like one where *thread-a* acquired *fast_mutex_1*, wants to acquire *fast_mutex_2*, and gets preempted. *Thread-b* in the meantime gets scheduled to execute, acquires *fast_mutex_2*, and now needs to acquire *fast_mutex_1*. This scenario would cause a deadlock condition.

Portable and hardware independent

The I/O subsystem is portable and hardware independent. Kernel-mode drivers developed for Windows NT environments are also required to be portable and hardware independent.

The NT Hardware Abstraction Layer (HAL) is responsible for providing an abstraction of the underlying processor and bus characteristics to the rest of the system. NT drivers must be careful to use the appropriate HAL, NT Executive, and I/O Manager support routines to ensure portability across Alpha, MIPS, PowerPC, and Intel platforms.

The vast majority of the code in the NT I/O subsystem is written in C, a high-level and portable language. NT currently also requires kernel-mode driver developers to write their code in the C language, though it is possible with some extra work to write and link drivers in assembly. However, development in low-level languages, such as assembly, is highly discouraged, because assembly languages are inherently processor/architecture specific, and therefore such drivers cannot execute on more than one type of processor architecture.*

Multiprocessor safe

The I/O subsystem is multiprocessor safe. Windows NT was designed from the ground up to be able to execute on symmetric multiprocessing environments.

Execution of NT kernel-mode code and drivers on multiprocessor machines requires careful synchronization by kernel designers to avoid data consistency problems. For example, on uniprocessor machines, a common practice used to avoid data consistency problems while servicing an interrupt is to disable all other interrupts on the same machine (e.g., via a `cli` assembly instruction on x86 architectures). However, this same mechanism will fail on symmetric multiprocessor systems, because it is possible to encounter an interrupt on another processor, even though all interrupts had been disabled on the current processor. Similarly, on uniprocessor systems, it can be guaranteed (e.g., via usage of a critical section) that only one thread at a time can access a particular data structure. However, on symmetric multiprocessor architectures, even if preemption of a thread from a single processor were temporarily suspended, other threads executing on other processors could conceivably try to simultaneously access the same data structure.

Typically, spin locks and other higher level (Executive) synchronization mechanisms must be used consistently and correctly in Windows NT drivers to ensure correct functionality on multiprocessor systems.

Modular

The NT I/O subsystem is modular. Any driver within the NT I/O subsystem can be easily replaced by another driver that provides support for the same dispatch entry points supported by the original driver. The use of I/O Request Packets to submit I/O requests and an object-based model where all I/O operations are invoked via standard methods (or well-defined dispatch routine entry points) allows easy replacement of one kernel-mode driver with another that responds appropriately to the same dispatch routines.

All drivers also invoke the services of the I/O Manager using a well-defined and consistent set of service and utility functions. Theoretically, therefore, the I/O Manager is also easily replaceable. In practice, however, the I/O Manager is an extremely complex and integral component of the core NT operating system, and

---

* There are third-party-provided libraries that claim to assist you in developing Windows NT device drivers in C++.

would be extremely difficult to replace easily, even by developers at Microsoft itself.

One obvious benefit of the modularity in the I/O subsystem, however, is the relative ease with which I/O Manager support functions and driver functionality can be reimplemented without affecting any clients that use the services of the I/O Manager or such drivers. As long as the interfaces are maintained consistently, the internals of any implementation can be changed whenever required.

Configurable

All components of the I/O subsystem are configurable. The I/O Manager and all components that comprise the I/O subsystem try to maximize run-time configurability. The NT I/O Manager works with the HAL to determine the set of peripherals connected to the system at boot time. It then initializes the appropriate data structures to support these connected devices. This process avoids any requirements for hardcoding device configurations into the operating system. Windows NT does not as yet support true plug-and-play, though it should in the near future.

Kernel-mode drivers can be developed to manipulate devices; each driver is dynamically loadable and unloadable, minimizing unnecessary kernel overhead. The I/O Manager determines the drivers to be loaded, and the order in which they should be loaded, based upon the entries in the Windows NT Registry. I/O Manager configuration parameters, as well as those required by kernel-mode drivers, are obtained from the Windows NT Registry.

Any drivers that you develop should be as configurable as possible. This includes avoiding any hardcoded values in the driver code and instead obtaining these values from the system Registry, maximizing user configurability.

Process and Thread Context

Before discussing other details specific to the I/O Manager and the I/O subsystem, it would be useful for you to understand the concepts underlying thread/process contexts and to realize why a good grasp of these concepts is essential to understanding the operation of the various components in the Windows NT Kernel. To design and develop kernel-mode drivers under Windows NT successfully, you will need a solid grasp of these issues.

Every process in a Windows NT operating environment is represented by a *process object* structure and has an *execution context* that is unique to that process. The execution context for the process includes the process virtual address space (described in greater detail in the next chapter), a set of resources visible to that process, and a set of threads that belong to the process. Examples of resources owned by a process include file handles for files opened by that process, any synchronization objects created by that process, and any other objects that are created either by the process or on behalf of that process. Each process has at least one thread that is created and belongs to the process, although the process certainly could have numerous threads that belong to it. Note that in Windows NT, the fundamental scheduleable entity is a thread object and not the process object.

Each process is described internally by the Windows NT Kernel by a Process Environment Block (PEB) structure, which is opaque to the rest of the system. The PEB contains process global context, such as startup parameters, image base address, synchronization objects for process-wide synchronization, and loader data structures. Upon creation, the process is also assigned an access token called the primary token of the process. This token is used, by default, by threads associated with the process to validate themselves when they access any Windows NT object.

An *object table* is created for each new process object structure. This object table is either empty or a clone of the parent process object table, depending upon the arguments supplied to the system's create process routine and the inheritance attributes (OBJ_INHERIT) for each of the objects contained within the object table for the parent process. The default access token and the base priority for a new process is the same as that of the parent process.

A *thread object* is the entity that actually executes program code and is scheduled for execution by the Windows NT Kernel. Every thread object is associated with a process object; several threads can be associated with a single process object, which enables concurrent execution of multiple threads in a single address space. On uniprocessor systems, threads can never be executed concurrently; however, on multiprocessor systems, concurrent execution is possible and does occur.

Each thread object has a *thread context* unique to it. This context is architecture-dependent and is typically composed of the following:

* Distinct user and kernel stacks for the thread, identified by a user stack pointer and a kernel stack pointer
* Program counter
* Processor status
* Integer and floating-point registers
* Architecture-dependent registers

You will notice that object handles and other related information about open object structures stored in the process' object table are global to all threads associated with the process. Therefore, all threads in a process can access all open handles for the process, even those opened by other threads within the process. Threads belonging to other processes can only access objects that belong to the process to which they are affiliated; any attempt to access a resource owned by another process will result in an error returned by the Object Manager component in Windows NT.*

Threads are typically referred to as *user-mode* or *kernel-mode* threads. Note that there is no difference in the internal representation of such threads, as far as the Windows NT operating system is concerned. The only conceptual difference between such threads is the mode of the processor when the thread typically executes code, and the virtual address range that is therefore accessible by the thread. For example, a Win32 application process contains threads that execute code while the processor is in user mode and therefore are referred to as user-mode threads. On the other hand, there is a global pool of worker threads created by the Windows NT Executive in the context of a special system process that are used to execute operating system or driver code when the processor is in kernel mode; these threads are typically referred to as kernel-mode threads.

Although user-mode threads typically execute code with the processor in user mode, they often request system services, such as file I/O, which result in the processor executing a *trap* and entering kernel mode to execute the file system code that will service the I/O request. Notice that the user-mode thread is now executing operating system (file system driver) code with the processor in kernel mode, with all the rights and privileges that exist while the processor in this state. While executing in kernel mode, the thread can access kernel virtual addresses and perform operations that are otherwise always denied while the processor is in user mode.

Execution contexts

Consider a kernel-mode driver that you develop. The fact that this is a *kernel-mode driver* tells us that, while the code is being executed, the processor will be in kernel mode and will therefore be able to access the kernel virtual address range. You might wonder which set of threads will execute the code that you develop. Will it be some special thread that you would have to create, or will it be a user-mode thread that requests services from your driver, or will it be a thread on loan from the pool of system worker threads I referred to earlier?

The answer is, it depends. Your driver might always execute code in the context of a special thread that you may have created at driver initialization time, or it

---

* Typically, if you write a kernel-mode driver that attempts to use a handle that is not valid within the execution context of the currently executing process, you will see an error status of STATUS_INVALID_ HANDLE returned to you.

might execute code in the context of a user thread that has requested I/O services, or it might be invoked in the context of system worker threads. It is quite possible that, if you develop a file system driver, your driver will execute code in the context of all three types of threads. Furthermore, if you develop device drivers or other lower-level drivers that have their dispatch routines invoked in response to interrupts, your code will execute in the context of whichever thread was executing on that processor at the particular instant when the interrupt occurs. This is referred to as execution of code in the context of an *arbitrary thread*, i.e., a thread whose context is unknown to your driver. The operating system temporarily "borrows" the execution context of this thread to execute your driver routines simply because this thread happened to be executing code on the processor at the time the interrupt occurred.

As a kernel-mode driver designer, you must, therefore, always be aware of the execution context in which your code will execute. This execution context is always one of the following:

The context of a user-mode thread that has requested system services

> If you develop a file system driver or a filter driver that resides above the file system in the driver hierarchy, then your code will often execute in the context of the user-mode thread that requested, say, a read operation. Your code will then be able to access the kernel virtual address range, as well as the virtual addresses in the lower 2GB of the virtual address space belonging to the user-mode process to which the requesting user-mode thread belongs.*

> Typically, only file system drivers or filter drivers that intercept file system requests should expect that their dispatch routines† will be executed directly in the context of user-mode threads. Other drivers cannot expect this, simply because higher-level drivers might have posted the user request to be executed asynchronously in the context of a worker thread, or your driver code might be executed in response to an interrupt as discussed previously.

The context of a dedicated worker thread created by your driver or by some kernel-mode component (typically a component belonging to the I/O subsystem)

> File system drivers sometimes create special threads in the context of the system process (using the `PsCreateSystemThread()` system service routine described in the DDK) that they subsequently use to perform operations that cannot otherwise be performed in the context of user-mode threads requesting I/O services. Filter drivers might also choose to create such dedi-

---

* See the next chapter for a detailed discussion on virtual address spaces.

† Dispatch routines are the entry points into a kernel-mode driver. Later in this chapter, I will describe the possible dispatch routines that a kernel-mode driver could have.

cated worker threads; or for that matter, any kernel-mode component can choose to create one or more worker threads.

If you write a file system driver, you might occasionally request that certain operations be carried out by such threads created by you. Your code will then execute in the context of your special threads. If, however, you write lower-level drivers, and if the file system uses a special thread to process I/O requests, your driver might now be invoked in the context of the special thread created by the file system driver. Either way, you can see that the code executes in the context of specially created threads belonging to the system process.

The context of system worker threads specially created by the I/O Manager to serve I/O subsystem components

It is possible for certain I/O operations to be performed in the context of system worker threads that are created by the I/O Manager. These worker threads are often used by file system driver implementations, or by device drivers or other kernel-mode components that need thread context to perform their operations. For example, consider asynchronous I/O requests from user-mode applications. Typically, a file system driver will service such a request by "posting" the request to be picked up and handled by a system worker thread. Control is immediately returned to the calling application once the request has been posted, and the I/O Manager will notify the application once the request has been serviced in the context of the system worker thread. In such a situation, all lower-level drivers will have their dispatch routines invoked in the context of the system worker thread. Note that a system worker thread belongs to the system process, just like the dedicated worker threads created by kernel-mode components described earlier.

The important point to note here is that once the request has been posted to the system worker thread, the virtual address space now accessible in the context of the system worker thread is not the same as the virtual address space that was accessible in the context of the original, user-mode thread that requested the I/O operation. Similarly, the resources that were valid in the context of the original user-mode thread are no longer valid in the context of the system worker thread. The reason for this is obvious: the system worker thread executes in the context of the system process, and the user-mode thread that requested the I/O operation belongs to a distinct application process with its own object table, virtual address space, and process environment block.

The context of some arbitrary thread

Consider now a device driver able to service one IRP at any given point in time. Typically, most device drivers respond to I/O requests by queuing the

IRP for delayed processing, and by returning control immediately to the driver above it in the hierarchy. The IRP will be processed later when the driver can get to it, which is when I/O Request Packets before it in the queue have been processed.

So how is an IRP taken off the queue? Once the current I/O operation is completed by the target device, the device informs the operating system via a hardware interrupt. The operating system responds to this interrupt by invoking the Interrupt Service Routines that various drivers have associated with that specific interrupt. One of these Interrupt Service Routines will be the ISR specified by your driver. As part of ISR execution, the current IRP will complete, and the next IRP will be taken off the device queue and scheduled for actual I/O.*

The point to note here is that the ISR is executed asynchronously, in the context of the currently executing thread—an arbitrary thread. Therefore, when responding to such an interrupt, the driver cannot assume that the virtual address space accessible to it is the same as that of the user thread that requested the IRP now being completed. Resources associated with that thread are not available to the driver code either, because the driver does not know which thread's context is being borrowed to execute the ISR code.

Importance of thread and process contexts

Your kernel-mode driver code will be invoked in one of the execution contexts described previously. The code you develop should be aware of the execution context in which it will be invoked, since that determines the restrictions under which your driver must operate.

Consider the case where you develop a kernel-mode driver that needs to open some object; for example, your driver may perform file I/O itself and may therefore open a file and receive a file handle in return.† If you open this file in your driver initialization code (the `DriverEntry()` routine that every kernel-mode driver must have), you should be aware that this handle will only be valid in the

---

* If you do develop device drivers, you will note that most processing described above is actually performed as a Deferred Procedure Call (DPC) initiated by the ISR. However, the DPC is also executed in the context of an arbitrary thread. Although I will not focus on DPCs and device driver development in this book, you can consult the DDK for more information.

† Although it may seem strange that a kernel-mode driver might want to perform file I/O, there are filter drivers that provide functionality that requires such capabilities. A strength of the object-based, layered model followed by Windows NT components is that kernel-mode drivers have a tremendous amount of flexibility in terms of services available to them. This leads to the design of very robust, and useful, kernel-mode drivers.

context of the kernel process and the threads associated with the kernel process. So, if you use this handle in the context of system worker threads, the handle will be valid. However, if you attempt to use the handle in the context of a user thread, or an arbitrary thread context, your handle will not be valid. Similarly, if your driver opens an object while servicing a read request in the context of a user thread, the handle can be used only in the context of that thread. Any attempt to use the handle in the context of a system worker thread, for example, will result in an error.

You must be also be aware of when you can safely use the user buffer address, passed to your driver, for a read or write I/O operation. The user specifies a virtual address pointer that is perfectly valid in the context of that particular user thread. However, if the I/O operation is not performed in the context of that user thread (e.g., the I/O operation is performed asynchronously), the virtual address passed in by the user application will no longer be valid and therefore cannot be used by the kernel-mode driver. The I/O Manager provides support for accessing user buffers in other contexts besides that of the requesting thread. I will discuss this support in detail later in this chapter.

As discussed above, there are certain restrictions on the resources that can be used by your driver, depending on the thread context in which your code executes. This thread context depends on the circumstances under which your code is invoked, and this context will determine the resources that your driver can utilize.

Objects and handles

All objects created by kernel-mode components in the Windows NT Executive can be referred to in two ways, either by using an object handle returned by the NT Object Manager when the object is created or opened, or by using a pointer to the object. Note that the pointer to an object allocated by a kernel-mode component will typically be valid in all execution contexts, because the virtual address referring to the object will be from the kernel virtual address range (more on this in the next chapter). However, as mentioned earlier, object handles are specific to the execution context in which the handle is obtained and hence are valid only in that particular execution context.

Remember that each object created by the NT Object Manager has a reference count associated with it. When the object is initially created, this reference count is set to 1. The reference count is incremented whenever a kernel-mode component requests the Object Manager to do so, typically via an invocation of `ObReferenceObjectByHandle()`, which is described in the DDK. The reference count is decremented whenever a close operation is performed on the object handle. Kernel-mode drivers use the `ZwClose()` system service routine to close a handle to any system-created object. The reference count is also decremented when a kernel-mode component invokes `ObDereferenceObject()`, which requires the object pointer to be passed in. When the object count goes to zero, the object will be deleted by the NT Object Manager.

In the course of this book, you will often find places where we open an object and receive a handle, then obtain a pointer to the object and stash it away someplace (possibly in global memory), reference the object, and close the handle. This allows us two advantages:

- By saving a pointer to the object, we can always reobtain a handle to the same object in the context of a thread other than the one that originally opened the object. You can find concrete examples of this later in the book.

- By referencing the object and closing the original handle, we are assured the object will not be deleted (until we finally dereference it for the last time), yet we are also assured that, once the last dereference operation is performed, the object will automatically be deleted.

Keep the above discussion in mind as you go through the discussion and code presented throughout this book. This methodology of working with objects and object handles will probably be used extensively by you when you develop your own kernel-mode driver.

Common Data Structures

Data structures are the heart of any computer application or operating system. The NT I/O Manager defines certain data structures that are important to kernel-mode driver designers and developers. Often, your driver will have to create and maintain one or more instances of these data structures to provide driver functionality. In this section, I will briefly discuss the structure and uses of some of the data structures that are important to file system driver and filter driver developers. Note that all of these structures are well documented in the Windows NT DDK. However, our objective here is to understand the reason for creating and working with these data structures, as well as to get a good understanding of the important fields that comprise these data structures.

Driver Object

The DRIVER_OBJECT structure represents an instance of a loaded driver in memory. Note that a kernel-mode driver can only be loaded once; i.e., multiple instances of the same driver will not be loaded by the Windows NT I/O Manager. The driver object structure is defined as follows:

```
typedef struct _DRIVER_OBJECT {
    CSHORT                          Type;
    CSHORT                          Size;
    /* a linked list of all device objects created by the driver */
    PDEVICE_OBJECT                  DeviceObject;
    ULONG                           Flags;
    PVOID                           DriverStart;
    ULONG                           DriverSize;
    PVOID                           DriverSection;
    /*****************************************************************
       the following field is provided only in NT Version 4.0 and later
    *****************************************************************/
    PDRIVER_EXTENSION               DriverExtension;
    /*****************************************************************
       the following field is only provided in NT Version 3.51 and before
    *****************************************************************/
    ULONG                           Count;
    /*****************************************************************/
    UNICODE_STRING                  DriverName;
    PUNICODE_STRING                 HardwareDatabase;
    PFAST_IO_DISPATCH               FastIoDispatch;
    PDRIVER_INITIALIZE              DriverInit;
    PDRIVER_STARTIO                 DriverStartIo;
    PDRIVER_UNLOAD                  DriverUnload;
    PDRIVER_DISPATCH                MajorFunction[IRP_MJ_MAXIMUM_FUNCTION + 1];
} DRIVER_OBJECT;
```

Earlier in this chapter, I discussed the NT packet-based I/O model. Each I/O Request Packet describes an I/O request. The major function of an I/O request packet is to request functionality from a driver.

We know that the IRPs will have to be dispatched to some I/O driver routines. If you examine the driver object structure, you will notice that it contains memory allocated for an array of function pointers called the `MajorFunction` array. It is the responsibility of the kernel-mode driver to initialize the contents of this array for each major function that the kernel-mode driver supports. There are no restrictions on the number of functions that your driver must support, nor are there any restrictions specifying that each function pointer should point to a unique function; you could initialize the entry points for all major functions to point to a single routine and this would work perfectly (as long as your driver routine handled all the IRPs that would be directed to it). If you develop a kernel-mode driver, you will probably support at least one major function and should therefore initialize the function pointers appropriately.

The `DriverStartIo` and the `DriverUnload` fields are also left for the driver to initialize. Lower-level Windows NT drivers typically provide a `StartIo` function, which is invoked either when an IRP is dispatched to the driver, or when an IRP has just been popped off a queue. The `DriverStartIo` field is initialized by lower-level drivers to point to this driver-supplied `StartIO` function. Typically, as you will see in code presented later in this book, file system drivers and filter drivers will not need a `DriverStartIo` routine, because such drivers manage their pending I/O Request Packets via other internal queue management implementations. The `DriverUnload` field should point to a routine that is executed just before the driver is unloaded. This allows your kernel-mode driver an opportunity to ensure that any on-disk information is in a consistent state, as well as to allow lower-level drivers to put the device(s) they control into a known state. Note that it is not required that your driver be unloadable; in particular, file system drivers are extremely difficult to design so that they can be unloaded on demand. If your driver cannot be unloaded, you must not initialize the `DriverUnload` field in the driver object structure (the field is initialized to NULL by the I/O Manager and therefore your driver entry routine need not do anything to this field).

Many kernel-mode drivers create one or more device object structures. These structures are linked in the `DeviceObject` field in the driver object structure. At driver load time, this linked list is empty. However, the NT I/O Manager fills the list with pointers to device objects created by your driver as such device objects are created using the `IoCreateDevice()` service routine.

To load a driver, the I/O Manager executes an internal routine called `IopLoadDriver()`. This routine performs the following functionality:

- Determines the name of the driver to be loaded and checks whether the driver has already been loaded by the system.

  The I/O Manager checks to see whether the driver has already been loaded by examining a global linked list of loaded kernel modules. If the driver is already loaded, the I/O Manager immediately returns success; otherwise, it continues with the process of loading the driver. To have your driver loaded, your installation utility must have created an appropriate entry in the Registry. See Part 3 for more information on how the Registry must be configured for kernel-mode file system and filter drivers.

- If the driver is not loaded, the I/O Manager requests the Virtual Memory Manager (VMM) to map in the driver executable. As part of mapping in the driver code, the VMM checks to see that the file contains a valid Windows NT executable format. If the driver was built incorrectly, the VMM will fail the map request and the I/O Manager, in turn, will fail the driver load request.

- Now the I/O Manager invokes the Object Manager, requesting that a new driver object be created. Note that the `DRIVER_OBJECT` type is an I/O Manager-defined object type, which was previously created by the I/O Manager at system initialization time; it is therefore recognized as a valid object type by the NT Object Manager. Note also that the returned driver object structure is allocated from nonpaged system memory and is, therefore, accessible at all IRQ levels.

- The I/O Manager zeroes out the driver object structure returned by the Object Manager. Each entry in the `MajorFunction` array is initialized to `IopInvalidDeviceRequest()`. This is the default dispatch routine for the various entry points. This routine simply sets a return status of `STATUS_INVALID_DEVICE_REQUEST` and returns control to the calling process.

- The I/O Manager initializes the `DriverInit` field to refer to the initialization routine in your driver (the `DriverEntry` routine). `DriverSection` is initialized to the section object pointer* for the mapped executable, `DriverStart` is initialized to the base address to which the driver image was mapped, and `DriverSize` is initialized to the size of the driver image.

- The I/O Manager requests that the object be inserted into the linked list of driver objects maintained by the NT Object Manager. In return, the I/O Manager gets a handle to the object. This handle is referenced by the I/O Manager and closed, thereby ensuring that the object will be deleted when dereferenced at driver unload time.

- The `HardwareDatabase` field is initialized with a pointer to the Configuration Manager's hardware configuration information; this field could be used by lower-level drivers to determine the hardware configuration for the current boot cycle. The I/O Manager also initializes the `DriverName` field so that it can be used by the error logging component when required.

- Finally, the I/O Manager invokes the driver initialization routine, which is where your driver gets the opportunity to initialize itself, including initializing the function pointers in the driver object structure. You should note that your driver initialization routine is always invoked at IRQL `PASSIVE_LEVEL`, allowing you to use pretty much all of the system services available. Furthermore, your initialization routine will be invoked in the context of the system process; this is especially important to keep in mind if you open any objects or create any objects resulting in a handle being returned to you. Any such handles will only be valid in the context of the system process. In order to be able to use such objects in the context of other threads, you will have to use the methodology described earlier in the chapter, where you obtain a pointer to the object and then subsequently obtain handles in the context of other threads as and when required.

If your driver fails the initialization routine it will automatically be unloaded by the Windows NT I/O Manager. Remember to deallocate any allocated

---

* Chapter 5, *The NT Virtual Memory Manager*, explains section objects and the process of mapping files in greater detail.

memory prior to returning control to the I/O Manager and also to close and dereference any open objects, or else you will leave a trail behind you that could lead to degraded or impaired system behavior.

The driver entry routine is the initialization routine for a kernel-mode driver and is invoked by the I/O Manager. Each kernel-mode driver can also register a re-initialization routine that is invoked after all other drivers have been loaded and the rest of the I/O subsystem, as well as other kernel-mode components, have been initialized. In NT 3.51 and earlier, the `Count` field in the driver object structure contained a count of the number of times the reinitialization routine had been invoked.

Beginning with NT 4.0 and later, the NT I/O Manager allocates an additional structure that is an extension of the original driver object structure. This *driver extension* structure is defined below and contains fields to support plug-and-play for lower-level drivers that manage hardware devices and peripherals. The `Count` field has been moved to the driver extension structure with the new release; however, it still provides the same functionality as it did in earlier releases. Plug-and-play support is provided by lower-level drivers and will not be covered in this book.

```
typedef struct _DRIVER_EXTENSION {
    // back pointer to driver object
    struct _DRIVER_OBJECT        *DriverObject;
    // driver routine invoked when new device added
    PDRIVER_ADD_DEVICE           AddDevice;
    ULONG                        Count;
    UNICODE_STRING               ServiceKeyName;
} DRIVER_EXTENSION, *PDRIVER_EXTENSION;
```

Finally, notice that there is a pointer to a *fast I/O dispatch table* in the driver entry structure. Currently, only file system driver implementations provide support via the fast I/O path. Essentially, the fast path is simply a way to avoid the abstract, clean, modular, yet relatively slow method of using packet-based I/O. Using the function pointers provided by the file system driver in this structure, the NT I/O Manager can either directly invoke the file system dispatch routines or call directly into the NT Cache Manager to request I/O without having to set up an IRP structure. The `FastIoDispatch` field should be initialized by the driver entry routine to refer to an appropriate structure containing initialized file system entry points. In the coverage of the NT Cache Manager, provided later in this book, you will see a detailed discussion of the entry points that comprise the fast I/O method of I/O.

Device Object

Device object structures are created by kernel-mode drivers to represent logical, virtual, or physical devices. For example, a physical device, such as a disk drive, is represented in memory by a device object. Similarly, consider the situation where you develop an intermediate driver that presents a large physical disk as three smaller disks or partitions. Now, there will be one device object, representing a large physical disk, that is created by the lower-level disk driver, and your intermediate driver should create three additional device objects, each of which represents a virtual disk. Finally, a driver might choose to create a device object to represent a logical device; for example, the file system drivers create a device object to represent the file system implementation. This device object can be opened by other processes and can be used to send specific commands targeted to the file system driver itself.

Without a device object, a kernel-mode driver will not receive any I/O requests, since there must be a target device for every I/O request dispatched by the I/O Manager. For example, if you develop a disk driver and do not create a device object structure representing this particular disk device, no user process can access this disk. Once you do create a device object for the disk, however, file system drivers can potentially mount any volumes present on the physical media and user-mode processes can try to read and write data from the disk.

Unnamed device objects are rarely created by kernel-mode drivers, since such device objects are not easily accessible to other kernel-mode or user-mode components. If you create an unnamed device object, none of the other components in the system will be able to open it, and therefore, no component will direct any I/O to it. However, one common example of unnamed device objects are those created by file system drivers to represent mounted file system volumes. In this case, there is a device object, created by the disk driver representing the physical or virtual disk, on which the file system volume resides, and a Volume Parameter Block (VPB) structure (described later) performs the association between the named physical disk device object and the unnamed logical volume device object created by the file system driver. I/O requests are sent to the device object representing the physical disk. However, the I/O Manger checks to see whether the disk has a mounted volume on it (mounted volumes are identified by an appropriate flag in the VPB structure for the device object that represents the physical disk), and if so, it redirects the I/O to the unnamed device object representing the instance of the mounted volume.

When your driver issues a call to `IoCreateDevice()` to request creation of a device object, it can specify an additional amount of nonpaged memory to be allocated and associated with the newly created device object. The reason is to have a global memory area reserved for and associated with that particular device object. This memory is called the device object extension and will be allocated by the I/O Manager on behalf of your driver. The I/O Manager initializes the `DeviceExtension` field to point to this allocated memory. There are no constraints mandated by the I/O Manager on how this memory object should be used by your driver. You may wonder what the difference is between requesting a device extension and declaring global static variables. The answer can be summed up as potentially cleaner code design. Another important benefit is that device-specific global variables stored in a device object extension become logically associated with the device object immediately, and therefore you can avoid unnecessary acquisition of synchronization resources before accessing this device-object-specific data.

Any static variables declared by your kernel-mode driver are global to the entire Windows NT operating system. They are also not logically associated with any particular device object, so if your driver creates and manages multiple device object structures, you will have to design some method where the global structures can be associated with specific device objects. Note, however, that both statically declared global variables and the device extensions are allocated from nonpaged pool, although you can request that your static variables be made pageable (typically, this is never done). Many kernel-mode drivers make use of both statically declared global variables that are required by the entire driver, and a driver extension containing global variables that are specific to the context of a certain device object structure.

The device object structure is defined as follows:

```
typedef struct _DEVICE_OBJECT {
    CSHORT                          Type;
    USHORT                          Size;
    LONG                            ReferenceCount;
    struct _DRIVER_OBJECT           *DriverObject;
    struct _DEVICE_OBJECT           *NextDevice;
    struct _DEVICE_OBJECT           *AttachedDevice;
    struct _IRP                     *CurrentIrp;
    PIO_TIMER                       Timer;
    ULONG                           Flags;
    ULONG                           Characteristics;
    PVPB                            Vpb;
    PVOID                           DeviceExtension;
    DEVICE_TYPE                     DeviceType;
    CCHAR                           StackSize;
    union {
        LIST_ENTRY                  ListEntry;
        WAIT_CONTEXT_BLOCK          Wcb;
    } Queue;
    ULONG                           AlignmentRequirement;
    KDEVICE_QUEUE                   DeviceQueue;
    KDPC                            Dpc;
    ULONG                           ActiveThreadCount;
    PSECURITY_DESCRIPTOR            SecurityDescriptor;
    KEVENT                          DeviceLock;
    USHORT                          SectorSize;
```

```
    USHORT                          Spare1;
/******************************************************************
     the following fields only exist in NT 4.0 and later
******************************************************************/
    struct _DEVOBJ_EXTENSION        *DeviceObjectExtension;
    PVOID                           Reserved;
/******************************************************************
     the following field only exists in NT 3.51 and earlier versions
******************************************************************/
    LARGE_INTEGER                   Spare2;
} DEVICE_OBJECT;
```

Any kernel-mode driver can direct the I/O Manager to create a device object using the `IoCreateDevice()` routine. This routine, if successful, will return a pointer to the device object structure that is allocated from nonpaged memory. Many of the fields in the device object structure are reserved for use by the I/O Manager. A brief description of the important fields is given below:

- As long as the `ReferenceCount` field is nonnull, two invariants hold true. First, the device object will never be deleted. Second, the driver object representing the driver that created this device object will never be deleted (i.e., the driver will never be unloaded as long as any of the device objects created by the driver has a positive reference count). The `ReferenceCount` field is manipulated at various times by the I/O Manager and can also be manipulated by the driver.* An example of this field being incremented by the I/O Manager is whenever a new file stream is opened on a mounted volume; the reference count for the device object representing the mounted volume is incremented by 1 to ensure that the volume is not dismounted as long as any file is open. This also ensures that the file system driver is not unloaded as long as any file is open, since unloading the driver could lead to a system crash. Similarly, whenever a new volume is mounted, the device object representing the logical volume has its reference count incremented to ensure that both the device object and the corresponding driver object are not deleted.

- The I/O Manager initializes the `DriverObject` field to refer to the driver object representing the loaded instance of the kernel-mode driver that invoked the `IoCreateDevice()` routine.

- All device objects created by a kernel-mode driver are linked together using the `NextDevice` field in the device object. Note that there is no particular order in which a kernel-mode driver, traversing this linked list, should expect to find created device objects. As it happens, the I/O Manager adds new

---

* Be careful if your driver manipulates the `ReferenceCount` field in the device object, because there is no method with which you can synchronize your operation with that of the I/O Manager. This could lead to inconsistent behavior.

device objects to the head of the linked list; therefore, you will probably find the last device object inserted at the beginning of the list.

- In this chapter, as well as in Chapter 12, *Filter Drivers*, you will be exposed to more detail about how filter drivers can be developed for Windows NT environments. These filter drivers are intermediate-level drivers that intercept I/O requests targeted to certain device objects by interjecting themselves into the driver hierarchy and by attaching themselves to the target device objects. The concept of attaching to a device object is simple, as illustrated in Figure 4-3.

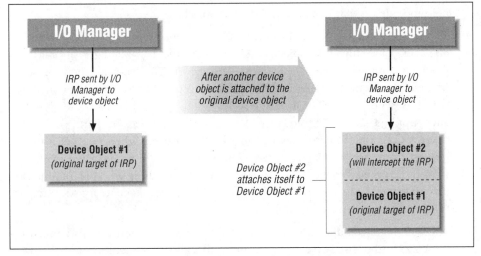

Figure 4-3. Illustration of a device object being attached to another

When a device object is attached to another (via the I/O-Manager-provided `IoAttachDevice()` or the `IoAttachDeviceByPointer()` routines), the `AttachedDevice` field in the device being attached to (device object #1 in Figure 4-3) will be set to the address of the device object being attached (device object #2).

- The `CurrentIrp` field is of interest to designers of device drivers or other lower-level drivers. Such drivers typically use the I/O-manager-supplied `IoStartNextPacket()` or `IoStartPacket()` routines to queue and dequeue an IRP from the driver queue of pending IRPs. Once the I/O manager dequeues a new IRP, it makes the dequeued IRP the current IRP to be processed by the driver. To do this, it inserts the IRP pointer in the `Current-Irp` field of the device object. The I/O manager subsequently passes a pointer to `DeviceObject->CurrentIrp` when invoking the device driver `StartIo()` dispatch routine.

This field is typically not of much interest to higher-level drivers.

- The `Timer` field is initialized when the driver invokes `IoInitialize-Timer()`. This allows the I/O Manager to invoke the driver-supplied timer routine every second.

- The device object `Characteristics` field describes some additional attributes for the physical, logical, or virtual device that the object represents. The possible values are `FILE_REMOVABLE_MEDIA`, `FILE_READ_ONLY_DISK`, `FILE_FLOPPY_DISK`, `FILE_WRITE_ONCE_MEDIA`, `FILE_REMOTE_DEVICE`, `FILE_DEVICE_IS_MOUNTED`, or `FILE_VIRTUAL_VOLUME`. This field is manipulated by the I/O Manager, as well as by the file system or kernel-mode driver that manages the device object.

- The `DeviceLock` is a synchronization-type event object allocated by the I/O Manager. Currently, this object is acquired by the I/O Manager prior to dispatching a mount request to a file system driver. This allows synchronization of multiple requests to mount the volume. You should only be concerned with this event object if you design a file system driver that uses the I/O-Manager-supplied `IoVerifyVolume()` routine (described in Part 3). In that case, you should be careful not to invoke that routine when you get a mount request from the I/O Manager, since the `DeviceLock` would have been previously acquired by the I/O Manager prior to sending you the mount IRP; invoking the verify routine would cause the I/O Manager to try to reacquire this resource and cause a deadlock.

- The I/O Manager allocates memory for the device extension and initializes the `DeviceExtension` field to point to this allocated memory.

I/O Request Packets (IRP)

As described earlier, the Windows NT I/O subsystem is packet-based. Kernel-mode drivers that comprise the I/O subsystem receive I/O Request Packets (IRP), which contain details of the operation being requested. The recipient of the IRP is responsible for processing the IRP, and either forwarding it on to another kernel-mode driver for additional processing, or completing the IRP, indicating that processing of the request described in the IRP has been terminated.

IRP allocation

All I/O requests are routed through the NT I/O Manager. Most often, a user process executes a Win32- or other subsystem-specific I/O request (e.g., `Create-File()`), and this request gets translated to an NT system service call to the I/O Manager. Upon receiving the I/O request, the I/O Manager identifies the driver that should service the I/O request. Most likely, this will be a file system driver that will have mounted the file system on the physical device to which the I/O request is targeted.

To dispatch the request to the kernel-mode driver, the I/O Manager allocates an I/O Request Packet using the routine `IoAllocateIrp()`.* This structure is always allocated from nonpaged pool. The method of allocation differs slightly in the various versions of Windows NT.

NOTE   A *zone* is a system-defined structure supported by the Windows NT Executive and is used to efficiently manage allocation and deallocation of fixed-sized chunks of memory. Allocating and freeing memory using zones is more efficient than asking for small chunks of memory from the VMM, which could also lead to some internal memory fragmentation. Using a zone requires your driver to perform two steps: first, allocate the memory that will comprise the zone and inform the NT Executive about this allocated pool, as well as the size of entries you will allocate from the zone; second, use the available `ExAllocateFromZone()` and other related support routines to allocate and free entries using the zone.

Read Chapter 2, *File System Driver Development*, for a discussion on how to use zones in your driver.

In NT version 3.51 and earlier, the I/O Manager first attempts to allocate the IRP from a zone composed of fixed-sized IRP structures. As you will read later in this discussion of IRPs, the size of the IRP depends upon the number of *stack locations* that are required for the IRP. Therefore, the I/O Manager keeps two zones available, one for IRPs with relatively fewer stack locations, and the other for I/O Request Packets with a larger number of stack locations. If the zone from which allocation is attempted is found empty (this can happen in high-load situations where an extremely large amount of concurrent I/O is in progress), the I/O Manager requests memory for the IRP directly from the VMM (actually, the I/O Manager uses the `ExAllocatePool()` support routine provided by the NT Executive). For I/O requests that originate in user-mode, if no memory is currently available, an error is returned to the user application indicating that the system is out of available resources. However, for I/O requests that originate in kernel-mode, the I/O Manager attempts to allocate memory for the IRP from the `NonPagedPoolMustSucceed` memory pool. If this memory allocation request does not succeed, the attempt will result in a system bugcheck.

The methodology used in NT version 4.0 is similar with one slight variation: the I/O Manager uses lookaside lists, a new structure used to manage fixed-sized pools of memory introduced in this new release, instead of zones. The reason for

---

* The `IoAllocateIrp()` routine is documented in the DDK. It can also be used by other kernel-mode drivers to request an IRP to be allocated. Supply a FALSE for the `ChargeQuota` argument required with this routine invocation.

this new structure is to gain some efficiency, because lookaside lists do not always use spin locks to perform synchronization; instead they use an atomic 8-byte compare exchange instruction on architectures where such support is possible.

Other kernel-mode components besides the I/O Manager can use the I/O-Manager-supplied routine `IoAllocateIrp()` to request a new IRP structure. This IRP can subsequently be used to send a I/O request to a kernel-mode driver. Other routines provided by the I/O Manager that also use `IoAllocateIrp()` to obtain a new IRP structure and then return these newly allocated IRPs after the initialization of certain fields are `IoMakeAssociatedIrp()`, `IoBuildSynchronousFsdRequest()`, `IoBuildDeviceIoControlRequest()`, and `IoBuildAsynchronousFsdRequest()`. Consult the DDK for more information on these routines. Part 3 also uses some of these routines in implementing filter drivers.

IRP structure

Logically, each I/O Request Packet is composed of the following:

- The IRP header
- I/O Stack Locations

The IRP header contains general information about the I/O request, useful to the I/O Manager as well as to the kernel-mode driver that is the target of the request. Many of the fields in the IRP header can be accessed by a kernel-mode driver; other fields exist solely for the convenience of the I/O Manager and should be considered off-limits by the drivers processing the IRP.

Here is a brief explanation of important fields that comprise the IRP header:

`MdlAddress`

A Memory Descriptor List (MDL) is a system-defined structure that describes a buffer in terms of the physical memory pages that back up the virtual address range comprising the buffer. There are different ways in which buffers used for I/O request handling can be passed down to the kernel-mode driver. Descriptions for the three methods will appear shortly. Remember for now, though, that if the *DirectIo* method is used, the `MdlAddress` field will contain a pointer to the MDL structure that can then be used in data transfer operations.

`AssociatedIrp`

This field is an union of three elements, defined as follows:

```
union {
    struct _IRP        *MasterIrp;
    LONG                IrpCount;
```

```
    PVOID                    SystemBuffer;
} AssociatedIrp;
```

Any IRP structure that has been allocated can be categorized as either a *master IRP* or an *associated IRP*. An associated IRP is, by definition, associated with some master IRP, and can be created only by a higher-level kernel-mode driver. By creating one or more associated IRPs, the highest-level driver can split up the original I/O request and send each associated IRP to lower-level drivers in the hierarchy for further processing.

For example, higher-level drivers sometimes execute the following loop:

```
while (more processing is required) {
    create an associated IRP using IoMakeAssociatedIrp();
    send the associated IRP to a lower-level driver using
    IoCallDriver();
    if (STATUS_PENDING is returned) {
        wait on an event for the completion of the associated IRP;
    } else {
        associated IRP was completed;
        check result and determine whether to continue;
    }
}
```

For an associated IRP, the union described here contains a pointer to the master IRP. For a master IRP, however, this union contains the count of the number of associated IRPs for this master IRP; or, if no associated IRPs have been created, the **SystemBuffer** pointer might be initialized to a buffer allocated in kernel virtual address space for data transfer. System buffers are allocated by the I/O Manager when a kernel-mode driver requests *buffered I/O* (described later in this book).

Note that the **IrpCount** field is manipulated under the protection of an internal I/O Manager resource. Therefore, external kernel-mode drivers must not attempt to manipulate or access the contents of this field directly.

ThreadListEntry

This field is typically manipulated by the I/O Manager. Before invoking a driver dispatch routine via **IoCallDriver()**, all I/O Manager routines insert the IRP into a linked list of IRPs for the thread in whose context the I/O operation is taking place. For example, if a user thread invokes a read request, the I/O Manager will allocate a new IRP structure, and insert it into the list of IRPs being processed by the user thread prior to invoking the file system read dispatch routine.

NOTE   There is a field in each thread structure called `IrpList`, which
              serves as the head of a linked list of pending I/O Request Packets.
              The `ThreadListEntry` field, described earlier, is used to queue
              the IRP to this linked list. This list is used to track all pending I/O
              Request Packets for the thread in question; this is especially useful
              when the I/O subsystem tries to cancel IRPs for a particular thread.

              Note that the `IoAllocateIrp()` routine does not queue the re-
              turned IRP to the linked list of outstanding IRPs for the current
              thread. Therefore, when a cancel request is posted, that IRP will not
              be found among the list of IRPs for the thread.

IoStatus

This field should be appropriately updated by your kernel-mode driver before
completing the I/O Request Packet. A description of the structure is provided
later in this chapter. Note that this field is part of the IRP structure, and not
part of the I/O status block structure passed in to the I/O Manager by the
thread requesting the I/O operation. It is the I/O Manager's responsibility to
transfer the results of the I/O operation from this field to the I/O status structure submitted by the requesting thread. This operation is performed by the
I/O Manager as part of the postprocessing of the IRP, once the IRP has been
completed by kernel-mode drivers.

RequestorMode

When code in your driver is executed, it would be useful if you knew
whether the caller was a user-mode thread (e.g., an application requesting an
I/O operation), or if the caller was a kernel component (some other driver
requesting your services in the context of a system worker thread).

You may wonder why such information could be useful. Think about the
case where the caller is a user-mode thread; you know then that you cannot
blindly assume that the arguments passed in to your driver are legitimate. If
your driver uses the direct-IO method of passing buffer pointers (explained
later), you will need to convert the passed-in addresses to something usable
by your kernel-mode code. This is especially true if the request will be
handled asynchronously by your driver.

On the other hand, if your driver is invoked from a system worker thread,
you could bypass these argument checks, because you could assume that
addresses passed in to you are legitimate and usable directly by your driver.

Similarly, the NT I/O Manager, as well as other kernel components such as
the Virtual Memory Manager, need to identify and differentiate whether
clients of their services are executing kernel-mode (operating system) code,
or whether the request came from a user-space component. This information

is used to check the legitimacy of the arguments passed in to these kernel-mode components.*

The solution used throughout the NT Executive is to identify the processor mode in which the calling thread executed prior to invoking the services of the kernel-mode component. Note that the key concept here is that the previous mode of the calling thread is important; the very fact that the thread is executing kernel-mode code at the instant when the check is made tells us that the current mode will always be kernel mode. To obtain the previous mode information, the I/O Manager directly accesses a field in the thread structure. The `ExGetPreviousMode()` function, declared in the DDK, provides the same functionality to third-party driver developers. This routine returns the previous mode of the thread being checked: user or kernel mode.

The I/O Manager puts the information about the previous mode of the requesting thread into the `RequestorMode` field prior to invoking the `IoCallDriver()` routine, which, in turn, invokes one of your driver dispatch routines. You should use this information both internally in your driver, as well as in invocations to system service routines such as `MmProbeAndLockPages()`.

PendingReturned

Each IRP is typically handled by more than one driver in the hierarchy. To process an IRP asynchronously, a kernel-mode driver must execute the following steps:

a. Mark the IRP pending by invoking the `IoMarkIrpPending()` function.

b. Queue the IRP internally.

Lower-level drivers may use a `StartIo()` function instead.

c. Return a status code of `STATUS_PENDING`.

The `IoMarkIrpPending()` call (implemented as a macro) simply sets the `SL_PENDING_RETURNED` flag in the `Control` field of the current I/O stack location.†

At the time of IRP completion processing, during the execution of the `IoCompleteRequest()` function, the I/O Manager traverses each stack location that had been used by drivers in the hierarchy, looking for any completion routines that may need to be invoked. This traversal of stack locations happens in reverse order from that used in processing the IRP. The most recently used stack location is processed first (the one used by the lowest-

---

* If the I/O Manager read system service (`NtReadFile()`) blindly assumed that the passed-in buffer address was a legitimate kernel-mode usable address, malicious users could have a field day overwriting operating system data with their own!

† Stack locations are discussed in detail later in this chapter. You may skip this discussion for the moment and come back to it after you have read that section.

level driver in the hierarchy that processed the IRP), followed by the next one, and so on.

As each stack location is unwound, the I/O Manager notes whether the SL_ PENDING_RETURNED flag had been set in the I/O stack location, and sets the PendingReturned flag to TRUE if the flag had been set. However, if the flag was not set in the stack location, the I/O Manager sets the Pending-Returned field to FALSE.

WARNING   The value of the PendingReturned field may change as the I/O stack locations are being traversed, while the I/O Manager looks for completion routines that may need to be invoked.

So why is the value of this field important? Well, later on in the IoCompleteRequest() function, the I/O Manager checks the value of the PendingReturned field to determine whether or not to queue a special kernel Asynchronous Procedure Call (APC) to the thread that originally requested the I/O operation. Your file system or filter driver will have to cooperate with the I/O Manager to ensure that the right course of action is adopted. You will see how your driver's actions affect the behavior of the I/O Manager later in this chapter.

Cancel, CancelIrql, and CancelRoutine

Kernel-mode drivers that process I/O Request Packets that might potentially require an indefinite time interval to be completed should provide appropriate IRP cancellation support. Our perspective is that of a file system driver or that of a filter driver. We would need to provide this functionality if we do not pass on IRPs to lower-level disk or network drivers but perform our own processing instead. Note that all three fields listed above are manipulated by either the driver or the I/O Manager to provide the capability to cancel pending I/O Request Packets when required.

ApcEnvironment

When an IRP is completed, the I/O Manager performs postprocessing on the IRP, the details of which are given below. The ApcEnvironment field is used internally by the I/O Manager in performing postprocessing on the IRP in the context of the thread that originally requested the I/O operation. This field is initialized by the I/O Manager when allocating the IRP and should not be accessed by driver designers.

Zoned/AllocationFlags

The Zoned field was replaced with the AllocationFlags field in NT version 4.0. Fundamentally, the field (called by whatever name) records internal bookkeeping information used by the I/O Manager during IRP completion to determine whether the IRP was allocated from a *zone/lookaside list,* or from system *nonpaged pool,* or from system *nonpaged-must-succeed pool.* This information is not useful from the kernel driver's perspective, except when debugging the driver and trying to locate all IRP structures allocated out of the global lookaside list or zone.

Caller-supplied arguments

The following are part of the IRP:

```
PIO_STATUS_BLOCK            UserIosb;
PKEVENT                     UserEvent;

union {
    struct {
        PIO_APC_ROUTINE     UserApcRoutine;
        PVOID               UserApcContext;
    } AsynchronousParameters;
    LARGE_INTEGER           AllocationSize;
} Overlay;
```

The `UserIosb` field in the IRP is set by the I/O Manager to point to the I/O status block supplied by the thread requesting I/O. As part of the postprocessing performed by the NT I/O Manager upon completion of an IRP, the I/O Manager copies the contents of the `IoStatus` field to the I/O status block pointed to by the `UserIosb` field.

Most NT I/O system service routines (documented in Appendix A) accept an optional event argument. This argument (if supplied by the caller) is initialized by the NT I/O Manager to the not-signaled state and is set to the signaled state by the I/O Manager upon completion of I/O. The I/O Manager fills in the `UserEvent` field with the address of the caller-supplied event object.

The `AllocationSize` field in the `Overlay` structure is only valid for file create requests. The user is allowed to specify an optional initial size for a file being created. The I/O Manager initializes the `AllocationSize` field with this caller-supplied size prior to invoking the file system driver create/open dispatch routine.

Many of the NT system services provided for I/O operations by the NT I/O Manager allow asynchronous operations. The caller thread can request that I/O be performed asynchronously and can also specify an APC to be invoked upon completion of the IRP. For these system services, the I/O Manager dutifully invokes the user-supplied APC, passing it the supplied APC context, as part of the postprocessing performed by the I/O Manager upon completion of the IRP by a kernel-mode driver. The I/O Manager stores the calling-thread-supplied APC function pointer in the `UserApcRoutine` field. The context is stored in the `UserApcContext` field. Some examples of asynchronous system services are directory control, read, write, and lock operations. Note that create/open requests are always processed synchronously, and therefore the `AllocationSize` field and the `AsynchronousParameters` form part of the `Overlay` union structure.

For I/O operations that involve transferring data, the caller supplies a data buffer. This buffer might serve as an input buffer, an output buffer, or both. In any case, the I/O Manager initializes the `UserBuffer` field with the caller-supplied buffer pointer before invoking `IoCallDriver()`. Upon IRP completion, if there is any data that needs to be copied back to the caller's buffer, the I/O Manager performs this function as part of postprocessing done on the IRP. If your driver does not specify either *direct I/O* or *buffered I/O* as the preferred method of user buffer manipulation, the I/O Manager will assume that you will handle the user-supplied buffer yourself and will therefore not allocate an MDL, or supply your driver with a system address. Your driver can subsequently use the buffer pointer in the `UserBuffer` field directly.*

Tail

An IRP has a `Tail` structure defined as follows:

```
union {
    struct {
        KDEVICE_QUEUE_ENTRY                 DeviceQueueEntry;
        PETHREAD                            Thread;
        PCHAR                               AuxiliaryBuffer;
        LIST_ENTRY                          ListEntry;
        struct _IO_STACK_LOCATION          *CurrentStackLocation;
        PFILE_OBJECT                        OriginalFileObject;
    } Overlay;
    KAPC                                    Apc;
    ULONG                                   CompletionKey;
} Tail;
```

This structure consists of fields that are manipulated and accessed directly only by the NT I/O Manager. It is not recommended that your driver try to directly access the contents of these fields.

The `DeviceQueueEntry` field is used to queue IRPs for a specific lower-level driver. Most lower-level drivers allow the NT I/O Manager to maintain a list of pending I/O Request Packets. The I/O Manager uses the `DeviceQueueEntry` field to queue the packet for the target device object, if the device object is found to be busy when `IoStartPacket()` is invoked by the device driver dispatch

---

* Note that the user-mode virtual address is valid only in the context of the user-mode thread requesting I/O. If your driver is a file system implementation, you will either complete the I/O immediately in the context of the user-mode thread, in which case you can use the passed-in virtual addresses directly, or your driver will have to obtain an appropriate system mode address for the user-supplied buffer, prior to queuing the IRP for later processing in the context of system worker threads.

routine. The DDK describes the `IoStartPacket()`, `IoStartNext-Packet()`, and `IoStartNextPacketByKey()` support routines, which manipulate this field. Kernel-mode drivers should not try to directly access or manipulate the contents of the `DeviceQueueEntry` field.

Before dispatching an IRP, the I/O Manager initializes the `Thread` field to point to the thread in whose context the dispatch will occur. This field is subsequently used by both lower-level drivers and file system drivers.

Consider the situation when a hard error occurs. File systems use the `IoRaiseInformationalHardError()` call to place a pop-up message box on the system console to notify the user of the error situation. This call is blocking and it displays the error by delivering a special kernel APC to the target thread. The problem is that the thread in whose context the message box is displayed is blocked until a user physically dismisses the error message from the system console. If, however, no thread is specified in the argument list to the `IoRaiseInformationalHardError()` routine, the error message is delivered in the context of a special (single) system worker thread.

Typically, if an error occurs, a kernel-mode driver will examine the `Overlay.Thread` field to determine if the thread is a system worker thread. If it is, then the driver will send in a NULL `Thread` argument to `IoRaiseInformationalHardError()`, because blocking system worker threads for an indefinite amount of time is clearly unacceptable.

Another instance when the `Thread` field assumes importance is in the handling of removable media. If a user-induced error occurs when reading/writing removable media, the lower level device driver uses the `IoSetHardErrorOrVerifyDevice()` routine to indicate that something unexpected has occurred and that higher-level drivers should either report an error to the user or verify that the media in the drive is correct. In response to this call, the I/O Manager simply stores the device object to be verified in the `DeviceToVerify` field for the thread object pointed to by the `Overlay.Thread` field in the IRP. The higher-level (file system) driver subsequently invokes `IoGetDeviceToVerify()`, supplying the thread object pointer obtained from the `Overlay.Irp` field, and the I/O Manager, in response, hands back the stored device object pointer.

Note that the `IoAllocateIrp()` I/O Manager service routine does not set the `Thread` object in the returned IRP. This is the responsibility of the caller of this routine.

The `AuxiliaryBuffer` exists supposedly to pass additional information to a kernel-mode driver that is not contained elsewhere in the IRP. However, at this point, none of the I/O Manager routines use this field to pass information to a kernel-mode driver.*

The `CurrentStackLocation` field is simply a pointer to the current stack location for the IRP. Stack locations are discussed later in this chapter. The important point to note for kernel-mode drivers is to always use I/O Manager-provided access functions to get the pointer to the current and the next stack locations in the IRP. To maintain portability, your driver should never try to access the contents of this field directly.

The `OriginalFileObject` field is initialized by the I/O Manager to the address of the file object to which an I/O operation is being targeted. The same information is available to the highest-level driver (typically, the file system driver) to which the I/O operation is sent from the current stack location. However, the I/O Manager keeps this information in the IRP header and can therefore access it independently of the manner in which stack locations are manipulated by lower-level drivers. The file object is used in the postprocessing of the IRP after it has been completed. For example, if the file object pointer is not NULL (i.e., the `OriginalFileObject` field is initialized at IRP allocation), the I/O Manager checks whether it needs to send a message to a completion port,† or dereference any event objects, or perform any similar notification or cleanup operation related to that file object. It is legitimate for this field to be NULL, in which case the I/O Manager will skip some of the postprocessing that it would otherwise perform.

The `Apc` field is used internally by the I/O Manager after the IRP has been completed, to queue an APC request for final postprocessing of the IRP in the context of the thread that issued the I/O request.

As mentioned earlier, each I/O Request Packet is composed of the IRP header, and the stack locations for that IRP. Some of the fields in the IRP structure such as `StackCount`, `CurrentLocation`, and `CurrentStackLocation` are related to stack location manipulation. IRP stack locations are discussed next.

Stack locations and reusing IRP structures

Windows NT I/O request packets are reusable. In a layered driver environment, such as in the Windows NT I/O subsystem, each higher-level driver in the hierarchy invokes the next lower-level driver, until some driver actually completes the

---

* If you write a file system driver, you might notice the value of this field is nonnull for directory-control IRPs. However, the same buffer pointer containing the directory name is accessible via the information obtained from the current stack location for the IRP, stored in the `Parameters.QueryDirectory.FileName` field.

† Consult the Win32 SDK for further information about I/O Completion Ports.

original IRP. It is quite possible, and is often the case, that the same IRP is passed down from driver to driver until it is completed.

Completing the IRP requires invoking `IoCompleteRequest()`; after such a call is issued, no component, other than the I/O Manager, can touch that IRP, since it can be deallocated at any time.

So how can a single IRP structure be reused cleanly? The solution provided by the NT I/O Manager is to use stack locations that contain descriptions of the I/O requests to the target device objects. When initially dispatching the IRP to a kernel-mode driver, the I/O Manager fills in one stack location with the parameters for the desired operation. Later, the driver to which the IRP is sent determines whether it can complete the IRP itself, or whether it needs to invoke another driver lower in the hierarchy. If it needs to invoke a lower-level driver, the current holder of the IRP can simply initialize the next IRP stack location, and then invoke the lower-level driver via `IoCallDriver()`, passing it the IRP. This process is repeated until a driver in the chain performs all of the required processing and decides to complete the IRP.

The NT I/O Manager allocates space for multiple associated stack locations when an IRP structure is allocated. Each of these stack locations can contain a complete description of an I/O request. For example, an IRP allocated for a *read* request should contain the following information:

- A function code, which will be examined by the kernel-mode driver to determine the type of request issued. In this example, the function code indicates a read request.

- An offset from which data should be read.

- The number of bytes that are requested.

- A pointer to the output buffer.

In addition to the above, other information relevant to the read request might also be passed to the driver that manages the device object that is the target of the read operation. All of this information is encapsulated into a single stack location structure.

The number of stack locations allocated for an IRP depends upon the `Stack-Size` field in the target device object to which the IRP is being issued. The `StackSize` field is initialized to 1 when the device object is created; it can then be set to any value by the driver managing the device object. The `StackSize` field is also changed when a device object is attached to another device object. As part of the attach process, the `StackSize` value is set to the value obtained from the device object being attached to, incremented by 1. The logic here is simple: an IRP sent to a device object needs one stack location for the initial target device object; it also needs one stack location for each filter and/or driver in the hierarchy that will perform some processing on the I/O Request Packet.

As shown in Figure 4-4, if a read request is sent to the file system driver that has a volume mounted on disk A, the I/O Manager will allocate four stack locations when creating the read IRP. These stack locations are used in reverse order, similar to the last-in-first-out usage of a stack structure. When invoking a driver, the I/O Manager always pushes the stack location pointer to point to the next stack location; when the called driver releases the IRP, the stack location pointer is popped to once again point to the previous stack location. Therefore, when invoking the filter driver dispatch routine in Figure 4-4 below, the I/O Manager uses stack location #4, the last stack location allocated.

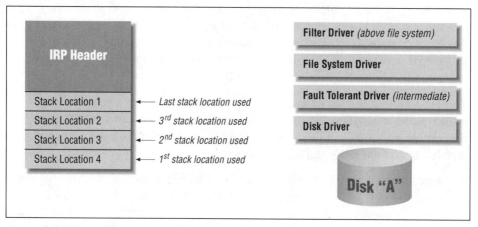

Figure 4-4. IRP stack locations used for a driver hierarchy

The NT I/O Manager initializes the `StackCount` field in the IRP header with the total number of stack locations allocated for that IRP. The `CurrentLocation` field in IRP header is initialized by the I/O Manager to (`StackCount + 1`). This value is decremented each time a driver dispatch routine is invoked via `IoCallDriver()`.

Therefore, if the `StackCount` is 4, the initial value of `CurrentLocation` is set to 5, which is an invalid stack location pointer value. The reason for this, however, is that to dispatch an IRP to the next driver in the hierarchy, the kernel component must always get a pointer to the next stack location and then fill in appropriate parameters for the request.

When an IRP is being dispatched to the first driver in the hierarchy, the next stack location will be (`CurrentStackLocation–1`) equal to 4, the correct value for the stack location used for the filter driver above.

The I/O Manager often performs sanity checks using this value to ensure that the IRP is being routed correctly through the I/O subsystem. For example, in `IoCallDriver()`, the I/O Manager first decrements the `CurrentLocation` field (since a new driver is being invoked, it requires the next IRP stack location), then checks to see if the `CurrentLocation` value is less than or equal to 0. If the value does become less than or equal to 0, it is obvious that `IoCall-Driver()` is being invoked once too often for the number of stack locations that were initially allocated (or that there is some stray pointer corrupting memory), and therefore the I/O Manager performs a bugcheck with the error code of `NO_MORE_IRP_STACK_LOCATIONS`.

NOTE   The reason for a bugcheck is that, by the time the `IoCallDriver()` is invoked, critical damage may have already been done, since the caller will in all likelihood have filled in the contents of the next stack location for the use of the driver being called. However, in this situation, the next stack location is some unallocated memory at the end of the IRP structure, which could literally be anything.

Continuing execution at this time could lead to all sorts of problems, including the possible corruption of user data.

The I/O Manager maintains a pointer to the current stack location, in addition to the `CurrentLocation` value mentioned previously. This pointer is maintained in the `CurrentStackLocation` field in the `Tail.Overlay` structure that is contained in the IRP header. Kernel-mode drivers should never try to manipulate the contents of either the `CurrentLocation` or the `CurrentStackLocation` fields themselves.* The I/O Manager does provide routines for a driver to get a pointer to the current stack location, via a call to `IoGetCurrentIrpStack-Location()`, to get a pointer to the next stack location using `IoGetNext-IrpStackLocation()` so that the driver can set up the contents of the stack location appropriately for the next driver in the hierarchy, and in rare cases to use `IoSetNextIrpStackLocation()` to set the stack location value.

The stack location structure defined in the NT DDK is composed of some fields that are independent of the nature of the I/O request being described by the stack location. Here are these fields:

MajorFunction

The NT I/O Manager defines a set of major functions, each of which identifies a generic function that a kernel-mode driver can implement. Functions are identified by function codes or numbers, and the set of functions is deliber-

---

* That being said, it is true that NT file systems themselves perform some underhanded operations on these fields. However, for most kernel-mode drivers, it is far more preferable to stick with the I/O Manager-supplied access methods to view and modify the contents of these fields.

ately comprehensive, since the function codes serve all types of NT kernel-mode drivers, including file system drivers, intermediate drivers, device drivers, and other lower level drivers.

When an IRP is delivered to a kernel-mode driver, the driver must examine the `MajorFunction` field in the current stack location to find out the functionality expected from the driver. The possible major function codes are shown below:

```
#define IRP_MJ_CREATE                      0x00
#define IRP_MJ_CREATE_NAMED_PIPE           0x01
#define IRP_MJ_CLOSE                       0x02
#define IRP_MJ_READ                        0x03
#define IRP_MJ_WRITE                       0x04
#define IRP_MJ_QUERY_INFORMATION           0x05
#define IRP_MJ_SET_INFORMATION             0x06
#define IRP_MJ_QUERY_EA                    0x07
#define IRP_MJ_SET_EA                      0x08
#define IRP_MJ_FLUSH_BUFFERS               0x09
#define IRP_MJ_QUERY_VOLUME_INFORMATION    0x0a
#define IRP_MJ_SET_VOLUME_INFORMATION      0x0b
#define IRP_MJ_DIRECTORY_CONTROL           0x0c
#define IRP_MJ_FILE_SYSTEM_CONTROL         0x0d
#define IRP_MJ_DEVICE_CONTROL              0x0e
#define IRP_MJ_INTERNAL_DEVICE_CONTROL     0x0f
#define IRP_MJ_SHUTDOWN                    0x10
#define IRP_MJ_LOCK_CONTROL                0x11
#define IRP_MJ_CLEANUP                     0x12
#define IRP_MJ_CREATE_MAILSLOT             0x13
#define IRP_MJ_QUERY_SECURITY              0x14
#define IRP_MJ_SET_SECURITY                0x15
#define IRP_MJ_QUERY_POWER                 0x16
#define IRP_MJ_SET_POWER                   0x17
#define IRP_MJ_DEVICE_CHANGE               0x18
#define IRP_MJ_QUERY_QUOTA                 0x19
#define IRP_MJ_SET_QUOTA                   0x1a
#define IRP_MJ_PNP_POWER                   0x1b
#define IRP_MJ_MAXIMUM_FUNCTION            0x1c
```

Function codes beginning at `IRP_MJ_DEVICE_CHANGE` and higher were introduced in NT version 4.0. Also, not all of the major function codes are implemented yet; for example, the quota-related function codes do not yet have any support from native NT file system drivers.

None of the major functions listed above is mandatory for a kernel-mode driver to implement, except for the ability to open and close objects managed by the driver. Open and close operations are very important because, if open operations fail, no I/O requests can be submitted, since there does not exist any object that would be the target of the requests. Similarly, if opens succeed, the close operations will eventually be invoked, and close operations cannot fail (the I/O Manager does not check the return code from a close operation). Therefore, if you do not implement a close operation to complement your open, the system might eventually run out of resources, depending on what operations were previously performed during the open, and also depending on the data structures created during the open operation.

The major function codes in the context of a file system driver and a filter driver are discussed in Part 3.

MinorFunction

Minor function codes provide more information specific to the major function code in the I/O stack location. For example, consider the IRP_MJ_ DIRECTORY_CONTROL major function code above. An IRP containing this major function code is sent by the I/O Manager to file system drivers. The intent is to perform some file directory operation. The question, however, is what directory control operation does the I/O Manager want the file system driver to perform?

The available operations include obtaining information about directory contents (IRP_MN_QUERY_DIRECTORY) and notifying the I/O Manager when certain attributes of files or directories contained within the target directory change (IRP_MN_NOTIFY_CHANGE_DIRECTORY).

Currently, only a few of the major functions have minor functions associated with them. However, for those few, the kernel-mode driver developer must examine this field to correctly determine the functionality it is expected to provide.

Flags

The Flags field also provides additional information that qualifies the functionality expected from the target driver. For example, consider the IRP_MJ_ DIRECTORY_CONTROL major function code previously discussed. If the minor function is IRP_MN_QUERY_DIRECTORY, the Flags field could contain additional information that might cause the file system to behave differently when returning the contents of the directory being queried.

For example, if the SL_RESTART_SCAN flag is set, the file system driver will restart the scan from the beginning of the directory being queried. Or if the SL_RETURN_SINGLE_ENTRY flag is set, the file system driver will return only the first entry matching the specified search criteria.

Lower-level drivers also have an interest in the settings for this flag. For example, removable media drivers will perform a read request dispatched to them from a file system driver if the SL_OVERRIDE_VERIFY_VOLUME flag has been set. If, however, the flag has not been set, and the device driver has recognized a media change (and informed the file system about it), it will fail all I/O requests, including all read requests.

Control

When a kernel-mode driver must process an IRP asynchronously, the driver can queue the IRP, mark it "pending" via a call to `IoMarkIrpPending()` and subsequently return control back to the caller. The call to `IoMarkIrp-Pending()` simply sets the `SL_PENDING_RETURNED` flag in the `Control` field for the current stack location. Any kernel-mode driver can examine the `Control` field for the existence of this flag.

This flag is also used internally by the NT I/O Manager to store information about whether a completion routine associated with the current stack location should be invoked if the return code supplied at IRP completion indicates a success, a failure, or a cancel operation. These flags are designated as `SL_INVOKE_ON_SUCCESS`, `SL_INVOKE_ON_FAILURE`, and `SL_INVOKE_ON_CANCEL`. Kernel-mode drivers typically should not need to be directly concerned with the state of these flags.

DeviceObject

This field is set by the NT I/O Manager as part of the processing performed in the `IoCallDriver()` routine. The contents are set to the device object pointer for the target device object (i.e., the device object to which the IRP is being dispatched).

FileObject

The I/O Manager sets this field to point to the file object that is the target of an I/O operation. Note that just calling `IoAllocateIrp()` from your driver will not result in this field being set. If you intend to use the returned IRP for an operation on a specific file object, your driver must set the field itself.

CompletionRoutine

The contents of this field are set by the I/O Manager when the `IoSetCom-pletionRoutine()` macro is invoked. The I/O Manager checks for a completion routine as part of the postprocessing performed during IRP completion. If a completion routine is specified, the routine is invoked in the context of the thread performing the postprocessing; typically this is in the context of the thread that invoked the `IoCompleteRequest()` routine. Since IRP completion is often performed by lower level drivers at a high IRQL, it is quite likely that the completion routine will be invoked at some high IRQL.

You should also note that completion routines are invoked in a *last-specified-first-invoked* order. Therefore, the highest-level driver's completion routine will be invoked after all other completion routines have been invoked. If any driver returns `STATUS_MORE_PROCESSING_REQUIRED` from an invocation to the driver-supplied completion routine, the I/O Manager immediately stops all postprocessing of the IRP. Freeing the memory for that IRP will then become the responsibility of the driver that returns the `STATUS_MORE_PROCESSING_REQUIRED` status.

If you develop a higher-level driver, like a file system driver or a filter driver, and if you specify a completion routine, always execute the following sequence of code in your completion routine:

```
if (PtrIrp->PendingReturned) {
    IoMarkIrpPending(PtrIrp);
}
```

If you fail to do this and if there are other drivers layered above yours in the calling hierarchy, the IRP may be processed incorrectly and you could experience a driver or process hang. The reason for the potential hang will be further explained later in this chapter.

`Context`

This field contains the context supplied by the kernel-mode driver when it specifies a completion routine for the IRP.

If you develop an intermediate driver, you will have to be careful about copying some of the values contained in the current I/O stack location into the next I/O stack location when you prepare to forward the IRP to the next driver in the hierarchy. For example, you must copy the contents of the `Flags` field, so the lower-level driver will know that it should perform an I/O read operation requested by a file system even though it had previously informed the file system about a media change.

Processing an IRP

Handling an IRP sent to your driver can be quite straightforward. The next four figures illustrate some of the common methods employed to handle an IRP dispatched to a kernel-mode driver.

In Figure 4-5, you can see that the target kernel-mode driver receives an IRP, obtains a pointer to the current stack location, performs some processing based on the contents of the I/O stack location, and, finally, completes the I/O request packet. Note, however, that there could be a delay between receiving the request and beginning the processing, since the driver might queue the IRP if it is currently busy processing other requests. The queued IRP would subsequently get processed asynchronously in the context of a worker thread.

Also note that once the driver gets control back from an invocation to `IoComplete-Request()`, it must not touch the IRP or any of the fields contained within the IRP again. Doing so could lead to data corruption and system crashes.

Figure 4-6 illustrates how a kernel-mode driver receives an IRP, obtains a pointer to the current stack location, and performs processing based upon the contents of

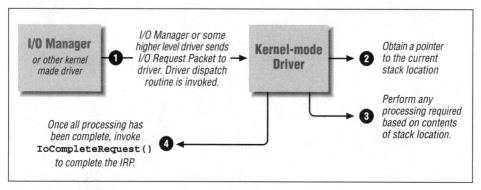

Figure 4-5. Simple IRP processing where invoked driver completes the IRP

the stack location. However, the driver might need to invoke the services of a lower-level driver before the requested functionality is declared completed. Therefore, the recipient of the IRP can initialize the next stack location in the IRP and forward the IRP to the next kernel-mode driver in the layered driver hierarchy.

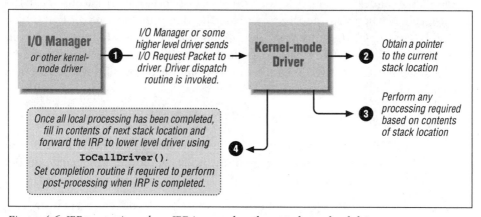

Figure 4-6. IRP processing where IRP is reused and sent to lower-level driver

If your driver forwards an IRP to another driver, it is no longer allowed to try to access that IRP, since it does not know when the lower-level driver will complete that particular IRP. Typically, forwarding of the IRP is done via a call to `IoCall-Driver()`. The I/O Manager will invoke the lower-level driver in the context of the thread that makes the call to `IoCallDriver()`; however, the lower-level driver that now receives the IRP might return `STATUS_PENDING` and complete the IRP asynchronously.

Figure 4-7 illustrates a sequence where a higher-level kernel-mode driver (e.g., a file system driver) uses associated I/O request packets to issue I/O requests to other lower-level drivers. This might be done if, for example, the higher-level driver wishes to split up an I/O request; it might even be required if the higher-level driver needs processing to be performed by more than one set of lower-level drivers.

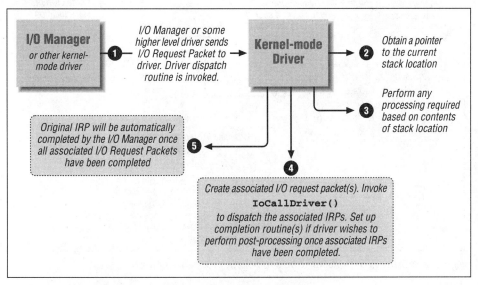

Figure 4-7. Using associated IRP structures to process an IRP

Note that the higher-level driver does not need to invoke `IoComplete-Request()` on the original IRP; the I/O Manager will automatically complete the original IRP once all associated IRPs have been completed by lower-level drivers. However, the higher-level driver can request that a completion routine be invoked when the associated IRP completes, thereby giving it the opportunity to perform some postprocessing, and also allowing itself the opportunity to complete the original IRP at its own convenience.

Figure 4-8 illustrates a variation of the method using associated IRPs; here the kernel-mode driver uses one of the I/O Manager-supplied functions to create new I/O Request Packets, which are then dispatched to other kernel-mode drivers. Once the newly created I/O Request Packets have been completed, the original IRP can be redispatched to lower-level drivers for further processing, or it can be immediately completed.

IRP completion and deallocation

Every I/O Request Packet must be completed in order for the I/O Manager to be informed that the request contained within the IRP has been completely processed. To complete an IRP, a kernel-mode driver has to invoke the `IoCompleteRequest()` I/O Manager support routine.

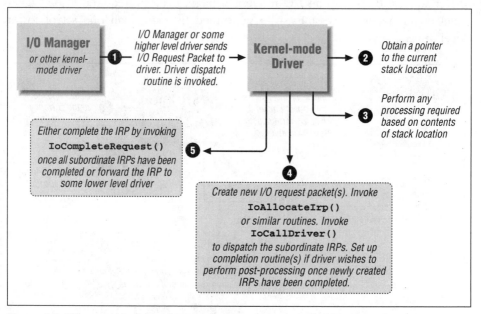

Figure 4-8. Using newly allocated IRPs to help in processing of an IRP

Once this routine is invoked, the NT I/O Manager performs some postprocessing on the I/O request packet being completed, as follows:

1. The I/O Manager performs some basic checks to ensure that the IRP is in a valid state. The value of the current stack location pointer is verified to ensure that it is less than or equal to (total number of stacks + 1). If the value is not valid, the system will bugcheck with an error code of **MULTIPLE_IRP_ COMPLETE_REQUESTS**. If you install the debug build of the operating system, the I/O Manager will execute some additional assertions, such as checking for a returned status code of **STATUS_PENDING** when completing the IRP, and checking other invalid return codes from the driver.

2. Now, the I/O Manager starts scanning through all stack locations contained in the IRP looking for completion routines that need to be invoked. Each stack location can have a completion routine associated with it, which should be called depending on whether the final return code was a success or a failure, or if the IRP was canceled. The I/O stack locations are scanned in reverse order, with the highest-valued I/O stack location being checked first. This results in completion routines invoked such that a completion routine supplied by a disk driver (the lowest-level driver) will be invoked first, while the completion routine for the highest-level driver (typically, the file system driver) will be invoked last.

   Completion routines are invoked in the context of the same thread that calls **IoCompleteRequest()**. If any completion routine returns **STATUS_MORE_**

PROCESSING_REQUIRED, the I/O Manager immediately stops all further postprocessing and returns control back to the routine that invoked IoCompleteRequest(). Now, it is the responsibility of the driver that returned STATUS_MORE_PROCESSING_REQUIRED to invoke IoFreeIrp() later.*

3. If the IRP being completed is an associated IRP, the I/O Manager will decrement the AssociatedIrp.IrpCount field in the master IRP. Then, the I/O Manager invokes an internal routine, IopFreeIrpAndMdls(), to free up memory allocated for the associated IRP and also to free any MDL structures allocated for the associated IRP. Finally, if this happens to be the last associated IRP outstanding for the master IRP, the I/O Manager recursively invokes IoCompleteRequest() on the master IRP itself.

4. A lot of the postprocessing performed by the I/O Manager occurs in the context of the thread that had originally requested the I/O operation. To do this, the I/O Manager queues a kernel-mode APC, which is subsequently executed in the context of the requesting thread. However, this methodology cannot be employed for certain types of IRP structures, used for the following types of operations:

Close operations

An IRP describing a close operation is generated by the I/O Manager and sent to the affected kernel-mode driver whenever the last reference to a kernel-mode object is removed. This might just as well occur while a special kernel-mode APC was already executing. To perform a close operation on objects defined by the I/O Manager, a special internal I/O Manager routine called IopCloseFile() is always invoked. IopCloseFile() is synchronous and therefore blocking. It allocates and issues a close IRP to the target kernel-mode driver and waits for an event object to complete the close operation. Therefore, when completing an IRP for a close operation, the I/O Manager simply copies over the return status (which incidentally is never checked by the requesting thread for a close operation), signals the event object for which the thread executing IopCloseFile() is waiting, and then returns control immediately. The IRP is subsequently deleted in IopCloseFile().

---

* The DDK assumes that STATUS_MORE_PROCESSING_REQUIRED will only be invoked by kernel-mode drivers for associated IRPs that they have created. There is nothing, however, that prevents your driver from returning this status code for a normal IRP request that was dispatched to you by the I/O Manager. The problem, though, is that there is a lot of postprocessing required on that IRP that will have been abruptly interrupted due to your returning such a status code from your completion routine. Your driver will then have to devise a method whereby such postprocessing can be resumed later; this is not a trivial task.

Paging I/O requests

Paging I/O requests are issued on behalf of the NT Virtual Memory Manager (VMM). In Chapters 5–8, you will read about the functionality provided by the NT VMM and the NT Cache Manager. For now, simply understand that the I/O Manager cannot afford to incur a page fault while completing a paging I/O request. That would cause a system crash. Therefore, the I/O Manager will do one of two things when completing a paging I/O request:

— For a synchronous paging I/O request, the I/O Manager will copy the returned I/O status into the caller-supplied I/O status block structure, signal the kernel event object for which the caller might be waiting, then free the IRP and return control, since there is no additional postprocessing to be performed.

— For an asynchronous paging I/O request, the I/O Manager will queue a special kernel APC to be executed in the context of the thread that requested paging I/O. This is the Modified Page Writer (MPW) thread, which is a component of the VMM subsystem. In the next chapter you will read a lot more about the MPW thread. For now, it is enough for you to know that the routine that executes in the context of the MPW thread (once the APC has been delivered), copies the status from the paging read operation to the I/O status block provided by the modified page writer, and subsequently invokes an MPW completion routine using another kernel APC.

Later, you will see that the I/O Manager typically frees up any Memory Descriptor Lists that are associated with the IRP, before freeing up the IRP itself. However, for paging I/O operations, the MDL structures that are used belong to the VMM (i.e., they are allocated by the VMM and will therefore be freed only by the VMM upon completion of I/O). That is the reason why the I/O Manager does not free up the MDL structures used in paging I/O requests.

Mount requests

If you examine the flags supplied in the NT DDK, indicating paging I/O requests and mount requests (`IRP_PAGING_IO` and `IRP_MOUNT_COMPLETION,` respectively), you will notice that they are both defined to the same value. This is because the I/O Manager treats the mount request exactly the same as a synchronous, paging I/O read request. Therefore, the I/O Manager performs exactly the same postprocessing for mount requests as described for a synchronous, paging I/O request.

5. If the IRP did not describe either a paging I/O, a close, or a mount request, the I/O Manager next unlocks any locked pages described by Memory

Descriptor Lists (MDLs) associated with the I/O Request Packet. Note that the MDL structures are not freed at this time; they are freed as part of the postprocessing performed in the context of the requesting thread.

6. At this point, the I/O Manager has completed as much of the postprocessing it can, without being in the context of the requesting thread. Therefore, the I/O Manager queues a special kernel APC to the thread that requested the I/O operation. The internal I/O Manager routine that is invoked in the context of the calling thread is called `IopCompleteRequest()`. It could happen, however, that there might not be any thread context to send the APC request to. This happens if the thread exited after starting an asynchronous I/O operation, the request had already been initiated by the lower level driver, and the driver could not complete the request within a fixed time-out period. In this scenario, the I/O Manager has given up on the request, and therefore, it simply frees up the memory allocated for the IRP at this point since no further postprocessing can be performed.

For synchronous I/O operations, the I/O Manager does not queue the special kernel APC but simply returns control immediately at this point. These IRP structures have the `IRP_DEFER_IO_COMPLETION` flag set in the `Flags` field in the IRP. Examples of IRP major functions for which IRP completion can be deferred are directory control operations, read operations, write operations, create/open requests, query file information, and set file information requests. By returning control immediately, the I/O Manager avoids the overhead associated with queuing kernel-mode APCs and the overhead of serving APC interrupts. Instead, the thread that originally requested the I/O operation by invoking `IoCallDriver()` invokes `IopCompleteRequest()` directly once control is returned to it. This is simply an optimization performed by the NT I/O Manager.

Note that the I/O Manager will perform two checks to determine whether the APC should be queued or not for the above situation:

— The `IRP_DEFER_IO_COMPLETION` flag should be set to TRUE.

— The `Irp->PendingReturned` field should be set to FALSE.

Only if both of the conditions above are TRUE will the I/O Manager simply return from the `IoCompleteRequest()` function at this stage.

The following situation may result in a problem if you are not careful in your driver:

— Your driver specifies a completion routine before forwarding a request to a lower-level driver.

— There is a driver layered above you in the calling hierarchy (e.g., a filter/intermediate driver).

— Your driver does not execute the instructions listed earlier about invoking `IoMarkIrpPending()` if `Irp->PendingReturned` is set to TRUE.

Now the I/O Manager may incorrectly believe that an APC should not be queued (thinking that the completion was being performed in the context of the requesting thread) and the original thread will stay blocked forever.

The other situation where the I/O Manager does not queue an APC is if the file object has a completion port associated with it, in which case the I/O Manager sends a message to this completion port instead.

At this time, all processing that could have been performed in `IoComplete-Request()` is complete.

The remaining steps described below occur in the context of the thread that had originally requested the I/O operation. The NT I/O Manager routine that performs these steps is the `IopCompleteRequest()` routine previously mentioned.

1. For buffered I/O operations, the I/O Manager copies any data returned as a result of the successful execution of the I/O request back into the caller's buffer. Details of buffered I/O operations are provided later in this chapter; however, note for now that if the driver returns an error or if the driver returns a code indicating that a verify operation is required in the IRP `IoStatus` structure, no copy will be performed.*

   Also, the number of bytes copied into the caller's buffer equals the value of the `Information` field in the `IoStatus` structure; therefore, if that field is not set correctly, the caller will not get back all or any of the returned data.

   The I/O Manager-allocated buffer is also deallocated once the copy operation is performed.

2. Any Memory Descriptor Lists associated with the IRP are freed at this time.

---

* You should understand that the NT I/O Manager treats warning status codes as if the operation succeeded; i.e., the I/O Manager will copy data into the caller's buffer even if the status code was not STATUS_SUCCESS, as long as it does not indicate an error.

TIP   It is possible for a file system driver to deliberately return a pointer to an MDL allocated by the Cache Manager when requested to do so by a caller for either a read or a write I/O request. Such requests are distinguished by the presence of the `IRP_MN_MDL` flag in the `MinorFunction` field of the IRP stack location in the IRP sent to the file system driver. Since all MDLs associated with an IRP are blindly freed at this point, it appears that there is not much point to a file system driver returning an MDL to the caller. However, currently the only kernel-mode client using the `IRP_MN_MDL` flag is the LAN Manager Server module, and this module typically circumvents the problem by returning `STATUS_MORE_PROCESSING_RE-QUIRED` from a completion routine. See Chapter 9, *Writing a File System Driver I*, for a discussion on how the file system driver processes MDL-read and MDL-write requests.

3. The I/O Manager copies the `Status` and `Information` fields into the caller-supplied I/O status block structure.

4. If the caller supplied an event object to be signaled, the I/O Manager signals that event object. The I/O Manager signals the event object in the `Event` field for any file object associated with the I/O Request Packet if either no event object was supplied by the caller or the I/O operation was executed synchronously because the file object was opened for synchronous access only.

5. Typically, the NT I/O Manager increments the reference count of any caller-supplied event object or any file object associated with an IRP before forwarding the IRP to a driver for processing. At this time, the I/O Manager dereferences both of these objects if they had been referenced before.

6. The I/O Manager dequeues the IRP from the list of I/O Request Packets pending for the current thread.

7. Memory for the I/O Request Packet is finally freed; if the I/O Request Packet has been allocated from a zone/lookaside list, memory for that packet is returned to the zone/lookaside list for reuse; otherwise, memory is returned back to the system.

Working with I/O request packets

There are a few key concepts that you must understand very well with regard to handling I/O Request Packets sent to your kernel-mode driver:

• Once your driver receives the IRP, no other component in the system, including the I/O Manager, can be concurrently accessing the same IRP. Until your driver either forwards the IRP to another kernel-mode driver, or completes the IRP, processing of the request described by the I/O Request Packet is solely the responsibility of your driver.

- Once your driver completes the IRP, or forwards it to another kernel-mode driver, your driver must give up control of the IRP and not attempt to access any of the fields contained within it again. The only time you can touch that IRP again is if you had specified a completion routine prior to forwarding the IRP. In that case, the I/O Manager will invoke your completion routine as part of its postprocessing performed during IRP completion.

- If you specify a completion routine to be invoked at the time of IRP completion, it can perform any postprocessing necessary. Keep in mind, though, that your completion routine might be called at an IRQL less than or equal to DISPATCH_LEVEL. If your completion routine is invoked at a high IRQL, you cannot incur any page faults while your code is executing. You do have the option of stopping any postprocessing of the IRP by returning STATUS_ MORE_PROCESSING_REQUIRED from your completion routine. Be careful, though, when doing this, especially from a lower-level driver, because some of the completion routines specified by other drivers higher in the chain, which normally would be invoked, will now not be called unless you play some tricks with the IRP later.

- No IRP can be completed more than once.* If you do try to do this either deliberately or erroneously, you might cause data corruption and/or system crashes. Although the I/O Manager checks for the possibility that an IRP is being completed more than once, the check is not completely foolproof, so be aware of this requirement when designing your driver.

- Your driver cannot blindly assume that it is being invoked to process an IRP in the context of the thread that originally requested the I/O operation. As a matter of fact, lower-level drivers, such as intermediate drivers and device drivers, will probably never have their dispatch routines invoked in the context of the issuing thread. Therefore, your driver must be careful when trying to access objects, handles, resources, and memory when processing the I/O Request Packet. Understand the context in which your dispatch routines can be invoked and only use resources that are available to you and that are valid in that particular context.

- Kernel-mode drivers have tremendous freedom in what they are able to do. At the same time, the responsibilities that are placed upon kernel-mode code are greater than for user-space applications. If your driver uses pointers to

---

* It is possible for a completion routine to return STATUS_MORE_PROCESSING_REQUIRED, perform some specialized postprocessing with the IRP, and then reissue the IoCompleteRequest() function on the IRP to make the I/O Manager correctly dispose of the IRP. This is the single exception to the rule mentioned above and results in the situation where an IRP is completed more than once.

buffers sent by user-space code, be careful about how you use such buffers. It is possible for kernel-mode drivers to easily compromise system integrity by misusing, or not carefully validating, any buffers and data contained within them, sent by unprotected, user-mode applications. Determine the mode of the caller in deciding whether or not to validate pointers sent to you. Use the previous mode of the caller in making your decision on whether or not to validate user-supplied buffers.

- Use only the I/O Manager-provided access methods to manipulate stack locations in an IRP. It is possible for a kernel-mode driver to modify IRP stack locations, which can affect both how IRP processing is done initially, as well as how IRP postprocessing is performed once the IRP has been completed. Try to resist the temptation to manipulate the contents of the stack locations in any undocumented fashion.

- Use your own I/O Request Packets if you wish to utilize services of other drivers above or below you in the hierarchy. Avoid using private communication channels that are not extensible. To create IRP structures, use one of the I/O Manager-supplied support routines (i.e., `IoAllocateIrp()`, `IoBuildSynchronousFsdRequest()`, `IoBuildAsynchronousFsdRequest()`, `IoBuildDeviceIoControlRequest()`, and `IoMakeAssociatedIrp()`). Use `IoInitializeIrp()`, in conjunction with `IoAllocateIrp()`, to initialize the common fields in the IRP header. Be careful, and reread the previous section to determine which additional fields you might wish to initialize. Also, realize that `IoFreeIrp()` may or may not need to be invoked, depending on the status code you return from any completion routine you may have specified.

- Some kernel-mode components, such as the LAN Manager server, allocate I/O Request Packets from internal pools, instead of requesting them from the NT I/O Manager. Be aware that these components may use some of the fields in the IRP in a manner different from the standard manner in which those fields are manipulated by the I/O Manager. Therefore, be careful when depending upon the contents of fields that the I/O Manager wants to keep private and that are not documented in the DDK, since there are no guarantees made by the system that the fields will always contain consistent values.

Furthermore, components like the LAN Manager server often have a maximum number of stack locations that they typically allocate for an I/O Request Packet. If you add one or more additional filter or intermediate drivers to the driver hierarchy, the number of stack locations required may then exceed the maximum that the LAN Manager server can deal with. There is a workaround to this problem, where you can instruct the user to specify additional stack locations that the LAN Manager server should allocate via a Registry parameter.

Volume Parameter Block (VPB)

The VPB is the link between the file system device object representing the mounted volume and the device object representing the physical or virtual disk that contains the physical file system data structures. Each time a file open request for an on-disk file stream is sent to a device object for a physical or virtual device,* the I/O Manager invokes an internal routine called `IopCheckVpb-Mounted()`. This routine is responsible for initiating a logical volume mount operation, if the VPB associated with the physical/virtual device that is the target of the request indicates that the volume has not been mounted. If, however, the volume is previously mounted, the I/O Manager redirects the open operation to the device object whose pointer is obtained using the `DeviceObject` field in the VPB.

Memory for a volume parameter block is automatically allocated from nonpaged pool by the Windows NT I/O Manager when a device object is created through a `IoCreateDevice()` call or when a file system driver invokes the `IoVerify-Volume()` call, for the following types of device objects:

- `FILE_DEVICE_DISK`

- `FILE_DEVICE_CD_ROM`

- `FILE_DEVICE_TAPE`

- `FILE_DEVICE_VIRTUAL_DISK` (used for RAM disks or any similar virtual disk structures that can hold a mountable volume)

Note that each of the these types of device objects can have a logical volume present on the device object, and each of these device objects typically also represents a single mountable partition for a device. The volume parameter block is used to map the file system (logical) volume device object to the physical device also represented by a device object. This structure is initially zeroed by the I/O Manager upon allocation. The following definition describes the VPB:

---

* Since the most commonly used subsystem on Windows NT platforms is the Win32 subsystem, consider the case when a user performs a file open operation on a file stream on drive letter *C:*. This drive letter is nothing but a Win32 subsystem-visible name that is actually a symbolic link to a Windows NT name, such as *\Device\HardDisk0\Partition1*. Therefore, accessing a file stream on *C:* is the same as accessing an on-disk file stream on the physical disk device object with the name *\Device\HardDisk0\Partition1*. Note that the Windows NT named object is **not** the device object representing the mounted volume; rather, it is the device object representing the physical/virtual disk drive. The VPB is used to perform the association between the named physical/virtual disk device object and the unnamed logical volume device object.

```
typedef struct _VPB {
    CSHORT                              Type;
    CSHORT                              Size;
    USHORT                              Flags;
    USHORT                              VolumeLabelLength;    // in bytes
    struct _DEVICE_OBJECT               *DeviceObject;
    struct _DEVICE_OBJECT               *RealDevice;
    ULONG                               SerialNumber;
    ULONG                               ReferenceCount;
    WCHAR           VolumeLabel[MAXIMUM_VOLUME_LABEL_LENGTH / sizeof(WCHAR)];
} VPB, *PVPB;
```

Each mounted volume can have a label associated with it with a maximum length of 32 characters. The `VolumeLabelLength` field is initialized by file system drivers to the actual length of the label for the volume, which is stored in the `VolumeLabel` field. Each file system volume can also have a serial number associated with it that should be read off the volume by the file system driver and placed in the `SerialNumber` field. As long as the reference count for the VPB is nonzero, the I/O Manager will not deallocate the VPB structure. The `RealDevice` field is initialized by the I/O Manager to point to the physical or virtual device object that contains the mountable logical volume. The `DeviceObject` field is initialized by the file system driver whenever a mount operation takes place. This field contains the address of the device object of type `FILE_DEVICE_DISK_FILE_SYSTEM`, created by the file system to represent the mounted volume.

The `Flags` field in the VPB can have one of three values:

VPB_MOUNTED

 This bit is set by the I/O Manager once a file system mounts the logical volume represented by the VPB. This happens after a file system driver returns `STATUS_SUCCESS` from an IRP sent to it with a major function of `IRP_MOUNT_COMPLETION`.

VPB_LOCKED

 This field can be set or cleared by the file system driver that has mounted the logical volume represented by the VPB. While this field is set, the NT I/O Manager will fail all subsequent open/create requests targeted to that logical volume. File systems may choose to set this field in response to application requests to lock the logical volume, or if they temporarily wish to prevent any create/open requests from proceeding. The FASTFAT file system responds to application IOCTL requests to lock a volume (**FSCTL_LOCK_VOLUME**) by setting this field in the VPB.

```
VPB_PERSISTENT
```

This field is also manipulated by file system drivers. If this field is set, the I/O Manager will not delete the VPB structure, even if the `ReferenceCount` in the VPB is 0.

The NT I/O Manager provides two routines that should be used by filter drivers and file system drivers to synchronize access to a VPB structure. These support routines are defined as follows:

```
VOID
IoAcquireVpbSpinLock(
    OUT PKIRQL        Irql
);

VOID
IoReleaseVpbSpinLock(
    IN KIRQL          Irql
);
```

Parameters:

`Irql`

For the `IoAcquireVpbSpinLock()` routine, this is a pointer that, upon return, will contain the IRQL to which the thread must be restored when the corresponding release function is invoked.

For the routine `IoReleaseVpbSpinLock()`, this argument contains the IRQL value returned when the spin lock was acquired.

Functionality Provided:

There is a global spin lock structure that is acquired by the I/O Manager internally while manipulating contents of the VPB. If your driver wishes to check or manipulate the `Flags`, `DeviceObject`, or `ReferenceCount` fields in any VPB, you should first invoke the `IoAcquireVpbSpinLock()` support routine to ensure data consistency. Note that this is a global spin lock and that, while this spin lock is acquired, not many I/O operations can continue (e.g., new create and open operations will be blocked). Therefore, be careful to acquire the lock only for the short period required while accessing the specified fields.

For more detailed information on the flow of execution leading to a mount operation, as well as for a detailed explanation of handling VPB structures for volumes mounted on removable media, consult Part 3.

I/O Status Block

The I/O Status Block is used to convey the results of an I/O operation. This structure is defined as follows:

```
typedef struct _IO_STATUS_BLOCK {
    NTSTATUS        Status;
    ULONG           Information;
} IO_STATUS_BLOCK, *PIO_STATUS_BLOCK;
```

Every I/O Request Packet (IRP) has an I/O Status Block associated with it. A kernel-mode driver should always insert the return code describing the results of processing the request in the `Status` field in the I/O status block structure. This field will, therefore, contain a return code denoting success (`STATUS_SUCCESS`), a return code denoting a warning, an informational message, or an error. Error status codes also include those indicating that an exception (which was handled by the driver) occurred while processing an I/O request. Consult the previous chapter for a discussion of the structure of NT return codes.

The `Information` field is typically filled with any additional information related to the requested I/O operation. For example, for a read request of 1024 bytes, the `Information` field upon return will contain the actual number of bytes read even if the Status field indicates `STATUS_SUCCESS`. Therefore, the `Information` field in this case would contain a value between 0 and 1024 bytes.

File Object

If you develop file system drivers in Windows NT, or if you develop filter drivers that reside above the file system driver in the driver hierarchy, you should become very familiar with the structure of a *file object*. A file object is the I/O Manager's in-memory representation of an open object. For example, if an open operation is successfully performed on an on-disk file, the I/O Manager creates a file object structure to represent that particular instance of the open operation. If another open operation is performed on the same file stream, the I/O Manager will allocate a new file object to represent this second open operation, even though both open operations were performed on the same underlying, on-disk file stream.

You should conceptualize a file object as the kernel equivalent of a *handle* created as a result of a successful open/create request. File objects are not limited to representing open file streams; rather, they are an abstraction used to represent any object opened by the NT I/O Manager. Therefore, if you open a logical volume or a disk drive device object, the open operation will result in the creation and initialization of a file object data structure.

All I/O operations targeted to on-disk file streams or logical volumes require a file object structure as the target for the request (you cannot perform a read request in a vacuum; you must have a target file object representing a previous successful open operation to which you can direct the read operation). The responsibility for

creating and maintaining a file object data structure is jointly shared by the NT I/O
Manager and the file system driver.

The file object structure is allocated by the I/O Manager before it passes the open
or a create request to a kernel-mode file system driver. The create/open IRP
contains a pointer to this newly allocated file object structure; it is the responsibility of the kernel-mode file system driver that processes the create/open request
to initialize certain fields in the file object structure.

The file object structure is defined by the NT I/O Manager:

```
typedef struct _FILE_OBJECT {
    CSHORT                          Type;
    CSHORT                          Size;
    PDEVICE_OBJECT                  DeviceObject;
    PVPB                            Vpb;
    PVOID                           FsContext;
    PVOID                           FsContext2;
    PSECTION_OBJECT_POINTERS        SectionObjectPointer;
    PVOID                           PrivateCacheMap;
    NTSTATUS                        FinalStatus;
    struct _FILE_OBJECT             *RelatedFileObject;
    BOOLEAN                         LockOperation;
    BOOLEAN                         DeletePending;
    BOOLEAN                         ReadAccess;
    BOOLEAN                         WriteAccess;
    BOOLEAN                         DeleteAccess;
    BOOLEAN                         SharedRead;
    BOOLEAN                         SharedWrite;
    BOOLEAN                         SharedDelete;
    ULONG                           Flags;
    UNICODE_STRING                  FileName;
    LARGE_INTEGER                   CurrentByteOffset;
    ULONG                           Waiters;
    ULONG                           Busy;
    PVOID                           LastLock;
    KEVENT                          Lock;
    KEVENT                          Event;
    PIO_COMPLETION_CONTEXT          CompletionContext;
} FILE_OBJECT;
```

The `DeviceObject` and `Vpb` fields in the file object structure are initialized by
the I/O Manager before sending a create or an open request to the file system
driver. The `DeviceObject` is initialized to the address of the target physical or
virtual device object to which the request is directed. The `Vpb` field is initialized
to the mounted VPB associated with the target device object.

The `FsContext`, `FsContext2`, `SectionObjectPointer`, and `Private-
CacheMap` fields are initialized and/or maintained by the file system driver
implementation and the NT Cache Manager. They will be discussed in greater
detail later in this book. The NT I/O Manager does not maintain the contents of

these fields, though it does check for and use the contents of the `FsContext` field; this will be discussed in Part 3.

The `FileName` field is initialized by the I/O manager to a string representing the file, volume, or physical device to be opened. This name can either be a *relative* pathname or an *absolute* pathname. A relative pathname is indicated by the presence of a nonnull value in the `RelatedFileObject` field. This field contains a pointer to a previously opened file object data structure. The relative pathname supplied in the `FileName` field must now be considered relative to the name of the file represented by the `RelatedFileObject`. Note that the `RelatedFile-Object` field is only valid in the context of a create request. At all other times, the contents of this field are undefined.

The `CurrentByteOffset` field is maintained by file systems for those file objects that were opened for synchronous access only. This field contains the current pointer position for the file stream, which is updated upon the successful completion of read and/or write I/O operations.

The `CompletionContext` field is used by the NT I/O Manager to send a message to a Local Procedure Call (LPC) port upon completion of an IRP. The `DeletePending` flag is set in the file object structure when a file system receives a set information IRP specifying that the file stream should be deleted.

The `LockOperation` field is set to TRUE by the I/O Manager if the thread that owns the file object structure invoked a byte-range lock operation at least once while the file was open. This field is later checked when the thread closes the file object to determine whether or not to send an unlock IRP to the file system driver.

The various access fields (`ReadAccess`, `WriteAccess`, and `DeleteAccess`) are set and cleared by the I/O Manager. So are the various share access related fields (`SharedRead`, `SharedWrite`, and `SharedDelete`). The state of these fields determines how the file is currently opened and also determines whether subsequent opens requesting certain specific types of access will be allowed to proceed or will be denied with an error code of `STATUS_SHARING_VIOLATION`. There exists an I/O Manager support routine called `IoCheckShareAccess()`, which maintains the state of these fields. This routine is typically only invoked by file system drivers and will be described later in this book.

Later in this chapter, you will read about synchronous and asynchronous I/O operations from the perspective of the file system drivers that must provide the code to implement such requests. A user can open a file object specifying that all operations performed on the opened object by that particular file object be executed synchronously. This is indicated by the presence of a `FO_SYNCHRONOUS_FLAG` in the `Flags` field of the file object structure, which is set by the I/O Manager as part of the create/open request. One of the effects of requesting synchronous I/O operations is that the I/O Manager always serializes all I/O operations performed using that particular file object. To implement this sequential behavior, the NT I/O Manager uses the `Busy` and the `Waiters` fields in the file object data structure. The `Busy` field is set when an I/O operation using that particular file object is in progress. The `Waiters` field denotes the number of threads waiting to perform I/O operations using the same file object. These fields should not be of much interest to other kernel-mode drivers.

The file object is a waitable kernel-mode object, i.e., threads can request asynchronous I/O, and subsequently wait for the completion of the I/O operation. The `Event` field in the file object is used by the I/O Manager to maintain the state of the wait object. This event object is set to the not-signaled state by the I/O Manager when an I/O operation begins using that file object. It is subsequently set to be signaled once the I/O is completed, though only if the caller had not explicitly supplied another event object to wait for.

The `Flags` field can reflect many values, one of has been described here, and each describes a state associated with the file object structure. I will defer discussion of each of the possible values of this field until later in the book, when the field is actually used in our code.

Determining Which Objects to Use

Here are a few simple rules to "put everything together" when developing your driver:

- When your driver loads, a driver object will be created and sent to your initialization routine by the I/O Manager. You must fill in certain fields in the driver object, such as the various dispatch routine function pointers, for the functionality you wish to support. If you do not fill in the function pointers, your driver will not receive any requests, because all requests will be handled by the default routine (`IopInvalidDeviceRequest()`).

- In order to provide any functionality, you will probably create at least one device object. More than likely, you will create one device object representing your driver and subsequent other device objects representing other virtual and/or physical devices you support. Most of the device objects you create will be named, unless you develop a file system driver, in which case, most of the device objects will represent logical volumes and will therefore be unnamed. When requesting a create operation for a device object, you should also specify a device extension in which you can store global data associated with each new device object.

- If you write a filter driver, you will create one device object for each target device object whose I/O requests you wish to intercept. You will then attach your device object to the target device object. This procedure of attaching to the target will actually cause all I/O requests directed to the target to be re-routed to your device object.*

- If you develop a file system driver, you will have to manipulate the Volume Parameter Block (VPB) for the physical device object on which you perform a *mount* operation. Performing a mount will cause the I/O Manager to make the physical device object accessible for read/write requests and those requests will be sent to your device object representing the mounted logical volume.

- Once you make a device object available for receiving I/O requests, requests will be sent to you in the form of I/O Request Packets (IRPs). If you develop a file system driver, you will also receive requests via the fast path (more on that later in this book).

- When you receive an IRP, you will determine the nature of the I/O operation your driver is being asked to perform. To do this, you should get a pointer to the current stack location in the IRP and use it to extract information pertaining to the I/O request. Your driver will then perform appropriate processing of the IRP, either synchronously or asynchronously.

- Your driver may be able to complete the IRP, or it might determine that the IRP needs to be forwarded to a driver that is lower in the hierarchy for some additional processing. In the latter case, you should obtain a pointer to the next stack location in the IRP and fill in the information that the next driver in the hierarchy can subsequently extract to determine the nature of processing it has to perform.

- If your driver will complete the IRP, it must return results of the I/O operation in the I/O status block structure. The `Status` field should contain the result, while the `Information` field should contain any additional information you wish to return to the caller.

- Last, but not least, if you develop a file system driver, you will access and possibly modify the file object structure as part of processing an open request (and subsequently when processing most IRPs). Each such structure represents an instance of a successful open operation.

In addition to the objects mentioned in this chapter, if you develop a device driver, you will be concerned with other objects as well, including controller objects, adapter objects, and interrupt objects.

Furthermore, your driver will undoubtedly create one or more object types of its own. For example, file system drivers will create some internal representation of a

---

* The process of attaching to a target device object is described in detail in Chapter 12.

file stream in memory. For those familiar with UNIX operating system environments, think about the *vnode* structure that is created and maintained by all file systems. The NT equivalent of this structure is a *File Control Block*, an object we will discuss at length in Part 3. In addition, file systems will create a context to internally represent an instance of a file open operation (similar to the system-defined file object structure). In Windows NT parlance, this structure is called a *Context Control Block*.

Once you start using these objects in your code development, they should become second nature to you and you will no longer have to spend time trying to figure out what a device object represents.

I/O Requests: A Discussion

The following discussion provides some additional information that you should keep in mind as we develop a higher-level kernel-mode driver. This information will be used not only in the sample drivers provided in this book, but also in any commercial kernel-mode drivers you design and develop.

Synchronous/Asynchronous Operations

Some I/O operations are always performed synchronously; therefore, any file system driver that you develop only has to design a synchronous method of processing IRPs for such types of requests. Other operations can be handled either synchronously or asynchronously; your file system driver must, therefore, provide both synchronous and asynchronous code paths for processing such I/O request packets.

How does a kernel-mode driver determine whether an IRP should be handled synchronously or asynchronously?

Before we address that question, it might be useful to see why handling asynchronous requests correctly is important. Consider a file system driver that you design that does not honor asynchronous requests but performs all requests synchronously. Your implementation should work correctly most of the time. The one problem that might occur is when your driver receives asynchronous paging I/O write requests. These requests typically originate from the NT Modified Page Writer. The number of worker threads available to the Modified Page Writer is fixed. It may be that the MPW uses only two threads to perform such paging I/O, one to the page files and the other to memory-mapped files.

In low-memory and high-stress situations, the VMM tries to quickly flush modified pages out to secondary storage to make room for other data in the system memory. The MPW does this by rapidly issuing asynchronous page write requests to file systems that manage one or more of the modified pages, either in mapped files or in page files. If your driver blocks the MPW thread until the I/O is completed, it slows down the whole process of flushing data out to disk, which can result in unacceptably long delays to the users of the system.

Therefore, if you develop a higher level kernel-mode driver, it would be prudent to provide support for asynchronous I/O operations.

Only some I/O system services can be processed asynchronously:

- Read requests
- Write requests
- Directory control requests
- Byte range lock/unlock requests
- Device I/O control requests
- File system I/O control requests

As you may have noticed, all of the types of requests listed above can potentially take a significant amount of time to complete. Therefore, it is logical that the caller be allowed to request asynchronous processing for such requests. All of the other IRP major functions should complete reasonably quickly.

Therefore, if your file system or higher-level filter driver (layered above a file system) receives an IRP with a major function other than the ones listed here, you can assume that you are allowed to block in the context of the calling thread.

For the major functions listed, the caller has the option of specifying whether the request should be performed synchronously or asynchronously. To find out what the caller wants, your kernel-mode driver can invoke the following I/O Manager support routine:

```
BOOLEAN
IoIsOperationSynchronous(
    IN PIRP        Irp
);
```

Parameters:

Irp

> The I/O request packet sent to your driver. This IRP has flags set by the I/O Manager that determine whether the IRP can be processed synchronously or asynchronously. Note that asynchronous operations can always be performed synchronously (with the slight caveat discussed above); however, even if your driver performs a synchronous operation asynchronously and therefore returns **STATUS_PENDING** to the I/O Manager, the NT I/O Manager will perform a wait operation in the kernel on behalf of the calling thread.

Functionality Provided:

This simple function call performs the following checks:

- If the `IRP_SYNCHRONOUS_IRP` flag has been set, the IRP should be executed synchronously. All IRP structures that describe major functions other than the ones listed above will have this flag set in the IRP. The presence of this flag causes `IoIsOperationSynchronous()` to return TRUE.

- As described earlier in this chapter, the caller may have opened the target file object for synchronous access only. This is denoted by the `FO_SYNCHRONOUS_IO` flag being set in the file object data structure; the presence of this flag causes the `IoIsOperationSynchronous()` routine to return TRUE.

- The IRP may be a paging I/O read or write request, denoted by the `IRP_PAGING_IO` flag in the IRP. Furthermore, even paging I/O requests can be synchronous or asynchronous. Synchronous paging I/O requests are indicated by the presence of the `IRP_SYNCHRONOUS_PAGING_IO` flag in the IRP. If the latter flag is not set, the I/O Manager knows that this is an asynchronous paging I/O request and returns FALSE; otherwise, the I/O Manager identifies the request as a synchronous paging I/O request and returns TRUE.

The NT I/O Manager provides different methods of informing callers when asynchronous I/O operations have been completed. Here are the possible methods:

- The file object structure is a waitable object in Windows NT. When an I/O operation is initiated on a file object, the object is initially set to the not-signaled state; when the I/O operation completes, the file object is set to the signaled state.

- The asynchronous NT system services provided by the I/O Manager accept an optional `Event` object that is initially set to the not-signaled state and is signaled when the I/O operation is completed. In the discussion on IRP completion, I mentioned that the I/O Manager signals a user-supplied event object when performing the final postprocessing upon IRP completion in the context of the calling thread. Note, however, that if an event object is supplied, the file object will not be signaled.

- Asynchronous NT system services provided by the I/O Manager also accept an optional caller-supplied APC routine. This routine is invoked via an Asynchronous Procedure Call by the I/O Manager as part of the postprocessing performed in the context of the calling thread.

One final note about synchronous requests; all synchronous requests made using the same file object structure are serialized, regardless of whether they are made by the same thread or by other threads that are part of the same process. The file system driver also has the responsibility of maintaining a current position pointer for each file object that is updated whenever a file object is opened for synchronous I/O.

Handling User-Space Buffer Pointers

When you create a device object that can receive and serve I/O requests, your driver gets the opportunity to specify how it will handle user-supplied buffer address pointers. You won't fully understand why this information is necessary until you read the next chapter on the NT Virtual Memory Manager. For now, however, note that the range of addresses that a user-mode thread can access is limited to the lower 2GB of the 4GB address space accessible to any process under Windows NT. Furthermore, this 2GB range of virtual address space is unique per process (i.e., the addresses used by *thread-A* do not necessarily refer to the same physical memory location as do similar addresses used by *thread-B*). Of course, threads belonging to the same process do share the same address space.

A user-mode application typically performs I/O to and from secondary storage using temporary buffers it has allocated in its own thread context. We will currently ignore the alternative method used by applications, which involves using shared memory or memory-mapped files.

For example, consider an application that needs to read some data for a file from disk. This application will typically allocate a buffer that should be large enough to contain the amount of requested data. The application will then invoke a read operation on the open file from which it wishes to obtain data, specifying the byte offset to read from and the amount of information to be read.

The read request from the application will eventually be translated into an NT system service call provided by the NT I/O Manager. Among the arguments received by the I/O Manager will be the pointer to the buffer, supplied by the user-mode application. This read request now is sent by the I/O Manager to the file system driver that manages the mounted logical volume on which the open file object resides.* It is at this point that the I/O Manager finds out how the file system driver will deal with the user-supplied buffer pointer. This buffer is valid only in the context of the user-mode thread and does not refer to locked (nonpaged) memory. The file system can choose from the following possible options:

---

* As you go through the rest of the book, you will find out that this statement is not completely true, since often the I/O Manager bypasses the file system driver completely and instead gets data directly from the system cache. Let us keep things simple and straightforward for now, though, and ignore that method of data transfer.

- Request that the I/O Manager always allocates a nonpaged system buffer that will subsequently be used by the file system driver in the data transfer. It would then be the responsibility of the I/O Manager to copy any data being written out to disk from the user-supplied buffer to the system buffer before dispatching the IRP to the file system driver. Similarly, for I/O operations where the user-mode application needs to obtain information from the file system driver or to read data from disk, the I/O Manager would have to copy the data back from the system buffer to the user-allocated buffer once the IRP had been completed.

This method of handling user-mode buffers by instructing the I/O Manager to always allocate a corresponding system buffer is called the *Buffered I/O* method.

The system buffer pointer is passed down to your driver in the `Associated-Irp.SystemBuffer` field in the IRP. Note that the I/O Manager will also often initialize the `UserBuffer` field in the IRP with the address of the caller-supplied buffer. Do not attempt to use the contents of this field in your kernel-mode driver, though, because the `SystemBuffer` field already contains the system buffer pointer you can use.

The disadvantage of using buffered I/O is the requirement for extra memory copies to be performed by the I/O Manager. This is not desirable when you wish to maximize system performance. However, buffered I/O is the simplest and therefore most widely utilized method of handling user-supplied buffers.

Another disadvantage of using the buffered I/O method is that the memory for the system buffer allocated by the I/O Manager is not paged. This results in unnecessary depletion of the nonpaged pool of memory reserved for the system. A third problem is that, although the memory is not paged out, if you wish to use Direct Memory Access to transfer data directly to/from memory and peripheral devices, a Memory Descriptor List will have to be created by either your driver or a lower-level driver to describe the physical pages that back the allocated buffer.

- If your driver wishes to avoid the overhead of allocating and copying data to and from a system buffer, you can instead specify that your driver will use the *direct I/O* method. If this method is specified, the I/O Manager will request an MDL from the VMM that describes the user buffer directly, and it will also request the VMM to allocate and lock physical pages for the user buffer. The resulting MDL pointer will be passed to your driver in the `MdlAddress` field in the IRP.

The direct I/O method is more efficient than the allocation of an extra buffer and the resulting copy operations that must be performed. The downside is that your driver must be capable of working with the MDL directly; i.e., there is no virtual address pointer that your driver can use when transferring data.

Now, this works fine when you simply pass the MDL down to a lower-level driver, which subsequently uses it in a DMA data transfer. However, if you need a virtual address pointer that is accessible in the context of the thread you process the IRP in, your driver will have to use the `MmGetSystemAddressForMdl()` support routine from the VMM. You must be careful when using this routine; freeing the Memory Descriptor List will cause all processors in the system to flush their caches. The reason for this is complex; simply stated though, obtaining a system virtual address for the MDL is done by *doubly mapping* the physical pages. This is also known as *aliasing*, a technique which, if not handled correctly, causes many cache consistency problems and resulting headaches for the VMM. If your driver does use the direct I/O method for handling user-supplied buffers, try to avoid using the `MmGetSystemAddressForMdl()` routine whenever possible.

- The third method is not to specify either direct I/O or buffered I/O as the preferred method for handling user-supplied buffers. If you do not specify either of these two methods, the I/O Manager will simply pass down the user address to your driver in the `UserBuffer` field in the IRP.

  The responsibility for manipulating the user buffer is on your driver if you choose this method. File system drivers often use this method, and then make a decision in their dispatch routines whether they will create an MDL themselves or internally allocate a system buffer they can use while processing the request. Most lower-level drivers, however, prefer to use the direct I/O method described above.

These methods do not apply to buffers passed in for device or file system IOCTL (I/O Control) requests. I will discuss IOCTL requests and the buffer manipulation performed by the I/O Manager for such requests in Part 3.

System Boot Sequence

Before you proceed to the remaining chapters in this book, it might be useful to understand the steps that are executed from the time you power-on your Windows NT system until the point where you see the logon screen on the console.

This information can prove quite useful when you design your driver, because it determines when your driver will be loaded and what part your driver might be called upon to play during this process. However, you should also note that the boot process is highly system-, processor-, operating-system-version-, and architecture-dependent, and the sole objective in listing some of the steps below is simply to provide you with generic information about "what really happens" when the system boots, not to prepare you to be able to adapt the boot sequence to a new processor architecture.* Therefore, be warned that the following description is highly simplified, though mostly correct.

The main problem in examining the system boot sequence is to determine the starting point. For the purposes of this section, our "beginning" will be the point at which code provided by Microsoft as part of the NT operating system gets executed:

1. The NT system startup routine is invoked by the system start-up module. This routine is passed a `BootRecord` structure, which contains basic machine and environment information used later by the OS Loader component.

   The NT system startup routine performs some global initialization and determines the disk drive and partition that the system is booting from. Part of the global initialization involves initializing memory descriptors for use during this initial system boot-up stage. The system startup routine also invokes a boot loader heap initialization routine, which sets up memory descriptors appropriately so that the boot loader can subsequently use that memory during the system load process.

   The boot sequence described so far comprises Phase 1 of the eight phases in the NT system boot process.

2. The boot loader startup routine is now invoked by the system startup routine. Note that system startup routine does not expect that the call to the boot loader startup routine will ever return, since that would indicate that system boot sequence has failed. However, if this does happen, you will probably see a hung system, where a hard power reset might be required to restart.

   The boot loader startup routine opens the boot partition, which had been previously identified by the caller, and reads the *boot.ini* file off it. As part of attempting to read this file, the boot loader startup routine uses code that has been compiled in to determine whether the boot partition contains an NTFS, CDFS, FAT, or HPFS partition. Note that the standard file system drivers have not been loaded yet, and the boot loader startup routine uses hardcoded support for only those file systems that Microsoft has chosen to provide boot support for; these happen to be the standard NT file system implementations. Since support for boot file systems has to be built into the NT boot loader startup code, providing a third-party bootable file system implementation is close to impossible without the active assistance of Microsoft.

---

* I have described the sequence that executes on the x86 processor architecture. Despite my warnings above, much of the code executed during system startup has been designed to be relatively portable across different architectures; therefore, the methodology and principles used are pretty much the same.

At this point, the boot loader startup routine makes a real-mode BIOS interrupt call to set the video adapter to 80*50, 16-color, alphanumeric mode. It also clears the display by writing blanks out to the screen.

The boot loader startup routine reads the entire contents of the *boot.ini* file and presents the list of bootable kernels available to the user, as listed in the *boot.ini* file. To read the file, the boot loader startup routine once again employs routines that can recognize NTFS, FAT, CDFS, and HPFS data structures, and can navigate successfully through the on-disk file system layout. If the *boot.ini* file is empty, the default option presented is NT (default) and the default directory path to boot from is *C:\winnt.*[*]

The boot loader startup routine now attempts to match the default boot location provided by the user in the [`boot loader`] section of the *boot.ini* file, with the options read from the [`operating systems`] section of the file. If no default option was specified, the default directory path is searched for. If the boot loader startup routine does not find a match between the default boot option and those options listed in the [`operating systems`] section, the default boot location chosen is *C:\winnt.*

The default boot location and the possible options are presented by the boot loader startup routine to the user using video display support routines. If the boot kernel path location selected by the user is *C:*, the NT loader startup code assumes that the user wishes to boot into DOS, Windows 3.x, Windows 95, or OS/2; therefore, it attempts to read in the *bootsect.dos* file and then reboots the machine into whichever alternative operating system is present.

If the boot location indicates that the user wishes to boot into Windows NT (this can happen because of a time-out in the selection process, or because of the user selecting a specific boot system), the boot loader startup routine attempts to read in the *ntdetect.com* executable from the root directory of the boot partition. If *ntdetect.com* is not found, or if the size of the file seems incorrect, or if any of the other consistency checks made by the OS loader startup code fail, the boot process will fail and you will have to reboot the system. If, however, a valid executable is found, it is read into memory, and the system attempts to use the services provided by the hardware manufacturer to detect the current hardware configuration.

Note that we are well into Phase 2 of the system boot initialization at this point. The OS loader startup routine now initializes the SCSI boot driver if required. The *ntldr.exe* OS loader is now loaded into memory.

---

[*] Note that the boot loader startup routine currently has a bug in that it cannot handle more than 10 entries in the *boot.ini* file. All entries exceeding this limit are simply ignored. Apparently, this bug has existed since Windows NT Version 3.5 (and probably since well before that).

3. The OS loader opens the console input and output devices, and also the system and boot partitions. It also displays the OS loader identification message on the console, `OS Loader V4.0`.

The loader uses the boot partition information to generate a complete pathname for the *ntoskrnl.exe* NT kernel system image file. Note that the system always expects to find this file in the *System32* directory under the boot partition location. Once the system image has been loaded into memory, the OS loader loads into memory the *hal.dll* system file. The HAL (Hardware Abstraction Layer) isolates platform dependent functionality for the rest of the Windows NT Executive.

At this point, all DLLs imported by the two loaded system files are identified and loaded into memory. Now, the OS loader attempts to load the *SYSTEM* hive from the NT Registry. At this time, the loader has already made the determination whether it should load the `LastKnownGood` control set or the *Default* control set from the Registry. This determination is important because the control set determines the set of boot drivers that will be loaded into the system.

To load the *SYSTEM* hive into memory, the OS loader attempts to open and read the *SYSTEM* file from the *System32\config* directory on the boot partition. If the attempt to open and read in the *SYSTEM* file fails, an attempt is made to read in the *SYSTEM.ALT* file. If neither of these attempts succeed, the OS loader fails the boot attempt. If the file can be successfully read, the contents of the file are verified, and in-memory data structures are initialized to reflect the contents of the on-disk file. Also, note that the system loader block, which is eventually passed to the loaded system image, is appropriately modified to point to the in-memory copy of the *SYSTEM* hive.

At this time, the OS Loader determines the list of boot drivers that need to be loaded into memory. Included among this list is the driver responsible for the boot partition file system. Note that boot drivers are identified by the `Start` value entry (should be equal to 0) associated with the driver's key in the control set that was loaded into memory. Once the list of boot drivers has been identified, the OS Loader sorts these drivers based upon the `Service-GroupOrder` specified in the Registry; subsequent drivers within a group are sorted based on the `GroupOrderList` specified in the Registry and the `Tag` value entry associated with each driver key in the Registry.

Once the driver load order has been determined, all boot drivers are loaded. In the event of an error while loading boot drivers, the `ErrorControl` value entry associated with the driver in the Registry is examined. If the driver was marked as a critical driver for the system boot process, the current boot fails; otherwise, the OS loader continues loading other boot drivers.

Finally, the OS Loader prepares to execute the loaded system image and transfers control to the entry point in the NT kernel.

4. During Phases 3-5 of the system boot process, the various NT Executive components and the NT kernel are initialized. Drivers that should be automatically loaded with a *Start* value entry of 1 are also loaded during Phase 5 of the system boot process.

   The NT kernel initialization routine, `KiInitializeKernel()`, is invoked during Phase 3 initialization by the kernel system startup routine (which is the entry point into the system image that was loaded into memory by the NT OS loader). This routine initializes the processor control block data structure, the kernel data structures, and the idle thread and process objects, and invokes the NT Executive initialization routine. Various spin locks protecting kernel data structures and kernel linked list structures are initialized here. The various kernel linked list heads (DPC queue list head, timer notification list head, various thread table lists, and other similar kernel data structures) are also initialized here.

   Once the kernel idle thread structure has been initialized, the Executive initialization routine is now invoked in the context of this idle thread. Initialization of the NT Executive and the various subcomponents of the Executive takes place in two phases.* During Phase 0 of the Executive initialization, the following subcomponents initialize their internal states:

   — The Hardware Abstraction Layer (HAL)

   — The NT Executive component

   — The Virtual Memory Manager (VMM)

     Memory Manager paged and nonpaged pools, the page frame database (explained in the next chapter), Page Table Entry (PTE) management structures, and various VMM resources, such as mutex and spin lock data structures, are initialized at this time. The VMM also initializes the NT system-cache-related data structures at this time, including the system cache working set and the various VMM data structures used to manage the system cache.

   — The NT Object Manager

   — The Security subsystem

---

* Do not confuse these phases with the system boot sequence Phases 1 through 8. These two phases are internal and specific to the initialization of the NT Executive and its various subcomponents.

— The Process Manager

During Phase 0 initialization of the NT Executive, the initial system process is created. Note that the idle process was hand crafted by the NT kernel before any of the Executive initialization began. The system process created at this time is distinct from the idle process that was created earlier. A system thread is also created in the context of the initial system process at this time. Phase 1, or the remainder of the NT Executive initialization, is now performed in the context of this newly created thread belonging to the initial system process.

During Phase 1 initialization of the NT Executive and various subcomponents, all interrupts are disabled and the priority of the thread in whose context the initialization is performed is raised to a high priority, effectively disabling any preemption. Also, during Phase 1 of the Executive initialization, the system is considered fully functional and subcomponents are now allowed to perform all required operations to complete their initialization. The following subcomponents are invoked (or their operations performed) during Phase 1 initialization of the NT Executive:

— The Hardware Abstraction Layer (HAL) is invoked to complete initialization.

— The system date and time are initialized.

— On an multiprocessor system, other processors are started at this time.

— The Object Manager, Executive subsystem, and the Security subsystem are invoked to perform the remainder of their initialization.

— The Virtual Memory Manager (VMM) Phase 1 initialization is performed.

At this time, the memory mapping functionality is initialized and becomes available to the rest of the system. VMM threads are also started now. The VMM can be considered fully functional and ready to service the remainder of the system after Phase 1 initialization.

— The NT Cache Manager is initialized after the VMM initialization has been completed.

You will read more about the NT Cache Manager and the functionality provided by it later in this book. Note for now, that during Cache Manager initialization, the number of worker threads required for asynchronous operations is determined and created, and the Cache Manager linked list structures and synchronization resources are initialized.

— The Configuration Manager is invoked to begin its initialization.

The Configuration Manager manages the NT Registry. During this phase of initialization, the Configuration Manager (CM) makes available the

\REGISTRY\MACHINE\SYSTEM and the *\REGISTRY\MACHINE\HARD-WARE* hives in the registry. To do this, all of the information obtained by *ntdetect.com* earlier, as well as information read into memory by the OS loader is filled into appropriate entries in the *SYSTEM* or *HARDWARE* hives. Once this phase of initialization has been completed, part of the Registry name space is available to other system components, particularly kernel-mode drivers that will soon be loaded; however, the CM will not write out modifications to the Registry at this time. The kernel-mode drivers that will soon be called upon to perform driver-specific initialization can use the standard Registry routines to access this information.

— The NT I/O Manager is called upon to perform its initialization.

The I/O Manager first initializes internal state objects, including synchronization data structures, linked lists, and memory pools (e.g., the IRP zone/lookaside lists). Then, the I/O Manager registers all of its internally defined object types (i.e. adapter objects, controller objects, device objects, driver objects, I/O completion objects, and file objects) with the Object Manager using an internal routine called `ObCreateObject-Type()`.* The I/O Manager also creates the *\Device*, *\DosDevices*, and the *\Driver* root directories in the object name-space at this time.

Next, the boot drivers loaded by the OS loader are initialized by the I/O Manager. This includes invoking the *driver entry* routines for each of these drivers to perform driver-specific initialization. The *raw file system* driver is also loaded at this time. The only other file system driver loaded is the *boot file system* driver. Drivers must adhere to the restrictions on interacting with the NT Registry. Finally, the drivers with a *Start* value entry value of 1 are loaded and their driver entry routines invoked for driver-specific initialization.

Driver reinitialization routines are subsequently invoked for all loaded drivers that have requested reinitialization. Following this, the NT I/O Manager assigns drive letters to recognized disk partitions. The drive letters *A:* and *B:* are reserved for floppy drives. The I/O Manager examines the registry for any "sticky" drive letter assignments that need to be maintained for CD-ROM drives and for hard disk drive partitions. These drive-letter assignments are internally reserved so that they will not be used subsequently when determining dynamic DOS drive letter assignments.

---

* Note that the Object Manager is not aware of these object types otherwise (i.e., information about I/O Manager-defined objects is not coded into the Object Manager design). This illustrates the philosophy of a layered and object-based system, followed by the NT development team.

Note that before reserving a drive letter for each of the hard disk drives, the I/O Manager performs an open operation on the physical drive. Therefore, if you develop a hard disk device driver or a lower-level filter or intermediate driver, you should expect an open request at this time. If the open request succeeds, a symbolic link to the device object is created in NT object name space; the name assigned to this link is of the form *DosDevices\PhysicalDrive%d* where *%d* represents the disk drive number in sequence. The NT I/O Manager also queries partition information from the disk driver at this time. The following method is used by the I/O Manager to determine the order in which drive letters are assigned to fixed disk partitions:

— The NT I/O Manager queries the Registry for any "sticky" drive letter assignments that need to be maintained.

— Bootable partitions are first assigned dynamic DOS-compatible drive letters (i.e., a symbolic link is created to the device object representing the partition, with the name *DosDevices\%c:* where *%c* represents the drive letter chosen by the NT I/O Manager for the partition).

— Primary partitions are next chosen for dynamically assigned drive letters.

— Extended partitions are subsequently assigned DOS drive letters.

— Other (enhanced) partitions are now assigned DOS drive letters. After drive letters have been assigned to hard disk drive and removable drive partitions, the NT I/O Manager assigns drive letters to all CD-ROM drives that were identified during hardware detection.

— The Local Procedure Call (LPC) subsystem and the Process Manager subsystem now complete their initialization.

— The Reference Monitor and Session Manager subsystem are invoked next to complete their initialization.

5. At this point, Phases 3-5 of the system boot process have been completed. Remember that NT Executive components were initialized in the context of the system worker thread belonging to the system process, which was created by the NT kernel. This thread now assumes the role of the Memory Manager *zero page thread*; this is a very low-priority thread used to asynchronously zero out pages that are placed on the free list by the VMM. As you will read in the next chapter, all pages need to be zeroed out before they can be reused to make the system conform to *C2* security defined by the US Department Of Defense (DOD).

6. The system has been initialized at this point. During Phases 6-8 of the system boot process, the various subsystems are initialized and other services are loaded by the Service Controller Manager. This includes the loading of kernel-mode drivers with a *Start* value of 2 in the Registry.

We have finished our bird's-eye view of the NT system boot process. This should have given you a reasonable understanding of the steps executed to bring the NT system to a stable state so that it can begin responding to user requests.

This chapter has introduced you to the Windows NT I/O Manager and the Windows NT I/O subsystem. Another important component of the NT Executive is the NT Virtual Memory Manager, which is the topic of the next chapter.

5

The NT Virtual Memory Manager

An important functionality provided by modern day operating systems is the management of physical memory on the node. Typically, the amount of available volatile RAM on a machine is less than that required by all the applications and by the operating system itself. Therefore, the operating system has to intervene and facilitate sharing this limited memory resource, given the often conflicting demands placed by all components on the node.

Furthermore, with multiple applications executing concurrently on the same machine, the operating system has the task of ensuring that these applications can perform their tasks independently of each other. Therefore, code and data structures for each of the applications must be managed such that they do not interfere with code and data from any other application. The operating system must also protect its own in-memory resources (both code and data), used to manage the system, from all of the applications executing on the system. This is required to guarantee the integrity and security of the machine itself. Finally, sophisticated applications on the same machine (and sometimes on networked clusters of machines) often need to share in-memory data with each other. The operating system has to facilitate orderly sharing of data such that only those applications that are given permission to access the shared data are allowed to do so.

The Virtual Memory Manager (VMM) has the responsibility for providing all of this functionality. The VMM is so named because it helps provide an abstraction to each application executing on the system: each application can perform its tasks believing all of the memory resources on that system are available for the sole use of that application. Furthermore, the application can execute believing that it has an infinite amount of memory resource available to it. This abstraction of an infinite amount of memory reserved solely for the use of a specific application is called virtual memory. The VMM is the kernel-mode component responsible for providing this abstraction.

Functionality

The NT VMM provides the following functionality to the other components of the system:

- The Virtual Memory Manager provides a demand-paged (with clustering support), virtual memory system. Each process has a private virtual address space associated with it.* This virtual address space is backed by physical pages, allocated on demand from the total pool of physical pages available on the machine.

- Management of the virtual address space associated with a process is separated from the manipulation of physical pages. The VMM provides support for application control of the virtual address space allocation, commitment, manipulation, and deallocation.

- Virtual memory support is provided with the help of the local file systems. In order to provide the illusion of a large amount of available memory (greater than the amount of actual RAM), the contents of memory are backed-up to storage allocated on secondary storage media. Memory backed by on-disk storage is called *committed memory*. Committed memory is backed either by page files, which can be dynamically resized, or by data/image files on secondary storage.

- The VMM provides support for memory-mapped files. These files can be arbitrarily large; files larger than 2GB can be mapped using partial *views* of the file.

- It supports sharing memory between different processes on the system. This is also used as a method of interprocess communication.

- It implements per-process quotas.

- It determines the policies for working-set management of physical memory allocated to processes.

---

* Currently (for Windows NT Version 4.0 and earlier), the Virtual Address Space associated with a process is limited to 4 GB. It is inevitable that this support will be extended to 2^{64} bytes when Windows NT becomes a true 64-bit operating system. At the time this book went to press, Microsoft announced its intention to support a 64-bit address space with Version 5.0 of the operating system.

Furthermore, all physical memory allocation/deallocation decisions are performed by the NT VMM. This is done irrespective of whether memory is allocated to user-mode applications or for kernel-mode file data caching.

- It provides support for the protection of memory using Access Control Lists (ACLs).

- It provides support for the POSIX *fork* and *exec* operations, thereby enabling compliance with the POSIX standard.

- It provides support for *copy-on-write* pages. It has the ability to establish guard pages and to set page level protection.*

Process Address Space

An address is simply a value that points to a memory location contained within system volatile memory. Every process that executes on a Windows NT system has a set of *virtual addresses* available for its use. From the perspective of the executing process, each element of the virtual address space conceptually refers to a byte of physical memory.† Windows NT is still a 32-bit operating system; that means all addresses pointing to memory are 32-bit quantities. This results in the limitation that each process can, at the most, access 4GB of virtual address space.

The reason for the term *virtual address space* is simple: although the range of addresses extends from *0x00000000* to *0xFFFFFFFF*, the amount of physical RAM on the machine is typically much less than 4GB. Assume that each element of the virtual address space really mapped to an equivalent physical address. Therefore, each system would have to install 4GB of memory for each process that would run on that system. Instead, the VMM tricks each process into believing that it has 4GB of addressable memory available for its usage. The process takes this proposition at face value and tries to access memory using the range of available virtual addresses. It is the responsibility of the VMM to translate (or map) each virtual address into a corresponding physical address.

Why does a process need to access memory? In order to provide any useful functionality, each process has most of the following components associated with it:

- Program text

- The process stack (local variables are stored here)

- Initialized global data

---

* Implementation of copy-on-write pages and support for page-level protection depends on the support provided by the underlying Memory Management Unit (MMU).

† *Word-oriented* commercial machines (where each address refers to a word of RAM storage space) are rare. We will ignore such beasts.

- Uninitialized global data

- Heap (dynamically allocated memory)

- Shared memory

- Shared libraries

These components must be stored somewhere in physical memory, though not all of these components need to always exist in physical memory all of the time. If these components are brought into physical memory when needed, the process must have some way of accessing the memory locations where this information is stored. Therefore, an address space (or a range of addresses) must be associated with each process.

Some amount of physical memory in the system must also be devoted to the operating system code and data. So now, not only does the VMM have to provide virtual addresses for process-specific information, it must provide virtual addresses to refer to operating system components, including addresses that refer to its own code used to manage the memory in the system. This is achieved by the creation of a special system process, which, like any other process, has 4GB of virtual memory available to it. However, creation of the system process is not sufficient in itself.

You know that user processes executing on the system often have to request services from the operating system. These requests might be related to I/O operations, allocation and manipulation of memory, creation of new processes and other similar operations. The NT operating system provides system services that receive user requests and execute code in kernel mode to handle such requests. This leads to the situation where operating system code executing in kernel mode must perform some tasks in the context of the user process that issued the request.

Figure 5-1 illustrates a typical process address space on an Intel x86 hardware platform.*

To perform such tasks, operating system code and data must be addressable from within the context of the user process; i.e., there must be a range of virtual addresses that refer to operating system code and data, but actually "reside" within the 4GB limit set by the underlying hardware. To achieve this, the NT VMM divides the 4GB range of addresses allocated to each process into two halves, a 2GB range dedicated to user-mode virtual addresses, called *user space* (a

---

* Some hardware platforms support a segmented addressing scheme, which divides physical memory into contiguous chunks known as *segments*. However, the view presented by the NT VMM to the entire system is that of a linear (or a *flat*) virtual address space. Any segmentation issues (if they exist on a particular architecture) are handled transparently by the VMM.

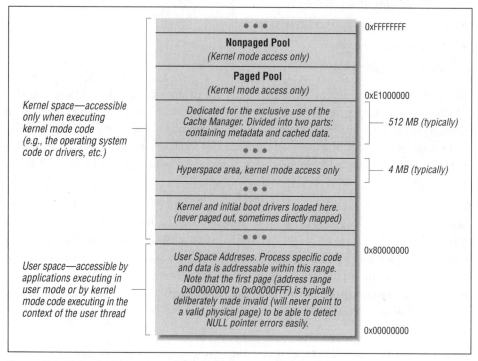

Kernel space—accessible
only when executing
kernel mode code
(e.g., the operating system
code or drivers, etc.)

User space—accessible by
applications executing in
user mode or by kernel
mode code executing in the
context of the user thread

Figure 5-1. Virtual address space for a typical process

user process executing in user mode can only access this 2GB range) and another
2GB range containing kernel-mode virtual addresses, called *kernel space*.

NOTE   Let me reiterate the following concept: a processor can execute code
in user mode (typically *Ring 3* on Intel x86 architectures) or it can execute code in kernel/privileged mode (typically *Ring 0* on Intel x86 architectures). Therefore, although stated otherwise, user-mode or
kernel-mode states are associated with a processor, not with any code
(or process) executing on that processor. The distinction, though subtle, must be well understood by all kernel developers.

Although the 2GB of user-mode virtual addresses refer to process-private data
(not accessible by other processes in the system), the 2GB of kernel-mode
addresses always refer to the same physical pages* on the system (regardless of
the thread context in which they are accessed) containing operating system code
and data.

---

* Pages are explained later in this chapter.

Another concept that you should understand is that of a *hyperspace area* within the 4GB virtual address space associated with each process. This hyperspace area is a range of virtual addresses actually reserved from within the 2GB kernel space area, but specially designated, since it typically contains process-specific internal data structures maintained by the NT VMM. Whenever a context switch occurs, the VMM refreshes this virtual address space to refer to information specific to the new process. These data structures include page table pages for the process, w, and other such VMM data structures.

If you develop kernel-mode drivers, you always have to be aware of the thread context in which your code operates. For example, if you design a file system driver, your dispatch entry points will typically be executed in the context of the user process that invoked the corresponding system call.* If this is the case, your driver can use addresses (passed in the IRP) within the lower 2GB of the process's virtual address space to refer to user-space memory (e.g., user buffers). However, if you write intermediate or lower-level drivers (e.g., device drivers), your dispatch routines will typically be invoked in the context of an arbitrary thread, defined as the thread that is executing on that processor at that particular time. In this case, you cannot assume that any user-space virtual addresses that might be contained in the I/O Request Packet are still valid, because your code is not executing in the context of the user thread originating the request; hence the lower 2GB of the virtual address space now map to physical pages belonging to some other process.

On the other hand, if you develop a kernel-mode driver and allocate memory, the returned memory pointer will typically be a virtual address in kernel space. Since the kernel-space virtual address is the same for all processes in the system, the allocated memory can be referred to (using the returned pointer) in the context of any thread in which your code might be executing.

How do you ensure that a user-space buffer pointer passed in via an IRP is accessible from within your driver, if code within your driver might execute in an arbitrary thread context? The VMM provides support to map user-space memory into kernel virtual address space precisely for this purpose (`MmGetSystemAddressForMdl()`).†

One final point: it might be necessary for your kernel-mode driver to occasionally access the virtual address space of some other process. One of the ways that this

---

* This is not always true. Sometimes, the subsystem (e.g., the Win32 subsystem) will invoke file system entry points in the context of a worker thread belonging to some Win32-specific process. Furthermore, the NT VMM and the NT Cache Manager often originate calls into the file system read/write routines in the context of a thread belonging to the system process.

† This routine is described in further detail later in this chapter.

can be accomplished is by using the `KeAttachProcess()` kernel support routine. This routine is not documented in the Windows NT DDK, but is defined as follows:

```
VOID
KeAttachProcess (
    IN PEPROCESS         Process
);
```

Parameters:

Process

A pointer to the process you wish to attach to. This can be obtained by an invocation to `IoGetCurrentProcess()`.

Functionality Provided:

The `KeAttachProcess()` call allows your kernel-mode thread to attach itself to the target process. Then your thread will execute in the context of that process, allowing it to access the entire virtual address space and all other resources belonging to that process.

NOTE   A reason you might wish to access the virtual address space of another process is if memory had been mapped into the virtual address space of the target process and you need to access it. Another reason is if you need to use any resources (e.g., file handles) that belong to the target process.

Be very careful though, since attaching to another process is an extremely expensive operation and will result in two context switches, at the very least, if the target process has been swapped out. Furthermore, it will probably result in flushing of *Translation Lookaside Buffers* on all processors in a symmetric multiprocessor (SMP) system, which can be detrimental to system performance.

Do not invoke this routine at an IRQL greater than `DISPATCH_LEVEL`. An executive spin lock used to protect internal data structures in the implementation of this routine is acquired at IRQL `DISPATCH_LEVEL`; therefore, invoking this function at a higher IRQL could lead to a deadlock scenario. Also, do not attempt to attach to a second process if you have already invoked the `KeAttachProcess()` function without invoking the corresponding detach routine, described next, or a bugcheck will occur.

The corresponding routine to detach from a process to which your thread is attached is defined as follows:

```
VOID
KeDetachProcess (
```

```
      VOID
);
```

Parameters:

None.

Functionality Provided:

The `KeDetachProcess()` function allows your kernel mode thread to detach itself from a previously attached process. Do not invoke this routine at an IRQL greater than `DISPATCH_LEVEL`.

Physical Memory Management

To write a kernel-mode driver (especially a file system driver), it helps to broadly understand the method used by the memory manager to manage physical memory. Once you understand how physical memory is manipulated, I will describe how virtual addresses are mapped to physical addresses. This knowledge can be invaluable when debugging NT systems and when attempting to understand why certain things work the way they do.

Page Frames and the Page Frame Database

The NT VMM must manage the available physical memory in the system. The method used by the VMM is the standard page-based scheme used by modern day commercial operating systems such as Solaris, HPUX, or other System V Revision 4 (SVR4)-based UNIX implementations.

The NT VMM divides the available RAM into fixed-size *page frames*. The size of the page frame (page size) supported can vary from 4K to 64K; on Intel x86 architectures, it is currently set to 4K bytes.* Each page frame is represented by an entry in a structure called the *page frame database* (*PFN database*).† The page frame database is simply an array of entries allocated in nonpaged system memory, one for each page frame of physical memory. For each page frame, the following information is maintained:

---

* Windows NT and most other commercial operation systems currently use fixed-sized pages. However, a considerable amount of research has been performed on the implementation of support for variable-sized pages by the underlying hardware architecture and the operating system. Support for variable-sized pages might someday be implemented in commercial operating systems, though one might conjecture that UNIX platforms are likely to implement it sooner than NT. With Windows NT Version 4.0, Microsoft does use 4 MB-sized pages (supported by the Intel Pentium processor *extensions*) to contain kernel mode code on Intel platforms. However, as stated here, truly variable-sized pages are not yet supported by the Windows NT platform.

† This is similar to the *core map* structure on 4.3 BSD-based systems.

- A physical address for the page frame represented by the entry in the PFN database. This physical address is currently limited to a 20-bit field. When combined with a 12-bit page offset, you can see that the resulting 32-bit quantity is limited to supporting a 4GB physical memory system.

- A set of attributes associated with the page frame. These are:

  — A modified bit that indicates whether the contents of the page frame were modified

  — Status indicating whether a read or write operation is underway for the page frame

  — A *page color* associated with the page (on some platforms)

NOTE   On systems that have a physically indexed direct-mapped cache, poor allocation of virtual addresses to physical addresses within page frames can lead to contention for the same cache line (i.e., 2 physical pages hash to the same cache line) and hence always cause cache misses if the pages happen to be part of the working set for one process or for two or more processes executing concurrently. Page coloring attempts to address this problem in software. Note that page coloring support is not provided by the NT VMM on x86 based machines. However, such support is provided, for example, for the MIPS R4000 processor.

  — Information on whether this page frame contains a shared page or a private page for a process

- A back pointer to the Page Table Entry/Prototype Page Table Entry (PTE/ PPTE)* that points to this page. This pointer is used to perform a reverse mapping from a physical address to the corresponding virtual address.

- Reference count for the page. The reference count value indicates to the VMM whether any PTE refers to the page in the page frame database.

- Forward and backward pointers for any hash lists on which the page frame might be linked.

- An event pointer that refers to an event whenever a paging I/O read operation is in progress; i.e., data is being brought into memory from secondary storage.

Valid page frames are those that have a nonzero reference count. These page frames contain a page of information actively being used by some process (or by the operating system). When a page frame is no longer pointed to by a PTE, the

---

* Page Table Entries and Prototype Page Table Entries are described in more detail later in this chapter.

reference count is decremented. When the reference count is zero, the page frame is considered unused. Each unused page frame is on one of five different lists, reflecting the state of the page frame:

- The bad page list, linking together page frames that have parity (ECC) errors

- The free list, indicating pages that are available for immediate reuse but have not yet been zeroed

  The NT VMM (in order to conform to C2 level security as defined by the US DOD) will not reuse a page frame unless the contents have been zeroed. However, in the interest of keeping low overhead, pages are not zeroed each time they are freed. Once a critical mass of free and not-zeroed pages has been reached, a system worker thread is awakened to asynchronously zero pages on the free list.

- The zeroed list, linking page frames that are available for immediate reuse

- The modified list, linking page frames that are no longer referenced but cannot be reclaimed until the contents of the page have been written to secondary storage

  Writing modified pages to secondary storage is typically performed asynchronously by the *Modified Page Writer/Mapped Page Writer*, a component that I will discuss in detail later in this chapter.

- The standby list, containing page frames with pages that were removed from the process's working set

  The NT VMM aggressively tries to decrease the number of page frames allocated to a given process, based upon the access pattern of the process. This number of pages allocated to the process at any given instant is called the *working set* for the process. By automatically trimming the working set for a process, the NT VMM tries to make better use of the physical memory. However, if a page frame allocated to a process is stolen due to this trimming of the working set, the VMM does not immediately reclaim the page frame. Instead, by placing the page frame on this standby list, the VMM delays the reuse of the page frame, giving the process an opportunity to regain the page frame by accessing an address contained within it. While a page frame is on this list, it is marked as being in a transitional state, since it is not yet free, nor does it really belong to a process.

The NT VMM keeps both a minimum and a maximum for the total of free and standby page frames on the system. Whenever a page frame is linked to the free or standby list and the total is below the minimum or above the maximum, an appropriate VMM global event is signaled. These events are used by the VMM to determine whether sufficient number of pages are available in the system.

Often, the VMM invokes an internal routine to check whether memory is available for a certain operation. For example, your driver might invoke a system routine called `MmAllocateNonCachedMemory()`. This routine needs free pages that it can allocate to your driver and therefore invokes an internal routine (not directly available to kernel developers) called `MiEnsureAvailablePageOrWait()` to check whether the number of required pages are available from either the free or the standby list. If not available, the `MiEnsureAvailablePageOrWait()` routine will block on the two events waiting for sufficient pages to become available. If neither of the two events is set within a fixed period of time, the system will panic by invoking `KeBugCheck()`.

Note that manipulation of the page frame database is a frequent operation. There has been considerable research on how VMM implementations can achieve greater concurrency by using fine-grained locking for the page frame database (or whatever the equivalent structure is called on some specific platform). However, the NT VMM does not follow any such model of using fine-grained locking. There is a global lock, an Executive spin lock, for the entire page frame database. This spin lock is acquired at an appropriate IRQL (`APC_LEVEL` or `DISPATCH_LEVEL`) when the PFN database is accessed. This might reduce concurrency, since it forces single threading whenever the PFN database must be accessed, but it definitely simplifies the code. Note that no I/O is ever performed (indeed no routine outside the VMM module is ever invoked) with the PFN lock acquired. However, since the lock is acquired at `DISPATCH_LEVEL` or less, you can now be completely convinced that any page fault by your code at a higher IRQL will lead to a system panic.

Virtual Address Support

The NT Virtual Memory Manager provides virtual address support to the remainder of the system:

- Virtual address ranges can be manipulated independently of the physical memory on the system.

- If a virtual address is backed by either physical memory or on-disk storage, the NT VMM assists the processor hardware in transparently translating the virtual address into the corresponding physical address.

- If the page containing the translated physical address needs to be read from secondary storage, the NT VMM initiates and manages the I/O operation.

  To achieve this transfer of data from disk to memory, the NT VMM uses the support of the appropriate file system driver.

- The VMM determines the paging policies used to control the transfer of information to and from disk and main memory to maximize system throughput.

As noted earlier in this chapter, the VMM provides each process with an address space larger than the amount of physical memory available on the system. Virtual addresses must eventually refer to some code or data residing in physical RAM on the system. Therefore, in order to support this large address space, the VMM and the system hardware must transparently translate virtual addresses into physical addresses. Furthermore, since the total memory requirements of all processes executing on the system will typically be in excess of the total physical memory available, the VMM must be able to move data and code to and from secondary storage as required.

The NT VMM is a core component that determines the perceived performance and cost of the system. RAM, although getting cheaper every day, is still not a costless component. At the same time, users are very demanding of their machines and a poor implementation of the VMM can significantly degrade the overall system throughput. Therefore, the VMM is extremely sensitive to the minimum memory requirements it imposes upon the system. As is the case with every design decision, certain tradeoffs have to be made. Later in this chapter, I will discuss an explicit tradeoff made by the designers of the NT VMM, resulting in problems for implementations of distributed file systems in the NT environment.

Virtual Address Manipulation

To provide a separate virtual address space for a process, the NT VMM maintains a self-balancing binary tree (splay tree) of Virtual Address Descriptors (VADs) for each process in the system. Every block of memory allocated for a process is represented by a VAD structure inserted into this tree. A pointer to the root of this tree is inserted into the process structure. A virtual address descriptor structure contains the following information:

- The starting virtual address for the range represented by the VAD
- The ending virtual address for the VAD range
- Pointers to other VAD structures in the splay tree
- Attributes determining the nature of the allocated virtual address range

  These attributes contain the following information:

  — Information on whether allocated memory has been committed

    For committed memory, the VMM allocates storage space from a page file to back up the allocated memory whenever it needs to be swapped to disk.

— Information specifying whether the range of allocated virtual addresses
  are private to the process, or whether the virtual address range is shared

— Bits describing the protection associated with the memory backing a
  range of virtual addresses

  The protection is composed of combinations of primitive protection
  attributes: PAGE_NOACCESS, PAGE_READONLY, PAGE_READWRITE,
  PAGE_WRITECOPY, PAGE_EXECUTE, PAGE_EXECUTE_READ, PAGE_
  EXECUTE_READWRITE, PAGE_EXECUTE_WRITECOPY, PAGE_GUARD,
  and PAGE_NOCACHE.

— Whether copy-on-write has been enabled for the range of pages

  The copy-on-write feature allows efficient support for POSIX-style
  fork() operations, in which the address space is initially shared by parent and child processes. If, however, either the parent or children try to
  modify a page, a private copy is created for the process performing the
  modification.

— Whether this range should be shared by a child process when a fork()
  occurs (VIEW_UNMAP = do not share, VIEW_SHARE = shared by parent
  and child)

  This information is valid only for mapped views of a file, which are discussed later in this chapter.

— Whether the VAD represents a mapped view of a section object

— The amount of committed memory associated with the VAD

Whenever memory is allocated on behalf of a process or whenever a process
maps a view of a file into its virtual address space, the NT VMM allocates a VAD
structure and inserts it into the splay tree. At allocation time, a process can specify
whether it requires committed memory, or whether it simply needs to reserve a
range of virtual addresses. Allocating committed memory results in the amount of
memory requested being charged against the quota allocated to the process.
Reserving a virtual address range, however, is a benign operation in that only a
VAD structure is created and inserted into the splay tree, and the starting virtual
address is returned to the requesting process. Note that memory must be
committed before it is actually used.

The NT VMM allows a process to allocate and deallocate purely virtual address
spaces, i.e., the memory need never be committed. If a process allocates a virtual
range of addresses and subsequently discovers that it needs to commit only a
subset of the range, the NT VMM also allows the process to do so.

There is a native allocation routine supplied by the NT VMM called `NtAllocate-VirtualMemory()`, which is not available to kernel developers. Kernel-mode drivers have access to the following routine instead:

```
NTSTATUS
ZwAllocateVirtualMemory(
    IN HANDLE               ProcessHandle,
    IN OUT PVOID            *BaseAddress,
    IN ULONG                ZeroBits,
    IN OUT PULONG           RegionSize,
    IN ULONG                AllocationType,
    IN ULONG                Protect
);
```

Parameters:

ProcessHandle

An open handle to the process in whose context the memory is being allocated. For NT kernel-mode drivers that call this routine, it is the context of the system process (e.g., at driver initialization time). You can use the macro `NtCurrentProcess()`, which simply returns a special handle value of (-1) which identifies the current process as the system process. Note that if you ask for memory to be allocated within the context of a process other than your current process, the `NtAllocateVirtualMemory()` routine will use the `KeAttachProcess()` routine described earlier, to attach your process to the target process before allocating the range of virtual addresses.

BaseAddress

Upon a successful return from this routine, the `BaseAddress` argument will contain the starting virtual address for the allocated memory.

If you supply a nonnull initial value, the VMM will attempt to allocate the memory at the address supplied by you, after rounding it down to a multiple of the page size. If, however, you supply a null initial value, the VMM will simply pick a base address for you.

Note that if the VMM cannot allocate memory at the base address supplied by you (the address has already been used or not enough contiguous memory is available beginning at that address), and if you have specified `MEM_RESERVE` as `AllocationType` (defined later), an error will be returned (`STATUS_CONFLICTING_ADDRESSES`). The same error will be returned if you supplied a base address without previously reserving it (using this same routine).

Finally, you cannot specify a base address greater than 2GB, and your specified range cannot exceed the 2GB virtual address limit. The important point to note, then, is that if you use this call, you will get a kernel-mode address that will not be valid in the context of any process except the process passed in (via the handle argument). This call is, therefore, not the preferred way to get kernel memory for your driver (use the `ExAllocatePool()` routines instead).

ZeroBits

This argument is only valid if the `BaseAddress` argument discussed above was passed in initialized to NULL (the VMM gets to pick the base address). You can specify the number of high-order bits that must be zero for the base address of the allocated memory.

By doing this, you can ensure that the returned starting address is below a specific value. This argument cannot be greater than 21 (since that would make the starting address less than 4096 bytes). A value of 0 is treated (at least) as a value of 2, since the returned virtual address will always be within the user-space-addressable 2GB of virtual address space.

RegionSize

Note that this is a pointer argument. You must supply the number of bytes to be allocated. You will receive the actual number of bytes allocated, which will be your number rounded up to a multiple of the page size.

AllocationType

You have a choice of `MEM_COMMIT`, `MEM_RESERVE`, or `MEM_TOP_DOWN`. The first option indicates that you wish space to be reserved in the page file (this memory is committed and therefore usable). The second option says that you simply want the virtual address range and that you might commit the memory later. The first two options are therefore mutually exclusive. The third option can be combined with either of the first two and it states that you want the highest possible starting virtual address allocated, given the constraints specified by the `ZeroBits` argument.

Protect

Your options are one or more of the following primitive protections: `PAGE_NOACCESS`, `PAGE_READONLY`, `PAGE_READWRITE`, `PAGE_NOCACHE` (cannot be placed into the data cache, this is not allowed for mapped pages), and `PAGE_EXECUTE`.

Functionality Provided:

This routine can only be used to allocate memory within the lower 2GB of the process virtual address space (even for the system process). Therefore, it is typically not used by kernel-mode drivers, unless you are quite sure that you will to access the memory only in the context of the specified process. If you need to allocate memory that is accessible within the context of any process, use the `ExAllocatePool()` routines instead.

This routine allows you to do one of three things:

- Reserve a range of virtual addresses but not commit them

- Reserve and commit a range of virtual addresses (in one call)

- Commit a previously reserved range of virtual addresses

The corresponding routine to free the allocated range is defined as follows:

```
NTSTATUS
NTAPI
ZwFreeVirtualMemory(
    IN HANDLE               ProcessHandle,
    IN OUT PVOID            *BaseAddress,
    IN OUT PULONG           RegionSize,
    IN ULONG                FreeType
);
```

Parameters:

ProcessHandle

An open handle to the process in whose context previously allocated memory is being freed.

BaseAddress

The first address of the virtual address range being freed. This value is rounded down to a multiple of the page size.

RegionSize

Note that this is a pointer argument. You must supply the number of bytes to be freed. You will receive the actual number of bytes freed, rounded up to a multiple of the page size.

FreeType

Your options are one of the following: **MEM_DECOMMIT** or **MEM_RELEASE**. These are mutually exclusive.

Functionality Provided:

You can use this routine to do the following:

- Decommit previously committed pages (but retain the virtual address range allocation)

- Release both the committed memory as well as the virtual address range that was previously allocated

This routine is fairly flexible, in the sense that it allows you to modify a subset of the address range previously allocated by you. Note, however, that you cannot expect to be able to free or release a range that spans two previous invocations to **ZwAllocateVirtualMemory()**; i.e., the entire range that you specify must be contained within a single, previously allocated VAD. If you specify a **Region-Size** value equal to 0, the VMM interprets this to mean that the entire VAD must be freed/decommited. However, in this case, you must specify the correct `BaseAddress` (equal to the starting `BaseAddress` of the VAD, or the `Base-Address` specified when you allocated the range earlier).

It might sound strange but there is a possibility that you might get an error indicating that you exceeded your quota for the target process if you try to free a subset of a previously allocated range. The reason for this is that the VMM splits a VAD, if required, into two VADs in order to accommodate your request to free up a range contained within the original allocated range. Of course, this requires allocating a new VAD structure which is charged to the quota assigned to the target process. If this pushes the allocated memory for that process to an amount greater than what is allowed, you will get an error returned.

Translation of Virtual Addresses

In this section, I will briefly discuss virtual to physical address translation. This topic is covered very well in the literature, and I recommend that you consult Appendix E, *Recommended Readings and References*, for further information.

Each virtual address in Windows NT is currently a 32-bit quantity. This virtual address must be transparently translated to refer to some physical byte in memory.* Two system components work together to achieve this translation:

- The Memory Management Unit (MMU) provided in hardware by the processor
- The Virtual Memory Manager implemented by the operating system in software

Translation is not necessarily performed only in one direction, for example, from virtual memory addresses to physical memory addresses. The VMM must also be able to translate in the reverse direction, from a physical address to any corresponding virtual addresses.† Whenever the contents of a physical page are written out to secondary storage to make room for some other data, the corresponding virtual addresses must be marked as "no longer valid in memory." This requires that the physical address be translated back to its corresponding virtual address.

Virtual address translation is typically performed by the MMU in hardware. The VMM is responsible for maintaining appropriate *translation maps* or *page tables* that can subsequently be used by the MMU to do the actual translation. Broadly

---

* Memory-mapped I/O device registers are also addressable via the virtual address space. Therefore, a virtual address could be translated to a physical address that actually corresponds to a mapped register on an I/O bus.

† It is possible for an operating system to implement aliasing, where more than one virtual address refers to the same physical address.

speaking, the following sequence of operations is typically performed to translate a physical address:

1. As part of the context switch procedure that causes a process to begin executing, the VMM sets up appropriate page tables that contain virtual-to-physical address translation information specific to that process.

2. When the executing process accesses a virtual address, the MMU attempts to perform virtual to physical address translation by either using a cache called the Translation Lookaside Buffer (TLB) or, if an entry is not found in the TLB, using the page tables set up by the VMM. Each translated address must be contained within a page that, in turn, might be present in one of the page frames on the system.

NOTE   Translating from a virtual to a physical address is a time-consuming operation. Since this operation must be performed for every memory access, most architectures provide efficient translation. One way of speeding up this process is by using an associative cache such as a Translation Lookaside Buffer (TLB). The TLB contains a list of the most recently performed translations, tagged by the process ID. Therefore, if a virtual address is located in the TLB, the corresponding physical address can be immediately obtained and the contents of that address are guaranteed to be in main memory. Software manipulation of the TLB is architecture dependent; some architectures allow the VMM to explicitly load, unload, and flush TLB entries (either one entry at a time or the entire TLB), while other architectures simply load or unload the TLB as a by-product of certain execution sequences.

---

3. If the byte referenced by the translated physical address is currently in main memory, the process is allowed access to the data.

4. If, however, the contents of the page are not contained within a page frame in memory, an exception is raised, a page fault occurs, and control is transferred to the VMM page fault handler that brings the appropriate data into the system memory. An exception could also be raised by hardware if the page protection conflicts with the attempted mode of access or for other similar reasons.

Note that the design of the MMU has far-reaching implications on the design of the VMM subsystem. Naturally, the portion of the VMM subsystem that interfaces with the MMU is very architecture-specific and inherently nonportable.

As described earlier, the VMM maintains a page frame database in nonpaged pool to manage the physical memory available on the system. This database is composed of page frame entries where each page frame represents a chunk of contiguous physical memory. Since each physical page frame in the system is numbered sequentially (from page frame *0* to page frame *(n-1)* for *n* page frames of physical RAM), computing the PFN database entry for a page frame is relatively trivial. Once a virtual address has been translated into a physical address (composed of a page frame and an offset into the frame), the page frame number is multiplied by the size of the PFN database entry and the resulting address is added to the physical base address assigned to the PFN database. The net result is a physical address pointer to the start of the entry describing the page frame in the PFN database for the translated physical address.

Consider the 32-bit virtual address on a Windows NT platform. Since the page size is 4096 bytes, computing an offset into a page requires 12 bits (the least significant 12 bits). This leaves the MMU with 20 bits to uniquely identify a page frame. Page frames are uniquely identifiable via Page Table Entries (PTEs) in a page table, where a page table is simply an array of PTEs. Note that many architectures (including the Intel x86 architecture) clearly define the structure of a PTE.*

On the Intel platform, each PTE must be 32 bits (or 4 bytes) wide. Given that there are a total of 2^{20} (1 million) possible PTEs and each PTE has a size of 2^2 bytes, the amount of memory required to store translation information for a single 4GB virtual address space is 2^{22} bytes (4MB). Since each page table can itself store one page-size worth of information (2^{12} bytes), 1024 page frames would be required simply to contain all the PTEs for the virtual address space for a single process.†

To avoid consuming this significant amount of memory for translation information,‡ page tables are also paged in and out of memory. To do this, the x86 processor defines a two-level page table scheme. Each process has a page directory that contains PTEs for page tables. This directory is a single page in size and therefore can contain 1024 PTEs, each referencing a page table. A typical virtual

---

* Other architectures, such as the MIPS R3000, provide no hardware support for page tables. Therefore, the MIPS R3000 does not mandate the structure of PTEs either, since the entire responsibility of translating virtual to physical addresses lies with the VMM.

† Note that the Intel x86 architecture is segmented, where a virtual address is actually composed of a segment and an offset. The Intel hardware converts this virtual address into a 32-bit linear address, which is subsequently translated into a physical address using the method described in this section. Since the Windows NT VMM presents a flat memory model to the system (hiding the segmentation details), we will neglect the virtual to linear address conversion process and assume that user addresses are virtual addresses that simply require a 1-step conversion to a physical address.

‡ Note that rarely will 4GB of virtual address space need to be completely translated, since most address spaces are sparse in nature, i.e., there exist gaps in the virtual address space for addresses that are never used. Reserving memory for PTEs that will probably never be utilized is therefore quite unnecessary.

address for a process has 10 bits reserved to identify a page table from a page directory associated with the process, 10 bits to identify a page frame given a page table, and 12 bits to get to the desired offset within a page.

Figure 5-2 graphically illustrates how virtual to physical address translation is performed on Windows NT systems. Note that even on systems such as the MIPS R3000 where the architecture places no limitations on the structure of the PTEs (and correspondingly provides no hardware virtual address translation support except for TLB lookups), the VMM maintains a similar set of data structures to simplify the design and maintenance of the VMM subsystem.

Everything so far seems to be relatively straightforward. The MMU checks the TLB and if it gets a TLB *hit*, it simply returns the translated physical address. On the other hand, if it gets a TLB *miss*, it must check the page tables for the process to locate the corresponding PTE that determines the physical page frame that might contain the accessed address. Now, if the PTE indicates that the page is resident in memory and the protection attributes match the access mode, the MMU allows the access to continue. Otherwise, an appropriate exception (page-fault or protection-violation) is raised and control transfers to the VMM. However, the observant reader must have noticed the presence of an additional table called the *Prototype Page Table* in Figure 5-2. So where exactly does the PPT fit into this clean model we understand so well by now?

Prototype Page Tables are used to contain page table entries for page frames that contain pages shared by more than one process. Sharing of pages and page frames occurs when more than one process maps in the same byte range for the same mapped object. Therefore, to understand the PPT, you must first understand the concept of shared memory and memory mapped files.

Shared Memory and Memory-Mapped File Support

Accessing memory seems so convenient to application developers these days. An application process can simply issue a `malloc` call (or its equivalent), receive a virtual address from the VMM, and begin using this virtual address to access the allocated block of memory. The operating system is responsible, along with the hardware, for managing physical memory and maintaining the appropriate translation between virtual addresses and physical addresses. Furthermore, the operating system can observe the behavior of all processes executing on the system, allowing it to make rational decisions concerning the allocation of physical memory to specific processes.

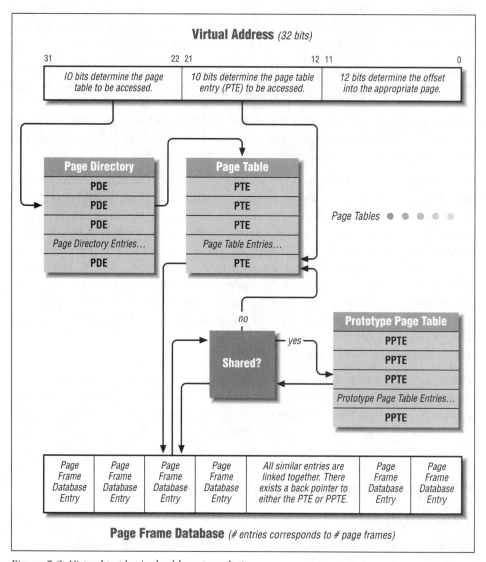

Figure 5-2. Virtual to physical address translation

At the same time, most applications must do other things besides computational activities requiring memory. Notably, all applications need to perform some I/O to and from secondary storage. In addition, sophisticated applications sometimes wish to share in-memory data with each other.

Traditionally, I/O has been performed via read/write system calls handled by the appropriate file system. Servicing these calls requires the execution of a system trap to switch the processor from user mode to kernel mode and vice versa. For a read request, the file system must first read data into system memory and then copy it into buffers allocated by the application. For a write request, the operating system must first copy data from the application's buffers into system memory. This copying of data to and from system buffers, combined with the overhead of making system calls for I/O requests, can lead to substantial execution overhead for application processes.

Consider now the case where two processes on the same system are accessing the same file. These processes might be accessing the same byte range, but since they have their own private buffers containing the data, where each buffer is backed by physical pages different from those backing the other buffer, each process has potentially a different view of the same data. *Process-1* might have read the data into memory and modified it but not yet written it out to disk; if *process-2* reads the same byte range, it will not see the modified data but will instead be given the original data obtained from disk. This can be a deterrent to efficient sharing of data between the two processes, because each process would have to ensure that its modifications are written out to disk before the other process reads-in the byte range.

Imagine now if each process could simply map the on-disk file into their virtual address space. The VMM provides virtual memory support by swapping data to and from an on-disk page file whenever required. An application allocates some memory, tries to access it and possibly gets a page fault. The page fault is resolved (we will see how later in this chapter), and magically the application can now access some physical memory reserved solely for its use.

Now consider the case where the data is originally read from an on-disk file and is destined to be written out to the same on-disk file. In this case, why not use the file itself as the backing store for data instead of a page file? Instead of making the application issue read/write system calls to access the data, simply let the application reserve a virtual address range associated with an on-disk byte range, try to access this memory (in reality, access the byte range with which the virtual addresses are associated) represented by the virtual address range, get a page fault, and then the operating system will resolve the page fault by allocating some physical memory and obtaining the appropriate data from the on-disk file. Similarly, the application can simply modify the data in-memory and the operating system will—whenever required—write out the modified data to the on-disk file and, possibly, release the physical memory to make room for another process.

The above method of mapping in a file has one additional benefit; all applications that try to map in the same file can now have their respective virtual addresses backed by the same physical pages, so all applications will always see a consistent view of the data, regardless of the fact that any application could modify the data at any time.*

The NT VMM supports file mapping. The mapped object is the on-disk file. When you execute a file (say Microsoft Word), the executable (the mapped object in this case) is mapped into your process's virtual address space and instructions are executed. Now, if some other user, on the same machine, tries to execute Microsoft Word as well, the same executable is mapped into his or her virtual address space, and since the physical pages backing the VADs are probably already in memory, the other user should see a relatively fast response time. See Figure 5-3 for an illustration of file mapping.

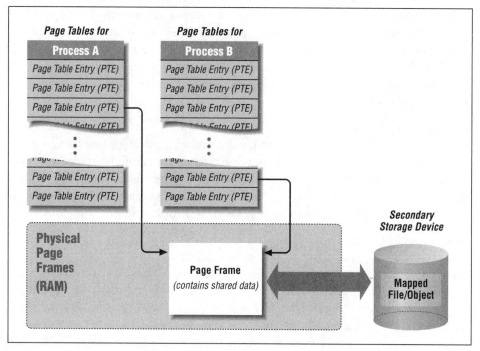

Figure 5-3. Two processes mapping the same page into their virtual address space

Note that file mapping is not the only way to share physical memory between two processes. Since Virtual Address Descriptors (VADs) are manipulated separately from the physical page frames backing the virtual addresses, it is entirely possible for the VMM to allow processes to share memory by simply ensuring that appropriate VADs for the two processes are backed by the same physical page frames. File mapping is simply an extension of this concept wherein the shared

---

* Each application must synchronize its changes, so that there are no unexpected consequences.

memory object is actually backed by an on-disk, permanent file object, instead of a page file. Just as you can create file-backed shared memory objects, it is also possible to create shared memory objects that will later be backed by one of the system page files. This is typically done when you wish to share memory between two modules or processes in the system. Often, kernel-driver designers need to share memory between some user-space helper processes and the kernel driver. The shared memory support provided by the VMM allows this functionality. When a shared memory object is created (one that is not backed by an on-disk file), the starting virtual address associated with the object represents *offset 0* into the shared object. Therefore, all processes sharing this object can index into the appropriate byte offset and manipulate data. You must note, however, that modifications to shared memory objects that are not backed by an on-disk file will not be permanent; i.e., such modifications will be lost once the shared object is closed by all processes using this object.

So how does mapping actually work? What data structures are created by the VMM to support mapped/shared objects. Before I address these questions, let me revisit the issue of the Prototype Page Table described back in Figure 5-2.

Prototype Page Table

Page frames that contain shared (mapped in) pages are described by a special structure—the Prototype Page Table (PPT). This structure can be allocated from paged or nonpaged memory.

Whenever the VMM creates a mapping or a shared object for a process, it allocates Prototype Page Table Entries (PPTEs) to describe the physical page frames that will back the file mapping. The PPT for a mapped object is shared by all processes that map in the same object. Each PPTE refers to a page that may or may not be present in memory; i.e., the page may be contained within a physical page frame, or it may need to be brought in from secondary storage when accessed. Since all processes have to use the same PPT (and corresponding PPTEs), it follows that all processes use the same physical page frame and therefore see the same view of the mapped data.

Whenever a page frame is assigned to a PPTE, the PPTE is marked as valid. The page frame entry within the PFN database is then initialized to point back to the PPTE. Note that neither the Intel x86 MMU nor the MIPS R3000 or similar architectures support prototype page tables. How does the VMM arrange things such that the MMU can work with shared memory?

Consider the Intel x86 architecture. The Intel x86 MMU strictly defines the structure of page tables and PTEs. The VMM creates a PPT (with PPTEs) in allocated memory whenever a process creates a file mapping. Imagine now that the process tries to access a virtual address that is part of a range backed by a mapped file object. The MMU will translate the virtual address into a page directory table offset and then offset into an appropriate page table. On the first access to this virtual address, the page table entry will indicate that the page is not backed by any physical memory.

This will result in a page fault and control will transfer to the VMM page fault handler. The page fault handler notices that the VAD containing the accessed virtual address is marked as being backed by a mapped object. The VMM can then find the appropriate PPTE and fault the page in. At this point, the PPTE is marked as valid and refers to a PFN database entry and correspondingly, a PFN database entry points back to the PPTE. At the same time, the VMM initializes the PTE as valid and makes it refer to the appropriate physical address. The net result is that both the PPTE and the PTE contain information about the physical address, but the corresponding PFN database entry only points back to the PPTE. Now, the memory access is retried, and, since the MMU finds the PTE initialized correctly (it does not know nor does it care about PPTEs), the translation from virtual address to a physical address can be performed.

A Small Problem with the PPT Design

You must note that, since the PFN database entry never refers back to the PTE, the VMM has no way of finding, from a PFN database entry, all the PTEs for all the processes that have mapped that shared object into their virtual address space. The best that the VMM can do is find the PPTE that refers to the PFN database entry (using the back pointer) and thereby manipulate the contents of the PPTE.

There is one serious flaw with this design: imagine that a kernel-mode component wanted to request the VMM to purge certain pages from physical memory.* Normally (for nonshared files), you can certainly ask the VMM to do this and the VMM will respond by marking the PFN database entry invalid. Furthermore, the VMM will use the information stored in the PFN database entry to find the appropriate PTE in the address space of some process that is currently referring to the PFN database entry. It will mark the PTE entry not valid, ensuring that the MMU will have to fault the page back in on the next access to an address contained within the page.

---

* You might ask why would anyone want to do this? Suppose you were implementing some complicated distributed data access method across multiple nodes where all consistency guarantees were maintained by your modules. Now, if some process on a remote machine modified shared data that was mapped in on a local node, you might wish to ensure that all nodes accessing this data refreshed their memory with the latest copy of the data. This is precisely what distributed file systems such as the OSF DFS attempt to do. There could be other similar scenarios that might be needed to support certain complicated functionality on distributed architectures.

However, if the page belongs to a mapped object, the VMM has no way of accessing all the PTEs that refer to the page frame containing the shared page. Therefore, if you requested that the VMM purge such a page from memory, the VMM will return an error saying that this functionality is not possible for mapped objects. This is a serious problem for any third-party developer that counts on being able to purge pages from system memory on demand.

Sections and Views

The Windows NT system tends to be strongly object-centric; i.e., most functionality is provided in the form of objects and methods that manipulate such objects. File mappings are created and accessed as a two-step process:

1. A *section object* is created by the VMM in response to a request for a file mapping or a shared memory object.

2. When the process actually needs to access a byte range for a mapped file or a shared memory object, the caller must request the VMM to map a *view* into the file. Conceptually, this view is like a window into the file, allowing access to a limited byte range. Of course, it is possible for a process to request multiple views for the same file concurrently, just as it is possible for multiple processes to have different views concurrently into the same mapped file.

Note that section objects have a set of protection attributes associated with them, just as all other objects in the Windows NT environment can. By specifying a set of protection attributes for the section object, a process can define the manner in which this object (and any data for a file object that might be mapped in and represented by the section object) is manipulated.

Section objects backed by on-disk files fall into two categories:

* Executable image file mappings
* File (nonimage) mappings

When you tell the VMM to create a section object representing a mapped file, you can specify how the mapped file should be treated. The system loader uses file mapping to run executables and specifies that the file mapping be treated as an executable image file mapping. However, it is entirely your prerogative to request that an executable (say, a copy of Microsoft Word) be mapped in as a nonimage file mapping.

Note that the VMM performs tests to verify that any section object created for an executable image file mapping actually does map in a valid executable. If you try to map in a simple text file as an executable image file mapping, you will get an error from the VMM. Also, it is entirely possible for the same executable file to be mapped both as an executable image file and as a simple file mapping; the address alignments for each of these mappings will probably be quite different though.

A major difference between how executable image file mappings and nonimage file mappings (or simple shared memory) are handled is in how modifications to the mapped range are managed by the VMM. When a nonimage file mapping is modified by a process, the modification is immediately seen by all processes mapping in the same file, because the contents of the shared physical page are changed by the VMM. These modifications will eventually be reflected in the on-disk mapped object when the modifications are flushed to secondary storage. However, when an image file mapping is modified, a private copy of the page is made for the process making the modification. This private page will now be backed by a page file, since the modifications to an image file mapping are never written out to the mapped object (the on-disk file). These modifications are eventually discarded when the process unmaps the file.

To create a shared memory object (a section object), the NT VMM provides a routine called `NtCreateSection()`. Though this routine is not exported to kernel developers, the `ZwCreateSection()` routine can be used instead. This routine is defined as follows:

```
NTSTATUS
NTAPI
ZwCreateSection (
    OUT PHANDLE                 SectionHandle,
    IN ACCESS_MASK              DesiredAccess,
    IN POBJECT_ATTRIBUTES       ObjectAttributes OPTIONAL,
    IN PLARGE_INTEGER           MaximumSize OPTIONAL,
    IN ULONG                    SectionPageProtection,
    IN ULONG                    AllocationAttributes,
    IN HANDLE                   FileHandle OPTIONAL
);
```

Parameters:

SectionHandle

If this routine returns a success status, a handle to the created section object is returned in this argument. Note that this handle is only valid in the context of the process that creates the section object. If you wish to access the section object in the context of other processes as well, you must use the `ObReferenceObjectByHandle()` object manager routine (described in the DDK) to get a pointer to the actual section object. Subsequently, you can use the `ObOpenObjectByPointer()` routine to get a handle in the context of some other process.

DesiredAccess

This argument allows you to specify the access desired to the section object: `SECTION_MAP_EXECUTE`, `SECTION_MAP_READ`, or `SECTION_MAP_WRITE`.

ObjectAttributes

This can be NULL, or you can specify an initialized structure (use the `InitializeObjectAttributes()` macro to do this). Note that if you need to share a piece of memory between two processes (or share memory between a module executed in user mode and a kernel-mode driver), you can use this structure to supply a name for the section object. This named section object can subsequently be opened by other processes, and thus sharing of in-memory data can be achieved without having to use a named file from secondary storage.

This structure can also be used to supply a security descriptor for the section object, which allows you to protect the section object appropriately.

MaximumSize

For a page-file-based section (i.e., you simply wish to create a shared memory object), this value cannot be NULL, since it represents the size of the section.

For a mapped file, it represents the maximum size to which the section might be extended. If the section is for a mapped file and the size of the file is less than this value, the file size is extended at this time.[*]

Note that any value supplied by you is rounded up to a multiple of the host page size. Finally, if this value is set to NULL for mapped files, the VMM will set the value to the end-of-file at that time (appropriately rounded up).

SectionPageProtection

This defines the protection to be placed on each page contained in the section. Here are the appropriate values:

— PAGE_READONLY

— PAGE_READWRITE

— PAGE_EXECUTE

— PAGE_WRITECOPY

AllocationAttributes

These attributes allow the caller to inform the VMM if this section object represents a shared piece of memory (backed by the page file), a file mapping for

---

[*] This is a very important point to note for developers of file systems, since you should be prepared to receive a request for extending the file size when the memory manager is in the process of creating a file mapping. I will discuss this more later in this chapter.

an executable, or a file mapping for some other type of file. Here are the options to use:[*]

— **SEC_IMAGE**, indicating that an executable is being mapped into a process virtual address space

— **SEC_FILE**, indicating that the supplied file handle refers to an open file that must be treated as a regular (nonimage) file mapping

— **SEC_RESERVE**, indicating that all pages allocated to the section object must be placed into the reserved state (only valid for a shared memory object not backed by an on-disk file)

— **SEC_COMMIT**, indicating that all pages allocated to the section object must be placed into the committed state (must also be set if **SEC_FILE** is set or if the shared memory object is not an executable image file mapping)

FileHandle

This optional argument indicates that the section object represents a mapped file (the handle must refer to an open file). Otherwise, the VMM will simply create a section object backed by a page file (simple piece of shared memory).

Functionality Provided:

This routine can be used by kernel-mode drivers to create a shared memory object (named or anonymous) or to create a file mapping for an on-disk file. Even if you are a file system driver developer implementing an on-disk or a network file system, you can use this call to create a shared memory object or mapped file object (do not try to create a mapped file object on your own file system using this call unless you really know what you are doing).

Sometimes, kernel-mode driver developers wish to share in-memory data with user-space modules. Or, if you design a kernel-mode driver that obtains data from across the network or transfers data across the network using the services of a user process, you may use this call to create either a simple shared memory object or a file-backed shared memory object in order to facilitate easy and efficient data transfer between the kernel driver and the user-space process (consider using a named object to allow for easy opening of the object by the user-mode service).

---

[*] These symbolic definitions do not exist in any of the supplied DDK include files, but you can use the symbolic names (or the actual values) in the *winnt.h* include file provided with the Win32 SDK. Since this routine is not documented by Microsoft, they must have figured that it was not necessary to define these symbols in any DDK header file.

TIP   In the description of the `ZwCreateSection()` routine, I mentioned the existence of an Object Manager routine that can be used
to obtain a handle to an object in the context of any arbitrary process, given a pointer to that object. This routine is called `ObOpe-`
`nObjectByPointer()` and is defined as follows (note that this
routine is not ordinarily documented in the DDK):

```
NTSTATUS
ObOpenObjectByPointer(
    IN PVOID              Object,
    IN ULONG              HandleAttributes,
    IN PACCESS_STATE      PassedAccessState OPTIONAL,
    IN ACCESS_MASK        DesiredAccess OPTIONAL,
    IN POBJECT_TYPE       ObjectType OPTIONAL,
    IN KPROCESSOR_MODE    AccessMode,
    OUT PHANDLE           Handle
);
```

Typically, you can pass in NULL for `PassedAccessState` and for
the `ObjectType`. Be careful to request only the type of access in
the `DesiredAccess` argument permitted by the original open operation (from which you obtained a pointer to the object). The `Han-`
`dleAttributes` can be obtained from the previous invocation to
`ObReferenceObjectByHandle()`. That routine returns `Han-`
`dleInformation`, which in turn contains the returned `Handle-`
`Attributes`.

There is also a routine called `ObReferenceObjectByPoint-`
`er()`, which simply increments the object reference count for the
specified object. This function is defined in the Windows NT IFS kit
as follows:

```
NTSTATUS
ObReferenceObjectByPointer(
    IN PVOID              Object,
    IN ACCESS_MASK        DesiredAccess OPTIONAL,
    IN POBJECT_TYPE       ObjectType OPTIONAL,
    IN KPROCESSOR_MODE    AccessMode,
);
```

There are other routines, well documented in the DDK, to open and close a previously created section object and to map and unmap a view using a section object.
Consult the available documentation for the following system support routines:

- `ZwOpenSection()`

- `ZwMapViewOfSection()`

- `ZwUnmapViewOfSection()`

File-Mapping Structures

When a process creates a file mapping, the process must specify whether an executable file or another type of file is being mapped. Although both types of file mappings eventually result in the file contents being mapped into the virtual address space of a process, the NT VMM treats the map requests differently.

As mentioned earlier, any modifications made to pages belonging to image file mappings will not be reflected in the on-disk mapped executable. The page will be backed by a page file instead, and all changes made to the page will be discarded once the mapping is closed.

Internally, the NT VMM maintains two types of section objects (and associated data structures) for each mapped file object. For each type of mapping, the VMM maintains a SEGMENT data structure that describes the mapping. Therefore, there are two possible segment data structures associated with each mapped file: the image segment and the data segment. Each segment data structure, in turn, points to the prototype page table for a mapped object.

Although the segment data structure is opaque to kernel-mode developers, the point to note here is that both types of mappings can exist concurrently. An executable can be mapped both as an image file and as a nonimage file. For each type of mapping, the VMM will create and maintain a segment data structure associated with the representation of the file in memory. Because there are two separate data structures created, depending on the type of mapping performed, the same byte range in a file contained within a page could exist in two separate page frames concurrently in memory! This is possible because each type of mapping has its own segment data structure and its own prototype page tables with different PPTEs.

Modified and Mapped Page Writer

As discussed earlier, the NT Virtual Memory Manager has the task of presenting the illusion of a large amount of available virtual memory to each process, even though the amount of physical memory on the system is limited. To perform this task, the NT VMM must use secondary storage devices as a backing store for in-memory data and page data in and out. This paging is performed transparently to the processes executing on the system.

The NT VMM automatically flushes dirty or modified pages to secondary storage to reclaim page frames for use by other threads in the system. Modified data within a page frame will be written either to one of the 16 possible page files, or to a named file on disk if the page frame was allocated to a mapped section object. Unless modified page frames are flushed to disk, the NT VMM cannot reuse the page frames, as doing so would cause data loss.

In order to ensure that sufficient RAM is available whenever required, the NT VMM always keeps a certain number of page frames available. These page frames must not contain any modified data and therefore, they can be reallocated whenever the VMM decides to do so. If the VMM did not maintain this pool of available page frames, it might need to make processes block, waiting for modified data to be flushed to secondary storage before it could reassign page frames to them. Making processes block is not conducive to good system performance.

Therefore, the NT VMM creates at least two special dedicated threads called *Modified* and *Mapped Page Writer* threads. Note that it is quite possible that the number of threads created could be greater than two. At least one modifier page writer thread is created to asynchronously write modified page frames to the page files. At least one other thread, called the mapped page writer thread, is assigned to asynchronously write out modified page frames to mapped files. Both of these threads essentially perform the same functionality and therefore throughout this book, the terms mapped page writer thread and modified page writer thread are used interchangeably.

The sole purpose of these dedicated threads is to flush modified page frames out to secondary storage, thereby keeping a certain number of page frames available for reassignment. Each of these threads is a real-time thread with a priority set to at least `LOW_REALTIME_PRIORITY + 1`.

The algorithm used by the modified page writer threads is shown below. Note that the following pseudocode is based on the operations performed by the mapped and modified page writer threads flushing page frames to memory-mapped or page files; differences in operations between these two threads is clearly indicated whenever required:

```
// The following routine summarizes the MPW code executed by a dedicated
// worker thread. Note, however, that although the specific method used
// in various versions of the operating system might be different, the
// fundamental methodology described here should be consistent.
MiModifiedPageWriterWorker() {
    for (;;) {
        // Wait for event to get set, indicating that insufficient "free"
        // (not modified) pages exist. This event is set when the system
        // is running low on available pages and the VMM wants some
        // modified pages written out so they can be reassigned.
        // This event is also set when the total number of modified pages
        // in the system becomes greater than a pre-determined
        // threshold value (the "threshold value" in turn depends on
        // whether the system is configured as a workstation or as a server
        // and on how much RAM is present on the system).
        KeWaitForSingleObject(ModifiedPageWriterEvent, ...);
```

```
// Now, lock the PFN database.

…

for (;;) {

    // The event was set indicating that some pages need to
    // be flushed. Pick a page frame to be flushed (the first on
    // the modified pages list from the PFN database?) and invoke
    // an appropriate routine.
    MiGatherMappedPages(PageFrameIndex, …);

    // The above routine is responsible for the actual flush.
    // To perform the flush I/O, the PFN database
    // lock will have been dropped and reacquired by the
    // MiGatherMappedPages() routine. Therefore, check whether
    // adequate clean pages are now available and if so, stop
    // flushing.
    if (enough free pages are available) {
        // Unlock PFN database.

        …

        break;
    }
} // End of loop in which the MPW thread flushed modified pages to
  // disk.

} // End of infinite loop awaiting event to be set so that the
  // MPW thread can begin flushing pages.

} // end of MiModifiedPageWriterWorker() routine

// The following routine is responsible for collecting a bunch of
// contiguous modified pages and writing them out to the page file.
// The similar routine responsible for writing out mapped file pages is
// called MiGatherMappedPages().
MiGatherMappedPages(…) / MiGatherPageFilePages(…) {
    // Find a paging file for page file backed pages only.
    if (paging file not available) {
        // Nothing can be done as some I/O is already in progress
        //    to all paging files.
        return;
    }

    //    Find a contiguous chunk of available paging file space using a
    //    bitmap per paging file.
    //    OR
    //    If this is a mapped file, ensure that the mapped file is not an
    //    image file.

    //    Initialize a MDL (Memory descriptor List) to be used in the
    //    I/O operation

    // Scan both backward and forward, starting from the sent-in page frame
```

```
//    index, to find a contiguous set of modified pages that can be
//    written out to the page file or to the mapped file.
for (each candidate PTE) {
    if (PTE is modified and backed by the page file or by the mapped
        file){
        // Increment reference count on this PTE
        PTE->reference_count++;

        // Mark this PTE as "not modified," anticipating that our write
        // will succeed.
        PTE->modified = FALSE;

        // Mark the fact that this PTE is being flushed. Any flush
        // requests for this PTE (say from a file system or from the
        // Cache Manager will be blocked until this I/O completes).
        PTE->being_flushed = TRUE;

        // Put the page file page address into the PTE.
        // Add this page frame into the physical page list described by
        // the MDL.
    }

// OK, so now we have a list of page frames that we wish to flush.

if (number of pages reserved in the page file > number of contiguous
        modified page frames encountered) {
    // Release extra space pre-allocated from the page file
    // (if any).
}

// Unlock the PFN database lock.
...


/********************************************************************/

// NOTE: If this were the routine handling mapped files, some
// additional processing would be performed here. This processing is
// as follows:
{
    // Only for mapped files.
    if (this file is marked as "fail all i/o," forget it and return) {
        return;
    }

    // Make a callback into the file system advising the file system
    // that a paging I/O is on its way.
    // THIS IS VERY IMPORTANT:
    // The file system must - in response to this callback - acquire
    // all resources that might be needed to satisfy the paging-IO
    // operation.  We will cover this call-back in detail later in
    // this chapter and in Part 3 of this book.
    if (FsRtlAcquireFileForModWrite(...)) {
        // Call-back succeeded, issue I/O here
        ...
```

```
                    IoAsynchronousPageWrite(…)
            } else {
                // Call-back failed.
                // Return error locally = STATUS_FILE_LOCK_CONFLICT;
                // Note that pages will stay marked dirty and the operation
                // will be retried sometime later.
            }

            // Return

        } // End of code that is executed only for mapped files.

        /*********************************************************************/

        // NOTE:  The following code is only executed for pagefile backed pages

        {
            // Perform an asynchronous, paging-IO operation. This operation is
            // a special request handled by the I/O manager who quickly
            // redirects it to the appropriate file system on which the page
            // file is located ...
            IoAsynchronousPageWrite(…);

            // Return;
        } // end of code executed only for page files.

        /*********************************************************************/

        // Lock the page frame database lock.
        …
} // end of MiGatherPageFilePages() / MiGatherMappedPages()

// The following routine is invoked as an Asynchronous Procedure Call
// (APC) when the asynchronous paging I/O is completed by the file system.
// Note that the file system might choose to handle the I/O
// synchronously though that is not recommended …

MiWriteComplete(Context, StatusOfOperation, Reserved) {
    BOOLEAN        FailAllIoWasSet = FALSE;

    // The Context is actually the MDL that was sent to the file system
    MdlPointer = Context;
    …
    // Lock the PFN database
    …

    for (each page that comprised the MDL that was written out) {

        // Set write-in-progress to false
        PTE->being_flushed = FALSE;

        // If an error was encountered …
        if (error AND this was a write to a mapped file AND the mapped
                file belongs to a networked file system) {
```

```
            // THIS IS IMPORTANT TO FILE SYSTEM DEVELOPERS WRITING
            // REDIRECTORS.
            // The VMM assumes that if a paging I/O to a file across the
            // network has failed, the network MUST BE DOWN.
            // In this case, the VMM marks the file as "fail all I/O" and
            // all modified data to the file will now be discarded!
            FailAllIOWasSet = TRUE;
        }

        // Dereference the page.
        PTE->reference_count-;

        if (error AND not file on networked file system) {
            // Mark page as modified once again so write will be retried
            //     later.
            PTE->modified = TRUE;
        }
    } // Loop for each page.

    // FOR MAPPED FILES ONLY …
    ReleaseFileResources(); // Resources acquired using file system
                            // callback

    // Unlock PFN database.
    …

    if (FailAllIOWasSet) {
        // The user sees the famous error message
        //    "system lost write-behind data" now.
        IoRaiseInformationalHardError(STATUS_LOST_WRITE_BEHIND_DATA,
                                          FileName, Status);
    }
} // end of MiWriteComplete()
```

Note that in this pseudocode, the VMM uses an I/O Manager function `IoAsynchronousPageWrite()` to flush modified data to secondary storage. This call will be quickly routed by the I/O Manager to the file system driver managing the mounted file system on which the target page file or mapped file resides.

The file system driver can easily recognize that the write request is a paging I/O request because the I/O Request Packet sent to the file system has the `IRP_PAGING_IO` and the `IRP_NOCACHE` flags set. Note that the file system is not permitted to take another page fault while resolving the paging I/O write request. The I/O Manager handles asynchronous page writes differently when performing postprocessing on IRP structures that described such paging I/O requests. Essentially, the I/O Manager invokes the `MiWriteComplete()` routine by means of a kernel APC upon completion of the asynchronous paging I/O IRP. The routine is invoked in the context of the MPW thread.

Page Fault Handling

The NT VMM is responsible for handling the case when contents referred to by a virtual address are not present in physical memory. Although the hardware MMU typically translates virtual addresses into physical addresses, when the MMU discovers that the PTE indicates that the page is not in memory, the MMU will turn the problem over to the VMM for resolution. The VMM routine invoked when a page fault occurs, either in kernel mode or in user mode, is called **MmAccessFault()**. This routine takes three arguments:

- The virtual address that caused the page fault

- A boolean argument that indicates whether a store/write operation caused the page fault (a FALSE value indicates that this was a read/load operation)

- The mode (kernel or user) in which the fault occurred

First, the **MmAccessFault()** routine checks the current IRQL. If it is greater than **APC_LEVEL**, and if either the page directory or the Page Table Entry indicates that the page is not valid, the VMM will bugcheck the system and the following message will be printed on your debugger screen:

```
MM:***PAGE FAULT AT IRQL > 1 Va %x, IRQL %x
```

The routine within the VMM that resolves page faults is appropriately called **MiDispatchFault()**. The **MmAccessFault()** routine invokes **MiDispatchFault()** to resolve the fault and make the contents of the page frame valid. This routine handles page faults for access to addresses in both system address space (the upper 2GB of the virtual address space) and in user process address space. Faults are dispatched for further processing to an appropriate subroutine based upon the nature of the faulting address:

- If the faulting address is backed by a page file, the routine **MiResolvePageFileFault()** is invoked.

    This routine performs the following tasks:

    — Allocate enough page frames in memory so that data can be read from the page file.

    — Note that this routine uses the **MiEnsureAvailablePageOrWait()** routine mentioned earlier in this chapter.

    — Figure out the page file to which the read operation should be directed from the PTE.

    — Build a Memory Descriptor List (MDL) containing the list of available physical pages.

— Mark the PTEs for the pages being brought into memory as being "in transition."

— Return a special status 0xC0033333 to the caller, `MiDispatchFault()`.

Because `MiResolvePageFileFault()` returned a status of 0xC0033333, `MiDispatchFault()` will then invoke a paging I/O read operation using the `IoPageRead()` call exported by the I/O Manager. Just as in the case of the paging I/O write request described in the Modified Page Writer discussion, the file system driver invoked by the I/O Manager to satisfy the page read request will recognize the request as a paging read, because of the presence of the `IRP_PAGING_IO` and the `IRP_NOCACHE` flags. Note that the file system cannot incur any page faults while trying to satisfy the paging I/O read request.

The VMM then waits for the page fault read request to be completed, and if successful, adds the page to the working set of the active process.

- If the PTE for the faulting address indicates that the page is in transition, then the `MiResolveTransitionFault()` routine is invoked. A transition page is marked as being in-transition for one of the following reasons:

  — The page frame contains valid data, but the page was placed on the free list because it was automatically trimmed.

  — The page frame contains valid data, but it was placed on the modified list as a result of being automatically trimmed from the working set of a process.

  — The page is being actively read from secondary storage; this is a *collided page fault*.

  This routine performs the following tasks:

  — For pages that are being actively read from secondary storage, the `MiResolveTransitionFault()` routine will block, awaiting I/O completion. If an error occurs, it will mark the PTE invalid and return success, forcing the caller to undergo another page fault, for which the PTE will now no longer be marked as *in-transition*.

  — Otherwise, this routine will mark the transition PTE valid and will add it to the working set for the current process.

  Note that this routine will not return the status 0xC0033333 since there is no page read operation to be initiated by `MiDispatchFault()`.

- The `MmAccessFault()` routine invokes `MiDispatchFault()` with a prototype PTE (PPTE) to fault into memory if the faulting virtual address belongs to a shared memory range or to a memory-mapped file. In this case, `MiDis-`

patchFault() invokes the MiResolveProtoPteFault() subroutine, which in turn performs the following tasks:

— If the PPTE belongs to a mapped file, the MiResolveMappedFile-Fault() routine is invoked to determine the set of pages to be faulted into memory, allocate an MDL and return 0xC0033333. Note that the VMM attempts to cluster pages together to improve performance.

— If the PPTE was created to back up shared memory contained within a page file, the MiResolvePageFileFault() routine is invoked. This routine determines the page file number from which to perform the paging I/O read operation, builds an MDL structure that will subsequently be used to perform the read, and returns 0xC0033333.

— If the PPTE indicates that it is in transition, this routine will itself invoke the MiResolveTransitionFault() subroutine discussed above.

— If a zeroed page is required, the MiResolveDemandZeroFault() subroutine is invoked.

Once an appropriate subroutine has been invoked successfully, the MiResolveProtoPteFault() routine will make the PTE reflect the contents of the PPTE. Now the PTE for the process will refer to the PFN database entry for the page frame whose contents either will be read in (if 0xC0033333 is returned) or are already valid if a transition fault was resolved.

• Sometimes, the VMM simply needs to materialize a page frame containing zeroes in response to a page fault. This may happen when a thread tries to extend a file on disk, or if a thread tries to access some newly allocated, committed memory. In this case, the MiDispatchFault() routine simply invokes the MiResolveDemandZeroFault() subroutine, which in turn allocates a zeroed page frame from the list of available page frames. If such a page frame is not available, the MiResolveDemandZeroFault() routine returns 0xC7303001, which simply causes the fault to recur and at that time a page should become available (remember that the MPW thread is always trying to ensure that there are enough free and unmodified page frames available to be reallocated).

As you can see, the NT VMM supports the MMU in resolving virtual addresses to physical addresses by faulting in pages that are not present in system memory. If you develop a kernel-mode driver that takes a page fault at an IRQL greater than or equal to DISPATCH_LEVEL, you will cause the system to bugcheck, since the VMM will not satisfy page faults at such a high IRQL. Ensure that all code and data that is accessed at high IRQLs has been previously locked into nonpageable system memory.

Interactions with File System Drivers

The NT Virtual Memory Manager and file system drivers have mutual dependencies between them. The VMM depends on file system drivers to provide support for page file I/O and also to provide support for section objects representing memory-mapped files. The file system, in turn, depends upon the NT VMM to resolve page faults that occur within the file system driver; to manipulate user and system buffers; to be able to allocate, manipulate, and deallocate memory; and to help cache file stream data.*

Here is a list of functionality provided by the VMM to the file system drivers on NT platforms:

- The file system driver is an executable, dynamically loadable driver that is loaded into system virtual address space with the assistance of the VMM and the file system driver that contains the executable. By default, code for the file system and other kernel-mode drivers is not pageable; i.e., these drivers reside in RAM as long as they are loaded. Similarly, all global memory associated with kernel-mode drivers is never paged-out by default. There is a compiler directive that your driver can specify that will cause portions of the driver code to be marked as pageable. This pragma is defined with any NT compatible compiler as follows:

  ```
  #pragma    alloc_text(PAGExxxx,    NameOfRoutine)
  ```

  Note that **xxxx** should be a unique sequence of four characters that identifies a pageable portion (also referred to a pageable section) of code. Furthermore, at run-time, it is possible for your driver to invoke the `MmLockPageable-DataSection()` or the `MmLockPageableCodeSection()` routines to dynamically lock code or data. These routines and the corresponding unlock routines are well documented in the DDK documentation. Some information on making drivers pageable is also provided in Chapter 2, *File System Driver Development.*

- File system drivers, filter drivers, and device drivers all need memory that they allocate at run-time. Typically, your driver will invoke a version of the `ExAllocatePoolWithTag()` routine to request pageable, nonpageable, or cache-aligned memory. You can even request memory with the condition that failure to allocate memory should result in an automatic system panic. Although the Executive support routines manage these *pools* from which your driver obtains memory, the physical memory and its manipulation is performed only by the VMM. Any virtual address pointers (for memory) returned

---

* Chapter 6, *The NT Cache Manager I*, defines file streams more formally. For now, you can substitute the word *file* for *file stream* if you like.

using one of the `ExAllocatePool()` routines is guaranteed to be in kernel virtual address space.

Note that your driver can also invoke the `ZwAllocateVirtualMemory()` routine to directly request memory from the VMM, although the returned virtual address will be in the lower 2GB of the process virtual address space; therefore, such memory will only be accessible in the context of the allocating thread/process.

- Since your kernel-mode driver must be accessible while executing in the context of any process in the system, the VMM manipulates the virtual address space of every process in the system such that the lower 2GB are unique (and private) to that process while the upper 2GB are reserved as the system virtual address space and are mapped to the same physical addresses in the context of all processes executing on the system.

- As a file system or as a kernel-mode driver, your code will often need to use buffers that are passed in from user-mode code (e.g., a thread that executes in user mode allocates memory and passes this buffer down to your driver). Your driver must use this buffer to transfer data either into or out of the buffer. However, there are two problems here that your kernel-mode driver must address:

  — Unless your driver is always guaranteed to execute in the context of the user-mode thread, your driver cannot use the virtual addresses passed in by the user-space thread, since they are only valid in that particular thread's context.

  — Sometimes, your driver might need to access the passed in buffer at an IRQL greater than `APC_LEVEL`. In this case, you must ensure that the buffer is backed by locked physical pages, because a page fault will certainly result in a system crash.

The VMM assists you in addressing both of the issues listed. Any buffer can have its associated physical pages locked in memory by invoking any of the VMM routines such as `MmProbeAndLockPages()`, `MmBuildMdl()`, and other similar routines. These request the VMM to create a Memory Descriptor List (MDL), an opaque structure that describes the list of physical page frames backing your allocated virtual address range. Optionally, depending upon the VMM routine invoked, the pages will also be locked in memory; the page frames allocated to the buffer will not be reclaimed until they are unlocked. If you need to map the passed in addresses into system virtual address space, you can use the `MmGetSystemAddressForMdl()` VMM routine.

TIP   A Memory Descriptor List (MDL) is a system-defined structure that
               describes a virtual address range (buffer) in terms of physical pages.
               It contains an array, each element of which refers to a page frame
               index for the frame backing the virtual address range. The array is
               allocated immediately after the MDL structure; i.e., the MDL struc-
               ture and the array (both of which are allocated from nonpaged
               pool) are physically contiguous in memory.

               Typically, your kernel-mode driver will often request the VMM to
               create such an MDL for a user buffer and will usually map the buff-
               er to system virtual address space. This ensures that the pages stay
               locked until you have finished processing them and that you can ac-
               cess the virtual addresses in the context of any arbitrary process.

               The *ntddk.h* include file, supplied as part of the DDK, contains the
               description of the MDL data structure. Note that your driver ideally
               must not access the fields within the data structure directly, since
               they could be changed by the system.

- The VMM manages the stack frames allocated to all threads executing in the
  system. The stack allocated to a thread executing in kernel mode is of fixed
  length. In NT 3.51 and previous versions, this stack was limited to two page-
  frames. In Windows NT 4.0, the stack has been expanded to three 4KB pages
  of RAM (12288 bytes).

- The VMM assists the file system (and the NT Cache Manager) in caching file
  data. All of the physical memory manipulation is concentrated in the NT
  VMM. Therefore, the support of the VMM is actively required in using physical memory to cache byte streams, which eventually enhances system throughput.

- The VMM provides support for clustering when satisfying page faults, which
  helps improve system performance.

  Typically, the VMM tries to cluster I/O operations into groups of 16 pages. On
  Intel x86 platforms, this leads to a 64KB I/O size, while on Alpha machines,
  this translates to 128KB I/O operations.

- Sometimes, filter drivers need to do unusual things, like caching data to a file
  on a local file system. Or, user-mode code and kernel-mode drivers might
  need to pass data buffers between them. To solve problems like these, kernel-
  mode drivers and user-mode applications can use the services of the VMM to
  create shared memory objects or memory-mapped files.

TIP   Although the focus of the book is not on designing and developing
NT device drivers, you should be aware that the NT VMM utility routines and data structures (the MDL data structure and routines that manipulate it) are also applicable to device driver designers. There are other supporting routines that the VMM provides to device driver developers, most notably `MmMapIoSpace()`, which maps a given physical address range into nonpaged system space. Consult the DDK for additional documentation on this routine as well as other supporting routines provided by the Hardware Abstraction Layer (HAL).

Remember, however, that regardless of the nature of the kernel-mode driver that you develop, you will need to understand the contents of this chapter.

- The NT Virtual Memory Manager provides the `MmQuerySystemSize()` support routine that can sometimes be useful to file system drivers.

The `MmQuerySystemSize()` function takes no arguments. It simply returns an enumerated type result that can take one of the following values:

— `MmSmallSystem` (enumerated type value = 0)

— `MmMediumSystem` (enumerated type value = 1)

— `MmLargeSystem` (enumerated type value = 2)

The value returned depends upon the amount of physical memory configured on the system. The VMM initializes a global variable, `MmSystemSize`, to one of these three values at system initialization time, after determining the amount of physical memory available on the node. `MmQuerySystemSize()` returns the contents of this global variable.

The actual amount of RAM that may result in one value being returned instead of another is subject to change between different versions of Windows NT. For example, if your system has less than 12MB of physical memory, you could expect to get back the `MmSmallSystem` value when you invoke the `MmQuerySystemSize()` function. Similarly, if you have less than 20MB of available physical memory, you could expect to get `MmMediumSystem` returned.

The `MmQuerySystemSize()` function call is typically made by kernel-mode components to guide them in making resource allocation decisions. For example, consider the case when the `MmSmallSystem` value is returned as a result of calling this function. Now your file system driver may not know exactly what a "small system" really means, but you can infer that, relatively speaking, the amount of available physical memory is less than what it would be on medium or large systems. Therefore, your driver could preallocate smaller-sized zones, or create fewer worker threads as compared to what it may do on medium or large systems. Use this routine to get additional information about the system to help determine the resource utilization within your driver.

There will undoubtedly be other factors that your driver will consider in making the final determination about the amount of resources (physical memory) your driver should consume.

The NT VMM also depends on the file system for the following functionality:

- Page files are created and manipulated on mounted file systems. Therefore, to implement virtual memory support, the VMM needs the file system to perform paging I/O read and write operations.

  As illustrated by sample code in Part 3, the file system driver must completely rely on the VMM when receiving I/O requests directed to a page file. Therefore, the file system should avoid acquiring any resources (to provide any synchronization), should never incur a page fault in processing the read/write request, should never defer the request for asynchronous processing, and should never block the request for any reason. It should simply forward the request immediately (after determining the on-disk parameters for the request) to the appropriate lower-level device drivers.

- In order to provide support for shared memory or for memory-mapped files, the VMM needs the active support of the underlying file system. First, the VMM requires that the file system provide appropriate callbacks to help maintain the locking hierarchy in the NT system. In addition, the VMM requires that the file system be prepared to receive page faults that occur as a direct consequence of the user process accessing mapped memory.

  The callbacks that must be implemented by the file system driver are the `AcquireFileForNTCreateSection()` and `ReleaseFileForNtCreateSection()`. The file system is expected to acquire all resources that might be needed while the NT VMM executes code in support of a *create section* request. I will discuss the implementation of these callbacks in detail in Part 3.

Support Routines Provided for FSD Implementations

The VMM provides two specific routines, `MmFlushImageSection()` and `MmCanFileBeTruncated()`, that are very important for file system designers, but they are not well documented. Part 3 has examples using these routines.

MmFlushImageSection()

This function is used by a file system driver to ask the VMM to discard pages in memory containing information associated with a specified image section object. For example, consider a copy of the Microsoft Word executable file that a user mapped in to memory and now wishes to delete, maybe to upgrade the copy to a later version of the software. The file system driver must ensure, before actually deleting the file, that all pages containing file data are flushed (discarded). During normal execution, these pages may contain file stream data even after all user handles to the file have been closed. However, the file system cannot allow such information to stay around in memory if it plans to delete the file stream.

NOTE   Note that the VMM enforces a restriction that a file can't be deleted
                as long as any user has actively mapped in the file stream; if the file
                is currently being executed, it cannot be deleted. However, from the
                discussions presented in this chapter, you have learned that the
                VMM keeps file data around in memory even after all handles to the
                mapped file stream have been closed, as long as it does not really
                need to reuse the physical memory. This helps achieve faster re-
                sponse if the user closes the file handle but reopens it soon after.

                It is precisely during these situations that the file system driver must
                flush the system pages before proceeding with the delete operation.

This function is also invoked by a file system driver before allowing a thread to open a file stream for write access. Also, the VMM will typically not allow a user to open a file for write access if another thread had previously mapped the file into memory as an executable.

The `MmFlushImageSection()` function is defined as follows:

```
BOOLEAN
MmFlushImageSection (
    IN PSECTION_OBJECT_POINTERS     SectionObjectPointer,
    IN MMFLUSH_TYPE                 FlushType
);
```

where

```
typedef enum _MMFLUSH_TYPE {
    MmFlushForDelete,
    MmFlushForWrite
} MMFLUSH_TYPE;
```

Resource Acquisition Constraints:

The file system driver must ensure that the file stream has been acquired exclusively before invoking this function. Typically, the `MainResource`* for the file stream is acquired exclusively before calling `MmFlushImageSection()`.

Parameters:

`SectionObjectPointer`
> In the next chapter, the `SECTION_OBJECT_POINTERS` structure will be described in detail. For now, note that a unique instance of this structure type is associated with each representation of the file stream in memory. The VMM expects a pointer to this structure to be passed in to the `MmFlushImageSection()` function.

`FlushType`
> This can assume one of two values, `MmFlushForDelete` or `MmFlushForWrite`. When checking whether a user open can be allowed to proceed during processing a create/open request for an on-disk file stream, the file system should pass in the `MmFlushForWrite` value. Before actually attempting to delete an on-disk file (in the *set file information* dispatch routine and in the *cleanup* dispatch routine, both of which are described in Part 3), the file system should pass in the `MmFlushForDelete` enumerated type value.

Functionality Provided:

- If the routine receives the argument `MmFlushForDelete`, and any user thread has mapped the file stream into its virtual address space as a regular data stream (memory-mapped file), the VMM will immediately return FALSE.

- In either case, whether `MmFlushForDelete` or `MmFlushForWrite` is passed in, if any thread has mapped the file stream into its virtual address space as an executable, the VMM will reject the request and return FALSE.

- Otherwise, the VMM will grab the page frame database lock and mark the image section object for deletion.

Once the VMM has determined that it is safe to proceed with flushing of the image section, the VMM will actually walk through the list of dirty pages contained within the section and flush them out to secondary storage if they are backed by an on-disk page file. Note that any dirty (modified) pages belonging to mapped files are simply discarded immediately. Before actually starting the flush operation, the VMM will ensure that all asynchronous modified page writer operations on the file stream have been stopped (and will actually block until any

---

* More information on synchronization objects associated with a file stream is provided in Part 3.

ongoing write operations have been completed). If your file system supports page files and if any of the dirty pages are backed by the page files residing on your file system, your driver should expect to receive recursive paging I/O write requests at this time.

Once the modified pages have been flushed (if required), the VMM will tear down the image section object for the file stream, making it safe for the file system to proceed with a delete or open operation.

There are two extremely important points you must be aware of before invoking this function:

- When trying to flush modified pages for the image section to a page file, the VMM will ignore any I/O errors encountered.

- The VMM will dereference the file object that was referenced when the image section object was created.

  To the file system designer, this means that your driver could receive a close request as part of the processing performed during this call. If your file system is in the middle of processing a create operation, do not be surprised to suddenly receive the last close operation on the file stream as a result of invoking this function.*

MmCanFileBeTruncated()

This routine is provided by the VMM to help a file system determine whether a truncate operation on a file stream should be allowed to proceed. The VMM imposes certain restrictions on when file size modifications and/or deletions are allowed to proceed. A user is not allowed to truncate a file stream if the file stream is mapped in as an executable; the truncate request will be denied if an image section object has been created by the VMM and is actively being used by a user thread. The rationale is that it would confuse the user executing the file tremendously if a page fault failed because the contents corresponding to the page no longer exist on disk due to the truncate operation, although the contents existed just a moment ago. Also, if any thread has mapped the file stream as a data file (not as an image section), and if the new file size would be less than the currently mapped view length of the file stream, the VMM will disallow the truncate request.

The `MmCanFileBeTruncated()` function is typically invoked by the file system before allowing a truncate request to proceed. An example using this function is

---

* Although you will appreciate this more when you actually develop your file system driver, this could cause all sorts of problems for your driver if you have to arbitrate between tearing down file system structures (as a result of the last close being received) and using them because you are processing a create/open request.

provided in Chapter 10, *Writing A File System Driver II*. The function is defined as follows:

```
BOOLEAN
MmCanFileBeTruncated (
IN PSECTION_OBJECT_POINTERS      SectionPointer,
IN PLARGE_INTEGER               NewFileSize
);
```

Resource Acquisition Constraints:

The file system driver must ensure that the file stream has been acquired exclusively before invoking this function. Typically, the **MainResource**[*] for the file stream is acquired exclusively before calling MmCanFileBeTruncated().

Parameters:

SectionObjectPointer

The **SECTION_OBJECT_POINTERS** structure is described in detail in the next chapter. Note for now that a unique instance of this structure type is associated with each representation of the file stream in memory.

NewFileSize

A pointer to a large integer containing the proposed new file size.

Functionality Provided:

- Internally, **MmCanFileBeTruncated()** invokes **MmFlushImageSection()**, supplying **MmFlushForWrite** as the reason for the flush request.

   If the **MmFlushImageSection()** function returns FALSE, the **MmCanFileBeTruncated()** function will also return FALSE and deny the truncate request.

- Otherwise, the function checks if any user thread-mapped views exist; if they do and the new file size would be less than the size of the mapped view, the **MmCanFileBeTruncated()** function returns FALSE.

- Otherwise, the function returns TRUE, allowing the truncate request.

The basic philosophy followed here is:

- If an image section is in use for the file stream, the VMM will return FALSE.
- If a user data section exists for the file stream, and if the new file size is less than the size of the currently mapped view, the VMM will return FALSE.
- If neither of the two conditions above are found to be TRUE, the VMM will return TRUE.

---

[*] More information on synchronization objects associated with a file stream is provided in Part 3.

This chapter presented the Virtual Memory Manager. The next three chapters will cover the NT Cache Manager, a kernel-mode component that assists file system drivers in caching data. This component depends heavily upon the NT VMM and is explicitly supported by it.

6

The NT Cache Manager I

Although constant advances in storage technologies have led to faster and cheaper secondary storage devices, accessing data off secondary storage media is still much slower than accessing data buffered in system memory. Therefore, to achieve greater performance with applications that manage large amounts of data (e.g., with database management applications), it becomes important to have data brought into system memory before it is accessed (*read-ahead functionality*), to retain such information in memory until it is no longer needed (*caching of data*), and possibly to defer writing of modified data to disk to obtain greater efficiency (*write-behind* or *delayed-write* functionality).

Most modern operating systems provide support for some form of file data caching.* This task is traditionally performed by individual file systems or by modules such as the systemwide buffer cache on UNIX systems. In the Windows NT operating system, the NT Cache Manager encapsulates the functionality required to cache file data.† In order to perform this task, the Cache Manager interacts with file system drivers and with the NT Virtual Memory Manager. The Cache Manager is an integral component of the Windows NT environment. By simply using Windows NT to access file data, each of us utilizes the services provided by the Cache Manager. If our requests to access data seem to be satisfied fairly quickly, without even accessing the disk drive, we know that the Cache Manager

---

* Even the maligned Microsoft DOS environment featured the (in)famous SmartDrive caching module.

† Actually, the Cache Manager caches *byte streams* (without interpretation), which can be stored on disk using any layout defined by the file system. Therefore, file system metadata can also be cached by the NT Cache Manager.

worked hard to preread our data into system memory. If requests to copy files or modify them return almost instantaneously, it is probably because the modified data was buffered in memory. When we notice that the hard disk shows activity periodically (every few seconds), we realize that modified data is being lazy-written to disk. And finally, when we lose data as a result of a system crash, it is quite evident that the Cache Manager must be to blame.*

In this chapter, as well as in the next two, I will present the NT Cache Manager in detail, focusing on the responsibilities of the Cache Manager, the methodology used by it to buffer data, and also the interactions of the Cache Manager with the NT file system drivers and the NT Virtual Memory Manager.

Functionality

The NT Cache Manager is a distinct component of the NT Executive, and it is closely affiliated with the Virtual Memory Manager.

It provides a consistent systemwide cache for data stored on secondary storage devices.

> This cache is managed in conjunction with the appropriate file system drivers, and with the cooperation of the Virtual Memory Manager and the I/O Manager.

It performs read-ahead on file data.

> The Cache Manager attempts to tune its read-ahead policy per file based on the pattern of data access performed by user applications. Since all I/O requests on buffered files get routed through the Cache Manager, the Cache Manager can keep track of the access pattern for the data belonging to the file. Therefore, if a user application reads (say) the first 10K bytes for a file, the NT Cache Manager will typically try to read ahead the next 64K bytes of the file into memory. Subsequently, if the application attempts to obtain this data, it can simply be copied over from the system cache, thereby avoiding making the user application wait until the data can be read from secondary storage. For sequentially accessed files, the *read-ahead* functionality provided by the Cache Manager can result in significant performance gains, since data will have already been read into system volatile memory before the application requests access to such data.

---

* By accepting (and requiring) greater throughput via caching in volatile system RAM, users accept the risks associated with such caching. Typically, unplanned system outages (perhaps due to failure of hardware components or errors in the software) result in the loss of modified data that had not been flushed to secondary storage. Although it is possible to use nonvolatile memory to cache data, the associated costs with such usage are prohibitive for most environments.

It provides delayed-write functionality for modified cached data.

By keeping modified data in memory for some time before actually writing it to disk, the Cache Manager provides greater responsiveness to the user applications that actually perform the write. It can also batch multiple contiguous write operations in memory and write all the modified bytes out in a single I/O operation, which is typically more efficient than performing each smaller write operation individually. Finally, it is possible that a user application may repeatedly modify the same byte range. By deferring I/O to disk, such modifications are made only in memory, avoiding completely the overhead of repeated write operations to the media.

File Streams

Each instance of an open file is represented by a file object structure in Windows NT. Any linear stream of bytes associated with a file object can be defined as a *file stream*. Examples of file streams include the data for the given file,* a directory (containing information about other files stored on disk), file system *metadata* (such as volume information), Access Control Lists (ACLs) associated with the file, and extended attributes stored with the file.

NT file systems create, delete, and manipulate file streams as the result of either externally generated user requests to read or write file data, or internally generated requests to manipulate file-system-specific data structures. File systems identify file streams that they wish to support and cache. For example, unless directed otherwise by a user, file systems cache user data contained within a file. For each file stream to be cached, the file system typically supports both cached and noncached access.

The Cache Manager provides support for the *caching of file streams* by using memory mapping, and it also integrates caching with the memory manager's policies for other uses of pageable memory. From the perspective of the Cache Manager, the stream is simply a random sequence of bytes representing information that should be kept in memory. Therefore, the same set of services offered by the Cache Manager can be used by file system drivers to cache user file data or file system metadata.

---

* Some files could have multiple data streams if the file system supports this feature. For example, NTFS supports multiple data streams. NTFS uses two distinct byte streams (for the same named file) to store the resource and data forks associated with Macintosh files stored on NTFS file systems on NT servers.

Virtual Block Caching

Some operating systems use physical offsets (or disk block addresses) to cache file data in system memory. Instead of using disk block addresses, the NT Cache Manager provides a *virtual block cache* by using the *file mapping method* for caching file streams. Figure 6-1 illustrates the difference between these two methods for data caching (for buffered data). Note that the numbering indicates the logical sequence in which the operations are performed.

In operating systems that use physical block addressing for cached data (the *old buffer cache* implementation in UNIX SVR4), the file system or caching module must first convert virtual byte offsets in a file to physical block offsets on disk before checking whether data is available in the system cache, since the caching module—the buffer cache—keeps track of cached data by using physical disk addresses. However, as shown in Figure 6-1, the NT Cache Manager only uses virtual byte offsets in a file to keep track of cached information. The Cache Manager does not need to understand physical block addresses for the data being accessed. Therefore, file system drivers in the Windows NT operating system generally translate virtual byte offsets in a file to physical block offsets on disk only if the data could not be obtained from the in-memory cache being managed by the Cache Manager.

The advantages of using a virtual block cache (as compared to a physical block cache) follow:

- Some applications may use native NT system calls to access file data, e.g., `NtReadFile()` or `NtWriteFile()`,[*] while other applications executing concurrently may map the file data into their address space for read or read/write access. By using virtual block caching, via file mapping, and by using proper synchronization, it is possible for all such applications to see the most current data.[†]

- Conceptually, there is no difference between file data mapped in by the NT Cache Manager compared to file data mapped in by an application. By using the file mapping model, all physical memory becomes available for data caching. As mentioned before, the allocation of physical memory is controlled by the NT Virtual Memory Manager; the number of physical pages allocated to

---

[*] Typically, applications use the interfaces provided by a subsystem (e.g., the `ReadFile()` interface provided by the Win32 subsystem) to perform read/write operations. Invoking such interface routines eventually results in calls to native NT system services. For a comprehensive listing of system services provided by the I/O Manager for data access, see Appendix A, *Windows NT System Services*.

[†] Note that neither the FASTFAT nor the NTFS native file system implementations currently **guarantee** that applications using conventional system calls will always obtain the most current data if other applications have also mapped the file for read/write access. However, in most cases, the file systems go to considerable lengths to ensure that this is indeed the case.

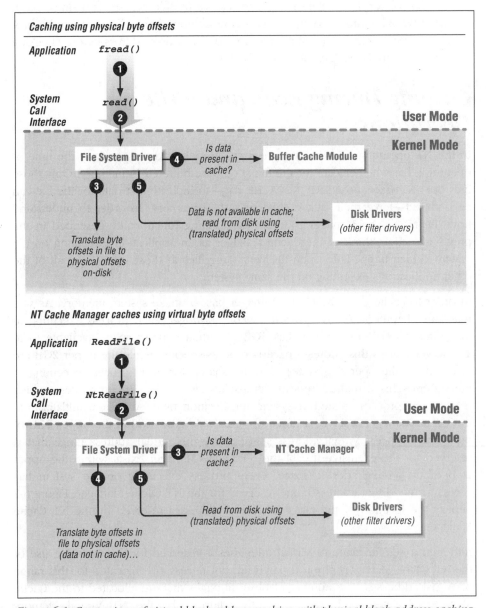

Figure 6-1. Comparison of virtual block address caching with physical block address caching

the Cache Manager depends on changing needs for memory by other components in the system (e.g., memory allocated for image file pages versus data file pages).

- Often, the I/O Manager invokes the Cache Manager directly, bypassing the file system driver or the network redirector driver completely. In such cases, it is possible for the Cache Manager to resolve the file access via a single hardware virtual address lookup.* This is considerably more efficient than the process of converting a virtual address to a physical disk address before checking whether data is available in system buffers.

Caching During Read and Write Operations

In the NT operating system, user processes are allowed to specify at the time of opening a file whether data for the file should be buffered in memory. Only those files opened without the IRP_NOCACHE flag—to indicate that data for the file can be buffered—have their data cached in system memory. In order to understand how the NT Cache Manager provides the caching functionality described in the previous section, think of the Cache Manager as an application, executing on the system, which happens to open the very same files as those opened by all of the other applications executing on the same system.

In order to cache data, the Cache Manager has to utilize system memory. As was noted in Chapter 5, *The NT Virtual Memory Manager,* each process executing in the Windows NT environment has 4GB of virtual address space available to it. The lower half of this address space is process-specific, while the upper 2GB are reserved for the operating system and are shared for every process executing in the system. This virtual address model applies also to the system process, which is a special process created at system initialization time. At system initialization, the Cache Manager reserves a range of virtual addresses within the upper 2GB of the system process virtual address space. Since this virtual address range that is reserved for the exclusive use of the NT Cache Manager exists within the upper 2GB of the virtual address space, every process executing on the system has access to the virtual address range reserved for the NT Cache Manager. Figure 6-2 depicts the location of the range of virtual addresses reserved by the NT Cache Manager.

Although a certain range of virtual addresses is reserved for the exclusive use of the NT Cache Manager, physical pages are not necessarily allocated for this range of virtual addresses. The number of physical pages that are allocated to the Cache Manager is determined, and constantly adjusted, by the NT Virtual Memory Manager. In the absence of demand for physical memory from other user processes or system components, the Virtual Memory Manager may choose to increase the amount of physical memory allocated to the Cache Manager. On the

---

* Virtual address translation can be immediately performed using the Translation Lookaside Buffer (TLB). A TLB hit results in extremely efficient translation to the corresponding physical memory address.

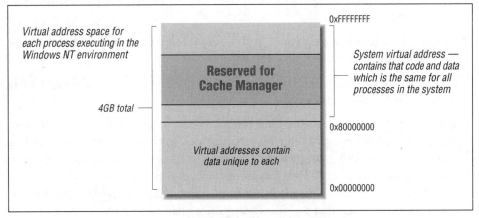

Figure 6-2 content labels:
- Virtual address space for each process executing in the Windows NT environment
- 4GB total
- Reserved for Cache Manager
- Virtual addresses contain data unique to each
- 0xFFFFFFFF
- System virtual address — contains that code and data which is the same for all processes in the system
- 0x80000000
- 0x00000000

Figure 6-2. Virtual address range reserved for the NT Cache Manager

other hand, on heavily loaded systems with scarce available physical memory, the memory manager may decrease the amount of physical memory allocated to the Cache Manager for caching file data.

It is important to note that these decisions concerning physical memory allocation are the sole prerogative of the NT Virtual Memory Manager.

The Cache Manager application uses *file mapping* to buffer file data. Caching is initiated on a file stream by a file system driver through a call to the Cache Manager. Upon receiving such a request, the Cache Manager, invokes the Virtual Memory Manager to create a section object representing the file mapping—this is done for the entire file stream. Subsequently, when a process attempts to access data belonging to the stream, the Cache Manager dynamically maps views of the file stream into portions of the virtual address space reserved for itself in the system virtual address space. Note that since the range of virtual addresses reserved for the Cache Manager is fixed, the Cache Manager may have to unmap one or more previously mapped views in order to be able to create a new view.

In order to better understand the role played by the Cache Manager in servicing I/O requests, let's examine the typical sequence of steps executed in response to user-initiated read and write operations.

Cached Read Operation

Consider a read operation initiated by a user application. This read operation is passed on to the file system by the NT I/O Manager.* Figure 6-3 illustrates the

---

* As shown later, the file system is bypassed by the I/O Manager in many cases. However, for simplicity, let's assume that I/O operations are first sent to the file system driver by the I/O Manager subsystem.

sequence of operations executed to satisfy the read request (using the *copy interface** provided by the Cache Manager).

An explanation for each step listed in the figure is provided below. Note that the arrows in the figure represent flow of control.

1. The user application executes a read operation, which causes control to be transferred to the I/O Manager in the kernel.

2. The I/O Manager directs the read request to the appropriate file system driver using an IRP. The user buffer may be mapped into the system virtual address space, or the I/O Manager may allocate a Memory Descriptor List representing the buffer and lock pages associated with this MDL, or the virtual address for the buffer may be passed-in unmodified by the I/O Manager. In Part 3 you will see that the file system driver has control over which of these operations is performed by the I/O Manager.

3. The file system driver receives the read request and notices that the read operation is directed to a file that is opened for buffered access. If caching has not yet been initiated for this file, the file system driver initiates caching on the file by invoking the Cache Manager. In turn, the Cache Manager requests the Virtual Memory Manager to create a file mapping (section object) for the file to be cached.

4. The file system driver passes the read request to the NT Cache Manager using the `CcCopyRead()`† Cache Manager call. The Cache Manager is now responsible for executing all the necessary steps to transfer data into the user's buffer.

5. The Cache Manager examines its data structures to determine whether there is a mapped view of the file containing the range of bytes requested by the user. If no mapped view exists, the Cache Manager creates one.

6. The Cache Manager simply performs a memory copy operation from the mapped view into the user's buffer.

7. If the mapped view of the file is not backed by physical pages containing the required data, a page fault occurs and control is transferred to the Virtual Memory Manager.

8. The VMM allocates physical pages that will be used to contain the requested data‡ for which the page fault occurred and then issues a *noncached paging I/O*

---

* Later in this chapter, I will discuss the various interface methods presented by the NT Cache Manager to other system components. The *copy interface* is one of the four available interfaces.

† See the next two chapters for a detailed discussion on all the routines exposed by the Cache Manager.

‡ In order to free up physical memory, the Virtual Memory Manager may need to write modified pages to disk. For now, assume that unmodified free pages are available.

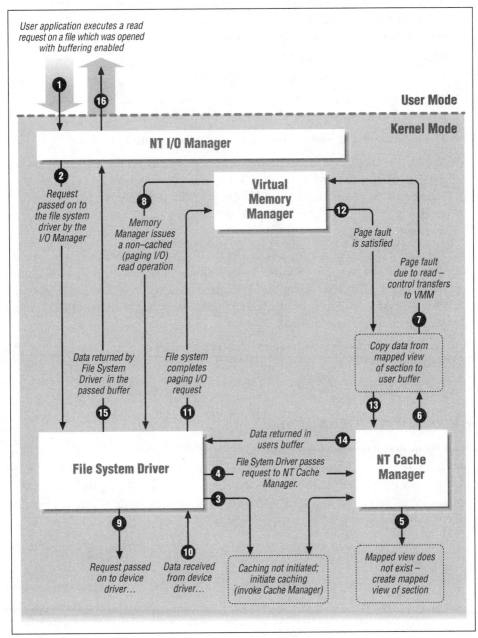

Figure 6-3. Sequence of steps executed to satisfy a user read request for a cached file

read operation to the file system driver via the NT I/O Manager. Note that although the figure above does not indicate that the paging I/O request is routed via the NT I/O Manager, that is indeed what happens.

9. Upon receiving the noncached read request, the file system driver creates a corresponding I/O request to obtain data off secondary storage media and sends this I/O request to the lower-layer drivers.

10. The device driver(s) below the file system obtain data from secondary storage (or from across the network) and complete the request.

11. The file system driver completes the paging I/O request from the NT Virtual Memory Manager.

12. The instruction that resulted in a page fault is reexecuted.

13. The Cache Manager completes the copy operation from the mapped view for the file to the user's buffer. This time, the copy should complete without incurring a page fault (although it is theoretically possible to have a page fault repeatedly on a page that has just been brought in, practically speaking, this does not occur).

14. The Cache Manager returns control to the file system driver after the cached data has been copied into the user's buffer. Note that this data will also remain cached in the virtual address space reserved for the Cache Manager (however, this data may be discarded from system memory by the NT Virtual Memory Manager at any time).

15. The file system driver completes the original IRP sent to it by the NT I/O Manager.

16. The I/O Manager completes the original user read request.

Cached Write Operation

Now, consider a write operation initiated by a user application. Figure 6-4 illustrates the sequence of operations executed to satisfy the write request (using the *copy interface* provided by the Cache Manager).* As you will see, the sequence of operations is similar to the read operation described previously. An explanation for each step listed in the figure is provided below:

1. The user application executes a write operation, which causes control to be transferred to the I/O Manager in the kernel.

2. The I/O Manager directs the write request to the appropriate file system driver using an IRP. As in the case of the read operation, the buffer may be mapped into the system virtual address space, or an MDL may be created, or

---

* The figure has been deliberately simplified for the sake of clarity. As you will see in Chapter 9, *Writing a File System Driver I*, in order to account for incomplete block transfers, write operations may cause the file system to actually read data from disk before executing the write.

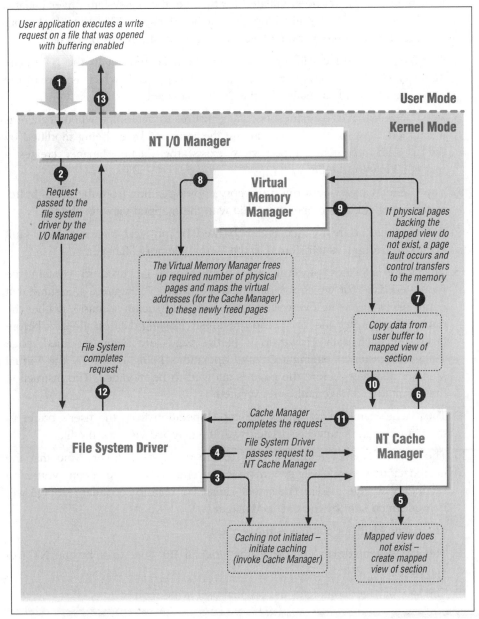

Figure 6-4. Sequence of steps executed to satisfy a write request for a cached file

the virtual address for the buffer may be passed to the file system driver without any modifications.

3. The file system driver notices that the write operation is directed to a file that is opened for buffered access. As shown in the example for a read operation,

if caching has not yet been initiated for this file, the file system driver initiates caching on the file by invoking the Cache Manager. The Virtual Memory Manager creates a file mapping (section object) for the file to be cached.

4. The file system driver simply passes on the write request to the NT Cache Manager via the `CcCopyWrite()` Cache Manager call, which is part of the copy interface made available by the Cache Manager.

5. The Cache Manager examines its data structures to determine whether there is a mapped view for the file containing the range of bytes being modified by the user. If no such mapped view exists, the Cache Manager creates a mapped view for the file.

6. The Cache Manager performs a memory copy operation from the user's buffer to the virtual address range associated with the mapped view for the file.

7. If this virtual address range is not backed by physical pages, a page fault occurs and control is transferred to the Virtual Memory Manager.

8. The VMM allocates physical pages, which will be used to contain the requested data (for which the page fault occurred). In Figure 6-4, assume that entire pages are being overwritten by the user. In such a scenario, neither the Cache Manager nor the VMM read previously existing data off the disk before modifying such data. However, if partial pages are being modified, page faults will result in paging I/O *read* operations being issued by the Virtual Memory Manager, before the page is allowed to be modified. The instruction that resulted in a page fault is reexecuted.

9. The Cache Manager completes the copy operation from the user's buffer to the virtual address range associated with the mapped view for the file.

10. The Cache Manager returns control to the file system driver. Note that the user data now resides in system memory and has not yet been written to secondary storage media. The actual transfer of data to secondary storage will be performed later by the Cache Manager.*

11. The Cache Manager completes the request.

12. The file system driver completes the original IRP sent to it by the NT I/O Manager.

13. The I/O Manager completes the original user write request.

---

* Either the lazy writer component of the Cache Manager or the modified page writer component of the Memory Manager may initiate the write to secondary storage media. Also, it is possible that a user request to flush system buffers or a flush initiated by the file system driver (due to some reason such as a cleanup operation) may be responsible for instigating the write operation to disk. The lazy writer component will be covered in greater detail in the next chapter. Refer to Chapter 5 for more details on the modified page writer.

Cache Manager Interfaces

Now that we have explored how caching is typically used by file system drivers, let us look at the different ways in which system components can use the NT Cache Manager. File system drivers and other components in the Windows NT operating system can use the services provided by the Cache Manager through four sets of interface routines. The first set of interface routines provides support for basic file stream access and manipulation, while the other three can be used as different access methods for the system cache.

The four sets of interfaces provided by the NT Cache Manager are file stream manipulation functions, the copy interface, the MDL interface, and the pinning interface.

File Stream Manipulation Functions

The Cache Manager provides support for initializing cached operations for a file stream, terminating caching, flushing cached data to disk (on demand), modifying file sizes, purging cached data, zeroing file data, support for logging file systems,[*] and other common maintenance functions. The functions provided by the Cache Manager within this interface set consist of the following:

- `CcInitializeCacheMap`
- `CcUninitializeCacheMap`
- `CcSetFileSizes`
- `CcPurgeCacheSection`
- `CcSetDirtyPageThreshold`
- `CcFlushCache`
- `CcZeroData`
- `CcGetFileObjectFromSectionPtrs`
- `CcSetLogHandleForFile`
- `CcSetAdditionalCacheAttributes`
- `CcGetDirtyPages`
- `CcIsThereDirtyData`
- `CcGetLsnForFileObject`

---

[*] Some file systems (e.g., the NTFS file system) use a method called *logging* to enable faster recovery and ensure metadata integrity upon a system crash (or any unexpected shutdown). These file systems need to ensure a certain sequence in which log entries and corresponding file metadata/data are written to disk. The Cache Manager provides support for such file system drivers via the routines listed above.

Copy Interface

The copy interface is the simplest form of cached access. The client module, using the Cache Manager, can utilize this interface to copy either a range of bytes from a buffer in memory to a specified virtual byte offset in the cached file stream, or a range of bytes from a specified virtual byte offset in the cached file stream to a buffer in memory.

This interface includes a call to initiate read-ahead and also includes calls to support *write throttling*. Write throttling allows the client of the Cache Manager (usually a file system driver) to defer certain write operations if the system is running low on available or unmodified pages. This condition can occur if some applications keep modifying data at an extremely rapid rate, greater than the rate at which the lazy writer or modified page writer can initiate the transfer of modified data to disk or across the network to a storage server. Note that it is also quite possible that the disk or network driver may not be able to keep pace with the rate at which I/O requests to write data to disk are being generated by the modified page writer or the lazy writer. This would also result in a decrease in the number of available, unmodified pages.

The functions provided by the Cache Manager within this interface set consist of the following:

- `CcCopyRead/CcFastCopyRead`
- `CcCopyWrite/CcFastCopyWrite`
- `CcCanIWrite`
- `CcDeferWrite`
- `CcSetReadAheadGranularity`
- `CcScheduleReadAhead`

MDL Interface

A Memory Descriptor List (MDL) is an opaque Memory-Manager-defined data structure that maps a particular virtual address range to one or more paged-based physical address ranges. The MDL interface to the Cache Manager allows direct access to the system cache via Direct Memory Access (DMA).* The set of routines comprising the MDL interface return an MDL to the caller, containing the byte range described in the request, which can be subsequently used by the caller to transfer data directly into or out of the system cache.

---

* DMA allows a device controller to transfer data directly between system memory and a secondary storage device. The processing unit doesn't get involved in the data transfer, resulting in better performance.

This interface is useful to subsystems that need direct access to the contents of the system cache. For example, network file servers that need to DMA across the network device directly into or out of the Cache Manager's virtual address range use the MDL interface to achieve higher performance. In the absence of this interface, a network driver transferring data out of the system cache might first have to allocate a temporary buffer, copy data from the system cache to this temporary buffer, let the network device perform the transfer, and, finally, deallocate the temporary buffer. The extraneous calls to allocate/deallocate the temporary buffer and the redundant copy can all be avoided if data can be transferred by the network device directly from the system cache across the network. This can indeed be achieved using the `CcMdlRead()` and `CcMdlReadComplete()` sequence of calls.[*]

Note that this interface shares the same read-ahead call as the copy interface. Also, routines comprising the MDL interface and those belonging to the copy interface can be used concurrently on the same file stream. The functions provided by the Cache Manager within this interface set consist of the following:

* `CcMdlRead`
* `CcMdlReadComplete`
* `CcPrepareMdlWrite`
* `CcMdlWriteComplete`

An interesting point to note here is that, while most of the other Cache Manager routines associated with data transfer (e.g., `CcMdlRead()`, `CcCopyRead()`) perform data transfer as part of the functionality provided by the routine, the `CcPrepareMdlWrite()` routine simply creates an MDL containing original data, which can be subsequently modified by the caller prior to invoking `CcMdl-WriteComplete()`. Therefore, although some data transfer might be performed by the Cache Manager when `CcPrepareMdlWrite()` is invoked (to obtain current file stream data from disk or across the network and place it in the pages described by the MDL), the routine acts more as an enabler routine, allowing the caller to transfer the new data later, using the returned MDL.

Pinning Interface

This interface provided by the Cache Manager can be used to perform two tasks:

* Map data into the system cache for direct access using a buffer pointer
* Pin (or lock) the physical pages that back the mapped data

---

[*] The terminology used here is important: `CcMdlRead()` is used when the client wishes to read from the system cache and write to the network (or disk). `CcPrepareMdlWrite()` is used when the client wishes to transfer directly from the network device (or disk) and write to the system cache.

In addition to being able to read data directly using a buffer pointer, the caller can also modify the data directly in the system cache.

When access to the mapped data is no longer required, the data can be unpinned. This will also result in locked pages being unlocked and made available for other uses. Once the data is unpinned, the pointer to the data should no longer be used.

Pinning data is typically used for efficiency reasons when file system drivers or other system components need to access frequently used data structures (or other data associated with the file stream) directly in memory. It is also used to ensure that the data being accessed cannot be removed from system memory. However, locking mapped data consumes physical memory and therefore decreases the amount of memory available to other system components.

Note that the pinning interface cannot currently be used in conjunction with either the copy interface or the MDL interface.

This interface is often used by file system drivers when dealing with cached file system metadata. The pinning interface consists of the following functions:

- `CcMapData`
- `CcPinMappedData`
- `CcPinRead`
- `CcSetDirtyPinnedData`
- `CcPreparePinWrite`
- `CcUnpinData`
- `CcUnpinDataForThread`
- `CcRepinBcb`
- `CcUnpinRepinnedBcb`
- `CcGetFileObjectFromBcb`

The above functions are described in greater detail in Chapter 7, *The NT Cache Manager II*.

Cache Manager Clients

The following components are typical users of the interfaces provided by the Cache Manager. These components are also known as *clients* of the Cache Manager.

- File system drivers such as NTFS, FASTFAT, CDFS, and other third-party file systems use the copy interface services of the Cache Manager to perform caching on user file data. This allows for greater performance, because once user data is cached in system memory, subsequent access to the data can be satisfied immediately without getting the data again from secondary storage media.

File system drivers also use the Cache Manager to cache file system metadata, including volume structures, directory information, bitmaps for free space on disk, extended attributes associated with a file, and other similar information. Many of these structures are often pinned in memory by the file system driver. Note that the Cache Manager does not interpret the type of data streams being cached; it only knows about file object data structures and data streams associated with such file objects.

File system drivers also typically use the read-ahead and delayed write functionality provided by the Cache Manager, although it is quite possible that certain sophisticated file system implementations may add their own support for read-ahead or delayed write operations. Finally, all file system drivers have to use the file stream manipulation functions provided by the Cache Manager to interface correctly with the Cache Manager.

- Network redirectors are similar to file system driver implementations; however, these modules obtain data from file servers across a network, instead of from a secondary storage medium directly attached to the host system. These components typically cache various data streams in the system cache to provide extremely fast performance comparable to local file systems.

  Network redirectors typically use the copy interface provided by the Cache Manager. They may also use the MDL interface to DMA data directly into or out of the system cache. These components also benefit from the read-ahead and write-behind functionality provided by the Cache Manager. In order to initiate or terminate caching on specific data streams or to perform other cache manipulation functions, network redirectors use the file stream manipulation functions.

- Network File Servers are indirect clients of the Cache Manager, since they use the local file systems to ultimately obtain access to file data. These drivers never invoke Cache Manager routines directly. File servers are often implemented as kernel-mode drivers for performance reasons. They use the copy interface via the file system drivers that serve their requests. Also, file servers typically use DMA to transfer data directly into (or out of) the system cache. To do this, file servers use the MDL interface to the Cache Manager. Since file servers cannot directly invoke the Cache Manager, they use special flags in read/write IRPs sent to file system drivers to request that a memory descriptor list be created for the specified virtual address range in the file stream. After data transfer has been completed, file servers inform file system drivers that previously created memory descriptor lists can now be deleted. Chapter 9, contains an explanation of the flags used by file servers to request the creation and deletion of MDLs for data buffered in the system cache.

- Filter drivers, or other drivers that use the NT file system interface for specialized purposes, are indirect clients of the Cache Manager. Consider a filter driver that provides hard disk caching for data stored on slower media such as magnetic tape or optical media. Such a driver uses the services of a local file system to store the cached information. Therefore, the filter driver is an indirect client of the Cache Manager, since the file system supporting the filter driver uses the copy interface to transfer data into and from system memory. Similarly, consider a filter driver that provides HSM* functionality. Such a driver has to migrate data from a relatively fast secondary storage device, such as a magnetic disk, to a slower device, such as tape. To help speed up the process, the filter driver uses DMA to transfer data directly from the system cache to tape and, therefore, uses the MDL interface (via special flags in read/write IRPs sent to the file system driver) provided by the Cache Manager. After the transfer process has completed, the filter driver will inform the file system driver that any previously created memory descriptor lists can now be deleted.

Table 6-1 summarizes the way clients of the Cache Manager use its various interfaces.

Table 6-1. Clients of the Cache Manager

	Local File Systems	Network Redirectors	Network File Servers	Filter Drivers
File Stream Manipulation	✓	✓		
Copy Interface	✓	✓	✓	✓
MDL Interface		✓	✓	✓
Pinning Interface	✓			

Some Important Data Structures

The services provided by the Cache Manager are most heavily utilized by file system drivers and network redirectors, which serve user I/O requests. The data

---

* HSM or Hierarchical Storage Management involves efficient management of available storage using configurations comprising faster and more expensive media along with slower but cheaper media, to minimize cost per byte of stored data and yet have data always available when required. Typically, this is performed by automatically transferring infrequently accessed data to slower, cheaper media, such as tape, from the faster (but more expensive) hard disks. When such data is subsequently accessed, the driver automatically transfers data back from tape to hard disk. There are other aspects to HSM that are outside the scope of this discussion.

structures and fields described below are important to understand to interface correctly with the Cache Manager.

Fields in the File Object

As explained in Chapter 4, *The NT I/O Manager*, each file stream, when created or opened, has a file object structure (of type **FILE_OBJECT**) created for it by the I/O Manager. Although most of the fields within the file object structure are filled in by the I/O Manager, the file system drivers and network redirectors that are the recipients of the I/O requests on the associated file stream are required to fill in certain specific fields. Three important fields that must be initialized follow:

- The **FsContext** field
- The **SectionObjectPointer** field
- The **PrivateCacheMap** field

This initialization is typically performed at file stream open (or create) time; it is possible, though, for a file system or network redirector to defer this operation to some other time before caching is first initiated for the file stream.

FsContext

If caching via the NT Cache Manager is required for an open file stream (represented by the file object structure), the **FsContext** field must be initialized to point to a structure of type **FSRTL_COMMON_FCB_HEADER**. This structure is defined as follows:

```
typedef struct _FSRTL_COMMON_FCB_HEADER {
 CSHORT         NodeTypeCode;
 CSHORT         NodeByteSize;
 UCHAR          Flags;
 UCHAR          IsFastIoPossible;
 // ****************************************************************
 // The following two fields are only present in Version 4.0+ of the
 // the Windows NT operating system.
 //   Second Flags Field.
 UCHAR          Flags2;
 // The following reserved field should always be 0.
 UCHAR          Reserved;
 // ****************************************************************
 PERESOURCE     Resource;
 PERESOURCE     PagingIoResource;
 LARGE_INTEGER  AllocationSize;
 LARGE_INTEGER  FileSize;
 LARGE_INTEGER  ValidDataLength;
} FSRTL_COMMON_FCB_HEADER;
```

The above structure will be referred to as the **CommonFCBHeader** structure. It has to be allocated by the file system or network driver from nonpaged kernel memory. As you will see in Chapter 9, each file stream is uniquely represented in memory by a File Control Block (FCB) structure.

NOTE   For readers with a UNIX background, note that a File Control Block is analogous to a UNIX *vnode* structure representing a file (or directory) in memory.

Although multiple concurrent open operations performed on the same file stream may result in multiple file object structures being created, there is only one unique FCB for the file, and all file object structures must refer to it.

Similarly, only one `CommonFCBHeader` structure can exist per file stream. Therefore, it is not uncommon to see file system driver or network driver implementations allocate the `CommonFCBHeader` structure as part of their FCB structure representing the file stream. Note, however, that the file system driver is not required to allocate the `CommonFCBHeader` as part of the FCB structure as long as a one-to-one (unique) logical association can be created between these two structures.

The first two fields in the `CommonFCBHeader`—`NodeTypeCode` and `NodeByteSize`—are unused by the Cache Manager. The fields comprising this structure are described below. Note that many of these fields require the understanding of concepts explained in later chapters (specifically Chapters 9-11); the issue of initialization of each of these fields will be revisited when all such required concepts have been presented:

Flags

> The `CommonFCBHeader` structure has pointers to two synchronization `ERESOURCE` type structures. The `PagingIoResource` is acquired by the modified page writer thread. By setting an appropriate value in the `Flags` field, the file system driver or network redirector is allowed to specify to the MPW thread that the `MainResource` (see below) should be acquired instead of the `PagingIoResource`. In Chapter 11, *Writing a File System Driver III*, reasons why a file system driver or a network redirector may set such a flag will be discussed.

Flags2

> This field was added with Version 4.0 of the operating system. As discussed later in this book, it is possible for an FSD to specify that lazy-write operations not be performed for a cached file stream. However, if the `Flags2` field has the `FSRTL_FLAG2_DO_MODIFIED_WRITE` flag set (defined as 0x01), the Cache Manager will ignore the FSD request to disallow delayed operations and perform lazy-write I/O for the file stream.

IsFastIoPossible

For efficiency reasons, the I/O Manager attempts to bypass the file system driver or network redirector for cached files and tries to obtain file data directly from the Cache Manager. This process is called the fast I/O process. The `IsFastIoPossible` field allows the file system driver or network redirector to control whether fast I/O operations should be allowed to proceed for the specific file stream. The contents of this field are set by the file system driver or network redirector and can be one of the following three enumerated types: `FastIoIsNotPossible`, `FastIoIsPossible`, or `FastIoIsQuestionable`.

Resource and PagingIoResource

Access to data associated with a file stream must be synchronized using these `ERESOURCE` structures.[*]

This is a requirement for file system drivers and network redirectors in order to be able to interface correctly with the Cache Manager and Memory Manager components.

Memory for both resources must be allocated by the file system or network redirector from nonpaged pool, and the fields in the `CommonFCBHeader` must be initialized to point to the allocated structures. These structures must also have been initialized by the FSD via the `ExInitializeResourceLite()` executive support routine.

Since these resources provide shared reader and exclusive writer semantics, the Cache Manager expects the file system driver or network redirector to synchronize all modifying operations for the file stream by obtaining the `MainResource` exclusively. Similarly, read operations can be synchronized by obtaining the `MainResource` shared.

AllocationSize

This is the actual amount of on-disk storage space allocated for the file stream. Typically, this is a multiple of the media sector size or file system cluster size.[†] This field must be initialized by the file system driver or network redirector to the appropriate value. Subsequently, the Cache Manager must be notified each time this value changes. In the next chapter, you will see how the file system driver notifies the Cache Manager of changes in the allocation size.

---

[*] See Chapter 3, *Structured Driver Development*, for a discussion on various synchronization structures available under Windows NT including a discussion on ERESOURCE type structures.

[†] Space is allocated on secondary storage devices in units called sectors. Each sector is composed of a fixed number of bytes—for example, one sector may equal 512 bytes. To avoid fragmentation, some file system drivers allocate storage space using clusters as units, where each cluster is some number of sectors. For example, one cluster may equal 8 physical sectors.

`FileSize`

>This is the size of the file as presented to the user; this value indicates the number of bytes contained within the file stream. Any read operations beyond this value will result in an end-of-file (`STATUS_END_OF_FILE`) error message being returned to the application process. Any read operations that overlap this value will be truncated at this value.

>For example, if the `FileSize` is 45 bytes and the reader wishes to obtain (say) 30 bytes beginning at offset 40 in the file stream, only 5 bytes will actually be returned to the reader by the file system driver (or the Cache Manager). However, if the same reader wishes to read 30 bytes beginning at offset 45 (assuming that offsets are counted beginning at offset 0), an error `STATUS_END_OF_FILE` will be returned to the reader.

>The file system driver or network redirector initializes this field to an appropriate value and informs the Cache Manager whenever this value changes.

`ValidDataLength`

>Consider a situation where the `FileSize` for a file stream is 100 bytes. However, only the first 10 bytes of the file stream have valid data and the last 90 bytes were never written to by any process. The `ValidDataLength` for this file stream is then set to 10. Any read operations that attempt to access bytes beyond this range will automatically get zeroes returned to them. This helps avoid unnecessary I/O operations from disk and also helps provide data security (since older information stored on the media from some previous file stream is not inadvertently returned to the user).

>Few file systems maintain the concept of a `ValidDataLength` stored on disk associated with a file stream. The NTFS and the HPFS file system drivers supplied with the NT operating system do support this concept. However, regardless of whether the file system driver supports the valid data length concept, the Cache Manager expects the file system driver or network redirector to initialize this field to an appropriate value.

SectionObjectPointer

This field has to be initialized to point to a structure of type `SECTION_OBJECT_POINTERS`.* This structure must be allocated from nonpaged kernel memory by the file system driver or network redirector and is shared by the Virtual Memory Manager and the Cache Manager. It stores file-mapping and caching-related information for a file stream. This structure has the following format:

```
typedef struct _SECTION_OBJECT_POINTERS {
```

---

* This structure is also required by the Virtual Memory Manager to provide support for memory-mapped files. See Chapter 5 for details on memory mapped files.

```
    PVOID        DataSectionObject;
    PVOID        SharedCacheMap;
    PVOID        ImageSectionObject;
} SECTION_OBJECT_POINTERS;
typedef SECTION_OBJECT_POINTERS *PSECTION_OBJECT_POINTERS;
```

Only one structure of this type can be associated with a given file stream at any time. However, it is entirely possible, and very probable in the case of user-opened files, that multiple file objects, each representing an open instance of a given file stream, can exist simultaneously on the node. In this case, all of the `SectionObjectPointer` fields in each file object structure must be initialized with the address of the single allocated structure of this type. Therefore, this structure is typically associated with the FCB for the file stream.

Upon allocation, it is the responsibility of the client of the Cache Manager to clear all fields within the `SECTION_OBJECT_POINTERS` data structure. After clearing the structure, the client does **not** need to be concerned anymore with the manipulation of any of the fields. An explanation of fields contained in this structure follows (remember that only the VMM or Cache Manager can manipulate these fields):

DataSectionObject

This pointer is used by the Virtual Memory Manager to refer to an internal data structure representing a data section object created for the file stream. Therefore, this field is initialized by the Virtual Memory Manager when caching is initiated for the file stream.

SharedCacheMap

The Cache Manager creates private data structures called cache maps to keep track of the views mapped for the specific data stream. This field is initialized by the Cache Manager with the address of the `SharedCacheMap` structure (described later in this section) when caching is initiated for the file stream.

ImageSectionObject

The Virtual Memory Manager initializes this field with the address of a private data structure whenever an image section is created for the file stream.

PrivateCacheMap

The client of the Cache Manager is expected to initialize this field to NULL for each file object structure. Note that multiple file object structures may exist concurrently in memory for a given file stream. It is also possible that caching may have been initiated by some, but not all, file object structures.

We know that file system drivers, network redirectors, and other clients of the Cache Manager work in cooperation with the Cache Manager to present a consistent view of the data to all users; this is done for those threads that access data using the cached path as well as for those who do not. The only way for a file system driver or network redirector to determine whether caching has been initiated using a specific file object for a given file stream is to examine whether the `PrivateCacheMap` field is nonnull. This check must only be performed after acquiring the `MainResource`, either shared or exclusively.

Information on whether caching has been initiated on a file stream via a specific file object cannot be maintained elsewhere by a client. This is because the Cache Manager retains the right to forcibly terminate caching via some or all file objects associated with the file stream. Therefore, as mentioned earlier, the fact that the `PrivateCacheMap` field is nonnull is the only reliable indicator for the client that caching is currently initiated via the file object structure being examined.

Cache Maps

The Cache Manager must maintain information about each file stream for which it helps to cache data. This information is maintained using *Cache Maps*. For each file stream, the Cache Manager allocates a *Shared Cache Map* structure that serves as the anchor for all information regarding views mapped for the file stream and other information associated with the file stream. This shared cache map structure is allocated when caching is first initiated for the file upon the request of a file system driver or a network redirector.

In addition to the shared cache map structure that is unique for each file stream and therefore allocated only when caching is first initiated for a file stream, each time a client issues a request to initiate caching using a specific file object structure, the Cache Manager allocates a *Private Cache Map* structure. This structure serves as a marker for the Cache Manager, establishing the fact that caching has been initiated using the specific file object. It also contains some private information for the Cache Manager for read-ahead control and other such data.

Note that both the private cache map structure and the shared cache map structure are allocated and maintained by the Cache Manager.

Buffer Control Blocks

One of the interfaces presented by the Cache Manager and mentioned previously is the pinning interface. Clients of the Cache Manager that use this interface must use the *Buffer Control Block* structure. This structure is divided into two parts: a *public BCB*, that is exposed to clients of the Cache Manager, and a *private BCB* that is internal to the Cache Manager.

The public BCB is defined as follows:

```
typedef struct _PUBLIC_BCB {
```

```
    CSHORT                  NodeTypeCode;
    CSHORT                  NodeByteSize;
    ULONG                   MappedLength;
    LARGE_INTEGER           MappedFileOffset;
} PUBLIC_BCB, *PPUBLIC_BCB;
```

The public BCB is extremely simple and serves as a context to the Cache Manager client—to be used in the pinning and subsequent unpinning of data. Upon return from a successful request to the Cache Manager by the file system driver or network redirector to pin data for a file stream, a pointer to the BCB structure is returned by the Cache Manager. Memory for this BCB structure is allocated by the Cache Manager.

The file system driver uses the pointer to the BCB structure in an opaque manner: the **MappedLength** and **MappedFileOffset** provide information to the client about the actual offset, beginning where the data has been pinned in memory and the number of bytes of data that were pinned.

Subsequent requests by the client to repin the memory structures or to unpin the memory must be performed using the BCB pointer as a context, which is returned to the Cache Manager. As will be explained in the next chapter, it's possible for the BCB returned by the Cache Manager to change across different Cache Manager invocations when the BCB is passed in as context. Therefore, the client must not attempt to make and use a copy of the returned BCB structure. The private portion of the BCB is not exposed by the Cache Manager.

File Size Considerations

There are three different file size values:

- The **AllocationSize** for a file stream is a value that reflects the actual on-disk space reserved for the file stream, which is a multiple of the minimum allocation unit for the media on which the file stream resides.

- The **FileSize** for a file stream is the value beyond which all read operations return an end-of-file error.[*]

- The **ValidDataLength** is the amount of valid data contained within a file stream.

  Any bytes accessed beyond this value (up to the **FileSize**) contain invalid data and should result in zeroes being returned to the application trying to read this information.

---

[*] Note that it is entirely possible that, for certain file system implementations, the **FileSize** may be greater than the **AllocationSize**. This happens when the file system driver supports sparse file implementations. None of the file systems supplied with Windows NT currently support sparse files.

There are two important considerations for Cache Manager clients who change one or more of these file sizes.

One cardinal rule all clients must follow is that changing the `AllocationSize` or the `FileSize` must be synchronized with other read/write requests and that the Cache Manager must be immediately informed of any changes.

Synchronizing changes in the `FileSize` with other read/write requests is accomplished by ensuring that the FCB for the file stream has been acquired exclusively while performing such a change. Both the `MainResource` as well as the `PagingIo-Resource` must be acquired exclusively before changing either of the file size values. The `CcSetFileSizes()` routine, which is invoked with the FCB for the file acquired will inform the Cache Manager.

The rationale behind the above rule is simple: the file system driver (or network redirector) is often bypassed by the I/O Manager, which tries to transfer data to or from a file stream directly, using the Cache Manager via the fast I/O path. In such cases, if the Cache Manager is not correctly notified of `FileSize` changes, invalid results may be returned to the application trying to perform the data transfer.* For example, if the current file size is extended by an application but the Cache Manager is not informed of the new file size, it is quite possible that the application will receive a `STATUS_END_OF_FILE` error when trying to read information from beyond the old end-of-file offset. This is incorrect and could result in data corruption.

A second important point to note is that changes in the `FileSize` are generally not synchronized with paging I/O read or write requests. Note that paging I/O requests generally originate either from the lazy writer or modified block writer components, or are a result of direct user read/write operations on mapped files. While paging I/O requests are dealt with in greater detail in Chapters 9-11, the reader should be cognizant of the following:

*   Paging I/O read requests starting beyond end-of-file are completed with a `STATUS_END_OF_FILE` error.

*   Paging I/O read requests that start before the current end-of-file but extend beyond current end-of-file are truncated to the current end-of-file byte offset. However, the client must be careful to set the number of bytes written to be the same as the number of bytes initially requested (although no I/O was actually performed).

---

* In certain cases, when the file is being truncated, the Cache Manager or the Memory Manager may refuse to allow the operation to proceed. This topic will be dealt with in greater detail in Chapter 10, *Writing A File System Driver II*. However, it is important to note that the file system driver or network redirector must coordinate changes in the file size for a file stream with the Cache Manager module.

- Paging I/O write requests that start beyond the current end-of-file must be voided by the file system driver or network redirector and `STATUS_SUCCESS` should be returned.

The `ValidDataLength` concept is supported by few file system drivers on disk. If the file system driver supports and records the `ValidDataLength` value on disk, it should initialize the `CommonFCBHeader` with the current value when the file stream is first opened. Subsequently, the Cache Manager will inform the file system driver when this value changes and the file system driver or network redirector can then record the modified value on disk. Note that the Cache Manager may have been invoked directly by the I/O Manager to service a user write request that could have resulted in a change in the valid data length.

The Cache Manager informs the client of the change in the valid data length via the `SetFileInformation` IRP. This IRP and the method used by the Cache Manager to notify the client will be discussed in greater detail in Chapter 10.

If the client does not support the concept of a valid data length on disk and therefore does not wish to receive notification from the Cache Manager about changes in this value, the client must initialize the `ValidDataLength` field as follows: the low 32 bits of the valid data length must be initialized to 0xFFFFFFFF and the high 32 bits of the field must be initialized to 0x7FFFFFFF.

Even if the client does not record the valid data length on disk, it might still be useful to the client to maintain the valid data length while the file stream stays open. Consider the situation where a user process extends the file length. Subsequently, the user process issues a write request beyond the old end-of-file byte offset. This request will be directed to the Cache Manager, which will first try to fault the page in while trying to get a page ready to receive the user data. This page fault will eventually need to be serviced by the file system driver or network redirector. If the file system driver maintains the concept of the valid data length in-memory, it could recognize that no read operation was required since the file stream had just been extended and zeroes can be returned immediately to complete the page fault request.

7

In this chapter:
- *Cache Manager
  Structures*
- *Interaction with
  Clients (File Systems
  and Network
  Redirectors)*
- *Cache Manager
  Interfaces*

The NT Cache Manager II

In the previous chapter, you were introduced to the NT Cache Manager module, which provides a global cache for file streams, along with read-ahead and delayed-write functionality. As was noted in that chapter, the Cache Manager cannot provide such functionality by itself, but must work in conjunction with the Virtual Memory Manager, the I/O Manager, and each file system or network redirector driver to boost throughput and increase system performance.

In this chapter, as well as in the next one, the interfaces presented by the Cache Manager are examined in much greater detail. First I present an overview of Cache Manager data structures used internally by the Cache Manager to maintain state information for cached file streams. You were exposed to some of these structures in the previous chapter; in this chapter, you will see how the Cache Manager tries to maintain a consistent in-memory representation of all information associated with the cached file streams.

Then I describe further the interactions between the Cache Manager and its clients, specifically file system drivers and network redirectors. This includes an introduction to the resource acquisition constraints that must be followed by the Cache Manager as well as by the client, followed by a detailed examination of the steps involved in initiating caching for file streams; code examples are used to make the material more concrete and applicable in real-world development environments.

Although the routines exported by the Cache Manager are the primary means of interaction between the Cache Manager and the file system drivers, there are also callback routines exported by Cache Manager clients, which are in turn invoked by the Cache Manager. I present some information on these routines in this chapter. Further discussion on callbacks exported by file system drivers will also be presented in Chapter 11, *Writing a File System Driver III*.

A detailed listing (with descriptions and examples) of the copy interface, the pinning interface, and the MDL interface concludes the chapter.

Cache Manager Structures

The Cache Manager maintains information for each file stream on which caching has been initiated. Before examining the interactions between the Cache Manager and other system components, it will be useful to understand some of the data structures used internally by the Cache Manager to maintain the required state information for cached file streams. Very little information is currently publicly available on the data structures used by the Cache Manager, and it is also likely that these data structures will continue to change and evolve in new releases of the Windows NT operating system. However, it is quite instructive to get an overall sense of the manner in which the Cache Manager keeps track of cached file streams.

The I/O Manager creates a file object structure for every successful open operation on a file stream. For every file object on which caching has been initiated, the Cache Manager maintains caching-related state information:

- A private cache map structure for each file object

- The shared cache map structure, which is shared by all file objects representing the same file stream

The private cache map structure is allocated by the Cache Manager for each file object when caching is initiated using that file object. It is unique to the file object, and therefore multiple private cache maps can exist concurrently for an open file stream. On the other hand, only one shared cache map structure is allocated by the Cache Manager when caching is first initiated for a file stream via some file object. This shared cache map is used by all open instances for the file stream. The shared cache map is accessible indirectly via the `SectionObject-Pointer` field in the file object structure.

Recall from the previous chapter that the Cache Manager provides caching services by mapping views of the file stream. Each mapped view of the file is represented internally by the Cache Manager in a structure called the *Virtual Address Control Block* (*VACB*). The mapping granularity—or the size of each mapped view for every file stream—is set to a constant value by the Cache Manager and therefore is the same for each VACB. This constant value determines how large the Cache Manager makes each *window* into the file stream. The Cache Manager maintains a global array of VACB structures and allocates VACBs to a specific file stream on an as-needed basis.

The shared cache map structure is the primary repository of caching information for a file stream and is maintained by the Cache Manager.

All VACBs associated with the same file stream are accessible to the Cache Manager using the shared cache map structure. Each VACB contains the virtual address associated with the view, as well as the starting offset in the file stream. This allows the Cache Manager to quickly determine whether a mapped view already exists containing the byte range requested by the user. If no such view exists, the Cache Manager can create a new view and allocate a VACB to represent it.* The list of VACBs associated with the file stream is accessible using an array of VACB pointers associated with the shared cache map. Since VACB structures are allocated from a fixed-size global pool of VACBs, it is possible that the Cache Manager may not have any free VACBs to allocate to a file stream when a view needs to be created. In this case, the Cache Manager may need to unmap a previously mapped view for a file stream (this could be from the same file stream that requires a new view to be mapped in or it could be from another file stream), remove the VACB from the linked list of VACBs allocated for the file stream, and then reassign the VACB to the new file stream. However, this operation is typically not required, since VACBs are freed whenever file close operations are performed, and a free VACB is generally available whenever required.

As shown in Figure 7-1, all private cache map structures for a cached file stream are linked together, and this list of private cache maps is anchored by a field in the shared cache map structure for the cached file stream.

This layout also allows the Cache Manager to keep track of all file objects that have the file stream cached, since the private cache map structure is always associated with a corresponding file object that represents an instance of the file stream opened for cached data access. As will be explained later in this chapter, in some situations the Cache Manager might need to forcibly terminate caching previously initiated using different file objects for a specific file stream. The Cache Manager must be able to get to each file object that has the file stream cached.

Now that you have some understanding of the structures used internally by the Cache Manager, we can examine the various routines exported by the Cache Manager and the interactions between the Cache Manager and file system drivers or network redirectors.

---

* Note that a byte range accessed by a user application may be quite large and may span multiple VACBs (since the size of the view associated with a VACB is a constant). However, the Cache Manager can still quickly determine what portions of the requested byte range are already contained in a mapped view of the file (if any such view exists) and what subset needs to be mapped in.

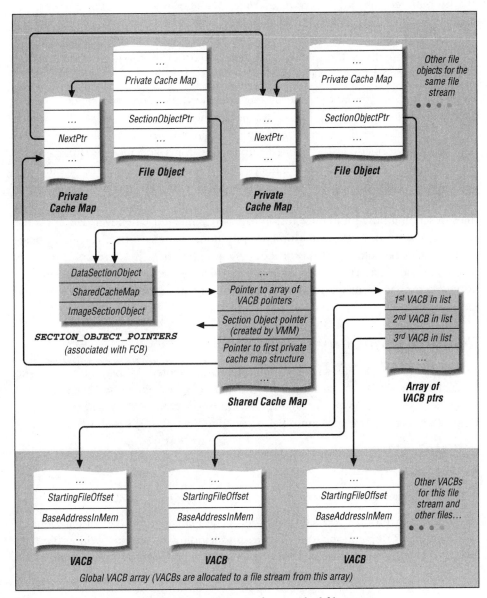

Figure 7-1. State maintained by Cache Manager for a cached file stream

Interaction with Clients (File Systems and Network Redirectors)

File system and network redirector drivers interact heavily with the Cache Manager; they must initiate caching for every file object for each file stream that can be buffered, use an appropriate Cache Manager interface routine to transfer data to and from the system cache, service page fault requests from the Virtual Memory Manager (caused by the Cache Manager), flush or purge data belonging to a file stream from the cache, and finally, terminate caching when the file stream is no longer being accessed.

To perform these operations, file system and network redirector clients use the interface routines made available by the Cache Manager. Nearly all interface routines available to file system or network redirector drivers result in an operation being performed on the cached information for a specific file stream. Since many threads could concurrently attempt to manipulate data for a file stream, any file system using Cache Manager services must correctly synchronize all such concurrent operations. Synchronization is maintained by following well-defined rules describing how mutual exclusion can be maintained whenever data for a file stream is modified. At the same time, applications that share data for read operations should be allowed to proceed concurrently only if no other thread is modifying the data. Therefore, many Cache Manager interface routines can also be invoked concurrently on behalf of multiple threads reading data for the same file stream.

Resource Acquisition

As you know, each file stream is uniquely represented in memory by a File Control Block (FCB) structure. In the previous chapter, you saw that each FCB must be associated with a unique structure of type `FSRTL_COMMON_FCB_HEADER`. There are two important fields contained within this structure:

- `MainResource`
- `PagingIoResource`

Both of these fields contain pointers to objects of type `ERESOURCE`.

In order to synchronize correctly with the Cache Manager and the Virtual Memory Manager, all I/O operations to a file stream, including reading or writing file data or file size changes, must be synchronized using one or both of these resources.*

---

* For some third-party file system or network driver implementations, there may be additional synchronization primitives associated with a file stream that may need to be acquired. Although the NT environment does not prohibit the existence of such additional primitives, these should be acquired (and released) in some manner compatible with the requirements placed by the Cache Manager on the two `ERESOURCE` type objects. For example, some file systems might have a third resource that may have to be acquired exclusively to provide mutual exclusion between threads when the file stream is being modified. In this case, this third resource would have to be acquired in addition to the predefined resources (i.e., the `MainResource` and/or the `PagingIoResource`) mentioned here.

NOTE   In any multithreaded or multiprocessor environment, shared objects that are accessed in the context of more than one thread or process must be protected using a synchronization primitive. This ensures that the state of the shared object does not change unexpectedly in the midst of an operation involving the object.

Synchronization primitives of type `ERESOURCE` (as described in Chapter 3, *Structured Driver Development*) are read/write locks that help provide multiple reader, single modifier semantics. By acquiring the synchronization primitive exclusively, a thread is able to ensure that no other thread can concurrently access the shared data object. On the other hand, by acquiring the synchronization primitive shared, multiple threads can concurrently read the data comprising the shared object, but no thread can acquire the synchronization primitive exclusively and modify the shared object.

Since starvation is a possibility for threads requiring exclusive access, the NT operating system typically grants waiting requests for exclusive access over requests for shared access.

A final note: in order to ensure data integrity and consistency, all threads accessing the shared data object must follow the resource acquisition rules described here. None of the synchronization is automatic and failure to observe the rules by any single thread could potentially lead to data corruption. Therefore, it is the file system driver's responsibility to ensure that resources are acquired correctly in the context of the thread requesting the cached I/O operation.

For each interface routine exported by the Cache Manager, there are well-defined options describing how the file stream should be acquired:

- Resources for the file stream should be acquired exclusively.

- Resources should be acquired shared.

- Resources should not be acquired (or should be *unowned*).

- The Cache Manager is not affected by the state of the resources.

Although the Cache Manager requires that synchronization be performed using the two resources associated with the FCB, there are not any clear, specific rules governing how these resources should actually be used to provide the required synchronization. For example, acquiring an FCB representing a file stream exclusively may consist of one of the following actions:

- Acquire the `MainResource` exclusively

- Acquire the `PagingIoResource` exclusively

- Acquire both the `MainResource` and the `PagingIoResource` exclusively

In this case, to prevent deadlock, a locking hierarchy must be defined between the two resources. Typically, most file systems define a hierarchy in which the `MainResource` must be acquired before the `PagingIoResource` is acquired.

Similarly, acquiring an FCB for shared access might be implemented by the Cache Manager client as acquiring any one or both of the resources shared. A determination of the exact usage of these resources is made by each file system or network redirector, based on the requirements of the particular driver.

Typically, the `PagingIoResource` is acquired only while servicing paging read operations or during delayed write (paging I/O write) operations. For example, if the file system driver read routine is invoked to service a page fault request, the FCB for the file stream is acquired shared, by acquiring the `PagingIoResource` shared. The `MainResource`, on the other hand, is typically used by the Cache Manager client to service requests that execute in the context of user threads (or as a result of direct user requests). For example, a write request executing in the context of the originating user thread is synchronized by acquiring the `MainResource` for the file exclusively.

NOTE   Each FSD has unique requirements that influence when and how resources should be acquired to ensure correct synchronization of FSD data structures. In general, however, the Windows NT environment appears to favor usage of the `PagingIoResource` to synchronize most modifications to file state (e.g., file size changes) while the `MainResource` appears to be used mostly to synchronize user-initiated I/O requests with each other.

Sometimes, the Cache Manager client may acquire both resources before performing an action of the file stream. For example, truncation of a file stream is performed only after both the `MainResource` and the `PagingIoResource` have been exclusively obtained. This prevents any unwanted side effects from taking place, since file size changes are typically not otherwise synchronized with background delayed-write or read-ahead activity that might be in progress. As mentioned previously, whenever both resources need to be acquired simultaneously, a well-defined locking hierarchy should dictate the order in which the two resources are acquired. For the remainder of this book, we will define the hierarchy such that the `MainResource` is acquired before the `PagingIoResource`.

In Part 3, the rules governing resource acquisition for file streams will be discussed in greater detail.

Prerequisites to Initiation of Caching

Now that you have a fair idea of how caching is provided by the Cache Manager, it is time to begin exploring the sequence of steps undertaken by Cache Manager clients to interact with the Cache Manager and provide higher performance to user applications. The previous chapter lists the various kinds of modules that interact with the Cache Manager; the two specific clients that use Cache Manager services directly are file systems and network redirector drivers.

Fundamentally, both disk-based file systems and network redirectors provide similar functionality to user applications, namely, access to data streams stored as files on media. The difference is that network redirectors obtain data from servers residing on other nodes across the network, while local file systems simply use the services of disk drivers to obtain data from media directly attached to the node on which the request was initiated. For the remainder of this chapter, we will not differentiate between the two kinds of modules, except where absolutely necessary, and will refer to both types of drivers generically as file system drivers.

At driver initialization: fast I/O support

Typically, I/O requests for a file are conveyed by the I/O Manager to the file system driver using I/O Request Packets (IRPs). However, the overhead associated with the creation, completion, and destruction of IRPs is sometimes an inhibitor of good performance. Also, if data is cached by the Cache Manager, it is possible that such data could be directly obtained from the system cache by directly issuing a request to the Cache Manager instead of going through the file system driver. Since the Cache Manager can then directly access data within the system cache, such access is as fast as a single hardware lookup (using the *Translation Lookaside Buffer* to convert the virtual address into a physical memory address), which is extremely efficient. The desire to achieve better system performance by taking into consideration the factors mentioned here led to the creation of the fast I/O method for obtaining cached file data in the Windows NT environment.*

Fast I/O is only performed if the file stream is cached and it is always a synchronous operation. An interesting point to note is that if data transfer is not possible using the fast I/O path for a specific operation on a file stream, the I/O Manager simply resorts to using the standard IRP method to retry the operation. This is no

---

* It could legitimately be argued that the entire fast I/O interface was a last minute hack or addition to the I/O subsystem in response to some serious performance problems encountered during testing by the Windows NT development group. Whether this is true is difficult to say, unless confirmed or denied by engineers at Microsoft. However, the fast I/O interface seems to have measurably enhanced throughput in the I/O path, and will continue to exist for the foreseeable future unless some major revamping of the Cache Manager module is undertaken by Microsoft.

worse than the original method of always creating an IRP to communicate with
the file system driver to service a user request. Figure 7-2 illustrates the flow of
execution when fast I/O is used to satisfy user requests.

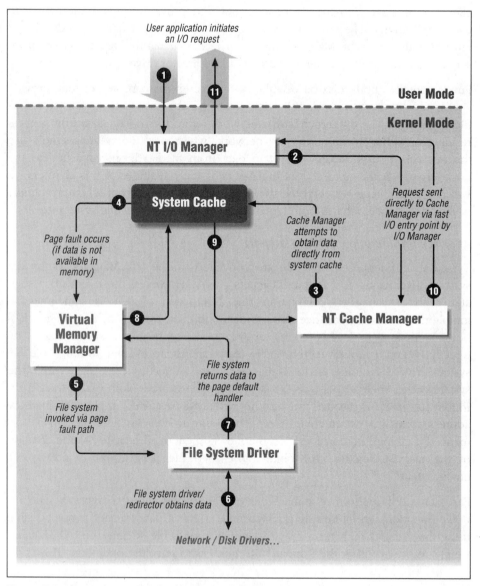

Figure 7-2. I/O requests using the fast I/O path

In Figure 7-2, the following steps are performed:

1. The I/O Manager receives a user request to read or write data for a specific file object. The file object represents an open instance for a file stream.

2. The I/O Manager invokes the fast I/O read or write entry point, which causes the corresponding Cache Manager entry point to be invoked. Note that typically the Cache Manager copy interface is used to obtain the data.

3. The Cache Manager attempts to transfer data from or to the system cache. If data exists in the system cache and is present in memory, Step 9 is executed. Otherwise, execution continues with Step 4 below.

4. A page fault occurs, causing the memory manager page fault handler routine to be invoked.

5. The page fault handler routine calls into the file system driver entry point using an I/O Request Packet. Although the figure does not show this, the actual call into the file system driver entry point is via the I/O Manager `IoCallDriver()` routine.

6. The file system driver uses the services of disk and network drivers to transfer data.

7. The file system satisfies the page fault request and control returns to the page fault handler.

8. The page fault is satisfied and the Cache Manager data transfer operation is restarted.

9. The Cache Manager completes the data transfer.

10. The Cache Manager returns control back to the I/O Manager (via the fast I/O entry point).

11. The I/O Manager completes the user request synchronously.

As you might have noticed, data that is physically present in memory can be transferred extremely quickly to or from the user's buffer. However, if data is not already physically present in memory, a trip through the file system will eventually result as a consequence of the page fault that must be resolved. This is not conducive to quick response times and is typically not required, due to the read-ahead performed by the Cache Manager.

Providing support for fast I/O is not required from file system drivers, and file systems have the option of not supporting fast I/O or of disabling fast I/O support for certain file streams dynamically. However, the resulting performance degradation is evident, especially when data transfer rates are compared with file systems that do provide fast I/O support.

To provide fast I/O support, the file system driver must perform the following actions, generally at driver initialization time:

- Initialize a global/static structure of type **FAST_IO_DISPATCH**. This structure contains a list of pointers that must be initialized to functions implementing each of the fast I/O entry points.

- Initialize a pointer within the **DRIVER_OBJECT** structure to refer to the fast I/O dispatch table described above.

There are specific operations that can be executed using the fast I/O method. The list of possible operations differs between the various NT versions. Specifically, Windows NT Version 4.0 supports more operations using the fast I/O method than Windows NT Version 3.51. Further information on the implementation of fast I/O support is given in Part 3.

The following code fragment illustrates the two steps described above:*

```
// Declare a static global fast I/O structure that contains function
// pointers. The fast I/O structure here is contained within a global
// data structure type declaration.
typedef struct _SFsdData {
    SFsdIdentifier              NodeIdentifier;

    // Other fields that you will read about in subsequent chapters.
    //  ....

    // The NT Cache Manager, the I/O Manager, and this code will
    // conspire to bypass IRP usage using the function pointers
    // contained in the following structure
    FAST_IO_DISPATCH            SFsdFastIoDispatch;

    // Still more fields ...
} SFsdData, *PtrSFsdData;

// Declare all the functions that we will implement to support the
// fast I/O path. In this example, only read and write operations are
// supported via the fast I/O method.
extern BOOLEAN SFsdFastIoCheckIfPossible (
    IN FILE_OBJECT              *FileObject,
    IN PLARGE_INTEGER           FileOffset,
    IN ULONG                    Length,
    IN BOOLEAN                  Wait,
    IN ULONG                    LockKey,
    IN BOOLEAN                  CheckForReadOperation,
    OUT PIO_STATUS_BLOCK        IoStatus,
    IN DEVICE_OBJECT            *DeviceObject
    );
extern BOOLEAN SFsdFastIoRead (
```

---

* All of the routines are prefixed with *SFsd* to conform to the convention used by the sample file system driver code provided in Part 3.

```
    IN FILE_OBJECT              *FileObject,
    IN PLARGE_INTEGER           FileOffset,
    IN ULONG                    Length,
    IN BOOLEAN                  Wait,
    IN ULONG                    LockKey,
    OUT PVOID                   Buffer,
    OUT PIO_STATUS_BLOCK        IoStatus,
    IN DEVICE_OBJECT            *DeviceObject
);
extern BOOLEAN SFsdFastIoWrite (
    IN FILE_OBJECT              *FileObject,
    IN PLARGE_INTEGER           FileOffset,
    IN ULONG                    Length,
    IN BOOLEAN                  Wait,
    IN ULONG                    LockKey,
    IN PVOID                    Buffer,
    OUT PIO_STATUS_BLOCK        IoStatus,
    IN DEVICE_OBJECT            *DeviceObject
);


// Driver Entry routine - this is where all of the initialization takes
// place.
NTSTATUS SFsdDriverEntry(
IN PDRIVER_OBJECT DriverObject,  // created by the I/O subsystem
IN PUNICODE_STRING RegistryPath) // path to registry key for the driver
{
    // Initialize the global data structure. Note that we will
    // end up zeroing out the fast I/O dispatch structure as well.
    // This will save us setting individual fields to NULL.
    RtlZeroMemory(&SFsdGlobalData, sizeof(SFsdGlobalData));

    // Other initialization operations ...

    // Initialize the IRP major function table, and the fast I/O table.
    SFsdInitializeFunctionPointers(DriverObject);

    // Still more initialization stuff ...
}


void SFsdInitializeFunctionPointers(
PDRIVER_OBJECT        DriverObject)        /* created by the I/O sub-
system */
{
    PFAST_IO_DISPATCH     PtrFastIoDispatch = NULL;

    // Initialize dispatch function table here. See Part 3
    // and accompanying disk for details.

    // Now, it is time to initialize the fast I/O stuff ...
    // Note that I am initializing the "FastIoDispatch" field in
    // the DriverObject below.
    PtrFastIoDispatch = DriverObject->FastIoDispatch =
        &(SFsdGlobalData.SFsdFastIoDispatch);
```

```
        // Initialize the global fast I/O structure
        // NOTE: The fast I/O structure has undergone a substantial
        // revision in Windows NT Version 4.0. The structure has been
        // extensively expanded.
        // Therefore, if your driver needs to work on both V3.51 and V4.0+,
        // you will have to be able to distinguish between the two versions
        // at compile time.
        PtrFastIoDispatch->SizeOfFastIoDispatch = sizeof(FAST_IO_DISPATCH);
        PtrFastIoDispatch->FastIoCheckIfPossible =
                                            SFsdFastIoCheckIfPossible;
        PtrFastIoDispatch->FastIoRead          = SFsdFastIoRead;
        PtrFastIoDispatch->FastIoWrite         = SFsdFastIoWrite;

        // See Part 3 for other initialization steps performed here.
}
```

In this example, the test driver only supports read and write operations using the fast I/O method. Therefore, other fields in the **FAST_IO_DISPATCH** data structure are initialized to NULL. An explanation for the SFsd**FastIoCheckIfPossible()** routine, as well as other information on the implementation of the fast I/O routines is provided in Part 3.

File open

In Windows NT, to access data for a file stream, the file stream must first be opened. The open* operation performed by an application returns a handle to the application. This handle is used by the application when reading or writing to the file stream and corresponds to a file object structure, created by the I/O Manager, representing an instance of a successful open operation.

From the perspective of the file system driver servicing the open request, a considerable amount of work is performed at file open time to support access to the file stream. The file system constructs all in-memory data structures required to support I/O operations to the file stream, including the construction of any data structures that might be required to support buffered access to file data. The file system driver must also fill in specific fields in the file object structure; these fields were described in the previous chapter.

The file system driver allocates and initializes a file control block (FCB) structure, which is a unique representation of the file stream in memory. This is done only if no such structure currently exists; as it would if the file stream had been previously opened and at least one reference to the FCB were still present. If a new

---

* Open operations requesting access to previously created file streams and close operations that create new file streams result in the same IRP being dispatched to a file system by the I/O Manager, with a major function of *IRP_MJ_CREATE*. Effectively, a create operation is simply a two-step process, where an entry representing the new file is first created, and subsequently opened. We will refer to both create and open operations together as requests to open a file stream.

file control block is created, most file system drivers also allocate memory for a structure of type FSRTL_COMMON_FCB_HEADER (see the previous chapter for an explanation of the various fields in the CommonFCBHeader structure). Often, this structure, which is required by the Cache Manager to be able to cache file data, is embedded by file system drivers within the file control block representing the file stream.

Note that even if the current open operation specifies noncached access to file data, the file system driver will still end up allocating the FSRTL_COMMON_FCB_ HEADER along with the FCB for the file, since subsequent concurrent open operations might require cached file access. Initialization of the individual fields within the structure is performed by the file system at this time as follows:

- The FSD initializes the two ERESOURCE type objects, allocated as part of the CommonFCBHeader from the nonpaged memory pool, with the ExInitializeResourceLite() system call.

  The two resource object fields are the MainResource and the PagingIoResource.

- The enumerated type field IsFastIoPossible is initialized to an appropriate value.

  Typically, FSDs set this to FastIoIsPossible. By doing so, the I/O Manager is encouraged to begin using the fast I/O method for accessing data for the file stream at the very earliest—typically, as soon as caching is initiated for the file.*

- Each of the file size fields—the AllocationSize, ValidDataLength, and FileSize—is initialized to their true values.

  If the file stream has been created as a result of the create operation, then the file size fields will all be initialized to 0. Otherwise, for an existing file stream or if the create operation requested preallocation of space for the file, the file size fields will be initialized to the correct values.

Once the CommonFCBHeader is allocated and initialized, the FsContext field in the file object is initialized to refer to the allocated CommonFCBHeader structure.

The PrivateCacheMap field in the file object structure is initialized by the file system driver to NULL.

Finally, the FSD must also allocate and initialize a structure of type SECTION_ OBJECT_POINTERS. A single (unique) instance of the structure is typically associ-

---

* Caching for the file stream is initiated when the FSD receives the first I/O request for the file stream. Therefore, the first I/O request for the file stream will always be described via an IRP by the I/O Manager.

ated with the FCB. Each of the fields within the structure is initialized to NULL. The `SectionObjectPointer` field in the file object structure is then initialized to refer to the allocated structure.

The following code extract from a file system driver implementation of a file open operation performs the operations described here (in the code extract, it's assumed that the `IRP_NOCACHE` flag has not been specified):

```
// There are some fields that must always be associated with an FCB
// to successfully interface with the Cache Manager. The sample FSD
// implementation has extracted these fields into a separate structure.
typedef struct _SFsdNTRequiredFCB {
    FSRTL_COMMON_FCB_HEADER         CommonFCBHeader;
    SECTION_OBJECT_POINTERS         SectionObject;
    ERESOURCE                       MainResource;
    ERESOURCE                       PagingIoResource;
} SFsdNTRequiredFCB, *PtrSFsdNTRequiredFCB;


// The actual FCB structure is defined by the sample FSD as shown below:
typedef struct _SFsdFileControlBlock {
    SFsdIdentifier                       NodeIdentifier;
    // We will go ahead and embed the "NT Required FCB" right here.
    //    Note that it is just as acceptable to simply allocate
    //    memory separately for the other half of the FCB and store a
    //    pointer to the "NT Required" portion here, instead of embedding
    //    it.
    SFsdNTRequiredFCB                    NTRequiredFCB;
    // Other fields go here. See subsequent chapters for details.
    // ...
    // Some state information for the FCB is maintained using the
    // Flags field
    uint32                               FCBFlags;
    // More fields here ...
} SFsdFCB, *PtrSFsdFCB;


// Some Flag definitions, see accompanying diskette for definitions
// of other flag values.
#define      SFSD_INITIALIZED_MAIN_RESOURCE        (0x00002000)
#define      SFSD_INITIALIZED_PAGING_IO_RESOURCE   (0x00004000)


// Our work is performed while servicing a create/open request.
// The parameters to the SFsdCommonCreate() function will be explained
// in Part 3.
NTSTATUS SFsdCommonCreate(
PtrSFsdIrpContext           PtrIrpContext,
PIRP                        PtrIrp)
{
    PtrSFsdFCB              PtrNewFCB = NULL;
    LARGE_INTEGER          FileAllocationSize, FileEndOfFile;
    PFILE_OBJECT           PtrNewFileObject = NULL;
    PtrSFsdVCB             PtrVCB = NULL;
    // Other declarations ...
```

```
    try {

        // As you will see in Chapter 9, a lot of information is obtained
        // from the IRP sent to the FSD for a create/open request.
        // The I/O-Manager-created file object structure pointer is also
        // obtained from the current I/O Stack Location in the FCB.
        PtrIoStackLocation = IoGetCurrentIrpStackLocation(PtrIrp);
        PtrNewFileObject   = PtrIoStackLocation->FileObject;

        // The Volume Control Block (VCB) pointer is obtained
        // from the target device object representing the mounted logical
        // volume.

        // ...

        // The create/open operation is fairly complex and is detailed in
        // Part 3. The FSD has to validate all arguments passed-in within
        // the IRP, and then traverse the path supplied within the IRP,
        // eventually leading to the file/directory/link that has to be
        // created/opened.

        // Assume that all the complicated processing has been done and
        // that we have decided to create a new FCB structure.
        // Note that a typical FSD gets the current file stream allocation-
        // size and EOF values from the directory entry for the file
        // stream (obtained from secondary storage).
        // In this example, we assume that this is the first instance of
        // an "open" operation for a specific file stream. Therefore, we
        // allocate the FCB structure for this file stream.
        RC = SFsdCreateNewFCB(&PtrNewFCB, &FileAllocationSize,
                                          &FileEndOfFile,
                                          PtrNewFileObject, PtrVCB);

        if (!NT_SUCCESS(RC)) {
            try_return(RC);
        }

    } finally {
        // All of the cleanup code is executed here.
        ...
    }

    return(RC);
}    // SFsdCommonCreate()

NTSTATUS SFsdCreateNewFCB(
PtrSFsdFCB                    *ReturnedFCB,
PLARGE_INTEGER                AllocationSize,
PLARGE_INTEGER                EndOfFile,
PFILE_OBJECT                  PtrFileObject,
PtrSFsdVCB                    PtrVCB)
{
    NTSTATUS                          RC = STATUS_SUCCESS;
    PtrSFsdFCB                        PtrFCB = NULL;
```

```
PtrSFsdNTRequiredFCB          PtrReqdFCB = NULL;
PFSRTL_COMMON_FCB_HEADER      PtrCommonFCBHeader = NULL;

try {
    // Obtain a new FCB structure.
    // The function SFsdAllocateFCB() will obtain a new structure
    // either from a zone or from memory requested directly from the
    // VMM.  Note that the sample FSD (described in greater detail in
    // Part 3 of this book) allocates the entire FCB from nonpaged pool
    // though you may choose to be "smarter" about your allocation
    // method and possibly break up the FCB into paged and nonpaged
    // portions.
    PtrFCB = SFsdAllocateFCB();
    if (!PtrFCB) {
        // Assume lack of memory.
        try_return(RC = STATUS_INSUFFICIENT_RESOURCES);
    }

    // Initialize fields required to interface with the NT Cache
    // Manager.  Note that the returned structure has already been
    // zeroed. This means that the SectionObject structure has been
    // zeroed, which is a requirement for newly created FCB structures.
    PtrReqdFCB = &(PtrFCB->NTRequiredFCB);

    // Initialize the MainResource and PagingIoResource structures now.
    ExInitializeResourceLite(&(PtrReqdFCB->MainResource));
    SFsdSetFlag(PtrFCB->FCBFlags, SFSD_INITIALIZED_MAIN_RESOURCE);

    ExInitializeResourceLite(&(PtrReqdFCB->PagingIoResource));
    SFsdSetFlag(PtrFCB->FCBFlags, SFSD_INITIALIZED_PAGING_IO_RESOURCE);

    // Start initializing the fields contained in the CommonFCBHeader.
    PtrCommonFCBHeader = &(PtrReqdFCB->CommonFCBHeader);

    // Allow fast I/O for now.
    PtrCommonFCBHeader->IsFastIoPossible = FastIoIsPossible;

    // Initialize the MainResource and PagingIoResource pointers in
    // the CommonFCBHeader structure to point to the ERESOURCE
    // structures we have allocated and already initialized above.
    PtrCommonFCBHeader->Resource = &(PtrReqdFCB->MainResource);
    PtrCommonFCBHeader->PagingIoResource =
                                &(PtrReqdFCB->PagingIoResource);

    // Ignore the Flags field in the CommonFCBHeader for now. Part 3
    // of the book describes it in greater detail.

    // Initialize the file size values here.
    PtrCommonFCBHeader->AllocationSize = *(AllocationSize);
    PtrCommonFCBHeader->FileSize = *(EndOfFile);

    // The following will disable ValidDataLength support. However,
    // your FSD may choose to support this concept.
    PtrCommonFCBHeader->ValidDataLength.LowPart  = 0xFFFFFFFF;
```

```
            PtrCommonFCBHeader->ValidDataLength.HighPart = 0x7FFFFFFF;

            // Initialize other fields for the FCB here.
            PtrFCB->PtrVCB = PtrVCB;
            InitializeListHead(&(PtrFCB->NextCCB));

            // Other similar initialization continues ...

            // Initialize fields contained in the file object now.
            PtrFileObject->PrivateCacheMap = NULL;
            // Note that we could have just as well taken the value of
            // PtrReqdFCB directly below. The bottom line, however, is that
            // the FsContext field must point to a FSRTL_COMMON_FCB_HEADER
            // structure.
            PtrFileObject->FsContext = (void *)(PtrCommonFCBHeader);

            // Other initialization continues here ...

        try_exit:     NOTHING;
    } finally {
        ;
    }

    return(RC);
}
```

Initiation of Caching

All file stream operations in NT require that the file stream first be opened. To avoid incurring unnecessary overhead, file system drivers do not initiate caching for a file stream until it can be determined that I/O (read/write of file data) will be performed on the file stream. Therefore, caching is typically initiated only when the first I/O operation (read/write) is received by the file system driver. Note that caching must be initiated for each file object on which I/O can be performed (only if buffered access is allowed by the user). To determine whether caching had been previously initiated for a specific file object, the **Private-CacheMap** field in the file object is checked as follows:

```
#define SFsdHasCachingBeenInitiated(PFileObject)     \
        ((PFileObject)->PrivateCacheMap ? TRUE : FALSE)
```

To initiate caching, the FSD uses the **CcInitializeCacheMap()** interface routine. This routine is defined as follows:

```
void CcInitializeCacheMap (
    IN PFILE_OBJECT               PtrFileObject;
    IN PCC_FILE_SIZES             FileSizes;
    IN BOOLEAN                    PinAccess;
    IN PCACHE_MANAGER_CALLBACKS   CallBacks;
    IN PVOID                      LazyWriterContext
);
```

where:

```
typedef struct _CC_FILE_SIZES {
    LARGE_INTEGER               AllocationSize;
    LARGE_INTEGER               FileSize;
    LARGE_INTEGER               ValidDataLength;
} CC_FILE_SIZES, *PCC_FILE_SIZES;

// The callbacks structure is defined as follows:
typedef struct _CACHE_MANAGER_CALLBACKS {
    PACQUIRE_FOR_LAZY_WRITE     AcquireForLazyWrite;
    PRELEASE_FROM_LAZY_WRITE    ReleaseFromLazyWrite;
    PACQUIRE_FOR_READ_AHEAD     AcquireForReadAhead;
    PRELEASE_FROM_READ_AHEAD    ReleaseFromReadAhead;
} CACHE_MANAGER_CALLBACKS, *PCACHE_MANAGER_CALLBACKS;
```

Resource Acquisition Constraints:

The above routine requires that the FCB for the file be acquired either shared or exclusive prior to invoking the routine.

Parameters:

PtrFileObject

This is the file object for which caching is being initiated.

FileSizes

The Cache Manager requires that the current file sizes be supplied at this time. Note that since the FCB for the file is acquired either shared or exclusively, none of the file size values can change while caching is being initiated for any file object associated with the file stream.*

PinAccess

The caller can specify if the pinning interface will be used to access data. Note that the pinning interface cannot be used concurrently with either the copy interface or the MDL interface to access data for the file stream. Typically, for user file open requests, you should set this to FALSE.

Callbacks

In the Windows NT environment, the file system, Virtual Memory Manager, and the Cache Manager are all highly dependent on each other. I/O operations can be initiated from the file system driver (on behalf of user processes), via the Virtual Memory Manager or from the Cache Manager. To avoid system

---

* It is highly recommended (in order to avoid data corruption) that the FCB for a file be acquired exclusively whenever there are any modifications resulting in changes to the data or attributes of the file stream. Therefore, if the FCB for the file stream has been acquired shared or exclusively while caching is being initiated, we can be certain that the file sizes will not change from underneath us.

deadlock, a well-defined hierarchy must set the order in which each of these components can acquire their respective resources associated with the file stream(s) on which I/O is being performed. This order is defined as follows:

— File system resources are acquired first.

— Cache Manager resources are acquired next.

— Virtual Memory Manager resources are acquired last.

To help maintain this hierarchy, the file system driver is required to supply the Cache Manager with callback routines that are utilized by the read-ahead and delayed-write threads in the Cache Manager. These callback routines are supplied when caching is initiated by the FSD using this argument. Further details on this topic will be presented in Part 3.

LazyWriterContext

This value is treated as an opaque pointer value by the Cache Manager. It is used as an argument supplied to the file system driver when the Cache Manager uses the `AcquireForLazyWrite()` and `AcquireForRead-Ahead()` callback routines. (The name of the argument is somewhat of a misnomer since the same context is used for both the read-ahead and write-behind callbacks; therefore it is not just the lazy writer context, but the read-ahead context as well.) Typically, the FSD will supply a pointer to a Context Control Block (CCB)* as the context.

Functionality Provided:

The `CcInitializeCacheMap()` routine is responsible for creating all data structures required for the Cache Manager to support caching for the concerned file stream. The first invocation of this routine results in the creation of the shared cache map structure for the file stream. It is extremely important to note that the Cache Manager also references the file object structure at this time to ensure that the file object stays around and that a corresponding uninitialize operation will occur sometime in the future. The Cache Manager also creates a file mapping (section) object for the file using the services of the Virtual Memory Manager. For all subsequent invocations of this routine for the same file stream (with different file object structures), the Cache Manager checks the current size of the mapping section object and extends it if required.

The Cache Manager also allocates a private cache map structure and initializes it. A pointer to the allocated `PrivateCacheMap` is stored in the `Private-CacheMap` field within the passed-in file object structure. Since the value of the

---

* The Context Control Block is a structure created by file system drivers to represent an open instance of a file stream. There is one CCB corresponding to each successful open operation; therefore there is a one-to-one mapping between file object structures created by the I/O Manager (representing a successful open operation on a file stream) and CCBs created by the file system driver. CCB structures are discussed in detail in Chapter 9, *Writing a File System Driver I*.

`PrivateCacheMap` field now becomes nonnull, subsequent I/O requests will check this field using the `SFsdHasCachingBeenInitiated()` macro, defined above, and determine that caching had been previously initiated for the file stream via the specific file object.

Note that the Cache Manager does not map in any views for the file stream at this time. These views into the file are created only when data transfer is requested using any of the three interfaces provided by the Cache Manager.

Since the initialization routine does not return any status back to the caller, the Cache Manager raises exceptions if something goes wrong while trying to perform the initialization for the file object. Exception handlers in the FSD should be capable of receiving such exceptions and returning an appropriate error back to the application that initiated the cached I/O operation.

WARNING   Using Structured Exception Handling is no longer optional if you write a file system driver that interacts with the Windows NT Cache Manager. I would advise that all kernel-mode drivers should incorporate SEH to ensure that system integrity and robustness is not compromised.

Example of Usage:

Caching is initiated by file system drivers when either a read or a write operation is invoked for a file stream. In this code snippet, caching is initiated when a read request is processed for a file stream.

```
// A pointer to a callbacks structure must be passed in to the Cache
// Manager when initializing caching for a file stream. Typically, file
// systems use a single global callbacks structure that has been
// initialized.
typedef struct _SFsdData {
    SFsdIdentifier              NodeIdentifier;
    // Some fields that will be discussed further in Part 3.
    ...
    // The NT Cache Manager uses the following callbacks to ensure
    // correct locking hierarchy is maintained.
    CACHE_MANAGER_CALLBACKS     CacheMgrCallBacks;

    // Some more fields that will also be discussed in Part 3.
    ...
} SFsdData, *PtrSFsdData;

// The arguments to the SFsdCommonRead() function (part of the sample FSD
// provided in this book) will be discussed in Part 3.
NTSTATUS    SFsdCommonRead(
PtrSFsdIrpContext                  PtrIrpContext,
PIRP                              PtrIrp)
```

```
{
    NTSTATUS                    RC = STATUS_SUCCESS;
    PFILE_OBJECT                PtrFileObject = NULL;
    PtrSFsdFCB                  PtrFCB = NULL;
    PtrSFsdCCB                  PtrCCB = NULL;
    PtrSFsdNTRequiredFCB        PtrReqdFCB = NULL;
    BOOLEAN                     NonBufferedIo = FALSE;
    LARGE_INTEGER               ByteOffset;
    uint32                      ReadLength = 0, TruncatedReadLength = 0;
    BOOLEAN                     CanWait = FALSE;
    void                        *PtrSystemBuffer = NULL;
    // Other declarations ...

    try {

        // As you will see in Chapter 9, a lot of information is obtained
        // from the IRP sent to the FSD for a read request.
        // The I/O-Manager-created file object structure pointer is also
        // obtained from the current I/O Stack Location in the FCB.
        PtrIoStackLocation = IoGetCurrentIrpStackLocation(PtrIrp);
        PtrFileObject      = PtrIoStackLocation->FileObject;

        // Get the FCB and CCB pointers.
        //     Typically the FsContext2 field in the file object refers to
        //     the Context Control Block associated with the file object.
        PtrCCB = (PtrSFsdCCB)(PtrFileObject->FsContext2);
        ASSERT(PtrCCB);
        PtrFCB = PtrCCB->PtrFCB;
        ASSERT(PtrFCB);

        // Other arguments are also obtained ...

        NonBufferedIo = ((PtrIrp->Flags & IRP_NOCACHE) ? TRUE : FALSE);
        ByteOffset    = PtrIoStackLocation->Parameters.Read.ByteOffset;
        ReadLength    = PtrIoStackLocation->Parameters.Read.Length;

        // Don't worry about how the following flag is set in the
        // PtrIrpContext structure at this time. Note, however, that
        // the CanWait value determines whether the caller is willing to
        // perform the operation synchronously (CanWait = TRUE), or if the
        // caller prefers asynchronous processing (CanWait = FALSE).
        CanWait = ((PtrIrpContext->IrpContextFlags &
                            SFSD_IRP_CONTEXT_CAN_BLOCK)
                                            ? TRUE : FALSE);

        PtrReqdFCB = &(PtrFCB->NTRequiredFCB);

        // A lot of preprocessing is typically performed that you will
        // read about later in this book.

        // Assume for now that this FSD does not have to worry about
        // paging I/O requests.

        // Try to acquire the FCB MainResource shared. Assume that the call
```

```
// cannot fail. Also assume that the caller does not mind blocking.
ExAcquireResourceSharedLite(&(PtrReqdFCB->MainResource), TRUE)

// More processing here that will be discussed later in Part 3 of
// this book.

// Branch here for cached vs. noncached I/O.
if (!NonBufferedIo) {

    // The caller wishes to perform cached I/O. Initiate caching if
    // this is the first cached I/O operation using this file
    // object
    if (!SFsdHasCachingBeenInitiated(PtrFileObject)) {
        // This is the first cached I/O operation. You must ensure
        // that the Common FCB Header contains valid sizes at this
        // time
        CcInitializeCacheMap(PtrFileObject, (PCC_FILE_SIZES)
                (&(PtrReqdFCB->CommonFCBHeader.AllocationSize)),
                    FALSE,      // We will not utilize pin access for
                                // this file
                    &(SFsdGlobalData.CacheMgrCallBacks), // callbacks
                    PtrCCB);        // The context used in callbacks
    }

    // Check and see if this request requires an MDL returned to
    // the caller.
    if (PtrIoStackLocation->MinorFunction & IRP_MN_MDL) {
        // Caller wants an MDL returned. Note that this mode
        // implies that the caller is prepared to block.
        // CcMdlRead() is discussed later in this chapter.
        CcMdlRead(PtrFileObject, &ByteOffset, TruncatedReadLength,
                    &(PtrIrp->MdlAddress),
                    &(PtrIrp->IoStatus));
        NumberBytesRead = PtrIrp->IoStatus.Information;
        RC = PtrIrp->IoStatus.Status;

        try_return(RC);
    }

    // This is a regular run-of-the-mill cached I/O request. Let
    // the Cache Manager worry about it.
    // First though, we need a buffer pointer (address) that is
    // valid.  More on this in Chapter 9.
    PtrSystemBuffer = SFsdGetCallersBuffer(PtrIrp);
    ASSERT(PtrSystemBuffer);
    if (!CcCopyRead(PtrFileObject, &(ByteOffset), ReadLength,
                CanWait, PtrSystemBuffer, &(PtrIrp->IoStatus))) {
        // The caller was not prepared to block and data is not
        // immediately available in the system cache.
        // Mark IRP Pending and prepare to post the request for
        // asynchronous processing. I am beginning to sound like a
        // broken record but more on this in Part 3 of the book.
        try_return(RC = STATUS_PENDING);
    }
```

```
        // We have the data
        RC = PtrIrp->IoStatus.Status;
        NumberBytesRead = PtrIrp->IoStatus.Information;

        try_return(RC);

    } else {
        // Noncached processing done here.
    }

    // Other processing ...

    try_exit:    NOTHING;

} finally {
    // A lot of processing done here before completing the IRP.
    ....
} // end of "finally" processing

return(RC);
}
```

Cache Manager Interfaces

Once caching has been initiated for a file stream using a file object, requests to read and write data are satisfied from the system cache. In the previous chapter, three interfaces provided by the Cache Manager to access cached data were listed. Each of the routines comprising the three interfaces is covered in this section.

TIP   You may find it useful simply to skim through the material present-
             ed below on your first reading and to refer back to it when required
             as you progress through Part 3 (describing FSD development) and
             also when you eventually design and debug your kernel-mode file
             system (or filter) driver.

Copy Interface

The copy interface is most commonly used by FSDs to access data within the system cache. The following routines comprise the copy interface.

CcCopyRead()/CcFastCopyRead()

```
BOOLEAN
CcCopyRead (
    IN PFILE_OBJECT          FileObject,
    IN PLARGE_INTEGER        FileOffset,
    IN ULONG                 Length,
```

```
        IN  BOOLEAN                  Wait,
        OUT PVOID                    Buffer,
        OUT PIO_STATUS_BLOCK         IoStatus
);


VOID
CcFastCopyRead (
        IN  PFILE_OBJECT             FileObject,
        IN  ULONG                    FileOffset,
        IN  ULONG                    Length,
        IN  ULONG                    PageCount,
        OUT PVOID                    Buffer,
        OUT PIO_STATUS_BLOCK         IoStatus
);
```

Resource Acquisition Constraints:

The FCB for the file must usually be acquired shared before invoking the routine. Acquiring the FCB exclusively will prevent multiple readers from being able to concurrently access file data and should therefore be avoided in the interest of efficiency.

Parameters:

FileObject

This is a pointer to the file object structure representing the open operation performed by the thread. Caching must have been previously initiated by the file system driver on this file object.

Note that if the file system driver has not initiated caching prior to invoking the CcCopyRead() or CcFastCopyRead() routines, an exception will be generated since the Cache Manager assumes that the private cache map and shared cache map structures exist and have been initialized correctly.

FileOffset

This is the starting offset in the file, from where the read operation should be performed.

For the CcCopyRead() routine, the starting offset can be anywhere within the allowable range of file offsets—a 64-bit quantity. However, the CcFast-CopyRead() expects the entire range being requested (starting offset + number of bytes) to be contained within 4GB (maximum range allowable for a 32 bit offset).

Length

This field specifies the number of bytes requested in the read operation.

Wait

This argument is only accepted by the CcCopyRead() routine. If the entire byte range requested is not present in the system cache (therefore, the data would have to read off media using the page fault mechanism), and if `Wait` is specified as FALSE, the `CcCopyRead()` routine returns a FALSE value to the caller. The caller can subsequently determine whether to restart the copy operation or to pursue some other course of action.

The `CcFastCopyRead()` routine assumes that the caller is prepared to wait for the data; i.e., the implied value of `Wait` is TRUE.

PageCount

This is the number of pages requested in the read operation. Argument is required only by the `CcFastCopyRead()` routine. The caller can use the `COMPUTE_PAGES_SPANNED()` macro supplied in the *ntddk.h* header file to determine the value to be passed in.

NOTE   It is surprising that the Cache Manager requires this argument, since computing the value could just as easily be done within the routine by the Cache Manager itself.

Buffer

This field contains a pointer to the buffer into which the copy operation should be performed is passed-in. If the buffer pointer becomes invalid (once the Cache Manager is invoked), an exception will be raised by the Cache Manager.

IoStatus

The Status field is generally set to `STATUS_SUCCESS` by the Cache Manager. The `Information` field contains the number of bytes that were actually transferred.

Functionality Provided:

Fundamentally, both the `CcCopyRead()` and the `CcFastCopyRead()` routines perform the same functionality: data is transferred from the system cache to the buffer passed in to either of the two routines. The Cache Manager also schedules *read-ahead* based upon the pattern of accesses detected during multiple invocations of either of these two routines.

The primary difference between the two routines is that the `CcFastCopy-Read()` routine assumes that the caller is always prepared to block, waiting for the data to be brought into the system cache if it is not already there. In the case of the `CcCopyRead()` routine, the caller is allowed to specify whether waiting for the data to be brought into the system cache is acceptable or not. If `Wait` is set to FALSE and file data is not already physically present in memory, the Cache Manager will simply return a status of FALSE to the caller. However, if data is already physically present in memory, or if `Wait` is supplied as TRUE, the Cache Manager will return as many bytes as it successfully reads, which can be less than or equal to the number of bytes requested (if the read extends beyond the end-of-file).

A second constraint for the `CcFastCopyRead()` routine is that it expects to work with byte ranges that are completely contained within a 32-bit quantity. Therefore, the `CcFastCopyRead()` routine will not accept a byte range with a starting offset greater than or equal to 4GB or an ending offset (= starting offset + length) greater than or equal to 4GB.

For both routines, the Cache Manager expects the file system to have checked that the byte range being requested does not extend beyond the end-of-file mark (based on the size of the file stream). Therefore, the only likely reason for the number of bytes in the `Information` field to be less than the number of bytes requested is if data was not present in the system cache and there was an error encountered faulting in the data from disk (or from across the network).

If the buffer pointer passed in to either routine is invalid, an exception is raised by the Cache Manager.

The implementation of both routines is conceptually very simple:

- The Cache Manager determines if a mapped view for the desired range exists. If no such view exists, the Cache Manager will create such a view.

- The Cache Manager checks to see if the requested data is already physically present in memory (using the services provided by the Virtual Memory Manager). If data is not already in memory and if `Wait` is supplied as FALSE (for the `CcCopyRead()` routine), the Cache Manager immediately returns to the caller with a return status of FALSE, indicating that data transfer was not performed. In the case of the `CcFastCopyRead()` routine, the Cache Manager expects that the caller is prepared to block, waiting for data to be brought into the system cache. If data is not already present, the Cache Manager also determines the number of pages that should be brought in using a single I/O operation, based upon the number of bytes requested. This information is then conveyed by the Cache Manager to the Virtual Memory Manager, which is responsible for handling the page fault (when it occurs) and actually obtaining data via the page fault path from the file system driver.

- The Cache Manager performs a simple copy operation from the system cache (using the mapped view of the file) to the buffer sent in by the caller. If data is already available in the system cache, the copy operation will immediately complete. Otherwise, a page fault will occur, and the page fault handler in the Virtual Memory Manager obtains the data from disk or from across the network. Note that this results in a recursive operation into the file system driver.

The Cache Manager returns the total number of bytes successfully transferred in the `Information` field in the `IoStatus` parameter.

CcCopyWrite()/CcFastCopyWrite()

```
BOOLEAN
CcCopyWrite (
    IN PFILE_OBJECT        FileObject,
    IN PLARGE_INTEGER      FileOffset,
    IN ULONG               Length,
    IN BOOLEAN             Wait,
    IN PVOID               Buffer
);

VOID
CcFastCopyWrite (
    IN PFILE_OBJECT        FileObject,
    IN ULONG               FileOffset,
    IN ULONG               Length,
    IN PVOID               Buffer
);
```

Resource Acquisition Constraints:

The FCB for the file must be acquired exclusively before invoking either of the two routines. This allows only a single thread to be able to access the file stream and modify it.

Parameters:

`FileObject`

> This argument contains a pointer to the file object structure representing the open operation performed by the thread. Caching must have been previously initiated by the file system driver on this file object.

> Note that if the file system driver has not initiated caching prior to invoking the `CcCopyWrite()` / `CcFastCopyWrite()` routines, an exception will be generated, since the Cache Manager assumes that the private cache map and shared cache map structures exist and have been initialized correctly.

`FileOffset`

> This is the starting offset in the file, from where the modification operation should be performed.

> For the `CcCopyWrite()` routine, the starting offset can be anywhere within the allowable range for file offsets, which is a 64-bit quantity. However, the `CcFastCopyWrite()` routine expects the entire range being modified (starting offset + number of bytes) to be contained within 4GB (maximum range allowable for a 32-bit offset).

Length

This is the number of bytes to be modified.

Wait

This argument is only accepted by the `CcCopyWrite()` routine. The caller can decide whether blocking for disk I/O is acceptable or not. For example, in order to modify a byte range in memory, free pages are required. To free up physical memory, some data may have to be transferred to disk. This involves disk (or network) I/O, which is a blocking operation. Similarly, if a page is being partially modified, the previous contents of the page must already be present in memory. If not, then the data has to be read off secondary storage. This, too, is a blocking operation.

If `Wait` is specified as FALSE to the `CcCopyWrite()` routine and blocking becomes necessary, the routine returns FALSE to the caller.*

The `CcFastCopyWrite()` routine assumes that the caller is prepared to block to achieve the data transfer; i.e., the (implied) value of `Wait` is TRUE.

If the file stream was opened for write-through operations, data will have been flushed to secondary storage media before this call returns. By definition, this call therefore will block and hence the `Wait` argument must be TRUE in this case. Otherwise, a return value of FALSE will result and no data transfer will occur.

Buffer

This argument contains a pointer to the buffer from which the copy operation should be performed. If the buffer pointer becomes invalid (once the Cache Manager is invoked), an exception will be raised by the Cache Manager.

Functionality Provided:

The `CcCopyWrite()` and the `CcFastCopyWrite()` functions are similar to their read counterparts. They are responsible for transferring modified data from the user's buffer into the system cache.

As mentioned above in the case of the routines providing read functionality, the primary difference between the `CcCopyWrite()` and `CcFastCopyWrite()` routines is that the latter routine assumes the caller is always prepared to block in the context of the requesting thread. The requesting thread may have to block due to any one of the following reasons:

---

* If FALSE is returned, the caller should assume that none of the data has been transferred.

- In the case of partial write requests,* data may first have to be obtained from disk (or from across the network) before it can be modified.

- The file stream may have been opened with write-through mode specified (the `FO_WRITE_THROUGH` flag was set in the file object structure). In this case, modified data will be physically written out to disk (or across the network) before either of these two routines return control back to the caller. Note that writing to disk is a blocking operation, since it involves a recursive call back into the file system driver (which will then forward the request to the disk drivers/network drivers responsible for the actual transfer of data).

- There may not be a sufficient number of available, unmodified pages of physical memory to contain the new data before it can be lazy-written to disk. To create space in memory for the data, the Virtual Memory Manager has to flush out other previously modified data to disk, discard the data, and reallocate the physical pages to contain the newly modified bytes.

If `CcCopyWrite()` is used, the caller can specify whether blocking is acceptable. If the caller is not prepared to block and data transfer cannot be immediately completed, the routine returns a FALSE status.

The `CcFastCopyWrite()` routine expects that the starting and ending offsets for the entire request are contained within a 32-bit quantity. It also assumes that the caller is prepared to block until the write operation can be successfully completed.

Just as in the case of `CcCopyRead()` described previously, an invalid buffer being passed in to the Cache Manager results in an exception condition being raised. Similarly, any errors encountered in either obtaining original data from secondary store (in the case of a partial write operation) or in writing the new data out (if write-through mode had been specified) will cause an exception to be raised. The exception values include the following:

`STATUS_INVALID_USER_BUFFER`
> This exception is raised if the user buffer is invalid or becomes invalid while the request is being processed.

---

* A *partial write* (as used in this context) is a write operation that does not begin and end on whole page boundaries. Note that the smallest unit of physical memory manipulated by the VMM is a page. The contents of a page are marked as either valid or not valid. It is too expensive for the VMM to keep track of valid ranges within a page. If an entire page is being overwritten (in a write request), the VMM optimizes by not obtaining the original byte range from secondary store—if the old data was not already present in memory. Instead, the VMM simply materializes an empty (zeroed) page into which the new data can be transferred and subsequently, the new contents of the page are marked as valid. If, however, an entire page is not being modified, the VMM must ensure that the original contents of the page have been brought into memory before the modification of a subset of the appropriate byte range is allowed to proceed. Transferring the affected byte range into memory from secondary storage (if it is not already present) is an expensive operation.

STATUS_UNEXPECTED_IO_ERROR or STATUS_IN_PAGE_ERROR

One of these two exceptions is raised if the Cache Manager received an error from the VMM when requesting data transfer. Note that the data transfer requested by the Cache Manager could be a read operation (in the event that the write request is a partial write), or it could be the attempt to write out the contents of the caller-supplied buffer.

STATUS_INSUFFICIENT_RESOURCES

This exception is raised if the Cache Manager could not allocate required memory to complete the request.

The implementation of both routines is similar to that for the read case described earlier:

- The Cache Manager determines if a mapped view for the desired range exists. If no such view exists, the Cache Manager creates such a view.

- The write request may either be contained completely within a page or span multiple pages. For those pages whose contents are being completely over-written, the Cache Manager recognizes that obtaining the original contents from disk (for the byte range associated with the pages) is not required. Therefore, the Cache Manager requests zeroed pages from the VMM (using a special call provided by the VMM) and transfers the new data there. For those pages that are not being completely overwritten, the Cache Manager will perform a simple copy operation from the user's buffer into the virtual address space associated with the mapped view.

  Note that as a result of the copy operation, a page fault may occur if the byte range being modified is not already present in physical memory. The Virtual Memory Manager will resolve the page fault by bringing the original contents (for the byte range) from disk and restarting the copy operation. The copy operation should then complete successfully.

CcCanIWrite()

This routine is defined as follows:

```
BOOLEAN
CcCanIWrite (
    IN PFILE_OBJECT          FileObject,
    IN ULONG                 BytesToWrite,
    IN BOOLEAN               Wait,
    IN BOOLEAN               Retrying
);
```

Resource Acquisition Constraints:

If `Wait` is TRUE, the file system should ensure that no resources have been acquired. Otherwise, the caller can choose to have the FCB resources unowned, or acquired shared or exclusively.

Parameters:

FileObject
This argument contains a pointer to the file object structure representing the open operation performed by the thread.

BytesToWrite
This is the number of bytes to be modified.

Wait
This argument is used by the Cache Manager to determine whether the caller is prepared to wait in the routine until it is acceptable for the caller to be allowed to perform the write operation.

Retrying
The file system may have to keep requesting permission to proceed with a write operation (if `Wait` is supplied as FALSE) until it is allowed to do so. This argument allows the file system to notify the Cache Manager if it had previously requested permission for the same write request or if the current instance was the first time permission was being requested for the specific write operation.

Functionality Provided:

This routine is part of a group of routines that allow the file system to defer executing a write request until it is appropriate to do so. There are a number of reasons why deferring a write operation is necessary. They include the following:

- The file system may need to restrict the number of dirty pages outstanding for each file stream at any time. This allows the file system to ensure that cached data for other file streams does not get discarded to make space for data belonging to a single file stream. Such a situation may arise if a process keeps modifying data for a specific file stream at a very fast rate.

- The Cache Manager tries to keep the total number of modified pages within a certain limit, for all files that have their data cached. This helps ensure that a sufficient number of free pages are available for other purposes, including memory for loading executable files, memory-mapped files, and memory for other system components.

- The Virtual Memory Manager sets certain limits on the maximum number of dirty pages within the system (based upon the total amount of physical memory present on the system). If the write operation causes the limit to be exceeded, the VMM would rather defer the write until the modified page writer has flushed some of the existing dirty data to disk.

In order to assist the Cache Manager and the Virtual Memory Manager in managing physical memory optimally, the file system driver can use the `CcCanI-Write()` routine to determine whether the current write operation should be allowed to proceed. Use of this routine is optional.

The `Wait` argument allows the file system to specify whether the thread can be blocked until the write can be allowed to proceed. If `Wait` is FALSE and the write operation should be deferred, the routine returns FALSE. The file system can then determine an appropriate course of action—this might be to postpone the operation using the `CcDeferWrite()` routine described next in this section.

Setting `Wait` to TRUE causes the Cache Manager to block the current thread (by putting it to sleep) until the write can be allowed to proceed. Note that the file system should ensure that no resources are acquired by the thread, since this may lead to a system deadlock.

The `Retrying` argument allows a file system to notify the Cache Manager whether permission is being requested either for the first time or in the case when permission had been previously requested (and denied) at least once before. If set to TRUE, the Cache Manager assigns a slightly higher priority to the current request while determining whether it should be allowed to proceed or not (e.g., if two write requests are pending and one of them is being retried, the Cache Manager will try to allow the one being retried to proceed first). Note, however, that there are no guarantees to ensure that a request being retried will indeed be allowed to proceed before other new requests.

Conceptually, the functionality provided by the Cache Manager in this routine is fairly simple:

- First, check whether the current write operation can proceed based upon criteria including whether the outstanding number of dirty pages associated with a file stream has been exceeded, whether the total number of dirty pages in the system cache has exceeded some limit, or whether the Virtual Memory Manager needs to block this write until enough unmodified pages are available in the system.

- If the write operation can proceed, return TRUE.

- Otherwise, if `Wait` is set to TRUE, put the current thread to sleep until the write operation can be allowed to proceed. Once the thread is awakened from the sleep, return TRUE. However, if `Wait` is FALSE, return FALSE immediately.

Note that a value of TRUE, if returned by this function, does not guarantee that conditions will continue to remain amenable to performing the write operation. Therefore, it is quite possible that `CcCanIWrite()` returns TRUE but by the time the write operation is actually submitted, conditions have changed (other writes may have caused many more pages to become dirty) such that the current write should really be deferred. However, since correctness of the operation is not affected, the caller should not really worry about this possible race condition.

To ensure that no other thread sneaks in to perform a write and thereby increase the number of outstanding modified pages, your FSD can acquire the FCB for the file stream exclusively before invoking `CcCanIWrite()`. However, `Wait` should then be set to FALSE.

CcDeferWrite()

```
VOID
CcDeferWrite (
    IN PFILE_OBJECT                    FileObject,
    IN PCC_POST_DEFERRED_WRITE         PostRoutine,
    IN PVOID                           Context1,
    IN PVOID                           Context2,
    IN ULONG                           BytesToWrite,
    IN BOOLEAN                         Retrying
);
```

where:

```
typedef
VOID (*PCC_POST_DEFERRED_WRITE) (
    IN PVOID            Context1,
    IN PVOID            Context2
);
```

Resource Acquisition Constraints:

No resources should be acquired before invoking this routine.

Parameters:

FileObject
> This argument contains a pointer to the file object structure representing the open operation performed by the thread.

PostRoutine
> The routine to be invoked whenever it is appropriate for the current write request to proceed. Typically, this is a recursive call into the file system write routine.

Context1 and **Context2**

> These are arguments that the **PostRoutine** will accept. Typically, if the post routine is the same as the generic write routine, these arguments are the **DeviceObject** and the IRP (for the current request).

BytesToWrite

> This is the number of bytes being modified.

Retrying

> This allows the file system to specify whether the check (should the write be allowed to proceed?) is being performed for the first time or has already been performed before.

Functionality Provided:

This routine is part of a group of routines that allows the file system to defer executing a write request. As discussed earlier, the **CcCanIWrite()** routine allows a file system driver to query the Cache Manager to see if the current write request can proceed immediately. If the **CcCanIWrite()** routine returns FALSE, the file system can use the **CcDeferWrite()** routine to queue the write until it is appropriate for it to proceed.

The **PostRoutine** argument allows the file system to specify the routine that will perform the actual write operation when invoked. It is quite possible that the Cache Manager might choose to invoke the post routine immediately (in the context of the thread invoking the **CcDeferWrite()** routine). Typically, however, the post routine is invoked asynchronously whenever a sufficient number of dirty pages have been flushed to disk.

CcSetReadAheadGranularity()

```
VOID
CcSetReadAheadGranularity (
    IN PFILE_OBJECT        FileObject,
    IN ULONG               Granularity
);
```

Resource Acquisition Constraints:

There are no special resource acquisition constraints associated with this routine.

Parameters:

FileObject

> This argument contains a pointer to the file object structure representing the open operation performed by the thread.

Granularity

This is the new granularity to be used in determining the number of additional bytes obtained by the read-ahead thread.

Functionality Provided:

The default read-ahead size is `PAGE_SIZE`. This simple routine allows the file system to determine an appropriate read-ahead granularity for a file stream. The new granularity should be a power of two and should be greater than or equal to the `PAGE_SIZE` value.

CcScheduleReadAhead()

```
VOID
CcScheduleReadAhead (
     IN PFILE_OBJECT          FileObject,
     IN PLARGE_INTEGER        FileOffset,
     IN ULONG                 Length
);
```

Resource Acquisition Constraints:

There are no special resource acquisition constraints associated with this routine.

Parameters:

FileObject

This argument contains a pointer to the file object structure representing the open operation performed by the thread.

FileOffset

This is the offset from which the last read was initiated.

Length

This is the number of bytes requested in the last read operation.

Functionality Provided:

The `CcScheduleReadAhead()` routine is shared by both the copy interface and the MDL interface. This routine allows the file system to request that read-ahead be performed (if appropriate) for a file stream.

Using this routine is optional, since read-ahead is automatically initiated by the Cache Manager (unless the file system has requested that read-ahead be disabled for a specific file stream) whenever a read operation is performed, using either the copy interface or the MDL interface. However, this routine allows a file system to initiate read-ahead itself whenever required.

The `FileOffset` and `Length` arguments typically describe a read operation that has just been completed (in the case of an MDL read, the read operation may have just been initiated). Since it has been determined empirically by Windows

NT designers that the read-ahead implementation on Windows NT is not particularly beneficial when the original read request is fairly small (performance might actually degrade in some cases where read-ahead is inappropriately invoked), the file system typically does not invoke the read-ahead routine directly. Instead, the file system can use the following system-defined macro to initiate read-ahead if required:

```
#define CcReadAhead(FO,FOFF,LEN) {                                  \
    if ((LEN) >= 256) {                                             \
        CcScheduleReadAhead((FO),(FOFF),(LEN));                     \
    }                                                              \
}
```

Whether read-ahead is actually performed depends on the following factors:

*   If the file stream had been opened for sequential access, the Cache Manager will typically read ahead aggressively to ensure that data is always present in the cache to satisfy the (expected) next read operation.

*   Even if the file stream is not open for sequential access, the Cache Manager maintains information, associated with the file stream, that allows it to determine the pattern of data access. If data is currently being accessed sequentially or if data is being accessed in a certain recognizable pattern, the Cache Manager will again attempt to read ahead enough data to satisfy the next read operations from the system cache.

The set of routines comprising the copy interface are the most commonly used by file systems when accessing cached data for file streams. Consult Part 3, as well as the accompanying diskette, for code fragments that illustrate the usage of these routines.

Pinning Interface

The pinning interface allows a client to map data into the system cache, lock the data into the system cache if required, and subsequently manipulate the data using a virtual address pointer. Data can be unpinned later when it is no longer required. The following routines comprise the pinning interface.

CcMapData()

```
BOOLEAN
CcMapData (
    IN PFILE_OBJECT         FileObject,
    IN PLARGE_INTEGER       FileOffset,
    IN ULONG                Length,
    IN BOOLEAN              Wait,
    OUT PVOID               *Bcb,
    OUT PVOID               *Buffer
);
```

Resource Acquisition Constraints:

There are no special resource acquisition constraints associated with this routine.

Parameters:

`FileObject`
> This argument contains a pointer to the file object structure representing the open operation performed by the thread.

`FileOffset`
> Data should be mapped in beginning at this offset in the file stream.

`Length`
> This is the number of bytes that should be mapped into the system cache.

`Wait`
> This is TRUE, if the caller wishes only that the data be mapped in (as opposed to requiring that the data be physically present in the system cache), otherwise, FALSE.

`Bcb`
> If this routine returns a success code, a pointer to a Buffer Control Block (BCB) structure (allocated by the Cache Manager) is returned in this argument. The memory allocated for the BCB structure is released by the Cache Manager when the `CcUnpinData()` routine is invoked for the last time. The BCB is also considered to be referenced whenever this routine is successfully invoked. A corresponding invocation of `CcUnpinData()` will dereference the BCB.

`Buffer`
> This contains the virtual address of the mapped data (if the routine is successful). The pointer is valid until a request to unmap or unpin the data is made.

Functionality Provided:

The `CcMapData()` routine allows the caller to request that a range of bytes associated with the file stream be mapped into the system cache. This range of bytes will not be unmapped until a subsequent call to `CcUnpinData()` is made. If successful, this routine returns two values:

- A pointer to a Buffer Control Block (BCB) structure. This pointer should be used by the caller as context to be supplied to the Cache Manager on subsequent calls to manipulate the mapped buffer.

- A virtual address pointer representing the start of the mapped range.

Note that this routine simply maps in the desired byte range—no guarantees are provided that the byte range will be pinned into memory. Therefore, it is entirely possible that subsequent attempts to access the byte range may cause page faults that will eventually result in the data being brought into memory from secondary storage.

It is important to note that the caller must not use the returned buffer pointer to modify the mapped range of bytes until a call either to `CcPinMappedData()` or `CcPreparePinWrite()` is made. Therefore, the caller can only use the returned buffer pointer to read the mapped range until the range is pinned in memory.

If `Wait` is TRUE, the Cache Manager will map the data into the cache and return. In this case, the data does not need to be physically present in the cache. If `Wait` is FALSE, the Cache Manager will return success only if the data is already physically present in the cache. The net result is that setting `Wait` to TRUE should result in quicker turnaround from the Cache Manager, since it must only ensure that data is mapped into the cache, as opposed to the alternative case, when the Cache Manager must ensure that data is physically present.

It is quite possible that this routine may pin the data into memory before returning a success code to the caller. However, the caller must be careful not to depend on this behavior and to explicitly invoke an appropriate routine to pin the mapped data when required.

Finally, the caller can invoke this routine multiple times for the same byte range. However, a corresponding invocation to `CcUnpinData()` must be made for each instance that the `CcMapData()` routine was successfully called.

CcPinMappedData()

```
BOOLEAN
CcPinMappedData (
    IN PFILE_OBJECT          FileObject,
    IN PLARGE_INTEGER        FileOffset,
    IN ULONG                 Length,
    IN BOOLEAN               Wait,
    IN OUT PVOID             *Bcb
);
```

Resource Acquisition Constraints:

There are no special resource acquisition constraints associated with this routine.

Parameters:

`FileObject`

   This argument contains a pointer to the file object structure representing the open operation performed by the thread.

FileOffset

Data is mapped in beginning at this offset in the file stream.

Length

This is the number of bytes that were mapped into the system cache.

Wait

This is TRUE if the caller can block, waiting for data to be brought into the system cache.

Bcb

When data was previously mapped into the system cache, a pointer to a BCB structure was returned by the Cache Manager. That pointer must now be used as context in this routine. It is quite possible that the Cache Manager might allocate a new BCB when this routine is invoked, and therefore return a new BCB pointer value to be used as context in subsequent calls for the pinned byte range.[*]

Functionality Provided:

Upon successful return from the `CcPinMappedData()` routine, the caller can be assured that the previously mapped data is now pinned in the system cache. Now, the caller is also permitted to modify the pinned data. However, if modifications are performed, the caller must inform the Cache Manager by using the `CcSetDirtyPinnedData()` routine, described later.

The `CcPinMappedData()` routine will not do anything and simply return success if any of the previous invocations to `CcMapData()` resulted in data being pinned in the system cache. Similarly, since it is legitimate to invoke the `CcPinMappedData()` routine multiple times for the same file stream, this routine will simply return a success if the requested byte range has been pinned before.

This routine is used only to pin previously mapped data. As was mentioned earlier, a successful return from a call to `CcMapData()` requires that a subsequent call to `CcUnpinData()` be made. However, note that no additional calls to `CcUnpinData()` are required if the `CcPinMappedData()` routine is successfully invoked for previously mapped data. Therefore, the following rules should be followed in this regard:

- If you invoke `CcMapData()` successfully for a specific byte range, you must subsequently invoke `CcUnpinData()`.

---

[*] If a new BCB pointer value is returned from this call, you (the caller) should assume that the old BCB has been dereferenced and deallocated.

- If you invoke CcMapData() and then you use CcPinMappedData(), you will invoke CcUnpinData() only once, to correspond to the CcMapData() call. Specifically, you should not invoke CcUnpinData() twice.

- If you invoke CcMapData() more than once for the same byte range (i.e., using the same BCB pointer), you must invoke CcUnpinData() for each instance when CcMapData() was successfully invoked.

- Regardless of the number of times you invoke CcPinMappedData() for the same byte range (i.e., using the same BCB pointer), you do not have to invoke CcUnpinData() to correspond to any of these calls (since the calls are effectively turned into NULL operations).

CcPinRead()

```
BOOLEAN
CcPinRead (
    IN PFILE_OBJECT         FileObject,
    IN PLARGE_INTEGER       FileOffset,
    IN ULONG                Length,
    IN BOOLEAN              Wait,
    OUT PVOID               *Bcb,
    OUT PVOID               *Buffer
);
```

Resource Acquisition Constraints:

There are no special resource acquisition constraints associated with this routine.

Parameters:

FileObject

This argument contains a pointer to the file object structure representing the open operation performed by the thread. The caller should have initialized caching for the file stream using this file object.

FileOffset

The caller wishes to have data pinned in memory beginning at this file offset.

Length

This is the number of bytes that should be pinned in the system cache.

Wait

This is TRUE if the caller can block, waiting for data to be brought into the system cache.

Bcb

If this routine returns a success code, a pointer to a BCB structure (allocated by the Cache Manager) is returned in this argument. The BCB structure must be used as context when invoking other routines for the buffer returned below. The memory allocated for the BCB structure is released by the Cache Manager when the `CcUnpinData()` routine is invoked for the last time.

`Buffer`

This contains the virtual address of the mapped data (if the routine is successful). The pointer is valid until a request to unmap or unpin the data is made.

Functionality Provided:

A call to `CcPinRead()` is functionally equivalent to calling `CcMapData()` followed by a call to `CcPinMappedData()`. The net result is that the requested byte range is pinned in the system cache. The caller is allowed to modify the byte range that is pinned, as long as the caller informs the Cache Manager that data has been modified (via the `CcSetDirtyPinnedData()` call).

The `CcPinRead()` routine returns TRUE if it successfully pins the requested byte range in the system cache. If successful, the routine also returns the following (just as in the case of the `CcMapData()` routine described earlier):

- A pointer to a Buffer Control Block (BCB) structure. This pointer should be used by the caller as context to be supplied to the Cache Manager on subsequent calls to manipulate the pinned buffer.

- A virtual address pointer representing the start of the pinned range.

If the `Wait` argument is set to FALSE, the `CcPinRead()` routine checks to see if the requested byte range is immediately available in the system cache. If the byte range is not present in the system cache, the routine will return an unsuccessful (FALSE) return code. However, if data is immediately available or if `Wait` is supplied as TRUE, this routine returns success.

This routine may be invoked multiple times for the same byte range belonging to the same file stream. However, each successful invocation of `CcPinRead()` must be later followed by a corresponding call to `CcUnpinData()`.

CcSetDirtyPinnedData()

```
VOID
CcSetDirtyPinnedData (
    IN PVOID            Bcb,
    IN PLARGE_INTEGER   Lsn OPTIONAL
);
```

Resource Acquisition Constraints:

There are no special resource acquisition constraints associated with this routine.

Parameters:

Bcb

> This is the BCB pointer used as context. This pointer was obtained from a previous invocation to either `CcPinMappedData()` or `CcPinRead()`.

Lsn

> This is a Logical Sequence Number (LSN)* associated with this dirty data.

Functionality Provided:

Once data has been pinned in memory using either `CcPinRead()` or `CcPin-MappedData()`, the file system is free to modify the data. However, once this data is modified, the Cache Manager must be informed that the byte range contains dirty (modified) data that has yet to be written to secondary media. The file system uses `CcSetDirtyPinnedData()` to inform the Cache Manager that the pinned data has been modified.

In the descriptions for `CcPinMappedData()` and `CcPinRead()`, it's mentioned that the BCB pointer returned by the Cache Manager should be used as context when invoking the Cache Manager to perform operations on the pinned byte range. The `CcSetDirtyPinnedData()` routine also requires the BCB pointer, so that the Cache Manager can identify the byte range that has to be marked dirty.

The Cache Manager allows the file system to request that a Logical Sequence Number (LSN) be associated with the modified, pinned byte range. If your driver wishes to associate a unique number with the pinned byte range, it can pass in the optional second argument to the Cache Manager. This number can be used to determine the sequence in which data is eventually written to secondary media.

When `CcSetDirtyPinnedData()` is invoked, the Cache Manager marks as dirty the BCB for the pinned byte range. This call also results in the lazy-writer thread being signaled if the lazy writer is not currently active. In time, the lazy-writer component will write the modified data out to secondary storage. There are two important points that must be noted here:

*   No I/O is attempted in the context of the thread invoking this routine.

---

* NT provides a Log File Service (LFS) component that can be used by file systems or other modules (apparently, the LFS has yet to be extended to become generically usable by components other than kernel-mode file systems). This component provides logging and recovery services to users. Currently, NTFS is the only client of the Log File Service. The LFS provides logging and recovery services to NTFS, via the use of log files associated with file objects. Records written by the LFS to the log files are identified using Logical Sequence Numbers (LSNs). These LSNs are used in a monotonically increasing fashion, and the file system can identify the oldest record describing a transaction that has not yet been updated on secondary media using the Logical Sequence Number associated with this record. The Cache Manager provides the service where a client can associate a Logical Sequence Number with a byte range that has been pinned in memory.

- None of the data that is pinned in memory will ever be written until it is unpinned (and no other references to pin the data are outstanding). Therefore, all data that is dirty and pinned will have to wait until it is completely unpinned before it can either be explicitly flushed or lazy-written to secondary storage.

Finally, if the byte range being marked dirty extends beyond current valid data length, the Cache Manager updates the valid data length for the file stream. At some point, the Cache Manager will then inform the file system that the valid data length for the file stream has been changed.

CcPreparePinWrite()

```
BOOLEAN
CcPreparePinWrite (
    IN PFILE_OBJECT      FileObject,
    IN PLARGE_INTEGER    FileOffset,
    IN ULONG             Length,
    IN BOOLEAN           Zero,
    IN BOOLEAN           Wait,
    OUT PVOID            *Bcb,
    OUT PVOID            *Buffer
);
```

Resource Acquisition Constraints:

There are no special resource acquisition constraints associated with this routine.

Parameters:

`FileObject`
This argument contains a pointer to the file object structure representing the open operation performed by the thread. The caller should have initialized caching for the file stream via this file object.

`FileOffset`
The caller wishes to have data pinned in memory beginning at this file offset. The caller will then begin writing the byte range, presumably beginning at this offset.

`Length`
This is the number of bytes that should be pinned in the system cache.

`Zero`
If TRUE, the Cache Manger will zero out the contents of the buffer before returning successfully from this routine.

`Wait`
This is TRUE if the caller can block, waiting for data to be brought into the system cache.

`Bcb`

> If this routine returns a success code, a pointer to a BCB structure (allocated by the Cache Manager) is returned in this argument. The BCB structure must be used as context when invoking other routines for the buffer returned below. The memory allocated for the BCB structure is released by the Cache Manager when the `CcUnpinData()` routine is invoked for the last time.

`Buffer`

> This contains the virtual address of the mapped data (if the routine is successful). The pointer is valid until a request to unmap or unpin the data is made.

Functionality Provided:

The `CcPreparePinWrite()` is used when the file system knows that it will modify a byte range for the file stream. Upon successful completion of this call, the file system can immediately begin transferring data into the buffer reserved for the byte range.

Functionally, this call is similar to the `CcPinRead()` routine; the Cache Manager maps in the desired byte range and then ensures that data is present in memory. If `Wait` is set to FALSE and the Cache Manager cannot return all the data requested within the byte range, the Cache Manager will return FALSE from this routine. However, if either `Wait` is set to TRUE or all the requested data is immediately available in the cache, the Cache Manager will pin the requested byte range in memory and return TRUE to the caller.

As a user of this routine, you should be aware of an important optimization performed by the Cache Manager: if the requested byte range contains pages that will be completely overwritten, the Cache Manager will not bother to read the original data contained in those pages from secondary media. Instead, the Cache Manager simply returns zeroed pages. Therefore, the caller of this routine must be careful not to use the `CcPreparePinWrite()` call in lieu of the `CcPinRead()` routine, since the buffer returned by the latter can indeed have data read from it. However, the buffer returned by `CcPreparePinWrite()` must only be used to transfer new data to secondary media.

Just as was described for the `CcPinRead()` routine, this function returns the following:

- A pointer to a Buffer Control Block (BCB) structure. This pointer should be used by the caller as context to be supplied to the Cache Manager on subsequent calls to manipulate the pinned buffer.

- A virtual address pointer representing the start of the pinned range.

This routine may be invoked multiple times for the same byte range belonging to the same file stream. However, each successful invocation of `CcPreparePin-Write()` must be later followed by a corresponding call to `CcUnpinData()`.

If `Zero` is set to TRUE, the Cache Manager will zero out the entire buffer before returning from this routine. Finally, the buffer returned by the Cache Manager is marked as dirty (internally). Therefore, at some time, the lazy-writer thread will begin writing the contents of the buffer to secondary storage. However, as noted in the description for `CcSetDirtyPinnedData()`, the modified byte range will be written to disk only after it has been unpinned.

CcUnpinData()/CcUnpinDataForThread()

```
VOID
CcUnpinData (
    IN PVOID    Bcb
);

VOID
CcUnpinDataForThread (
    IN PVOID                Bcb,
    IN ERESOURCE_THREAD     ResourceThreadId
);
```

Resource Acquisition Constraints:

There are no special resource acquisition constraints associated with these routines.

Parameters:

Bcb
    BCB pointer used as context. This pointer was obtained from a previous invocation to `CcMapData()`, `CcPinRead()`, or `CcPreparePinWrite()`.

ResourceThreadId
    This is only used in `CcUnpinDataForThread()`. It identifies the thread performing the operation.

Functionality Provided:

It is extremely important that each successful invocation of `CcMapData()`, `CcPinRead()`, and `CcPreparePinWrite()` be followed by a corresponding call to `CcUnpinData()`; this should be done after the operation requiring that data be pinned has been completed. This routine simply unpins (unlocks) the byte range from the system cache.

The byte range is unmapped from memory only after all invocations of `CcUnpin-Data()` have been made—one for each invocation of `CcMapData()`, `CcPinRead()`, or `CcPreparePinWrite()`. Data that was modified in the system cache and has been marked dirty will be written to secondary storage by the lazy-writer thread after the BCB has been completely unmapped. Note that no I/O is performed in the context of the thread invoking the `CcUnpinData()` routine (all I/O will be performed asynchronously). This can be a problem when the client (file system driver) needs to ensure that all data has indeed been written to secondary storage when the BCB has been completely unmapped (unpinned). A solution to this problem is described later (see `CcUnpin-RepinnedBcb()`).

Functionally, there is no difference between the `CcUnpinData()` and the `CcUn-pinDataForThread()` routines.

CcRepinBcb()

```
VOID
CcRepinBcb (
    IN PVOID    Bcb
);
```

Resource Acquisition Constraints:

There are no special resource acquisition constraints associated with this routine.

Parameters:

Bcb

> This is the BCB pointer used as context. This pointer was obtained from a previous invocation to either `CcMapData()`, `CcPinRead()`, or `CcPreparePin-Write()`.

Functionality Provided:

After the BCB has been completely unpinned (i.e., `CcUnpinData()` has been invoked for each successful invocation of `CcMapData()`, `CcPinRead()`, or `CcPreparePinWrite()`), the modified data will be asynchronously written to disk via the lazy-writer module. However, this presents a problem for file streams that have also been opened by users with write-through access specified (FO_WRITE_THROUGH set in the flags for the associated file object).

Since the user requires that the data be synchronously written to disk, file systems have to ensure that such write-through functionality is indeed performed before returning to the requesting user process. To ensure this, file systems use the `CcRepinBcb()` and the `CcUnpinRepinnedBcb()` routines.

The `CcRepinBcb()` routine simply references the BCB an additional time. This ensures that the BCB will not be deleted when a subsequent call to `CcUnpin-Data()` is made.

NOTE   The BCB is deleted only after all references to the BCB are re-
              moved. Typically, a BCB is referenced when one of the `Cc-`
              `MapRead()`, etc. routines are invoked. The reference is only
              removed when `CcUnpinData()` is subsequently called.

The significance of this operation is explained below (see `CcUnpinRe-`
`pinnedBcb()`).

CcUnpinRepinnedBcb()

```
VOID
CcUnpinRepinnedBcb (
     IN PVOID                    Bcb,
     IN BOOLEAN                  WriteThrough,
     OUT PIO_STATUS_BLOCK        IoStatus
);
```

Resource Acquisition Constraints:

The caller must ensure that no client resources have been acquired when
invoking this routine (otherwise, a system deadlock is possible).

Parameters:

`Bcb`

> This is the BCB pointer used as context. This pointer was obtained from a
> previous invocation to either `CcMapData()`, `CcPinRead()`, or to `CcPre-`
> `parePinWrite()`.

`WriteThrough`

> If set to TRUE, the Cache Manager will synchronously flush modified data to
> secondary storage before returning from this call.

`IoStatus`

> This is set to **STATUS_SUCCESS** if **WriteThrough** is FALSE (i.e., since there
> was nothing to flush synchronously, the return status must be **STATUS_**
> **SUCCESS**). Otherwise, it returns the actual result of the flush operation.

Functionality Provided:

In the earlier description for `CcUnpinData()`, it's mentioned that modified,
pinned data will be asynchronously written to secondary storage by the lazy-
writer component of the Cache Manager when the BCB is completely unpinned/
unmapped. This happens after the reference count for the BCB structure is equal
to 0; i.e., for every successful invocation of `CcMapData()`, `CcPinRead()`,
`CcPreparePinWrite()`, a corresponding invocation of `CcUnpinData()` has
been performed.

Consider the case, however, when a user process that has opened the file stream with write-through access makes a write request for the byte range that has been pinned in memory. Alternatively, the user process may request a write-through operation when the file system has pinned metadata for the file stream in memory (metadata includes file stream date, time, and size information, along with other information pertaining to the file stream). To perform write-through, the file system must ensure that the data has been written to secondary storage before control is returned to the user process.

The file system achieves this by using the `CcRepinBcb()` and `CcUnpinRe-pinnedBcb()` sequence of calls to the Cache Manager. The `CcRepinBcb()` call adds a reference to the BCB structure, ensuring that the BCB will not be deleted when `CcUnpinData()` is invoked (which will be done by the file system as part of processing the user request). Subsequently, before completing the IRP describing the user's write request (typically, the file system does this by requesting that it be invoked by the I/O Manager before the IRP is completed), the file system will invoke `CcUnpinRepinnedBcb()`. Note that the file system must ensure that no resources have been acquired by the file system when this routine is invoked.

If `WriteThrough` is set to TRUE by the file system, the Cache Manager will synchronously write the modified data to secondary storage before returning from the routine. This ensures that the resource acquisition hierarchy is maintained, yet the file system can honor the user's desire for write-through operation.

Although there is a Cache Manager interface routine to flush cached data (described in the next chapter), pinned buffers are not flushed when that routine is invoked. Therefore, by using the method described here, the file system can achieve its objective of ensuring synchronous flush/write-through of user data.

CcGetFileObjectFromBcb()

```
PFILE_OBJECT
CcGetFileObjectFromBcb (
    IN PVOID    Bcb
);
```

Resource Acquisition Constraints:

There are no special resource acquisition constraints associated with this routine.

Parameters:

`Bcb`

> This is the BCB pointer used as context. This pointer was obtained from a previous invocation to either `CcMapData()`, `CcPinRead()`, or to `CcPreparePinWrite()`.

Functionality Provided:

The Cache Manager returns a pointer to the file object that was used when caching was first initiated for the file stream. Note that the file object is not returned referenced (i.e., the Cache Manager does not reference the file object structure an extra time when returning a pointer to the structure from this routine) and hence the Cache Manager cannot guarantee that the file object structure will not be deallocated at any instant.

MDL Interface

The Memory Descriptor List (MDL) interface is used by clients of the Cache Manager so that they can perform I/O directly into or out of the system cache. This interface can be used concurrently with the copy interface; however, neither the copy interface nor the MDL interface can be used in conjunction with the pinning interface. The following routines comprise the MDL interface.

CcMdlRead()

```
VOID
CcMdlRead (
    IN PFILE_OBJECT          FileObject,
    IN PLARGE_INTEGER        FileOffset,
    IN ULONG                 Length,
    OUT PMDL                 *MdlChain,
    OUT PIO_STATUS_BLOCK     IoStatus
);
```

Resource Acquisition Constraints:

The FCB for the file must usually be acquired shared before invoking the routine Acquiring the FCB exclusively will prevent multiple readers from being able to concurrently access file data.

Parameters:

`FileObject`

This argument contains a pointer to the file object structure representing the open operation performed by the thread. Caching must have been previously initiated by the file system driver on this file object.

Note that if the file system driver did not initiate caching prior to invoking the `CcMdlRead()` routine, an exception is generated, because the Cache Manager assumes that the private cache map and shared cache map structures exist and have been initialized correctly.

`FileOffset`

This is the starting offset in the file. This offset denotes the file position from which the data will be transferred from the system cache. Note that the Cache

Manager does not require that the starting offset be aligned on some boundary (e.g., page boundary or sector boundary). However, the device that eventually uses the returned MDL to perform data transfer may have certain alignment restrictions that the caller should keep in mind.

Length

This is the number of bytes that will be transferred from the system cache.

MdlChain

If this routine does not generate an exception condition and if the status field in the returned **IoStatus** argument is set to TRUE, then the Cache Manager will return a pointer to an allocated MDL, describing the requested byte range in this field.

IoStatus

The Cache Manager returns the status code for this operation—in the **Status** field—as well as the number of bytes that are described by the MDL in the **Information** field. Typically, if the **CcMdlRead()** routine does not generate an exception condition, the **Status** field will be set to **STATUS_SUCCESS**.

Functionality Provided:

The **CcMdlRead()** routine returns a Memory Descriptor List (MDL) that describes physical pages allocated for the passed-in byte range. This allows the client to read data directly from the system cache and write it either across the network or to some secondary storage device (that typically supports DMA).

Note that the returned pages are locked; i.e., the specified byte range is guaranteed to continue to be backed by the physical pages described in the MDL. The pages are available for reuse only after the caller invokes the **CcMdlReadComplete()** routine to signify that the caller no longer has any use for the MDL. Also note that the returned MDL is not necessarily mapped into the system virtual address space. If the caller does require that the pages be mapped into the system virtual address space, the caller can invoke the **MmGetSystemAddressForMdl()** function to do so. (Note that **MmGetSystemAddressForMdl()** is actually a macro defined in the *ntddk.h* header file.)

As part of creating an MDL describing the byte range (requested by the caller), the Cache Manager ensures that data is physically present in the requested pages. This is done by faulting the requested byte range into the system cache.

If this routine fails to allocate an MDL or if the data cannot be read-in, an exception will be generated by this routine. Therefore, the client must ensure that an exception handler is prepared to handle any exceptions generated as a result of invoking this routine (a rare, though typical exception is STATUS_INSUFFICIENT_ RESOURCES).

CcMdlReadComplete()

```
VOID
CcMdlReadComplete (
    IN PFILE_OBJECT         FileObject,
    IN PMDL                 MdlChain
);
```

Resource Acquisition Constraints:

There are no special resource acquisition constraints associated with this routine.

Parameters:

FileObject

This argument contains a pointer to the file object structure used when CcMdlRead() was invoked.

MdlChain

This is the pointer to the MDL chain that was returned by the Cache Manager when CcMdlRead() was invoked.

Functionality Provided:

Once the client has transferred data from the system cache using the MDL created by the Cache Manager (see description of CcMdlRead()), the client must invoke this routine to allow the Cache Manager to deallocate the MDL and unlock the physical pages associated with the byte range.

If multiple calls to CcMdlRead() are made for different byte ranges for a file stream, it is not necessary that the calls to CcMdlReadComplete() be made in the same order (or in any particular order) to release the various MDL chains. However, to avoid serious memory leaks, among other problems, the client must ensure that a call to CcMdlRead() is always followed by a corresponding call to CcMdlReadComplete().

CcPrepareMdlWrite()

```
VOID
CcPrepareMdlWrite (
    IN PFILE_OBJECT           FileObject,
    IN PLARGE_INTEGER         FileOffset,
    IN ULONG                  Length,
    OUT PMDL                  *MdlChain,
    OUT PIO_STATUS_BLOCK      IoStatus
);
```

Resource Acquisition Constraints:

The FCB for the file must at least be acquired shared before invoking the routine. Typically, the FCB for the file stream is acquired exclusively by the file system to ensure that data consistency is maintained.

Parameters:

FileObject

> This argument contains a pointer to the file object structure representing the open operation performed by the thread. Caching must have been previously initiated by the file system driver on this file object.

> Note that if the file system driver has not initiated caching prior to invoking the `CcPrepareMdlWrite()` routine, an exception is generated, because the Cache Manager assumes that the private cache map and shared cache map structures exist and have been initialized correctly.

FileOffset

> This is the starting offset in the file. This offset denotes the file position at which the data will be transferred into the system cache. Note that the Cache Manager does not require that the starting offset be aligned on some boundary (e.g., page boundary or sector boundary). However, the device that eventually uses the returned MDL to perform data transfer may have certain alignment restrictions that the caller should keep in mind.

Length

> This is the number of bytes that will be transferred into the system cache.

MdlChain

> If this routine does not generate an exception condition and if the status field in the returned `IoStatus` argument is set to TRUE, then the Cache Manager will return a pointer to an allocated MDL, describing the requested byte range in this field.

IoStatus

> The Cache Manager returns the status code for this operation in the `Status` field, as well as the number of bytes that are described by the MDL in the `Information` field. Typically, if the `CcPrepareMdlWrite()` routine does not generate an exception condition, the Status field will be set to `STATUS_SUCCESS`.

Functionality Provided:

The `CcPrepareMdlWrite()` routine is analogous to the `CcMdlRead()` routine in that it returns a list of locked physical pages that can subsequently be used by the client to transfer data directly into the system cache. Typically, data is transferred directly from across the network or from a secondary storage device that supports DMA.

The pages comprising the returned MDL are guaranteed to be resident (locked in memory) until the caller invokes the `CcMdlWriteComplete()` routine to signify that data has been transferred into the system cache. Just as in the case of `CcMdlRead()`, the caller must not assume that the pages backing the requested byte range have been mapped into system virtual address space. However, the caller may choose to map these pages into the system virtual address space explicitly as a separate step.

Since the Cache Manager assumes that the byte range for which an MDL has been requested will be modified by the caller, the Cache Manager tries to optimize for the case when entire pages are being overwritten by returning zeroed pages instead of attempting to fault the original data into the system cache. Typically this is done only when the requested byte range extends beyond the current valid data length.*

If this routine fails to allocate an MDL or if the data cannot be read in, it will generate an exception. Therefore, the client must ensure that an exception handler is prepared to handle any exceptions generated as a result of invoking this routine (a rare exception is `STATUS_INSUFFICIENT_RESOURCES`; this exception would be raised if the Cache Manager could not allocate an MDL or some other similar scenario).

CcMdlWriteComplete()

```
VOID
CcMdlWriteComplete (
    IN PFILE_OBJECT        FileObject,
    IN PLARGE_INTEGER      FileOffset,
    IN PMDL                MdlChain
);
```

Resource Acquisition Constraints:

The caller must ensure that no client resources have been acquired when invoking this routine, or a system deadlock is possible.

---

* Though the Cache Manager could further optimize for the case when entire pages are presumably being overwritten by returning zeroed pages spanning a byte range contained within current valid data length, it appears as though the Cache Manager does not do so. One possible explanation for this is the fact that if the write operation does not successfully complete, the Cache Manager would then overwrite perfectly valid data with zeroes! The conservative option, in this case, is to fault in all data that is contained within the current valid data length for the file and to return zeroed pages only for that portion of the byte range that extends beyond the valid data length.

Parameters:

`FileObject`
> This argument contains a pointer to the file object structure used when `CcPrepareMdlWrite()` was invoked.

`FileOffset`
> This is a starting offset passed in to the `CcPrepareMdlWrite()` routine.

`MdlChain`
> This is the pointer to the MDL chain that was returned by the Cache Manager when `CcPrepareMdlWrite()` was invoked.

Functionality Provided:

After data has been transferred into the system cache following a call to `CcPrepareMdlWrite()`, the client must invoke the `CcMdlWriteComplete()` routine to inform the Cache Manager that it is now safe to unlock the pages comprising the MDL. In turn, the Cache Manager will unlock the pages backing the requested byte range and also ensure that the modified data is written to disk.

If the file stream was opened with write-through specified, the Cache Manager will not return control from this routine until the data has been written to secondary storage. In this case, any error in writing the data out to media is returned in the form of a raised exception. However, if the file stream was not opened for write-through access, the Cache Manager simply initiates an asynchronous write operation via the lazy writer component. This data will then be written to disk at a later time.

In order to avoid system deadlock (especially in the case where write-through has been specified), it is extremely important that this routine be invoked with none of the client's resources acquired.

In the next chapter, we will continue our detailed exploration of the Cache Manager and examine issues related to termination of caching, flushing and purging of file streams, cleanup and close operations, and truncation of cached streams. We'll also review the interaction of the Cache Manager with the Virtual Memory Manager, the lazy-writer, and the read-ahead components of the Cache Manager.

8

The NT Cache Manager III

This chapter explains the remaining file stream manipulation functions that were listed in Chapter 6, *The NT Cache Manager I.* These include flushing the cache on demand, purging pages from the system cache, changing file sizes (and informing the Cache Manager of such changes), and terminating caching for a file object.

Following the description of the file stream manipulation functions, I describe some of the interactions the Cache Manager has with both the Virtual Memory Manager and the I/O Manager. I then present a discussion of the lazy-writer and the read-ahead components of the Cache Manager.

Flushing the Cache

Modified cached data is typically written asynchronously to secondary storage media by the lazy-writer component. Also, if the system is running low on available physical memory, the Virtual Memory Manager may flush modified pages to secondary storage. However, any thread that opens a file stream for write access can request that cached data be flushed, and it then has the option of waiting until the flush operation completes before continuing with further processing.

Another method that a thread can use to force modified data to be written to secondary storage is to use write-through operations. This is accomplished by specifying the FILE_WRITE_THROUGH flag when the file stream is opened.

An interesting situation arises when multiple open operations are concurrently
performed on a file stream, some requesting cached access and others specifying
write-through mode. Typically, when the file system receives a write request
using a file object that specifies write-through, the file system has to ensure that
all modified data for the file stream in the system cache is written to secondary
storage, including the newly modified data.* Therefore, requests for access to data
using file objects that were created with write-through specified typically result in
frequent flush operations performed on the file stream.

The routine used by file systems to request that file stream data be flushed is
defined as follows:

```
VOID
CcFlushCache (
    IN PSECTION_OBJECT_POINTERS        SectionObjectPointer,
    IN PLARGE_INTEGER                  FileOffset OPTIONAL,
    IN ULONG                           Length,
    OUT PIO_STATUS_BLOCK               IoStatus OPTIONAL
);
```

Resource Acquisition Constraints:

The file system can choose from one of two acquisition options:

- The FCB for the file stream can be acquired exclusively.

- The FCB for the file stream is left unowned. The file system should guarantee
  in this case that no resources are acquired before invoking the Cache Manager.

---

* It is indeed possible that a file system may flush only the region specified in the write-through request.
Typically, however, most files are relatively small (many are less than 64KB in length), and it might make
sense for the file system to request that the entire file be flushed out to secondary storage—hopefully, in
a single I/O operation. Only modified pages will ever be written out; therefore, most file systems simply
request that the Cache Manager flush the entire file and subsequently let the Cache Manager and the Virtual Memory Manager figure out the pages to be actually written.

Parameters:

SectionObjectPointer

The file system allocates a section object pointer structure when caching is first initiated for the file stream. As noted in Chapter 6, the **Shared-CacheMap** field is used by the Cache Manager to store a pointer to an allocated shared cache map structure uniquely associated with the file stream. The Cache Manager can uniquely identify the file stream that should be flushed using this pointer.

Since a pointer to the section object pointers structure is required, caching must have been previously initiated on the file stream.

FileOffset

This is an optional argument. If supplied, the offset specifies the starting offset of the byte range to be flushed. If not supplied, the Cache Manager assumes that the starting offset is *byte 0* in the file stream. Also, if the file offset argument is omitted, the Cache Manager ignores the **Length** argument and also assumes that the entire file should be flushed to secondary storage.

Note that the large integer structure is not pushed onto the stack and that a pointer to the large integer structure is required instead.

Length

This is the number of bytes that should be flushed. This argument is ignored if no file offset is supplied to the Cache Manager.

IoStatus

The Cache Manager returns the status code for this operation in the **Status** field of the **IoStatus** structure. This is an optional argument and the caller can supply a NULL pointer if the client does not need to know the result of the operation.

Functionality Provided:

The **CcFlushCache()** routine accepts a request to flush the modified in-memory data to secondary storage. The flushing is performed synchronously, and hence the calling thread should be prepared to block, waiting for the I/O operation to complete.

The implementation of this routine is conceptually very simple: the Cache Manager receives this request and decides if the entire file (beginning at *file offset 0*) should be flushed or if a specific byte range in the file should be flushed. This is determined based on whether the caller supplied a file offset argument or not. If a file offset is supplied, then the requested byte range is flushed; otherwise, the entire file is flushed. If a byte range is supplied, the Cache Manager checks that a valid range has been requested.

The Cache Manager then asks the Virtual Memory Manager to flush the section object (representing the file stream mapping object) to secondary storage. The results of the operation are then returned to the caller, if the caller supplies an `IoStatus` argument.

Note that modified buffers that are currently pinned in memory are not flushed when this routine is invoked. These buffers are flushed asynchronously by the lazy-writer thread after they are unpinned.

Termination of Caching

Once caching has been initiated for a file object, the user can access data directly out of the system cache and also enjoy the benefits obtained from read-ahead and lazy-write operations on the cached data. As was noted in the previous chapter, in response to a file system request to initiate caching, the Cache Manager allocates the shared cache map data structure. Once all processes in the system complete processing data for the file stream, this structure should be deallocated by the Cache Manager and memory pages used to cache data for the file stream should be freed.

After I/O operations on the file stream have ceased, a close operation is performed on the file handle representing the file stream. This operation indicates that the particular process no longer needs to access the data for that file stream, and the file system should terminate caching of data using the associated file handle.

After all processes that opened the file stream close their respective handles to the file, all references to file objects for the file stream are removed. At this time, all data structures used to maintain cache state information can be deallocated and data for the file stream can be purged from system memory.

To understand the sequence of operations that leads to termination of caching for a file stream, let us examine the cleanup and close requests handled by file system drivers.

Once a process completes all desired I/O operations on a file stream, it performs a close operation on the handle representing that file stream. When the last user handle corresponding to the file object is closed, the I/O Manager invokes the file system driver with an IRP containing the major function `IRP_MJ_CLEANUP`. This is known as a cleanup request to the file system driver.

NOTE   The terminology is a little confusing here; you may wonder why a *close* operation by a process on a handle to the file stream results in a *cleanup* request (IRP) to the file system. And then, at some point, the file system receives a *close* request (IRP) as well for the file stream. The simple answer: someone at Microsoft picked these non-intuitive names! Alternative names for these IPRs could include `IRP_MJ_FILE_OBJ_USERS_HANDLES_CLOSED`hmn, for the cleanup request, and `IRP_MJ_FILE_ALL_REFERENCES_GONE` for the close request. Hopefully, the discussion in this chapter and in Part 3 will help clarify the situation.

The cleanup request notifies the file system that no additional user processes will attempt to access the file stream using the specific file object (an argument to the file system receiving the cleanup request). In response, the file system performs a well-defined sequence of operations; these operations are explained in further detail in Part 3. However, regarding interfacing with the Cache Manager, the file system driver typically does the following:

- The file system flushes all the buffers associated with the file stream.*

    Once the IRP for the cleanup request is completed by the file system, the calling process expects that modified data should have been written to secondary storage, or at the very least, it should be scheduled to be written fairly soon.

- The file system terminates caching for the passed-in file object.

You have already seen the Cache Manager routine used by the file system to flush buffers for a file stream. The routine to terminate caching for a file object associated with a file stream is defined as follows:

```
BOOLEAN
CcUninitializeCacheMap (
    IN PFILE_OBJECT                     FileObject,
    IN PLARGE_INTEGER                   TruncateSize OPTIONAL,
    IN PCACHE_UNINITIALIZE_EVENT        UninitializeCompleteEvent OPTIONAL
);
```

The `CACHE_UNINITIALIZE_EVENT` structure is defined below:

```
typedef struct _CACHE_UNINITIALIZE_EVENT {
    struct _CACHE_UNINITIALIZE_EVENT        *Next;
    KEVENT                                  Event;
} CACHE_UNINITIALIZE_EVENT, *PCACHE_UNINITIALIZE_EVENT;
```

---

* The Cache Manager routine to uninitialize the cache map for a file object also ensures that data for the file stream gets flushed to secondary storage. However, that flush operation is typically performed asynchronously, and invoking the flush call explicitly could be useful to file systems that wish to ensure that modified buffers are written to secondary storage each time a user handle is closed.

Resource Acquisition Constraints:

The FCB for the file stream must be acquired exclusively before invoking this routine.

Parameters:

`FileObject`

> This is a pointer to the file object structure for which caching is being terminated by the file system.

`TruncateSize`

> This is an optional argument. If the file stream has been deleted, the delete actually occurs only when the final cleanup call for the file stream is received by the file system driver, i.e., when the last user handle is closed.* At this time, the Cache Manager purges all pages from the system cache and forces the section representing the file mapping to be closed if the value of the `TruncateSize` argument is set to 0.

> Alternatively, the file system may wish to truncate the file stream even when there are other open handles for the file stream. In this case, specifying a valid truncate size results in this truncation and pages are purged when the last user handle is closed.

`UninitializeCompleteEvent`

> The name for this optional argument is somewhat of a misnomer (maybe `UninitializeAndFlushCompleteEvent` might have been a better choice). Since the Cache Manager might choose to lazy-write the file stream data to secondary storage and/or lazy-delete the section object representing the file mapping, this argument allows the caller to request that it be notified when the actual flush of cached data and the subsequent uninitialization of the cache map is completed.

Functionality Provided:

The `CcUninitializeCacheMap()` routine is used by file systems for each file object when a cleanup IRP is received for a file object. Note that this routine should be invoked for every file object, regardless of whether caching had ever been invoked for the file object. This is because truncation related to deletion of a

---

* This is a peculiarity of the Windows NT system. As you will see in Chapter 10, *Writing A File System Driver II*, to delete a file stream (more specifically, to delete a link/name-entry in a directory associated with a file stream), a process must first open the link for the file stream, mark it for deletion, and finally close the handle. When all file handles for the file stream are closed, the directory entry will actually be deleted (and so will the file stream if the link count for the file was 1). For cached files, when the last user handle for the file stream is closed, the Cache Manager purges all the pages associated with the file stream from system memory and also forces the section to be closed. In other operating systems, it is not always required that a file stream be opened in order to delete it.

file is only performed when the last cleanup operation is invoked for a file stream; i.e., when all user file handles (and therefore all corresponding file objects) have been closed. Similarly, truncation specified for a file stream opened by other processes is performed when all user handles to the file stream have been closed.

Invoking this routine for a file object on which caching has not been initialized has a benign effect.

WARNING   Although the above statement is mostly true, if you write a file system driver, be careful to ensure that the `SectionObjectPointer` field in the file object structure has been initialized prior to invoking this routine. Failure to do so might lead to an exception being raised because the Cache Manager dereferences this field to get to the shared cache map field within the structure. The shared cache map structure in turn is used to determine whether caching is in progress at all for the file stream associated with the file object.

You should ensure that the file control block for the file stream has been acquired exclusively prior to invoking the routine. If caching has been initiated for the file object on which this operation is being performed, caching will be uninitialized. You should note that after returning from this operation, the `PrivateCacheMap` field in the file object structure will have been reset to NULL.

If the last open user handle to the file stream is being closed, invoking this routine will result in the following:

- If a valid `TruncateSize` argument was supplied, the pages starting at the supplied offset will be purged from the system cache.

- Modified (but unpurged) pages in the system cache are flushed to secondary storage.

- The shared cache map for the file stream is deleted (actually a lazy-delete will be initiated, since modified pages may be lazy-flushed to secondary storage).

As was noted in Chapter 6, the Cache Manager does not interpret the contents of the byte streams that it caches for other system components. In particular, the Cache Manager is used by file systems to cache not only user data but also file system metadata, such as volume information, extended attributes, directory contents, and other similar information. To initiate caching for such file streams, file systems use the `IoCreateStreamFileObject()` routine to request that the I/O Manager create a file object representing the file stream. Once this file object has been created, the file system can itself initiate caching on the returned file object and use the system cache to cache nonuser data.

The `IoCreateStreamFileObject()` routine creates a file object and references it. It then executes a close operation on the referenced file object before
returning the file object pointer to the caller. This close operation on the handle
for the newly created file object results in a cleanup IRP being dispatched to the
file system. The file system should recognize that this is a cleanup request for a
special stream file object data structure and simply no-op the call (instead of
trying to uninitialize caching for the file object).

You should also note that receipt of a cleanup request on a file object by the file
system does not mean that no further I/O requests will be received by the file
system using that file object. Although the cleanup request does indicate that all
user handles associated with the file object have been closed, it is indeed possible
that the Cache Manager (and/or the Virtual Memory Manager) may have referenced the file object and might send read or write-behind requests to the file
system using that file object.

Typically, once a file system receives a cleanup request on a file object, further
I/O requests should be expected if the following conditions hold true:

- The file object was the first one used to initiate caching for the file stream
  (i.e., this was the first file object—corresponding to the first open instance
  among many possible file open instances—that was used in a call to `CcIni-`
  `tializeCacheMap()` to initiate caching).

- The file system did not invoke `CcFlushCache()` explicitly when receiving
  the cleanup IRP and there is modified data in the system cache (you should
  note that the lazy-writer would then try to write-behind this modified data),
  or there are other open instances for the same file stream and one or more is
  resulting in modified data in the system cache (this means that some other
  thread/process seems to be modifying data for the file stream).

Close Request

When the last user handle associated with a file object is closed, the file system
receives a cleanup request. In response, the file system flushes the cached file
stream data, uninitializes the cache map, and performs other housekeeping functionality for that file object.

It is important to note that, although all user handles associated with a file object
may be closed, there may be references to the particular file object. As long as
one or more references exist to a file object, the file object structure cannot be
deallocated. However, once the last reference to the file object structure has been
removed, the file system receives a close IRP (`IRP_MJ_CLOSE`). At this time, the
file system can perform any final housekeeping associated with the file object
before it gets deallocated.

Although most file systems do not interact with the Cache Manager when a close IRP is received for a file stream, it is important to note that the Cache Manager retains a reference to the first file object for a file stream on which caching has been initiated. This may result in a close operation on a file object being delayed until after the cleanup request for the file object has been received and completed.

To clarify this further, consider a file stream for a file *foo* on disk. When *process-1* opens this file, a file object is created to represent the open instance for the file stream. Now, imagine that *process-2* also opens file *foo*. At this time, another file object representing the second open for the file stream is created. Now, let *process-1* initiate the first I/O operation (either read or write) on the file stream. The file system driver initiates caching for the file object, and this request to initiate caching is received by the Cache Manager. While initiating caching for the file object, the Cache Manager notices that this is the first occurrence of caching being initiated for the file stream *foo*. Therefore, the Cache Manager retains a reference to the file object. Although, at some later time, *process-2* might also perform buffered I/O, which causes caching to be initiated for the second file object associated with the file stream *foo*, the Cache Manager does not reference any other file object for the same file stream.

After both processes have closed their respective handles, the file system will get a close IRP only when the Cache Manager (and any other component that references the file object) releases its reference to the file object structure.

NOTE   You know that the Cache Manager invokes the Virtual Memory Manager to create a section object representing the file mapping for each file that is cached. When the VMM is invoked for the first time on a file stream (to create a section object or file mapping), the VMM also references the passed-in file object. Therefore, the first file object on which caching is initiated for a file stream is referenced at least twice due to the act of caching being initiated—once by the Cache Manager and a second time by the Virtual Memory Manager. Both of these references need to be removed before a close IRP is received by the file system for this particular file object.

This method of referencing the file object and thereby delaying the close operation for a file object results in cached data being kept around in the system cache across user file open and close operations. Therefore, if you open a Microsoft Word document, then close it and then quickly open it once again, the second open and subsequent I/O operations will typically access cached data, and should be a lot quicker than the first one.

Miscellaneous File Stream Manipulation Functions

In Chapter 7, *The NT Cache Manager II*, as well as in this chapter, I presented in detail some file stream manipulation functions used by Cache Manager clients. For example, you now know how to request that the Cache Manager initialize caching for a file stream, how to flush the cache, and how to uninitialize caching. In this section, the remaining file stream manipulation functions made available by the Cache Manager are presented.

CcSetFileSizes()

```
VOID
CcSetFileSizes (
    IN PFILE_OBJECT         FileObject,
    IN PCC_FILE_SIZES       FileSizes // See the previous chapter
                                      // for the type definition
);
```

Resource Acquisition Constraints:

The FCB for the file must be acquired exclusively before invoking this routine.

Parameters:

`FileObject`

    This argument contains a pointer to a file object structure associated with the file stream whose size is being modified.

`FileSizes`

    This is an initialized structure with the correct `AllocationSize` (may be different from the current one), `FileSize` (i.e., the end-of-file value, which might be changed), and the `ValidDataLength`. Note that the value in the `ValidDataLength` field is not used.

Functionality Provided:

When the file system changes either the allocation size for a file or the current end-of-file mark for a file stream on which caching has been initiated, it must inform the Cache Manager of the new sizes. This is done using the `CcSetFileSizes()` routine.

By acquiring the file stream exclusively, the file system ensures that no other thread can concurrently access the data contained within the stream until the file size change operation has been completed. This ensures that users see a consistent view of the data.

The functionality provided by this routine is as follows:

1. If the new allocation size is greater than the previous allocation size, the Cache Manager will extend the section size for the mapped data section object created for the file stream.

   Remember that the Cache Manager provides caching services by mapping the file stream data. Mapping of a file stream is performed by requesting that the Virtual Memory Manager create a section object for the file stream. Therefore, the Cache Manager (once again) asks the VMM to increase the size of the section object to correspond to the new allocation size for the file stream.

   Note that this section object extension operation could result in a recursive callback into the file system.

2. The Cache Manager will update the end-of-file with the new file size value.

   If the valid data length value is being maintained (remember that the file system can decide whether valid data length should be maintained or not), the Cache Manager will also update the valid data length field for the file stream. If the new end-of-file mark is less than the previous end-of-file value, the Cache Manager may purge the cache of all extraneous pages.

   You should note that in certain cases, the NT Cache Manager may actually flush some dirty data to disk before purging the pages from the cache. These flush operations typically cause a recursion back into the file system driver at this time. The flush operations are usually performed when the file system driver has not yet initiated caching on the file stream, yet the user has mapped the file into the process' virtual address space.

CcPurgeCacheSection()

```
BOOLEAN
CcPurgeCacheSection (
      IN PSECTION_OBJECT_POINTERS       SectionObjectPointer,
      IN PLARGE_INTEGER                 FileOffset OPTIONAL,
      IN ULONG                          Length,
      IN BOOLEAN                        UninitializeCacheMaps
);
```

Resource Acquisition Constraints:

The FCB for the file must be acquired exclusively before invoking this routine.

Parameters:

SectionObjectPointer
   The Cache Manager uses the **SectionObjectPointer** to uniquely identify the cached file stream on which the purge operation is being performed.

FileOffset

> The caller can specify that data be purged beginning at this file offset. If the **FileOffset** value is nonnull, the **Length** argument (described below) will be used; otherwise the **Length** argument will be ignored. Note that if the **FileOffset** pointer value is set to NULL, all cached pages associated with the file stream will be purged from memory.

Length

> The client file system can request that the supplied number of bytes should be purged, beginning at the **FileOffset** value described above. Note that the **Length** field is ignored if the value of the **FileOffset** pointer is set to NULL. If the supplied **Length** is not a multiple of the **PAGE_SIZE** for the system, then the value will be adjusted upward to a multiple of the page size.

> For example, if the **FileOffset** is 0, signifying that the purge should begin at the beginning of the file stream, and the **Length** is 5, then at least one page will be purged. Note that typically the page size is 4K bytes or greater.

UninitializeCacheMaps

> If set to TRUE, the Cache Manager will force uninitialization of caching for all file objects associated with the file stream.

Functionality Provided:

A file system uses this routine when a file stream is being truncated, but not deleted. This routine causes previously written data to be discarded from memory without being flushed to secondary storage (although a flush might have taken place already due to asynchronous I/O initiated by either the lazy-writer or the modified page/block writer).

The file system supplies a pointer to the section object structure associated with the file stream. The Cache Manager purges the entire file (i.e., all pages in memory for the file stream) if the supplied **FileOffset** pointer is NULL or if the **FileOffset** value is 0 and **Length** is 0. Otherwise, it purges beginning at the supplied offset value for **Length** number of bytes. Note that if **Length** is set to 0, then the remainder of the file, beginning at **FileOffset**, will be purged from memory.

An important point to note here is that user-mapped files cannot be purged or truncated as long as the file is mapped by some process. Therefore, if a user process previously mapped the file (see Chapter 5, *The NT Virtual Memory Manager*, for details), the purge request fails and potentially stale data continues to reside in the system cache. If the purge is unsuccessful, this routine returns FALSE; otherwise it returns TRUE.

The client can also request that all file objects with caching initiated for this file stream have their cache maps uninitialized. Note that typically, uninitialization of a cache map is only performed by a file system upon receiving a cleanup request. Uninitialization of the cache maps forces all file objects to reinitiate caching whenever new I/O operations are received. If `UninitializeCacheMaps` is set to TRUE, the Cache Manager will force uninitialization of all cache maps on all file objects associated with this file stream, regardless of whether the purge operation succeeds or fails.

CcSetDirtyPageThreshold()

```
VOID
CcSetDirtyPageThreshold (
    IN PFILE_OBJECT         FileObject,
    IN ULONG                DirtyPageThreshold
);
```

Resource Acquisition Constraints:

There are no special resource acquisition constraints associated with this routine.

Parameters:

`FileObject`
>   This is a file object associated with the file stream on which a restriction is being placed. The file object must have caching initialized.

`DirtyPageThreshold`
>   This is the maximum number of modified pages that can be outstanding at any time for this file stream.

Functionality Provided:

In order to help provide good overall system performance, a file system may restrict the maximum total number of outstanding modified pages associated with a file stream. An example of when this may be necessary is if some process starts rapidly modifying pages for a file stream at a rate faster than the system can cope with, resulting in pages for other file streams being discarded from memory, to make room for this one particular file stream. This situation leads to unnecessary thrashing of pages in and out of memory and degrades overall system responsiveness and performance to other processes.

By restricting the total number of outstanding modified pages for a file stream, and subsequently using the `CcCanIWrite()` and `CcDeferWrite()` routines described in the previous chapter, the file system can ensure that no rogue process can seriously degrade overall system performance by flooding the system cache with data belonging to a single file stream.

CcZeroData()

```
BOOLEAN
CcZeroData (
IN PFILE_OBJECT         FileObject,
IN PLARGE_INTEGER       StartOffset,
IN PLARGE_INTEGER       EndOffset,
IN BOOLEAN              Wait
);
```

Resource Acquisition Constraints:

The FCB for the file must be acquired exclusively before invoking this routine.

Parameters:

`FileObject`
This argument contains a pointer to a file object structure for which a range of bytes should be zeroed.

`StartOffset`
This is the starting offset for the range of bytes to be zeroed.

`EndOffset`
This is the corresponding ending offset.

`Wait`
This is set to TRUE if the file system is prepared to block in the context of the thread used to invoke this routine. Otherwise, it should be set to FALSE.

Functionality Provided:

This routine can be used by the Cache Manager client to zero a range of bytes within a file stream. The `StartOffset` and `EndOffset` arguments determine the actual range of bytes that will be modified (set to zero).

The `CcZeroData()` routine can be invoked regardless of whether or not caching has been initiated on the concerned file object. If caching has not been previously initiated on the file object or if the file object has been marked for write-through, i.e., the `FO_WRITE_THROUGH` flag was set, then the byte range is zeroed directly on-disk.

Note that it is possible that other file objects for the same file stream may have caching initiated (even though the one being used to zero data might not), or that other file objects for the same file stream may not have write-through specified. In such situations, the cached byte range might not be consistent with the newly zeroed range on disk. Therefore, file system developers should be especially careful when invoking this routine if they want to present a consistent view of data to all processes accessing the file stream.

The `Wait` argument allows the file system to specify whether the file system is prepared to block in the context of the thread used to invoke the `CcZero-Data()` routine. Writing to secondary storage is potentially a blocking operation, and if write-through is set or if the file object does not have caching initiated and if `Wait` is set to FALSE, no zeroing of data will be performed. In general, if `Wait` is set to FALSE, the Cache Manager will be able to successfully zero the specified byte range only if the required space for the byte range is immediately accessible in the system cache. If `Wait` is set to TRUE, however, the Cache Manager attempts to zero as much of the byte range in the system cache as possible, and the remainder of the specified byte range is zeroed directly on disk.

File systems should note that if the Cache Manager decides to zero data directly on disk, invoking this routine leads to a recursive callback into the file system in the form of a paging I/O write operation. See Chapter 10 for a discussion of the implications on FSD processing when the zeroing operation is performed directly on-disk.

If the Cache Manager successfully zeroes the specified byte range, the call to this routine returns TRUE; otherwise the Cache Manager returns FALSE. This routine raises an exception (e.g., `STATUS_INSUFFICIENT_RESOURCES`) in the event of an error while allocating resources or while performing I/O to secondary storage.

CcGetFileObjectFromSectionPtrs()

```
PFILE_OBJECT
CcGetFileObjectFromSectionPtrs (
    IN PSECTION_OBJECT_POINTERS     SectionObjectPointer
);
```

Resource Acquisition Constraints:

There are no special resource acquisition constraints associated with this routine.

Parameters:

`SectionObjectPointer`
> This is a pointer to the section object associated with the FCB representing the file stream.

Functionality Provided:

The Cache Manager returns a pointer to the file object used when caching was first initiated for the file stream. Note that the Cache Manager does not reference the file object structure an extra time when returning a pointer to the structure from this routine, and hence, the Cache Manager cannot guarantee that the file object structure will not be deallocated at any instant.

This routine is typically used when the file system needs to perform an operation requiring a file object pointer that might not be conveniently available at that time.

CcSetLogHandleForFile()

```
VOID
CcSetLogHandleForFile (
    IN PFILE_OBJECT          FileObject,
    IN PVOID                 LogHandle,
    IN PFLUSH_TO_LSN         FlushToLsnRoutine
);
```

where:

```
typedef
VOID (*PFLUSH_TO_LSN) (
    IN PVOID                 LogHandle,
    IN LARGE_INTEGER         Lsn
);
```

Resource Acquisition Constraints:

There are no special resource acquisition constraints associated with this routine.

Parameters:

`FileObject`
> This is a file object for a file stream with which the log handle is being associated.

`LogHandle`
> This is an opaque value (from the Cache Manager's perspective) associated with the file stream identified by the passed-in file object.

`FlushToLsnRoutine`
> This routine is invoked before the Cache Manager flushes buffers (or any BCB) for the file.

Functionality Provided:

As described in the previous chapter, the Cache Manager helps the Log File Service assist file systems that use on-disk logging to help guarantee data consistency and to provide fast recovery from system crashes. The file system can associate a handle with a file stream for a data file using this routine; typically this handle represents a log file associated with the data file.

The file system can also specify a callback routine, which is invoked before the Cache Manager flushes a BCB (Buffer Control Block) to disk. By specifying a callback routine, the file system is informed of the newest Logical Sequence Number (associated with a data record) being flushed, giving the file system an opportunity to ensure that the contents of the log file are written to before the data is written out. Typically, this is required by logging file systems to guarantee data consistency in the event of system crashes. See the previous chapter, especially the discussion on `CcSetDirtyPinnedData()`, for additional information.

CcSetAdditionalCacheAttributes()

```
VOID
CcSetAdditionalCacheAttributes (
    IN PFILE_OBJECT        FileObject,
    IN BOOLEAN             DisableReadAhead,
    IN BOOLEAN             DisableWriteBehind
);
```

Resource Acquisition Constraints:

There are no special resource acquisition constraints associated with this routine.

Parameters:

`FileObject`

>   This is a pointer to a file object structure for the file stream for which read-ahead and/or write-behind is being disabled. Caching must have been initiated for the file stream using the passed-in file object, or an exception will be raised.

`DisableReadAhead`

>   If set to TRUE, read-ahead is being disabled.

`DisableWriteBehind`

>   If set to TRUE, write-behind (or lazy-write) will be disabled.

Functionality Provided:

Typically, read-ahead and lazy-write (or write-behind) are enabled for all file streams for which caching is initiated. In the event that a file system wishes to disable one or both of these features for a particular file stream, this routine can be used to do so.

CcGetDirtyPages()

```
LARGE_INTEGER
CcGetDirtyPages (
    IN PVOID                        LogHandle,
    IN PDIRTY_PAGE_ROUTINE          DirtyPageRoutine,
    IN PVOID                        Context1,
    IN PVOID                        Context2
);
```

where:

```
typedef
VOID (*PDIRTY_PAGE_ROUTINE) (
    IN PFILE_OBJECT                 FileObject,
    IN PLARGE_INTEGER               FileOffset,
    IN ULONG                        Length,
    IN PLARGE_INTEGER               OldestLsn,
    IN PLARGE_INTEGER               NewestLsn,
    IN PVOID                        Context1,
    IN PVOID                        Context2
);
```

Resource Acquisition Constraints:

There are no special resource acquisition constraints associated with this routine.

Parameters:

LogHandle

This is a log handle, previously associated with the file stream, for which dirty pages should be returned.

DirtyPageRoutine

This is the callback routine to be invoked for each dirty page that is found for the file stream identified by the **LogHandle** input parameter.

Context1

This is an opaque (from the Cache Manager's perspective) value to be passed in to the dirty page callback routine.

Context2

This is a second opaque value to be passed in to the dirty page callback routine.

Functionality Provided:

For logging file systems, the Cache Manager provides this routine to obtain a list of dirty pages for file streams associated with the specified log handle. Cached file streams may have been previously associated with a log handle. Each of these cached file streams may also have one or more byte ranges cached in memory, with modified data that has not yet been written to secondary storage.

The Cache Manager checks all cached byte ranges in memory, and if it finds any such range that has dirty data for a file stream that was associated with the specified log handle, the Cache Manager immediately invokes the supplied dirty page routine for this byte range. The dirty page routine is given the starting file offset, length of the cached range (in memory), the oldest and newest logical sequence numbers associated with this range, and the two opaque context values that the file system supplied in the call to `CcGetDirtyPages()`.

The file system should be aware that the callback is invoked at high IRQL with a spin lock acquired. Therefore, the callback is not allowed to take a page fault and it must perform its tasks quickly before returning control back to the Cache Manager. Also, since the Cache Manager invokes the callback for each modified byte range, the callback could be invoked multiple times for every file stream associated with the specified log handle.

The call to `CcGetDirtyPages()` returns 0 if no dirty pages are encountered, or else it returns the value of the oldest logical sequence number found for a modified byte range for a file stream associated with the supplied log handle.

CcIsThereDirtyData()

```
BOOLEAN
CcIsThereDirtyData (
    IN PVPB      Vpb
);
```

Resource Acquisition Constraints:

There are no special resource acquisition constraints associated with this routine.

Parameters:

Vpb
  This is a pointer to a mounted Volume Parameter Block structure.

Functionality Provided:

In response to this call, the Cache Manager simply scans through all the cached file streams, looking for those that are associated with the supplied VPB and have some modified—but not flushed—data in the system cache. If any such cached file stream is encountered, the Cache Manager returns TRUE.

Note that this is a quick way for a file system to determine whether dirty data for any file stream on a particular volume exists in the system cache.

So how does the Cache Manager determine whether a cached file stream belongs to the specified volume? Recall that the Cache Manager stores a pointer to the referenced file object used in the very first `CcInitializeCacheMap()` invocation for a file stream. Also, recall from Chapter 4, *The NT I/O Manager*, that each file object has a pointer to the VPB for the volume on which the file stream for the file object resides. Therefore, the Cache Manager can always obtain the pointer to the VPB from the file object for that file stream.

CcGetLsnForFileObject()

```
LARGE_INTEGER
CcGetLsnForFileObject(
    IN PFILE_OBJECT        FileObject,
    OUT PLARGE_INTEGER     OldestLsn OPTIONAL
);
```

Resource Acquisition Constraints:

There are no special resource acquisition constraints associated with this routine.

Parameters:

`FileObject`

This is the file object for the file stream for which information is being requested.

`OldestLsn`

This is an optional argument. If the oldest logical sequence number is also required, this argument will be filled in.

Functionality Provided:

This routine simply returns the newest logical sequence number associated with a file stream among dirty byte ranges. If caching has not been initiated for the file stream, or if all data for the file stream has already been flushed to secondary storage, this routine returns 0.

If the `OldestLsn` argument is supplied, and if there is any dirty data cached in memory, the routine will also return the oldest logical sequence number for the file stream.

Interactions with the VMM

The Cache Manager depends on the services provided by the Virtual Memory Manager to provide caching functionality. Specifically, all policies related to actual memory management, such as allocation of physical memory, creation of file mappings, destruction of file mappings (section objects), and flushing data cached in memory are performed with the active assistance of the VMM subsystem.

Dependencies upon the VMM exist throughout the Cache Manager implementation; most of these dependencies are resolved by internal calls to the VMM. Unfortunately, most of the Cache Manager calls to the VMM use routines that are not exposed to other kernel developers. Still, in order to understand the Cache Manager, it is useful to be aware of the dependencies that the Cache Manager has on the VMM. This allows you to be more aware of the dependencies within the NT Executive as a whole, and if you design or develop a kernel-mode driver, you will undoubtedly see stack traces during system crashes that indicate that both the Cache Manager and VMM were involved in calls that ended up in your code.* Let us examine the various points where the Cache Manager requires the assistance of the Virtual Memory Manager.

At system initialization time, the Cache Manager requires a range of addresses within the system virtual address space to be reserved for its exclusive use. This is performed by the VMM automatically, and therefore the Cache Manager can be guaranteed an available fixed-size virtual address byte range.

When the Cache Manager initializes, it needs to determine the number of threads it should create, the maximum number of dirty pages that the entire system cache can contain, and other such configuration parameters. To determine absolute values, the Cache Manager uses a VMM routine called `MmQuerySystemSize()` (see Chapter 5 for the definition of this routine).

Assume that a file system invokes the `CcInitializeCacheMap()` routine described earlier to initiate caching for a file stream using a specific file object. To service this request, the Cache Manager checks whether caching was previously initiated for the file stream using any other file object. If this is the first instance of caching being initiated for the file stream using any file object, the Cache Manager has to map the file stream into memory (specifically, into the reserved virtual address range set aside for the Cache Manager). The Cache Manager achieves this by using the `MmCreateSection()` routine, and although this routine is not exported by the Windows NT Executive for use by any external kernel drivers, the routine is amazingly similar to the `NtCreateSection()` (also known as the `ZwCreateSection()`†) system call. The `MmCreateSection()` routine results in the creation of a section object that represents a file stream mapping to the

---

* My apologies for insinuating that newly developed kernel code by readers could lead to system crashes. Unfortunately, this is a fact of life that all kernel developers either learn to accept and so become better designers/developers, or deny stoically forever, resulting in their customers finding out the effects of the designers intransigence the hard way.

† This routine is defined in Chapter 5.

VMM. A pointer to the section object can subsequently be used by the Cache Manager whenever it needs to manipulate the section or its contents.

When the allocation size of a file stream is extended, the Cache Manager must extend the section associated with the specific file stream if the file stream was previously mapped into the system cache. This is achieved, once again, by invoking the VMM via a routine called `MmExtendSection()`. Unfortunately, this routine is not defined or exposed by the NT Executive and hence the arguments supplied to this routine are subject to change.

Whenever a file system tries to perform I/O to a cached byte range and the request is transferred to the Cache Manager, the Cache Manager must map a view of the affected byte range into the system virtual address space (using the section object created earlier when caching was initiated). This is achieved by invoking the VMM routine called `MmMapViewInSystemCache()`. Note that, although this routine is not exposed, the functionality provided is similar to that of `ZwMap-ViewOfSection()`. The difference, however, is that the requested view is mapped into the specific reserved virtual address range set aside for the Cache Manager.

Correspondingly, whenever the Cache Manager wishes to discard a previously mapped view, it uses the VMM routine `MmUnmapViewInSystemCache()`.*

Now, when the Cache Manager has to flush the data associated with a file stream, the actual flush is performed by invoking the `MmFlushSection()` call. The interesting point to note is that, for any data present in the system cache, the Cache Manager never directly invokes the file system or the I/O Manager to write data out, instead, the Cache Manager always requests that the VMM flush out the associated section (and more specifically, a byte range within the section), thereby always synchronizing with the modified page writer thread within the VMM. This is true even when the lazy-writer component within the Cache Manager performs asynchronous write-behind of data.

---

* Unmapping a mapped view is almost never a cheap operation. If pages are physically assigned to some addresses within the mapped view, invoking this routine leads to TLB (Translation Lookaside Buffer) flushes. This degrades performance somewhat.

NOTE   The way a file system eventually sees this request to write data out is in the form of a noncached, paging I/O write request that comes via the VMM and the I/O Manager. Again, if you were to see the stack trace, you might be able to see the Cache Manager routine (`CcFlushCache()`) in the trace. Sometimes, if the modified page writer is already in the process of asynchronously flushing out the same byte range, you may not even see the Cache Manager in the trace, since the Cache Manager's request to the VMM would be blocked waiting for the asynchronous flush to complete.

When the Cache Manager has to read data into the system cache, it does not even have to invoke the VMM explicitly. It simply attempts to copy data from the mapped view in the system cache into the user-supplied buffer. This causes a page fault, which is automatically (and normally) handled by the page fault handler component of the VMM. Note that when the read-ahead component of the Cache Manager wishes to bring data asynchronously into the system cache, it, too, simply tries to touch (or access) a byte from each page that is being brought into the system cache. Once again, the act of accessing a byte leads to a page fault (if the data is not already in physical memory) and this page fault is resolved by the VMM. Remember that the page fault will eventually be resolved by a noncached, paging I/O read request to the file system by the VMM, although the file system cannot tell whether the page fault is due to the Cache Manager touching a page that was not in memory or some other process doing so.

NOTE   File system drivers (especially those for the Windows NT operating system) have to be fully aware of how an I/O request arrives at either the read or write dispatch entry point. Therefore, file systems work very hard to determine the sequence of operations that caused the dispatch entry point to be invoked. This applies equally well to paging I/O operations. Part 3 discusses this topic extensively.

There are other VMM routines that are available only to the Cache Manager for use during normal operations. For example, the Cache Manager can check whether an address is backed by a physical page (and if not, request that the page be made resident and zeroed) using the `MmCheckCachedPageState()` routine. The Cache Manager can set an address range to modified (causing the data to be flushed out) using a routine called `MmSetAddressRangeModified()`. Also, the Cache Manager can force pages to be purged from the system cache using the `MmPurgeSection()` routine.[*]

---

[*] The request to purge might be failed by the VMM if the section is mapped by a user process as well as by the Cache Manager.

Note that the Cache Manager is treated as any other (though slightly special) client by the VMM. This means that the VMM maintains a working set for the pages allocated to the Cache Manager and trims or expands the physical memory that is assigned to the Cache Manager, based upon demands made by the Cache Manager and other modules in the system. This allows the VMM to make global allocation decisions wisely and prevents file data caching from overwhelming the system to the extent that all other work becomes impossible.

Although routines listed in this section might not be exported and described in detail for use by other kernel-mode subsystems, it is obvious that special support is provided by the VMM to the Cache Manager. This makes the Cache Manager unique within the NT Executive and allows it, in turn, to provide caching support to other modules, such as file systems.

One final note: although the Cache Manager uses the services of the NT VMM, the VMM never needs to utilize services provided by the Cache Manager.* Therefore, the relationship is mostly a one-directional, client-server relationship.

Interactions with the I/O Manager

The Cache Manager uses the services of the I/O Manager, just like other system modules. For example, the Cache Manager must request that the I/O Manager allocate an IRP for it using the `IoAllocateIrp()` system call. The Cache Manager uses `IoCallDriver()` when it invokes the file system to notify the file system about changes in the file size. Other I/O Manager routines such as `IoAllocateMdl()` and `IoRaiseInformationalHardError()` are also used by the Cache Manager.

An important point to note about the interactions between the Cache Manager and the I/O Manager is the existence of the fast I/O path described in the previous chapter. The I/O Manager tries to increase system throughput by bypassing the file system completely and invoking the Cache Manager directly to satisfy user I/O requests for cached file streams. If this fails, the I/O Manager defaults to using the standard I/O path through the file system driver. The fast I/O path is described in detail in the previous chapter and further information is also available in Chapter 11, *Writing a File System Driver III*.

---

* As with everything else, this is almost true. It appears that the VMM uses a single routine, `CcZeroEndOfLastPage()`, provided by the Cache Manager, when mapping a section on behalf of a user process. The purpose of this routine is to check for uninitialized pages at the end of the file stream being mapped, and if found, to zero these pages by freeing them. This routine is exported for use by other kernel developers, but the lack of sufficient documentation explaining this routine seems to deter usage by any other module.

The Read-Ahead Module

The Cache Manager helps enhance system responsiveness and throughput by providing read-ahead functionality. This means that the Cache Manager tries to bring data from secondary storage into the system cache before it is even requested by a user process. Subsequently, when the user process tries to access the byte range that was read-ahead into the system cache, the user I/O request can be immediately satisfied from the data present in the cache, avoiding a time consuming read operation to obtain data from secondary storage or from across the network.

In order to provide read-ahead, the Cache Manager must be able to answer the following questions:

- Should read-ahead be performed for a specific file stream?
- If it is determined that read-ahead should be performed for a cached file stream, when should read-ahead be initiated?
- What should be read-ahead into the system cache?
- Given a user request that was recently satisfied, what would be the byte range that the user process is likely to access in the near future?
- Who does the actual read-ahead operation—one thread, many threads, specially reserved threads, or simply system worker threads?
- If errors occur while trying to read-ahead data into the system cache, what should the Cache Manager do in response to these error conditions?

Let us examine each of the issues listed here to see how the Cache Manager implements read-ahead functionality.

Should Read-Ahead Be Attempted for a File Stream?

The default answer to this question is yes. Read ahead is generally attempted by the Cache Manager for all file streams that are cached in memory. The exception is that read-ahead is not attempted for file streams on which caching was initiated specifying that `PinnedAccess` would be used to access cached data.

It is possible for file systems to request that read-ahead be disabled for specific file streams. This can be achieved by the `CcSetAdditionalCacheAttributes()` routine described earlier in this chapter.

When Should the Cache Manager Try Read-Ahead?

Read-ahead is attempted by the Cache Manager either at the explicit request of file system drivers or automatically when I/O requests are serviced by the Cache

Manager. A file system can request that read-ahead be performed by using the following system defined macro:

```
#define CcReadAhead(FO,FOFF,LEN) {                               \
    if ((LEN) >= 256) {                                          \
        CcScheduleReadAhead((FO),(FOFF),(LEN));                  \
    }                                                            \
}
```

where:

> FO = file object pointer
> FOFF = file offset from where last read request was initiated
> LEN = length in bytes of last read request

As you can see, the system will perform read-ahead (at the explicit request of a module such as a file system) only if the last read operation was greater than 256 bytes. Apparently, invoking read-ahead for smaller read operations actually results in degraded system performance.[*]

The CcScheduleReadAhead() routine is automatically invoked by the Cache Manager whenever CcCopyRead(), CcFastCopyRead(), or CcMdlRead() are invoked. The Cache Manager checks read-ahead is not currently active for the file stream and, if not active, will invoke CcScheduleReadAhead(). Of course, if read-ahead is disabled for the file stream, it will not be attempted.

NOTE   The Cache Manager often schedules read-ahead concurrently with trying to read in the current user request. Typically though, the Cache Manager will not get ahead of itself and the user request will be received by the file system before the read-ahead request makes it to the file system.

What Does the Cache Manager Read-Ahead?

The function of read-ahead is to try to anticipate the byte range the user process might next access and preread into memory. The Cache Manager relies on the property of *locality of reference* to make educated guesses about the byte range that the user process might access next, following the current read request.

Simply stated, this means that a user process is likely to access a byte range that is within a few bytes of the byte range that was just accessed. Therefore, say that a process accessed bytes 1000–5000 within a file with length of 2MB. There is a

---

[*] The caller is not required to use the read-ahead macro; it's simply a good idea.

greater probability that the process will next try to access byte offset 10,000 than that the process will next try to access byte offset (1MB + 1).

A process can specify when opening a file whether the file stream will be accessed in a sequential manner by means of the `FO_SEQUENTIAL_ONLY` flag in the file object. This flag serves as a valuable hint to the Cache Manager, which then tries to keep at least two read-ahead granularities ahead of the current read operation (although the default read-ahead granularity is one `PAGE_SIZE`, it can be changed using the `CcSetReadAheadGranularity()` routine described earlier). This means that if the user process has just accessed the first page length in the file stream, approximately two additional pages beyond the ending offset of the first page will be read-ahead by the Cache Manager.

Even if the sequential-only flag is not supplied by a process when opening a file stream, the Cache Manager keeps track of read requests performed via the copy or the MDL interfaces. If the Cache Manager detects a sequential nature in the read operations being performed (e.g., if the previous two read requests were close enough to be considered sequential), the Cache Manager will attempt to read-ahead from the offset where the last read request ended (rounded up to a multiple of the page size).

NOTE   The Cache Manager masks off certain *noise bits* when trying to characterize two or more read operations as being sequential or not. For example, if read operation #1 starts at offset 0 and has a length of 4096 bytes, and read operation #2 starts at offset 5002 and has a length of 1500 bytes, the Cache Manager will disregard the fact that operation #2 starts 6 bytes beyond the end of the first request and will consider the two read requests to be sequential in nature. Therefore, read-ahead will be attempted.

Note that the Cache Manager keeps track of whether sequential accesses are being performed in the forward or in the reverse direction. Read-ahead will also be performed if a process begins reading from the end of a file stream sequentially toward the beginning of the file.

Who Performs the Actual Read-Ahead Operation?

The read-ahead is performed in the context of a system worker thread. As you know, there are worker threads available to asynchronously perform operations that are not time-critical. Therefore, the Cache Manager simply posts a request using the `ExQueueWorkItem()` system call. Note that the Cache Manager specifies that the request be posted onto the critical work queue.

This `ExQueueWorkItem()` routine is defined in the documentation for the Device Driver's Kit. It allows a work request to be queued to a global system queue. The work item is subsequently performed in the context of a system worker thread when such a thread becomes available.

There are three categories of work requests that can be queued: *delayed work requests*, *critical work requests*, and *hypercritical work requests*. The read-ahead operation is queued onto the critical work queue. Note also that, when invoking this routine, the caller has to specify the actual function call that the worker thread must invoke, and the caller must also supply an opaque context pointer that will be supplied as an argument to the specified function call.

In Chapter 7, I mentioned that a file system has to supply callback routines when initiating caching on a file stream. These callback routines are used to maintain locking hierarchy between the Cache Manager, the VMM, and the file system driver. One of the callback routines that a file system must supply (`AcquireFor-ReadAhead()`) allows the Cache Manager to acquire file system resources before initiating read-ahead. This callback is invoked by the thread that actually performs the read-ahead operation on a file stream. Upon completion of the read-ahead operation, the thread invokes `ReleaseFromReadAhead()` to inform the file system that resources previously acquired should now be released.

Further information on the implementation of these callback routines is given in Chapter 11.

What If There Are I/O Errors in Attempting the Read-Ahead?

If there are I/O errors during the read-ahead, the Cache Manager ignores them and simply aborts the current read-ahead operation. It is possible that read-ahead might be retried in the future.

Lazy-Write Functionality

Just as in the case of read-ahead operations, the Cache Manager tries to help enhance system responsiveness and provide greater throughput by implementing write-behind (or lazy-write) functionality. Here, the Cache Manager does not write modified data supplied by a user process, either directly to disk or across the network to a file server. Instead, the Cache Manager buffers the data in memory and periodically flushes modified data asynchronously to nonvolatile storage. This asynchronous, periodic flushing of data is called write-behind (or delayed-write or lazy-write) functionality.

As in the case of read-ahead operations, the Cache Manager must be able to answer the following questions:

- Should lazy-write be performed for a specific file stream?
- If it is determined that lazy-write should be performed for a cached file stream, how is the lazy-write functionality initiated?
- Who does the actual lazy-write operation?
- If errors occur during trying to lazy-write data from the system cache, what should the Cache Manager do in response to these error conditions?

Let us examine each of the issues listed above to see how the Cache Manager implements lazy-write functionality.

Should Lazy-Write Be Attempted for a File Stream?

By default, all cached file streams are lazy-written unless lazy-write has been disabled for a specific file stream, using the `CcSetAdditionalCacheAttributes()` routine described earlier in this chapter. However, data that is currently pinned in memory is not flushed until the data is unpinned.*

Furthermore, temporary files are not written to secondary storage, since the application has specified that the file be deleted anyway once the last user handle to the file has been closed.

How Is Lazy-Write Functionality Initiated?

The lazy-writer is invoked in one of the following ways:

- The Cache Manager has a DPC (Deferred Procedure Call) timer that pops once every few seconds (between 1–3 seconds). When this timer pops, it schedules a scan through the cache to find candidates that should be flushed to secondary storage.
- The Cache Manager explicitly schedules a scan of all cached byte ranges to search for modified ranges that can be flushed to secondary storage.

Once a scan is initiated, the Cache Manager sets a target amount of data that it would like to flush in that instance. Typically, the Cache Manager determines that one quarter of the currently modified (or dirty) data in the system cache should be flushed. This allows the Cache Manager to sweep through all of the dirty data in four scans through the cache. Note that the scan always begins at the point at

---

* This is different from the read-ahead case where file streams that specified `PinAccess` as TRUE would simply not have read-ahead initiated for them. Lazy-write, in contrast, is performed on these file streams, but pinned byte ranges are skipped until unpinned.

which the last scan terminated; this ensures that all dirty pages in the system cache are flushed out to secondary storage in a round-robin fashion.

When searching the cache for candidates to be flushed, the Cache Manager simply looks at each shared cache map that has dirty pages outstanding and schedules an asynchronous write operation for the shared cache map. The Cache Manager continues to schedule such write operations until the targeted limit of 1/4 of the total dirty pages has been exceeded or the Cache Manager runs out of dirty pages to be flushed.

The Cache Manager also tries to adapt the rate at which it flushes data to disk. For example, if the Cache Manager notices that modified pages are being produced at a fast rate, it will try to flush out more data in the current scan to keep the total number of outstanding dirty pages constant in the system cache.

Who Performs the Actual Lazy-Write Operation?

As noted in the preceding section, the Cache Manager periodically scans through all the shared cache maps and schedules asynchronous write operations for those that contain dirty data. Just as in the case of the read-ahead functionality, the actual write-behind operation is performed in the context of a system worker thread. The write-behind requests are posted to the global critical work queue and are picked up by available system worker threads assigned to service that queue.

Before actually posting the write to the file system, via a synchronous call internally to `CcFlushCache()`, the thread performing the write-behind will invoke the file system callback for `AcquireForLazyWrite()`. After completion of the flush operation, the Cache Manager will invoke a corresponding callback `ReleaseFromLazyWrite()` to inform the file system that it can release its resources.

The thread performing the write-behind will also check to see if the write operation extended the `ValidDataLength` associated with the file stream. If the current `ValidDataLength` is exceeded, the file system will be invoked via the `IRP_MJ_SET_INFORMATION` I/O Request Packet (the `AdvanceOnly` Boolean flag will be set to TRUE),* and informed of the new valid data length for the file stream.

Finally, the thread that performs the lazy-write operation also performs a lazy/delete operation of the shared cache map for the file stream if such a delete had

---

* A description of this IRP is presented in Part 3. There, you will also find an explanation of this special flag that exists solely to inform the file system that the `ValidDataLength` for the file stream must be changed.

been requested earlier by the file system. Of course, no file object should be actively referencing the shared cache map so that the delete operation is attempted. If any thread is awaiting the deletion of the shared cache map, the appropriate event will be set in order to inform the thread that the shared cache map was deleted.

What If There Are I/O Errors in Attempting the Write-Behind?

Consider a situation where the system worker thread, performing a lazy-write, encounters an error during the actual write operation. In this case, the thread attempts to retry the write operation—one page at a time. The theory here is to try to write out as much data as possible.

Once the retry operation has been attempted (one write per page being flushed to secondary storage), any I/O errors encountered while retrying are essentially ignored. The thread marks the pages as clean and thereby effectively loses all data that could not be flushed to secondary storage. This is a nasty side effect of the delayed-write method because a user process that opened the file stream wrote data that was buffered, received a successful return code, closed the file stream, and exited can lose the data that it thought had been successfully written out, due to the failure of the write-behind attempt!

However, the Cache Manager does pop up a message on the system console, and also writes out the message to the error log, stating that some data for the specific file stream was lost in the write-behind process. Unfortunately, by the time the system operator receives this message, it is already too late to save the data, since the pages have been marked clean.[*]

With this chapter, we have concluded our discussion of the NT Cache Manager. In Part 3, you will find code examples and discussions of how file systems and filter drivers take advantage of the services provided by the NT Cache Manager.

---

[*] It would be wise for system administrators to invest in high availability software (and redundant hardware) that provide for mirrored copies to avoid such nasty surprises. However, this still does not guarantee that such data loss will never occur.

III

The Drivers

Part III is a detailed examination of the implementation issues in file system and filter driver development.

9

Writing a File System Driver I

Most of you reading this book will never design a file system implementation; as a matter of fact, the number of people who do design and implement complete commercially available file systems are truly very few. However, a lot of you probably have a strong desire or at the very least some amount of curiosity to learn about how file systems fit into the Windows NT operating system; many of you might even design some functionality that incorporates file-system-like features. For example, you may choose to design a source code management system as a pseudo-file system implementation;* or you may choose to design a filter driver that intercepts file system requests to examine or possibly modify them before passing them on to the file system driver. In either case, an understanding of the implementation of file systems in the Windows NT environment will be a good investment. Also, if you simply wish to learn a little bit more about what really happens when your I/O is received by the native NT file systems (e.g., FASTFAT, NTFS), the discussions on the various FSD dispatch routines should give you a fairly good overview.†

This chapter, as well as most of the remaining chapters in this book, focuses on the implementation of a file system in the Windows NT environment. The method of presentation is fairly simple: first, file system data structures are covered, followed by each of the dispatch routines that a file system would typically implement. To understand the implementation better, I first describe the functionality expected from the file system for the dispatch routine; this is typically accompa-

---

* A good example of this is the *ClearCase* source code control system from Atria Systems, Inc.

† Unfortunately, I cannot discuss the myriad details that the native FSD implementations have to take care of and which are dependent on the specifics on the on-disk layout used by the FSD implementation. Documenting all of that (if indeed such information were ever made public) would occupy a whole book by itself. You can, however, purchase the IFS kit from Microsoft, which seems to contain some modified source to at least two file system implementations (FASTFAT and CDFS).

nied by code or pseudo-code (if required) that illustrates the concepts followed by an explanation of the code (pseudocode) fragment provided.

This chapter starts off with some of the very basic functionality expected from a file system; file system driver initialization, create, read, and write operations are covered here. Some of the more advanced concepts for the read and write dispatch routines (as well as other dispatch entry points) will also be covered in the next two chapters.

File System Design

No file system implementation can be successful without a sound design serving as its base. To construct a sound design, you should have a very good understanding of the goals that your file system is being designed to achieve. For instance, some file systems are deliberately developed to be simple and fast; their fundamental design goal is to provide a reliable, easily maintainable, and uncomplicated means of managing stored data. These file systems make no guarantees about ensuring data consistency in the presence of software or hardware failures; neither do they provide some of the advanced functionality, such as data security, and compression features that you might expect from more sophisticated file systems. A prime example of a relatively simple, yet very reliable file system is the FAT file system implemented in Windows NT.

Other file system implementations are considerably more sophisticated. For example, the NTFS file system implementation under Windows NT is a log-based file system. This file system design stresses fast recoverability from system failures, ensuring data consistency in the presence of hardware or software failures, providing security for user data, and providing other useful functionality, including flexible byte-range locking and data compression.

There are other file system designs that are even more sophisticated and distributed in nature. The Distributed File System (DFS)* from the Open Software Foundation is an example of a considerably more complex file system implementation. This file system comprises local disk-based file systems that provide features similar to NTFS, and also client-server components that provide consistent, global accessibility with the benefits of a single name space across geographically distributed locations. The long-awaited Object File System (OFS) implementation from Microsoft is also an example of a distributed and complex file system implementation, which should provide sophisticated functionality such as online logical volume replication and location independence.

---

* The predecessor to DFS is the famous Andrew File System (AFS) implementation from Carnegie Mellon University. Commercial versions of both DFS and AFS are now available from Transarc Corporation.

For more information about some of the file system implementations mentioned here, consult the references provided at the end of this book.

Sample File System Code

The design goals for the sample file system implementation code provided in this book are to acquaint you with the interactions between the Windows NT operating system components and a file system driver. Therefore, I focus only on these interactions and exclude coverage of other file-system-specific implementation details.

Every file system implementation must interact intimately with the rest of the operating system. After all, the file system does not exist in a vacuum, and the only generic way for a user to access data managed by the file system is by using some well-defined system services.

All file systems must also manage the on-disk data structures that allow them to store user data. Figure 9-1 illustrates how a file system design can be composed of multiple layers to address the various functional requirements expected of the implementation. The *veneer* serves as the upper-level interface between the file system implementation and the remainder of the operating system environment. This layer is the most operating-system-specific layer. The *core* can be designed to serve the requirements of the veneer by managing on-disk data structure accesses; this layer can be designed to be relatively free from any operating-system-specific constraints. The *driver interface layer*, once again, must deal with lower-level disk or network drivers in the operating system and therefore has to conform to the interface presented by such drivers.

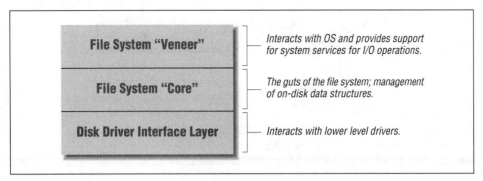

Figure 9-1. File system components in a layered file system driver (FSD) design

Most file systems, including the native NT FSD implementations, conform to the high-level design illustrated in Figure 9-2. The FSD code samples in this book also use the same methodology. However the code samples ignore the two lower layers illustrated in Figure 9-1 and focus exclusively on the veneer. Therefore, you will not see any code that deals with the actual retrieval and manipulation of data to and from secondary storage; this book does not present any discussion of these topics either. Naturally, the code fragments provided in this book should only be used as a starting point for your development efforts. They do, however, illustrate the important aspects of interacting with the NT I/O Manager, the NT Cache Manager, and the NT Virtual Memory Manager. You can design the lower levels of your commercial file system driver and plug your implementation into the driver model presented here to get yourself a fully functional, "native" file system driver under Windows NT.

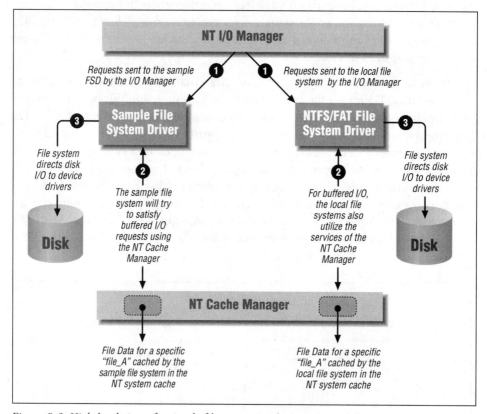

Figure 9-2. High-level view of a simple file system implementation architecture

Logistics

The sample code will get you started understanding, designing, and developing a commercial NT file system or filter driver. Although not complete by any means, the code should serve as a framework, using which you can innovate and build in the functionality for your commercial file system driver. Keep the following points in mind as you read through the code samples and explanations accompanying the code:

Maintain focus on interactions between the NT operating system and the FSD.

For a commercial FSD implementation, there are a lot of conflicting design choices that must be made. Some of the more obvious ones include choosing between fast (*tuned*) implementations or cleaner, more abstract, though relatively slower designs. Or you might consider the tradeoffs involved in incorporating strict security requirements in your design as opposed to the inevitable resulting inconvenience caused to users. You may choose to increase concurrency at the expense of a complex design that is relatively more difficult to maintain and enhance; or you may choose a less parallel model, which might be quicker to design and implement and also be more easily maintainable.

The sample code in this book does not even attempt to enumerate the various choices available to the FSD designer, let alone provide solutions for such complex issues. Therefore, while reading through the sample FSD implementation, focus on learning about the interactions with the NT operating system, and consult the literature listed at the back of this book for additional information on the issues involved in developing file system drivers.

Note that all data structures and function names are prefixed by the letters SFsd.

This allows for easy identification of those function calls and data structures that are implemented by the sample FSD. NT driver conventions require that you should prefix your function and data structure names with an appropriate identifier unique to your driver.

Exception handling is built into the sample code (or code fragments).

The sample FSD implementation presented in this book utilizes structured exception handling. You may disregard some of the details pertaining to structured exception handling if you believe that providing this support is unnecessary from your perspective. However, I would strongly encourage you to consider incorporating SEH into your implementation at the onset of file system design, since the resulting benefits in terms of code robustness far outweigh the cost of the time commitments required for such support.

Comments are interspersed in the implementation.

Some people believe that comments included with source code are useful, while others do not. I have liberally interspersed comments in the sample code included with this book. Please read these comments, because much of the information they contain is not repeated in the accompanying text.

Look for alternative methods for implementation.

Designing and implementing kernel-mode drivers requires a certain amount of on-the-job experience and is often an iterative process. The sample implementations presented in this book should not be construed as the only way the desired functionality can be implemented. Alternatives typically abound, and you should always explore any such alternative methods if you can think of them. Use the implementation presented here as a general guideline, but always keep an eye out for alternative designs.

Be aware of memory allocation issues.

Kernel-mode drivers, including file system drivers or filter drivers, should be cognizant of their memory requirements. Your goal should always include efficient usage of system memory. If you require nonpaged memory (and you typically will), you should always carefully monitor your requirements and attempt to minimize your usage of these scarce resources.

Even if you are careful and separate your memory requirements into nonpaged memory required by your driver, as well as paged memory you can work with, remember that paging is not a cheap operation. Excessive page faults or TLB faults caused by your kernel-mode driver will lead to degraded performance by the entire system. Therefore, always be careful, to the point of being stingy, with your memory needs.

Having said all of that, you should note that the code you see in this book makes no attempt at efficient memory usage, except for an example in which zone structures are utilized.[*] That is something you must work at in your commercial implementations.

Be aware of synchronization issues.

Chapter 3, *Structured Driver Development*, explained the various objects that can be used to synchronize access to shared data structures in Windows NT. The sample code in this book uses one or more of these objects. For certain shared data structures, it may sometimes be possible to modify the synchronization methodology used in the code samples, such that performance is enhanced. Typically, this is done by carefully examining the various situations under which a particular shared data structure is accessed, and then possibly lowering the synchronization requirements associated with the shared data only if you have determined that data integrity will still be preserved. No such attempts at enhancing performance have been made in the sample code presented in the book. I have used a simpler, cleaner design that always uses synchronization primitives to monitor access to shared data structures. You can, however, analyze any drivers that you develop based on code samples provided in this book for obtaining performance gains using such methods.

---

[*] If your software only executes on Windows NT Version 4.0 and later, consider using lookaside lists instead of zones.

Remember, though, to always be conservative in your analysis; otherwise, you may inadvertently cause data corruption.

Registry Interaction

A typical file system implementation requires the creation of a number of keys and associated value-entries in the Windows NT Registry:

- HKEY_LOCAL_MACHINE\SYSTEM\CurrentControlSet\Services\SampleFSD

  Table 9-1 shows the subkeys and value entries that should be created.

Table 9-1. Subkeys and Value Entries

Subkey/Value Entry	Type	Value	Description
ErrorControl	REG_DWORD	0x1	Log an error and display a message box if driver fails to load, but continue initialization (if driver is being loaded automatically).
Group	REG_SZ	"File System"	This indicates the driver belongs to the group of file system drivers. If you develop a network redirector instead, replace the value with *Network Provider*.
ImagePath	REG_EXPAND_SZ	"%System-Root%\System32\drivers\sfsd.sys"	The complete path name of the driver image.
Start	REG_DWORD	0x2 or 0x3	A value of 0x2 specifies automatic start; 0x3 specifies manual start only.
Type	REG_DWORD	0x2	Indicates that this is a file system driver.
Parameters	–	–	This subkey contains driver required configurable parameters. For a list of parameters accepted by the sample FSD, see Table 9-2.

Table 9-2 lists the possible configurable parameters accepted by the sample FSD. In your driver, you can add other value entries under the *Parameters* subkey.

Table 9-2. Configurable Parameters Accepted by the Sample FSD

Value Entry	Type	Value	Description
PreAllocated-NumStructures	REG_DWORD	0 (Default)	Specifies the number of structures for which to preallocate memory (this illustrates how an FSD could use the Registry to obtain user-configurable information).

- HKEY_LOCAL_MACHINE\...\CurrentControlSet\Services\EventLog\System\SampleFSD

  This key is added to allow any event log viewer application to decipher the messages logged by the sample FSD implementation to the NT Event Log.

  Table 9-3 shows the value entries that are created.

Table 9-3. Value Entries

Value Entry	Type	Value	Description
EventMessageFile	REG_EXPAND_SZ	%System-Root%\System32\sfsdevnt.dll	The complete path-name for the message catalog containing textual descriptions of events recorded by the sample FSD in the NT system event log.
TypesSupported	REG_DWORD	0x7	*Informational, Warning,* and *Error* messages will be logged.

- HKEY_LOCAL_MACHINE\SOFTWARE\SampleFSD

  Information contained below this key is not available at system load time. However, it is often useful to keep nonessential information about the driver itself, the manufacturer, or other information here.

The sample FSD implementation will create the following value entries and sub-keys as shown in Table 9-4.

Table 9-4. Value Entries and Subkeys

Value Entry	Type	Value	Description
VendorName	REG_SZ	"Rajeev Nagar"	Any string that uniquely identifies your organization. This field is simply informational in nature.
CurrentVersion	–	–	This subkey contains information pertaining to the current version of the driver.

The `CurrentVersion` subkey listed in Table 9-4 could contain the following value entries:

— `VersionMajor`

— `VersionMinor`

— `VersionBuild`

— `InstallDate`

The Windows NT Software Developers Kit and the Device Drivers Kit provide ample documentation and recommendations on these optional value entries.

Data Structures

At the core of any file system driver design are the data structures that together define the file system; these include the *on-disk* data structures that determine the management of the actual stored data, as well as the *in-memory* data structures that facilitate orderly access to such data. If you understand the data structures that might be required for a particular type of driver or kernel component, you have probably won half of the battle in your attempts at successfully designing such a component.

In an ideal world, the operating system should be completely independent of the on-disk data structures and layout maintained by a specific file system driver; the operating system should also be indifferent to the in-memory structures that a FSD implementation might implement, since these in-memory structures exist simply to help the implementation provide file-system-specific functionality. Windows NT is not an ideal operating system environment, and neither, for that matter, is any other commercially available operating system. However, Windows NT is relatively indifferent to the on-disk data structures maintained by a file system. Typically though, it would confuse a user of your file system tremendously if the FSD did not maintain expected information for files stored on physical media. For example, if your FSD did not maintain *last write time, last access time,* or a *file name* on disk, your file system could seem fairly strange to a Windows NT user, since such users have come to expect and depend on the existence of these attributes associated with file streams.

The native file systems supplied with Windows NT vary greatly in the features provided to users of the file system. The FASTFAT file system does not provide any security attributes for files (typically stored as Access Control Lists); it does not support multiple hard links to files, file compression, or fast recovery from system failures. The NTFS implementation does, however, support all of the features listed above, and therefore the on-disk data structures maintained by the NTFS implementation differ greatly from those maintained by the FAT file system implementation.

As mentioned earlier, the goals that you set for your file system will determine the on-disk data structures that you need to maintain. In the remainder of this book, we won't discuss on-disk structures any further, since they do not need to conform to any specific model for you to successfully implement a file system driver under Windows NT. However, as you design your file system, you should carefully study the various alternatives available to you in the format of the on-disk layout and associated structures for your file system.

The interesting structures from our perspective, therefore, are the in-memory data structures that your FSD should implement. Although Windows NT does not mandate that any specific structures be maintained, here are the two structures you should become familiar with:

- The File Control Block (FCB) structure

- The Context Control Block (CCB) structure

An FCB uniquely represents an open, on-disk object in system memory. Notice that I said that an FCB represents an on-disk object, not just an on-disk file. Directories, files, volume structures, and practically any other object that your FSD maintains and that can be opened by a user of your file system would be represented as an FCB.* If you have some background in UNIX implementations, you can easily draw an analogy between UNIX *vnode* structures, which are simply

---

* Some file system implementations, including the native file systems denote in-memory representations of directory structures as DCB objects (Directory Control Blocks). DCBs are not any different (functionally) from FCBs and the sample FSD (as well as the discussion provided throughout the course of the book) uses the FCB to represent both files and directories.

abstract representations of files in memory, and Windows NT file control block (FCB) structures. They both serve the same purpose of representing of the on-disk object in memory.

A CCB is simply a handle or the context created and maintained by the FSD to represent an open instance of an on-disk object. For example, when a user application performs an *open* operation on a file, it receives a handle from the operating system if the open request was successful. Corresponding to this handle, a Windows NT FSD creates a CCB structure, which is simply the kernel equivalent of the user handle. Is your FSD required to maintain a CCB for each open instance and an FCB to uniquely represent an open on-disk object? My answer to this is yes, it is. If you are not convinced of the necessity for maintaining these data structures, I would advise you to reserve judgment on this question until you have read through the next few chapters.

Representation of a File in Memory

You already know of the file object structure created by the I/O Manager to represent successful open operations on files and directories. To see how file objects, FCB structures, CCB structures, and VCB structures fit together, refer to Figure 9-3.

I would recommend that, to better understand the figure, you should start at the bottom of the illustration. Here is a description of its various components.

Physical device object

At the very bottom of the illustration, you see two device objects: the physical device object and the logical device object. The physical device object structure is typically a media-type object with a `DeviceType` of `FILE_DEVICE_DISK`, `FILE_DEVICE_VIRTUAL_DISK`, `FILE_DEVICE_CD_ROM`, or some such type.

This structure is created by a device driver, via the `IoCreateDevice()` routine, to represent the physical or virtual disk object that it manages. At creation time, a VPB (Volume Parameter Block) structure is allocated and associated with media type objects by the NT I/O Manager. Initially, the VPB flags indicate that the physical media does not have any logical volume mounted on it, via the absence of the `VPB_MOUNTED` flag value. Later though, some file system implementation might verify the data structures on the physical media and decide to *mount* a logical volume on that physical device object.

This leads us to the next object depicted in the illustration, the logical volume device object.

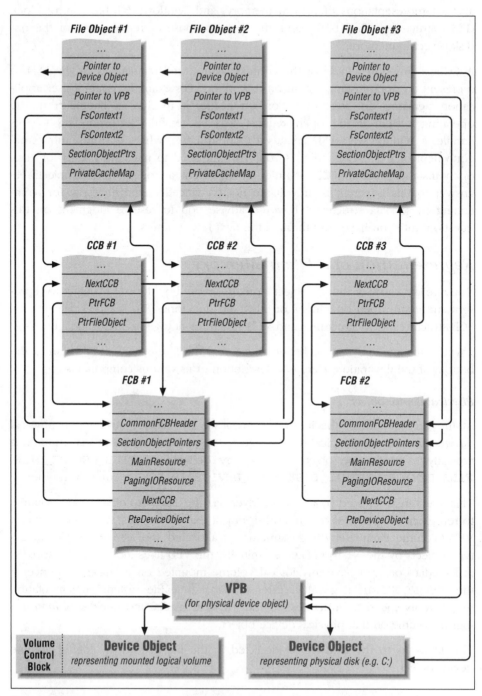

Figure 9-3. Representation of files in memory

Logical volume device object

The volume device object represents an instance of a mounted logical volume. This device object is created by a file system driver implementation; our sample FSD will also create volume device objects.

A *mount* operation is typically required on most operating systems before users are allowed to access file system data on secondary storage devices. This logical mount operation is performed by a file system driver implementation on that platform. The process of mounting a volume exists simply to allow a file system driver the opportunity to prepare the volume for subsequent access.

Most of the steps that a file system might undertake as part of mount operation are file-system-specific and the operating system does not interfere much during the process. Typically, a file system driver will first check the on-disk data structures to determine whether the medium to be mounted contains valid file system information. If these checks pass, the file system will then read in basic volume information such as volume size, root directory location, free block map, allocated cluster map, and so on, and then create the requisite in-memory structures that will be used to support access to the volume.

As part of mounting the logical volume, most operating systems (including Windows NT) do require that certain system-defined data structures be created and/or initialized, to establish linkage between the rest of the I/O Manager structures and the in-memory representation of the mounted logical volume. Therefore, file system designers must always understand the requirements that the operating system places upon the file system implementation and ensure that the correct data structures are initialized as required.

Under Windows NT, the I/O Manager requires that a device object representing the mounted logical volume be created, and for physical media, the VPB associated with the device object representing the physical media be correctly initialized.

Each volume device object is logically associated with a physical device object using the VPB structure belonging to the physical device object. This association occurs at volume mount time, which happens when the very first create/open request is received by the I/O Manager for an object residing on the physical device object.

The pseudocode fragment below illustrates how a logical volume device object structure is associated with the physical device object structure. This logical volume device object is important, because it is created by the FSD that mounts the logical volume and is used by the I/O Manager to determine the target driver/ device object for a create/open request.

The sequence follows:

```
I/O Manager receives an open/create request for an object residing on the
physical device object (e.g., an open for "C:\dir1");
I/O Manager obtains a pointer to the VPB structure associated with the
physical device object representing "C:";
I/O Manager checks the "Flags" field in the VPB to see if a mounted
logical volume exists for the physical device object;
if (no mounted volume exists, i.e., VPB_MOUNTED is not set) {
        I/O Manager requests each of the file systems to check whether
        they wish to perform a mount on the physical device object;
        One of the file system drivers performs a mount operation;
        As part of the "mount" process, the FSD will create a device object
        of type FILE_DEVICE_DISK_FILE_SYSTEM or the network equivalent;
     .  Now, the DeviceObject field in the VPB will point to the logical
        volume device object (this is done by the FSD that performs the
        mount);

When some file system has returned STATUS_SUCCESS for a mount request,
the I/O Manager will set the VPB_MOUNTED flag in the Flags field for
the VPB;
}
```

Now the I/O Manager can proceed with other instructions pertaining to the create/ open request (described later in the book).

VPB

Immediately above the two device objects depicted in Figure 9-3 is the VPB structure. This structure performs the important task of creating a logical association between the physical disk device object and the logical volume device object. A VPB structure only exists for device objects that represent physical, virtual, and/or logical media that can be mounted. Therefore, if you design network redirectors and/or servers, you will not interact directly with the VPB structure.

Note that there is no physical association between the physical device object and the logical device object representing the mounted volume (i.e., there is no pointer leading from a logical volume device object directly to the physical device object or vice versa, as would typically happen when two device objects are connected via an *attach* operation); for example, later in this book, we'll discuss a routine called `IoAttachDevice()` used by intermediate or filter drivers to create an association between their own device object and a target device object. Such attachments are performed with the intent of intercepting requests targeted to the original device object (the one being attached to).

For file system mount operations, however, the only association between the two device objects is the logical connection via the VPB structure. The I/O Manager is aware of this logical association between the two device objects, and always checks the VPB structure on receipt of a create/open request for an on-disk object to determine the file system volume device object to which the request should actually be directed.

Also note that each file object structure representing a successful open operation on an on-disk object points to the VPB structure belonging to the physical device on which the opened on-disk object resides.

Volume control block (VCB)

As mentioned earlier, as part of the mount process, each file system implementation creates appropriate in-memory data structures that will enable the file system to permit orderly and correct access to data contained in the logical volume. One of the structures maintained by the sample FSD to assist in this process is the Volume Control Block structure.

The VCB structure contains such essential information as a pointer to the in-memory root directory structure (i.e., the FCB for the root directory), a count of the number of file streams that are currently open on the logical volume, some flags representing the state of the logical volume at any given instant, synchronization structures used to maintain the integrity of the VCB structure itself, and other similar information. However, just as with all other structures defined by the sample FSD, the VCB structure is slightly less comprehensive then it would be if we were developing a full-fledged physical-media-based file system driver implementation. In that case, the VCB would also typically contain pointers to structures containing information about available free clusters on disk, a list of allocated clusters, and any such on-disk structure management related information.

Note that the Windows NT I/O Manager does not require that a file system maintain a structure like the VCB structure. However, most file system implementations (including the native NT file system implementations) maintain some variant of such VCB data structures.

The sample FSD code allocates the VCB as part of the device object extension for the device object created to represent the mounted logical volume. This seems like a very logical manner in which to allocate the VCB structure, since this method of allocation creates the association between the mounted logical volume representation known to the rest of the system (i.e., the device object) and the file system internal representation (i.e., the VCB structure). This also implies that the VCB structure is allocated by the I/O Manager from nonpaged system memory (since a device extension is allocated by the I/O Manager on behalf of the caller when the device object is being created).

If you study the VCB structure, defined below by the sample FSD, you will see that it contains fields used in obtaining services of the NT Cache Manager. Many Windows NT FSD implementations use the Cache Manager to cache on-disk volume metadata structures. This is accomplished by creating a stream file object to represent the open on-disk volume information and then initiating caching for this file object. The data is mapped into the system cache using `CcMapData()`, and it can be easily accessed, just as cached file stream data is typically accessed by user threads.

The VCB structure defined by the sample FSD is shown below:

```
typedef struct _SFsdVolumeControlBlock {
    SFsdIdentifier                      NodeIdentifier;
    // a resource to protect the fields contained within the VCB
    ERESOURCE                           VCBResource;
    // each VCB is accessible on a global linked list
    LIST_ENTRY                          NextVCB;
    // each VCB points to a VPB structure created by the NT I/O Manager
    PVPB                                PtrVPB;
    // a set of flags that might mean something useful
    uint32                              VCBFlags;
    // A count of the number of open files/directories
    // As long as the count is != 0, the volume cannot
    // be dismounted or locked.
    uint32                              VCBOpenCount;
    // we will maintain a global list of IRPs that are pending
    // because of a directory notify request.
    LIST_ENTRY                          NextNotifyIRP;
    // the above list is protected only by the mutex declared below
    KMUTEX                              NotifyIRPMutex;
    // for each mounted volume, we create a device object. Here then
    // is a back pointer to that device object
    PDEVICE_OBJECT                      VCBDeviceObject;
    // We also retain a pointer to the physical device object, which we
    // have mounted ourselves. The I/O Manager passes us a pointer to this
    // device object when requesting a mount operation.
    PDEVICE_OBJECT                      TargetDeviceObject;
    // the volume structure contains a pointer to the root directory FCB
    PtrSFsdFCB                          PtrRootDirectoryFCB;
    // For volume open operations, we do not create a FCB (we use the VCB
    //    directly instead). Therefore, all CCB structures for the volume
    //    open operation are linked directly to the VCB
    LIST_ENTRY                          VolumeOpenListHead;
    // Pointer to a stream file object created for the volume information
    // to be more easily read from secondary storage (with the support of
    // the NT Cache Manager).
    PFILE_OBJECT                        PtrStreamFileObject;
    // Required to use the Cache Manager.
    SECTION_OBJECT_POINTERS             SectionObject;
    // File sizes required to use the Cache Manager.
    LARGE_INTEGER                       AllocationSize;
    LARGE_INTEGER                       FileSize;
    LARGE_INTEGER                       ValidDataLength;
} SFsdVCB, *PtrSFsdVCB;

// some valid flags for the VCB
```

```
#define          SFSD_VCB_FLAGS_VOLUME_MOUNTED          (0x00000001)
#define          SFSD_VCB_FLAGS_VOLUME_LOCKED           (0x00000002)
#define          SFSD_VCB_FLAGS_BEING_DISMOUNTED        (0x00000004)
#define          SFSD_VCB_FLAGS_SHUTDOWN                (0x00000008)
#define          SFSD_VCB_FLAGS_VOLUME_READ_ONLY        (0x00000010)
#define          SFSD_VCB_FLAGS_VCB_INITIALIZED         (0x00000020)
```

File control blocks (FCB)

Figure 9-3, shown earlier, depicts two FCB structures, each of which represents a file stream in memory.

Just as an application needs to maintain in-memory data structures to provide services to users, file systems must maintain some in-memory data structures. Traditional file systems typically manipulate two types of on-disk objects: *files* and *directories*. A file, as we understand it, simply represents a stream of bytes stored on disk. A directory is a file-system-defined structure that contains information about files; i.e., a directory is not useful in itself except as a means to locate files, which, in turn, contain the user's data. In database terms, the directory simply comprises an index for the actual data, where the data is defined as the individual file streams. Files and directories are examples of *persistent objects*, objects that persist across system reboots, since they are stored on nonvolatile secondary storage media.

Files are simply named objects contained within directories. An important concept is the logical separation between a *directory entry* (a named file object) and any data associated with the file object. For example, consider a file *foo*, contained in directory *dir1*. File *foo* is identified within directory *dir1* by the presence of a directory entry created within *dir1* representing file *foo*. Regardless of how much data is associated with the file, there will typically exist one directory entry of a fixed size within the directory *dir1* that names file *foo* as a valid object contained in the directory.

Further, if the file *foo* has 2 bytes associated with it, and now if you *truncate* the size to 0 bytes, the directory entry within the directory *dir1* will still exist, except that now it will be updated to reflect the new size. Truncating the file may have caused any on-disk storage assigned to the file to be released, but it does not free up the directory entry for the file. Deleting the file, however, will free the directory entry for the file and the storage allocated for the data will also (in this case) be freed.

Finally, if an FSD supports multiple linked files, the logical separation between a file name and the storage space allocated for file data becomes even more obvious. Now, you may have two separate directory entries referring to the same on-disk stored data. For example, file *foo* in directory *dir1* and file *bar* in directory *dir2* may simply be synonyms for the same on-disk data. Now, even if you delete a directory entry (say, the entry for *foo* in directory *dir1*), the storage allocated for the data will not be released, since the directory entry for *bar* in directory *dir2* still points to the allocated data. Space allocated for data will only be freed after all directory entries referring to the allocated storage space for data on secondary media are deleted.

When a user tries to access a file or a directory object, which exists on secondary storage, the file system must obtain information from secondary storage to satisfy the user request. Typically, this information will be the actual data stored on disk; sometimes, though, a user might want *control* information (also known as *metadata*), such as the last time any process actually modified the contents of the file, or the last time a process tried to read the contents of the file. Therefore, all file systems should also be able to provide such information on request.

When a file system obtains data from secondary storage, it must keep this data in system memory somewhere to make it accessible to the user. If file data is stored somewhere in system memory, the file system is responsible for maintaining appropriate pointers to this data. Also, if multiple users try to access the same data, the file system should be able to consistently satisfy these concurrent requests. This requires that the file system assume some responsibility for providing appropriate synchronization when a thread tries to access on-disk data.

To provide the functionality just described, file systems create and maintain an abstract representation of open files and directories; i.e., each file system defines for itself the in-memory control data structures that it must maintain to satisfy user requests for access to persistent on-disk objects. Note that these in-memory representations of files and directories are not themselves persistent; they exist simply to facilitate access to on-disk data and can always be recreated from the data stored on secondary storage.

On most UNIX implementations, an in-memory abstraction of a file or directory is commonly called a *vnode*. On Windows NT systems, it is called a *File Control Block*. Regardless of the term used to identify this representation (we'll stick with the Windows NT terminology in the rest of the book), the important thing to note is that an on-disk object must always be represented by one, and only one, FCB. Therefore, even if your file system were to support multiple linked file streams, you should only create one FCB to represent this file stream in memory, regardless of the fact that two different processes may have used different path names or identifiers to open the same on-disk object.*

Here is the FCB defined by the sample FSD:

---

* Multiple hard links are simply alternate names for the same file stream. For example, a file *\directory1\foo* could also be identified by the path *\directory2\directory3\bar*, as long as both path names referred to the same on-disk byte stream; an FSD will represent the file by a single FCB structure.

```
typedef struct _SFsdNTRequiredFCB {
    // see Chapters 6-8 for an explanation of the fields here
    FSRTL_COMMON_FCB_HEADER              CommonFCBHeader;
    SECTION_OBJECT_POINTERS              SectionObject;
    ERESOURCE                           MainResource;
    ERESOURCE                           PagingIoResource;
} SFsdNTRequiredFCB, *PtrSFsdNTRequiredFCB;

typedef struct _SFsdDiskDependentFCB {
    // although the sample FSD does not maintain on-disk data structures,
    // this structure serves as a reminder of the logical separation that
    // your FSD can maintain between the disk-dependent and the disk-
    // independent portions of the FCB.
    uint16                              DummyField;        // placeholder
} SFsdDiskDependentFCB, *PtrSFsdDiskDependentFCB;

typedef struct _SFsdFileControlBlock {
    SFsdIdentifier                      NodeIdentifier;
    // We will embed the "NT Required FCB" right here.
    // Note though that it is just as acceptable to simply allocate
    // memory separately for the other half of the FCB and store a
    // pointer to the "NT Required" portion here instead of embedding it
    // ...
    SFsdNTRequiredFCB                   NTRequiredFCB;
    // the disk-dependent portion of the FCB is embedded right here
    SFsdDiskDependentFCB                DiskDependentFCB;
    // this FCB belongs to some mounted logical volume
    struct _SFsdLogicalVolume          *PtrVCB;
    // to be able to access all open file(s) for a volume, we will
    // link all FCB structures for a logical volume together
    LIST_ENTRY                          NextFCB;
    // some state information for the FCB is maintained using the
    // flags field
    uint32                              FCBFlags;
    // all CCBs for this particular FCB are linked off the following
    // list head.
    LIST_ENTRY                          NextCCB;
    // NT requires that a file system maintain and honor the various
    // SHARE_ACCESS modes ...
    SHARE_ACCESS                        FCBShareAccess;
    // to identify the lazy writer thread(s) we will grab and store
    // the thread id here when a request to acquire resource(s) arrives …
    uint32                              LazyWriterThreadID;
    // whenever a file stream has a create/open operation performed,
    // the Reference count below is incremented AND the OpenHandle count
    // below is also incremented.
    // When an IRP_MJ_CLEANUP is received, the OpenHandle count below
    // is decremented.
    // When an IRP_MJ_CLOSE is received, the Reference count below is
    // decremented.
    // When the Reference count goes down to zero, the FCB can be
    // de-allocated.
    // Note that a zero Reference count implies a zero OpenHandle count.
    // This must always hold true ...
```

```
    uint32                              ReferenceCount;
    uint32                              OpenHandleCount;
    // if your FSD supports multiply linked files, you will have to
    // maintain a list of names associated with the FCB
    SFsdObjectName                      FCBName;
    // we will maintain some time information here to make our life easier
    LARGE_INTEGER                       CreationTime;
    LARGE_INTEGER                       LastAccessTime;
    LARGE_INTEGER                       LastWriteTime;
    // Byte-range file lock support (we roll our own).
    SFsdFileLockAnchor                  FCBByteRangeLock;
    // The OPLOCK support package requires the following structure.
    OPLOCK                              FCBOplock;
} SFsdFCB, *PtrSFsdFCB;
```

Notice that the FCB in the sample FSD is divided into two main logical components:

- The **SFsdFCB** structure, which is operating system independent

- The **SFsdNtRequiredFCB** structure, which contains fields required to interact with the rest of the system

Additionally, the disk-dependent data structures can also be carved out into a separate data structure to provide increased portability and modularity, as is illustrated by the structures defined previously.

SFsdFCB. The first thing you should note about file control block structures is that the operating system does not determine the contents of this structure. Therefore, each file system implementation has complete flexibility over the fields contained in the FCB structure. The fields that exist in the **SFsdFCB** structure shown here are simply representative of the contents of typical FCB structures, defined by the various file system driver implementations under Windows NT. Usually, most file systems will maintain some information about the object names (hard links) associated with the FCB structure. Similarly, most FCB structures defined by file system drivers will maintain a field representing the current **ReferenceCount** for the FCB, and another field representing the current **OpenHandleCount** for the FCB. In this chapter and in the next two chapters, I will present code examples that manipulate the fields contained in the sample FCB structure. These code examples will assist you in understanding why such fields are helpful to file system drivers.

Another noteworthy aspect of the FCB defined in the sample FSD is the lack of any information about on-disk structures; e.g., there is no information about the actual on-disk clusters occupied by the file stream represented by the FCB. As mentioned earlier, we'll ignore those aspects of FSD implementations that require creating and maintaining on-disk data structures. A real file system, however, does not have this luxury and will contain far more information about on-disk file stream layout than shown in the sample FSD. If you wish to adapt the sample FSD for your own file system driver implementation, I would recommend that you isolate the on-disk format-related information into a separate data structure and then associate that separate structure with the FSD shown here, either via a pointer embedded in the FCB or by embedding the data structure itself into the FCB. This method will allow you to maintain a clean logical separation between the disk-independent and the disk-dependent parts of the FCB structure. For example, you can create a FCB structure as shown in Figure 9-4.

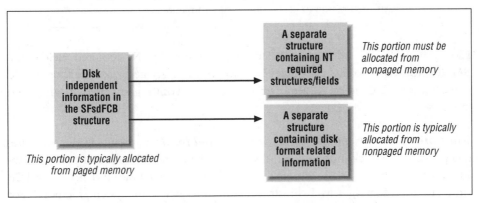

Figure 9-4. A logical breakdown of the components of an FCB

This separation is illustrated by the presence of a `DiskDependentFCB` field of type `SFsdDiskDependentFCB` structure, embedded in the `SFsdFCB` structure shown above.

SFsdNtRequiredFCB. Although Windows NT allows an FSD considerable latitude in how it wishes to define its own FCB structures, successful integration with the Cache Manager and the Virtual Memory Manager requires that certain NT-defined structures also be associated with the FCB. Integration with the NT Cache Manager and the VMM is essential if an FSD needs to use the NT system cache and also support memory mapped files.

There are four fields that must be associated with each FCB as a prerequisite for successful integration:

- A single structure of type `FSRTL_COMMON_FCB_HEADER` (called the `CommonFCBHeader` field in the sample FCB above)

- A single structure of type `SECTION_OBJECT_POINTERS` (called the `SectionObject` field in the sample FCB)

- Two synchronization structures of type `ERESOURCE` (named as the `MainResource` and the `PagingIoResource` by the sample FSD)

Just as there must be only one FCB representing the file stream in memory, there must be only one instance of each of these NT-defined structures associated with a particular FCB. Typically, these fields do not need to be associated with FCB structures representing directory objects; however, you can still create them to maintain consistency.

TIP   You will also require these structures for FCBs representing directo-
               ry objects if you intend to use the `IoCreateStreamFileOb-`
               `ject()` function to cache directory information.

File system drivers have to allocate memory for the NT-required fields; the `ERESOURCE` type objects can never be allocated from paged pool, neither should you allocate the `CommonFCBHeader` or the `SectionObject` fields from paged memory.

When are in-memory FCB structures created and freed? A new FCB structure, composed of the disk-independent, disk-dependent, and NT-required parts, is allocated when a byte stream is being opened for the first time and no other FCB structure representing this byte stream currently exists in system memory. For example, if an application decides to open a file *foo* for the very first time since the system was booted up, the FSD managing the logical volume on which *foo* resides creates an FCB structure in response to the caller's open request (i.e., as part of processing an `IRP_MJ_CREATE` request). Subsequent requests to open the file *foo*, however, will not result in the creation of a new in-memory FCB structure, as long as the previously created FCB structure is still retained in memory by the FSD. The factor that determines whether an FCB is still retained by an FSD is the value of the `ReferenceCount` field (or its equivalent), maintained by the FSD in the FCB structure. See the discussion on FCB reference counts presented below for more information. If, however, the FCB for the file *foo* has already been discarded by the FSD when the new open request is received, the FSD will once again create a new FCB structure to represent file *foo* in memory.

This file control block structure serves as the single unique representation of the open byte stream in system memory. The FCB is retained as long as any NT component maintains a reference for it. The reference count for an FCB is contained in the `ReferenceCount` field in the sample FCB shown here; your file system driver is free to name an analogous field whatever it may choose. A `ReferenceCount` value of zero implies that the FCB can be safely deallocated, because no component in the system is actively accessing the byte stream associated with the byte stream represented by the FCB at that instant.

ReferenceCount and OpenHandleCount fields. Two fields in the `SFsdFCB` structure are the `ReferenceCount` field and the `OpenHandleCount` field. It is extremely important that you understand the significance of these two fields.

Both the *reference count* and the *open handle count* are **internal counts** maintained by the FSD in the FCB structure and are therefore not externally visible to any other kernel-mode or user-mode component. Both counts help to determine when a FSD can safely deallocate the FCB structure.

The reference count is simply a number that indicates the total number of outstanding references to this FCB structure, known to the file system driver. As long as the reference count is not zero, the FSD knows that some component is using the FCB and therefore, memory for the FCB structure cannot be deallocated. The reference count field is incremented by 1 whenever a successful create/open operation is processed by the FSD in response to an `IRP_MJ_CREATE` request. The contents of this field are decremented by 1 whenever a close operation is processed for the FCB in response to an `IRP_MJ_CLOSE` request. Note that the key concept here is that the open count is simply the number of references known to the FSD; if some external component stores away the pointer to a FCB without the FSD's knowledge, the open count associated with the FCB will not have been incremented, and therefore there is no guarantee made by the FSD that it will be retained once the reference count is 0.

You should also note that the NT I/O Manager expects the FSD to maintain a reference count that is incremented during a create request and decremented during a close request. Furthermore, the I/O Manager also expects that the FSD will free the memory for the FCB only after this count is equal to zero. This knowledge is used by the I/O Manager and other Windows NT components because although neither the I/O Manager nor other system components manipulate the reference count directly, they can and do indirectly manipulate when the counter is decremented, by controlling when a close IRP request (with major function `IRP_MJ_CLOSE`) is issued. Therefore, NT system components can be reasonably certain of the FSD's behavior and can manipulate how long a FCB structure is retained by the FSD.

The open handle count simply indicates the number of outstanding user open handles for the FCB. This field is also incremented as part of processing an `IRP_MJ_CREATE` request; it is, however, decremented only in response to an `IRP_MJ_CLEAN` request issued to the FSD. The `IRP_MJ_CLEAN` request is issued by the I/O Manager to the FSD whenever a user process closes a file handle for the last time (i.e., when the system open handle count for a file object representing all user open instances is equal to zero).

File object type structures, just like other Windows NT Executive-defined data structures, are maintained by the NT Object Manager. For file object structures, the Object Manager maintains two counts, a `ProcessHandleCount` for each process that has one or more open handles associated with the file object, and a `SystemHandleCount` that is the sum total of all `ProcessHandleCount` values associated with the file object. In addition to these two handle count values, the NT Object Manager maintains an `ObjectReferenceCount` for all objects.* This reference count is always incremented whenever either the `ProcessHandle-Count` or the `SystemHandleCount` value is incremented. However, it is possible that the `ObjectReferenceCount` will be incremented even if neither the `ProcessHandleCount` nor the `SystemHandleCount` are incremented (e.g., a kernel-mode component references the object but does not request a new handle for the object).

When a process closes a open handle (i.e., when `ZwClose()` or `NtClose()` is invoked), the NT Object Manager decrements both the `ProcessHandleCount` and the `SystemHandleCount` for the object. It then invokes any *object-close method* associated with the object being closed; in the case of file objects, the close routine, called `IopCloseFile()`, is supplied by the Windows NT I/O Manager. The Object Manager supplies the `ProcessHandleCount` and the `SystemHandleCount` values to the `IopCloseFile()` function.

The `IopCloseFile()` function issues an `IRP_MJ_CLEANUP` request to the FSD if and only if all outstanding user handles for the file object have been closed and if the passed-in `SystemHandleCount` for the file object is equal to 1, meaning there was only one outstanding reference on the file object at the time the `NtClose()` operation was invoked.

Once `IopCloseFile()` has completed processing (i.e., the FSD has completed processing the cleanup request, if invoked), the Object Manager decrements the `ObjectReferenceCount` for the file object structure. If this reference count value is 0, the Object Manager deletes the object and, prior to doing so, invokes the *delete method* (`IopDeleteFile()`) associated with the file object. `IopDeleteFile()`, in turn, issues an `IRP_MJ_CLOSE` request to the FSD managing the file object structure.

Although an FSD receives a cleanup IRP whenever a user handle is closed, the FSD knows that it cannot free up the FCB until the last `IRP_MJ_CLOSE` request is received for that FCB.

---

* I have made up the symbolic names presented here since the field names for an object structure are not exposed by the Windows NT Object Manager. However, the actual symbolic names used by the Object Manager are relatively uninteresting from our perspective, as long as we understand the logic used by the Object Manager to determine how objects are retained in system memory and when they should be deleted.

For readers with a UNIX background, you can create the analogy where a `IRP_MJ_CLEANUP` request corresponds to a UNIX *vnode close* operation, and the *last* `IRP_MJ_CLOSE` request signifies that an *inactivate* operation should be performed on the *vnode* structure.

The reference count and the open handle count maintained internally by the FSD in the FCB structure together help the FSD determine the answer to the following two questions:

How many user handles are outstanding for the FCB?

In other words, the FSD should have some idea about the total number of `IRP_MJ_CREATE` requests that were successful, and for which a corresponding `IRP_MJ_CLEANUP` has not yet been received. As long as this number is nonzero, the FSD knows that at least one thread has a valid open handle to the file stream represented by the FCB, and the FCB structure should be retained in memory. Note that this is in addition to the requirement that the FCB cannot be deleted as long as the `ReferenceCount` is not 0.

You should also note that, although the `OpenHandleCount` in the FCB is incremented in response to the create operation (when a new file object is created by the I/O Manager), the count does not necessarily correspond to the system-wide handle count on the corresponding file object, which is maintained by the NT Object Manager. Each time a user file handle is duplicated (say between threads in the same process), or inherited (by a child of a parent process), or whenever some process requests a new handle from a file object pointer, the Object Manager increments the `SystemHandleCount` on the file object representing the open file instance. Since an FSD is not informed when such duplication or inheritance of file handles occurs, the `OpenHandleCount` maintained internally by the FSD does not get incremented at such occasions. However, this does not cause any problems for the FSD, since the NT I/O Manager will not invoke an `IRP_MJ_CLEANUP` request on the particular file object unless all user threads that had an open handle for that file object have also invoked a close operation on it. Therefore, the FSD will always see one cleanup operation corresponding to one create/open request and will decrement the open handle count in response to the cleanup request.

How many outstanding references exist for the FCB structure?

The `ReferenceCount` field helps determine the total number of outstanding references for the FCB. It is entirely possible, and indeed very probable, that the `ReferenceCount` will be nonzero long after the `OpenHandleCount` has gone down to zero. This simply means that, although all user handles for the FCB have been closed, some kernel-mode component wishes to retain the FCB in memory.

Typically, this situation arises when the NT Cache Manager and the NT VMM together conspire to keep file data cached in memory, even after a user application process has closed the file, indicating that it has finished processing the file stream. The reason that the Cache Manager and/or the VMM wish to retain the file data in memory (and remember that they cannot have file data retained in memory unless the FCB is also present) is to be able to provide relatively fast response if the user application needs to access the contents of the file stream once again. This may seem a bit silly to you but, quite often, application processes open and close the same file multiple times within the span of a few minutes, and retaining file contents in memory to help speed up the second and subsequent accesses to the same file stream's data enhances system throughput.

To sum up, how would the VMM or any component ensure that an FCB is retained by the FSD in memory? Here's the answer: if, for example, the VMM wishes to ensure that an FCB will stay around, it references some file object associated with the FCB. By referencing the file object, the VMM prevents the NT Object Manager from issuing a close request on that file object, even if all user handles for that particular file object are closed. Therefore, the FCB reference count is not decremented to 0 and the FCB is retained in memory.

Context control blocks (CCB)

A CCB structure is used by the FSD to store state information for a specific open operation performed on a file stream. As discussed earlier, each file stream is uniquely represented in memory by an FCB structure. The FCB structure, however, only contains information that assists in managing user accesses to the file stream as a whole; it does not contain any information about specific user open operations. The CCB structure is used instead for this purpose.

There is one CCB structure created by the FSD for each successful open operation on the file stream. Each CCB structure is typically associated in some way with the unique FCB structure representing the file stream; in the sample FSD, all CCB structures associated with a FCB structure are linked together and accessible from the FCB structure. Also, each CCB structure contains a pointer back to its associated FCB.

The CCB defined by the sample FSD is shown below:

```
typedef struct _SFsdContextControlBlock {
    SFsdIdentifier                          NodeIdentifier;
    // Pointer to the associated FCB
    struct _SFsdFileControlBlock        *PtrFCB;
    // all CCB structures for a FCB are linked together
    LIST_ENTRY                              NextCCB;
    // each CCB is associated with a file object
```

```
        PFILE_OBJECT                        PtrFileObject;
        // flags (see below) associated with this CCB
        uint32                              CCBFlags;
        // current byte offset is required sometimes
        LARGE_INTEGER                       CurrentByteOffset;
        // if this CCB represents a directory object open, we may
        // need to maintain a search pattern
        PSTRING                             DirectorySearchPattern;
        // we must maintain user specified file time values
        uint32                              UserSpecifiedTime;
} SFsdCCB, *PtrSFsdCCB;
```

Figure 9-3 shows three CCB structures, each created by an FSD in response to an **IRP_MJ_CREATE** request. Two of the CCB structures are for the same file stream (*file #1*), and they are therefore linked together on FCB #1. The other CCB structure represents an instance of a successful open operation on FCB #2.

Note carefully that there is a one-to-one mapping between a file object structure created by the I/O Manager in response to an open/create request and the CCB structure created by the FSD. Therefore, there may be only one FCB structure created for an open file stream, but there can potentially be many CCB structures created for the same file stream, each of which serves as the FSD's context for a successful open operation on the file stream.

Why would a file system wish to create a CCB structure representing each successful open operation? There are quite a few situations when the file system wishes to maintain some state that is not global to the entire file stream (i.e., a state that is not common to all open instances of the file). As an example, the CCB could be used to maintain information about byte-range locks requested by a thread using a particular file object; if the thread closes the file handle without unlocking all of the outstanding byte-range locks for that handle, the FSD can automatically perform the unlock operation upon receipt of an **IRP_MJ_ CLEANUP** request on the file object by checking for the outstanding locks on the CCB associated it. Similarly, the CCB is often also used by an FSD to store information about the next offset from which to resume a directory search operation in response to *find-first* and *find-next* requests issued by an application.

As you can see, it is quite useful to have context maintained by the FSD for each outstanding open operation, thereby avoiding cluttering up the FCB with nonglobal state information.

The I/O Manager puts no requirements on the FSD about the contents of a CCB structure; the FSD is allowed complete control about whether it wishes to maintain such a structure in the first place. Also, if the FSD does maintain a CCB structure, the contents are completely opaque to the I/O Manager. All of the current NT file system implementations maintain one CCB structure per open operation.

File objects

Finally, Figure 9-3 also depicts three file object structures; two of these file objects represent open operations performed on *file #1* while the third file object represents an open operation performed on *file #2*. Each of these file object structures is allocated and maintained by the I/O Manager in response to an open request by a thread on a file stream. Chapter 4, *The NT I/O Manager*, describes the file object structure in considerable detail.

As was mentioned in Chapter 4, the file system driver is responsible for initializing the `FsContext` and the `FsContext2` fields in the file object structure. In Figure 9-3, you will observe that the `FsContext2` field seems to be pointing to the CCB structure. As you read earlier, each instance of an open operation is represented by a CCB structure and, in order to be able to correctly associate a file object with the corresponding CCB, most file system implementations under Windows NT initialize the `FsContext2` field as part of processing an `IRP_MJ_CREATE` request to refer to the CCB structure that is newly allocated during the open operation. Note that this type of association is not mandated by the NT I/O Manager. If, however, you do develop a filter driver that attaches itself to a device object representing a mounted logical volume for one of the native NT file systems (e.g., FASTFAT, NTFS, or CDFS), you should expect that the `FsContext2` field will have been initialized by the file system implementation to refer to a CCB structure internal to the FSD.

Unfortunately, though, a file system driver does not have an equivalent amount of flexibility with respect to manipulating the `FsContext` field. Although, theoretically, this field also exists solely for driver use, the NT Cache Manager, I/O Manager, and the Virtual Memory Manager make certain assumptions about what this field points to; therefore, in order to integrate your FSD correctly with the rest of the system, your driver must initialize the `FsContext` field to point to the common FCB header structure associated with the FCB. This initialization is performed by the FSD as part of processing an `IRP_MJ_CREATE` request.

Other Data Structures

In addition to the data structures described above, a file system driver typically maintains other data structures that assist in providing standard file system functionality to the system. These data structures include the following:

Support for byte-range locking

Many file system implementations support byte-range locks. These locks can either be mandatory or advisory in nature. Mandatory locks are part of the specification to which NT FSD implementations must conform; i.e., if a thread acquires a lock on a certain byte range, the FSD implementation on the

Windows NT operating system should enforce the semantics associated with that lock for all other threads attempting to use the same byte range for the same file stream. On the other hand, advisory byte-range locks are a synchronization mechanism for different cooperating processes that need to coordinate concurrent access to the same byte range for a specific file stream. Advisory byte-range file locks are not really supported on the Windows NT platform, although your FSD does have the option of implementing advisory lock support instead of mandatory locks. Be careful if you do this, though, since most Windows-based applications expect locks to be mandatory.

If you design an FSD that supports byte range locking (as do all native NT file system driver implementations), you will undoubtedly maintain certain data structures associated with the FCB/CCB to support this functionality. The sample FSD code presented in this book implements some support for byte-range locking, a topic that is discussed in Chapter 11, *Writing a File System Driver III.*

Support for a Dynamic Name Lookup Cache (DNLC) implementation

You may be familiar with the concept of a DNLC if you have studied file systems on the UNIX platform; if you are not, the DNLC is simply a per-directory cache of the files that were recently accessed within that directory. This list of recently accessed filenames with their on-disk metadata information, which is typically implemented as a hashed list, simply helps the FSD quickly look up a particular file within a specific directory. Normally, most FSD implementations use linear searching to look up specific file names within a directory; the DNLC helps speed things up by skipping the tedious linear search for the more recently accessed files.

Implementation of a DNLC is not mandatory; in fact, the NT system (or any operating system for that matter) does not care whether your FSD uses a DNLC or not. However, you should be aware of the term in case you happen to run into a FSD implementation that does implement this functionality.

Note that the sample FSD presented in this book does not implement any sort of DNLC functionality.

Support for file stream or directory quotas

Although the NT operating system does not yet support quotas associated with file streams, directories, or logical volumes, NT Version 5.0 is expected to provide such support. If you design an FSD that implements quota management, similar to the disk quota implementation on the BSD UNIX operating system, your FSD will have to maintain appropriate data structures to support this quota management functionality. These data structures will include both on-disk structures as well as in-memory representations of the data structures.

Quotas will not be discussed further in this book, though you should certainly be able to add support for this feature for the native FSD implementations on the current NT releases, using the filter driver information provided in Chapter 12, *Filter Drivers.*

Support for opportunistic locking (oplock) functionality in Windows NT

Opportunistic locks are a characteristic of the LAN Manager networking protocol implemented in the Windows family of operating system environments. Basically, *oplocks* are guarantees made by a server for a shared logical volume to its clients. These guarantees inform the client that the contents of a certain file stream will not be allowed to be changed by the server, or if some change is imminent, the client will be notified before the change is allowed to proceed.

The guarantees made by the server node are helpful in improving client response performance to requests accessing remote file streams, since the client can safely cache the file stream data, knowing that the data will not be changed behind its back, leading to data inconsistency across nodes.

Oplocks are not required for NT FSD implementations. However, if you expect logical volumes, managed by your FSD implementation, to be shared using the LAN Manager protocol shipped with the Windows NT operating system (typically, this does not apply if you are designing a network redirector), then you should get familiar with the requirements for successfully implementing oplock support. Otherwise, you may have to assuage unhappy clients who will complain that accessing shared logical volumes managed by your FSD over the LAN Manager network is slower that accessing (say) a shared NTFS logical volume.

Later in this book, we'll explore oplock support in greater detail.

Support for directory change notification

Directory change notification is another neat feature that was implemented in the Windows NT operating system by the native file system drivers and the I/O Manager. Basically, directory change notification functionality works somewhat like the following: a component (either user-mode or kernel-mode) needs to monitor changes to a specific directory or to a directory tree. This component can specify exactly which changes to monitor; e.g., it may be interested in being notified if new files get added to the directory, or it may only need to be notified if a specific file is accessed or modified. The I/O Manager receives a request from the component specifying the type of access the component wishes to monitor and the directory or directory tree that it wishes to monitor. In response to this request, the I/O Manager asks the FSD to asynchronously invoke a specific I/O Manager notification function when the to-be-monitored changes occur.

This feature is very powerful, since it allows a lot of applications to do away with the inefficient polling methodology used before in monitoring changes to particular directories, and to use this notification methodology instead. Supporting this functionality requires the active participation of the I/O Manager and the FSD. Supporting the directory change notification feature is not mandatory; however, all of the native NT FSD implementations support it and you should at least understand the requirements that your FSD would have to meet in order to provide this kind of support.

Directory change notification support is discussed further in the next chapter.

Support for data compression

NTFS provides data compression functionality. Your FSD might also implement online data compression. This would require that your FSD maintain on-disk and in-memory structures that indicate whether a file stream has been compressed or not, and if it has been compressed, store information such as the original file length and other such control information.

The NT I/O Manager provides support for FSD implementations that support data compression by providing system call interfaces allowing a user process to specify whether it expects to receive compressed or uncompressed data back (for read operations). Similarly, Version 4.0 of the operating system allows processes to request that compressed data be written out. In addition, the NT I/O Manager allows a user process to query control information, such as the compressed length, as well as the uncompressed length, of the file stream.

Support for encryption/decryption of data

Some sophisticated file system implementations could potentially provide support for dynamic encryption/decryption of stored data. If you design an FSD that provides such functionality, you will undoubtedly create appropriate data structures that help you manage the encrypted data and decrypt it when required.

It is also quite likely that you might choose to design a filter driver that layers itself on top of the native NT file system implementations and provides support for data encryption and decryption.

Support for logging for fast recovery

NTFS is an example of an FSD implementation that uses in-memory and on-disk logging to be able to provide quick recovery from unexpected system failures. A lot of research has been performed on the design and development of log-based and/or logging file system implementations. If you design such a log-based file system implementation, you will have to maintain appropriate on-disk and in-memory log file streams and also other supporting data structures that will allow you to provide the logging feature to users.

Maintain support for on-disk data structures

Typically, a disk-based file system, or a network redirector, will maintain support for the on-disk data structures, such as an on-disk file stream representation (i.e., on-disk FCB/vnode/inode), a directory entry structure (e.g., the `dirent` structure) used in obtaining the contents of a directory, on-disk bitmaps, volume information, and other similar structures. Your FSD may also need to provide appropriate translation routines that would convert the in-memory information to on-disk formats for storage on physical media or for transmitting across a network.

Dispatch Routine: Driver Entry

All kernel-mode drivers are required to have a driver entry routine. This routine is invoked by the NT I/O Manager in the context of a system worker thread at IRQL `PASSIVE_LEVEL`.

Functionality Provided

File system drivers typically perform the steps listed below in their driver entry routines. Note that these steps are not much different from those performed by other lower-level drivers in their initialization routines:

1. Allocate memory for global data structures and initialize these data structures.

2. Read Registry information if required.

   Although most file system implementations will not provide many configurable parameters, redirectors and servers (e.g., the LAN Manager software) do allow users to specify the values of many configurable parameters.

3. Create a device object to which requests targeted to the FSD itself (as opposed to requests targeted to logical volumes managed by the FSD) can be sent.

   This device object will be one of the following types of device objects:

   — `FILE_DEVICE_DISK_FILE_SYSTEM`

     This is used by disk-based FSD implementations such as NTFS (device object name is *Ntfs*) and FAT (device object name is *Fat*).

   — `FILE_DEVICE_NETWORK`

     This is used by network servers, e.g., the LAN Manager Server.

   — `FILE_DEVICE_TAPE_FILE_SYSTEM`

   — `FILE_DEVICE_NETWORK_FILE_SYSTEM`

> This is used by the LAN Manager redirector, and other third-party NFS/ DFS implementations.

4. Initialize the function pointers for the dispatch routines that will accept the different IRP requests.

5. Initialize the function pointers for the fast I/O path and the callback functions used for synchronization across modules.

6. Initialize any timer objects and associated DPC objects, that your FSD might require.

   Some FSD implementations use timer interrupts to perform asynchronous processing. This requires using timer objects.

7. Initiate asynchronous initialization, if required.

   For example, if your driver needs to create worker threads that perform some initialization asynchronously, the threads can be created either in the context of the `DriverEntry()` routine or as an asynchronous operation.

8. Physical-media-based file system drivers will invoke `IoRegisterFile-System()` to register the current loaded instance of the driver.

   Note that the physical-media-based FSDs supported by the NT I/O Manager are disk-, virtual disk-, CDROM-, and tape-based FSD implementations. By registering the FSD with the I/O Manager, your FSD will ensure that it is on the list of file system drivers asked by the I/O Manager to examine and potentially perform a mount operation on media accessed for the first time in a boot cycle.

9. Network file system implementations that support Universal Naming Convention (UNC) names will invoke `FsRtlRegisterUncProvider()` to register themselves with the MUP component.

10. Network redirectors and servers will also register a shutdown notification function using the `IoRegisterShutdownNotification()` routine, ensuring that the FSD has an opportunity to flush modified data before the system goes down, as well as perform any other necessary processing.

Code Fragment

The following `DriverEntry()` code sample performs the previously listed steps. The code fragment contains conditionally compiled code for disk-based file system drivers as well as for network redirectors:

```
NTSTATUS DriverEntry(
PDRIVER_OBJECT          DriverObject,       // created by the I/O subsystem
PUNICODE_STRING         RegistryPath)       // path to the Registry key
{
```

```
NTSTATUS            RC = STATUS_SUCCESS;
UNICODE_STRING      DriverDeviceName;
BOOLEAN             RegisteredShutdown = FALSE;
try {
    try {
        // initialize the global data structure
        RtlZeroMemory(&SFsdGlobalData, sizeof(SFsdGlobalData));

        // initialize some required fields
        SFsdGlobalData.NodeIdentifier.NodeType =
                                    SFSD_NODE_TYPE_GLOBAL_DATA;
        SFsdGlobalData.NodeIdentifier.NodeSize =
                                    sizeof(SFsdGlobalData);

        // initialize the global data resource and remember the fact
        // that the resource has been initialized
        RC =
        ExInitializeResourceLite(&(SFsdGlobalData.GlobalDataResource));
        ASSERT(NT_SUCCESS(RC));
        SFsdSetFlag(SFsdGlobalData.SFsdFlags,
            SFSD_DATA_FLAGS_RESOURCE_INITIALIZED);

        // store a pointer to the driver object sent to us by the I/O
        // Mgr.
        SFsdGlobalData.SFsdDriverObject = DriverObject;

        // initialize the mounted logical volume list head
        InitializeListHead(&(SFsdGlobalData.NextVCB));

        // before we proceed with any more initialization, read in
        // user supplied configurable values ...
        if (!NT_SUCCESS(RC = SFsdObtainRegistryValues(RegistryPath))) {
            // in your commercial driver implementation, it would be
            // advisable for your driver to print an appropriate error
            // message to the system error log before leaving
            try_return(RC);
        }

        // we have the Registry data, allocate zone memory
        // This is an example of when FSD implementations
        // try to preallocate some fixed amount of memory to avoid
        // internal fragmentation and/or waiting later during runtime
        // ...
        if (!NT_SUCCESS(RC = SFsdInitializeZones())) {
            // we failed, print a message and leave ...
            try_return(RC);
        }

        // initialize the IRP major function table, and the fast I/O
        // table
        SFsdInitializeFunctionPointers(DriverObject);

        // create a device object representing the driver itself
        // so that requests can be targeted to the driver ...
```

```
                    // e.g., for a disk-based FSD, "mount" requests will be sent to
                    // this device object by the I/O Manager.
                    // For a redirector/server, you may have applications
                    // send "special" IOCTLs using this device object ...
                    RtlInitUnicodeString(&DriverDeviceName, SFSD_FS_NAME);
                    if (!NT_SUCCESS(RC = IoCreateDevice(
                            DriverObject,        // our driver object
                            0,               // don't need an extension for this object
                            &DriverDeviceName,
                        // name - can be used to "open" the driver
                        // see the book for alternate choices
                            FILE_DEVICE_DISK_FILE_SYSTEM,
                            0,                             // no special characteristics
                        // do not want this as an exclusive device, though you might
                            FALSE,
                            &(SFsdGlobalData.SFsdDeviceObject)))) {
                      // failed to create a device object, leave ...
                      try_return(RC);
                    }

#ifdef      _THIS_IS_A_NETWORK_REDIR_OR_SERVER_

                    // since network redirectors/servers do not register
                    // themselves as "file systems," the I/O Manager does not
                    // ordinarily request the FSD to flush logical volumes at
                    // shutdown. To get some notification at shutdown, use the
                    // IoRegisterShutdownNotification() instead ...
                    if (!NT_SUCCESS(RC =
                            IoRegisterShutdownNotification(
                                SFsdGlobalData.SFsdDeviceObject))) {
                      // failed to register shutdown notification ...
                      try_return(RC);
                    }
                    RegisteredShutdown = TRUE;

                    // Register the network FSD with the MUP component.
                    if (!NT_SUCCESS(RC = FsRtlRegisterUncProvider(
                                            &(SFsdGlobalData.MupHandle),
                                            &DriverDeviceName,
                                            FALSE))) {
                        try_return(RC);
                    }

#else          // This is a disk-based FSD

                    // register the driver with the I/O Manager, pretend as if
                    // this is a physical-disk-based FSD (or in other words, this
                    // FSD manages logical volumes residing on physical disk
                    // drives)
                    IoRegisterFileSystem(SFsdGlobalData.SFsdDeviceObject);

#endif      // _THIS_IS_A_NETWORK_REDIR_OR_SERVER_

        } except (EXCEPTION_EXECUTE_HANDLER) {
```

```
                        // we encountered an exception somewhere
                        RC = GetExceptionCode();
                    }

                    try_exit:     NOTHING;
            } finally {
                // start unwinding if we were unsuccessful
                if (!NT_SUCCESS(RC)) {

#ifdef     _THIS_IS_A_NETWORK_REDIR_OR_SERVER_
        if (RegisteredShutdown) {
            IoUnregisterShutdownNotification(SFsdGlobalData.SFsdDeviceObject);
        }
#endif     // _THIS_IS_A_NETWORK_REDIR_OR_SERVER_

                    // Now, delete any device objects, etc. we may have created
                    if (SFsdGlobalData.SFsdDeviceObject) {
                        IoDeleteDevice(SFsdGlobalData.SFsdDeviceObject);
                    SFsdGlobalData.SFsdDeviceObject = NULL;
                    }

                    // free up any memory we might have reserved for zones/
                    // lookaside lists
                    if (SFsdGlobalData.SFsdFlags
                            & SFSD_DATA_FLAGS_ZONES_INITIALIZED) {
                    SFsdDestroyZones();
                    }

                    // delete the resource we may have initialized
                    if (SFsdGlobalData.SFsdFlags
                            & SFSD_DATA_FLAGS_RESOURCE_INITIALIZED) {
                        // uninitialize this resource
                        ExDeleteResourceLite(&(SFsdGlobalData.GlobalDataResource));
                        SFsdClearFlag(SFsdGlobalData.SFsdFlags,
                            SFSD_DATA_FLAGS_RESOURCE_INITIALIZED);
                    }
                }
            }
        }

    return(RC);
}


void SFsdInitializeFunctionPointers(
PDRIVER_OBJECT          DriverObject)           // created by the I/O subsystem
{
    PFAST_IO_DISPATCH     PtrFastIoDispatch = NULL;

    // initialize the function pointers for the IRP major
    // functions that this FSD is prepared to handle ...
    // NT Version 4.0 has 28 possible functions that a
    // kernel mode driver can handle.
    // NT Version 3.51 (and earlier) has only 22 such functions,
    // of which 18 are typically interesting to most FSDs.
```

```
// The only interesting new functions that a FSD might (currently)
// want to respond to beginning with are the
// IRP_MJ_QUERY_QUOTA and the IRP_MJ_SET_QUOTA requests.

// The code below does not handle quota manipulation; neither
// does the NT Version 4.0 operating system (or I/O Manager).
// However, you should be on the lookout for any such new
// functionality that your FSD might have to implement in
// the near future.

// The functions that your FSD might wish to consider implementing
// (and are not covered below) are:

// Note that the "IRP_MJ_CREATE_NAMED_PIPE", and the "IRP_MJ_CREATE_
// MAILSLOT" requests won't be directed toward any FSD you would
// develop.
DriverObject->MajorFunction[IRP_MJ_CREATE]                = SFsdCreate;
DriverObject->MajorFunction[IRP_MJ_CLOSE]                 = SFsdClose;
DriverObject->MajorFunction[IRP_MJ_READ]                  = SFsdRead;
DriverObject->MajorFunction[IRP_MJ_WRITE]                 = SFsdWrite;
DriverObject->MajorFunction[IRP_MJ_QUERY_INFORMATION]     = SFsdFileInfo;
DriverObject->MajorFunction[IRP_MJ_SET_INFORMATION]       = SFsdFileInfo;
DriverObject->MajorFunction[IRP_MJ_FLUSH_BUFFERS]         = SFsdFlush;
DriverObject->MajorFunction[IRP_MJ_QUERY_VOLUME_INFORMATION]
                                                          = SFsdVolInfo;
DriverObject->MajorFunction[IRP_MJ_SET_VOLUME_INFORMATION]
                                                          = SFsdVolInfo;
DriverObject->MajorFunction[IRP_MJ_DIRECTORY_CONTROL]
                                                        = SFsdDirControl;
DriverObject->MajorFunction[IRP_MJ_FILE_SYSTEM_CONTROL]
                                                        = SFsdFSControl;
DriverObject->MajorFunction[IRP_MJ_DEVICE_CONTROL]
                                                      = SFsdDeviceControl;
DriverObject->MajorFunction[IRP_MJ_SHUTDOWN]            = SFsdShutdown;
DriverObject->MajorFunction[IRP_MJ_LOCK_CONTROL]
                                                      = SFsdLockControl;
DriverObject->MajorFunction[IRP_MJ_CLEANUP]            = SFsdCleanup;
DriverObject->MajorFunction[IRP_MJ_QUERY_SECURITY]     = SFsdSecurity;
DriverObject->MajorFunction[IRP_MJ_SET_SECURITY]
                                                      = SFsdSecurity;
DriverObject->MajorFunction[IRP_MJ_QUERY_EA]
                                                    = SFsdExtendedAttr;
DriverObject->MajorFunction[IRP_MJ_SET_EA]
                                                    = SFsdExtendedAttr;

// Now, it is time to initialize the fast I/O stuff ...
PtrFastIoDispatch = DriverObject->FastIoDispatch
                            = &(SFsdGlobalData.SFsdFastIoDispatch);

// initialize the global fast I/O structure
// NOTE: The fast I/O structure has undergone a substantial revision
// in Windows NT Version 4.0. The structure has been extensively
// expanded.
```

```
        // Therefore, if your driver needs to work on both V3.51 and V4.0+,
        // you will have to be able to distinguish between the two versions
        // at compile time.
        PtrFastIoDispatch->SizeOfFastIoDispatch    = sizeof(FAST_IO_DISPATCH);
        PtrFastIoDispatch->FastIoCheckIfPossible

                                                   = SFsdFastIoCheckIfPossible;
        PtrFastIoDispatch->FastIoRead              = SFsdFastIoRead;
        PtrFastIoDispatch->FastIoWrite             = SFsdFastIoWrite;
        PtrFastIoDispatch->FastIoQueryBasicInfo    = SFsdFastIoQueryBasicInfo;
        PtrFastIoDispatch->FastIoQueryStandardInfo = SFsdFastIoQueryStdInfo;
        PtrFastIoDispatch->FastIoLock              = SFsdFastIoLock;
        PtrFastIoDispatch->FastIoUnlockSingle      = SFsdFastIoUnlockSingle;
        PtrFastIoDispatch->FastIoUnlockAll         = SFsdFastIoUnlockAll;
        PtrFastIoDispatch->FastIoUnlockAllByKey    = SFsdFastIoUnlockAllByKey;
        PtrFastIoDispatch->AcquireFileForNtCreateSection
                                                   = SFsdFastIoAcqCreateSec;
        PtrFastIoDispatch->ReleaseFileForNtCreateSection
                                                   = SFsdFastIoRelCreateSec;

        // the remaining are only valid under NT Version 4.0 and later
#if(_WIN32_WINNT >= 0x0400)
        PtrFastIoDispatch->FastIoQueryNetworkOpenInfo = SFsdFastIoQueryNetInfo;
        PtrFastIoDispatch->AcquireForModWrite      = SFsdFastIoAcqModWrite;
        PtrFastIoDispatch->ReleaseForModWrite      = SFsdFastIoRelModWrite;
        PtrFastIoDispatch->AcquireForCcFlush       = SFsdFastIoAcqCcFlush;
        PtrFastIoDispatch->ReleaseForCcFlush       = SFsdFastIoRelCcFlush;

        // MDL functionality
        PtrFastIoDispatch->MdlRead                 = SFsdFastIoMdlRead;
        PtrFastIoDispatch->MdlReadComplete         = SFsdFastIoMdlReadComplete;
        PtrFastIoDispatch->PrepareMdlWrite         = SFsdFastIoPrepareMdlWrite;
        PtrFastIoDispatch->MdlWriteComplete        = SFsdFastIoMdlWriteComplete;

        // although this FSD does not support compressed read/write
        // functionality, NTFS does, and if you design a FSD that can provide
        // such functionality,
        // you should consider initializing the fast I/O entry points for
        // reading and/or writing compressed data ...
#endif    // (_WIN32_WINNT >= 0x0400)

        // last but not least, initialize the Cache Manager callback functions
        // which are used in CcInitializeCacheMap()
        SFsdGlobalData.CacheMgrCallBacks.AcquireForLazyWrite
                                                   = SFsdAcqLazyWrite;
        SFsdGlobalData.CacheMgrCallBacks.ReleaseFromLazyWrite
                                                   = SFsdRelLazyWrite;
        SFsdGlobalData.CacheMgrCallBacks.AcquireForReadAhead
                                                   = SFsdAcqReadAhead;
        SFsdGlobalData.CacheMgrCallBacks.ReleaseFromReadAhead
                                                   = SFsdRelReadAhead;

        return;
}
```

Notes

The two routines listed comprise the bulk of the driver entry code for the sample FSD driver. The code fragment doesn't initiate any asynchronous initialization; neither does it initialize any timer or DPC objects. However, your FSD can certainly perform such functions in its driver entry routine. Otherwise, the code pretty much follows the logical steps listed earlier that most FSD implementations perform in the initialization routine.

For additional details on some of the supporting functions invoked by the driver entry routine, consult the disk that accompanies this book.

Dispatch Routine: Create

As a file systems designer, you will probably count the "create" routine as one of the more difficult routines to design and implement. This routine forms the very core of your FSD, since in order to perform any operation on on-disk objects, the object must first be created and/or opened. Therefore, not only are create routines required to be robust, but the design and implementation of the create routine can also contribute significantly to overall system performance, because badly designed or implemented "create" routines can become a bottleneck very easily during frequent (high stress) file system manipulation operations.

Logical Steps Involved

The I/O stack location contains the following structure relevant to processing a create/open request issued to an FSD:

```
typedef struct _IO_STACK_LOCATION {

    // ...

    union {

        //...

        // System service parameters for:  NtCreateFile
        struct {
            PIO_SECURITY_CONTEXT SecurityContext;
            ULONG Options;
            USHORT FileAttributes;
            USHORT ShareAccess;
            ULONG EaLength;
        } Create;

        // ...
```

```
} Parameters;

// ...

} IO_STACK_LOCATION, *PIO_STACK_LOCATION;
```

Create routines are conceptually not very difficult. Unfortunately, however, the details involved in processing a create request sometimes become overwhelming. Logically, you need to perform the following operations when processing a create or an open request on an object stored on secondary storage:*

1. First, you would have to obtain the caller-supplied path that leads you to the object of interest.

   Note that most of the common, commercially available operating systems are equipped only to handle inverted-tree-based file system organizations. In this kind of file system arrangement, there is a *container object,* such as a directory structure, which in turn leads you to the actual *named data objects,* also known as file streams. Container objects typically also contain other container objects in addition to file streams, thereby leading to the inverted-tree structured file system layout.

   On some operating system platforms such as most commercial UNIX implementations, the FSD is not supplied with the entire path leading to a specific named file stream. Instead, the operating system performs the task of parsing the path leading to the target file stream, and only supplies the FSD with a handle to the container object and the name of an object to open within the container. See Figure 9-5 for an illustration of a file system layout. For example, if a thread wished to open an object *dir1**dir2*\\...*foo* on such a platform, the operating system would first request the FSD to open \\ (or the *root* of the tree), then request the FSD to open *dir1* given a handle to \\ (received from the just concluded open request), then move on to *dir2* given a handle to *dir1* and so on, until the operating system finally requests the FSD to open the object *foo*—the actual target of the create/open request

   On Windows NT platforms, however, the I/O Manager (which happens to be the component that invokes the FSD *create* dispatch entry point) does not perform such name parsing. Instead, the I/O Manager supplies the FSD with the entire caller-supplied path and then expects the FSD to perform any required processing that might be required, including parsing the pathname supplied; i.e., the I/O Manager would give the FSD the complete name, *dir1**dir2*\\...*foo* in the example discussed earlier, for processing in the

---

* Note that a request to create a new object always implies that the caller wishes to open the object as well. Therefore, when I use the term *create* in this section, I do so generically, implying that this is either some form of *open* request, or a *create and open* request.

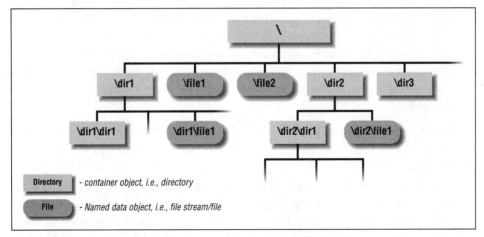

Figure 9-5. Simple representation of an inverted-tree file system layout

create dispatch routine. This is both a blessing and a curse: it affords considerable latitude to the FSD on how it can structure on-disk names and paths leading to on-disk objects, but the complete responsibility for parsing the caller-supplied name is the responsibility of the FSD implementation.

One final point should be mentioned here is that the NT I/O Manager supports the concept of relative open operations, where the pathname supplied by the caller is assumed to be relative to a container (directory) object opened earlier, instead of being a path beginning at the root of the file system tree. Your FSD must be able to distinguish between these two kinds of create/open operations and be able to deal with each of them correctly.

2. Now, your FSD can obtain other arguments supplied by the caller that will determine how you process the create/open request. These arguments include information on whether the caller has specified that the target must be created (and the FSD should return an error if the target already exists), whether the target must be opened only (and the FSD should return an error if the target object does not exist), or whether the target should be created conditionally (opened if it exists but created if it does not). Note that the caller may also request the creation of a hard link to an existing object. However, in the Windows NT operating system environment, this does not happen via the create entry point so we will discuss it later.*

Other caller-supplied arguments include any specifications on the type of object being created or opened (e.g., whether the caller wishes to create or

---

* The method used to create a hard link in Windows NT is via the IRP_MJ_SET_INFORMATION request, which is described in the next chapter.

open a container object or a file-stream object). Furthermore, the caller can specify attributes to associate with the object if a new one is being created; e.g., a caller might specify that the *delete-on-close* attribute be associated with the object, to make it a temporary object that is automatically deleted by the FSD once the object has been closed for the last time. Other attributes include the sharing mode that a caller might wish to enforce with the object being opened.

3. Once your FSD has obtained all of the caller-supplied information, all it needs to do is to try to locate the target object, given the user-supplied pathname leading to this object.

   Your driver may or may not be successful in locating the target object, given the path to that object. If the object is found and the caller has requested that a new object must be created (`CreateDisposition` in sample code below is `FILE_CREATE`), your driver must return an *object exists* error code. If however the object is not found—i.e., it does not exist, but the caller has specified that the object must only be opened and not created (`CreateDisposition` is `FILE_OPEN`)—your driver must return an *object not found* error. Finally, the *create-if-not-found* or *open-if-found* option (`CreateDisposition` is `FILE_OPEN_IF` or `FILE_OVERWRITE_IF`) is the most flexible since it allows your driver to return success more often than not. Regardless, you will either decide to return an error at this point or move on to the next step.

4. At this time, your driver can check whether the caller can be allowed to create/open the object, given the caller's identity, the operation requested, and the sharing mode requested. The sharing mode assumes greater importance if another thread already has the target object open, in which case the new request must not conflict with the sharing mode allowed by the previous open operations.

   If your FSD provides access-checking functionality, you can use the caller's subject context to validate whether the caller has appropriate privileges to perform the desired operation on the target file/directory object. You may also be required to perform traverse access checking while parsing the pathname leading up to the target object.

5. If your FSD is successful in creating and/or opening the target object, it will have to create appropriate in-memory data structures that can be used later in accesses to the object. For example, if no FCB describing this object currently exists in memory, the FSD must create one. More likely than not, the FSD will also create a CCB structure at this time to maintain some context for this particular instance of a create request.

   Both of these structures, as well as any supporting structures, will have to be initialized appropriately by the FSD.

6. The Windows NT I/O Manager expects that, for a successful create/open operation, the FSD will initialize certain fields in the file object structure as described earlier. Your FSD should do so at this point if the create/open operation does succeed.

7. Lastly, your FSD must convey the results of the create/open request to the I/O Manager, which in turn will forward the results to the caller.

As long as your driver understands the steps, described here, that it must perform in response to a create request and implements them systematically, you should be able to handle create requests correctly.

Synchronization Issues

There are other, more advanced considerations that file systems often have to deal with in designing the create/open dispatch entry point, as well as other dispatch entry points.

One of the issues that you should understand well is the synchronization that your file system driver must perform to process create requests correctly and efficiently. For example, your FSD must be cognizant of the fact that multiple concurrent create/open operations could potentially be happening in the same file system and possibly in the same directory. All of these concurrent operations should be handled consistently. For example, consider the situation when two threads request that the target file \dir1\foo be created if it does not exist and opened if it does exist. Assume that the file does not exist. Unless your FSD is careful about synchronizing both requests correctly, it might actually allocate a new directory entry for the file twice in directory dir1 and assign the same name foo to both the directory entries. The inconsistent result can be avoided, however, by serializing both requests with respect to each other.

Another consideration that your FSD must take into account is that delete and/or file close operations (leading to the possible destruction of a FCB) could also be happening concurrently with other create/open requests. In this case, your FSD must be careful to correctly synchronize concurrent operations, such that a consistent view of file system data structures is always maintained. For example, two threads may both be manipulating an object \dir1\foo concurrently. One thread might request that the object be deleted, while the other thread may wish to create/open the object. Your FSD must again be very careful to always maintain internal consistency. Note that it is not important to guarantee which thread is allowed access first; i.e., should the thread trying to delete be allowed to go first or should the thread performing the create/open be allowed to go first? No file system guarantees any such ordering to its clients. Regardless of which operation happens first, however (and yes, it might be possible for one of the user requests to get an error code returned, depending on the sequence in which the threads are allowed to proceed), it is important that both not be allowed to proceed together or file system internal data structures will surely become corrupted.

At other times, your FSD will have to synchronize between multiple threads performing I/O to the same file control block concurrently. For example, a thread could be performing a read operation at the same time as another thread is attempting a write.* In such cases, it is the FSD implementation's responsibility to ensure that the read and write requests are serialized with respect to each other. It is not the responsibility of the FSD to ensure that the read and write occur in some specific sequence; the caller can ensure such order using other methods, such as byte-range locking on the file stream. As long as the read and write routines do not overlap within the FSD (i.e., once the FSD has begun processing the read in `SFsdRead()`, the write is blocked in `SFsdWrite()` until the thread executing `SFsdRead()` completes processing, or vice versa), the FSD will have succeeded in maintaining its responsibilities.

You will also need to synchronize multiple threads attempting other directory manipulation operations concurrently. For example, one thread might be querying the contents of a directory while another might be in the process of deleting an object within the directory.

Regardless of which operation is being performed on a particular FCB, your file system driver will surely have to utilize some sort of synchronization mechanism to ensure orderly access. If you are developing a significantly more complex FSD, such as one that is inherently networked (e.g., NFS) and/or distributed in nature (e.g., DFS), your task is now made even more complicated by the fact that your create/open operations must now be made consistent across nodes as well.

Note that, in most situations, synchronization attempts described here and practiced throughout the sample code are fairly fine-grained; the FSD attempts to synchronize at the level of each FCB. If two concurrent operations proceed independently on two different FCB structures (on two different file streams or directories), the FSD will not serialize the two operations. At this point, you may be wondering why you should not simply disallow concurrent operations to the same logical volume? Although such synchronization might be a little bit coarser than that performed at the level of an FCB, it seems as if that would make life a

---

* Often, you may encounter the case where a delayed-write from the NT Cache Manager on an FCB proceeds concurrently with a user read request on the same FCB. At other times, a user write may be received at the same time as a Cache Manager read-ahead operation. In most such cases (unless the user has requested direct disk I/O), such operations will be allowed to proceed concurrently. This is in contrast to the situations where two concurrent user write requests on an FCB will be serialized with respect to each other or a write and a read operation proceeding concurrently and independently will also be serialized with respect to each other. This is discussed in detail later in the book as well.

lot simpler. Unfortunately, although serializing all accesses to a logical volume may make an FSD developer's life easier, generally speaking, for any file system, preventing concurrent access to different files within the same logical volume is simply not a viable option. Imagine how upset you might become if a file system made you wait two hours to respond to a `dir` request simply because it serialized all accesses to files within a logical volume! As a matter of fact, in order to enhance response time and throughput, you should always be looking for ways in which your FSD can safely increase parallelism and concurrency. For example, you should always allow multiple threads to concurrently read data for the same file stream, even though for write operations you would have to serialize across different threads.

Note that a file system driver typically never keeps any resources acquired across invocations of a particular dispatch routine. For example, if the create dispatch routine is invoked and the thread acquires some resources as part of the processing performed in the create, these resources must be released before the thread exits file system code (from the create entry point). Not doing this will lead either to a system crash or to a hang/deadlock. Resources are only acquired while processing some file system code within a particular dispatch routine.

Here is a set of general synchronization rules followed by the sample FSD to ensure consistent access to an FCB. Your driver is free to determine appropriate synchronization rules specific to your situation:

- The sample FSD will use the **MainResource** and the **PagingIoResource** as the two synchronization resources for each file control block structure representing a file stream. These are read/write locks and will be acquired either shared or exclusively, depending upon the specific situation.

  Note once again that your FSD is free to use other synchronization primitives in addition to the **MainResource** and the **PagingIoResource**. You can choose from any of the mutex/executive mutex primitives available or use counting semaphores.

- Since two resources will be used by the FSD to synchronize access to an FCB, a locking hierarchy must be maintained for these two resources. The locking hierarchy I will follow is that, if both resources need to be acquired, the **MainResource** will always be acquired before the **PagingIoResource** is acquired.

  Whenever multiple synchronization primitives are used to synchronize access to an object, you must determine a hierarchy between such primitives to avoid deadlock scenarios. For example, consider the case where no hierarchy was defined and two threads tried to concurrently manipulate the same FCB. For some reason, both threads determine that they must acquire both the resources to completely shut out all other operations on the FCB. One of the threads may now acquire the `MainResource` and then try to acquire the `PagingIoResource`. The other thread, in the meantime, might have already acquired the `PagingIoResource` and could now be attempting to acquire the `MainResource`. Both threads will now block on each other, and neither can subsequently make any headway. This situation will not occur if the locking hierarchy described above is followed, since only one thread will be able to acquire the `MainResource` and that thread can continue on to acquire the `PagingIoResource`.

• Typically, the sample FSD will acquire the `MainResource` only to perform synchronization between multiple user threads accessing the same FCB structure. For example, if two user threads perform a *query directory* operation on an FCB representing a directory (container object), the `SFsdDirControl()` dispatch routine implementation will first attempt to acquire the `MainResource` exclusively for the target FCB on behalf of each thread. This will ensure that accesses will be serialized across both threads within the specific dispatch routine.

Similarly, as described earlier, if multiple user threads try to perform I/O on the same file stream (FCB) concurrently, each of threads will use the `MainResource` to synchronize access to the FCB. All threads attempting a read I/O operation will acquire the `MainResource` shared, allowing multiple reads to proceed concurrently on the file stream. All threads attempting a write operation, however, will do so having acquired at least the `MainResource` exclusively, thereby preventing any other read or write operation to proceed concurrently.

• The sample FSD will typically acquire the `PagingIoResource` only when performing read or write operations that have the `IRP_PAGING_IO` flag set in the IRP structure.* This will simply allow the FSD to synchronize across multiple concurrent paging I/O operations. However, user read/write operations and paging I/O operations will typically not be serialized with respect to each other (since user requests use the `MainResource` while the NT VMM-initiated requests use the `PagingIoResource`) and will therefore proceed concurrently.

• On some occasions, the sample FSD will acquire both the `MainResource` and the `PagingIoResource` on behalf of the same thread, while ensuring

---

* The presence of this flag indicates that this request comes to the FSD via the NT VMM. The FSD must be extremely careful in handling paging I/O requests, since page faults are not allowed at that time. Also, most consistency checks will be bypassed by the FSD when a paging I/O request is directed to page files. The FSD implementation will simply trust the VMM to submit a valid request and pass on the request to the underlying lower-level device drivers for completion (by reading/writing the requested byte range from/to secondary storage devices).

that the resource acquisition hierarchy is always maintained (i.e., the `MainRe-`
`source` is always acquired before the attempt to acquire the `PagingIo-`
`Resource`). This will be done for specific situations only; e.g., both
resources will be acquired when the size of file stream changes (a file is trun-
cated/extended).

TIP   It is difficult to present any sort of cookbook on how and when resources should be acquired by all FSDs since each FSD has unique
requirements that dictate the synchronization methodology adopted
by it. However, in general, keep in mind that many critical in-memory fields contained in the FCB data structure are synchronized using
the `PagingIoResource`. That said, however, file create operations and all user-initiated operations are usually synchronized using
the `MainResource`. Finally, as mentioned, some operations (e.g.,
an `IRP_MJ_CREATE` that also specifies a certain file allocation size)
will require both resources to be acquired.

As noted, it is certainly not easy and will require considerable
thought on your part to determine the correct synchronization methodology that will ensure data consistency for your FSD.

Consider the create dispatch entry point. When processing the create/open
request, the FSD has to examine the contents of each directory that comprises the
pathname leading up to the target object. When examining the contents of a directory object in the path, the FSD must ensure that the contents of the directory do
not unexpectedly change. To do this, the FSD will block changes by acquiring the
`MainResource` for the directory object's FCB. Your FSD can determine whether
the `MainResource` needs to be acquired exclusively or shared. Acquiring the
resource exclusively ensures that no other create or lookup operation can
proceed concurrently in the same directory, while acquiring it shared does allow
other create or lookup operations to proceed concurrently in the same directory.

One final note: often FSD implementations are fairly coarse-grained in the
synchronization employed while processing create/open requests. For example, it
appears that the Windows NT CDFS implementation simply acquires a resource
associated with the volume control block exclusively for the logical volume on
which the create operation is being performed. This ensures that no other create/
open can proceed while the current request is being processed. There are,
however, some FSD implementations that do not lock out all other create/open
operations when processing any one of them. You can determine the appropriate
locking for your FSD.

Simple Algorithm to Process a Create/Open Request

Before you examine the code/pseudocode provided here, understand the following simple algorithm used to process a create/open request of an on-disk file object. You know that the NT I/O Manager depends upon the FSD to parse a complete pathname in the create dispatch routine.* Assume that the I/O Manager has given a pathname *dir1**dir2**dir3**foobar* to be processed. The following simple terms and rules are important:

- The *pathname* supplied is composed of individual components.

- Each component is identified by a string composed of characters, e.g., *dir2*.

  Your FSD can determine the range of characters and symbols that would be acceptable to it.

- Components are demarcated by the presence of a valid separator character; the convention on Windows platforms is to use the \ character.

- The last component in the pathname string is the actual *target* of the create/open operation.

- Each component in the pathname string preceding the last component must be a valid subdirectory.

The algorithm used to parse the pathname can be implemented as follows:

```
determine the starting directory from which to begin processing;
get current component and next component by parsing pathname
    (using the \ as the path separator);
current component = starting directory (= \ in example given);
open current component;
next component = string obtained from the pathname (= dir1)
while (TRUE) {
    perform traverse access checks if required, i.e., check whether
        caller has appropriate privileges to read contents of the
        directory identified by the current component;

    if (entire path has been parsed) {
        // we are down to the last token/component.
        //    In our example, we are at the point where current
        // component = dir3 and next component = foobar
        final component = next component;
        break;
    }
    lookup† next component in current component
```

---

* If you are familiar with UNIX file system structures and implementations, this is simply a `namei()` (name-to-inode) type of routine that a file system must implement.

† A lookup operation simply means checking whether the named object exists within the specified directory. To perform the lookup, most FSD implementations read in the list of entries that comprise the directory and perform a string comparison of the name being looked up with all of the entries in the directory in a linear fashion. If a match is found, the object exists in the directory; otherwise, the FSD determines that the object does not exist.

```
        (may involve I/O to obtain directory contents);
    if (not found) {
        return (STATUS_OBJECT_PATH_NOT_FOUND);
    }
    if (next component looked-up != directory) {
        return(STATUS_OBJECT_PATH_NOT_FOUND);
    }
    close current component;
    open next component;
    current component = next component;
    next component = get next string identifier from pathname;
}
lookup final component;
if (not found) {
    if (create requested) {
        perform create …;
      } else {
        return(STATUS_OBJECT_NAME_NOT_FOUND);
      }
} else {
      if (create only request) {
          return (STATUS_OBJECT_NAME_COLLISION);
      }
}
open final component;
initialize various internal (FCB/CCB) and external (file object)
    data structures;
return (results);
```

This algorithm is the general methodology used by file systems in response to a create/open request. Basically, the algorithm starts parsing the given pathname, beginning at the user-supplied starting point. This could either be the root of the file system, or in the case of relative file opens, it would begin at the directory identified by the `RelatedFileObject` field, initialized by the NT I/O Manager in the newly created file object for the target of the open.

Once the starting point has been determined, the file system driver simply iterates through all of the components that comprise the pathname leading to the target file/directory object. If the FSD is security conscious, it will always check whether the caller has appropriate privileges to traverse and/or read the directories in the pathname.

After the FSD has successfully traversed the user-supplied pathname, the FSD will look for the target file/directory object. Depending on whether the object already exists or not, and also on the type of create/open operation requested by the user, the FSD will either complete the request or return an appropriate error code to the caller. The code fragments later provide you with some more information about how to process create/open requests on the Windows NT platform.

More About the Name Supplied to the FSD

Before you examine the following code fragment, you may still be wondering about the composition of a pathname when it is sent to you by the I/O Manager. You might also wonder how the I/O Manager determines that a create/open request should be sent to your FSD.

Let me briefly summarize the answer to the latter question first. Consider physical-disk-based FSD implementations. Remember from Chapter 4, that the I/O Manager assigns drive letters to each physical disk in the system. When a thread decides to create/open an object, it must supply a path leading to the object. Typically this path will look like *D:\dir1\dir2....\target_file*. Now, this create/open request gets directed to the I/O Manager,* which determines that the target device object for this request is the physical disk represented by the letter *D:*. (Note that *D:* and other such symbolic identifiers are simply symbolic links that point to a particular physical device object; in this case, to a SCSI disk drive.)

The I/O Manager then checks the volume parameter block (VPB) associated with the device object for the physical disk to see whether any logical volume has been mounted on the physical disk identified by the device object. If no mount operation has been performed, the I/O Manager will attempt a new mount sequence, which is explained in further detail in the next chapter. If a logical mount had been previously performed or after a successful mount operation is completed, the I/O Manager will send the complete pathname excluding the portion that has already been parsed, i.e., excluding *D:*, to the FSD as an argument to the create/open dispatch routine. The logic here is simple: the NT Object Manager and the I/O Manager have already parsed (processed) some portion of the user-supplied pathname to determine the target FSD for the request. The FSD should not need that portion of the string. The remainder of the user-supplied string, however, has not yet been parsed/processed, and it is sent in its entirety to the FSD.

For network redirectors, the situation is not very different conceptually. Requests are directed to specific network redirectors, identified by the symbolic name associated with a device object created by the redirector. For example, a hypothetical redirector might create a symbolic link *F:* that points to a device object that handles all I/O-related requests for a remote, shared network drive. Once again, the actual pathname sent by the I/O Manager to the redirector device object dispatch routine will be the portion that has not been parsed by the I/O Manager or the Object Manager (i.e., everything excluding the string used to identify the target device object and therefore, everything excluding *F:)*.

---

* In the next chapter, I will explain the mount process in a little more detail. At that time, I will also mention how the create/open request gets directed to the NT I/O Manager in the first place.

Code Fragment

```
NTSTATUS SFsdCommonCreate(
PtrSFsdIrpContext            PtrIrpContext,
PIRP                         PtrIrp)
{
    // Declarations go here …

    ASSERT(PtrIrpContext);
    ASSERT(PtrIrp);

    try {

        AbsolutePathName.Buffer = NULL;
        AbsolutePathName.Length = AbsolutePathName.MaximumLength = 0;

        // First, get a pointer to the current I/O stack location
        PtrIoStackLocation = IoGetCurrentIrpStackLocation(PtrIrp);
        ASSERT(PtrIoStackLocation);

        // If the caller cannot block, post the request to be handled
        // asynchronously
        if (!(PtrIrpContext->IrpContextFlags
                & SFSD_IRP_CONTEXT_CAN_BLOCK)) {
                // We must defer processing this request, since we could
                // block anytime while performing the create/open ...
            RC = SFsdPostRequest(PtrIrpContext, PtrIrp);
         DeferredProcessing = TRUE;
            try_return(RC);
        }

        // Now, we can obtain the parameters specified by the user.
        // Note that the file object is the new object created by the
        // I/O Manager, in anticipation that this create/open request
        // will succeed.
        PtrNewFileObjec t    = PtrIoStackLocation->FileObject;
        TargetObjectNam e    = PtrNewFileObject->FileName;
        PtrRelatedFileObject = PtrNewFileObject->RelatedFileObject;

        // If a related file object is present, get the pointers
        // to the CCB and the FCB for the related file object
        if (PtrRelatedFileObject) {
            PtrRelatedCCB = (PtrSFsdCCB)(PtrRelatedFileObject->FsContext2);
            ASSERT(PtrRelatedCCB);
            ASSERT(PtrRelatedCCB->NodeIdentifier.NodeType
                    == SFSD_NODE_TYPE_CCB);
            // each CCB in turn points to a FCB
            PtrRelatedFCB = PtrRelatedCCB->PtrFCB;
            ASSERT(PtrRelatedFCB);
            ASSERT((PtrRelatedFCB->NodeIdentifier.NodeType
                    == SFSD_NODE_TYPE_FCB)
                        ||
                    (PtrRelatedFCB->NodeIdentifier.NodeType
                        == SFSD_NODE_TYPE_VCB));
```

```
        RelatedObjectName = PtrRelatedFileObject->FileName;
}

// Allocation size is only used if a new file is created
// or a file is superseded.

AllocationSize = PtrIrp->Overlay.AllocationSize.LowPart;

// Note: Some FSD implementations support file sizes > 2GB.
// The following check is only valid if your FSD does not support
// a large file size. With NT version 5.0, 64-bit support will
// become available and your FSD ideally should support large files
if (PtrIrp->Overlay.AllocationSize.HighPart) {
    RC = STATUS_INVALID_PARAMETER;
    try_return(RC);
}

// Get a pointer to the supplied security context
PtrSecurityContext =
    PtrIoStackLocation->Parameters.Create.SecurityContext;

// The desired access can be obtained from the SecurityContext
DesiredAccess = PtrSecurityContext->DesiredAccess;

// Two values are supplied in the Create.Options field:
// (a) the actual user-supplied options
// (b) the create disposition
RequestedOptions =
    (PtrIoStackLocation->Parameters.Create.Options &
                        FILE_VALID_OPTION_FLAGS);

// The file disposition is packed with the user options ...
// Disposition includes FILE_SUPERSEDE, FILE_OPEN_IF, etc.
RequestedDisposition =
    ((PtrIoStackLocation->Parameters.Create.Options >> 24)
        && 0xFF);

FileAttributes    =
    (uint8)(PtrIoStackLocation->Parameters.Create.FileAttributes
                    & FILE_ATTRIBUTE_VALID_FLAGS);
ShareAccess    = PtrIoStackLocation->Parameters.Create.ShareAccess;

// If your FSD does not support EA manipulation, you might return
// invalid parameter if the following are supplied.
// EA arguments are only used if a new file is created or a file is
// superseded
PtrExtAttrBuffer    = PtrIrp->AssociatedIrp.SystemBuffer;
ExtAttrLength = PtrIoStackLocation->Parameters.Create.EaLength;

// Get the options supplied by the user

// User specifies that returned object MUST be a directory.
// Lack of presence of this flag does not mean it *cannot* be a
// directory *unless* FileOnlyRequested is set (see below)
```

```
// Presence of the flag however, does require that the returned
// object be a directory (container) object.
DirectoryOnlyRequested =
    ((RequestedOptions & FILE_DIRECTORY_FILE) ? TRUE : FALSE);

// User specifies that returned object MUST NOT be a directory.
// Lack of presence of the flag below does not mean it cannot be a
// file unless DirectoryOnlyRequested is set (see above).

// Presence of the flag, however, does require that the returned
// object be a simple file (noncontainer) object.
FileOnlyRequested =
    ((RequestedOptions & FILE_NON_DIRECTORY_FILE) ? TRUE : FALSE);

// We cannot cache the file if the following flag is set.
// However, things do get a little bit interesting if caching
// has been already initiated due to a previous open ...
// (maintaining consistency then becomes a little bit more
// of a headache - see read/write file descriptions)
NoBufferingSpecified =
    ((RequestedOptions & FILE_NO_INTERMEDIATE_BUFFERING)
        ? TRUE : FALSE);

// Write-through simply means that the FSD must not return from
// a user write request until the data has been flushed to
// secondary storage (either to disks directly connected to the
// node, or across the network in the case of a redirector)
WriteThroughRequested =
    ((RequestedOptions & FILE_WRITE_THROUGH) ? TRUE : FALSE);

// Not all of the Windows NT file system implementations support
// the delete-on-close option. The presence of this flag implies
// that after the last close on the FCB has been performed, your
// FSD should delete the file. Specifying this flag saves the
// caller from issuing a separate delete request. Also, some FSD
// implementations might choose to implement a Windows NT
// idiosyncratic behavior where you could create such "delete-on-
// close"-marked files under directories marked for deletion.
// Ordinarily, an FSD will not allow you to createa new file under
// a directory that has been marked for deletion.
DeleteOnCloseSpecified =
    ((RequestedOptions & FILE_DELETE_ON_CLOSE) ? TRUE : FALSE);


NoExtAttrKnowledge =
    ((RequestedOptions & FILE_NO_EA_KNOWLEDGE) ? TRUE : FALSE);

// The following flag is only used by the LAN Manager redirector
// to initiate a "new mapping" to a remote share.
// Third-party FSD implementations will not see this flag.
CreateTreeConnection =
    ((RequestedOptions & FILE_CREATE_TREE_CONNECTION)
        ? TRUE : FALSE);
```

```
// The NTFS file system, for example, supports the OpenByFileId
// option. Your FSD may also be able to associate a unique
// numerical ID with an on-disk object. Any thread can then obtain
// this ID via a "query file information" call to your FSD.
// Later, the caller might decide to reopen the object; this time,
// though, it may supply your FSD with the file identifier instead
// of a file/pathname.
OpenByFileId =
    ((RequestedOptions & FILE_OPEN_BY_FILE_ID) ? TRUE : FALSE);

// Are we dealing with a page file? Page files are not very
// different from any other kind of on-disk file stream though you
// should allocate the FCB, CCB, and other structures for a page
// file from nonpaged pool.
PageFileManipulation =
    ((PtrIoStackLocation->Flags & SL_OPEN_PAGING_FILE)
        ? TRUE : FALSE);

// The open target directory flag is used as part of the sequence
// of operations performed by the I/O Manager is response to a
// file/dir rename operation. See the explanation in the book for
// details.
OpenTargetDirectory =
    ((PtrIoStackLocation->Flags & SL_OPEN_TARGET_DIRECTORY) ?
                            TRUE : FALSE);

// If your FSD supports case-sensitive file name checks, you may
// choose to honor the following flag. It is not mandatory for your
// FSD to support case-sensitive name matching (e.g., FAT/CDFS do
// not support case-sensitive name comparisons.
IgnoreCaseWhenChecking =
    ((PtrIoStackLocation->Flags & SL_CASE_SENSITIVE)
        ? TRUE : FALSE);

// Ensure that the operation has been directed to a valid VCB ...
PtrVCB = (PtrSFsdVCB)(PtrIrpContext->TargetDeviceObject->
                                    DeviceExtension);
ASSERT(PtrVCB);
ASSERT(PtrVCB->NodeIdentifier.NodeType == SFSD_NODE_TYPE_VCB);

// Use coarse-grained locking and acquire the VCB exclusively. This
// will lock out all other concurrent create/open requests.
ExAcquireResourceExclusiveLite(&(PtrVCB->VCBResource), TRUE);
AcquiredVCB = TRUE;

// Disk-based file systems might decide to verify the logical
// volume (if required and only if removable media are supported)
// at this time.

// Implement your own volume verification routine ...
// Read the DDK for more information on when a FSD must verify a
// volume (this is typically done when a lower-level disk driver
// for removable drives reports that the media in the drive might
// possibly have been changed; i.e., user ejected and inserted some
```

```
// media). Chapter 11 also describes the volume verification
// process in considerable detail.

// If the volume has been locked, fail the request. Users may have
// locked the volume to issue a dismount request
if (PtrVCB->VCBFlags & SFSD_VCB_FLAGS_VOLUME_LOCKED) {
    RC = STATUS_ACCESS_DENIED;
    try_return(RC);
}

// If a "volume open" is requested, satisfy it now.
if ((PtrNewFileObject->FileName.Length == 0) &&
    ((PtrRelatedFileObject == NULL) ||
     (PtrRelatedFCB->NodeIdentifier.NodeType
         == SFSD_NODE_TYPE_VCB))) {
    // If the supplied file name is NULL and either there exists
    // no related file object or a related file object was supplied
    // but it refers to a previously opened instance of a logical
    // volume, this open must be for a logical volume.

    // Note: your FSD might decide to do special things (whatever
    // they might be) in response to an open request for the
    // logical volume.

    // Logical volume open requests are done primarily to get/set
    // volume information, lock the volume, dismount the volume
    // (using the IOCTL FSCTL_DISMOUNT_VOLUME), etc.

    // If a volume open is requested, perform checks to ensure that
    // invalid options have not also been specified ...
    if ((OpenTargetDirectory) || (PtrExtAttrBuffer)) {
        RC = STATUS_INVALID_PARAMETER;
        try_return(RC);
    }

    if (DirectoryOnlyRequested) {
        // a volume is not a directory
        RC = STATUS_NOT_A_DIRECTORY;
        try_return(RC);
    }

    if ((RequestedDisposition != FILE_OPEN) &&
        (RequestedDisposition != FILE_OPEN_IF)) {
        // cannot create a new volume, I'm afraid …
        RC = STATUS_ACCESS_DENIED;
        try_return(RC);
    }

    RC = SFsdOpenVolume(PtrVCB, PtrIrpContext, PtrIrp,
                ShareAccess, PtrSecurityContext, PtrNewFileObject);
    ReturnedInformation = PtrIrp->IoStatus.Information;

    try_return(RC);
}
```

```
// Your FSD might implement the open-by-id option. The "id"
// is an FSD-defined unique numerical representation of the on-
// disk object. The caller can subsequently give you this file id
// and your FSD should be completely capable of opening the object.
if (OpenByFileId) {
    // perform the open ...
    // RC = SFsdOpenByFileId(PtrIrpContext, PtrIrp ....);
    // try_return(RC);
}

// Now determine the starting point from which to begin the parsing
if (PtrRelatedFileObject) {
    // We have a user-supplied related file object.
    // This implies a relative open; i.e., relative to the
    // directory represented by the related file object ...

    // Note: The only purpose FSD implementations ever have for
    // the related file object is to determine whether this
    // is a relative open or not. At all other times (including
    // during I/O operations), this field is meaningless from
    // the FSD's perspective.
    if (!(PtrRelatedFCB->FCBFlags & SFSD_FCB_DIRECTORY)) {
        // we must have a directory as the "related" object
        RC = STATUS_INVALID_PARAMETER;
        try_return(RC);
    }

    // So we have a directory, ensure that the name begins with
    // a \ (i.e., begins at the root and does *not* begin with a
    // \\).
    // NOTE: This is just an example of the kind of pathname string
    // validation that an FSD must do. Although the remainder of
    // the code may not include such checks, any commercial
    // FSD *must* include such checking (no one else, including
    // the I/O Manager will perform checks on your FSD's behalf).
    if ((RelatedObjectName.Length == 0) ||
        (RelatedObjectName.Buffer[0] != L'\\')) {
        RC = STATUS_INVALID_PARAMETER;
        try_return(RC);
    }

    // Similarly, if the target file name starts with a \, it
    // is wrong, since the target file name can no longer be
    // absolute if a related file object is present.
    if ((TargetObjectName.Length != 0) &&
        (TargetObjectName.Buffer[0] == L'\\')) {
        RC = STATUS_INVALID_PARAMETER;
        try_return(RC);
    }

    // Create an absolute pathname. You could potentially use
    // the absolute pathname if you cache previously opened
    // file/directory object names.
    {
```

```
            AbsolutePathName.MaximumLength = TargetObjectName.Length +
                    RelatedObjectName.Length + sizeof(WCHAR);
            if (!(AbsolutePathName.Buffer =
                        ExAllocatePool(PagedPool,
                            AbsolutePathName.MaximumLength))) {
                RC = STATUS_INSUFFICIENT_RESOURCES;
                try_return(RC);
            }

            RtlZeroMemory(AbsolutePathName.Buffer,
                                AbsolutePathName.MaximumLength);

            RtlCopyMemory((void *)(AbsolutePathName.Buffer),
                            (void *)(RelatedObjectName.Buffer),
                            RelatedObjectName.Length);
            AbsolutePathName.Length = RelatedObjectName.Length;
            RtlAppendUnicodeToString(&AbsolutePathName, L"\\");
            RtlAppendUnicodeToString(&AbsolutePathName,
                    TargetObjectName.Buffer);
        }

    } else {

        // The supplied pathname must be an absolute pathname.
        if (TargetObjectName.Buffer[0] != L'\\') {
            RC = STATUS_INVALID_PARAMETER;
            try_return(RC);
        }

        {
            AbsolutePathName.MaximumLength = TargetObjectName.Length;
            if (!(AbsolutePathName.Buffer =
                        ExAllocatePool(PagedPool,
                            AbsolutePathName.MaximumLength))) {
                RC = STATUS_INSUFFICIENT_RESOURCES;
                try_return(RC);
            }

            RtlZeroMemory(AbsolutePathName.Buffer,
                                AbsolutePathName.MaximumLength);

            RtlCopyMemory((void *)(AbsolutePathName.Buffer),
                            (void *)(TargetObjectName.Buffer),
                            TargetObjectName.Length);
            AbsolutePathName.Length = TargetObjectName.Length;
        }
    }

    // Go into a loop parsing the supplied name
    // Use the algorithm supplied in the book to implement this loop.

    // Note that you may have to open intermediate directory objects
    // while traversing the path. You should try to reuse existing code
    // whenever possible; therefore, you should consider using a common
```

```
// open routine regardless of whether the open is on behalf of the
// caller or an intermediate (internal) open performed by your
// driver.

// But first, check if the caller simply wishes to open the root
// of the file system tree.
if (AbsolutePathName.Length == 2) {
    // This is an open of the root directory, ensure that
    // the caller has not requested a file only
    if (FileOnlyRequested ||
        (RequestedDisposition == FILE_SUPERSEDE)
        || (RequestedDisposition == FILE_OVERWRITE) ||
        (RequestedDisposition == FILE_OVERWRITE_IF)) {
        RC = STATUS_FILE_IS_A_DIRECTORY;
        try_return(RC);
    }

    // Insert code to open root directory here.
    // Include creation of a new CCB structure.

    try_return(RC);
}

if (PtrRelatedFileObject) {
    // Insert code such that your "start directory" is
    // the one identified by the related file object
} else {
    // Insert code to start at the root of the file system
}

// NOTE: If your FSD does not support access checking (i.e.,
// your FSD does not check traversal privileges), you could
// easily maintain a prefix cache containing pathnames and
// open FCB pointers. Then, if the requested pathname is already
// present in the cache, you can avoid the tedious traversal
// of the entire pathname performed below and described in the
// book.

// If you do not maintain such a prefix table cache of previously
// opened object names, or if you do not find the name to be opened
// in the cache, then get the next component in the name to be
// parsed. Note that obtaining the next string component is
// similar to the strtok library routine where the separator is a
// \.

// Your FSD should also always check the validity of the token
// to ensure that only valid characters comprise the path/file
// name.

// Insert code to open the starting directory here.

while (TRUE) {
    // Insert code to perform the following tasks here:
```

```
//      (a) acquire the parent directory FCB MainResource
//          exclusively.
//      (b) ensure that the parent directory in which you will
//          perform a lookup operation is indeed a directory.
//      (c) if there are no more components left after this one
//          in the pathname supplied by the user, break.
//      (d) attempt to lookup the subdirectory in the parent.
//      (e) if not found, return STATUS_OBJECT_PATH_NOT_FOUND.
//      (f) otherwise, open the new subdirectory and make it
//          the new parent.
//      (g) close the current parent directory (after releasing
//          resources that were acquired in step (a) above.
//      (h) go back and repeat the loop for the next component in
//          the path.

//      NOTE: If your FSD supports it, you should always check
// that the caller has appropriate privileges to traverse
// the directories being searched.
}

// Now we are down to the last component, check it out to see if it
// exists …
// Even for the "open target directory" case below, it is important
// to know whether the final component specified exists.

// If "open target directory" was specified:
if (OpenTargetDirectory) {
    if (NT_SUCCESS(RC)) {
        // File exists, set this information in the Information
        // field.
        ReturnedInformation = FILE_EXISTS;
    } else {
        RC = STATUS_SUCCESS;
        // Tell the I/O Manager that file does not exist.
        ReturnedInformation = FILE_DOES_NOT_EXIST;
    }

    // Now, do the following:
    // (a) Replace the string in the FileName field in the
    //     PtrNewFileObject to identify the target name
    //     only (i.e., the final component string without the path
    //     leading to the object).
    // (b) Return with the target's parent directory opened.
    // (c) Update the file object FsContext and FsContext2 fields
    //     to reflect the fact that the parent directory of the
    //     target has been opened.

    try_return(RC);
}

// We make the check here to see if the file stream already exists.
// Assume that RC will contain the status (success/failure) for our
// check.
```

```
if (!NT_SUCCESS(RC)) {
    // Object was not found, create if requested
    if ((RequestedDisposition == FILE_CREATE) ||
        (RequestedDisposition == FILE_OPEN_IF) ||
        (RequestedDisposition == FILE_OVERWRITE_IF)) {
        // Create a new file/directory here.

        // Open the newly created object.

        // Note that a FCB structure will be allocated at this time
        // and so will a CCB structure. Assume that these are
        // called PtrNewFCB and PtrNewCCB respectively.
        // Further, note that since the file is being created, no
        // other thread can have the file stream open at this time.

        // Set the allocation size for the object is specified.

        // Set extended attributes for the file.

        // Set the Share Access for the file stream.
        // The FCBShareAccess field will be set by the I/O Manager.
        IoSetShareAccess(DesiredAccess, ShareAccess,
                          PtrNewFileObject,
                          &(PtrNewFCB->FCBShareAccess));

        RC = STATUS_SUCCESS;
        ReturnedInformation = FILE_CREATED;
    }

    try_return(RC);

} else {

    // File stream does exist. Now we must perform some additional
    // error checking.

    if (RequestedDisposition == FILE_CREATE) {
        ReturnedInformation = FILE_EXISTS;
        RC = STATUS_OBJECT_NAME_COLLISION;
        try_return(RC);
    }

    // Insert code to open the target here, return if failed.

    // The FSD will allocate a new FCB structure if no such
    // structure currently exists in memory for the file stream.
    // A new CCB will always be allocated.
    // Assume that these structures are named PtrNewFCB and
    // PtrNewCCB respectively.
    // Further, you should obtain the FCB MainResource exclusively
    // at this time.

    // Once you have opened the file stream and created an FCB,
    // you should perform some additional checks to verify whether
```

```
// the user open request should be succeeded.

// Check if caller wanted a directory only and target object
// not a directory, or caller wanted a file only and target
// object not a file.
if (FileOnlyRequested && (PtrNewFCB->FCBFlags
                            & SFSD_FCB_DIRECTORY)) {
    // Close the new FCB and leave
    // SFsdCloseCCB(PtrNewCCB);
    RC = STATUS_FILE_IS_A_DIRECTORY;
    try_return(RC);
}

// Check whether caller-specified flags are incompatible
// with the type of object being returned.
if ((PtrNewFCB->FCBFlags & SFSD_FCB_DIRECTORY) &&
     ((RequestedDisposition == FILE_SUPERSEDE) ||
      (RequestedDisposition == FILE_OVERWRITE) ||
      (RequestedDisposition == FILE_OVERWRITE_IF))) {
    // SFsdCloseCCB(PtrNewCCB);
    RC = STATUS_FILE_IS_A_DIRECTORY;
    try_return(RC);
}

if (DirectoryOnlyRequested &&
        !(PtrNewFCB->FCBFlags & SFSD_FCB_DIRECTORY)) {
    // Close the new FCB and leave
    // SFsdCloseCCB(PtrNewCCB);
    RC = STATUS_NOT_A_DIRECTORY;
    try_return(RC);
}

// Check share access and fail if the share conflicts with an
// existing open.
if (PtrNewFCB->OpenHandleCount > 0) {
    // The FCB is currently in use by some thread.
    // We must check whether the requested access/share access
    // conflicts with the existing open operations.

    if (!NT_SUCCESS(RC = IoCheckShareAccess(DesiredAccess,
                            ShareAccess,
                            PtrNewFileObject,
                            &(PtrNewFCB->FCBShareAccess),
                            TRUE))) {
        // SFsdCloseCCB(PtrNewCCB);
        try_return(RC);
    }
} else {
        // Store the fact that an open is being satisfied with
        // the specified share access.
        IoSetShareAccess(DesiredAccess, ShareAccess,
                            PtrNewFileObject,
                            &(PtrNewFCB->FCBShareAccess));
}
```

```
        ReturnedInformation = FILE_OPENED;

        // If a supersede or overwrite was requested, do it now.
        // Your FSD may need to determine whether any byte-range
        // locks exist on the file stream. For overwrite requests (as
        // opposed to requests to supersede the file stream), your FSD
        // may wish to deny the request if a conflicting byte-range
        // lock has been obtained by another process.
        if (RequestedDisposition == FILE_SUPERSEDE) {
            // Attempt the operation here ...
            // RC = SFsdSupersede(...);
            if (NT_SUCCESS(RC)) {
                ReturnedInformation = FILE_SUPERSEDED;
            }
        } else if ((RequestedDisposition == FILE_OVERWRITE) ||
                    (RequestedDisposition == FILE_OVERWRITE_IF)){
            // Attempt the operation here ...
            // RC = SFsdOverwrite(...);
            if (NT_SUCCESS(RC)) {
                ReturnedInformation = FILE_OVERWRITTEN;
            }
        }
    }

    try_exit:    NOTHING;

} finally {
    // Complete the request unless we are here as part of unwinding
    // when an exception condition was encountered, OR
    // if the request has been deferred (i.e., posted for later
    // handling)
    if (RC != STATUS_PENDING) {
        // If we acquired any FCB resources, release them now.

        // If any intermediate (directory) open operations were
        // performed, implement the corresponding close (do not
        // however close the target you have opened on behalf of the
        // caller).

        if (NT_SUCCESS(RC)) {
            // Update the file object such that:
            // (a) the FsContext field points to the NTRequiredFCB
            //     field in the FCB
            // (b) the FsContext2 field points to the CCB created as a
            //     result of the open operation

            // If write-through was requested, then mark the file
            // object appropriately.
            if (WriteThroughRequested) {
            PtrNewFileObject->Flags |= FO_WRITE_THROUGH;
            }

            // Release the PtrNewFCB MainResource at this time.
        } else {
```

```
                    // Perform failure-related postprocessing now.
            }

            // As long as this unwinding is not being performed as a
            // result of an exception condition, complete the IRP.
            if (!(PtrIrpContext->IrpContextFlags
                    & SFSD_IRP_CONTEXT_EXCEPTION)) {
                PtrIrp->IoStatus.Status = RC;
                PtrIrp->IoStatus.Information = ReturnedInformation;

                // Free up the IRP Context.
                SFsdReleaseIrpContext(PtrIrpContext);

                // complete the IRP.
                IoCompleteRequest(PtrIrp, IO_DISK_INCREMENT);
            }
        }

        if (AcquiredVCB) {
            ASSERT(PtrVCB);
          SFsdReleaseResource(&(PtrVCB->VCBResource));
            AcquiredVCB = FALSE;
        }

        if (AbsolutePathName.Buffer != NULL) {
            ExFreePool(AbsolutePathName.Buffer);
        }
    }

    return(RC);
}
```

Notes

The FSD implementation can receive a create/open request for one of the
following objects:

The FSD device object itself

This open will typically be received by the FSD if a process sends an IOCTL
to the FSD to affect the behavior of the driver. This request can be implemented by your driver in any manner appropriate to your driver
implementation. The sample FSD simply succeeds such a request immediately
(see the accompanying diskette).

A mounted logical volume

If a process wants to request that a volume be dismounted, the process must
first open the logical volume itself, as opposed to opening an object
contained on the mounted logical volume. Similarly, processes may wish to
perform query and/or set label operations on the logical volume, in which
case they might request an open of the logical volume. Finally, some threads

might wish to read the volume information directly off media for which they would need to open the volume device object directly.

A file or directory object on the logical volume

These are the more commonly received create/open requests. A user process may wish to open either a file object or a directory object, both of which are supported by all FSD implementations. Open operations on directories are performed to query the contents of the directory. Normal file open operations are performed to be able to access/modify file stream data or control information.

The preceding code fragment above is mostly self-explanatory. Read the comments to understand the code better. The first thing you will notice is that a lot of the routines have been commented out. These are placeholders for you to replace with appropriate functionality suitable for your FSD implementation.

Basically, the implementation follows the logical steps, listed earlier, that an FSD should perform upon receiving a create/open request. The objective is to try to find the target object, given a path leading to that object. If the object exists and the user wishes to open it, the FSD will create a file control block (if none currently exists), create a context control block, and initialize the I/O Manager file object appropriately. If the object does not exist and the user wants to create it, the FSD will first create the object on secondary storage (on the logical volume) and then open the object for the caller, creating an FCB, a CCB, and initializing the file object structure. If a new object is created, the FSD may also set an allocation size for the created object if the caller has specified such a size.

The code fragment describes a special type of request from the NT I/O Manager indicated by the presence of the **SL_OPEN_TARGET_DIRECTORY** flag in the current I/O stack location. This flag is slightly unusual and quite specific to the Windows NT environment. Basically, when the I/O Manager receives a request to move or rename a file or directory, it sends this request to the FSD, supplying the target name in the rename/move request. For example, if a user requests that file *dir1**dir2**dir3**foo* be renamed/moved to *dir1**dir4**bar*, the I/O Manager will send the latter string to the FSD with the **SL_OPEN_TARGET_DIRECTORY** flag set. The FSD must respond as follows when this flag is set:

- The FSD must first check to see if the target object (i.e., *bar*) exists on the path leading to *bar*.

  The presence or absence of the target should be conveyed back to the I/O Manager.

- The FSD must replace the pathname in the file object with the last component; i.e., replace *dir1**dir4**bar* in our example with the string *bar*.

This replace operation is required due to the manner in which the I/O Manager subsequently invokes the FSD `SFsdFileInfo()` dispatch entry point. In Chapter 10, *Writing A File System Driver II*, this routine is described in further detail.

- Instead of opening/creating the actual target (*bar* in our example), the FSD must open the parent directory (in our example, the FSD must return with *dir4* having been opened for the caller).

Note that although an FCB structure is initialized as part of the processing performed for a successful create/open operation, the FSD does not invoke `CcInitializeCacheMap()` at this time for the file object and the FCB representing the open file. The reason for this is fairly simple; often commonly used applications open file objects simply to perform a query-file-information operation on them and subsequently close the file stream without ever attempting any I/O. Therefore, requesting the Cache Manager to perform any initialization in anticipation of buffered I/O would simply degrade performance in such situations. Therefore, it is recommended in Windows NT that the FSD implementation defer any Cache Manager–related initialization until the time when a read or write operation is actually attempted for the first time.

Although it is not discussed in the code fragment, it is possible for an FSD to replace the name supplied with the file object created by the I/O Manager and return `STATUS_REPARSE` to the I/O Manager. Be careful, though, to free the memory allocated by the I/O Manager for the original file name buffer and allocate new memory from paged pool. Also, if applicable, you may wish to set the `RelatedFileObject` pointer to NULL in this situation.

If your FSD does not support page file create requests, you can return an error when such a request is received by your driver. Page file create requests will only be initiated by the NT VMM internal routine called (`NtCreatePagingFile()`, which invokes the I/O Manager internal routine (not exported) called `IoCreate-File()` with an attribute that specifies that the file to be created is a page file. Page files are not really different from any other ordinary file created on a logical volume. However, most NT FSD implementations return `STATUS_ACCESS_DENIED` or `STATUS_SHARING_VIOLATION` if a thread tries to open an already-opened page file. Also, you should ensure that all in-memory representations of a page file are allocated from nonpaged pool; this includes the FCB and the CCB structure for the file. The rationale is simply to allow your FSD to safely access these in-memory structures without incurring a page fault when a paging I/O is received by your driver, because page faults at that time will crash the system.

Finally, you will have noticed that the code fragment checks the access requested and whether the caller is allowed to open the file for the desired access. An I/O

Manager routine `IoCheckShareAccess()` is used to determine whether the desired access and the specified share access conflict with any previous open for the file stream. If no such conflict is present, the I/O Manager updates the `FCBShareAccess` field (this is a result of the last argument, called `Update-ShareAccess`, to the routine being set to TRUE). Of course, if this is the first open operation on the file stream (or if all previous open handles have been closed), then the FSD directly invokes the `IoSetShareAccess()` function to set the share access in the `FCBShareAccess` field in the FCB structure. In the next chapter, you will see that the share access stored in the FCB will be removed when the last file handle corresponding to the file object is closed (i.e., when the `IRP_MJ_CLEANUP` request is received by the FSD).

Dispatch Routine: Read

The read dispatch entry point is invoked in response to user requests to access file data. Most FSD implementations allow users to access data for ordinary file streams only, and any attempt to directly access directory contents will typically be rejected with a `STATUS_ACCESS_DENIED` error.

All NT FSD implementations support two kinds of read I/O requests:

- Buffered read operations
- Nonbuffered read operations satisfied directly from secondary storage

By default, an FSD will attempt to satisfy the read request using buffered (cached) data. All of the native Windows NT FSD implementations use the services of the NT Cache Manager in caching file data in memory. You can, however, choose some other caching module with your FSD implementation, though the NT Cache Manager does a fairly good job and you should at least seriously consider using it instead.

In order for the caller to request that the read be satisfied directly from secondary storage, the file object used in the read operation should have been opened with `FILE_NO_INTERMEDIATE_BUFFERING` set. The only other read operations that are directly satisfied from secondary storage by the FSD are those marked as paging I/O. These operations come to the FSD from the NT VMM and cannot be satisfied by a recursive call back to the NT Cache Manager, but should be sent to the underlying disk driver for further processing.

Logical Steps Involved

The I/O stack location contains the following structure relevant to processing a read request issued to an FSD:

```
typedef struct _IO_STACK_LOCATION {

    // ....

    union {

        //....

        // System service parameters for:  NtReadFile
        struct {
            ULONG Length;
            ULONG Key;
            LARGE_INTEGER ByteOffset;
        } Read;

        // ....
    } Parameters;

// …

} IO_STACK_LOCATION, *PIO_STACK_LOCATION;
```

An FSD performs the following simple tasks upon receiving a read request on a file object:

1. Get a pointer to the CCB and FCB for the file stream.

2. Verify that the read operation is allowed.

   Typically, FSD implementations on any operating system platform will reject user read requests directed to directory objects.

3. Identify the type of read operation: a paging I/O operation, a normal non-cached operation, a non-MDL cached read operation, or an MDL read operation.

   This is probably the most important task that your FSD will perform in the read operation. You should be able to identify whether the read is a recursive operation, or whether the read request comes to your FSD directly from a user thread, from the VMM, or from the NT Cache Manager. Furthermore, your FSD should be able to identify whether the read is as a result of read-ahead being performed by the Cache Manager. For more discussion on this topic, read through the next chapter.

4. Obtain any resources that are appropriate to ensure consistency of data.

   Most FSD implementations, including the sample code provided here, acquire the **MainResource** shared if the read request has been received directly from a user thread. This prevents other write operations from proceeding concurrently, but does allow concurrent read operations. If, however, the read request is due to a page fault, the FSD will acquire the **PagingIoResource** shared instead.

5. Obtain the starting offset, length, and buffer pointer supplied by the caller.

   The starting offset and length uniquely determine the byte range requested by the caller. The caller provides a buffer for the FSD to return data. In Chapter 4, I explained the various buffering mechanisms that can be used by callers of kernel-mode drivers. Most NT FSD implementations and the sample code provided here choose `METHOD_NEITHER` as the buffering option for the device objects created to represent mounted logical volumes. The result is that the I/O Manager does not manipulate the caller buffer, but sends it down as-is to the FSD.

6. Lock the user's buffer if required, and also create a Memory Descriptor List (MDL) for requests that must be directed to lower-level drivers.

7. Check if the byte range requested by the caller has been locked; it is possible with Windows NT, however, for the caller to provide a key that would still allow the read request to proceed.

   If the byte range desired by the user has a byte-range lock that does not permit read access by other processes, the FSD will return an error to the caller.

8. Determine whether the byte range specified by the caller is valid, and if not, return an appropriate error code to the caller.

9. If this is a buffered I/O request and caching has not yet been initiated on the FCB, invoke `CcInitializeCacheMap()` to initiate caching at this time.

10. If this is a buffered non-MDL I/O request, forward the request on to the NT Cache Manager via an invocation to `CcCopyRead()`, or if this is a nonbuffered (direct I/O or paging I/O request), forward it on to the lower-level driver for further processing.

    If this is an MDL read request, use the `CcMdlRead()` function, provided by the Cache Manager, to return an MDL containing file data to the caller.

11. Once data has been obtained either from the Cache Manager or from lower-level drivers, release FCB resources acquired and return the results to the caller.

Code Fragment

```
NTSTATUS      SFsdCommonRead(
PtrSFsdIrpContext                PtrIrpContext,
PIRP                            PtrIrp)
{
    // Declarations go here ...

    try {
        // First, get a pointer to the current I/O stack location.
        PtrIoStackLocation = IoGetCurrentIrpStackLocation(PtrIrp);
```

```
        ASSERT(PtrIoStackLocation);

        // If this happens to be an MDL read complete request, then
        // there is not much processing that the FSD has to do.
        if (PtrIoStackLocation->MinorFunction & IRP_MN_COMPLETE) {
            // Caller wants to tell the Cache Manager that a previously
            // allocated MDL can be freed.
            SFsdMdlComplete(PtrIrpContext, PtrIrp,
                                    PtrIoStackLocation, TRUE);
            // The IRP has been completed.
            CompleteIrp = FALSE;
            try_return(RC = STATUS_SUCCESS);
        }

        // If this is a request at IRQL DISPATCH_LEVEL, then post
        // the request (your FSD may process it synchronously
        // if you implement the support correctly).
        if (PtrIoStackLocation->MinorFunction & IRP_MN_DPC) {
            CompleteIrp = FALSE;
            PostRequest = TRUE;
            try_return(RC = STATUS_PENDING);
        }

        PtrFileObject = PtrIoStackLocation->FileObject;
        ASSERT(PtrFileObject);

        // Get the FCB and CCB pointers.
        PtrCCB = (PtrSFsdCCB)(PtrFileObject->FsContext2);
        ASSERT(PtrCCB);
        PtrFCB = PtrCCB->PtrFCB;
        ASSERT(PtrFCB);

        // Get some of the parameters supplied to us.
        ByteOffset = PtrIoStackLocation->Parameters.Read.ByteOffset;
        ReadLength = PtrIoStackLocation->Parameters.Read.Length;

        CanWait =
            ((PtrIrpContext->IrpContextFlags & SFSD_IRP_CONTEXT_CAN_BLOCK)
                ? TRUE : FALSE);
        PagingIo = ((PtrIrp->Flags & IRP_PAGING_IO) ? TRUE : FALSE);
        NonBufferedIo = ((PtrIrp->Flags & IRP_NOCACHE) ? TRUE : FALSE);
        SynchronousIo =
            ((PtrFileObject->Flags & FO_SYNCHRONOUS_IO) ? TRUE : FALSE);

        // A 0 byte read can be immediately succeeded.
        if (ReadLength == 0) {
            try_return(RC);
        }

        // NOTE: if your FSD does not support file sizes > 2GB, you
        // could validate the start offset here and return end-of-file
        // if the offset begins beyond the maximum supported length.

        // Is this a read of the volume itself?
```

```
if (PtrFCB->NodeIdentifier.NodeType == SFSD_NODE_TYPE_VCB) {
    // Yup, we need to send this on to the disk driver after
    // validation of the offset and length.
    PtrVCB = (PtrSFsdVCB)(PtrFCB);

    // Acquire the volume resource shared.
    if (!ExAcquireResourceSharedLite(&(PtrVCB->VCBResource),
                                     CanWait)) {
        // Post the request to be processed in the context of a
        // worker thread.
        CompleteIrp = FALSE;
        PostRequest = TRUE;
        try_return(RC = STATUS_PENDING);
    }
    PtrResourceAcquired = &(PtrVCB->VCBResource);

    // Insert code to validate the caller-supplied offset here.

    // Lock the caller's buffer.
    if (!NT_SUCCESS(RC = SFsdLockCallersBuffer(PtrIrp,
                                  TRUE, ReadLength))) {
        try_return(RC);
    }

    // Forward the request to the lower-level driver.

    // For synchronous I/O wait here, else return STATUS_PENDING.
    // For asynchronous I/O support, read the discussion in
    // Chapter 10.

    try_return(RC);
}

// If the read request is directed to a page file (if your FSD
// supports paging files), send the request directly to the disk
// driver. For requests directed to a page file, you have to trust
// that the offsets will be set correctly by the VMM. You should
// not attempt to acquire any FSD resources either.
if (PtrFCB->FCBFlags & SFSD_FCB_PAGE_FILE) {
    IoMarkIrpPending(PtrIrp);
    // You will need to set a completion routine before invoking
    // a lower-level driver.
    // Forward request directly to disk driver.
    // SFsdPageFileIo(PtrIrpContext, PtrIrp);

    CompleteIrp = FALSE;

    try_return(RC = STATUS_PENDING);
}

// If this read is directed to a directory, it is not allowed
// by the sample FSD. Note that you may choose to create a stream
// file for FSD (internal) directory read/write operations, in
// which case you should modify the check below to allow reading
```

```
// (directly from disk) directories as long as the read originated
// from within your FSD. Your driver will have to be smart enough
// to recognize that the read originated in your FSD (e.g., via
// the contents of the TopLevelIrp field in TLS described in the
// next chapter).
if (PtrFCB->FCBFlags & SFSD_FCB_DIRECTORY) {
    RC = STATUS_INVALID_DEVICE_REQUEST;
    try_return(RC);
}

PtrReqdFCB = &(PtrFCB->NTRequiredFCB);

// This is a good place for oplock-related processing.
// Chapter 11 expands upon this topic in greater detail.

// Check whether the desired read can be allowed depending
// on any byte-range locks that might exist. Note that for
// paging I/O, no such checks should be performed.
if (!PagingIo) {
    // Insert code to perform the check here ...
    //    if (!SFsdCheckForByteLock(PtrFCB, PtrCCB, PtrIrp,
    //        PtrCurrentIoStackLocation)) {
    //    try_return(RC = STATUS_FILE_LOCK_CONFLICT);
    // }
}

// There are certain complications that arise when the same file
// stream has been opened for cached and noncached access. The FSD
// is then responsible for maintaining a consistent view of the
// data seen by the caller.
// Also, it is possible for file streams to be mapped in both as
// data files and as an executable. This could also lead to
// consistency problems since there now exist two separate
// sections (and pages) containing file information.
// Read Chapter 10 for more information on the issues involved in
// maintaining data consistency.
// Insert appropriate code here.

// Acquire the appropriate FCB resource shared.
if (PagingIo) {
    // Try to acquire the FCB PagingIoResource shared.
    if (!ExAcquireResourceSharedLite(&(PtrReqdFCB->
                                        PagingIoResource),
                    CanWait)) {
        CompleteIrp = FALSE;
        PostRequest = TRUE;
        try_return(RC = STATUS_PENDING);
    }
    // Remember the resource that was acquired.
 PtrResourceAcquired = &(PtrReqdFCB->PagingIoResource);
} else {
    // Try to acquire the FCB MainResource shared.
    if (!ExAcquireResourceSharedLite(&(PtrReqdFCB->MainResource),
                    CanWait)) {
```

```
                CompleteIrp = FALSE;
                PostRequest = TRUE;
                try_return(RC = STATUS_PENDING);
        }
            // Remember the resource that was acquired.
     PtrResourceAcquired = &(PtrReqdFCB->MainResource);
    }


    // Validate start offset and length supplied.
    // If start offset is > end-of-file, return an appropriate
    // error. Note that since an FCB resource has already been
    // acquired, and since all file size changes require acquisition
    // of both FCB resources (see Chapter 10), the contents of the FCB
    // and associated data structures can safely be examined.

    // Also note that I am using the file size in the Common FCB
    // Header to perform the check. However, your FSD might keep a
    // separate copy in the FCB (or some other representation of the
    // file associated with the FCB).
    if (RtlLargeIntegerGreaterThan(ByteOffset,
            PtrReqdFCB->CommonFCBHeader.FileSize)) {
        // Starting offset is > file size.
        try_return(RC = STATUS_END_OF_FILE);
    }


    // We can also truncate the read length here
    // such that it is contained within the file size.

    // This is a good place to set whether fast I/O can be performed
    // on this particular file or not. Your FSD must make its own
    // determination on whether or not to allow fast I/O operations.
    // Commonly, fast I/O is not allowed if any byte-range locks exist
    // on the file or if oplocks prevent fast I/O. Practically any
    // reason chosen by your FSD could result in your setting
    // FastIoIsNotPossible
    // OR FastIoIsQuestionable instead of FastIoIsPossible.
    //
    // PtrReqdFCB->CommonFCBHeader.IsFastIoPossible = FastIoIsPossible;


    //    Branch here for cached vs. noncached I/O.
    if (!NonBufferedIo) {

        // The caller wishes to perform cached I/O. Initiate caching if
        // this is the first cached I/O operation using this file
        // object.
        if (PtrFileObject->PrivateCacheMap == NULL) {
            // This is the first cached I/O operation. You must ensure
            // that the Common FCB Header contains valid sizes at this
            // time.
            CcInitializeCacheMap(PtrFileObject,
                (PCC_FILE_SIZES)(&(PtrReqdFCB->
                                        CommonFCBHeader.AllocationSize)),
                    FALSE,          // We will not utilize pin access for
```

```
                                // this file
                    &(SFsdGlobalData.CacheMgrCallBacks), // callbacks
                    PtrCCB);          // The context used in callbacks
        }

        // Check and see if this request requires an MDL returned to
        // the caller.
        if (PtrIoStackLocation->MinorFunction & IRP_MN_MDL) {
            // Caller does want an MDL returned. Note that this mode
            // implies that the caller is prepared to block.
            CcMdlRead(PtrFileObject, &ByteOffset, TruncatedReadLength,
                            &(PtrIrp->MdlAddress),
                            &(PtrIrp->IoStatus));
            NumberBytesRead = PtrIrp->IoStatus.Information;
            RC = PtrIrp->IoStatus.Status;

            try_return(RC);
        }

        // This is a regular run-of-the-mill cached I/O request. Let
        // the Cache Manager worry about it.
        // First though, we need a buffer pointer (address) that is
        // valid.
        PtrSystemBuffer = SFsdGetCallersBuffer(PtrIrp);
        if (!CcCopyRead(PtrFileObject, &(ByteOffset), ReadLength,
                    CanWait, PtrSystemBuffer, &(PtrIrp->IoStatus))) {
            // The caller was not prepared to block and data is not
            // immediately available in the system cache.
            CompleteIrp = FALSE;
            PostRequest = TRUE;
            // Mark IRP Pending ...
            try_return(RC = STATUS_PENDING);
        }

        // We have the data
        RC = PtrIrp->IoStatus.Status;
        NumberBytesRead = PtrIrp->IoStatus.Information;

        try_return(RC);

    } else {

        // Send the request to lower-level drivers.

        // For paging I/O, the FSD has to trust the VMM to do the right
        // thing.

        // First, mark the IRP as pending, then invoke the lower-level
        // driver after setting a completion routine.
        // Meanwhile, this particular thread can immediately return a
        // STATUS_PENDING return code.
        // The completion routine is then responsible for completing
        // the IRP and unlocking appropriate resources.
```

```
                    // Also, at this point, your FSD might use the
                    // information contained in the ValidDataLength field to simply
                    // return zeroes to the caller for reads extending beyond
                    // current valid data length.

                    IoMarkIrpPending(PtrIrp);

                    // Invoke a routine to read disk information at this time.
                    // You will need to set a completion routine before invoking
                    // a lower-level driver.

                    CompleteIrp = FALSE;

                    try_return(RC = STATUS_PENDING);
                }

            try_exit:    NOTHING;

        } finally {
            // Post IRP if required.
            if (PostRequest) {
                // Implement a routine that will queue-up the request to be
                // executed later (asynchronously) in the context of a system
                // worker thread. See Chapter 10 for details.

                if (PtrResourceAcquired) {
                    SFsdReleaseResource(PtrResourceAcquired);
                }
            } else if (CompleteIrp && !(RC == STATUS_PENDING)) {
                // For synchronous I/O, the FSD must maintain the current byte
                // offset.
                // Do not do this however, if I/O is marked as paging I/O.
                if (SynchronousIo && !PagingIo && NT_SUCCESS(RC)) {
                    PtrFileObject->CurrentByteOffset =
                        RtlLargeIntegerAdd(ByteOffset,
                        RtlConvertUlongToLargeInteger((unsigned
                                                    long)NumberBytesRead));
                }

                // If the read completed successfully and this was not a
                // paging I/O operation,* you should modify the time stamp for
                // the file stream indicating that an access operation was
                // performed. You can do this in one of two ways:
                // (a) You could set a flag in the CCB indicating that the file
                //        stream was accessed and in the cleanup routine
                //        (described in the next chapter), you would update the
                //        time value.
```

---

* Paging I/O requests are either asynchronous requests initiated by the VMM or the NT Cache Manager, or recursive requests from the FSD to the Cache Manager, back to the FSD. Therefore, most FSD implementations do not update the file access/modification time upon processing such requests. Paging I/O requests can also occur due to page faults on a user-mapped file stream. Unfortunately, by choosing not to update the access time for all paging I/O requests, your FSD will be unable to mark the fact that some user application accessed the file albeit via the memory-mapped file method.

```
            // (b) Or, you could simply get the current time and insert it
            //     into FCB structure now. Then at file cleanup time, you
            //     would update the directory entry for the file.
            if (NT_SUCCESS(RC) && !PagingIo) {
                // The following is method (a) above. If you wish to be
                // more accurate, then update the time in the FCB now.
                // Also remember in this case to remove the
                // FO_FILE_FAST_IO_READ flag from the the file object.
                SFsdSetFlag(PtrCCB->CCBFlags, SFSD_CCB_ACCESSED);
            }

            if (PtrResourceAcquired) {
                SFsdReleaseResource(PtrResourceAcquired);
            }

            // Can complete the IRP here if no exception was encountered.
            if (!(PtrIrpContext->IrpContextFlags
                    & SFSD_IRP_CONTEXT_EXCEPTION)) {
                PtrIrp->IoStatus.Status = RC;
                PtrIrp->IoStatus.Information = NumberBytesRead;

                // Free up the IRP Context.
                SFsdReleaseIrpContext(PtrIrpContext);

                // Complete the IRP.
                IoCompleteRequest(PtrIrp, IO_DISK_INCREMENT);
            }
        } // can we complete the IRP?
    } // end of "finally" processing.

    return(RC);
}

NTSTATUS SFsdLockCallersBuffer(
PIRP            PtrIrp,
BOOLEAN         IsReadOperation,
uint32          Length)
{
    NTSTATUS      RC = STATUS_SUCCESS;
    PMDL          PtrMdl = NULL;

    ASSERT(PtrIrp);

    try {
        // Is an MDL already present in the IRP?
        if (!(PtrIrp->MdlAddress)) {
            // Allocate an MDL.
            if (!(PtrMdl = IoAllocateMdl(PtrIrp->UserBuffer, Length, FALSE,
                    FALSE, PtrIrp))) {
                RC = STATUS_INSUFFICIENT_RESOURCES;
                try_return(RC);
            }

            // Probe and lock the pages described by the MDL.
```

```
            // We could encounter an exception doing so, swallow the
            // exception.
            // NOTE: The exception could be due to an unexpected (from our
            // perspective), invalidation of the virtual addresses that
            // comprise the passed-in buffer.
            try {
                MmProbeAndLockPages(PtrMdl, PtrIrp->RequestorMode,
                        (IsReadOperation ? IoWriteAccess:IoReadAccess));
            } except(EXCEPTION_EXECUTE_HANDLER) {
                RC = STATUS_INVALID_USER_BUFFER;
            }
        }

        try_exit:    NOTHING;

    } finally {
        if (!NT_SUCCESS(RC) && PtrMdl) {
            IoFreeMdl(PtrMdl);
            // You must NULL the MdlAddress field in the IRP after freeing
            // the MDL, or else the I/O Manager will also attempt to free
            // the MDL pointed to by that field during I/O completion. The
            // pointer becomes invalid once you free the allocated MDL and
            // you will encounter a system crash during IRP completion.
            PtrIrp->MdlAddress = NULL;
        }
    }

    return(RC);
}

void *SFsdGetCallersBuffer(
PIRP                    PtrIrp)
{
    void                *ReturnedBuffer = NULL;

    // If an MDL is supplied, use it.
    if (PtrIrp->MdlAddress) {
      ReturnedBuffer = MmGetSystemAddressForMdl(PtrIrp->MdlAddress);
    } else {
        ReturnedBuffer = PtrIrp->UserBuffer;
    }

    return(ReturnedBuffer);
}

void SFsdMdlComplete(
PtrSFsdIrpContext            PtrIrpContext,
PIRP                        PtrIrp,
PIO_STACK_LOCATION          PtrIoStackLocation,
BOOLEAN                     ReadCompletion)
{
    NTSTATUS                RC = STATUS_SUCCESS;
    PFILE_OBJECT            PtrFileObject = NULL;
```

```
        PtrFileObject = PtrIoStackLocation->FileObject;
        ASSERT(PtrFileObject);

        // Not much to do here.
        if (ReadCompletion) {
            CcMdlReadComplete(PtrFileObject, PtrIrp->MdlAddress);
        } else {
            // The Cache Manager needs the byte offset in the I/O stack
            // location.
          CcMdlWriteComplete(PtrFileObject,
                &(PtrIoStackLocation->Parameters.Write.ByteOffset),
                PtrIrp->MdlAddress);
        }

        // Clear the MDL address field in the IRP so the IoCompleteRequest()
        // does not try to play around with the MDL.
        PtrIrp->MdlAddress = NULL;

        // Free up the Irp Context.
        SFsdReleaseIrpContext(PtrIrpContext);

        // Complete the IRP.
        PtrIrp->IoStatus.Status = RC;
        PtrIrp->IoStatus.Information = 0;
        IoCompleteRequest(PtrIrp, IO_NO_INCREMENT);

        return;
}
```

Notes

This code fragment follows the list of logical steps, described earlier, that a file system driver typically implements to satisfy a read request. In response to the request, the FSD must first obtain the parameters supplied by the caller. Validation of the starting offset and the read length is typically not required for requests issued by the VMM.

Notice that the sample FSD conditionally acquires either the volume control block resource, the file control block `MainResource`, or the FCB `PagingIoResource`, depending upon the nature of the request. The various ways in which the read routine can be invoked are discussed in greater detail in the next chapter.

The buffer supplied by the caller is passed directly to the FSD by the I/O Manager. The FSD, in turn, creates a memory descriptor list (MDL) and locks pages in memory before forwarding the request to a lower-level disk driver. This allows the disk driver to obtain the data in the context of any arbitrary thread, directly into the locked pages. The routine `SFsdLockCallersBuffer()` illustrates the method used in creating a memory descriptor list and locking pages in memory so that lower-level drivers can subsequently access the buffer in the context of any arbitrary thread, even at a high IRQL.

Before a read request is allowed to proceed, the FSD should also ensure that there are not any conflicting byte locks on the range requested by the caller. If conflicting locks do exist, the caller should get an appropriate error code returned to it. Note, however, that byte lock checks are not performed for requests marked as paging I/O, since these requests originate from the VMM in response to a page fault incurred by the thread trying to access the data, it is assumed that the checks must have been performed at some earlier point in time. Unfortunately, though, you will notice that the byte-range lock check will also be skipped for page faults incurred when accessing data mapped into the virtual address space of a process (memory-mapped file).

The caller of the read routine can request either cached or noncached I/O. When a request for buffered I/O is received by the FSD, the driver checks if caching had previously been initiated on the file stream using that particular file object. If this happens to be the first cached I/O request received for that particular file object, the FSD initiates caching by invoking the `CcInitializeCacheMap()` function call. Chapter 7, *The NT Cache Manager II*, describes this routine in greater detail. Once caching has been initiated, the FSD can simply forward the cached I/O request to the NT Cache Manager for further processing. Note that it is quite possible that invoking `CcCopyRead()` might result in a page fault incurred by the Cache Manager, which causes the FSD read routine to be recursed into, this time for paging I/O. The FSD will then handle the page fault by obtaining data directly from disk or from across the network (for redirectors) and complete the paging I/O request.

The preceding code fragment doesn't elaborate on the steps taken by an FSD to forward an I/O request to the lower-level disk driver to get data from secondary storage. The methodology used by your FSD depends upon the specific requirements for your driver. However, some common steps are performed by all FSD implementations before forwarding a request to lower-level drivers:

- Your FSD will determine the logical block offset and number of logical blocks that need to be read.

- The FSD may be able to obtain data in a single I/O operation or, for discontiguous data, your FSD might need to make multiple requests.

  Your FSD may initiate multiple I/O requests concurrently to the disk driver to handle the discontiguous data case.

- If a single I/O request is being sent to the lower-level disk driver, the FSD will initialize the next IRP stack location in the IRP sent to it and will also set a completion routine before forwarding the IRP down to the next driver in the hierarchy.

It is important for the FSD to set a completion routine so that the correct status can be returned to the caller and also to ensure that all resources acquired during the read operation are released before the request is returned to the caller. Furthermore, the FSD can respond to errors returned by the lower-level disk drivers by initiating appropriate processing from the completion routine.

- If multiple I/O requests are required to read all of the data from secondary storage, the FSD can initiate all I/O requests concurrently or sequentially.

  The FSD can initiate concurrent read operations by creating multiple associated IRP structures, initializing the IRPs appropriately, creating partial MDLs for each of the concurrent requests, setting a completion routine for each associated IRP, and sending the associated IRP requests down to the lower-level drivers.*

For read I/O requests, a caller can specify that an MDL be returned containing the file data. This request for an MDL-read operation can be identified by checking for the `IRP_MN_MDL` flag value in the `MinorFunction` field of the current I/O stack location. The code fragment above invokes the `CcMdlRead()` function, which results in an MDL being allocated by the Cache Manager. Once the caller has completed processing the data contained in the MDL, a second read request is issued to the FSD. This special read request is only issued to inform the Cache Manager that the MDL structure can now be freed (and pages reallocated, if required) and is identified by the `IRP_MN_COMPLETE` flag value in the `MinorFunction` field. The FSD must simply invoke the `CcMdlReadComplete()` Cache Manager function in response to this request as is illustrated in the `SFsdMdlComplete()` function.

Dispatch Routine: Write

The steps involved in processing a write request are very similar to those performed in processing read requests.

---

* Note that the `IoMakeAssociatedIrp()` routine can be used to request that the I/O Manager allocate an associated IRP structure for the FSD while the `IoBuildPartialMdl()` routine will create the partial MDL for the FSD. One side effect of creating associated IRP structures is that the I/O Manager will automatically complete the master IRP once all associated IRPs have been completed. To prevent this from happening, simply increment the `AssociatedIrp` count in the master IRP before sending requests to the lower-level driver. This trick will cause the I/O manager to believe that there is some associated IRP pending (even after the last one has been completed), and your FSD can subsequently complete the master IRP itself (remember, though, to decrement the `AssociatedIrp` count before completing the master IRP yourself).

Logical Steps Involved

The I/O stack location contains the following structure relevant to processing a write request issued to a FSD:

```
typedef struct _IO_STACK_LOCATION {

    // ....

    union {

        //....

        // System service parameters for:  NtWriteFile
        struct {
            ULONG Length;
            ULONG Key;
            LARGE_INTEGER ByteOffset;
        } Write;

        // ....
    } Parameters;

    // ....

} IO_STACK_LOCATION, *PIO_STACK_LOCATION;
```

An FSD performs the following simple tasks upon receiving a write request for a file object:

1. Get a pointer to the CCB and the FCB for the file stream.

2. Verify that the write operation is allowed.

    Most FSD implementations will reject user write requests directed to directory objects.

3. Identify the type of write operation: a paging I/O operation, a normal non-cached operation, or a cached write operation. Also determine if the write request was initiated by the lazy-writer thread or by the modified page/block writer thread.

    It is extremely important that your dispatch routine know the caller initiating the write request. In Windows NT, paging I/O asynchronous requests are not synchronized with user file size changes, and therefore, your FSD should be able to always determine whether a write operation should be allowed to proceed or should be disregarded.

4. Obtain any resources that are appropriate to ensure consistency of data.

    The sample FSD implementation provided here acquires the **MainResource** exclusively if the write request has been received directly from a user thread. This prevents all other user-initiated read or write requests from proceeding concurrently. If, however, the write request has been marked as paging I/O, the FSD will acquire the `PagingIoResource` exclusively as well.*

5. Obtain the starting offset, length, and buffer pointer supplied by the caller.

    The starting offset and length uniquely determine the byte range requested by the caller. The caller provides a buffer, as well, for the FSD to transfer data from.

6. Lock the user's buffer, if required, and also create a memory descriptor list (MDL) for requests that must be directed to lower-level drivers.

7. Check that the byte range requested by the caller has been locked; it is possible with Windows NT, however, for the caller to provide a key that would still allow the write request to proceed.

8. Determine whether the byte range specified by the caller is valid.

    In the case of write requests, a starting offset beyond end-of-file for a user-initiated request implies that the user is extending the file size.

9. If this is a buffered I/O request and caching has not yet been initiated on the FCB, invoke `CcInitializeCacheMap()` to initiate caching at this time.

10. If this is a buffered I/O request, forward the request to the NT Cache Manager via an invocation to `CcCopyWrite()`; if this is a nonbuffered (direct I/O or paging I/O) request, forward it on to the lower-level driver for further processing.

11. Once data has been transferred either to the Cache Manager buffers, or to secondary storage using lower-level drivers, release FCB resources acquired and return the results to the caller.

Code Fragment

```
NTSTATUS    SFsdCommonWrite(
PtrSFsdIrpContext           PtrIrpContext,
PIRP                        PtrIrp)
{
    // Declarations go here

    try {
        // First, get a pointer to the current I/O stack location.
        PtrIoStackLocation = IoGetCurrentIrpStackLocation(PtrIrp);
        ASSERT(PtrIoStackLocation);
```

---

* Actually, the native NT implementations appear to use a different philosophy when determining how to acquire the resources for the FCB. They tend to acquire the resource shared, unless the write operation extends beyond the current end-of-file. The reason for acquiring the paging I/O resource shared is based on the philosophy that the VMM will correctly serialize paging I/O write operations to any specific byte range, and that it is better to provide greater concurrency in writing dirty pages quickly to secondary storage. This method of acquisition is slightly more difficult to implement.

```
// If this is an MDL write complete request, then
// there is not much processing that the FSD has to do.
if (PtrIoStackLocation->MinorFunction & IRP_MN_COMPLETE) {
    // Caller wants to tell the Cache Manager that a previously
    // allocated MDL can be freed. This may cause a recursive write
    // back into the FSD.
    SFsdMdlComplete(PtrIrpContext, PtrIrp,
                                PtrIoStackLocation, FALSE);
    // The IRP has been completed.
    CompleteIrp = FALSE;
    try_return(RC = STATUS_SUCCESS);
}
// If this is a request at IRQL DISPATCH_LEVEL, then post
// the request (your FSD may process it synchronously
// if you implement the support correctly).
if (PtrIoStackLocation->MinorFunction & IRP_MN_DPC) {
    CompleteIrp = FALSE;
    PostRequest = TRUE;
    try_return(RC = STATUS_PENDING);
}

PtrFileObject = PtrIoStackLocation->FileObject;
ASSERT(PtrFileObject);

// Get the FCB and CCB pointers.
PtrCCB = (PtrSFsdCCB)(PtrFileObject->FsContext2);
ASSERT(PtrCCB);
PtrFCB = PtrCCB->PtrFCB;
ASSERT(PtrFCB);

// Get some of the other parameters supplied to us.
ByteOffset = PtrIoStackLocation->Parameters.Write.ByteOffset;
WriteLength = PtrIoStackLocation->Parameters.Write.Length;

CanWait = ((PtrIrpContext->IrpContextFlags
                & SFSD_IRP_CONTEXT_CAN_BLOCK)
          ? TRUE : FALSE);
PagingIo = ((PtrIrp->Flags & IRP_PAGING_IO) ? TRUE : FALSE);
NonBufferedIo = ((PtrIrp->Flags & IRP_NOCACHE) ? TRUE : FALSE);
SynchronousIo = ((PtrFileObject->Flags & FO_SYNCHRONOUS_IO) ?
                                TRUE : FALSE);

// You might wish to check at this point whether the file object
// being used for write really did have write permission requested
// when the create/open operation was performed. Of course, for
// paging I/O write operations, the check is not valid, since
// paging I/O (via the VMM) could use any file object (likely the
// first one with which caching wasinitiated on the FCB) to
// perform the write operation.

// A 0-byte write can be immediately succeeded.
if (WriteLength == 0) {
    try_return(RC);
}
```

```
// NOTE: if your FSD does not support file sizes > 2GB, you
// could validate the start offset here and return end-of-file
// if the offset begins beyond the maximum supported length.

// Is this a write of the volume itself?
if (PtrFCB->NodeIdentifier.NodeType == SFSD_NODE_TYPE_VCB) {
    // Yup, we need to send this on to the disk driver after
    // validation of the offset and length.
    PtrVCB = (PtrSFsdVCB)(PtrFCB);

    // Acquire the volume resource exclusively
    if (!ExAcquireResourceExclusiveLite(&(PtrVCB->VCBResource),
                                        CanWait)) {
        // Post the request to be processed in the context of a
        // worker thread.
        CompleteIrp = FALSE;
        PostRequest = TRUE;
        try_return(RC = STATUS_PENDING);
    }
    PtrResourceAcquired = &(PtrVCB->VCBResource);

    // Insert code to validate the caller-supplied offset here.

    // Lock the caller's buffer.
    if (!NT_SUCCESS(RC = SFsdLockCallersBuffer(PtrIrp,
                                    TRUE, WriteLength))) {
        try_return(RC);
    }

    // Forward the request to the lower-level driver.

    // For synchronous I/O wait here, else return STATUS_PENDING.
    // For asynchronous I/O support, read the discussion in
    // Chapter 10.

    try_return(RC);
}

// Your FSD should check whether it is
// convenient to allow the write to proceed by utilizing the
// CcCanIWrite() function call. If it is not convenient to perform
// the write at this time, you should defer the request for a
// while. The check should not, however, be performed for
// noncached write operations. To determine whether we are
// retrying the operation or not, use the IrpContext structure we
// have created (see the accompanying diskette to this book for a
// definition of the structure).
IsThisADeferredWrite =
    ((PtrIrpContext->IrpContextFlags
        & SFSD_IRP_CONTEXT_DEFERRED_WRITE) ? TRUE : FALSE);
if (!NonBufferedIo) {
    if (!CcCanIWrite(PtrFileObject, WriteLength, CanWait,
            IsThisADeferredWrite)) {
        // Cache Manager and/or the VMM does not want us to perform
```

```
            // the write at this time. Post the request.
            SFsdSetFlag(PtrIrpContext->IrpContextFlags,
                SFSD_IRP_CONTEXT_DEFERRED_WRITE);
            CcDeferWrite(PtrFileObject, SFsdDeferredWriteCallBack,
                PtrIrpContext, PtrIrp, WriteLength,
                IsThisADeferredWrite);
            CompleteIrp = FALSE;
            try_return(RC = STATUS_PENDING);
        }
    }


    // If the write request is directed to a page file (if your FSD
    // supports paging files), send the request directly to the disk
    // driver. For requests directed to a page file, you have to trust
    // that the offsets will be set correctly by the VMM. You should
    // not attempt to acquire any FSD resources either.
    if (PtrFCB->FCBFlags & SFSD_FCB_PAGE_FILE) {
        IoMarkIrpPending(PtrIrp);
        // You will need to set a completion routine before invoking
        // a lower-level driver
        // forward request directly to disk driver
        // SFsdPageFileIo(PtrIrpContext, PtrIrp);

        CompleteIrp = FALSE;

        try_return(RC = STATUS_PENDING);
    }


    // We can continue. Check whether this write operation is targeted
    // to a directory object, in which case the sample FSD will
    // disallow the write request. Once again though, if you create a
    // stream file object to represent a directory in memory, you
    // could come to this point as a result of modifying the directory
    // contents internally by the FSD itself. In that case, you should
    // be able to differentiate the directory write as being an
    // internal, noncached write operation and allow it to proceed.
    if (PtrFCB->FCBFlags & SFSD_FCB_DIRECTORY) {
        RC = STATUS_INVALID_DEVICE_REQUEST;
        try_return(RC);
    }


    PtrReqdFCB = &(PtrFCB->NTRequiredFCB);

    // There are certain complications that arise when the same file
    // stream has been opened for cached and noncached access. The FSD
    // is then responsible for maintaining a consistent view of the
    // data seen by the caller.
    // If this happens to be a nonbuffered I/O, you should try to
    // flush the cached data (if some other file object has already
    // initiated caching on the file stream). You should also try to
    // purge the cached information, though the purge will probably
    // fail if the file has been mapped into some process's virtual
    // address space.
    // Read Chapter 10 for more information on the issues involved in
```

```
            // maintaining data consistency.
            // Insert appropriate code here ...
            // CcFlushCache(...
            // CcPurgeCacheSection(...

            // Acquire the appropriate FCB resource exclusively.
            if (PagingIo) {
                // Try to acquire the FCB PagingIoResource exclusively.
                if (!ExAcquireResourceExclusiveLite(&(PtrReqdFCB->
                                                    PagingIoResource),
                                                    CanWait)) {
                    CompleteIrp = FALSE;
                    PostRequest = TRUE;
                    try_return(RC = STATUS_PENDING);
                }
                // Remember the resource that was acquired.
             PtrResourceAcquired = &(PtrReqdFCB->PagingIoResource);
            } else {
                // Try to acquire the FCB MainResource exclusively.
                if (!ExAcquireResourceExclusiveLite(&(PtrReqdFCB->
                                                    MainResource),
                            CanWait)) {
                    CompleteIrp = FALSE;
                    PostRequest = TRUE;
                    try_return(RC = STATUS_PENDING);
                }
                // Remember the resource that was acquired.
             PtrResourceAcquired = &(PtrReqdFCB->MainResource);
            }

            // Validate start offset and length supplied.
            // Here is a special check that determines whether the caller
            // wishes to begin the write at current end-of-file (whatever the
            // value of that offset might be).
            if ((ByteOffset.LowPart == FILE_WRITE_TO_END_OF_FILE) &&
                (ByteOffset.HighPart == 0xFFFFFFFF)) {
             WritingAtEndOfFile = TRUE;
            }

            // Paging I/O write operations are special. If paging I/O write
            // requests begin beyond end-of-file, the request should be no-
            // op'ed (see the next two chapters for more information). If
            // paging I/O requests extend beyond current end of file, they
            // should be truncated to current end-of-file.
            // Insert code to do this here.

            // This is also a good place to set whether fast I/O can be
            // performed on this particular file or not. Your FSD must make
            // its own determination whether or not to allow fast I/O
            // operations. Commonly, fast I/O is not allowed if any byte-range
            // locks exist on the file or if oplocks prevent fast I/O. Many
            // reasons could result in setting FastIoIsNotPossible
            // OR FastIoIsQuestionable instead of FastIoIsPossible.
            //
```

```
PtrReqdFCB->CommonFCBHeader.IsFastIoPossible = FastIoIsPossible;

// This is also a good place for oplock-related processing.
// Chapter 11 expands upon this topic in greater detail.

// Check whether the desired write can be allowed, depending
// on any byte-range locks that might exist. Note that for
// paging I/O, no such checks should be performed.
if (!PagingIo) {
    // Insert code to perform the check here ...
    // if (!SFsdCheckForByteLock(PtrFCB, PtrCCB, PtrIrp,
    // PtrCurrentIoStackLocation)) {
    // try_return(RC = STATUS_FILE_LOCK_CONFLICT);
    // }
}

// Check whether the current request will extend the file size,
// or the valid data length (if your FSD supports the concept of a
// valid data length associated with the file stream). In either
// case, inform the Cache Manager using CcSetFileSizes() about
// the new file length. Note that real FSD implementations will
// have to first allocate enough on-disk space before they
// inform the Cache Manager about the new size to ensure that the
// write will subsequently not fail due to lack of disk space.

// if ((WritingAtEndOfFile) ||
//      ((ByteOffset + TruncatedWriteLength) >
//          PtrReqdFCB->CommonFCBHeader.FileSize)) {
//      we are extending the file;
//      allocate space and inform the Cache Manager
// } else if (same test as above for valid data length) {
//      we are extending valid data length, inform Cache Manager;
// }


//    Branch here for cached vs. noncached I/O.
if (!NonBufferedIo) {

    // The caller wishes to perform cached I/O. Initiate caching if
    // this is the first cached I/O operation using this file
    // object.
    if (PtrFileObject->PrivateCacheMap == NULL) {
        // This is the first cached I/O operation. You must ensure
        // that the Common FCB Header contains valid sizes.
        CcInitializeCacheMap(PtrFileObject,
            (PCC_FILE_SIZES)(&(PtrReqdFCB->
                                CommonFCBHeader.AllocationSize)),
            FALSE,          // We will not utilize pin access for
                            // this file.
            &(SFsdGlobalData.CacheMgrCallBacks), // Callbacks.
            PtrCCB);        // The context used in callbacks.
    }
```

```
        // Check and see if this request requires an MDL returned to
        // the caller.
        if (PtrIoStackLocation->MinorFunction & IRP_MN_MDL) {
            // Caller does want an MDL returned. Note that this mode
            // implies that the caller is prepared to block.
            CcPrepareMdlWrite(PtrFileObject, &ByteOffset,
                        TruncatedWriteLength,
                        &(PtrIrp->MdlAddress), &(PtrIrp->IoStatus));
            NumberBytesWritten = PtrIrp->IoStatus.Information;
            RC = PtrIrp->IoStatus.Status;

            try_return(RC);
        }

        // This is a regular run-of-the-mill cached I/O request. Let
        // the Cache Manager worry about it.
        // First though, we need a valid buffer pointer (address).
        // More on this in Chapter 10.

        // Also, if the request extends the ValidDataLength, use
        // CcZeroData() first to zero out the gap (if any) between
        // current valid data length and the start of the request.
        PtrSystemBuffer = SFsdGetCallersBuffer(PtrIrp);
        ASSERT(PtrSystemBuffer);
        if (!CcCopyWrite(PtrFileObject, &(ByteOffset),
                        TruncatedWriteLength,
                        CanWait, PtrSystemBuffer)) {
            // The caller was not prepared to block and data is not
            // immediately available in the system cache.
            CompleteIrp = FALSE;
            PostRequest = TRUE;
            // Mark IRP Pending ...
            try_return(RC = STATUS_PENDING);
        } else {
            // We have the data
            PtrIrp->IoStatus.Status = RC;
            PtrIrp->IoStatus.Information
                    = NumberBytesWritten = WriteLength;
        }

    } else {

        // If the request extends beyond valid data length, and if the
        // caller is not the lazy-writer, then utilize CcZeroData() to
        // zero out any blocks between current ValidDataLength and the
        // start of the write operation. This method of zeroing data
        // is convenient since it avoids any unnecessary writes to
        // disk. Of course, if your FSD makes no guarantees about
        // reading uninitialized data (native NT FSD implementations
        // guarantee that read operations will receive zeroes if the
        // sectors were not written to, thereby ensuring that old data
        // cannot be reread unintentionally or maliciously), you can
        // avoid performing the zeroing operation altogether. You
        // must, however, be careful about correctly determining the
```

```
                    // top-level component for the IRP so as to be able to extend
                    // valid data length only when appropriate and also avoid any
                    // infinite, recursive loops.
                    // See Chapter 10 for a discussion on this topic.

                    // Send the request to lower-level drivers.
                    // Here is a common method used by Windows NT file system
                    // drivers that are in the process of sending a request to the
                    // disk driver. First, mark the IRP as pending, then invoke
                    // the lower-level driver after setting a completion routine.
                    // Meanwhile, this particular thread can immediately return
                    // a STATUS_PENDING return code.
                    // The completion routine is then responsible for completing
                    // the IRP and unlocking appropriate resources.

                    IoMarkIrpPending(PtrIrp);

                    // Invoke a routine to write information to disk at this time.
                    // You will need to set a completion routine before invoking
                    // a lower-level driver.

                    CompleteIrp = FALSE;

                    try_return(RC = STATUS_PENDING);
                }

            try_exit:    NOTHING;

            // If a synchronous I/O write request succeeded, and if the file
            // size has changed as a result, you may wish to update the file
            // size and the modification time for the file stream in the
            // directory entry for the link at this time.

        } finally {
            // Post IRP if required.
            if (PostRequest) {
                // Implement a routine that will queue-up the request to be
                // executed later (asynchronously) in the context of a system
                // worker thread. See Chapter 10 for details.

                if (PtrResourceAcquired) {
                    SFsdReleaseResource(PtrResourceAcquired);
                }
            } else if (CompleteIrp && !(RC == STATUS_PENDING)) {
                // For synchronous I/O, the FSD must maintain the current byte
                // offset. Do not do this however, if I/O is marked as paging
                // I/O.
                if (SynchronousIo && !PagingIo && NT_SUCCESS(RC)) {
                    PtrFileObject->CurrentByteOffset =
                        RtlLargeIntegerAdd(ByteOffset,
                        RtlConvertUlongToLargeInteger((unsigned
                                                    long)NumberBytesWritten));
                }
```

```
                    // If the write completed successfully and this was not a
                    // paging I/O operation, set a flag in the CCB that indicates
                    // that a write was performed and that the file time should be
                    // updated at cleanup. The other option would be to set the
                    // access time in the FCB directly now.
                    if (NT_SUCCESS(RC) && !PagingIo) {
                        SFsdSetFlag(PtrCCB->CCBFlags, SFSD_CCB_MODIFIED);
                    }

                    // If the file size was changed, set a flag in the FCB
                    // indicating that this occurred.

                    // If the request failed, and we had done some nasty stuff like
                    // extending the file size (including informing the Cache
                    // Manager about the new file size), and allocating on-disk
                    // space etc., undo it at this time.

                    // Release resources.
                    if (PtrResourceAcquired) {
                        SFsdReleaseResource(PtrResourceAcquired);
                    }

                    // Can complete the IRP here if no exception was encountered.
                    if (!(PtrIrpContext->IrpContextFlags
                            & SFSD_IRP_CONTEXT_EXCEPTION)) {
                        PtrIrp->IoStatus.Status = RC;
                        PtrIrp->IoStatus.Information = NumberBytesWritten;

                        // Free up the IRP Context.
                        SFsdReleaseIrpContext(PtrIrpContext);

                        // Complete the IRP.
                        IoCompleteRequest(PtrIrp, IO_DISK_INCREMENT);
                    }
                } // Can we complete the IRP?
            } // End of "finally" processing.

        return(RC);
}

void SFsdDeferredWriteCallBack (
void                        *Context1,            // Should be
PtrIrpContext
void                        *Context2)            // Should be PtrIrp
{
        // You should typically simply post the request to your internal
        // queue of posted requests (just as you would if the original write
        // could not be completed because the caller could not block).
        // Once you post the request, return from this routine. The write
        // will then be retried in the context of a system worker thread.
}
```

Notes

This code fragment provides you with a sound framework that you should follow when implementing a dispatch routine to process file system write requests. Conceptually, write requests are not very different from read operations, and can be handled simply by forwarding the request to the NT Cache Manager, or by forwarding the request down to a disk or network driver to transfer information to secondary storage (either locally or across the network).

Some of the issues that you should be concerned about when implementing the write dispatch routine include correctly identifying the caller of the entry point, ensuring that data consistency is maintained if the same file stream is opened for both cached and noncached access, and keeping the Cache Manager informed about any changes to the file size. We will discuss some of these issues further in the next chapter.

10

Writing A File System Driver II

In this chapter, we'll continue to discuss how a file system driver can be conceived and implemented. First, discuss the read and write dispatch routines that you were introduced to in the previous chapter, focusing on the different ways in which these two entry points can be invoked. When you design a file system driver, knowing the different ways in which a particular dispatch routine can be invoked is essential to creating a robust design. I intend to help you understand better the logic described by the code and comments presented in the previous chapter, as well as to plug in the gaps left by the sample code presented earlier. In order to understand the context in which these two routines can be invoked, you must first understand the concept of the *top-level component* for any I/O request dispatched to an FSD. I discuss this concept at length here.

Next I look at some of the issues that you must deal with in providing support for asynchronous I/O, including the file information dispatch routines (both query and set file information) and the directory control, cleanup, and close entry points. By this time, you should have a very good understanding of the issues involved in providing some of the basic functionality expected from a Windows NT file system driver.

I/O Revisited: Who Called?

Throughout the course of this book, I have repeatedly mentioned that the FSD read and write dispatch routines can be invoked by all sorts of different components on a Windows NT system and that these invocations can occur due to different direct or indirect actions initiated by processes. Here is a formal list of the different ways in which the read and write entry points for a file system driver can be invoked:

- From a user- or kernel-mode thread that requests I/O using one of the NT system services, e.g., `NtReadFile()`, `NtWriteFile()`, `ZwReadFile()`, `Zw-WriteFile()`, or `NtFlushBuffers()`

- From a user- or kernel-mode thread as a result of a page fault on a byte range that is part of a mapped view of a named file stream (i.e., page faults on virtual addresses backed by named file objects):

  — From the NT Cache Manager as a result of asynchronous read-ahead operations being performed

  — Recursion into the FSD dispatch routines, due to page faults incurred by the NT Cache Manager when servicing a buffered I/O request

  — Due to page faults in files mapped by user application processes (typically page faults on mapped-in, executable files)

- From the NT Virtual Memory Manager as a result of servicing a page fault that was incurred by some user-mode or kernel-mode process for allocated buffers (i.e., page faults on virtual addresses backed by paging files)

- From the NT Virtual Memory Manager as a result of asynchronous flushing of modified pages (modified page write operations)*

- From the NT Cache Manager as a result of asynchronous flushing of Cache Manager buffers (lazy-write of data)

Regardless of the caller and of the situation leading up to the invocation of the read/write entry points, the implementation of these two important dispatch entry points should try to achieve the following goals:

- Satisfy cached (buffered) I/O requests by forwarding the I/O request to the NT Cache Manager

- Satisfy nonbuffered I/O requests by directly accessing secondary storage devices

- Return a consistent view of file stream data, regardless of whether the request is a buffered or nonbuffered I/O request

- Try to maintain consistency between views of file data mapped in as an executable and as a regular data stream

---

* For the purposes of discussions in this book, there is conceptually no difference between VMM-initiated flushing of pages belonging to a page file and VMM-initiated flushing of pages belonging to a named on-disk (mapped) file.

- Ensure correct synchronization by following a strict, well-defined resource acquisition hierarchy

Figure 10-1 illustrates the manner in which the NT file system drivers, the NT Cache Manager, and the NT VMM interact.* This figure also serves to demonstrate the various ways in which an FSD read/write dispatch entry point can be invoked. In order to better understand how the FSD achieves the goals listed earlier, you should understand the concept of a top-level component for an IRP.

Top-Level Component for an IRP

From the figure, you can see that an I/O request in Windows NT can be one of the following three types:

- The I/O request is directly issued to an FSD.
- The I/O request either originates in the Cache Manager component or is handed directly to the Cache Manager by the I/O Manager (bypassing the FSD).
- The I/O request originates in the VMM component, or is directly handled by the VMM in the kernel in the case of a page fault.

Depending on which category a given I/O request falls into, the FSD always identifies a top-level component that is associated with the IRP representing the request. The top-level component is defined as the kernel-mode component that initiates the processing for a specific I/O request.†

Note carefully that identification of a top-level component is **not** restricted to read/write I/O requests. Rather, your FSD must consistently be aware of the top-level component associated with any functionality invoked in your FSD implementation; either the FSD itself, or the NT VMM could be a top-level component for query/set file size requests.

According to our definition, therefore, the FSD will identify itself as the top-level component when a user read request is directly forwarded by the NT I/O Manager to the read dispatch routine in the FSD, because all of the processing for that IRP is initiated in the FSD dispatch routine. If instead, the I/O request for a read operation originates in the NT Cache Manager (due to read-ahead being

---

* Note that the shaded areas represent modules that initiate asynchronous I/O in the context of system worker threads or dedicated kernel-mode worker threads.

† Microsoft Windows NT developers have previously defined a top-level component as the kernel-mode component that directly receives the user I/O request. I believe that this definition is not complete, since read-ahead and lazy-write calls originating in the NT Cache Manager do not originate as a result of any particular user request, yet the Cache Manager should be considered the top-level component for these I/O operations. We will therefore use the definition presented here to identify top-level components.

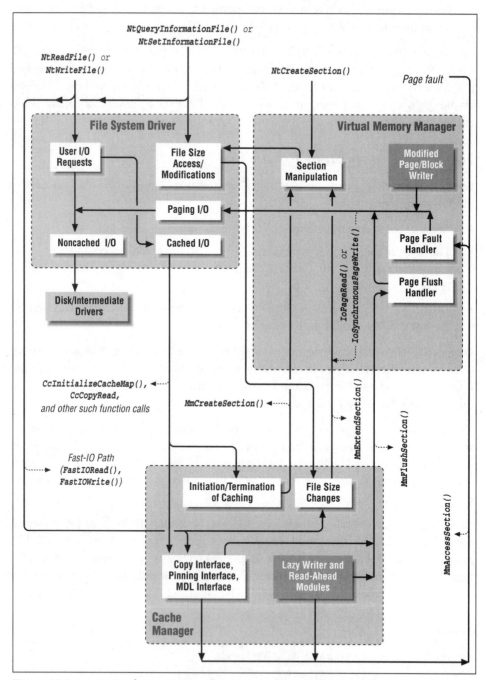

Figure 10-1. Interaction between FSDs, the VMM, and the Cache Manager

performed), the FSD identifies the Cache Manager as being the top-level component handling the particular IRP. Again, the rationale for classifying the Cache Manager as the top-level component is that all of the processing for the particular I/O operation originates in the Cache Manager. Finally, requests that originate in the VMM for flushing modified pages to secondary storage are identified by the FSD by noting that the VMM is the top-level component associated with the request.

Setting and querying the top-level component value

To identify the top-level component for a particular I/O request, the FSD, the NT Cache Manager, and the NT VMM use Thread-Local Storage (TLS). A thread is represented within the Windows NT Executive by a structure called **ETHREAD**. Although the structure is opaque to most of the NT Executive components, including FSDs, you should note that this structure contains a field called **TopLevelIrp**. The **TopLevelIrp** field is large enough to store a pointer value. An FSD typically stores the pointer to the current IRP being processed in the context of a particular thread in this field. This, however, is only done if the FSD is the top-level component for the IRP.

There are a few constant values that are used to identify the fact that some other component may be top-level for a particular IRP. For example, the fact that the NT Cache Manager is top-level for a particular I/O request is noted by storing a constant value defined as **FSRTL_CACHE_TOP_LEVEL_IRP** in this field. Here is a list of the constant values that could be stored in the top-level IRP field:

```
#define    FSRTL_FSP_TOP_LEVEL_IRP          (0x01)
#define    FSRTL_CACHE_TOP_LEVEL_IRP        (0x02)
#define    FSRTL_MOD_WRITE_TOP_LEVEL_IRP    (0x03)
#define    FSRTL_FAST_IO_TOP_LEVEL_IRP      (0x04)
#define    FSRTL_MAX_TOP_LEVEL_IRP_FLAG     (0x04)
```

The constant value **FSRTL_FSP_TOP_LEVEL_IRP** is stored by an FSD in the TLS only when an IRP has been posted to be processed in the context of a worker thread and only if some other component (other than the FSD) happens to be top-level for that particular I/O request. In other words, when processing a request for deferred processing in the context of a worker thread, the FSD performs the following tests:

- Was the FSD the top-level component for the original request? If so, set the IRP pointer in TLS, since the FSD will still continue to be the top-level component even while processing the request in the context of the current worker thread.

- Otherwise, set the constant `FSRTL_FSP_TOP_LEVEL_IRP` in the TLS for the worker thread, to indicate that some other component is actually top-level for this particular IRP.

The constant value `FSRTL_CACHE_TOP_LEVEL_IRP` is stored in the TLS by the FSD when a callback is received by the FSD to preacquire FSD resources for read-ahead, lazy-write and/or flush operations initiated by the Cache Manager. You have already been introduced to the Cache Manager callbacks provided by a file system driver in Chapter 7, *The NT Cache Manager II.*

When the FSD receives the callback to preacquire resources, it should set the `FSRTL_CACHE_TOP_LEVEL_IRP` constant flag value in the TLS. Later, when the IRP is received by the FSD, it can easily identify that the Cache Manager happens to be the top-level component for the request.

The constant value `FSRTL_MOD_WRITE_TOP_LEVEL_IRP` is stored in the TLS by the modified/mapped page writer threads themselves at thread creation time. This is because the modified/mapped page writer threads are dedicated worker threads that initiate write-behind requests and are therefore always top-level components for IRPs that result from their actions. The FSD can check for the existence of this value, but does not need to set the value itself.

The constant value `FSRTL_FAST_IO_TOP_LEVEL_IRP` is set in the TLS by the File System run-time library (FSRTL) fast I/O routines. The FSRTL routines are not typically exported in the DDK. You have to buy a separate IFS Kit license from Microsoft to get header files that define all of the FSRTL routines that Microsoft wishes to export.

Note that the FSRTL exports certain routines that your FSD can use to service the fast I/O calls to your FSD. For example, the FSRTL exports a function called `FsRtlCopyRead()`, to which Microsoft I/O designers recommend your fast I/O read function pointer should be initialized. This function provides the expected preamble before passing the fast I/O request directly to the NT Cache Manager and bypassing the FSD in the process. We will discuss the fast I/O path in greater detail later in the next chapter, but note for now that the `FsRtlCopyRead()` helper routine and others like it automatically set the `FSRTL_FAST_IO_TOP_LEVEL_IRP` flag in the TLS for the thread performing fast I/O. This flag indicates to the FSD that some other component (in this case, the NT Cache Manager), is top-level, since the fast path bypassed the FSD dispatch routines.

An FSD uses the following two routines to access and/or modify the contents of this field in the TLS:

- `IoSetTopLevelIrp()`

```
VOID
IoSetTopLevelIrp(
    IN PIRP    Irp
);
```

Resource Acquisition Constraints:

None.

Parameters:

`Irp`

    This is either a pointer to an IRP structure or a constant value. If the FSD happens to be the top-level component for the IRP, it supplies the pointer to the IRP as an argument to this routine.

Functionality Provided:

This routine will simply set the passed-in value into the `TopLevelIrp` field in the thread structure for the currently executing thread in whose context the routine is invoked.

- `IoGetTopLevelIrp()`

```
PIRP
IoGetTopLevelIrp(
    VOID
);
```

Resource Acquisition Constraints:

None.

Parameters:

None

Return Value:

An IRP pointer or the constant value that was stored in the TLS. You can always identify whether or not this is a valid IRP pointer by checking whether the returned value, cast to an unsigned long, is less than the constant *FSRTL_ MAX_TOP_LEVEL_IRP_FLAG.*

Functionality Provided:

This routine returns the contents of the `TopLevelIrp` field in the thread structure for the currently executing thread in whose context the routine is invoked.

Code sample

Here is a code fragment from the sample FSD that illustrates how an FSD would check and/or set the top-level component field in the TLS.

```
NTSTATUS SFsdRead(
PDEVICE_OBJECT          DeviceObject,      // the logical volume device object
PIRP                    Irp)               // I/O Request Packet
{
    NTSTATUS                 RC = STATUS_SUCCESS;
    PtrSFsdIrpContext        PtrIrpContext = NULL;
    BOOLEAN                  AreWeTopLevel = FALSE;

    FsRtlEnterFileSystem();
    ASSERT(DeviceObject);
    ASSERT(Irp);

    // set the top level context
    AreWeTopLevel = SFsdIsIrpTopLevel(Irp);

    try {

        // get an IRP context structure and issue the request
        PtrIrpContext = SFsdAllocateIrpContext(Irp, DeviceObject);
        ASSERT(PtrIrpContext);

        RC = SFsdCommonRead(PtrIrpContext, Irp);

    } except (SFsdExceptionFilter(PtrIrpContext, GetExceptionInformation()))
    {

        RC = SFsdExceptionHandler(PtrIrpContext, Irp);

        SFsdLogEvent(SFSD_ERROR_INTERNAL_ERROR, RC);
    }

    if (AreWeTopLevel) {
        IoSetTopLevelIrp(NULL);
    }

    FsRtlExitFileSystem();

    return(RC);
}

BOOLEAN SFsdIsIrpTopLevel(
PIRP            Irp)                   // the IRP sent to our dispatch routine
{
    BOOLEAN            ReturnCode = FALSE;

    if (IoGetTopLevelIrp() == NULL) {
        // OK, so we can set ourselves to become the "top level" component.
        IoSetTopLevelIrp(Irp);
        ReturnCode = TRUE;
    }

    return(ReturnCode);
}
```

Notes

The code fragment illustrates the processing performed in the FSD read dispatch routine entry point before the FSD invokes the `SFsdCommonRead()` routine, shown in the previous chapter. Here, you can see that the FSD invokes a routine to determine whether the FSD can be the top-level component for the current IRP. The invoked routine is called `SFsdIsIrpTopLevel()`. This routine simply checks the current value of the `TopLevelIrp` field in the TLS to determine whether it has already been set. If the field contains a nonzero value, the FSD assumes that some other component is top-level for the current request; otherwise, the FSD sets the IRP pointer value in the TLS to indicate that the FSD itself is top-level for the current request.

Although this processing is adequate for the sample FSD (and for that matter, the FAT and CDFS file system implementations in NT also do pretty much the same thing), NTFS and other more sophisticated file systems may manipulate the TLS storage area differently. Fundamentally though, the above concepts can be used to determine the top-level component for any I/O request dispatched to the FSD.

How information about the top-level component is used

This concept of identifying the top-level component for each request is used as follows:

In determining the flow of execution when processing a request. Consider a file stream mapped by some thread that has the file stream opened for nonbuffered I/O. Write operations performed by this thread will eventually be dispatched to the FSD write routine via the NT VMM in the form of paging I/O write operations. If such a modification performed by the user extends beyond current valid data length for the file, most FSD implementations will attempt to zero the range between the current valid data length and the start of the new write operation.

Figure 10-2 illustrates the byte range being modified in such a situation.

The reason an FSD might wish to zero the "hole" represented by the byte range between the current valid data length and the starting offset for the current request is to avoid returning old data that might be present on disk for the sectors backing this range.

To ensure consistency between cached and buffered data for a file stream, the FSD should use `CcZeroData()` to zero the resulting hole. Upon receiving the request to zero data, the Cache Manager checks for a write-through file object, and directly flushes data to disk in such a scenario. This flush is performed synchronously by the Cache Manager.

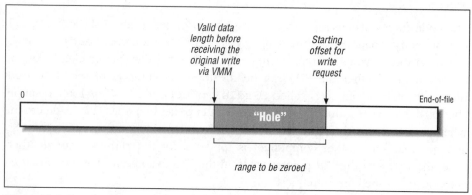

Figure 10-2. Range to be zeroed for write extending beyond valid data length

The flush operation is also dispatched to the FSD write routine as a synchronous, paging I/O write operation. Now, the FSD must distinguish this synchronous flush for the original write-through request from the original request itself. The only reliable method to do this is to check the top-level component for the new request. Since the flush is a recursive call in the context of the thread performing the original write-through operation, the FSD can identify that it cannot be top-level with respect to the flush IRP. This identification allows the FSD to perform the right processing in response to the flush, and the FSD will now not attempt to change the valid data length again (it was already done when the original write was received), nor will the FSD try to recursively invoke the Cache Manager to zero any holes (since that would lead to a deadlock, and/or infinite recursive loop condition).

There are other file systems (e.g., distributed file systems) that might be required to perform some special processing when the FSD is top-level for a request, and they could safely avoid such processing in the case of recursive requests. These FSD implementations also find it useful to identify the top-level component for an IRP, and they modify their processing appropriately.

Last but not least, an FSD must always be careful about dealing with asynchronous I/O requests if some other component is top-level for a request. As discussed below, the top-level component for the IRP ensures that resource acquisition hierarchies across the FSD, VMM, and Cache Manager are maintained. Therefore, when an FSD receives an I/O request for which it is not top-level, and when it is a recursive I/O request or an I/O request that requires synchronous processing, the FSD should never post the request to be handled in the context of some other worker thread, since this could lead to a deadlock situation. This issue is addressed once again in the discussion on asynchronous I/O processing below.

In performing synchronization. Earlier in this book, we discussed the resource acquisition hierarchy that must be maintained by FSD implementations, the NT Cache Manager, and the NT VMM in order to avoid deadlocks. The hierarchy follows:

- File system driver resources must always be acquired first.
- The NT Cache Manager resources are acquired next, if required.
- The NT VMM resources are acquired last.

To help maintain this hierarchy, the Cache Manager, as well as the VMM, are careful to preacquire FSD resources in situations when they are top-level for an I/O operation. This ensures that the resource acquisition hierarchy is always maintained. Earlier in Chapter 7, as well as in Chapter 8, *The NT Cache Manager III*, we discussed the four Cache Manager callbacks that an FSD should be cognizant of. In the next chapter, we'll see a sample implementation of the callback routines that the FSD is expected to provide.

For now, note that since the top-level component for any IRP operation is careful to preacquire FSD resources before sending the request down to the FSD, the file system implementation must always be careful of which resources it then tries to acquire recursively (remember that **ERESOURCE** type synchronization objects, as well as normal **KMUTEX** objects, can be recursively obtained) and of the manner in which it then tries to acquire such resources. If your FSD uses other resources that are not recursively acquirable (e.g., **FAST_MUTEX** structures), the FSD must be careful not to attempt such acquisition when it is not top-level for the IRP (since the top-level component must have presumably preacquired the resource).

The bottom line is that the FSD should be aware that the top-level component typically has a whole bunch of resources acquired before sending the request to the FSD dispatch routine entry point, and it is therefore the FSD's responsibility to proceed carefully.

In file size modifications. There are two rules you must always follow with respect to file size modifications:

- The valid data length for a file stream can only be extended by the top-level component for any I/O request, and only directly in response to user modifications of file stream data.
- The end-of-file value cannot be extended or changed by paging I/O operations. Chapter 6, *The NT Cache Manager I*, explains in greater detail the behavior expected from an FSD in this regard.

The first rule is straightforward if you understand the concept of a *top-level writer*, which can be defined as the component that is performing a write operation directly as a result of a user thread modification of file stream data. Now, it becomes simple to restate the above rule as only the top-level writer component can modify the valid data length for a file stream.

When a user I/O write request extending the valid data length is received by the FSD, the file system is the top-level writer and therefore extends the valid data length.* For fast I/O write requests, the FSRTL package is typically the top-level component, the request is not a recursive request, and therefore the valid data length is extended. If a user maps in a file, and modifies that mapped view for the file, extending the valid data length in the process, the FSD once again is the top-level writer and extends the value appropriately when the modifications are received by the FSD via paging I/O.

Note, however, that Cache Manager lazy-write operations can never cause the valid data length to be extended, because lazy-write operations are never directly a result of user modifications. However, VMM-initiated modified page write operations can and do cause the valid data length to be extended by the FSD, just as it is entirely possible for an FSD to receive other paging I/O write operations extending wholly beyond valid data length. The reason for this is that paging I/O operations are decoupled from normal user thread synchronization.

The FSD has a small problem in determining whether or not it should extend the valid data length for a paging I/O write operation. As I mentioned earlier, if the paging I/O write is due to a user modification of a mapped view of a file, the FSD receives a paging I/O write request and must extend the valid data length. However, if the paging I/O write beyond the current valid data length value is due to lazy-writing by the Cache Manager, the FSD does not have to extend the valid data length, since this will be done by the Cache Manager itself at some appropriate time. Unfortunately, it is difficult to distinguish between these two conditions. Therefore, the native Windows NT FSD implementations, as well as other installable FSDs, typically use the following workaround. When the FSD receives a callback from the lazy-writer thread requesting resources be acquired for lazy-write operations via the `AcquireForLazyWrite()` callback function, the FSD stores the lazy-writer thread ID (using the `PsGetCurrentThread()` support function call) in the FCB for the file stream. Later, when a paging I/O write request is received, the FSD checks the current thread ID with the stored value. A match indicates that the write is due to lazy-writing performed by the

---

* As mentioned earlier in this book when discussing the NT Cache Manager, it is extremely important for the FSD to keep the Cache Manager informed when any file size value changes. Therefore, if the FSD determines that the valid data length should be extended, it must inform the Cache Manager, using the `CcSetFileSizes()` routine (invoked by the FSD write dispatch routine processing the user write request), before actually transferring modified data from the user-supplied buffer either to the system cache via `CcCopyWrite()`, or directly to disk.

Cache Manager, and the FSD knows that it must not modify the valid data length. Subsequently, when preacquired FSD resources are released by the Cache Manager via another callback (`ReleaseFromLazyWrite()`), the stored thread ID value is zeroed.

In reporting unrecoverable hard error conditions. It is possible that a data transfer cannot be completed due to some unrecoverable error condition. The top-level component for an IRP uses the `IoRaiseInformationalHardError()` support routine (explained in the DDK) to report an appropriate error message to the user. For example, the modified page writer component will report failures in flushing modified pages to disk by specifying `STATUS_LOST_WRITEBEHIND_DATA` as the error code when invoking this routine. Similarly, the NT Cache Manager lazy-writer thread will use the same error code if it received an error when trying to lazily-write modified cached data for a file stream.

Achieving I/O-Related Goals

In Chapter 9, *Writing a File System Driver I*, the code samples for read and write IRP processing demonstrated how I/O requests for cached data transfer are forwarded to the Cache Manager via the `CcCopyRead()` and the `CcCopy-Write()` function calls.

As mentioned, the FSD must ensure consistency between cached and noncached I/O to the same file stream. The FSD must also maintain a consistent view of the file data, given the fact that two separate sections can possibly exist for a file stream, if it is mapped both as an executable and as a regular data section object. There are two kinds of consistency problems that arise depending upon the type of I/O operation:

- If the caller attempts to read file data requesting nonbuffered I/O, the FSD should try to avoid returning stale data to the user if the file stream has also been cached in system memory. Also, you probably recall from earlier chapters that the NT VMM maintains separate section objects for the same file stream mapped in both as an executable and as a data section object. Your FSD must, therefore, also attempt to maintain consistency between these two different section objects; if a thread modifies the data for the file stream, the image section object should also get the most recent modifications.*

---

* As discussed in Chapter 5, *The NT Virtual Memory Manager*, this policy of maintaining two different section objects leads to considerable headaches for FSD designers. If the same file stream is indeed mapped in both as an executable and as a data section object, and is modified while the executable is being executed, returning the latest modifications when servicing page faults will probably cause the executable to crash anyway. Therefore, you could legitimately argue that providing a consistent view of the data has dubious benefits in this case.

When the FSD receives a noncached read request on a file stream that is currently being cached by the Cache Manager, most FSD implementations simply perform a flush operation on the accessed byte range using the `CcFlush-Cache()` call. However, the invocation of `CcFlushCache()` is typically done by NT FSD implementations before acquiring any resources in the context of the thread requesting nonbuffered read access. The implication here is that no guarantees are made by the FSD in this case to always return the latest data—it is still theoretically possible for some other thread to quickly modify the accessed byte range in the system cache between completion of the flush operation and the instant when the FSD acquires FCB resources shared to satisfy the noncached read.

If your FSD needs to guarantee that the most recently modified data is always returned, it can do so either by preacquiring resources exclusively before initiating the flush operation or by purging data from the system cache, as in the noncached write access described below.

In the code sample presented in the previous chapter for the read dispatch entry point, you would have to add the following code to achieve the flush:

```
// The test below flushes the data cached in system memory if the
// current request mandates noncached access (file stream must be
// cached) and
// (a) the current request is not paging I/O, which indicates it is not
//     a recursive I/O operation OR originating in the Cache Manager
// (b) OR the current request is paging I/O BUT it did not originate
//     via the Cache Manager (or is a recursive I/O operation) and we
//     do have an image section that has been initialized.

// Note that the MmIsRecursiveIoFault() macro below is defined in the
// IFS Kit as follows:
// #define MmIsRecursiveIoFault()                                      \
//         ((PsGetCurrentThread()->DisablePageFaultClustering) |      \
//          (PsGetCurrentThread()->ForwardClusterOnly))
//
#define    SFSD_REQ_NOT_VIA_CACHE_MGR(ptr)                            \
    (!MmIsRecursiveIoFault() && ((ptr)->ImageSectionObject != NULL))

if (NonBufferedIo &&
    (PtrReqdFCB->SectionObject.DataSectionObject != NULL)) {
    if    (!PagingIo ||
        (SFSD_REQ_NOT_VIA_CACHE_MGR(&(PtrReqdFCB->SectionObject)))) {
        CcFlushCache(&(PtrReqdFCB->SectionObject),
                                    &ByteOffset, ReadLength,
                                    &(PtrIrp->IoStatus));
        // If the flush failed, return error to the caller
        if (!NT_SUCCESS(RC = PtrIrp->IoStatus.Status)) {
            try_return(RC);
        }
    }
}
```

- If the caller requests a noncached write operation on a file stream that is also currently being cached, the FSD must ensure that the cached data is consistent with the new (to-be-written) on-disk information.

The FSD has to avoid the situation where it writes new information to disk, and subsequently, the older information, when flushed by the lazy-writer or modified page writer threads overwrites the latest data.

To prevent such problems from occurring, I would suggest that your FSD implementation flush the currently cached information for the affected byte range and also purge it from the system cache, thereby forcing the Cache Manager to reload the latest information from secondary storage. This is also the approach followed by most existing Windows NT file system drivers.

One point that you must be aware of is that the NT VMM will fail a purge request if any process has the file stream mapped in its virtual address space. This will result in stale data being returned to the caller, but unfortunately, given the current design of the NT VMM, all FSD implementations have to learn to live with this restriction.

Finally, be careful about how you acquire file control block resources when performing such a purge operation. The Cache Manager requires that the FCB resources be acquired exclusively when requesting a purge. However, if you acquire FCB resources exclusively, perform the purge, and then release the FCB resources, you still run the risk of having another thread sneak in and perform another cached write on the file stream data, thereby invalidating all you just tried to achieve via the purge.

The following code fragment demonstrates how the cache flush and subsequent purge can be achieved:

```
if (NonBufferedIo && !PagingIo &&
    (PtrReqdFCB->SectionObject.DataSectionObject != NULL)) {
    // Flush and then attempt to purge the cache
    CcFlushCache(&(PtrReqdFCB->SectionObject),
                        &ByteOffset, WriteLength,
                        &(PtrIrp->IoStatus));
    // If the flush failed, return error to the caller
    if (!NT_SUCCESS(RC = PtrIrp->IoStatus.Status)) {
        try_return(RC);
    }


    // Attempt the purge and ignore the return code
    CcPurgeCacheSection(&(PtrReqdFCB->SectionObject),
                            (WritingAtEndOfFile ?
                            &(PtrReqdFCB->
                                CommonFCBHeader.FileSize) :
                            &(ByteOffset)),
                            WriteLength, FALSE);
    // We are finished with our flushing and purging
}
```

Resource acquisition hierarchies across the NT Cache Manager, the VMM, and the FSD are maintained by the presence of FSD callbacks, which are invoked by the Cache Manager and the NT VMM, to preacquire FSD resources before they initiate an I/O operation. Later in the next chapter, you will see sample code for such a callback operation. Similarly, when the I/O Manager uses the fast I/O method to bypass the FSD and directly request data from the NT Cache Manager, either the FSRTL routine or the FSD fast I/O routine must ensure that the correct file system resources are acquired before passing the request on to the Cache Manager.

The Cache Manager and the VMM are also extremely careful not to invoke routines exported by the respective modules in any manner that could lead to deadlock.

Asynchronous I/O Processing

FSD dispatch routines can be invoked either for synchronous or for asynchronous processing. Synchronous processing implies that the I/O request can be processed and completed in the context of the requesting thread, even if the requesting thread must be made to block, awaiting completion of processing of the request. Asynchronous processing, on the other hand, requires that the request either be completed in the context of the thread that invoked the FSD dispatch routine entry point, or if processing requires blocking of the original thread, be processed asynchronously in the context of some worker thread.

Two situations can result in a thread being blocked when processing an I/O request:

- When a thread tries to acquire some synchronization resource (e.g., a mutex or a read/write lock)

   The thread requesting the resource may be put into the blocked state, awaiting release of the resource by another thread that already has this resource acquired.

- When transferring data to/from secondary storage

   Most lower-level disk drivers queue I/O requests for subsequent, asynchronous processing if they are actively processing other I/O requests when the new request is received.

Although you can design an FSD that always performs synchronous processing, this can lead to system stability problems, especially in the case when your FSD tries to synchronously service asynchronous paging I/O requests from the VMM.

WARNING It is important that your FSD honor requests for asynchronous processing. As was explained in Chapter 5, the NT VMM modified page writer and mapped page writer threads aggressively try to write out modified pages when the system is running low on available physical memory. To achieve their objectives of flushing out pages quickly, each of these routines sends asynchronous paging I/O requests to the different FSDs in the system. If your FSD attempts to process such I/O requests synchronously, you are essentially thwarting the memory manager's attempts to respond quickly to the system's requirements for free pages. Not only do you prevent additional write requests from being queued to your FSD for processing, you also prevent write requests from being queued to any other FSD in the system. Worse, if your FSD were to block for a long time, it is almost certain that the VMM would eventually bugcheck the system.

Note that you will never block while attempting to acquire FSD resources for asynchronous mapped page writer requests, since these will have been preacquired by the NT VMM via a callback to the FSD before issuing the write request.

To provide support for asynchronous processing, your FSD must perform the following operations:

- Determine whether the caller has requested synchronous or asynchronous processing.

  Your FSD can use the `IoIsOperationSynchronous()` routine to find out whether an operation should be performed synchronously. This routine is defined as follows:

```
BOOLEAN
IoIsOperationSynchronous(
    IN PIRP        Irp
);
```

Resource Acquisition Constraints:

None.

Parameters:

Irp
  Pointer to the I/O Request Packet sent by the I/O Manager to the FSD.

Return Value:

TRUE if the current request should be processed synchronously; FALSE if the request is an asynchronous I/O request.

Functionality Provided:

The NT I/O Manager checks the following conditions to determine whether the operation is synchronous. If this is not an asynchronous paging I/O operation,[*] and one of the following is true, the operation is synchronous.

— The file object used in the IRP specifies that the file was opened for synchronous access.

— The NT I/O Manager API is an inherently synchronous API (e.g., the "create/open" operation is inherently synchronous).

— The IRP indicates that this is a synchronous paging I/O operation.

If the above checks evaluate to TRUE, the I/O Manager returns TRUE to indicate that the operation should be performed synchronously; otherwise, the I/O Manager returns FALSE, indicating that this I/O request should not be processed synchronously.

• If the caller is not prepared to block, always attempt to acquire resources in a nonblocking manner only. If resources cannot be acquired without blocking, post the request to a queue to be picked up later and processed in the context of a worker thread routine.

• When invoking the Cache Manager for accesses to buffered data, always inform the Cache Manager of whether the caller is prepared to block. Often, the Cache Manager may not be able to satisfy the request immediately and for nonblocking callers will return a FALSE value from the function call, indicating that the request processing should be deferred and retried later.

Most Windows NT file system drivers do not create dedicated worker threads to process asynchronous requests. Rather, the FSDs use the services of a pool of global system worker threads. The Windows NT Executive provides a set of supporting structure definitions and utilities that allow the FSD to initialize a work queue item for deferred processing and post the request to an appropriate queue supplying a callback function that can subsequently be invoked in the context of the worker thread.

Earlier in this chapter, we saw some sample code for a typical read dispatch routine entry point in the FSD. The `SFsdRead()` routine allocates an `IrpContext` structure. This `IrpContext` structure serves as an encapsulation of the current I/O request, and turns out to be useful when preparing the IRP for deferred processing and the subsequent posting of the IRP. Here is a sample `IrpContext` structure as defined by the FSD:

---

[*] Even if the file object was opened specifying synchronous I/O operations, the modified/mapped page writer will try to write data out asynchronously. Therefore, the last clause in the list of checks performed above is important.

```
typedef struct _SFsdIrpContext {
    SFsdIdentifier                      NodeIdentifier;
    uint32                              IrpContextFlags;
    // copied from the IRP
    uint8                               MajorFunction;
    // copied from the IRP
    uint8                               MinorFunction;
    // to queue this IRP for asynchronous processing
    WORK_QUEUE_ITEM                     WorkQueueItem;
    // the IRP for which this context structure was created
    PIRP                                Irp;
    // the target of the request (obtained from the IRP)
    PDEVICE_OBJECT                      TargetDeviceObject;
    // if an exception occurs, we will store the code here
    NTSTATUS                            SavedExceptionCode;
} SFsdIrpContext, *PtrSFsdIrpContext;
#define     SFSD_IRP_CONTEXT_CAN_BLOCK          (0x00000001)
#define     SFSD_IRP_CONTEXT_WRITE_THROUGH      (0x00000002)
#define     SFSD_IRP_CONTEXT_EXCEPTION          (0x00000004)
#define     SFSD_IRP_CONTEXT_DEFERRED_WRITE     (0x00000008)
#define     SFSD_IRP_CONTEXT_ASYNC_PROCESSING   (0x00000010)
#define     SFSD_IRP_CONTEXT_NOT_TOP_LEVEL      (0x00000020)
#define     SFSD_IRP_CONTEXT_NOT_FROM_ZONE      (0x80000000)
```

The `IrpContext` structure is used by the sample FSD implementation to encapsulate the current I/O request. Your FSD can utilize a similar structure, if it proves to be convenient. Notice that the `IrpContext` structure has a flag, `SFSD_IRP_CONTEXT_CAN_BLOCK`, that indicates to the FSD if the current caller of the dispatch routine can block during I/O processing. This flag is set when the `IrpContext` structure is allocated, to indicate whether synchronous processing can be performed. Furthermore, the `WorkQueueItem` field in the `IrpContext` structure is used by the FSD to post the request for deferred processing in the context of a system worker thread.

The following code fragment demonstrates the implementation of a simple (though typical) `IrpContext` allocation routine:

```
PtrSFsdIrpContext SFsdAllocateIrpContext(
PIRP                    Irp,
PDEVICE_OBJECT          PtrTargetDeviceObject)
{
    PtrSFsdIrpContext           PtrIrpContext = NULL;
    BOOLEAN                     AllocatedFromZone = TRUE;
    KIRQL                       CurrentIrql;
    PIO_STACK_LOCATION          PtrIoStackLocation = NULL;

    // first, try to allocate out of the zone
    KeAcquireSpinLock(&(SFsdGlobalData.ZoneAllocationSpinLock),
                        &CurrentIrql);
    if (!ExIsFullZone(&(SFsdGlobalData.IrpContextZoneHeader))) {
        // we have enough memory
        PtrIrpContext =
```

```
                        (PtrSFsdIrpContext)ExAllocateFromZone
                               (&(SFsdGlobalData.IrpContextZoneHeader));

        // release the spin lock
        KeReleaseSpinLock(&(SFsdGlobalData.ZoneAllocationSpinLock),
                                       CurrentIrql);
    } else {
        // release the spin lock
        KeReleaseSpinLock(&(SFsdGlobalData.ZoneAllocationSpinLock),
                                       CurrentIrql);

        // if we failed to obtain from the zone, get it directly from the
        // VMM
        PtrIrpContext = (PtrSFsdIrpContext)ExAllocatePool(NonPagedPool,
                                  SFsdQuadAlign(sizeof(SFsdIrpContext)));
      AllocatedFromZone = FALSE;
    }


    // if we could not obtain the required memory, bugcheck.
    // Do NOT do this in your commercial driver, instead handle
    // the error gracefully (e.g., by returning STATUS_INSUFFICIENT_
    // RESOURCES to the caller and also logging the error condition).
    if (!PtrIrpContext) {
        SFsdPanic(STATUS_INSUFFICIENT_RESOURCES,
                SFsdQuadAlign(sizeof(SFsdIrpContext)), 0);
    }


    // zero-out the allocated memory block
    RtlZeroMemory(PtrIrpContext, SFsdQuadAlign(sizeof(SFsdIrpContext)));

    // set up some fields ...
    PtrIrpContext->NodeIdentifier.NodeType   = SFSD_NODE_TYPE_IRP_CONTEXT;
    PtrIrpContext->NodeIdentifier.NodeSize   =
                        SFsdQuadAlign(sizeof(SFsdIrpContext));


    PtrIrpContext->Irp = Irp;
    PtrIrpContext->TargetDeviceObject = PtrTargetDeviceObject;

    // copy over some fields from the IRP and set appropriate flag values
    if (Irp) {
        PtrIoStackLocation = IoGetCurrentIrpStackLocation(Irp);
        ASSERT(PtrIoStackLocation);

        PtrIrpContext->MajorFunction = PtrIoStackLocation->MajorFunction;
        PtrIrpContext->MinorFunction = PtrIoStackLocation->MinorFunction;

        // Often, an FSD cannot honor a request for asynchronous processing
        // of certain critical requests. For example, a "close" request on
        // a file object can typically never be deferred. Therefore, do not
        // be surprised if sometimes your FSD (just like all other FSD
        // implementations on the Windows NT system) has to override the
        // flag below.
        if (IoIsOperationSynchronous(Irp)) {
```

```
                SFsdSetFlag(PtrIrpContext->IrpContextFlags,
                    SFSD_IRP_CONTEXT_CAN_BLOCK);
        }
    }

    if (!AllocatedFromZone) {
        SFsdSetFlag(PtrIrpContext->IrpContextFlags,
                        SFSD_IRP_CONTEXT_NOT_FROM_ZONE);
    }

    // Are we top-level? This information is used by the dispatching code
    // later (and also by the FSD dispatch routine)
    if (IoGetTopLevelIrp() != Irp) {
        // We are not top-level. Note this fact in the context structure
        SFsdSetFlag(PtrIrpContext->IrpContextFlags,
                        SFSD_IRP_CONTEXT_NOT_TOP_LEVEL);
    }

    return(PtrIrpContext);
}
```

The `IrpContext` allocation routine determines whether the FSD can be considered top-level for the original invocation of the FSD dispatch routine and remembers this fact by setting an appropriate flag value.

A work queue item must be initialized by the FSD to post a request for deferred processing. This initialization can be performed by using the `ExInitialize-WorkItem()` Executive support function, which accepts the following arguments:

- A pointer to the work item to be initiated

  You can pass in a pointer to the `WorkQueueItem` field in the `IrpContext` structure.

- A pointer to the callback function

  Note that the sample FSD implementation uses a common callback function called `SFsdAsyncDispatch()`, shown later.

- A context for which you should simply pass in the pointer to the IRP context structure itself

The following expanded code fragment from the `SFsdCommonRead()` function, originally presented in the previous chapter, illustrates how the FSD can post an item for subsequent (deferred) processing:

```
NTSTATUS        SFsdCommonRead(
PtrSFsdIrpContext               PtrIrpContext,
PIRP                           PtrIrp)
{
    // Declarations go here …

    try {
```

```
    // Chapter 9 has more information on processing performed here.

    ....

    // Acquire the appropriate FCB resource shared.
    if (PagingIo) {
        // Try to acquire the FCB PagingIoResource shared
        if (!ExAcquireResourceSharedLite(&(PtrReqdFCB->
                                        PagingIoResource),
                                        CanWait)) {
            CompleteIrp = FALSE;

            // This is one instance where we have decided to defer
            // processing ...
            PostRequest = TRUE;
            try_return(RC = STATUS_PENDING);
        }
        // Remember the resource that was acquired.
        PtrResourceAcquired = &(PtrReqdFCB->PagingIoResource);
    } else {
        // Try to acquire the FCB MainResource shared.
        if (!ExAcquireResourceSharedLite(&(PtrReqdFCB->MainResource),
                        CanWait)) {
            CompleteIrp = FALSE;

            // Defer processing ...
            PostRequest = TRUE;
            try_return(RC = STATUS_PENDING);
        }
        // Remember the resource that was acquired.
        PtrResourceAcquired = &(PtrReqdFCB->MainResource);
    }

    // There are other situations that could require us to post
    // the request.
    ...

    try_exit:    NOTHING;

} finally {
    // Post IRP if required.
    if (PostRequest) {

        // Release any resources acquired here ...
        if (PtrResourceAcquired) {
            SFsdReleaseResource(PtrResourceAcquired);
        }

        // Implement a routine that will queue up the request to be
        // executed later (asynchronously) in the context of a system
        // worker thread.

        // Lock the caller's buffer here. Then invoke a common routine
        // to perform the post operation.
```

```
                    if (!(PtrIoStackLocation->MinorFunction & IRP_MN_MDL)) {
                        RC = SFsdLockCallersBuffer(PtrIrp, TRUE, ReadLength);
                        ASSERT(NT_SUCCESS(RC));
                    }

                    // Perform the post operation, which will mark the IRP pending
                    // and will return STATUS_PENDING back to us.
                    RC = SFsdPostRequest(PtrIrpContext, PtrIrp);

                } else if (CompleteIrp && !(RC == STATUS_PENDING)) {

                    // More information in Chapter 9 ...

                } // can we complete the IRP?
            } // end of "finally" processing.

        return(RC);
}
```

In this code fragment, you can see that the request is posted for deferred
processing if appropriate resources cannot be acquired without blocking and if
the caller had specified no blocking. Before sending the request to be queued,
the FSD is careful to create a memory descriptor list (MDL), describing the caller-
supplied buffer and also to lock the pages comprising this MDL. Then, the FSD
invokes the **SFsdPostRequest()** routine to post the request. This routine is
shown below:

```
NTSTATUS SFsdPostRequest(
PtrSFsdIrpContext           PtrIrpContext,
PIRP                        PtrIrp)
{
    NTSTATUS            RC = STATUS_PENDING;

    // mark the IRP pending; a flag SL_PENDING_RETURNED is set in the
    // current stack location.
    IoMarkIrpPending(PtrIrp);

    // queue up the request.
    ExInitializeWorkItem(&(PtrIrpContext->WorkQueueItem),
                            SFsdCommonDispatch,
                            PtrIrpContext);

    ExQueueWorkItem(&(PtrIrpContext->WorkQueueItem), CriticalWorkQueue);

    // return status pending.
    return(RC);
}
```

The **SFsdPostRequest()** function shown here is very simple; it marks the I/O
Request Packet pending, queues the request for processing by a system worker
thread, and returns the **STATUS_PENDING** code to the caller. Each of these steps

is important to successfully process the request asynchronously. Here's what each of the steps in the `SFsdPostRequest()` routine achieves:

- The I/O Manager checks for the presence of the `SL_PENDING_RETURNED` flag when the IRP is eventually completed.

  This flag is an indicator to the I/O Manager that your driver must have returned `STATUS_PENDING` to the caller of a dispatch routine, and that the IRP could have been processed asynchronously.

  If this flag is set in the current stack location (the stack location of the driver that invokes `IoCompleteRequest()`), the I/O Manager remembers not to take the shortcut method, described in Chapter 4, *The NT I/O Manager*, of performing IRP completion postprocessing directly in the context of the thread that originated the I/O request; instead, the I/O Manager queues a kernel asynchronous procedure call to the originating thread and performs the requisite postprocessing when the APC is delivered.

- Invoking `ExQueueWorkItem()` queues the request in a global system queue for asynchronous handling by an available worker thread.

- Returning `STATUS_PENDING` informs the caller that your driver will process the request asynchronously.

  When the caller receives this return status, it knows that the request will be completed asynchronously and that the caller can wait for the request completion immediately, or after performing some concurrent processing. It is quite possible that the request can be completed even before your `STATUS_PEND-ING` gets returned to the caller if the thread that invoked your FSD dispatch routine is preempted. However, that is not a race condition that you have to worry about. The pseudocode below demonstrates how FSD dispatch routines are invoked:

```
// The FSD dispatch routine is invoked as shown here:
RC = IoCallDriver(PtrDeviceObject, PtrIrp);
if (RC != STATUS_PENDING) {
    // Check the return status and react appropriately, since the
    // request has been processed synchronously.
    ...
} else {
    // We received a STATUS_PENDING. Optionally, perform some
processing
    // and then wait for the request completion.
    ...
    KeWaitForSingleObject(...);
    // Now, the wait was completed; therefore IoCompleteRequest()
    // must have been invoked on the IRP.
    ...
}
```

In this pseudocode, the caller simply waits for an event object to be signaled when `STATUS_PENDING` is returned. The worst that could happen if the request gets completed before the caller begins the wait is that the event object may have already been signaled (when `IoCompleteRequest()` was processed), and the caller will find the event object in the signaled state in the `KeWaitForSingleObject()` function call; this will result in no wait actually being performed.

Once the request has been posted by the FSD, a system worker thread picks up the request from the appropriate queue. There is a fixed pool of system worker threads, and they exist for the sole purpose of performing work for the different Windows NT Executive components. When your FSD initializes the work item for subsequent queuing, it specifies a function that the worker thread must execute. The sample FSD supplies a pointer to the `SFsdCommonDispatch()` routine. Also note that the sample FSD uses a pointer to the `IrpContext` structure as the context to be supplied to the callback routine. This is convenient, since the `IrpContext` structure contains a pointer to the original IRP, and also additional information, such as whether the FSD was top-level for the IRP request to be processed. The following code fragment demonstrates a typical callback dispatch routine that your FSD could implement:

```
void SFsdCommonDispatch(
void                        *Context)    // actually a SFsdIrpContext
                                         // structure
{
    NTSTATUS                     RC = STATUS_SUCCESS;
    PtrSFsdIrpContext            PtrIrpContext = NULL;
    PIRP                         PtrIrp = NULL;

    // The context must be a pointer to an IrpContext structure.
    PtrIrpContext = (PtrSFsdIrpContext)Context;
    ASSERT(PtrIrpContext);

    // Assert that the context is legitimate.
    if ((PtrIrpContext->NodeIdentifier.NodeType !=
            SFSD_NODE_TYPE_IRP_CONTEXT)
        || (PtrIrpContext->NodeIdentifier.NodeSize !=
            SFsdQuadAlign(sizeof(SFsdIrpContext)))) {
        // This does not look good!
        SFsdPanic(SFSD_ERROR_INTERNAL_ERROR,
            PtrIrpContext->NodeIdentifier.NodeType,
            PtrIrpContext->NodeIdentifier.NodeSize);
    }

    // Get a pointer to the IRP structure.
    PtrIrp = PtrIrpContext->Irp;
    ASSERT(PtrIrp);

    // Now, check if the FSD was top level when the IRP was originally
```

```
// invoked and set the thread context (for the worker thread)
// appropriately.
if (PtrIrpContext->IrpContextFlags & SFSD_IRP_CONTEXT_NOT_TOP_LEVEL) {
    // The FSD is not top-level for the original request.
    // Set a constant value in the TLS to reflect this fact.
    IoSetTopLevelIrp((PIRP)FSRTL_FSP_TOP_LEVEL_IRP);
}

// Since the FSD routine will now be invoked in the context of this
// worker thread, we should inform the FSD that it is perfectly OK to
// block in the context of this thread.
SFsdSetFlag(PtrIrpContext->IrpContextFlags,
            SFSD_IRP_CONTEXT_CAN_BLOCK);

FsRtlEnterFileSystem();

try {

    // Preprocessing has been completed; check the Major Function code
    // value either in the IrpContext (copied from the IRP), or
    // directly from the IRP itself (we will need a pointer to the
    // stack location to do that).
    // Then, switch, based on the value on the Major Function code.
    switch (PtrIrpContext->MajorFunction) {
    case IRP_MJ_CREATE:
        // Invoke the common create routine.
        (void)SFsdCommonCreate(PtrIrpContext, PtrIrp);
        break;
    case IRP_MJ_READ:
        // Invoke the common read routine.
        (void)SFsdCommonRead(PtrIrpContext, PtrIrp);
        break;
    // Continue with the remaining possible dispatch routines.
    default:
        // This is the case where we have an invalid major function.
        PtrIrp->IoStatus.Status = STATUS_INVALID_DEVICE_REQUEST;
        PtrIrp->IoStatus.Information = 0;

        IoCompleteRequest(PtrIrp, IO_NO_INCREMENT);
        break;
    }
} except (SFsdExceptionFilter(PtrIrpContext,
            GetExceptionInformation())) {

    RC = SFsdExceptionHandler(PtrIrpContext, PtrIrp);

    SFsdLogEvent(SFSD_ERROR_INTERNAL_ERROR, RC);
}

// Enable preemption
FsRtlExitFileSystem();
```

```
    // Ensure that the top-level field is cleared.
    IoSetTopLevelIrp(NULL);

    return;
}
```

The callback routine shown here performs some simple preprocessing before forwarding the request to the appropriate FSD dispatch routine, including indicating to the FSD (via a flag in the `IrpContext` structure) that it can now block in the context of the worker thread. Furthermore, if the FSD was not top-level when the IRP was originally dispatched to the driver, the worker thread callback routine indicates this by setting the `FSRTL_FSP_TOP_LEVEL_IRP` flag in the TLS for the system worker thread.

There is one additional, and extremely important, point you must be aware of when determining whether to post a request for asynchronous processing. Synchronous I/O requests for which the FSD is not top-level and recursive I/O requests should typically never be posted by the FSD, since attempting to acquire FSD resources when processing the request in a worker thread context could lead to a system deadlock (because resources would have been preacquired in the context of the original thread that initiated the request). If you do decide to handle such requests asynchronously, your FSD must be capable of some pretty sophisticated processing in the dispatch routines (e.g., `SFsdCommonRead()`) to determine if it is allowed to acquire resources or to skip such acquisition. Modified/mapped page writer requests can therefore never be posted, although they are asynchronous requests. However, you can be assured that your FSD will never block on file system resources for such requests, since the VMM preacquires these resources.

Here are a few specific dispatch entry points for which the FSD should be able to provide asynchronous processing capabilities:

- Read file stream
- Write file stream
- Query directory contents
- Notify when directory contents are changed
- Byte-range lock/unlock requests
- Device IOCTL requests
- File system IOCTL requests

All of the other possible FSD requests are *inherently synchronous.* Remember that the caller must use the API provided by the NT I/O Manager (or native NT I/O services like `NtReadFile()`) to obtain and modify file system data. The NT I/O Manager classifies all APIs, excluding the ones corresponding to the listed request types, as synchronous APIs and will therefore perform a wait in the invoking thread's context, even if the caller has requested asynchronous processing. Therefore, the file system can process these other types of requests in the context of the invoking thread.

For synchronous I/O requests, the NT I/O Manager serializes the I/O. Therefore, if *thread-A* requests synchronous I/O using a file object opened for synchronous I/O, and concurrently, *thread-B* issues an I/O request using the same file object, the I/O request arriving later in the I/O Manager (say, *thread*-B's request) will be forced to wait by the I/O Manager until the first request has been completed.

Typically, a thread issuing asynchronous I/O requests can synchronize with the completion of the request using one of the three methods listed below:

Waiting for the file object handle itself
> The NT I/O Manager sets the file object handle to a not-signaled state when the I/O is requested and then signals the file object after `IoComplete-Request()` has been invoked for the IRP representing the I/O request. This method is not error-proof, however, because if two asynchronous I/O requests are issued concurrently, the file handle is signaled when one of them finishes, and it is then not possible for the caller to determine which of the two requests actually completed.

Waiting for an event object supplied by the caller when requesting the I/O
> This method is mutually exclusive with waiting for the file object (i.e., if the caller supplies an event object when requesting the I/O, the NT I/O Manager will signal the event instead of signaling the file object). This method is more robust if multiple, concurrent, asynchronous I/O requests will be issued.

Specifying an APC to be invoked when the I/O is completed
> Each of the potentially asynchronous I/O APIs listed accepts the address of an optional APC routine that will be invoked by the I/O Manager after the IRP has been completed. This APC is invoked with the caller-supplied context and the address of the I/O status block containing the results of the I/O operation.

Now that you have a fairly good understanding of how to determine the top-level component for a request and how to asynchronously process FSD requests, we'll discuss other important FSD dispatch routine implementations. Let's start with the *set and query file information* requests.

Dispatch Routine: File Information

It is quite typical for a user to want to query and manipulate information about file streams such as the current file size, the date that the file stream was last accessed, the date that the file stream was last modified, the number of links to the data associated with the filename entry, and other similar information.

Since a filename entry in a directory is considered an attribute associated with the file stream data, the Windows NT operating system allows the user to delete and add filename entries (links) to the file stream via the set file information routine. In fact, the only method allowed by the NT I/O Manager to delete filenames is to open the file stream, modify the file attributes by specifying that the filename entry be deleted using the set file information dispatch routine, and then closing the file handle.*

One of the peculiarities of the Windows NT I/O Manager and FSD interface is the method mandated by the I/O subsystem in processing user requests to rename file streams. A rename operation can be logically decomposed into the following two steps:

1. Remove the original filename entry from the source directory.

2. Add a new filename entry to the destination directory; this entry must refer to the same on-disk data stream that was pointed to by the original (source) filename.

As you can see, there are four objects that potentially need to be manipulated in a rename operation (if the source and target directories are the same, then you have only three objects to worry about):

- The filename being deleted
- The source directory that contains the filename being deleted
- The filename being added
- The target directory, which will contain the new filename entry

In the case where the source and target directories are different, the NT I/O Manager performs the following sequence of operations:

1. First, request the FSD to open the target directory and determine whether the target filename exists.

   This special create request sent to the FSD is recognizable by the presence of the `SL_OPEN_TARGET_DIRECTORY` flag in the `Flags` field of the current I/O stack location of the create IRP. In Chapter 9, you saw the response from the FSD in the create dispatch routine entry point.

---

* This sequence is performed transparently by Windows NT subsystems when a user application process requests that the file entry be deleted. The actual deletion of the file name entry is only performed by the FSD in the cleanup dispatch routine, which in turn is invoked after all of the user handles corresponding to a particular file object have been closed. You will see this in the description for the cleanup dispatch routine entry point provided later in this chapter.

The FSD is expected to respond by determining whether the target filename exists or not, and then by opening the parent directory of the target file. The FSD must also replace the name supplied in the create request (which is the complete path and filename leading to the target file) with only the name of the target file itself. For example, if the I/O Manager supplies a pathname *directory1\directory2\directory3\source_dir\foo*, the FSD should replace this name with the name *foo* in the `FileName` field of the file object structure created by the I/O Manager.

The following code fragment from the create dispatch routine entry point, describing the steps listed previously, was originally presented in Chapter 9 and is expanded upon and included here for completeness:

```
// Now we are down to the last component, check it out to see if it
// exists ...
// Even for the "open target directory" case below, it is important
// to know whether the final component specified exists (or not).

// If "open target directory" was specified:
if (OpenTargetDirectory) {
    if (NT_SUCCESS(RC)) {
        // file exists, set this information in the Information
        // field.
        ReturnedInformation = FILE_EXISTS;
    } else {
        RC = STATUS_SUCCESS;
        // Tell the I/O Manager that file does not exit.
        ReturnedInformation = FILE_DOES_NOT_EXIST;
    }

    // Now, do the following:
    // (a) Replace the string in the FileName field in the
    //     PtrNewFileObject to identify the target name
    //     only (i.e. the final component string without the path
    //     leading to the object).

    {
        unsigned int Index =
            ((AbsolutePathName.Length / sizeof(WCHAR)) - 1);

        // Back up until we come to the last '\'.
        // But first, skip any trailing '\' characters.

        while (AbsolutePathName.Buffer[Index] == L'\\') {
            ASSERT(Index >= sizeof(WCHAR));
            Index -= sizeof(WCHAR);
            // Skip this length also.
            PtrNewFileObject->FileName.Length -= sizeof(WCHAR);
        }

        while (AbsolutePathName.Buffer[Index] != L'\\') {
            // Keep backing up until we hit one.
```

```
                ASSERT(Index >= sizeof(WCHAR));
                Index -= sizeof(WCHAR);
        }

        // We must be at a '\' character.
        ASSERT(AbsolutePathName.Buffer[Index] == L'\\');
        Index++;

        // We can now determine the new length of the filename
        // and copy the name over.
        PtrNewFileObject->FileName.Length -=
                (unsigned short)(Index*sizeof(WCHAR));
        RtlCopyMemory(&(PtrNewFileObject->FileName.Buffer[0]),
                &(PtrNewFileObject->FileName.Buffer[Index]),
                PtrNewFileObject->FileName.Length);
    }

    // (b) Return with the target's parent directory opened.
    // (c) Update the file object FsContext and FsContext2 fields
    //     to reflect the fact that the parent directory of the
    //     target has been opened.

    try_return(RC);
}
```

2. If the FSD returns **FILE_EXISTS**, and the original rename request does not request file replacement, the I/O Manager will return a **STATUS_OBJECT_NAME_COLLISION** error to the caller.

3. Now, the I/O Manager issues the **IRP_MJ_SET_INFORMATION** request to the FSD, passing in the target directory file object pointer, the full pathname of the source file, and the request to rename the file.

   A description of the processing performed by the FSD upon receiving the **IRP_MJ_SET_INFORMATION** request is described later in this chapter.

NOTE   You may be wondering why the I/O Manager issues the "open target directory" request to the FSD prior to issuing the rename (and also link) IRPs. Remember that, in order to issue the **IRP_MJ_SET_INFORMATION** request, the I/O Manager requires an open file object pointer. Therefore, the logical choice for file stream to be opened (for which a file object will be created) is the target (parent) directory in which the rename (or link) will be performed since this is the directory whose contents will definitely be modified as a result of processing the rename/link request.

You should note that the method used by the I/O Manager to create a new hard link for a file stream across directories is exactly the same as the rename operation previously described.

It is not required that an FSD use the same dispatch routine for both the `IRP_MJ_QUERY_INFORMATION` and the `IRP_MJ_SET_INFORMATION` major functions. However, that is the approach taken by the sample FSD driver. It can be easily changed, if you so desire, in your driver implementation.

Logical Steps Involved

The I/O stack location contains the following structures relevant to processing the query file information and the set file information requests issued to a FSD:

```
typedef struct _IO_STACK_LOCATION {

    // ....

    union {

        //....

        // System service parameters for:  NtQueryInformationFile
        struct {
            ULONG Length;
            FILE_INFORMATION_CLASS FileInformationClass;
        } QueryFile;

        // System service parameters for:  NtSetInformationFile
        struct {
            ULONG Length;
            FILE_INFORMATION_CLASS FileInformationClass;
            PFILE_OBJECT FileObject;
            union {
                struct {
                    BOOLEAN ReplaceIfExists;
                    BOOLEAN AdvanceOnly;
                };
                ULONG ClusterCount;
                HANDLE DeleteHandle;
            };
        } SetFile;

        // ....
    } Parameters;

    // ....

} IO_STACK_LOCATION, *PIO_STACK_LOCATION;
```

The following logical steps are executed by the FSD upon receiving a query/set file information IRP. Note that to query or modify file attribute information, the caller must have previously opened the file stream. Therefore, the FSD is guaranteed to receive a pointer to a file object that was created during the open operation, from which it can obtain pointers to the internal associated CCB and FCB data structures.

If your FSD does not support any of the query/set file information types described below, the FSD should return STATUS_INVALID_PARAMETER when asked to process the unsupported type.

IRP_MJ_QUERY_INFORMATION

The I/O Manager can request different types of information about the file stream. The Parameters.QueryDirectory.FileInformationClass field in the current I/O stack location in the IRP contains the type of information requested by the caller. The information requested is one of the following:

FileBasicInformation (FILE_BASIC_INFORMATION)

```
typedef struct _FILE_BASIC_INFORMATION {
    LARGE_INTEGER    CreationTime;
    LARGE_INTEGER    LastAccessTime;
    LARGE_INTEGER    LastWriteTime;
    LARGE_INTEGER    ChangeTime;
    ULONG            FileAttributes;
} FILE_BASIC_INFORMATION, *PFILE_BASIC_INFORMATION;
```

The possible file attribute values that your FSD might return will be one or more of FILE_ATTRIBUTE_READONLY, FILE_ATTRIBUTE_HIDDEN, FILE_ATTRIBUTE_DIRECTORY (to indicate a directory type file stream), and other similar values defined in the DDK.

Fundamentally, the basic information requested includes the various time attributes associated with the file stream, as well as information on the type of the file. If your FSD does not support certain time values requested (e.g., your FSD may not support the concept of a separate CreationTime for the file stream), you should return a 0 value in the corresponding field.

The CreationTime is defined as the date and time that the file stream was created. The LastAccessTime specifies the date and time that the contents of the file stream were last accessed, the LastWriteTime specifies the date and time that the file stream was last written to, and the ChangeTime specifies the date and time that one or more attributes of the file stream were changed.

All time values are specified in the standard Windows NT system-time format, in which the absolute system time is the number of 100 nanosecond intervals since January 1, 1601.

The LastAccessTime value is initialized when a file stream is created. It is typically updated when the file data is read. For directories, this value is updated when query directory requests are received by the FSD.

The `LastWriteTime` is initialized when a file stream is created, superseded, or overwritten (during a create operation). For an ordinary file, it is typically updated when write requests are received by the FSD. For directories, the value is updated when a new file is created or superseded in a directory, or when a set file information request is received that affects the contents of the directory. These requests include the `FileDispositionInformation`, `FileRenameInformation` (affects the `LastWriteTime` for both the source and target directories), and the `FileLinkInformation` request.

The `ChangeTime` is initialized when a file stream is created. It is modified whenever the `LastWriteTime` for a file stream is modified. In addition, the `ChangeTime` should be updated when a set file information request of type `FileAllocationInformation` or `FileEndOfFileInformation` is received for an ordinary file. The `FileDispositionInformation` request (if successful) results in the `ChangeTime` being updated for the affected file as well as the directory containing the file; the `FileRenameInformation` type request results in the change time being modified for both the source and target directories, and the `FileLinkInformation` request results in the `ChangeTime` being modified for the file being linked to as well as the directory containing the file.

FileStandardInformation (FILE_STANDARD_INFORMATION)

```
typedef struct _FILE_STANDARD_INFORMATION {
    LARGE_INTEGER     AllocationSize;
    LARGE_INTEGER     EndOfFile;
    ULONG             NumberOfLinks;
    BOOLEAN           DeletePending;
    BOOLEAN           Directory;
} FILE_STANDARD_INFORMATION, *PFILE_STANDARD_INFORMATION;
```

The structure shown here is mostly self-explanatory. The **NumberOfLinks** field refers to the number of directory entries that point to the data for the file stream. This field has a value that is typically set to 1 but can have a value greater than 1 if your FSD supports multiply linked file streams. The **Delete-Pending** field is set to TRUE if some thread had previously invoked the set file information dispatch entry point, requesting that the file be marked for deletion. The **AllocationSize** and the **EndOfFile** size definitions were introduced in Chapter 6.

FileNetworkOpenInformation (FILE_NETWORK_OPEN_INFORMATION)

```
typedef struct _FILE_NETWORK_OPEN_INFORMATION {
    LARGE_INTEGER CreationTime;
    LARGE_INTEGER LastAccessTime;
    LARGE_INTEGER LastWriteTime;
    LARGE_INTEGER ChangeTime;
    LARGE_INTEGER AllocationSize;
    LARGE_INTEGER EndOfFile;
    ULONG         FileAttributes;
} FILE_NETWORK_OPEN_INFORMATION, *PFILE_NETWORK_OPEN_INFORMATION;
```

This particular form of file information request was added with Windows NT version 4.0 to speed-up network file information requests served by the LAN Manager Server. The Server Message Block (SMB) protocol, used by the LAN Manager Server and the LAN Manager Redirectors, contains a request to get *standard information* about a file stream. This standard information structure, as defined in the SMB protocol, consists of both the information obtained via `FILE_BASIC_INFORMATION` and the file size values normally obtained by issuing a second request for `FILE_STANDARD_INFORMATION`. To avoid making two separate trips through the I/O Manager to the FSD, the Windows NT operating system designers decided to add this optimization of having a single call provide the necessary information in Version 4.0.

FileInternalInformation (FILE_INTERNAL_INFORMATION)

```
typedef struct _FILE_INTERNAL_INFORMATION {
    LARGE_INTEGER IndexNumber;
} FILE_INTERNAL_INFORMATION, *PFILE_INTERNAL_INFORMATION;
```

If your FSD can associate a unique numerical value with a particular file stream, you should return this value when *file internal information* is requested from you. The native FASTFAT implementation returns the cluster number index value in the logical volume for the on-disk FCB structure. The native NTFS implementation returns the on-disk index entry (record index) in the Master File Table (MFT) for the file stream.

The caller can subsequently supply the file identifier in a create/open request sent to your FSD, instead of a complete pathname leading to the file to be created. Your FSD should then be capable of identifying the file to be opened using the file identifier value. NTFS, for example, reads the particular MFT record identified by the file identifier into memory, and then continues processing the create/open request. Note that opening a file stream using the file identifier can be a lot quicker than doing so by supplying the entire pathname to be traversed.

FileEaInformation (FILE_EA_INFORMATION)

```
typedef struct _FILE_EA_INFORMATION {
    ULONG EaSize;
} FILE_EA_INFORMATION, *PFILE_EA_INFORMATION;
```

If your FSD supports extended attributes associated with a file stream, you should return the size of these extended attributes. Return 0 if no extended attributes are associated with the particular file stream.

FileNameInformation/FileAlternateNameInformation (FILE_NAME_INFORMATION)

```
typedef struct _FILE_NAME_INFORMATION {
    ULONG FileNameLength;
    WCHAR FileName[1];
} FILE_NAME_INFORMATION, *PFILE_NAME_INFORMATION;
```

Your FSD must return the complete pathname for the open file stream (the name beginning with the root directory in the logical volume on which the file stream resides). If your FSD supports the DOS-style 8.3 names on-disk (in addition to the regular, long filename), and if the request is for `FileAlternateNameInformation`, you should return that name instead. However, it is not required that all FSD implementations support an alternate name for a file stream.

FileCompressionInformation (FILE_COMPRESSION_INFORMATION)

```
typedef struct _FILE_COMPRESSION_INFORMATION {
    LARGE_INTEGER CompressedFileSize;
} FILE_COMPRESSION_INFORMATION, *PFILE_COMPRESSION_INFORMATION;
```

If your FSD supports compressed file streams, here is your opportunity to return the true on-disk size (compressed size) for the file.

FilePositionInformation (FILE_POSITION_INFORMATION)

```
typedef struct _FILE_POSITION_INFORMATION
    LARGE_INTEGER CurrentByteOffset
} FILE_POSITION_INFORMATION, *PFILE_POSITION_INFORMATION;
```

If the file object was opened for synchronous I/O, the I/O Manager does not even bother to call the FSD when file position information is requested, but instead fills in the information directly from the `CurrentByteOffset` field in the file object data structure. If, however, the file object was not opened for synchronous I/O, the I/O Manager invokes the FSD to satisfy the request. Unfortunately, though, the caller is not guaranteed, in this case, to have any valid information returned to it, unless the file position had been explicitly set at some prior time. The reason is that all of the current NT FSD implementations also appear to obtain the current file position from the file object structure; however, this structure is only guaranteed to be updated during synchronous I/O operations, and therefore contains a valid current file position value only if the file object had been opened for synchronous I/O.

FileAllInformation (FILE_ALL_INFORMATION)

```
typedef struct _FILE_ALL_INFORMATION {
    FILE_BASIC_INFORMATION       BasicInformation;
    FILE_STANDARD_INFORMATION    StandardInformation;
    FILE_INTERNAL_INFORMATION    InternalInformation;
    FILE_EA_INFORMATION          EaInformation;
    FILE_ACCESS_INFORMATION      AccessInformation;
    FILE_POSITION_INFORMATION    PositionInformation;
    FILE_MODE_INFORMATION        ModeInformation;
    FILE_ALIGNMENT_INFORMATION   AlignmentInformation;
    FILE_NAME_INFORMATION        NameInformation;
} FILE_ALL_INFORMATION, *PFILE_ALL_INFORMATION;
```

The FSD combines information that might otherwise be requested separately and returns it in this call. Take note of the fact that you do not need to worry about the `AccessInformation`, `ModeInformation`, and `AlignmentIn` formation requested. See the note below on how this information is filled into the user-supplied buffer.

FileStreamInformation (FILE_STREAM_INFORMATION)

```
typedef struct _FILE_STREAM_INFORMATION {
    ULONG               NextEntryOffset;
    ULONG               StreamNameLength;
    LARGE_INTEGER       StreamSize;
    LARGE_INTEGER       StreamAllocationSize;
    WCHAR               StreamName[1];
} FILE_STREAM_INFORMATION, *PFILE_STREAM_INFORMATION;
```

This particular type of query file information call is supported only by NTFS, out of all the native file systems supported under Windows NT. The NTFS implementation supports multiple named/unnamed data streams for any on-disk file. This particular call can be used by the caller to obtain name and stream-length information for all the data streams for a named file object. The caller typically supplies a buffer that is of some appropriate size. NTFS determines all of the valid data streams for the file represented by the FCB and fills in information (using the structure defined previously) for each such stream into the caller-supplied buffer. If the buffer turns out to be too small to contain information on all streams, an appropriate error (**STATUS_BUFFER_OVERFLOW**) is returned to the caller. Each entry in the buffer contains information for a data stream, is quad-aligned (4 byte aligned), and contains the offset in the **NextEntryOffset** field for the next entry. The last entry contains a value of 0 in the **NextEntryOffset** field. Typically, a named data stream supported by NTFS has a name such as *:Joes_Book:$DATA*, while an unnamed data stream will have a name such as *::$DATA*. If your FSD supports multiple byte streams, then you should also implement support for this query information call.

In addition to the information types previously described, a user may request **FileAccessInformation** (for information on the type of access to the file stream granted via the file object), **FileModeInformation** (information on whether the file object was opened with write-through specified, whether no intermediate buffering had been requested during the open, and so on), or **FileAlignmentInformation** (for the alignment mandated by the device object for the logical volume on which the file stream resided). This kind of requested information is considered FSD-independent by the I/O Manager, since it can be immediately obtained by the I/O Manager without having to invoke the FSD. Therefore, the NT I/O Manager fills in this information itself and returns control to the caller. In the case of **FileAllInformation**, the I/O Manager fills in the information contained in these FSD-independent categories and then forwards the request to the FSD.

When the FSD receives an IRP requesting information for the file stream, it performs the following simple logical steps to process the request:

- Obtain a pointer to the I/O-Manager-supplied system buffer

- Acquire the `MainResource` shared, to synchronize with any user requested changes

- Determine the type of information requested and copy it over into the supplied buffer

Note that the information requested is typically available immediately in memory from the file control block structure for the file stream. Most file system driver implementations update their FCB with the on-disk metadata associated with the file stream when it is first opened, and then subsequently keep the information updated in memory as long as the FCB is retained.

IRP_MJ_SET_INFORMATION

The following types of requests can be issued to modify file attributes:

FileBasicInformation (FILE_BASIC_INFORMATION)

This request type is used to modify file time and dates. Your FSD must determine whether to use caller-supplied values or values determined by your driver based upon any I/O performed by the caller.

FileDispositionInformation (FILE_DISPOSITION_INFORMATION)

```
typedef struct _FILE_DISPOSITION_INFORMATION {
    BOOLEAN DeleteFile;
} FILE_DISPOSITION_INFORMATION, *PFILE_DISPOSITION_INFORMATION;
```

This structure is used to mark a filename entry for deletion. Note that in the Windows NT I/O subsystem model, the caller must open a file stream using a link (name) associated with the file stream, mark the file name (link) for deletion using this set file information request, and then close the file handle. When the last `IRP_MJ_CLEANUP` request is received by the FSD (only after all user handles have been closed), the filename directory entry will actually be deleted. This means that any directory query operations issued in the interim will continue to see the filename entry.[*]

FilePositionInformation (FILE_POSITION_INFORMATION)

This request is issued to set the byte offset field in the file object structure. The byte offset is used by the FSD to determine the position to read/write for file objects that are opened for synchronous access. Note that the FSD must

---

[*] Readers who have a UNIX file system background, or even those who have used UNIX file systems, will recognize that this is different from the method used there. In UNIX file systems, the filename directory entry is immediately removed when an `unlink()` operation is performed on the directory entry.

check for and deny any requests to set the byte offset to a value that is not aligned appropriately for the physical device object on which the logical volume resides, if the file object was opened with no intermediate buffering specified.

FileAllocationInformation (FILE_ALLOCATION_INFORMATION)

```
typedef struct _FILE_ALLOCATION_INFORMATION {
    LARGE_INTEGER AllocationSize;
} FILE_ALLOCATION_INFORMATION, *PFILE_ALLOCATION_INFORMATION;
```

This request is used by the caller to increase or decrease the allocation size of a file stream. Note that this request does not affect the end-of-file position for the file stream. Increasing the allocation size does not pose any problems; your FSD can do whatever it needs in order to reserve additional on-disk space for the file stream.

Decreasing the file stream allocation size requires a little bit more effort on the part of the FSD. The NT VMM does not allow file size decreases if any process has mapped the file stream into its virtual address space; this, however, does not apply to the mapping performed by the NT Cache Manager. Therefore, before attempting to decrease the allocation size for a file stream, the FSD must first request permission to proceed from the VMM. If the VMM agrees, then the file size modification can proceed; otherwise, the FSD is required to fail the request.

Whenever the allocation size is changed, the FSD must be careful to immediately inform the NT Cache Manager of any such changes.

FileEndOfFileInformation (FILE_END_OF_FILE_INFORMATION)

```
typedef struct _FILE_END_OF_FILE_INFORMATION {
    LARGE_INTEGER EndOfFile;
} FILE_END_OF_FILE_INFORMATION, *PFILE_END_OF_FILE_INFORMATION;
```

A change in the end-of-file position implies that the allocation size for the file stream could also be changed. Specifically, if the new end-of-file has a value that is larger than the current allocation size for the file stream, most FSD implementations will change the allocation size as well and reserve additional on-disk space at this time. It is not mandated by the NT I/O Manager that you do this; however, it would be prudent to avoid a nasty situation where your FSD successfully extends the current end-of-file, does not prereserve new space corresponding to the extended file stream, and later gets and returns a disk out-of-space error when the user actually attempts to write to the file.*

---

* In general, it is wise to report error conditions to users when they expect errors and are able to respond to them sensibly. In the scenario described above, a user of the FSD can possibly try to workaround the error condition if you return an out-of-disk-space error when the caller attempts to extend the file size. Not doing so at this time, but failing a subsequent write request because the space is simply not available on disk will lead to a very confused caller (since the caller probably deduced from the success of the file extend operation that sufficient disk space should be available).

The FSD must follow the rule described earlier when truncating the file stream. The FSD must first request permission from the NT VMM before proceeding; if such permission is denied because another process has the file stream mapped in its virtual address space, the NT VMM will deny the request.

FileRenameInformation/FileLinkInformation
(FILE_RENAME_INFORMATION/FILE_LINK_INFORMATION)

```
typedef struct _FILE_LINK_INFORMATION {
    BOOLEAN         ReplaceIfExists;
    HANDLE          RootDirectory;
    ULONG           FileNameLength;
    WCHAR           FileName[1];
} FILE_LINK_INFORMATION, *PFILE_LINK_INFORMATION;

typedef struct _FILE_RENAME_INFORMATION {
    BOOLEAN         ReplaceIfExists;
    HANDLE          RootDirectory;
    ULONG           FileNameLength;
    WCHAR           FileName[1];
} FILE_RENAME_INFORMATION, *PFILE_RENAME_INFORMATION;
```

Both the rename and the link operations are fairly complex to implement. The following steps must be taken to successfully process a rename or a link request:*

a. First, the source directory must be opened.

b. The I/O Manager supplies the file object pointer representing the opened target directory. The FSD should once again check whether the target filename already exists, and reject the request if it does and if the caller did not request replacement of the target filename.

c. The source filename directory entry must be deleted in the case of a rename operation (this is not required for link operations).

d. The new filename entry must then be added.

When the FSD receives an IRP requesting modifications to the file metadata, it performs the following logical steps to process the request:

* Obtain a pointer to the I/O-Manager-supplied system buffer containing the parameters defining the request.

* If the FSD supports opportunistic locking (described in the next chapter), check whether the caller can be allowed to proceed based upon the state of the oplocks for the file stream.

---

* The FASTFAT implementation supplied with the Windows NT operating system does not support multiple links to a file stream. NTFS does, however. Whether you have to worry about link requests depends upon the capabilities provided by your file system.

- Acquire the `MainResource` for the FCB exclusively, to synchronize with other threads.

- Determine whether any other resources need to be acquired for operations such as rename/link on the file stream (typically, your FSD will acquire the VCB resource exclusively and the `PagingIoResource` for the FCB exclusively as well).

- Determine the nature of the request and invoke an appropriate routine to perform the requested functionality.

Code Fragment

```
NTSTATUS    SFsdCommonFileInfo(
PtrSFsdIrpContext            PtrIrpContext,
PIRP                        PtrIrp)
{
    // Declarations go here ...

    try {
        // First, get a pointer to the current I/O stack location.
        PtrIoStackLocation = IoGetCurrentIrpStackLocation(PtrIrp);
        ASSERT(PtrIoStackLocation);

        PtrFileObject = PtrIoStackLocation->FileObject;
        ASSERT(PtrFileObject);

        // Get the FCB and CCB pointers.
        PtrCCB = (PtrSFsdCCB)(PtrFileObject->FsContext2);
        ASSERT(PtrCCB);
        PtrFCB = PtrCCB->PtrFCB;
        ASSERT(PtrFCB);
        PtrReqdFCB = &(PtrFCB->NTRequiredFCB);

        CanWait = ((PtrIrpContext->IrpContextFlags
                    & SFSD_IRP_CONTEXT_CAN_BLOCK)
                ? TRUE : FALSE);

        // If the caller has opened a logical volume and is attempting to
        // query information for it as a file stream, return an error.
        if (PtrFCB->NodeIdentifier.NodeType == SFSD_NODE_TYPE_VCB) {
            // This is not allowed. Caller must use get/set volume
            // information instead.
            RC = STATUS_INVALID_PARAMETER;
            try_return(RC);
        }

        ASSERT(PtrFCB->NodeIdentifier.NodeType == SFSD_NODE_TYPE_FCB);

        // The NT I/O Manager always allocates and supplies a system
        // buffer for query and set file information calls.
        // Copying information to/from the user buffer and the system
```

```
                // buffer is performed by the I/O Manager and the FSD need not
                // worry about it.
                PtrSystemBuffer = PtrIrp->AssociatedIrp.SystemBuffer;

            if (PtrIoStackLocation->MajorFunction == IRP_MJ_QUERY_INFORMATION)
            {
                // Now, obtain some parameters.
                BufferLength = PtrIoStackLocation->Parameters.QueryFile.Length;
            FunctionalityRequested =
                PtrIoStackLocation->Parameters.QueryFile.FileInformationClass;

                // Acquire the MainResource shared (NOTE: for paging I/O on a
                // page file, we should avoid acquiring any resources and
                // simply trust the VMM to do the right thing, or else we
                // could possibly run into deadlocks).
                if (!(PtrFCB->FCBFlags & SFSD_FCB_PAGE_FILE)) {
                    // Acquire the MainResource shared.
                    if (!ExAcquireResourceSharedLite(&(PtrReqdFCB->
                                                        MainResource),
                                                        CanWait)) {

                        PostRequest = TRUE;
                        try_return(RC = STATUS_PENDING);
                    }
                    MainResourceAcquired = TRUE;
                }

                // Do whatever the caller asked us to do.
                switch (FunctionalityRequested) {
                case FileBasicInformation:
                    RC = SFsdGetBasicInformation(PtrFCB,
                                    (PFILE_BASIC_INFORMATION)PtrSystemBuffer,
                                    &BufferLength);
                    break;
                case FileStandardInformation:
                    // RC = SFsdGetStandardInformation(PtrFCB, PtrCCB, ...);
                    break;
                // Similarly, implement all of the other query information
                // routines that your FSD can support.
#ifdef   _NT_VER_40_PLUS_
                case FileNetworkOpenInformation:
                    // RC = SFsdGetNetworkOpenInformation(...);
                    break;
#endif   // _NT_VER_40_PLUS_
                case FileInternalInformation:
                    // RC = SFsdGetInternalInformation(...);
                    break;
                case FileEaInformation:
                    // RC = SFsdGetEaInformation(...);
                    break;
                case FileNameInformation:
                    // RC = SFsdGetFullNameInformation(...);
                    break;
                case FileAlternateNameInformation:
                    // RC = SFsdGetAltNameInformation(...);
```

```
           break;
    case FileCompressionInformation:
        // RC = SFsdGetCompressionInformation(...);
           break;
    case FilePositionInformation:
        // This is fairly simple. Copy over the information from
        // the file object.
        {
     PFILE_POSITION_INFORMATION          PtrFileInfoBuffer;

            PtrFileInfoBuffer =
                (PFILE_POSITION_INFORMATION)PtrSystemBuffer;

            ASSERT(BufferLength >=
                sizeof(FILE_POSITION_INFORMATION));
            PtrFileInfoBuffer->CurrentByteOffset =
                               PtrFileObject->CurrentByteOffset;
            // Modify the local variable for BufferLength
            // appropriately.
            BufferLength -= sizeof(FILE_POSITION_INFORMATION);
        }
           break;
    case FileStreamInformation:
        // RC = SFsdGetFileStreamInformation(...);
           break;
    case FileAllInformation:
        // The I/O Manager supplies the Mode, Access, and Alignment
        // information. The rest is up to us to provide.
        // Therefore, decrement the BufferLength appropriately
        // (assuming that the above 3 types of information are
        // already in the buffer)
        {
     PFILE_POSITION_INFORMATION          PtrFileInfoBuffer;
     PFILE_ALL_INFORMATION               PtrAllInfo =
                        (PFILE_ALL_INFORMATION)PtrSystemBuffer;

            BufferLength -= (sizeof(FILE_MODE_INFORMATION) +
                        sizeof(FILE_ACCESS_INFORMATION) +
                   sizeof(FILE_ALIGNMENT_INFORMATION));

            // Fill in the position information.

            PtrFileInfoBuffer = (PFILE_POSITION_INFORMATION)
                    &(PtrAllInfo->PositionInformation);

            PtrFileInfoBuffer->CurrentByteOffset =
                               PtrFileObject->CurrentByteOffset;

            // Modify the local variable for BufferLength
            // appropriately.
            ASSERT(BufferLength >=
                    sizeof(FILE_POSITION_INFORMATION));
            BufferLength -= sizeof(FILE_POSITION_INFORMATION);
```

```
                // Get the remaining stuff.
                if (!NT_SUCCESS(RC =
                        SFsdGetBasicInformation(PtrFCB,
                            (PFILE_BASIC_INFORMATION)
                                &(PtrAllInfo->BasicInformation),
                            &BufferLength))) {
                    // Another method you may wish to use to avoid the
                    // multiple checks for success/failure is to have
                    // the called routine simply raise an exception
                    // instead.
                    try_return(RC);
                }
                // Similarly, get all of the others ...
            }
            break;
        default:
            RC = STATUS_INVALID_PARAMETER;
            try_return(RC);
        }

        // If we completed successfully, return the amount of
        // information transferred.
        if (NT_SUCCESS(RC)) {
            PtrIrp->IoStatus.Information =
                PtrIoStackLocation->Parameters.QueryFile.Length
                                                - BufferLength;
        } else {
            PtrIrp->IoStatus.Information = 0;
        }

    } else {
        ASSERT(PtrIoStackLocation->MajorFunction ==
                                    IRP_MJ_SET_INFORMATION);

        // Now, obtain some parameters.
        FunctionalityRequested =
            PtrIoStackLocation->Parameters.SetFile.FileInformationClass;

        // If your FSD supports opportunistic locking (described in
        // Chapter 11), then you should check whether the oplock state
        // allows the caller to proceed.

        // Rename and link operations require creation of a directory
        // entry and possibly deletion of another directory entry.
        // Since, we acquire the VCB resource exclusively during
        // create operations, we should acquire it exclusively for
        // link and/or rename operations as well.
        // Similarly, marking a directory entry for deletion should
        // cause us to acquire the VCB exclusively as well.
        if ((FunctionalityRequested == FileDispositionInformation) ||
            (FunctionalityRequested == FileRenameInformation) ||
            (FunctionalityRequested == FileLinkInformation)) {
            if (!ExAcquireResourceExclusiveLite(&(PtrVCB->
                                            VCBResource),
```

```
                                                         CanWait)) {
            PostRequest = TRUE;
            try_return(RC = STATUS_PENDING);
        }
        // We have the VCB acquired exclusively.
        VCBResourceAcquired = TRUE;
    }

    // Unless this is an operation on a page file, we should
    // acquire the FCB exclusively at this time. Note that we will
    // pretty much block out anything being done to the FCB from
    // this point on.
    if (!(PtrFCB->FCBFlags & SFSD_FCB_PAGE_FILE)) {
        // Acquire the MainResource exclusively.
        if (!ExAcquireResourceExclusiveLite(&(PtrReqdFCB->
                                        MainResource),
                                        CanWait)) {

            PostRequest = TRUE;
            try_return(RC = STATUS_PENDING);
        }
        MainResourceAcquired = TRUE;
    }

    // The only operations that could conceivably proceed from
    // this point on are paging I/O read/write operations. For
    // delete link (rename), set allocation size, and set EOF,
    // should also acquire the paging I/O resource, thereby
    // synchronizing with paging I/O requests. In your FSD, you
    // should ideally acquire the resource only when processing
    // such requests; here, however, I will block out all paging I/
    // O operations at this time (for convenience). However, be
    // careful when doing this, since if your callback for
    // NtCreateSection() (described in the next chapter), does not
    // also acquire the paging I/O resource appropriately, you
    // could cause a deadlock situation.*
    if (!ExAcquireResourceExclusiveLite(&(PtrReqdFCB->
                                    PagingIoResource),
                                    CanWait)) {

        PostRequest = TRUE;
        try_return(RC = STATUS_PENDING);
    }

    // Do whatever the caller asked us to do
    switch (FunctionalityRequested) {
    case FileBasicInformation:
        RC = SFsdSetBasicInformation(PtrFCB, PtrCCB, PtrFileObject,
                        (PFILE_BASIC_INFORMATION)PtrSystemBuffer);
        break;
```

---

* It is unlikely that a deadlock would occur even in such a situation because the paging I/O resource is typically designated as an end-resource (by definition, your driver must not attempt to acquire any other resource object once an *end-resource* has been acquired) and should ideally not be held by any thread for a long period of time. However, it might be better to be prudent and understand the ramifications of this particular resource acquisition method shown in the code sample.

```
    case FilePositionInformation:
        // Check    if no intermediate buffering has been
        // specified. If it was specified, do not allow nonaligned
        // set file position requests to succeed.
        {
    PFILE_POSITION_INFORMATION            PtrFileInfoBuffer;

            PtrFileInfoBuffer =
                      (PFILE_POSITION_INFORMATION)PtrSystemBuffer;

            if (PtrFileObject->Flags &
                  FO_NO_INTERMEDIATE_BUFFERING) {
                if (PtrFileInfoBuffer->CurrentByteOffset.LowPart &
                    PtrIoStackLocation->DeviceObject->
                                        AlignmentRequirement) {
                    // Invalid alignment.
                    try_return(RC = STATUS_INVALID_PARAMETER);
                }
            }

            PtrFileObject->CurrentByteOffset =
                PtrFileInfoBuffer->CurrentByteOffset;
        }
        break;
    case FileDispositionInformation:
        RC = SFsdSetDispositionInformation(PtrFCB, PtrCCB, PtrVCB,
                    PtrFileObject, PtrIrpContext, PtrIrp,
                    (PFILE_DISPOSITION_INFORMATION)PtrSystemBuffer);
        break;
    case FileRenameInformation:
    case FileLinkInformation:
        // When you implement your rename/link routine, be careful
        // to check the following two arguments:
        // TargetFileObject =
        //   PtrIoStackLocation->Parameters.SetFile.FileObject;
        // ReplaceExistingFile =
        //   PtrIoStackLocation->Parameters.SetFile.ReplaceIfExists;

        // The TargetFileObject argument is a pointer to the
        // "target directory" file object obtained during the
        // "create" routine invoked by the NT I/O Manager with the
        // SL_OPEN_TARGET_DIRECTORY flag specified. Remember that
        // it is quite possible that if the rename/link is
        // contained within a single directory, the target and
        // source directories will be the same. The
        // ReplaceExistingFile argument should be used by you to
        // determine if the caller wishes to replace the target
        // (if it currently exists) with the new link/renamed
        // file. If this value is FALSE, and if the target
        // directory entry (being renamed-to, or the target of the
        // link) exists, you shouldreturn a STATUS_OBJECT_NAME_
        // COLLISION error to the caller.

        // RC = SFsdRenameOrLinkFile(PtrFCB, PtrCCB, PtrFileObject,
```

```
        //      PtrIrpContext,
        //      PtrIrp, (PFILE_RENAME_INFORMATION)PtrSystemBuffer);

        // Once you have completed the rename/link operation, do
        // not forget to notify any "notify IRPs" about the
        // actions you have performed.
        // An example is if you renamed across directories, you
        // should report that a new entry was added with the
        // FILE_ACTION_ADDED action type. The actual modification
        // would then be reported as either
        // FILE_NOTIFY_CHANGE_FILE_NAME (if a file was renamed) or
        // FILE_NOTIFY_CHANGE_DIR_NAME (if a directory was
        // renamed).
        break;
    case FileAllocationInformation:
        RC = SFsdSetAllocationInformation(PtrFCB, PtrCCB, PtrVCB,
                    PtrFileObject,
                    PtrIrpContext, PtrIrp, PtrSystemBuffer);
        break;
    case FileEndOfFileInformation:
        // RC = SFsdSetEOF(...);
        break;
    default:
        RC = STATUS_INVALID_PARAMETER;
        try_return(RC);
    }
}

try_exit:   NOTHING;

} finally {

    if (PagingIoResourceAcquired) {
        SFsdReleaseResource(&(PtrReqdFCB->PagingIoResource));
        PagingIoResourceAcquired = FALSE;
    }

    if (MainResourceAcquired) {
        SFsdReleaseResource(&(PtrReqdFCB->MainResource));
        MainResourceAcquired = FALSE;
    }

    if (VCBResourceAcquired) {
        SFsdReleaseResource(&(PtrVCB->VCBResource));
        VCBResourceAcquired = FALSE;
    }

    // Post IRP if required
    if (PostRequest) {

        // Since, the I/O Manager gave us a system buffer, we do not
        // need to "lock" anything.

        // Perform the post operation which will mark the IRP pending
```

```
                // and will return STATUS_PENDING back to us
                RC = SFsdPostRequest(PtrIrpContext, PtrIrp);

        } else {

                // Can complete the IRP here if no exception was encountered
                if (!(PtrIrpContext->IrpContextFlags
                        & SFSD_IRP_CONTEXT_EXCEPTION)) {
                    PtrIrp->IoStatus.Status = RC;

                    // Free up the Irp Context
                    SFsdReleaseIrpContext(PtrIrpContext);

                    // complete the IRP
                    IoCompleteRequest(PtrIrp, IO_DISK_INCREMENT);
                }
        } // can we complete the IRP ?
    } // end of "finally" processing

    return(RC);
}


NTSTATUS     SFsdGetBasicInformation(
PtrSFsdFCB                    PtrFCB,
PFILE_BASIC_INFORMATION       PtrBuffer,
long                          *PtrReturnedLength)
{
    NTSTATUS            RC = STATUS_SUCCESS;

    try {
        if (*PtrReturnedLength < sizeof(FILE_BASIC_INFORMATION)) {
            try_return(RC = STATUS_BUFFER_OVERFLOW);
        }

        // Zero-out the supplied buffer.
        RtlZeroMemory(PtrBuffer, sizeof(FILE_BASIC_INFORMATION));

        // Note: If your FSD needs to be even more precise about time
        // stamps, you may wish to consider the effects of fast I/O on the
        // file stream. Typically, the FSD/FSRTL package simply sets a flag
        // indicating that fast I/O read/write has occurred. Time stamps
        // are then updated when a cleanup is received for the file
        // stream. However, if the user performs fast I/O and subsequently
        // issues a request to query basic information, your FSD could
        // query the current system time using KeQuerySystemTime(), and
        // update the FCB time stamps before returning the values to the
        // caller. This gives the caller a slightly more accurate value.

        // Get information from the FCB.
        PtrBuffer->CreationTime = PtrFCB->CreationTime;
        PtrBuffer->LastAccessTime = PtrFCB->LastAccessTime;
        PtrBuffer->LastWriteTime = PtrFCB->LastWriteTime;
        // Assume that the sample FSD does not support a "change time."
```

```
        // Now fill in the attributes.
     PtrBuffer->FileAttributes = FILE_ATTRIBUTE_NORMAL;

        if (PtrFCB->FCBFlags & SFSD_FCB_DIRECTORY) {
            PtrBuffer->FileAttributes |= FILE_ATTRIBUTE_DIRECTORY;
        }

        // Similarly, fill in attributes indicating a hidden file, system
        // file, compressed file, temporary file, etc. if your FSD supports
        // such file attribute values.

        try_exit: NOTHING;
    } finally {
        if (NT_SUCCESS(RC)) {
            // Return the amount of information filled in.
            *PtrReturnedLength -= sizeof(FILE_BASIC_INFORMATION);
        }
    }
    return(RC);
}

NTSTATUS     SFsdSetBasicInformation(
PtrSFsdFCB                  PtrFCB,
PtrSFsdCCB                  PtrCCB,
PFILE_OBJECT                PtrFileObject,
PFILE_BASIC_INFORMATION     PtrBuffer)
{
    NTSTATUS            RC = STATUS_SUCCESS;
    BOOLEAN            CreationTimeChanged = FALSE;
    BOOLEAN            AttributesChanged = FALSE;

    try {

        // Obtain a pointer to the directory entry associated with
        // the FCB being modified. The directory entry is
        // part of the data associated with the parent directory that
        // contains this particular file stream.
        // Note that no other modifications
        // are currently allowed to the directory entry, because we have
        // the VCB resource exclusively acquired (as a matter of fact,
        // NO directory on the logical volume can be currently modified).
        // PtrDirectoryEntry = SFsdGetDirectoryEntryPtr(...);

        if (RtlLargeIntegerNotEqualToZero(PtrBuffer->CreationTime)) {
            // Modify the directory entry time stamp.
            // ...

            // Also note that fact that the time stamp has changed
            // so that any directory notifications can be performed.
            CreationTimeChanged = TRUE;

            // The interesting thing here is that the user has set certain
            // time fields. However, before doing this, the user may have
            // performed I/O, which in turn could have caused your FSD to
```

```
                  // mark the fact that write/access time should be modified at
                  // cleanup (this is especially true for fast I/O read/write
                  // operations). You might wish to mark the fact that such
                  // updates are no longer required since the user has
                  // explicitly specified the values to be associated with the
                  // file stream.
                  SFsdSetFlag(PtrCCB->CCBFlags, SFSD_CCB_CREATE_TIME_SET);
              }

              // Similarly, check for all the time stamp values that your
              // FSD cares about. Ignore the ones that you do not support.
              // ...


              // Now come the attributes.
              if (PtrBuffer->FileAttributes) {
                  // We have a nonzero attribute value.
                  // The presence of a particular attribute indicates that the
                  // user wishes to set the attribute value. The absence
                  // indicates the user wishes to clear the particular attribute.

                  // Before we start examining attribute values, you may wish
                  // to clear any unsupported attribute flags to reduce
                  // confusion.

                  SFsdClearFlag(PtrBuffer->FileAttributes,
                                        ~FILE_ATTRIBUTE_VALID_SET_FLAGS);
                  SFsdClearFlag(PtrBuffer->FileAttributes,
                                        FILE_ATTRIBUTE_NORMAL);

                  // Similarly, you should pick out other invalid flag values.
                  // SFsdClearFlag(PtrBuffer->FileAttributes,
                  //     FILE_ATTRIBUTE_DIRECTORY|FILE_ATTRIBUTE_ATOMIC_WRITE...);


                  if (PtrBuffer->FileAttributes & FILE_ATTRIBUTE_TEMPORARY) {
                      SFsdSetFlag(PtrFileObject->Flags, FO_TEMPORARY_FILE);
                  } else {
                      SFsdClearFlag(PtrFileObject->Flags, FO_TEMPORARY_FILE);
                  }

                  // If your FSD supports file compression, you may wish to
                  // note the user's preferences for compressing/not compressing
                  // the file at this time. If the user requests that the file
                  // be compressed and the file is currently not compressed,
                  // your FSD will probably have to initiate a fairly complex
                  // execution sequence at this time.
              }

          try_exit: NOTHING;
      } finally {
          ;
      }
      return(RC);
}
```

```
NTSTATUS       SFsdSetDispositionInformation(
PtrSFsdFCB                      PtrFCB,
PtrSFsdCCB                      PtrCCB,
PtrSFsdVCB                      PtrVCB,
PFILE_OBJECT                    PtrFileObject,
PtrSFsdIrpContext               PtrIrpContext,
PIRP                            PtrIrp,
PFILE_DISPOSITION_INFORMATION   PtrBuffer)
{
    NTSTATUS            RC = STATUS_SUCCESS;

    try {
        if (!PtrBuffer->DeleteFile) {
            // "un-delete" the file.
            SFsdClearFlag(PtrFCB->FCBFlags, SFSD_FCB_DELETE_ON_CLOSE);
            PtrFileObject->DeletePending = FALSE;
            try_return(RC);
        }

        // The easy part is over. Now, we know that the user wishes to
        // delete the corresponding directory entry (if this
        // is the only link to the file stream, any on-disk storage space
        // associated with the file stream will also be released when the
        // only link is deleted.)

        // Do some checking to see if the file can even be deleted.

        if (PtrFCB->FCBFlags & SFSD_FCB_DELETE_ON_CLOSE) {
            // All done.
            try_return(RC);
        }

        if (PtrFCB->FCBFlags & SFSD_FCB_READ_ONLY) {
            try_return(RC = STATUS_CANNOT_DELETE);
        }

        if (PtrVCB->VCBFlags & SFSD_VCB_FLAGS_VOLUME_READ_ONLY) {
            try_return(RC = STATUS_CANNOT_DELETE);
        }

        // An important step is to check if the file stream has been
        // mapped by any process. The delete cannot be allowed to proceed
        // in this case.
        if (!MmFlushImageSection(&(PtrFCB->NTRequiredFCB.SectionObject),
                        MmFlushForDelete)) {
            try_return(RC = STATUS_CANNOT_DELETE);
        }

        // It would not be prudent to allow deletion of either a root
        // directory or a directory that is not empty.
        if (PtrFCB->FCBFlags & SFSD_FCB_ROOT_DIRECTORY) {
            try_return(RC = STATUS_CANNOT_DELETE);
        }
```

```
        if (PtrFCB->FCBFlags & SFSD_FCB_DIRECTORY) {
            // Perform your check to determine whether the directory
            // is empty or not.
            // if (!SFsdIsDirectoryEmpty(PtrFCB, PtrCCB, PtrIrpContext)) {
            //         try_return(RC = STATUS_DIRECTORY_NOT_EMPTY);
            // }
        }

        // Set a flag to indicate that this directory entry will become
        // history at cleanup.
        SFsdSetFlag(PtrFCB->FCBFlags, SFSD_FCB_DELETE_ON_CLOSE);
        PtrFileObject->DeletePending = TRUE;

        try_exit: NOTHING;
    } finally {
        ;
    }
    return(RC);
}

NTSTATUS     SFsdSetAllocationInformation(
PtrSFsdFCB                    PtrFCB,
PtrSFsdCCB                    PtrCCB,
PtrSFsdVCB                    PtrVCB,
PFILE_OBJECT                  PtrFileObject,
PtrSFsdIrpContext             PtrIrpContext,
PIRP                         PtrIrp,
PFILE_ALLOCATION_INFORMATION  PtrBuffer)
{
    NTSTATUS          RC = STATUS_SUCCESS;
    BOOLEAN           TruncatedFile = FALSE;
    BOOLEAN           ModifiedAllocSize = FALSE;

    try {
        // Increasing the allocation size associated with a file stream
        // is relatively easy. All you have to do is execute some FSD-
        // specific code to check whether you have enough space available
        // (and if your FSD supports user/volume quotas, whether the user
        // is not exceeding quota), and then increase the file size in the
        // corresponding on-disk and in-memory structures.
        // Then, all you should do is inform the Cache Manager about the
        // increased allocation size.

        // First, do whatever error checking is appropriate here (e.g.,
        // whether the caller is trying the change size for a directory,
        // etc.).

        // Are we increasing the allocation size?
        if (RtlLargeIntegerLessThan(
                PtrFCB->NTRequiredFCB.CommonFCBHeader.AllocationSize,
                PtrBuffer->AllocationSize)) {

            // Yes. Do the FSD-specific stuff; i.e., increase reserved
            // space on disk.
```

```
            // RC = SFsdTruncateFileAllocationSize(...)

        ModifiedAllocSize = TRUE;

    } else if (RtlLargeIntegerGreaterThan(
                    PtrFCB->NTRequiredFCB.CommonFCBHeader.AllocationSize,
                        PtrBuffer->AllocationSize)) {
        // This is the painful part. See if the VMM will allow us to
        // proceed. The VMM will deny the request if:
        // (a) any image section exists OR
        // (b) a data section exists and the size of the user mapped
        //     view is greater than the new size
        // Otherwise, the VMM should allow the request to proceed.
        if (!MmCanFileBeTruncated(&(PtrFCB->
                                    NTRequiredFCB.SectionObject),
                &(PtrBuffer->AllocationSize))) {
            // VMM said no way!
            try_return(RC = STATUS_USER_MAPPED_FILE);
        }

        // Perform your directory entry modifications. Release any on-
        // disk space you may need to in the process.
        // RC = SFsdTruncateFileAllocationSize(...);

        ModifiedAllocSize = TRUE;
        TruncatedFile = TRUE;
    }

try_exit:

    // This is a good place to check if we have performed a
    // truncate operation. If we have performed a truncate
    // (whether we extended or reduced file size), you should
    // update file time stamps.

    // Last, but not the least, you must inform the Cache Manager
    // of file size changes.
    if (ModifiedAllocSize && NT_SUCCESS(RC)) {
        // Update the FCB Header with the new allocation size.
        PtrFCB->NTRequiredFCB.CommonFCBHeader.AllocationSize =
            PtrBuffer->AllocationSize;

        // If we decreased the allocation size to less than the
        // current file size, modify the file size value.
        // Similarly, if we decreased the value to less than the
        // current valid data length, modify that value as well.
        if (TruncatedFile) {
            if (RtlLargeIntegerLessThan(
                    PtrFCB->NTRequiredFCB.CommonFCBHeader.FileSize,
                    PtrBuffer->AllocationSize)) {
                // Decrease the file size value.
                PtrFCB->NTRequiredFCB.CommonFCBHeader.FileSize =
                    PtrBuffer->AllocationSize;
            }
```

```
                    if (RtlLargeIntegerLessThan(
                        PtrFCB->
                            NTRequiredFCB.CommonFCBHeader.ValidDataLength,
                            PtrBuffer->AllocationSize)) {
                    // Decrease the valid data length value.
                    PtrFCB->
                        NTRequiredFCB.CommonFCBHeader.ValidDataLength =
                                    PtrBuffer->AllocationSize;
                    }
                }


                // If the FCB has not had caching initiated, it is still
                // valid for you to invoke the NT Cache Manager. It is
                // possible in such situations for the call to be no-op'ed
                // (unless some user has mapped in the file).

                // NOTE: The invocation to CcSetFileSizes() will quite
                // possibly result in a recursive call back into the file
                // system. This is because the NT Cache Manager will
                // typically perform a flush before telling the VMM to
                // purge pages, especially when caching has not been
                // initiated on the file stream, but the user has mapped
                // the file into the process's virtual address space.
                CcSetFileSizes(PtrFileObject,
                    (PCC_FILE_SIZES)
                        &(PtrFCB->
                            NTRequiredFCB.CommonFCBHeader.AllocationSize));

                // Inform any pending IRPs (notify change directory).
            }

    } finally {
        ;
    }
    return(RC);
}
```

Notes

Read the comments provided above for information on the approach taken to implement some of the set/query file information routines.

An interesting point, not illustrated in the code example, pertains to the **File-EndOfFileInformation** request. In earlier chapters, we saw that the NT Cache Manager issues this call if the **ValidDataLength** for the file stream has been extended (due to a user writing beyond the current valid data length). This call can be distinguished by the fact that the **AdvanceOnly** field will be set to TRUE. When your FSD receives this special set end-of-file file information call, it should change the directory entry (on-disk) valid data length for the file stream

only if the new valid data length value is greater than the current value. This type
of request is only utilized by the NT Cache Manager.

You should also be aware that both the query and the set file information calls
can and do originate in the NT VMM when a process tries to create a section
object for a file stream to prepare to map-in views for the file. Before issuing
these calls, though, the NT VMM will invoke the FSD callback routine to acquire
FSD resources for the FCB. An example of providing support for such a callback
routine is given later in the next chapter.

Dispatch Routine: Directory Control

There are two kinds of directory control requests that are issued to a file system
driver:

- Requests to obtain the contents of a directory
- Requests to inform the caller when specified changes occur to the files/directories contained within a directory (and in all directories recursively below the target directory)

The first type of request is by far the most common operation for which an FSD
provides support. Users of file system routinely ask for a listing of the contents of
a target directory. The type of information that a caller might be interested in is
quite varied though; some callers may wish to find out all metadata information
for all of the files and directories contained in the target directory, while other
callers may be looking for a specific directory entry, and /or may wish to get
some specific information only for objects that they search for in a directory.

The other type of directory control operation is the *notify change directory*
request. This request is relatively uncommon and provides a transparent method
for callers (both in kernel and user mode) to monitor a directory tree for specific
actions that they might be interested in. As an example, consider the Windows
Explorer utility provided with Windows NT. This application attempts to always
list the most updated contents of a particular directory that might be actively
accessed. If any changes occur (e.g., file additions, deletions, rename operations,
and so on) while a user is browsing the contents of a directory, the application
automatically updates the information presented to the user. In order to avoid
having to constantly poll the file system to determine whether a directory tree has
been modified, the Windows NT operating system instead provides the notification method where the caller can simply request that a specific callback be issued
when the interesting changes occur.

Providing support for the notify change directory control request is not mandatory
for a file system; and it is quite possible for a file system to return a **STATUS_**

NOT_IMPLEMENTED error upon receiving the notify change directory control request; however, it is a rather nice feature to support from the user's perspective.

Both the query directory contents and the notify change directory control requests are issued to the same dispatch routine servicing the IRP_MJ_DIRECTORY_CONTROL I/O request packet. However, the specific functionality requested can be determined by the minor function code that is supplied in the IRP. The IRP_MN_QUERY_DIRECTORY minor function value clearly indicates that the caller wishes to obtain some information on entries contained within the target directory, whereas the IRP_MN_NOTIFY_CHANGE_DIRECTORY minor function indicates that the caller is interested in monitoring events that affect the contents of the directory.

Logical Steps Involved

The I/O stack location contains the following structures relevant to processing the directory control request issued to an FSD:

```
typedef struct _IO_STACK_LOCATION {

    // ...

    union {

        //...

        // System service parameters for: NtQueryDirectoryFile
        struct {
            ULONG Length;
            PSTRING FileName;
            FILE_INFORMATION_CLASS FileInformationClass;
            ULONG FileIndex;
        } QueryDirectory;

        // System service parameters for:  NtNotifyChangeDirectoryFile
        struct {
            ULONG Length;
            ULONG CompletionFilter;
        } NotifyDirectory;

        // ...
    } Parameters;

    // ...

} IO_STACK_LOCATION, *PIO_STACK_LOCATION;
```

The following logical steps are executed by the FSD upon receiving a directory control IRP. The caller must supply a valid file object pointer to a directory that was previously opened.

IRP_MN_QUERY_DIRECTORY

Conceptually, this routine is extremely simple to understand. The caller supplies a pointer to a file object for an open target directory, a search pattern that could be used when listing the contents of a target directory, and a specification on the type of information requested. The FSD is expected to simply perform a search of the directory for all entries that match the caller-supplied search pattern, and return information on one or more matching entries in the caller's buffer.

The following types of information can be requested by the caller:[*]

`FileDirectoryInformation (FILE_DIRECTORY_INFORMATION)` [†]

```
typedef struct _FILE_DIRECTORY_INFORMATION {
    ULONG                   NextEntryOffset;
    ULONG                   FileIndex;
    LARGE_INTEGER           CreationTime;
    LARGE_INTEGER           LastAccessTime;
    LARGE_INTEGER           LastWriteTime;
    LARGE_INTEGER           ChangeTime;
    LARGE_INTEGER           EndOfFile;
    LARGE_INTEGER           AllocationSize;
    ULONG                   FileAttributes;
    ULONG                   FileNameLength;
    WCHAR                   FileName[1];
} FILE_DIRECTORY_INFORMATION, *PFILE_DIRECTORY_INFORMATION;
```

For each of the directory entries that match the user-supplied search pattern, the FSD is expected to return all of the information defined by the `FILE_DIRECTORY_INFORMATION` structure. You may notice that the information requested is a combination of the `FILE_BASIC_INFORMATION` and the `FILE_STANDARD_INFORMATION` query file information structures. The `FileName` field should contain the name of the entry contained in the target directory.

When information on multiple directory entries is returned by the FSD in the caller-supplied buffer, the FSD is expected to align each returned entry on a 8-byte (quadword-aligned) boundary. The `NextEntryOffset` field should contain either 0, indicating that there are no more entries in the buffer, or the byte offset to the next `FILE_DIRECTORY_INFORMATION` entry in the caller-supplied buffer.

---

[*] For each type of information requested, the caller may request information on a single entry in the directory (that matches the optional search pattern supplied) or on multiple entries, limited by the size of the buffer supplied and the size of the directory itself.

[†] If you develop a distributed/networked file system, it would be advisable if your distributed protocol supported bulk *stat* features, for obtaining detailed information on multiple directory entries. The alternative of individually querying properties for each directory entry could become quite time consuming.

The `FileIndex` field should contain the index of the entry within the directory. Note that the `FileNameLength` field should contain the length of the filename in bytes; the `FileName` field expects a name in the UNICODE character set. The `FileName` should simply be appended to the end of the `FILE_DIRECTORY_INFORMATION` structure and the length of the filename appropriately filled in.

NOTE   The `FileIndex` is simply an FSD-specific value that your FSD can subsequently use (in the next request to get directory contents) to determine the offset from which to begin scanning the target directory. As an example, you could return the byte offset of the next entry in the directory and use this byte offset to begin searching the directory when the next *query directory* request is received.

FileFullDirectoryInformation (FILE_FULL_DIR_INFORMATION)

```
typedef struct _FILE_FULL_DIR_INFORMATION {
    ULONG               NextEntryOffset;
    ULONG               FileIndex;
    LARGE_INTEGER       CreationTime;
    LARGE_INTEGER       LastAccessTime;
    LARGE_INTEGER       LastWriteTime;
    LARGE_INTEGER       ChangeTime;
    LARGE_INTEGER       EndOfFile;
    LARGE_INTEGER       AllocationSize;
    ULONG               FileAttributes;
    ULONG               FileNameLength;
    ULONG               EaSize;
    WCHAR               FileName[1];
} FILE_FULL_DIR_INFORMATION, *PFILE_FULL_DIR_INFORMATION;
```

This request is similar to the `FILE_DIRECTORY_INFORMATION` request; the only additional information requested is the total length of the extended attributes associated with the file stream (if any). For most third-party file systems, this request will be returned with the `EaSize` field set to 0.

FileBothDirectoryInformation (FILE_BOTH_DIR_INFORMATION)

```
typedef struct _FILE_BOTH_DIR_INFORMATION {
    ULONG               NextEntryOffset;
    ULONG               FileIndex;
    LARGE_INTEGER       CreationTime;
    LARGE_INTEGER       LastAccessTime;
    LARGE_INTEGER       LastWriteTime;
    LARGE_INTEGER       ChangeTime;
    LARGE_INTEGER       EndOfFile;
    LARGE_INTEGER       AllocationSize;
    ULONG               FileAttributes;
    ULONG               FileNameLength;
    ULONG               EaSize;
    CCHAR               ShortNameLength;
```

```
        WCHAR                    ShortName[12];
        WCHAR                    FileName[1];
} FILE_BOTH_DIR_INFORMATION, *PFILE_BOTH_DIR_INFORMATION;
```

This request is a superset of the `FileFullDirectoryInformation` request. Note that although native Windows NT applications support long filenames (255 characters or less), the older DOS-based applications often have difficulty with filenames that do not fit into the 8.3 format* mandated by that operating environment. The Windows NT I/O Manager attempts to support such legacy applications by working in tandem with file systems sensitive to their needs, which are prepared to maintain an abbreviated, unique alternate name that fits into the 8.3 format and can therefore be used by the older applications. The native NT file system implementations do support these alternate names and will provide such an alternate name in the `FILE_BOTH_DIR_INFORMATION` structure, in the `ShortName` field.

Note that it is not required that a file system support alternate names for directory entries.

FileNamesInformation (FILE_NAMES_INFORMATION)

```
    typedef struct _FILE_NAMES_INFORMATION {
        ULONG                    NextEntryOffset;
        ULONG                    FileIndex;
        ULONG                    FileNameLength;
        WCHAR                    FileName[1];
} FILE_NAMES_INFORMATION, *PFILE_NAMES_INFORMATION;
```

This request type requires the least amount of information for each directory entry. The FSD simply has to supply the `FileIndex` for each entry in the directory, and the name for that entry. This is typically invoked in response to a DOS *dir /w* command.

All disk-based file systems, and for that matter, even networked file systems, have some internal representation of a directory entry structure (i.e., a structure that describes the on-disk or network-protocol-defined format representing a directory entry). When a directory control request is received by the FSD, your file system should obtain the contents of the directory, either by reading them from secondary storage, or by obtaining them from a server node across the network. Then it becomes a relatively simple matter of searching (typically sequentially) through all entries in the directory, looking for a match with the specified search pattern. Information on the matching entry can then be provided to the caller by

---

* For those readers that have somehow (luckily) managed to avoid using the DOS system, you may be amused to note that it could only support filenames that had a maximum name length of 8 characters, followed by an optional period, followed by an optional suffix that had a maximum length of 3 characters. This peculiar filename format has become well-known as the DOS 8.3 filename format.

converting the internal directory entry representation to one of the NT-defined structures described previously.*

NOTE   Many current Windows NT file system implementations use the NT Cache Manager to cache directory contents just as file data is normally cached. To achieve this, they use the `IoCreateStreamFileObject()` routine. This routine accepts two arguments (you need to supply just one of the two and the other can be NULL): a pointer to a file object structure and a pointer to a device object. Note that the pointer to the device object is ignored (and a device object pointer is obtained from the file object supplied) if a file object pointer is provided.

The implementation of the `IoCreateStreamFileObject()` routine is quite simple: it creates and initializes a new file object structure, just as would have been created had an open operation been performed on the directory. As a side effect, it increments the `ReferenceCount` in the VPB structure associated with the device object to ensure that the logical volume cannot be dismounted as long as the stream file object is kept open.

Once a stream file object has been created representing the directory, the native NT file systems initialize it with appropriate pointers to the CCB and FCB structures for the directory. Now, caching can be initiated on this file object; typically, this is done by specifying `PinAccess` set to TRUE. This allows the FSD to read the directory contents directly into the system cache and access them using a virtual address pointer and appropriate offsets into the byte stream based on the internal directory entry representation. Furthermore, since the data in pinned into the system cache, the FSD is guaranteed that the information will always be accessible and will not be discarded.

The stream file object can be closed by simply performing an `ObDereferenceObject()` operation on the file object structure. The FSD will receive a close request at this time on the file object that was dereferenced.

---

* There are some file systems that I have worked with, and that readers may be aware of, that do not store file attributes such as the file date and time stamps in the directory entry along with the file name. In these file system layouts, the FSD must obtain the address of the on-disk sector from the directory entry that contains it and read this information into memory to fill in the caller-supplied buffer. There is a large performance penalty due to the extra read operation for each directory entry for which information has to be returned. Such file systems cache a lot of information to avoid being discarded because of such poor on-disk file system layouts.

IRP_MN_NOTIFY_CHANGE_DIRECTORY

As described earlier, this functionality is not really mandated for an NT FSD. However, for users of the file system, this is a rather nice feature that file systems may be able to support.* This functionality allows file system users to specify that they be told when certain events occur to change the contents of a directory in some specified manner. For example, the caller may wish to be notified if file *foo* in directory *dir1* is deleted. Or, the user may wish to be notified if any file in directory *dir1* is deleted, or even if any file in the directory *dir1* or any directory under it is deleted or modified in some manner. Therefore, as you can see, this functionality can be a very powerful tool for file system clients who wish to monitor the file system.

Although it may seem a little difficult to implement, the Windows NT File System Runtime Library (FSRTL) does a rather nice job of providing supporting routines that your FSD can use.

WARNING   The FSRTL routines providing support for the directory change notify support have not been officially exported by Microsoft. The function prototypes described here can be changed by Microsoft at will. Therefore, you could decide to use the routines described below or you can examine the description of the routines listed below to determine how to develop your own supporting routines that provide similar functionality.

The native NT FSD implementations have the support of the FSRTL package, however, and utilize the routines described below.

Basically, your FSD is responsible for executing the following steps to support this feature:

- When your FSD receives such a request, and after it has validated the user's request, it must invoke the `FsRtlNotifyFullChangeDirectory()` function to queue the user request. The FSD should then return **STATUS_PENDING** to the caller, which indicates that the IRP has been queued and will be completed when the desired event occurs.

---

* For distributed or networked file systems, it becomes practically impossible to support this feature, unless the networked/distributed protocol supports something that can be adapted to provide such functionality. The reason is simple: users can make directory changes from any node in a distributed file system. If the clients and servers do not have some means of being notified when specific changes occur, redirectors on the Windows NT client systems cannot possibly accurately support the notify change directory functionality (without resorting to extremely inefficient polling methods).

The implication is that notify change directory IRPs are held by the FSD (or the FSRTL package) until an event occurs that causes the FSD to report a monitored change to the caller.

- When changes occur to any directory, the FSD should invoke the `FsRtlNo-tifyFullReportChange()` FSRTL support routine to inform the library about the changes. The library routine is then responsible for scanning through all the notify requests that have been queued up and performing appropriate processing for those waiting for the occurrence of the particular event.

- Whenever a cleanup is performed on a particular file object (indicating that all user handles corresponding to the file object have been closed), the FSD should notify the FSRTL using the `FsRtlNotifyCleanup()` routine. The library routine will then dequeue and complete any IRPs that were using the particular file object.

One of the peculiarities of the notify change directory request type is that it is a one-shot kind of request. Therefore, if an application wants to continuously monitor changes to a directory tree, it must keep reissuing the request whenever the request is satisfied because a watched-for modification occurs. However, it is possible for changes to occur to a directory in the period between the time when a notify change directory IRP is completed and the next notify change directory request arrives. In order not to lose information about such changes, the FSD (or the FSRTL package, if you use it) is responsible for keeping information about changes to the directory (or directory tree) during the period between completion of a notify change directory request and the arrival of the next such IRP.

To achieve this objective, either the FSD or the FSRTL package allocates an internal buffer and associates it with the file object structure (using appropriate internal structures) to keep information about any changes that may occur. This buffer is only released (and monitoring consequently terminated) after the cleanup operation is received for the file object, indicating that all user handles have been closed.

The run-time library needs a list anchor from which it can queue all of the pending IRPs. The expectation is that the FSD will use one such list head for each mounted logical volume on which notify change directory requests could be issued. Furthermore, for synchronization, the library requires that the FSD allocate and initialize one **MUTEX** structure associated with the list head on which the notify requests can be queued.

```
VOID
FsRtlNotifyFullChangeDirectory (
IN PNOTIFY_SYNC                    NotifySync,
```

```
IN PLIST_ENTRY                       NotifyList,
IN PVOID                             FsContext,
IN PSTRING                           FullDirectoryName,
IN BOOLEAN                           WatchTree,
IN BOOLEAN                           IgnoreBuffer,
IN ULONG                             CompletionFilter,
IN PIRP                              NotifyIrp,
IN PCHECK_FOR_TRAVERSE_ACCESS        TraverseCallback OPTIONAL,
IN PSECURITY_SUBJECT_CONTEXT         SubjectContext OPTIONAL
);

where

typedef PVOID PNOTIFY_SYNC;

typedef
BOOLEAN (*PCHECK_FOR_TRAVERSE_ACCESS) (
IN PVOID          NotifyContext,
IN PVOID          TargetContext,
IN PSECURITY_SUBJECT_CONTEXT     SubjectContext
);
```

Resource Acquisition Constraints:

None. Typically, though, you should acquire the FCB **MainResource** shared (at least) before invoking this routine.

Parameters:

NotifySync

> This should be a pointer to a FSD-allocated **KMUTEX** structure. The sample FSD volume control block (VCB) structure has a field called **NotifyIRP-Mutex** that is used for this purpose. This mutex should be used to protect the list of queued notify requests for the logical volume. Do not be misled into thinking that this can be any other synchronization object because of the definition of **PNOTIFY_SYNC**.

NotifyList

> This should be a pointer to the list head for queued notify IRP structures. The library expects that you maintain one such list for each mounted logical volume. The sample FSD uses the **NextNotifyIRP** field for this purpose.

FsContext

> This is determined by the FSD and is used to uniquely identify the notify structure. You should use the CCB pointer as the argument for this particular field. This becomes particularly useful when a cleanup is received on the file object, and the FSD can supply the CCB pointer to the run-time library to notify it to complete all pending requests for the file object.

FullDirectoryName

> Exactly as its name implies, this is a complete pathname for the directory the caller wishes to monitor. Do not deallocate the memory for this string until the pending request has been completed. The FSRTL routine accepts either a Unicode or ASCII name string.

WatchTree

> To monitor all directories that are children of the directory being monitored, set this variable to TRUE.

> The FSD can determine whether the caller wishes to monitor the directory tree by checking for the presence of the **SL_WATCH_TREE** flag in the IRP flags field.

IgnoreBuffer

> When a user asks to be notified of specific changes to the contents of a directory, the caller can also supply a buffer to contain the specific changes that occurred. (For example, the user process may be monitoring for any file entry that is deleted; when such a deletion occurs, it would like to know which directory entry was deleted.) The other option for the caller is simply to request to be notified whenever some change occurs, without requiring the FSD to list the specific changes that caused the notification. The caller will subsequently reenumerate the directory contents.

> Providing a list of changes is slower than simply telling the user to reenumerate the directory upon being notified. The FSRTL routine allows the FSD to decide whether it wishes to speed up operations by setting the **Ignore-Buffer** value to TRUE and forcing the user to reenumerate the directory.

CompletionFilter

> The **CompletionFilter** is provided by the caller issuing the notify change directory request and is invoked when the monitored event occurs.

TraverseCallback

> Remember that the caller has the option of specifying that all subdirectories within a directory also be monitored for changes. If your FSD is security conscious like NTFS, you would want to ensure that the caller has appropriate permissions to monitor changes in a specific subdirectory. Therefore, your FSD has the option of supplying a callback function that is invoked by the runtime library before notifying the caller. If your callback returns FALSE, the runtime library will not notify the user of the changes that have occurred.

SubjectContext

> If your FSD supplies a **TraverseCallback** function pointer, you need to know what the calling process is in order to check whether it has appropriate privileges. The **SubjectContext** is one of the arguments passed in to your

callback routine and you can obtain it (when queuing the notify request) by using the `SeCaptureSecurityContext()` function, which takes a pointer to an FSD-allocated `SECURITY_SUBJECT_CONTEXT` structure.[*]

Functionality Provided:

This routine will enqueue the IRP in the list of pending notify structures, if no such notify request already exists (remember that notify requests are uniquely identified by the `FsContext` field). Here is a logical list of steps that this function goes through:

- The `FsRtlNotifyFullChangeDirectory()` routine obtains the current stack location pointer from the IRP and also obtains a pointer to the file object structure used in the current request.

- It then waits to acquire the supplied `KMUTEX` object to ensure synchronization.

- If the file object has already undergone cleanup (while the runtime library was waiting), then it immediately completes the IRP with a `STATUS_NOTIFY_CLEANUP` return code. The runtime library checks for the presence of the `FO_CLEANUP_COMPLETE` flag in the file object structure to determine whether the file object has undergone cleanup.

- If there is a notify pending, then it completes the IRP.

    As mentioned earlier, once the first notify change directory request has been received for a specific file object, it becomes the responsibility of the FSD (or the FSRTL package in the case when the FSD uses it) to maintain information about changes to the directory being monitored, even if there is no current notify change directory request pending. This is because the FSD expects that the caller will soon reissue the notify request and therefore does not want to lose any intermediate changes between the time when the last request was completed and a new request is received. Therefore, the `FsRtlNotify-FullChangeDirectory()` maintains state about whether any changes had occurred and immediately completes the new notify change directory request if information about any intermediate changes is already present in its internal buffer.

- If the IRP has been canceled, then it completes the IRP.

- Otherwise, if no other notify structure exists in the queue, it queues up this request.

Note that the implication is that a thread can only have one pending notify IRP per file object.

---

[*] This structure is defined in the DDK.

The `FsRtlNotifyFullReportChange()` routine is defined as follows:

```
VOID
FsRtlNotifyFullReportChange (
IN PNOTIFY_SYNC          NotifySync,
IN PLIST_ENTRY           NotifyList,
IN PSTRING               FullTargetName,
IN USHORT                TargetNameOffset,
IN PSTRING               StreamName OPTIONAL,
IN PSTRING               NormalizedParentName OPTIONAL,
IN ULONG                 FilterMatch,
IN ULONG                 Action,
IN PVOID                 TargetContext
);
```

where `Action` is one of the following:

```
#define FILE_ACTION_ADDED               0x00000001
#define FILE_ACTION_REMOVED             0x00000002
#define FILE_ACTION_MODIFIED            0x00000003
#define FILE_ACTION_RENAMED_OLD_NAME    0x00000004
#define FILE_ACTION_RENAMED_NEW_NAME    0x00000005
#define FILE_ACTION_ADDED_STREAM        0x00000006
#define FILE_ACTION_REMOVED_STREAM      0x00000007
#define FILE_ACTION_MODIFIED_STREAM     0x00000008
```

and `FilterMatch` is one of the following:

```
#define FILE_NOTIFY_CHANGE_FILE_NAME     0x00000001
#define FILE_NOTIFY_CHANGE_DIR_NAME      0x00000002
#define FILE_NOTIFY_CHANGE_NAME          0x00000003
#define FILE_NOTIFY_CHANGE_ATTRIBUTES    0x00000004
#define FILE_NOTIFY_CHANGE_SIZE          0x00000008
#define FILE_NOTIFY_CHANGE_LAST_WRITE    0x00000010
#define FILE_NOTIFY_CHANGE_LAST_ACCESS   0x00000020
#define FILE_NOTIFY_CHANGE_CREATION      0x00000040
#define FILE_NOTIFY_CHANGE_EA            0x00000080
#define FILE_NOTIFY_CHANGE_SECURITY      0x00000100
#define FILE_NOTIFY_CHANGE_STREAM_NAME   0x00000200
#define FILE_NOTIFY_CHANGE_STREAM_SIZE   0x00000400
#define FILE_NOTIFY_CHANGE_STREAM_WRITE  0x00000800
#define FILE_NOTIFY_VALID_MASK           0x00000fff
```

Resource Acquisition Constraints:

None.

Parameters:

`NotifySync`

> This should be a pointer to the FSD-allocated KMUTEX structure used in the preceding `FsRtlNotifyFullChangeDirectory()` routine.

NotifyList

This is a pointer to the list head for all pending notify IRPs for the mounted logical volume.

FullTargetName

This is the name of the target file or directory that had its attributes modified.

TargetNameOffset

This is the byte offset of the last component in the name supplied in the **FullTargetName** field. The notify change directory call returns only the relative target name (relative to the directory on which the notify change directory IRP is pending).

StreamName

This optional argument can be used to supply a stream name in addition to the filename. This is used by FSDs that support multiple data streams for a named file object. If supplied, the FSRTL package appends the **StreamName** to the stored target name.

NormalizedParentName

This is the name of the parent directory for the target file or directory (optional argument).

FilterMatch

FilterMatch can have any one or more of the values listed above to indicate what directory actions have occurred. This field is compared with the **CompletionFilter** field in the pending notify IRP structures. If any of the bit positions match, then the caller for that pending IRP is notified.

Action

If a user buffer was supplied with the pending IRP, this **Action** value will be stored there along with the relative file/directory name for the object modified.

TargetContext

The second argument to be passed to the FSD in the traverse access check callback.

Functionality Provided:

This routine performs the following functionality. It walks through the list of pending notify IRP structures, searching for one that matches the **FilterMatch** argument supplied (i.e., one or more bit values are the same), and checking whether the found entry is an exact match or an ancestor of the target file/directory name.*

---

* Either the matching entry has a directory name that matches the parent directory name for the target file, or the matching entry has a directory name that is some ancestor of the target file.

The caller of a notify change directory request has two options:

- All pending notify IRP structures that match the above criteria are completed at this time.

- Supply a buffer in which the names of the modified objects and actions performed on them will be returned.

Not supply any buffer, in which case the notify change directory IRP will simply be completed with the `STATUS_NOTIFY_ENUM_DIR` status.*

The `FsRtlNotifyFullReportChange()` routine simply completes a matching, pending IRP with the `STATUS_NOTIFY_ENUM_DIR` status immediately if no buffer was provided by the caller.

NOTE   Note that since the FSD (or the FSRTL package) must maintain information about a directory, even if no pending IRPs exist (as long as one instance of a notify change directory request was received), the FSD/FSRTL package maintains state about whether the caller had supplied a buffer the first time the notify request is made for a file object. Even if subsequent requests do not supply a buffer, the FSD/FSRTL package will continue to maintain an internally allocated buffer with information on changes to objects in the directory tree being monitored.

If the caller has supplied a buffer, however, the caller expects to receive information about objects that have changed and the actual changes performed on the modified objects. Once again, though, if the changes are numerous and cannot fit into the buffer, the FSD/FSRTL package always has the option of returning `STATUS_NOTIFY_ENUM_DIR` to the caller.

If you do decide to develop your own notify change directory support routines, be extremely careful about handling user-supplied buffers correctly. you should have your FSD create a memory descriptor list to describe the user buffer and obtain a system address for the MDL before queuing the IRP and returning `STATUS_PENDING` to the caller. This will allow your FSD to copy information into the user's buffer in the context of any thread (typically the one performing the modifications leading to the completion of the pending notify change directory IRP).

The structure returned by the FSD to the caller of the notify change directory request is defined below:

---

* If you check the actual value of this symbolic name, you will see that the `NT_SUCCESS()` macro will treat this value equivalent to `STATUS_SUCCESS`.

```
typedef struct _FILE_NOTIFY_INFORMATION {
    ULONG       NextEntryOffset;
    ULONG       Action;
    ULONG       FileNameLength;
    WCHAR       FileName[1];
} FILE_NOTIFY_INFORMATION, *PFILE_NOTIFY_INFORMATION;
```

The fields in the **FILE_NOTIFY_INFORMATION** structure shown here are fairly self-explanatory. Note that there are no special alignment restrictions on the entries returned in the user buffer (i.e., none of the returned entries require any padding bytes).

Some explanation is probably in order for two of the notify actions listed, namely, **FILE_ACTION_RENAMED_OLD_NAME** and **FILE_ACTION_RENAMED_NEW_NAME**. These two notify actions are reported by the file system driver when processing a rename operation. The rules used in reporting these events are as follows:

- The FSD reports two notification events as part of processing the rename operation:

  — The first event is reported when the source directory entry is deleted for the object being renamed.

  — The second event is reported when the target directory entry is added, i.e., the rename has been completed.

- When the first notification event has to be reported, the FSD has a choice of reporting either the **FILE_ACTION_RENAMED_OLD_NAME** action type or simply **FILE_ACTION_REMOVED**.

  If the rename operation will be performed within the same directory and if the target of the rename operation does not exist, the FSD should report **FILE_ACTION_RENAMED_OLD_FILE**, else the FSD should report **FILE_ACTION_REMOVED**.*

- When the second notification event has to be reported, the FSD has a choice between **FILE_ACTION_RENAMED_NEW_NAME**, **FILE_ACTION_MODIFIED**, and **FILE_ACTION_ADDED**.

  If the target file name existed before the rename operation and was replaced as a result of the rename, the FSD should report **FILE_ACTION_MODIFIED** for the target of the rename operation. Otherwise, if the rename operation was performed across directories, the FSD should report **FILE_ACTION_**

---

* I did not make the rules here but am simply reporting them! The reason for giving you this information is to simply assist you in reporting events in a manner similar to that employed by the existing Windows NT FSD implementations.

ADDED. Finally, if neither of the above conditions holds TRUE, the FSD should report `FILE_ACTION_RENAMED_NEW_NAME`.

The `FsRtlNotifyCleanup()` routine is defined as follows:

```
VOID
FsRtlNotifyCleanup (
IN PNOTIFY_SYNC          NotifySync,
IN PLIST_ENTRY           NotifyList,
IN PVOID                 FsContext
);
```

Resource Acquisition Constraints:

None.

Parameters:

`NotifySync`

> This should be a pointer to the FSD allocated KMUTEX structure used in the `FsRtlNotifyFullChangeDirectory()` routine.

`NotifyList`

> This is a pointer to the list head for all pending notify IRPs for the mounted logical volume.

`FsContext`

> This is the unique identifier used to locate all pending notify IRP structures. Typically, this is a pointer to the CCB structure.

Functionality Provided:

This routine simply walks the list of pending notify IRP structures, finds those that match the supplied `FsContext` value, and processes these IRPs. The processing consists of removing any cancel routine that the FSRTL package may have set, and completing the IRP with a status of `STATUS_NOTIFY_CLEANUP`.

Code sample

Here is a code fragment from the sample FSD that illustrates how an FSD processes a directory control request (notify change directory requests, illustrated later, use the routines exported by the FSRTL package):

```
NTSTATUS    SFsdCommonDirControl(
PtrSFsdIrpContext             PtrIrpContext,
PIRP                         PtrIrp)
{
    // Declarations go here ...

    // First, get a pointer to the current I/O stack location
    PtrIoStackLocation = IoGetCurrentIrpStackLocation(PtrIrp);
    ASSERT(PtrIoStackLocation);
```

```
    PtrFileObject = PtrIoStackLocation->FileObject;
    ASSERT(PtrFileObject);

    // Get the FCB and CCB pointers
    PtrCCB = (PtrSFsdCCB)(PtrFileObject->FsContext2);
    ASSERT(PtrCCB);
    PtrFCB = PtrCCB->PtrFCB;
    ASSERT(PtrFCB);

    // Get some of the parameters supplied to us
    switch (PtrIoStackLocation->MinorFunction) {
    case IRP_MN_QUERY_DIRECTORY:
        RC = SFsdQueryDirectory(PtrIrpContext, PtrIrp,
                    PtrIoStackLocation,
                       PtrFileObject, PtrFCB, PtrCCB);
        break;
    case IRP_MN_NOTIFY_CHANGE_DIRECTORY:
        RC = SFsdNotifyChangeDirectory(PtrIrpContext, PtrIrp,
                    PtrIoStackLocation,
                       PtrFileObject, PtrFCB, PtrCCB);
        break;
    default:
        // This should not happen.
        RC = STATUS_INVALID_DEVICE_REQUEST;
        PtrIrp->IoStatus.Status = RC;
        PtrIrp->IoStatus.Information = 0;

        // Free up the Irp Context
        SFsdReleaseIrpContext(PtrIrpContext);

        // complete the IRP
        IoCompleteRequest(PtrIrp, IO_NO_INCREMENT);
        break;
    }

    return(RC);
}


NTSTATUS     SFsdQueryDirectory(
PtrSFsdIrpContext           PtrIrpContext,
PIRP                        PtrIrp,
PIO_STACK_LOCATION          PtrIoStackLocation,
PFILE_OBJECT                PtrFileObject,
PtrSFsdFCB                  PtrFCB,
PtrSFsdCCB                  PtrCCB)
{
    // Declarations go here ...

    try {

        // Validate the sent-in FCB
        if ((PtrFCB->NodeIdentifier.NodeType == SFSD_NODE_TYPE_VCB) ||
            !(PtrFCB->FCBFlags & SFSD_FCB_DIRECTORY)) {
            // We will only allow notify requests on directories.
```

```
                RC = STATUS_INVALID_PARAMETER;
        }

        PtrReqdFCB = &(PtrFCB->NTRequiredFCB);
        CanWait = ((PtrIrpContext->IrpContextFlags
                        & SFSD_IRP_CONTEXT_CAN_BLOCK)
                ? TRUE : FALSE);
    PtrVCB = PtrFCB->PtrVCB;

        // If the caller does not wish to block, it would be easier to
        // simply post the request now.
        if (!CanWait) {
            PostRequest = TRUE;
            try_return(RC = STATUS_PENDING);
        }

        // Obtain the caller's parameters
        BufferLength =
            PtrIoStackLocation->Parameters.QueryDirectory.Length;
        PtrSearchPattern =
            PtrIoStackLocation->Parameters.QueryDirectory.FileName;
        FileInformationClass =
            PtrIoStackLocation->
                        Parameters.QueryDirectory.FileInformationClass;
        FileIndex =
            PtrIoStackLocation->Parameters.QueryDirectory.FileIndex;

        // Some additional arguments that affect the FSD behavior
        RestartScan        = (PtrIoStackLocation->Flags & SL_RESTART_SCAN);
        ReturnSingleEntry = (PtrIoStackLocation->Flags
                                        & SL_RETURN_SINGLE_ENTRY);
        IndexSpecified     = (PtrIoStackLocation->Flags
                                        & SL_INDEX_SPECIFIED);

        // I will acquire exclusive access to the FCB.
        // This is not mandatory, however, and your FSD could choose to
        // acquire the resource shared for increased parallelism.
        ExAcquireResourceExclusiveLite(&(PtrReqdFCB->MainResource), TRUE);
        AcquiredFCB = TRUE;

        // We must determine the buffer pointer to be used. Since this
        // routine could be invoked directly either in the context of the
        // calling thread or in the context of a worker thread, here is
        // a general way of determining what we should use.
        if (PtrIrp->MdlAddress) {
            Buffer = MmGetSystemAddressForMdl(PtrIrp->MdlAddress);
        } else {
            Buffer = PtrIrp->UserBuffer;
        }

        // The method of determining where to look from and what to look
        // for is unfortunately extremely confusing. However, here is a
        // methodology you can broadly adopt:
        // (a) You have to maintain a search buffer per CCB structure.
```

```
// (b) This search buffer is initialized the very first time
//      a query directory operation is performed using the file
//      object.
// (For the sample FSD, the search buffer is stored in the
// DirectorySearchPattern field)
// However, the caller still has the option of "overriding" this
// stored search pattern by supplying a new one in a query
// directory operation.
//
if (PtrSearchPattern == NULL) {
    // User has supplied a search pattern
    // Now validate that the search pattern is legitimate; this is
    // dependent upon the character set acceptable to your FSD.

    // Once you have validated the search pattern, you must
    // check whether you need to store this search pattern in
    // the CCB.
    if (PtrCCB->DirectorySearchPattern == NULL) {
        // This must be the very first query request.
    FirstTimeQuery = TRUE;

        // Now, allocate enough memory to contain the caller-
        // supplied search pattern and fill in the
        // DirectorySearchPattern field in the CCB
        // PtrCCB->DirectorySearchPattern = ExAllocatePool(...);
    } else {
        // We should ignore the search pattern in the CCB and
        // instead use the user-supplied pattern for this
        // particular query directory request.
    }

} else if (PtrCCB->DirectorySearchPattern == NULL) {
    // This MUST be the first directory query operation (else the
    // DirectorySearchPattern field would never be NULL. Also, the
    // caller has neglected to provide a pattern so we MUST invent
    // one. Use "*" (following NT conventions) as your search
    // pattern and store it in the PtrCCB->DirectorySearchPattern
    // field.

    PtrCCB->DirectorySearchPattern = ExAllocatePool(PagedPool,
                        sizeof(L"*"));
    ASSERT(PtrCCB->DirectorySearchPattern);

    FirstTimeQuery = TRUE;
} else {
    // The caller has not supplied any search pattern that we are
    // forced to use. However, the caller had previously supplied
    // a pattern (or we must have invented one) and we will use it.
    // This is definitely not the first query operation on this
    // directory using this particular file object.

    PtrSearchPattern = PtrCCB->DirectorySearchPattern;
}
```

```
        // There is one other piece of information that your FSD must store
        // in the CCB structure for query directory support. This is the
        // index value (i.e., the offset in your on-disk directory
        // structure) from which you should start searching.
        // However, the flags supplied with the IRP can make us override
        // this as well.

        if (FileIndex) {
            // Caller has told us where to begin.
            // You may need to round this to an appropriate directory
            // entry alignment value.
         StartingIndexForSearch = FileIndex;
        } else if (RestartScan) {
         StartingIndexForSearch = 0;
        } else {
            // Get the starting offset from the CCB.
            // Remember to update this value on your way out from this
            // function. But, do not update the CCB CurrentByteOffset
            // field if you reach the end of the directory (or get an
            // error reading the directory) while performing the search.
         StartingIndexForSearch = PtrCCB->CurrentByteOffset.LowPart;
        }

        // Now, your FSD must determine the best way to read the directory
        // contents from disk and search through them.

        // If ReturnSingleEntry is TRUE, please return information on only
        // one matching entry.

        // One final note though:
        // If you do not find a directory entry OR while searching you
        // reach the end of the directory, then the return code should be
        // set as follows:

        // (a) If any files have been returned (i.e., ReturnSingleEntry
        //     was FALSE and you did find at least one match), then return
        //     STATUS_SUCCESS
        // (b) If no entry is being returned then:
        //     (i) If this is the first query, i.e., FirstTimeQuery is TRUE
        //         then return STATUS_NO_SUCH_FILE
        //     (ii) Otherwise, return STATUS_NO_MORE_FILES

        try_exit:    NOTHING;

        // Remember to update the CurrentByteOffset field in the CCB if
        // required.

        // You should also set a flag in the FCB indicating that the
        // directory contents were accessed.

    } finally {
        if (PostRequest) {
            if (AcquiredFCB) {
                SFsdReleaseResource(&(PtrReqdFCB->MainResource));
            }
```

```
                    // Map the user's buffer and then post the request.
                    RC = SFsdLockCallersBuffer(PtrIrp, TRUE, BufferLength);
                    ASSERT(NT_SUCCESS(RC));

                    RC = SFsdPostRequest(PtrIrpContext, PtrIrp);

            } else if (!(PtrIrpContext->IrpContextFlags &
                                    SFSD_IRP_CONTEXT_EXCEPTION)) {
                if (AcquiredFCB) {
                    SFsdReleaseResource(&(PtrReqdFCB->MainResource));
                }

                // Complete the request.
                PtrIrp->IoStatus.Status = RC;
                PtrIrp->IoStatus.Information = BytesReturned;

                // Free up the Irp Context
                SFsdReleaseIrpContext(PtrIrpContext);

                // complete the IRP
                IoCompleteRequest(PtrIrp, IO_DISK_INCREMENT);
            }
        }

    return(RC);
}

NTSTATUS    SFsdNotifyChangeDirectory(
PtrSFsdIrpContext               PtrIrpContext,
PIRP                            PtrIrp,
PIO_STACK_LOCATION              PtrIoStackLocation,
PFILE_OBJECT                    PtrFileObject,
PtrSFsdFCB                      PtrFCB,
PtrSFsdCCB                      PtrCCB)
{
    // Declarations go here ...

    try {

        // Validate the sent-in FCB
        if ((PtrFCB->NodeIdentifier.NodeType == SFSD_NODE_TYPE_VCB) ||
            !(PtrFCB->FCBFlags & SFSD_FCB_DIRECTORY)) {
            // We will only allow notify requests on directories.
            RC = STATUS_INVALID_PARAMETER;
            CompleteRequest = TRUE;
        }

        PtrReqdFCB = &(PtrFCB->NTRequiredFCB);
        CanWait = ((PtrIrpContext->IrpContextFlags &
                        SFSD_IRP_CONTEXT_CAN_BLOCK)
                            ? TRUE : FALSE);
        PtrVCB = PtrFCB->PtrVCB;

        // Acquire the FCB resource shared
```

```
        if (!ExAcquireResourceSharedLite(&(PtrReqdFCB->MainResource),
                    CanWait)) {
            PostRequest = TRUE;
            try_return(RC = STATUS_PENDING);
        }
    AcquiredFCB = TRUE;

        // Obtain some parameters sent by the caller
        CompletionFilter =
            PtrIoStackLocation->Parameters.NotifyDirectory.CompletionFilter;
        WatchTree = (PtrIoStackLocation->Flags
                    & SL_WATCH_TREE ? TRUE : FALSE);

        // If you wish to capture the subject context, you can do so as
        // follows:
        // {
        //        PSECURITY_SUBJECT_CONTEXT SubjectContext;
        //         SubjectContext = ExAllocatePool(PagedPool,
        //                            sizeof(SECURITY_SUBJECT_CONTEXT));
        //        SeCaptureSubjectContext(SubjectContext);
        //    }

        FsRtlNotifyFullChangeDirectory(&(PtrVCB->NotifyIRPMutex),
                        &(PtrVCB->NextNotifyIRP),
                        (void *)PtrCCB,
                        (PSTRING)(PtrFCB->FCBName->ObjectName.Buffer),
                        WatchTree, FALSE, CompletionFilter, PtrIrp,
                        NULL,        // SFsdTraverseAccessCheck(...)?
                        NULL);   // SubjectContext?

        RC = STATUS_PENDING;

        try_exit:    NOTHING;

    } finally {

        if (PostRequest) {
            // Perform appropriate post-related processing here
            if (AcquiredFCB) {
                SFsdReleaseResource(&(PtrReqdFCB->MainResource));
                AcquiredFCB = FALSE;
            }
            RC = SFsdPostRequest(PtrIrpContext, PtrIrp);
        } else if (CompleteRequest) {
            PtrIrp->IoStatus.Status = RC;
            PtrIrp->IoStatus.Information = 0;

            // Free up the Irp Context
            SFsdReleaseIrpContext(PtrIrpContext);

            // complete the IRP
            IoCompleteRequest(PtrIrp, IO_DISK_INCREMENT);
        } else {
            // Simply free up the IrpContext, since the IRP has been queued
```

```
            SFsdReleaseIrpContext(PtrIrpContext);
    }

    // Release the FCB resources if acquired.
    if (AcquiredFCB) {
        SFsdReleaseResource(&(PtrReqdFCB->MainResource));
        AcquiredFCB = FALSE;
    }

}

    return(RC);
}
```

Dispatch Routine: Cleanup

The cleanup dispatch routine entry point is invoked for each file object created as part of a successful create/open request. Therefore, for each create/open operation that succeeds, your FSD will receive a corresponding cleanup request.

Invoking the FSD Cleanup Entry Point

The cleanup entry point is invoked by the NT I/O Manager. Threads executing on the Windows NT platform cannot really invoke the cleanup routine directly; all they can do is open or close handles to file streams, or reference/dereference file objects that are the I/O-Manager-created structures representing open file streams.

In Chapter 4, we discussed file object structures in detail. You may recall that file object structures are managed by the NT Object Manager. One question that may occur to you is how does that Object Manager know about I/O-Manager-defined structures, such as the file object structure?

The answer is: at system initialization time, the NT I/O Manager registers all the different I/O Manager objects (including the file object structure) with the NT Object Manager. The `ObCreateObjectType()` Object Manager routine is used for this purpose. Although this routine is not exposed by the NT Executive, it serves to make the NT Object Manager aware of a new object type. When invoking this routine, the I/O Manager also supplies the functions that must be invoked by the Object Manager to manipulate the object being defined. For file object structures, the I/O Manager supplies an internal routine called `IopClose-File()` to be invoked whenever any handle associated with the file object has been closed.

The `IopCloseFile()` routine is fairly simple in its implementation. It performs the following logical steps whenever invoked (i.e., whenever a handle to the file object is closed).

- If the process closing the handle has other handles open for the file object, the I/O Manager does not do anything, but simply returns.[*]

- The I/O Manager checks whether it needs to issue a request to the FSD to unlock any byte-range locks obtained by the current process.

  It is possible that the process performing the close handle operation may have requested byte-range locks on the file stream associated with the file object structure. In the next chapter, we'll discuss byte-range locking in more detail, but note for now that the I/O Manager remembers when a process has requested byte-range locks and uses this information when the process is closing the last handle to the file object structure. The I/O Manager then creates a `IRP_MJ_LOCK_CONTROL` IRP, with a minor function of `IRP_MN_UNLOCK_ALL`, requesting the FSD to unlock any byte ranges locked by the particular process.[†]

  Note that the I/O Manager issues this request to unlock all byte ranges previously locked by the process only if other processes in the system still have open handles to the file object structure. If all handles to the file object have been closed, the I/O Manager does not explicitly issue an unlock request, but instead directly issues an `IRP_MJ_CLEANUP` request. The implicit expectation is that, as part of performing cleanup-related processing, the FSD will unlock any byte-range locks acquired by the current process.

- Now, if all handles to the file object have been closed (the system-wide handle count for the file object is 0), the I/O Manager creates an IRP with a major function of `IRP_MJ_CLEANUP` and invokes the FSD entry point.

  Note that the I/O Manager does not really care about the results of a cleanup request, except to perform a wait in the context of the thread closing the handle if the FSD returns `STATUS_PENDING`. Therefore, a cleanup request is an inherently synchronous request. Even if your FSD returns an error code from the cleanup routine, the I/O manager will ignore the error and proceed. Remember that cleanup operations must continue even in the face of errors; there are no second chances here!

---

[*] There is a handle count associated with a file object structure that is specific to each process that has an open handle to the file object. Also, there is a system-wide handle count, which is the sum of all process-specific handle counts. Here, the I/O Manager checks whether the process-specific handle count is equal to 0, or whether the process still has other open handles for the file object.

[†] Actually, the I/O Manager will first attempt to use the fast I/O path to issue this request and will use an IRP if the fast I/O method does not work.

Logical Steps Involved

Now that you know how the cleanup routine is invoked in your file system driver, here are the steps that most FSD implementations take in processing such a request:

- Synchronize cleanup requests with create requests by acquiring the volume control block resource exclusively during a cleanup operation.

  This also serializes all cleanup requests for the particular logical volume. If the VCB resource cannot be acquired immediately, the FSD can post the request for asynchronous processing (remember that the I/O Manager will still be waiting for the cleanup operation to complete in the context of the requesting thread).

- Your FSD should also acquire the `MainResource` for the file object exclusively to synchronize with other user-initiated I/O operations on the file stream (remember that other processes may still have open references/handles to the file stream).

  If you cannot acquire the `MainResource` for the FCB, you should post the request to be handled asynchronously.

- If the cleanup request is for a regular file and if your FSD supports opportunistic locking, you should invoke the FSRTL-supplied oplock package, informing it about the cleanup request, thereby allowing it to perform any cleanup that it needs to at this time.

- If the cleanup operation is for a directory, the cleanup routine now invokes the `FsRtlNotifyCleanup()` routine, described earlier, to complete any pending notify IRPs for the file object.

- For cleanup operations on files, the FSD must now unlock any byte-range locks acquired by the process in whose context the cleanup routine was invoked.

- If the file was accessed or modified, your FSD should update appropriate time stamp values for the file stream (in the directory entry for the file stream) at this time. You may also need to update the file size value in the directory entry if it has changed and the directory entry does not reflect the current value for the file stream.

  Note that your FSD may use a different approach to updating time stamp values (e.g., your FSD might update time stamp values at the time when the access/modification actually occurred, in which case you would not need to do anything at cleanup time). If, however, you do change some time stamp values, you should invoke the FSRTL `FsRtlNotifyFullReport-`

`Change()` routine once all the modifications have been done locally in the FCB/directory entry for the file stream.

Note that for fast I/O read/write operations, your FSD may not have had the opportunity to update the access/modify/change time stamp values. However, you can determine that such I/O occurred by the presence of the `FO_FILE_FAST_IO_READ` flag in the file object structure (indicating that at least one fast I/O read operation was processed), or by the presence of `FO_FILE_MODIFIED` (some thread performed a modification, implying that the modification time should be updated), and/or by the presence of the `FO_FILE_SIZE_CHANGED` flag (indicating that the file size was changed in the FCB header, and the FSD might need to modify the directory entry for the file stream appropriately).

- If this is the last cleanup request that you expect for the file stream, you should check for any pending file stream truncate requests.

  Remember that with the NT I/O Manager–mandated model for file stream deletion (for directories as well as for regular files), the FSD actually deletes the directory entry for a file stream only when the last user handle has been closed. In this case, if the link count for the file stream is also 0 (if your FSD does not support multiply linked files, then any delete operation will always cause the link count to equal 0), the FSD must also free up all of the on-disk space for the file stream. Therefore, the FSD must do two things if the file has been marked for deletion:

  — Check if the link count is equal to 0. If so, then acquire the `PagingIoResource` exclusively (blocking if you have to in the process), and set the file size and valid data length fields to 0.

    Now, the FSD can release the `PagingIoResource`, and release the on-disk space reserved for the file stream. However, there is one important step that the FSD must perform before actually deallocating the on-disk space reserved for the file stream; the FSD must invoke `MmFlushImageSection()` to ensure that the VMM purges any pages containing mapped data for the file stream.

  — If the current link is being deleted, the FSD should remove the directory entry corresponding to the current link at this time.

    Remember to invoke the `FsRtlNotifyFullReportChange()` routine to notify pending IRPs about the fact that an entry has been deleted.

- Decrement the `OpenHandleCount` in the FCB structure.

- Invoke `CcUninitializeCacheMap()` for all FCB structures, regardless of whether or not caching had been initiated using the file object on which the cleanup is being performed.

If the file stream was truncated, supply the new size for the file stream in the `TruncateSize` argument to the `CcUninitializeCacheMap()` function call. This will result in the Cache Manage purging the truncated pages from the system cache.

- Be sure to set the `FO_CLEANUP_COMPLETE` flag in the `Flags` field of the file object structure.

- Invoke the I/O Manager routine `IoRemoveShareAccess()` to update the share access associated with the FCB.

  The reason for updating the share access at cleanup time instead of in a close operation, is because the close could theoretically take a very long time to be issued, and it would be unfriendly to prevent fresh user open operations simply because of some stale, conflicting share access value set in the FCB.

  Note that the `IoRemoveShareAccess()` routine accepts two arguments: a pointer to the file object structure on which the cleanup is being performed and a pointer to the unique share access value stored in the FCB structure (the address of the `FCBShareAccess` field in the sample FSD).

The steps listed here are simply a checklist of items that the FSD is expected to perform as part of processing a cleanup request. Many sophisticated file systems may need to perform additional operations to ensure data consistency on disk. For example, some file systems may make certain guarantees about the validity of the on-disk data once a file handle has been closed, and therefore they will undoubtedly have file-system-specific operations to perform, including flushing file data and/or writing log files to disk at this time.

I have not provided a code fragment for the cleanup or close routine, since they are quite FSD-specific. However, as long as your FSD follows the steps listed here, you should be able to derive such a routine successfully.

Dispatch Routine: Close

Just as a cleanup request will always be issued for a file object structure representing an open file stream, a close request will always be issued for the file object some time after the cleanup has been processed.

The fundamental rule is that the file object is not really closed until the `IRP_MJ_CLOSE` is received. The `IRP_MJ_CLEANUP` means that all user file handles for the file object have been closed; however, if the file object has any references pending, then the `IRP_MJ_CLOSE` will be delayed until the reference count on the file object structure (maintained by the NT Object Manager) is equal to 0.

Invoking the FSD Close Entry Point

Just as is the case for the cleanup request, the close entry point is invoked by the NT I/O Manager. Threads executing on the Windows NT platform cannot directly issue a close request to the FSD; the best they can do is to dereference a file object structure that they might have previously referenced. Note that there are two methods exposed by the Object Manager to reference a file object, and correspondingly, there are two methods to dereference the file object. To reference a file object, a thread can create a file handle for the file object either by opening the file object, (NtCreateFile(), NtOpenFile(), ZwCreateFile()), or by requesting a new handle from the file object pointer (ObReferenceObjectBy-Handle()). Similarly, the thread can also cause the reference count on the file object to be incremented by invoking the ObReferenceObjectByPointer() routine (described in Chapter 5).

To dereference a previously referenced file object, the thread can either close a file handle using ZwClose() or NtClose(), or dereference the file object directly by invoking ObDereferenceObject() on the file object pointer.

Whenever a user closes a file handle, the NT Object Manager invokes the IopCloseFile() routine for the particular file object structure on which that close has been invoked. From the previous discussion, you know that the IopCloseFile() routine could lead to an IRP_MJ_CLEANUP being issued to the FSD. Once the I/O Manager returns control back to the Object Manager, it invokes ObDereferenceObject() internally. The ObDereferenceObject() routine decrements the reference count in the object header by 1, and invokes the delete routine associated with the object, if such a routine has been provided and if the reference count maintained by the Object Manager is equal to 0. In the case of file object structures, the I/O Manager supplies an internal (not exposed) delete routine called IopDeleteFile().

The IopDeleteFile() routine performs the following operations:

- It creates an IRP with a major function of IRP_MJ_CLOSE and invokes the FSD close dispatch routine.

- Once the FSD returns control from the close dispatch routine, the I/O Manager frees any file name string allocated for the file object structure.

- The I/O Manager closes any completion ports associated with the file object.

- The I/O Manager decrements a reference count on the FSD driver object (the count is incremented by the I/O Manager as part of processing a create/open request, to ensure that the driver can't be unloaded while open file objects are present).

- If the driver reference count is equal to 0 and if the driver had an unload operation pending, the driver is unloaded at this time.

Just as in the case of a cleanup request, the I/O Manager doesn't expect an FSD close routine to return any errors. Also, it's important to note that the I/O Manager doesn't expect close requests to return STATUS_PENDING (i.e., the I/O Manager expects the close operation to be performed synchronously).*

Logical Steps Involved

Here are the steps most FSD implementations take in processing an IRP_MJ_ CLOSE request:

- Obtain a pointer to the FCB and CCB structures.
- Synchronize with other close/create/cleanup requests by acquiring the VCB resource exclusively.
- Delete the CCB structure and free any other associated memory objects.
- If this is the last close operation for the file, delete the in-memory FCB structure as well.

These steps are extremely simplified, although accurate. Close requests can often occur at some inconvenient moments, and it is quite probable that your FSD may not be able to acquire the required resources without blocking. However, blocking a close request will lead to some very unexpected deadlock conditions. Therefore, you should, as a rule, never make a close request block, waiting for resources to be acquired. The best thing to do in such situations is to simply obtain any necessary information from the file object structure, make a local copy of such information, and post a request to perform the close asynchronously. Your FSD can then immediately return success to the caller.

Note that if you do such asynchronous processing of a close request, you should be extremely careful when creating new FCB structures later to ensure that any subsequent create/open operations are well synchronized with the asynchronous delayed close operations. Similarly, if a user requests that a volume be dismounted and if the dismount is pending because of open file streams, your FSD should be able to perform appropriate processing when the last file object is closed for the last time to perform the dismount operation.

Note again that it is not a wise decision to post a close request and if your FSD expects to perform some sophisticated processing during a close operation, you should try to do it asynchronously.

---

* If you have to do something that can't be done synchronously, you will have to perform the operation asynchronously after obtaining whatever context is required from the file object structure; remember, though, that you simply must return STATUS_SUCCESS to the I/O Manager.

11

Writing a File System Driver III

Before continuing with some of the remaining file system dispatch routines, it would be useful to understand the fast I/O execution path defined by the NT I/O Manager. Because the FSD must provide support for callback routines that allow other NT components to preacquire FSD resources, an example of such a callback routine is provided and discussed in this chapter. Then, we'll discuss some of the remaining FSD dispatch routines that you should become familiar with before designing your file system, including the flush file entry point, get/set volume information support, support for byte-range locks on a file stream, and file system IOCTL support. We'll also see the NT LAN Manager opportunistic locking protocol, which you may wish to support in your FSD. I will conclude this chapter with a short overview of the file system driver load process, implemented by using a file system recognizer module.

Handling Fast I/O

The fast I/O execution path was apparently developed in response to a recognition by NT file system driver and I/O subsystem designers that the normal IRP dispatch mechanism did not meet some of the performance criteria they had set out to achieve. Although it was originally conceived to handle user read/write requests more efficiently, the fast I/O method has evolved to encompass the many different FSD requests that a user could issue, including requests to get or set file information, request byte-range locks, and request device IOCTLs. It has also become somewhat of a catch-all mechanism for issuing requests to preacquire FSD resources, although this does not appear to be part of the original fast I/O design.

Chapter 7, *The NT Cache Manager II*, provides an introduction to the fast I/O method of data access. Refer to that chapter before proceeding with the following discussion.

Why Fast I/O?

Let's recall how a typical file system buffered I/O (read/write) request is handled:

1. First, the I/O Manager creates an IRP describing the request.

2. This IRP is dispatched to the appropriate FSD entry point, where the driver extracts the various parameters that define the I/O request (e.g., the buffer pointer supplied by the caller and the amount of data requested) and validates them.

3. The FSD acquires appropriate resources to provide synchronization across concurrent I/O requests and checks whether the request is for buffered or nonbuffered I/O.

4. Buffered I/O requests are sent by the FSD to the NT Cache Manager.

5. If required, the FSD initiates caching before dispatching the request to the NT Cache Manager.

6. The NT Cache Manager attempts to transfer data to/from the system cache.

7. If a page fault is incurred by the NT Cache Manager, the request will recurse back into the FSD read/write entry point as a paging I/O request.

   You should note, that in order to resolve a page fault, the NT VMM issues a paging I/O request to the I/O Manager, which creates a new IRP structure (marked for noncached, paging I/O) and dispatches it to the FSD. The original IRP is not used to perform the paging I/O.

8. The FSD receives the new IRP describing the paging I/O request and transfers the requested byte range to/from secondary storage.

   Lower-level disk drivers assist the FSD in this transfer.

There were two observations that NT designers made that will help explain the evolution of the fast I/O method:

- Most user I/O requests are synchronous and blocking (i.e., the caller does not mind waiting until the data transfer has been achieved).

- Most I/O requests to read/write data can be satisfied directly by transferring data from/to the system cache.

Once they had made the two observations listed, the NT I/O Manager developers decided that the sequence of operations used in a typical I/O request could be further streamlined to help achieve better performance. Certain operations appeared to be redundant and could probably be discarded in order to make user I/O processing more efficient. Specifically, the following steps seemed unnecessary:

Creating an IRP structure to describe the original user request, especially if the IRP was not required for reuse

> Assuming that the request would typically be satisfied directly from the system cache, it is apparent that the original IRP structure, with its multiple stack locations and with all of the associated overhead in setting up the I/O request packet, is not really required or fully utilized. It seems to make more sense to dispense with this operation altogether and simply pass the I/O request parameters directly to the layer that would handle the request.

Invoking the FSD

> This may seem a little strange to you but a legitimate observation made by the NT designers was that, for most synchronous cached requests, it seems to be redundant to get the FSD involved at all in processing the I/O transfer. After all, if all that an FSD did was route the request to the NT Cache Manager, it seemed to be more efficient to have the I/O Manager directly invoke the NT Cache Manager and bypass the FSD completely.

> This can only be done if caching is initiated on the file stream, so that the Cache Manager is prepared to handle the buffered I/O request.

Becoming Efficient: the Fast I/O Solution

Presumably, after pondering the observations listed here, NT I/O designers decided that the new, more efficient sequence of steps in processing user I/O requests should be as follows:

1. The I/O Manager receives the user request and checks if the operation is synchronous.

2. If the user request is synchronous, the I/O Manager determines whether caching has been initiated for the file object being used to request the I/O operation.*

---

* The check made by the I/O Manager is simply whether the `PrivateCacheMap` field in the file object structure is nonnull. This field is set to a nonnull value by the Cache Manager as part of initializing caching for the particular file object structure.

For asynchronous operations, the I/O Manager follows the normal method of creating an IRP and invoking the driver dispatch routine to process the I/O request.

3. If caching has been initiated for the file object as determined in Step 2, the I/O Manager invokes the appropriate fast I/O entry point.

    The important point to note here is that the I/O Manager assumes that the fast I/O entry point must have been initialized if the FSD supports cached file streams. If you install a debug version of the operating system, you will actually see an assertion failure if the fast I/O function pointer is NULL.

    Note that a pointer to the fast I/O dispatch table is obtained by the I/O Manager from the `FastIoDispatch` field in the driver object data structure.

4. The I/O Manager checks the return code from the fast I/O routine previously invoked.

    A TRUE return code value from the fast I/O dispatch routine indicates to the I/O Manager that the request was successfully processed via the fast I/O path. Note that the return code value TRUE does not indicate whether the request succeeded or failed; all it does is indicate whether the request was processed or not. The I/O Manager must examine the `IoStatus` argument supplied to the fast I/O routine to find out if the request succeeded or failed.

    A return code of FALSE indicates that the request could not be processed via the fast I/O path. The I/O Manager accepts this return code value and, in response, simply reverts to the more traditional method of creating an IRP and dispatching it to the FSD.

    This point is very important for you to understand. The NT I/O subsystem designers did not wish to force an FSD to have to support the fast I/O method of obtaining data. Therefore, the I/O Manager allows the FSD to return FALSE from a fast I/O routine invocation and simply reissues the request using an IRP instead.

5. If the fast I/O routine returned success, the I/O Manager updates the `CurrentByteOffset` field in the file object structure (since this is a synchronous I/O operation) and returns the status code to the caller.

The advantage of using the new sequence of operations is that synchronous I/O requests can be processed without having to incur the overhead of either building an IRP structure (and the associated overhead of completion processing for the IRP), or routing the request via the FSD dispatch entry point.

Possible Problems in Bypassing the FSD

Not all file system implementations are alike; as a matter of fact, nearly all file systems have unique characteristics, requirements, and processing needs, specific to the particular implementation. Therefore, although bypassing the FSD completely and directly obtaining data from the Cache Manager appears, on the surface, to be a highly efficient method of data transfer, the following issues must be considered:

Acquiring FSD resources

It would be nice not to have to worry about FSD resources and simply obtain data from the Cache Manager. However, as you well know, the FSD tries to ensure data consistency usually by providing a shared (multiple) reader and single writer model to file system clients. To do this, the FSD typically acquires the `MainResource` either shared or exclusively, and in some cases (especially if the file size is to be modified), also synchronizes with paging I/O requests by acquiring the `PagingIoResource` exclusively.

Even if the I/O Manager does bypass the FSD dispatch entry point when performing fast I/O, appropriate FSD resources should always be somehow acquired.

Presence of byte-range locks

This is a very obvious problem in the implementation and support of fast I/O routines that bypass the FSD dispatch entry points. In Chapter 9, *Writing a File System Driver I*, the code fragments presented for read/write operations noted that the FSD dispatch entry points always check to see whether the caller should be allowed to proceed with the I/O operation, or whether the operation should be denied, because some or all of the byte range being accessed/modified has a byte-range lock associated with it.

Since the typical Windows NT byte-range locking model implements mandatory byte-range locks, such checks should also be performed in the fast I/O case. The other alternative is to prevent fast I/O operations if the file stream has any byte-range locks associated with it.

Opportunistic locks

Opportunistic locking support is discussed in greater detail later in this chapter. However, just as in the case of byte-range locks, the FSD may wish to be careful about allowing fast I/O operations to proceed, depending on the state of the oplocks associated with the file stream.

Other FSD-specific issues

Consider a file system that must perform certain preprocessing before allowing file write operations to proceed on the file stream. For example, certain distributed file systems (e.g., DFS) may employ token-based or other similar methods of ensuring data consistency across geographically dispersed nodes. For such complex file system implementations, the FSD may not allow fast I/O support without ensuring that the requisite preprocessing has been performed.

The first three concerns listed here can be placed into two categories:

- Ensuring acquisition of file system resources for the file stream being accessed
- Allowing the FSD to determine whether fast I/O should be allowed to proceed on a file stream or not

NT I/O subsystem designers seem to have thought through these issues and have provided support to FSD designers to address such problems. The solutions include providing generic fast I/O intermediate routines in the FSRTL package that always acquire appropriate FSD resources, and also allowing the FSD to specify, on a per-file-stream basis, whether fast I/O should be allowed for the file stream.

However, for more complex FSD implementations that always need to perform preprocessing before allowing any sort of I/O to proceed, the FSD designer must devise an FSD-specific method to also allow fast I/O access to file streams. There is no easy solution in such a situation.

Ensuring Correct FSD Resource Acquisition

You should either initialize the fast I/O dispatch routine function pointers in the fast I/O dispatch table to point to *intermediate* routines in your driver that perform appropriate FCB acquisition, or use the Windows NT FSRTL-provided generic routines instead.

In the sample FSD initialization code presented in Chapter 9, you will notice that I have initialized the fast I/O dispatch routine function pointers to sample FSD-provided routines (e.g., `SFsdFastIoRead()`, `SFsdFastIoWrite()`, and so on). The theory is that these intermediate routines will not allow the I/O Manager to bypass the FSD completely, but instead will perform any required preprocessing, such as resource acquisition, before passing the request on to the Cache Manager (if appropriate).

You will find that this is still a lower overhead I/O operation (even though the FSD is not being completely bypassed) than the corresponding IRP-based I/O operation.

There are also some FSRTL-provided intermediate support routines that perform appropriate FSD resource acquisition and forward the fast I/O request to the NT Cache Manager. The two most widely used (and Microsoft recommended) are the `FsRtlCopyRead()` and `FsRtlCopyWrite()` utility functions described later. If you decide to use these functions, you should understand the assumptions made by them and the nature of the processing that they perform. Some file systems that have a lot of complex preprocessing required before they forward a request to the Cache Manager may wish to use a combination of their own fast I/O dispatch routines and the FSRTL-provided functions (one way of doing this is to have your FSD's fast I/O dispatch routine perform appropriate preprocessing, and *then* invoke the FSRTL routine).

Allowing Fast I/O on a File Stream

You must set the `IsFastIoPossible` field, in the `CommonFCBHeader` for the file stream, appropriately. You should also provide a callback function and initialize the `FastIoCheckIfPossible` function pointer field in the `CommonFCBHeader` to invoke this callback function when required.

One of the methods for an FSD to disable the fast I/O method for a specific file stream is by initializing the `IsFastIoPossible` field in the `CommonFCBHeader` to `FastIoIsNotPossible`. The other method is to set `IsFastIoPossible` to `FastIoIsQuestionable`, and then, after appropriate processing, return FALSE from the `FastIoCheckIfPossible()` function callback invocation.

Here are the three enumerated type values the `IsFastIoPossible` field can contain:

- `FastIoIsPossible` (enumerated type value = 0)
- `FastIoIsNotPossible` (enumerated type value = 1)
- `FastIoIsQuestionable` (enumerated type value = 2)

The `FastIoIsNotPossible` value results in fast I/O being disabled for the particular file stream until the contents of the `IsFastIoPossible` field are changed.

If the `IsFastIoPossible` field is initialized to `FastIoIsPossible`, the intermediate routine (whether your own or that provided by the FSRTL) proceeds with fast I/O processing for the request. If, however, the `IsFastIoPossible` field is initialized to `FastIoIsQuestionable`, then the FSRTL-provided intermediate routine issues a callback to the FSD to determine whether the fast I/O operation should be allowed to proceed or not (your internal intermediate routine can follow the same model). The callback function must be provided by the FSD and the callback function address must be initialized in the `FastIoCheckIfPossible` field of the fast I/O dispatch table (the sample FSD initializes this value to the `SFsdFastIoCheckIfPossible()` function address).

The FSD can determine, in the callback routine, whether the fast I/O operation should be allowed to proceed. If the FSD returns FALSE from the `FastIoCheck-IfPossible` field, the FSRTL-provided intermediate routines (and also your own) will stop processing the fast I/O request and return FALSE to the NT I/O Manager; otherwise, the intermediate function will continue with processing the fast I/O request (since the FSD has essentially granted permission for the current fast I/O operation to proceed).

The following code fragment illustrates the implementation of a typical `FastIo-CheckIfPossible` function callback implementation:

```
BOOLEAN SFsdFastIoCheckIfPossible(
IN PFILE_OBJECT             FileObject,
IN PLARGE_INTEGER           FileOffset,
IN ULONG                    Length,
IN BOOLEAN                  Wait,
IN ULONG                    LockKey,
IN BOOLEAN                  CheckForReadOperation,
OUT PIO_STATUS_BLOCK        IoStatus,
IN PDEVICE_OBJECT           DeviceObject)
{
    BOOLEAN                 ReturnedStatus = FALSE;
    PtrSFsdFCB              PtrFCB = NULL;
    PtrSFsdCCB              PtrCCB = NULL;
    LARGE_INTEGER           IoLength;

    // Obtain a pointer to the FCB and CCB for the file stream.
    PtrCCB = (PtrSFsdCCB)(FileObject->FsContext2);
    ASSERT(PtrCCB);
    PtrFCB = PtrCCB->PtrFCB;
    ASSERT(PtrFCB);

    // Validate that this is a fast I/O request to a regular file.
    // The sample FSD, for example, will not allow fast I/O requests
    // to volume objects or to directories.
    if ((PtrFCB->NodeIdentifier.NodeType == SFSD_NODE_TYPE_VCB) ||
        (PtrFCB->FCBFlags & SFSD_FCB_DIRECTORY)) {
        // This is not allowed.
        return(ReturnedStatus);
    }

    IoLength = RtlConvertUlongToLargeInteger(Length);

    // Your FSD can determine the checks that it needs to perform.
    // Typically, an FSD will check whether there are any byte-range
    // locks that would prevent a fast I/O operation from proceeding.

    // ... (FSD specific checks go here).

    if (CheckForReadOperation) {
        // It would be nice to be able to use the FSRTL's services
        // for file lock operations. However, this chapter describes how
```

```
            // to design and implement your own file lock support routines.
            // Check here whether or not the read I/O can be allowed.
            ReturnedStatus = SFsdCheckLockReadAllowed(&(PtrFCB->
                                                       FCBByteRangeLock),
                             FileOffset, &IoLength, LockKey, FileObject,
                             PsGetCurrentProcess());

    } else {
            // This is a write request. Invoke the appropriate support routine
            // to see if the write should be allowed to proceed.
            ReturnedStatus =
                SFsdCheckLockWriteAllowed(&(PtrFCB->FCBByteRangeLock),
                                 FileOffset, &IoLength, LockKey, FileObject,
                                 PsGetCurrentProcess());
    }

        return(ReturnedStatus);
}
```

A legitimate question that you should have is, when should you modify/update the `IsFastIoPossible` field in the `CommonFCBHeader`?

The answer is—it depends. You should initialize the field when creating the FCB for the file stream, which is when the first open operation is performed on the file stream. Subsequent updates should always be made after acquiring the `MainResource` for the file stream exclusively. Typically, if byte-range locks have been granted on the file stream, or if opportunistic locks have been granted such that they would prevent fast I/O access, then you should set the `IsFastIoPossible` field value to either `FastIoIsNotPossible` or `FastIoIsQuestionable`.

A common method that sets the `IsFastIoPossible` field is shown in this pseudocode fragment:

```
if ((no opportunistic locks have been granted for the file stream) ||
        (if the caller has an exclusive opportunistic lock on the stream) ||
        (if my FSD-specific checks tell me that fast I/O is not a good
             idea)) {
    if ((there are any byte-range file locks) ||
            (if my FSD-specific checks tell me that fast I/O is
                 questionable)) {
            // Force the FSD to be queried for permission before fast
            // I/O is allowed to proceed.
            IsFastIoPossible = FastIoIsQuestionable;
    } else {
        // Fast I/O seems safe at this time.
        IsFastIoPossible = FastIoIsPossible;
    }
} else {
    // Allowing fast I/O would not be a good idea. Force the IRP route
    // instead.
    IsFastIoPossible = FastIoIsNotPossible;
}
```

Note that there are no set rules that an FSD must follow in determining whether to allow fast I/O operations or not; the issue is highly FSD-specific. If, however, you do plan to use the methodology presented here, as opposed to simply refusing fast I/O outright, then there are a multitude of occasions during file system execution that you will have to execute the fragment and reevaluate if fast I/O should be allowed to proceed without question, allowed on a per-occasion basis, or never allowed.

The specific occasions on which you should reevaluate the status of fast I/O for a specific file stream include the following:

- At file stream open time
- Whenever read or write requests are dispatched to the file system
- Whenever byte-range lock/unlock requests are processed by the FSD
- Whenever file stream attributes are modified via a set file information request
- Whenever opportunistic locks are granted/broken
- At file stream cleanup
- For removable media, whenever a volume needs to be reverified due to media change

Of course, your FSD may have some very specific situations, in addition to those listed, when it may need to reevaluate the status of fast I/O vis-à-vis a specific file stream.

FSRTL Support for Fast I/O

The NT I/O subsystem designers recommend that FSD implementations use FSRTL-supplied routines to perform appropriate preprocessing (including acquiring FSD resources), before invoking the NT Cache Manager to complete a fast I/O read/write request. Specifically, the following generic support routines have been provided:[*]

- `FsRtlCopyRead()`
- `FsRtlCopyWrite()`

There are other fast I/O support routines that the NT FSRTL provides (e.g., `FsRtlQueryBasicInformation()`, `FsRtlQueryStandardInformation()`, and so on). The NT IFS kit lists all of the fast I/O support routines that

---

[*] The native NT file system implementations follow recommendations and use these FSRTL routines to perform fast I/O related preprocessing. Therefore, during file system initialization, they initialize the `FastIoRead` and `FastIoWrite` (function pointer) fields in the fast I/O dispatch table with `FsRtlCopyRead()` and `FsRtlCopyWrite()`, respectively.

your FSD can use. We will discuss the two I/O-related routines in greater detail here, because they encapsulate some of the most complex processing related to fast I/O support. The FSRTL routines provided for file-lock support are also discussed later in this chapter.

In the initialization code for the sample FSD implementation provided in Chapter 9, you will have noticed that the `FastIoRead` function pointer is initialized to `SFsdFastIoRead()`, and the `FastIoWrite()` function pointer is initialized to `SFsdFastIoWrite()`. This is not in keeping with the recommendation made by the NT I/O subsystem designers that these function pointers should be directly initialized to `FsRtlCopyRead()` and `FsRtlCopyWrite()`. The reason for not following these recommendations is simply to illustrate to the reader that it is possible for more complex file system implementations to perform any required pre-processing in their own routines (e.g., `SFsdFastIoRead()` for the sample FSD implementation), and then invoke the appropriate FSRTL routine directly from the FSD fast I/O function. This method is especially useful for more complex file system implementations such as distributed/networked file system drivers.

Of course, for your FSD implementation, you may choose to initialize the function pointers with the appropriate FSRTL routines directly.

The `FsRtlCopyRead()` function is defined as follows:

```
BOOLEAN
FsRtlCopyRead (
IN PFILE_OBJECT             FileObject,
IN PLARGE_INTEGER           FileOffset,
IN ULONG                    Length,
IN BOOLEAN                  Wait,
IN ULONG                    LockKey,
OUT PVOID                   Buffer,
OUT PIO_STATUS_BLOCK        IoStatus,
IN PDEVICE_OBJECT           DeviceObject
);
```

The arguments accepted by the `FsRtlCopyRead()` function match those required in the function type definition for a fast I/O read function defined in the NT DDK. Notice that all of the relevant parameters supplied by the user thread when invoking the `NtReadFile()` system service routine are passed directly to the fast I/O (FSRTL) read routine instead of being inserted into an IRP structure.[*]

Functionality Provided:

The `FsRtlCopyRead()` routine executes the following steps:

---

[*] Although I did not talk about the `LockKey` user-supplied argument in Chapter 9 when discussing read/write dispatch entry point implementations, note for now that it is possible for a user to read/write a locked byte range if the locker had associated a key with the byte-range lock, and if the reader/writer knows the key value. Byte-range locks are discussed in greater detail later in this chapter.

- It attempts to acquire the `MainResource` for the file stream shared.

  In case you are wondering how the FSRTL can get to the FCB `MainResource` pointer, remember that the `FsContext` field in the file object structure is always initialized to point to a common FCB header structure of type `FSRTL_COMMON_FCB_HEADER`. This structure contains the `Resource` field, which is initialized by the FSD to the address of the `MainResource` (`ERESOURCE` type) structure.

  If the caller is not prepared to block (i.e., the `Wait` argument has been set to FALSE), and if the `MainResource` cannot be acquired immediately without blocking, the FSRTL routine will simply return FALSE. The I/O Manager will then reissue the read request to the FSD via the traditional IRP method.

- If the `IsFastIoPossible` field in the `CommonFCBHeader` is set to `FastIoIsNotPossible`, the `FsRtlCopyRead()` routine returns FALSE to the I/O Manager.

- If the `IsFastIoPossible` field in the `CommonFCBHeader` is set to `FastIoIsQuestionable`, the `FsRtlCopyRead()` routine queries the FSD (as described earlier in this chapter) whether it should proceed with fast I/O or return FALSE to the caller.

- Once the `FsRtlCopyRead()` has determined that it is safe to proceed, it invokes the `CcCopyRead()`/`CcFastCopyRead()` function to transfer data to/from the system cache.

  The FSRTL is careful about setting itself as the top-level component for the request. It sets the `TopLevelIrp` field in the TLS to the `FSRTL_FAST_IO_TOP_LEVEL_IRP` constant value. Once the read operation has completed, the `FsRtlCopyRead()` function sets the `FO_FILE_FAST_IO_READ` flag in the file object structure.

- The `FsRtlCopyRead()` function releases the `MainResource` for the file stream and returns TRUE to the I/O Manager.

  The I/O Manager performs appropriate postprocessing (described earlier in this chapter) and returns control to the caller.

The `FsRtlCopyWrite()` function is defined as follows:

```
BOOLEAN
FsRtlCopyWrite (
IN PFILE_OBJECT          FileObject,
IN PLARGE_INTEGER        FileOffset,
IN ULONG                 Length,
IN BOOLEAN               Wait,
IN ULONG                 LockKey,
IN PVOID                 Buffer,
OUT PIO_STATUS_BLOCK     IoStatus,
IN PDEVICE_OBJECT        DeviceObject
);
```

Functionality Provided:

The `FsRtlCopyWrite()` routine executes the following steps:

- If the file object has been opened with write-through specified, or if the Cache Manager `CcCanIWrite()` function call returns FALSE, this routine returns FALSE immediately.

  The I/O Manager will reissue the write request via the normal IRP method.

- The `FsRtlCopyWrite()` routine acquires the FCB `MainResource` either shared or exclusive.

  This routine acquires the `MainResource` shared, unless the caller wishes to append to the file stream, or if the write will extend the valid data length for the file stream. If the `FsRtlCopyWrite()` routine cannot acquire the `Main-Resource` immediately and if `Wait` is set to FALSE, this routine returns FALSE to the NT I/O Manager.

- A check is made to determine whether fast I/O write should even be attempted.

  Just as in the case of the `FsRtlCopyRead()` routine, this function invokes the FSD to make the final determination on whether fast I/O should be attempted if `IsFastIoPossible` is set to `FastIoIsQuestionable`.

- The `FsRtlCopyWrite()` routine also returns FALSE immediately to the I/O Manager if the file is being extended such that the new file size would exceed the current allocation size for the file stream, or if the new file size results in a wrap-around of the allocation size for the file stream from a 32-bit value to a 64-bit value.*

- If the file size is being extended, the `FsRtlCopyWrite()` routine will acquire the `PagingIoResource` exclusively, modify the file size in the `CommonFCBHeader`, and release the paging I/O resource.

- A `CcZeroData()` is performed, if required (i.e., if the current write operation results in a hole between the current valid data length before the new write operation was attempted and the starting offset of the new write request).

---

* There are valid reasons for these checks. First, allowing a write to proceed without having adequate disk space preallocated could result in an unexpected out-of-disk-space error code being returned during a subsequent lazy-write/modified page write operation; this could even happen well after a user process had closed the file handle and exited, expecting that all of the data had made it (or would) to secondary storage. Second, some file systems (e.g., FASTFAT) do not currently support 64-bit file sizes, while others (e.g., NTFS) do; therefore, the FSRTL package is unsure whether to allow such file I/O operations to proceed or not.

- The `FsRtlCopyWrite()` request issues a `CcCopyWrite()`/`CcFastCopy-Write()` request to actually transfer the data to the system cache.

  Just as in the case of the fast I/O read operation, the `FsRtlCopyWrite()` routine is careful to mark itself as the top-level component for the write request.

- Once the write operation has completed, the `FsRtlCopyWrite()` routine marks the fact that a fast I/O write operation was performed by setting the `FO_FILE_MODIFIED` flag in the file object structure.

  If the file was extended, or if valid data length was changed, the routine also sets the `FO_FILE_SIZE_CHANGED` flag in the file object structure.

- The `FsRtlCopyWrite()` function releases the `MainResource` for the file stream and returns TRUE to the I/O Manager.

  The I/O Manager performs appropriate postprocessing (described earlier in this chapter) and returns control to the caller.

Rolling Your Own Fast I/O Routine

Now that you understand the methodology used by the FSRTL in providing generic fast I/O read/write support routines, you should be able to easily replace them with your own if required, and also supplement them with appropriate routines to support the other fast I/O entry points.

There are a couple of issues you should keep in mind when developing your own fast I/O support routines:

- It would be prudent for your driver to provide appropriate exception handling in your fast I/O routines.

  The `FsRtlCopyRead()` and the `FsRtlCopyWrite()` functions do provide exception handlers since it is quite possible for a malicious user thread (or even a carelessly written application) to send in an invalid buffer, or to deallocate the buffer while the I/O is in progress using another thread, or to change the buffer permissions in such a way so as to cause an access violation error condition when the data transfer is attempted by the Cache Manager. Failure on your part to provide an exception handler could cause the system to crash.

- Your routine should encapsulate the fast I/O support within `FsRtlEnterFileSystem()` and `FsRtlExitFileSystem()` calls.

  This is simply a reminder to you that, just as in the case of the regular IRP dispatch routines, your FSD should not allow kernel-mode APCs to be delivered while executing file system code. This will prevent nasty priority inversion situations, which could lead to a system deadlock.

NOTE   The `FsRtlEnterFileSystem()` macro is simply defined to `KeEn-`
                `terCriticalRegion()`, while the `FsRtlExitFileSystem()`
                macro is defined to `KeLeaveCriticalRegion()`.

Also remember that the fast I/O path started off as a more efficient method to transfer data; if you find that certain situations would result in your fast I/O routine having to perform an inordinate amount of extraneous processing simply to support this method of data transfer, it could be more efficient to just return FALSE from the fast I/O routine, since the I/O Manager will then issue a regular IRP-based request back to your driver.

The Pseudo Fast I/O Routines

You may have rightly noticed that the fast I/O dispatch table contains entries such as `FastIoQueryBasicInfo`, `FastIoQueryStandardInfo`, and others that do not quite follow the original fast I/O model of bypassing the FSD and obtaining data from the NT Cache Manager. As explained earlier, there were two goals that the fast I/O method was designed to accomplish: avoiding the overhead associated with the creation and completion of an IRP structure and attempting to obtain data directly from the best source for the data, the NT Cache Manager.

The basic design goal for the fast I/O method is to achieve faster (better) performance. To achieve this goal, NT I/O subsystem designers seem to be providing fast entry points for some of the most frequently used FSD entry points. This is the reason behind the inclusion of most of the (non-I/O) fast I/O entries, including those previously listed.

There are also certain callbacks that have been lumped together with the regular fast I/O entry points in the fast I/O dispatch table, simply because the table seemed like a good, extensible container for these callback routines. Here are the specific callbacks:

- `AcquireFileForNtCreateSection` and `ReleaseFileForNtCreate-` `Section`
- `FastIoDetachDevice`
- `AcquireForModWrite` and `ReleaseForModWrite`
- `AcquireForCcFlush` and `ReleaseForCcFlush`

Only the first pair of callbacks, acquire/release for create section, existed in Windows NT Version 3.51. The others have been added with Version 4.0.

I presume it's harder for the NT designers to justify the inclusion of these call-backs in the fast I/O dispatch table. The only rational explanation for including them where they currently reside is that these seem to be last-minute solutions to synchronization/deadlock-related problems encountered during late testing, and the only extensible place where such callbacks could possibly reside, without breaking existing file system drivers, seemed to be the fast I/O dispatch table.

NOTE   Recall from earlier chapters that the fast I/O dispatch table contains a field called `SizeOfFastIoDispatch`, which is initialized by an FSD to the size of the structure it knows about (when the driver was implemented). Since new fast I/O entry points are always added at the end of the dispatch table (thereby increasing its size), it is relatively easy for the caller of a fast I/O routine to check whether the underlying FSD knows about the new entries, by comparing the size of the dispatch table with the new entries in it to the size value initialized by the FSD. If the FSD specifies a size that would include the particular fast I/O entry, the caller can proceed with the fast I/O operation; otherwise, the caller can assume that it is dealing with an older driver and simply skip the particular fast I/O call.

Unfortunately, this isn't a method your driver can use to skip fast I/O support altogether, since a basic assumption made by the NT I/O Manager is that your driver at least knows the initial fast I/O table, introduced with Version 3.51 of the operating system.

AcquireFileForNtCreateSection/ReleaseFileForNtCreateSection

To map a file stream into its virtual address space, a process must first create a section object for the file by invoking the `NtCreateSection()` system call.* This call is provided by the NT VMM, which performs all of the required processing to create the appropriate image/data section object for the caller.

The process requesting the create section operation specifies the length (in bytes) of the section object to be created. As part of processing the request, the VMM must query the FSD for the current file size associated with the file stream, and modify the file size as well, if the requested length is greater than the current end-of-file position. There are other operations that the VMM must perform, which could also cause the VMM to issue I/O requests to the underlying FSD managing the mounted logical volume on which the file stream resides.

When issuing file system get/set file size requests, the `MmExtendSection()` internal routine in the VMM acquires certain VMM resources, in order to synchro-

---

* This routine (actually the kernel-equivalent, `ZwCreateSection()`) is explained in detail in Chapter 5, *The NT Virtual Memory Manager*.

nize with other threads trying to perform another create section operation concurrently.

Unfortunately, though, it is still quite possible for another user thread to concurrently issue a cached read request for which the file system initiates caching, which, in turn, results in the `CcInitializeCacheMap()` routine in the Cache Manager possibly invoking the `MmExtendSection()` internal support routine provided by the VMM.

Similarly, other user threads trying to change the file size concurrently could invoke the set file information dispatch routine in the FSD; the FSD, in turn, would issue a `CcSetFileSizes()` request, and the Cache Manager would possibly invoke the `MmExtendSection()` routine internally.

Here, the stage is being set for a classic deadlock situation. For the thread performing the create section request, the VMM has acquired some global internal resources preventing other concurrent operations that could possibly result in any modifications to the section object. Then, the VMM invokes the FSD get/set file information entry point. As part of processing this request, the FSD attempts to acquire the `MainResource` exclusively, and later, tries to acquire the `Paging-IoResource`. However, the FSD can be forced to block when attempting the acquisition of the `MainResource` if some other thread either performing cached I/O or changing the file length acquired it first.

The thread performing a cached I/O or file size modification operation would, in turn, be blocked in the VMM on the same resource that the `MmExtendSec-tion()` routine acquired to prevent concurrent modifications to the file stream size.

The result is deadlock; the reason is simply because the VMM broke the resource acquisition hierarchy of acquiring FSD resources for the file object *first*, before acquiring its internal resources.

After the NT I/O subsystem designers encountered this problem, they added the two callbacks to the fast I/O dispatch table. Now the VMM invokes the FSD `AcquireForNtCreateSection()` callback before acquiring its internal resources when processing a create section request. After all of the processing requiring interaction with the FSD has been completed, the VMM invokes the `ReleaseForNtCreateSection()` callback, to request the FSD to release FCB resources.

Here is the code fragment illustrating the implementation of the `AcquireForNt-CreateSection` and `ReleaseForNtCreateSection` in the sample FSD:

```
void SFsdFastIoAcqCreateSec(
IN PFILE_OBJECT          FileObject)
{
```

```
    PtrSFsdFCB              PtrFCB = NULL;
    PtrSFsdCCB              PtrCCB = NULL;
    PtrSFsdNTRequiredFCB    PtrReqdFCB = NULL;

    // Obtain a pointer to the FCB and CCB for the file stream.
    PtrCCB = (PtrSFsdCCB)(FileObject->FsContext2);
    ASSERT(PtrCCB);
    PtrFCB = PtrCCB->PtrFCB;
    ASSERT(PtrFCB);
    PtrReqdFCB = &(PtrFCB->NTRequiredFCB);

    // Acquire the MainResource exclusively for the file stream
    ExAcquireResourceExclusiveLite(&(PtrReqdFCB->MainResource), TRUE);

    // Although this is typically not required, the sample FSD will
    // also acquire the PagingIoResource exclusively at this time
    // to conform with the resource acquisition described in the set
    // file information routine.
    ExAcquireResourceExclusiveLite(&(PtrReqdFCB->PagingIoResource), TRUE);

    return;
}

void SFsdFastIoRelCreateSec(
IN PFILE_OBJECT         FileObject)
{

    PtrSFsdFCB .            PtrFCB = NULL;
    PtrSFsdCCB              PtrCCB = NULL;
    PtrSFsdNTRequiredFCB    PtrReqdFCB = NULL;

    // Obtain a pointer to the FCB and CCB for the file stream.
    PtrCCB = (PtrSFsdCCB)(FileObject->FsContext2);
    ASSERT(PtrCCB);
    PtrFCB = PtrCCB->PtrFCB;
    ASSERT(PtrFCB);
    PtrReqdFCB = &(PtrFCB->NTRequiredFCB);

    // Release the PagingIoResource for the file stream
    SFsdReleaseResource(&(PtrReqdFCB->PagingIoResource));

    // Release the MainResource for the file stream
    SFsdReleaseResource(&(PtrReqdFCB->MainResource));

    return;
}
```

The **FastIoDetachDevice** callback will be covered in the next chapter when we discuss filter driver design and implementation.

AcquireForModWrite/ReleaseForModWrite

Before NT Version 4.0 was released, this callback did not exist. As discussed in detail in earlier chapters, it is extremely important for the NT VMM, the NT Cache

Manager, and the FSD implementations to ensure that resources are acquired in the correct order. This callback exists precisely to ensure that the resource acquisition hierarchy is maintained.

In Chapter 5, we discussed the design and philosophy of the modified/mapped page writer threads used by the NT VMM to asynchronously flush dirty pages, allowing the VMM to reuse these pages for other applications. When an asynchronous I/O request is issued to the FSD, the file system implementation may need to acquire the `MainResource` and/or the `PagingIoResource`. To pre-acquire the appropriate resources and maintain the locking hierarchy across modules, the NT VMM issues a call to the FSRTL `FsRtlAcquireFileForModWrite()` support routine.

In Windows NT Version 3.51, the FSRTL routine simply acquired the file resources directly. In order to determine which resource to acquire (`MainResource` or `PagingIoResource`) and if the resource needed to be acquired shared or exclusively, the FSRTL package depended on the following flag values set by the FSD in the `CommonFCBHeader` associated with the file stream:

```
#define FSRTL_FLAG_ACQUIRE_MAIN_RSRC_EX (0x08)
#define FSRTL_FLAG_ACQUIRE_MAIN_RSRC_SH (0x10)
```

If the flag `FSRTL_FLAG_ACQUIRE_MAIN_RSRC_EX` is set by an FSD in the `CommonFCBHeader` for the file stream, the `FsRtlAcquireFileForModWrite()` routine acquires the `MainResource` exclusively; a flag value of `FSRTL_FLAG_ACQUIRE_MAIN_RSRC_SH` results in the routine acquiring the `MainResource` shared. If neither flag is set, the routine acquires the `PagingIoResource` shared if the a resource is present. Finally, in the most degenerate case of no flag having been set and the `PagingIoResource` pointer in the `CommonFCBHeader` being NULL, the routine does not acquire any resource at all.

The fundamental rule that an FSD is supposed to follow in setting appropriate flag values is that the flag value cannot be changed unless the FSD acquired both resources before attempting the change; or in other words, if the FSRTL package managed to acquire either of the two resources, it is guaranteed that the flag value would stay constant.

You may wish to note that the FASTFAT file system does not appear to set any flag values at all in Version 3.51, (preferring to rely on the default behavior instead), and the only native FSD implementation that seems to care about these flag values and actively modify them is the NTFS file system. Furthermore, it should not surprise you to know the `FsRtlAcquireFileForModWrite()` jumps through a lot of hoops to acquire the right resource. It initially examines the flag values in an unsafe fashion and attempts to acquire the designated resource (without waiting). Once a resource is acquired, it reexamines the flag values—since they could have changed between the time they were examined in an unsafe fashion and when the resource was actually acquired—and retries the resource acquisition after releasing the original resource, if the flag values have changed. All of this is done within a `while(TRUE) {...}` loop construct.

There were other problems with this implementation as well. It was sometimes possible for the VMM to want to acquire the FSD resource for write operations that would extend the valid data length. Unfortunately, if the FSD indicated that the `MainResource` should be acquired shared, following the FSD's instructions possibly leads to a deadlock situation when the write request is actually dispatched to the FSD. Therefore, the `FsRtlAcquirefFileForModWrite()` routine checks for the condition where the ending offset (starting-offset + write-length −1) exceeds the current valid data length, and internally ignores the FSD's instructions, preferring instead to acquire the `MainResource` exclusively.

It appears as though with Version 4.0 of the operating system, the I/O subsystem designers have realized just how messy, and FSD-dependent, the preceding implementation is.* Therefore, they implemented the `AcquireForModWrite()` callback, invoked by the `FsRtlAcquireFileForModWrite()` routine. Your FSD should acquire the appropriate resources in response to the callback and also return a pointer to the resource acquired in the `ResourceToRelease` argument passed in to your callback. The `ReleaseForModWrite()` callback will be invoked later by the VMM and your FSD can use the `ResourceToRelease` argument to determine which resource should be released.†

AcquireForCcFlush/ReleaseForCcFlush

This callback was added with Windows NT Version 4.0. It supports invocations to `CcFlushCache()` for a file stream by a component other the FSD. As described in Chapter 8, *The NT Cache Manager III*, the `CcFlushCache()` routine can be invoked (by an FSD) with driver resources either acquired exclusively, or left unowned. However, if the routine is invoked by a component other than an FSD, the potential for deadlock exists if FSD resources are not acquired before Cache Manager or VMM resources.

---

* The older method implicitly places a lot of faith in the FSRTL's judgment of what is the correct action to take under the different scenarios in which the routine can be invoked. This is not a particularly extensible policy, especially with the development of third-party file system implementations whose requirements could be very different from what the FSRTL expects. Therefore, letting the FSD determine what to do in response to the VMM request to preacquire resources is a step in the right direction.

† There is an additional benefit to having a callback into your FSD. You can now safely determine the thread ID of the modified/mapped page writer thread when the `AcquireForModWrite()` callback is issued and store it in the FCB, if you need such information.

Your FSD should ensure that appropriate resources have been acquired to support a subsequent paging I/O, synchronous write operation that will presumable soon follow.

Callback Example

In addition to the fast I/O dispatch routines and the fast I/O callbacks to pre-acquire FSD resources, the FSD also provides callbacks specifically for the use of the NT Cache Manager read-ahead thread and the lazy-writer thread. A pointer to an initialized **CACHE_MANAGER_CALLBACKS** structure is passed in by the FSD when invoking the **CcInitializeCacheMap()** routine (described earlier in Chapter 8). The callback's structure is defined as follows:

```
typedef struct _CACHE_MANAGER_CALLBACKS {
    PACQUIRE_FOR_LAZY_WRITE    AcquireForLazyWrite;
    PRELEASE_FROM_LAZY_WRITE   ReleaseFromLazyWrite;
    PACQUIRE_FOR_READ_AHEAD    AcquireForReadAhead;
    PRELEASE_FROM_READ_AHEAD   ReleaseFromReadAhead;
} CACHE_MANAGER_CALLBACKS, *PCACHE_MANAGER_CALLBACKS;
```

where:

```
typedef
BOOLEAN (*PACQUIRE_FOR_LAZY_WRITE) (
    IN PVOID        Context,
    IN BOOLEAN      Wait
);

typedef
VOID (*PRELEASE_FROM_LAZY_WRITE) (
    IN PVOID        Context
);

typedef
BOOLEAN (*PACQUIRE_FOR_READ_AHEAD) (
    IN PVOID        Context,
    IN BOOLEAN      Wait
);

typedef
VOID (*PRELEASE_FROM_READ_AHEAD) (
    IN PVOID        Context
);
```

The **AcquireForLazyWrite** and **ReleaseFromLazyWrite** callbacks are invoked by the NT Cache Manager lazy-writer thread to maintain resource acquisition hierarchy across the Cache Manager and the FSD modules. Similarly, the **AcquireForReadAhead** and **ReleaseFromReadAhead** callbacks are invoked by the read-ahead component of the NT Cache Manager.

By now, you should have a very good understanding of the motivating forces behind the design and implementation of these callback functions (i.e., to avoid deadlock situations due to the incorrect sequence of resource acquisitions). Here are examples of the `AcquireForLazyWrite` and `ReleaseFromLazyWrite` callback functions for the sample FSD:

```
BOOLEAN SFsdAcqLazyWrite(
IN PVOID                        Context,
IN BOOLEAN                      Wait)
{
    BOOLEAN                 ReturnedStatus = TRUE;

    PtrSFsdFCB              PtrFCB = NULL;
    PtrSFsdCCB              PtrCCB = NULL;
    PtrSFsdNTRequiredFCB    PtrReqdFCB = NULL;

    // The context is whatever we passed to the Cache Manager when invoking
    // the CcInitializeCacheMaps() function. In the case of the sample FSD
    // implementation, this context is a pointer to the CCB structure.

    ASSERT(Context);
    PtrCCB = (PtrSFsdCCB)(Context);
    ASSERT(PtrCCB->NodeIdentifier.NodeType == SFSD_NODE_TYPE_CCB);

    PtrFCB = PtrCCB->PtrFCB;
    ASSERT(PtrFCB);
    PtrReqdFCB = &(PtrFCB->NTRequiredFCB);

    // Acquire the MainResource in the FCB exclusively. Then, set the
    // lazy-writer thread id in the FCB structure for identification when
    // an actual write request is received by the FSD.
    // Note: The lazy-writer typically always sets WAIT to TRUE.
    if (!ExAcquireResourceExclusiveLite(&(PtrReqdFCB->MainResource),
                                                    Wait)) {
        ReturnedStatus = FALSE;
    } else {
        // Now, set the lazy-writer thread id.
        ASSERT(!(PtrFCB->LazyWriterThreadID));
        PtrFCB->LazyWriterThreadID = (unsigned int)(PsGetCurrentThread());
    }

    // If your FSD needs to perform some special preparations in
    // anticipation of receiving a lazy-writer request, do so now.

    return(ReturnedStatus);
}

void SFsdRelLazyWrite(
IN PVOID                        Context)
{
    BOOLEAN                 ReturnedStatus = TRUE;

    PtrSFsdFCB              PtrFCB = NULL;
```

```
PtrSFsdCCB             PtrCCB = NULL;
PtrSFsdNTRequiredFCB   PtrReqdFCB = NULL;

// The context is whatever we passed to the Cache Manager when invoking
// the CcInitializeCacheMaps() function. In the case of the sample FSD
// implementation, this context is a pointer to the CCB structure.

ASSERT(Context);
PtrCCB = (PtrSFsdCCB)(Context);
ASSERT(PtrCCB->NodeIdentifier.NodeType == SFSD_NODE_TYPE_CCB);

PtrFCB = PtrCCB->PtrFCB;
ASSERT(PtrFCB);
PtrReqdFCB = &(PtrFCB->NTRequiredFCB);

// Remove the current thread id from the FCB and release the
// MainResource.
ASSERT((PtrFCB->LazyWriterThreadID) ==
                        (unsigned int)PsGetCurrentThread());
PtrFCB->LazyWriterThreadID = 0;

// Release the acquired resource.
SFsdReleaseResource(&(PtrReqdFCB->MainResource));

// Your FSD should undo whatever else seems appropriate at this time.

return;
}
```

Typically, the Cache Manager lazy-writer and read-ahead threads always set `Wait` to TRUE before invoking the FSD callback routines.

Dispatch Routine: Flush File Buffers

The flush file buffers dispatch routine is invoked by a user process to try to ensure that all of the cached information for a file stream or for a group of files has been either written out to secondary storage or flushed across the network to the server node.

Logical Steps Involved

The following logical steps are executed by a file system upon receiving a flush file buffers request:

1. The file system driver must obtain pointers to internal data structures for the object on which the flush file buffers operation has been requested.

   The flush file buffers invocation can be made for three types of objects:

— An open file stream (ordinary file)

— An open directory

— An open volume object representing the mounted logical volume

The FSD typically has different responses for a flush request on each of these object types.

2. If the flush buffers request is for an open file stream, the FSD should typically acquire the FCB exclusively and request that the Cache Manager flush the system cache for the file stream synchronously.

3. If the flush buffers request is on an open directory object, most FSD implementations simply return success without really doing anything.

   The exception to this is if the flush request is made for the root directory of the mounted logical volume. In this case, an FSD should treat the request as if it were a flush request for all open files on the mounted volume. The next step outlines the FSD's response in this situation.

4. If the flush buffers request is made for an open volume object, the FSD should try to flush all open file streams on the mounted logical volume to secondary storage devices.

   Typically, the caller would like to ensure that cached information for modified files residing on the logical volume being flushed is written out to secondary storage before this routine returns control. This is the behavior implemented by the native NT file system drivers as well. Note that a flush buffers request on the root directory is always treated in the same manner as a flush buffers request on the volume object representing a mounted logical volume.

5. Finally, it would be prudent for the FSD to pass the flush file buffers request on to the lower-level disk/network drivers, ensuring that any requests queued there would be processed immediately.

The following pseudocode illustrates how your FSD could implement the flush file buffers dispatch routine. Note that the code assumes the data structures to be those defined by the sample FSD. You can, however, substitute your own data structures (and associated fields) quite easily instead:

```
get pointer to FCB/VCB from file object;
if (VCB) {
    flush the volume;
    (this involves flushing all open file streams (see below for example),
     updating the directory entries, updating timestamp values,
     flushing directories, flushing log files, flushing bitmaps,
     and any other in-memory information that you may wish to write
     to disk)
} else {
```

```
    if (PtrFCB->FCBFlags & SFSD_FCB_ROOT_DIRECTORY) {
        // Treat this exactly the same as a flush volume request.
        flush the volume;
    } else if (!(PtrFCB->FCBFlags & SFSD_FCB_DIRECTORY)) {
        // Flush the file stream from the system cache.
        // Note that the following operation is inherently synchronous;
        // therefore, if the caller did not wish to block, you should
        // have posted the request earlier.
        PtrReqdFCB = &(PtrFCB->NTRequiredFCB);
        CcFlushCache(&(PtrReqdFCB->SectionObject), NULL, 0,
                        &(PtrIrp->IoStatus));
        // Results of the operation are returned by the Cache Manager
        // in the IoStatus structure.
        RC = PtrIrp->IoStatus.Status;
        // All done as far as the Cache Manager is concerned.
        // Now, you may wish to update the associated directory
        // entry for the file stream (e.g., with the latest file
        // size, timestamp values, etc.) and flush that to disk.
    }
    // We ignore flush requests for normal directories (just as the
    // native FSD implementations do).
}

// Now that the FSD has completed performing its processing, you
// should forward the flush request to lower-level drivers.
// CAUTION: Some drivers will return STATUS_INVALID_DEVICE_REQUEST
// to you. You should "eat-up" that error and simply return the actual
// status from your flush attempts to the caller. To do this you will
// also have to set a completion routine before invoking the lower-level
// driver.
```

Dispatch Routine: Volume Information

There are two kinds of volume information requests that your FSD should handle:

- Requests to get (query) volume information
- Requests to set (modify) volume information

Let us examine the logical steps involved in processing each of these two types of volume information requests.

Logical Steps Involved

The I/O stack location contains the following structures relevant to processing the query volume information and the set volume information requests issued to an FSD:

```
typedef struct _IO_STACK_LOCATION {

    // ...
```

```
union {

    //...

    // System service parameters for:  NtQueryVolumeInformationFile
    struct {
        ULONG Length;
        FS_INFORMATION_CLASS FsInformationClass;
    } QueryVolume;

    // System service parameters for:  NtSetVolumeInformationFile
    struct {
        ULONG Length;
        FS_INFORMATION_CLASS FsInformationClass;
    } SetVolume;

    // ...
} Parameters;

// ...

} IO_STACK_LOCATION, *PIO_STACK_LOCATION;
```

The type of volume information request dispatched to an FSD can be determined by examining the major function code contained in the request packet. The two major function codes of interest are `IRP_MJ_QUERY_VOLUME_INFORMATION` and `IRP_MJ_SET_VOLUME_INFORMATION`. Of course, your FSD could have separate dispatch routines to handle each kind of volume information request, unlike the sample FSD presented in this book, in which case the appropriate request type would be dispatched to the correct file system driver function.

IRP_MJ_QUERY_VOLUME_INFORMATION

The I/O Manager identifies the kind of information requested in the `FS_INFORMATION_CLASS` enumerated type value, supplied in the current stack location of the query volume information IRP. Note that the Windows NT I/O subsystem allows any caller to obtain logical volume information. Furthermore, the caller can supply a handle to any open object associated with the logical volume (i.e., a file object representing an open instance of the logical volume itself, a file object representing an open instance of a file or directory contained in the logical volume, or a file object representing an open instance of the target device on which the logical volume has been mounted).

The following volume information request types should be supported by your FSD:

`FileFsVolumeInformation` (enumerated type value = 1)

The caller expects information about the volume to be returned in the `FILE_FS_VOLUME_INFORMATION` structure:

```
typedef struct _FILE_FS_VOLUME_INFORMATION {
    LARGE_INTEGER               VolumeCreationTime;
    ULONG                       VolumeSerialNumber;
    ULONG                       VolumeLabelLength;
    BOOLEAN                     SupportsObjects;
    WCHAR                       VolumeLabel[1];
} FILE_FS_VOLUME_INFORMATION, *PFILE_FS_VOLUME_INFORMATION;
```

The fields are quite self-explanatory. The serial number is expected to be a unique integer value identifying the mounted logical volume. The volume label can be any string identifier associated with the logical volume. Note that it is possible that the buffer supplied by the caller may not be large enough to contain the entire volume label, in which case your FSD should copy over as much of the label as it can and return a status code of **STATUS_BUFFER_OVERFLOW**, indicating to the caller that not all of the information could be returned.

FileFsSizeInformation (enumerated type value = 3)

The caller expects information about the volume to be returned in the **FILE_FS_SIZE_INFORMATION** structure:

```
typedef struct _FILE_FS_SIZE_INFORMATION {
    LARGE_INTEGER               TotalAllocationUnits;
    LARGE_INTEGER               AvailableAllocationUnits;
    ULONG                       SectorsPerAllocationUnit;
    ULONG                       BytesPerSector;
} FILE_FS_SIZE_INFORMATION, *PFILE_FS_SIZE_INFORMATION;
```

As you can see, the kind of information expected by the caller is fairly generic and your FSD should be able to return some kind of sensible values that can translate into a valid total volume size.*

FileFsDeviceInformation (enumerated type value = 4)

The caller expects to receive information about the type of physical or logical device on which the logical volume has been mounted:

```
typedef struct _FILE_FS_DEVICE_INFORMATION {
    DEVICE_TYPE     DeviceType;
    ULONG           Characteristics;
} FILE_FS_DEVICE_INFORMATION, *PFILE_FS_DEVICE_INFORMATION;
```

The **DeviceType** field value can be set by your FSD to an appropriate device type. For example, CDFS specifies the **DeviceType** value as **FILE_DEVICE_CD_ROM**, while FASTFAT and NTFS use **FILE_DEVICE_DISK** instead. For a network redirector, the **DeviceType** field can be set to an appropriate value depending upon the type of connection made. If, for example, the query volume information request is issued using a file object

---

* For read-only volumes (e.g., for those managed by CDFS), the AvailableAllocationUnits value is set to 0.

representing an open instance of the network redirector itself, the value could well be set to FILE_DEVICE_NETWORK_FILE_SYSTEM.

The Characteristics field should be set to an appropriate value from the following (one or more flag values can be set):

```
// Volume mounted on removable media.
#define FILE_REMOVABLE_MEDIA        0x00000001
#define FILE_READ_ONLY_DEVICE       0x00000002
#define FILE_FLOPPY_DISKETTE        0x00000004
#define FILE_WRITE_ONCE_MEDIA       0x00000008
#define FILE_REMOTE_DEVICE          0x00000010
#define FILE_DEVICE_IS_MOUNTED      0x00000020
#define FILE_VIRTUAL_VOLUME         0x00000040
```

Note that if you have designed a network redirector and if you set the FILE_REMOTE_DEVICE flag in the Characteristics field, the logical volume cannot be reshared across the LAN Manager Network.

FileFsAttributeInformation (enumerated type value = 5)

The structure used to request file system attribute information is defined as follows:

```
typedef struct _FILE_FS_ATTRIBUTE_INFORMATION {
    ULONG           FileSystemAttributes;
    LONG            MaximumComponentNameLength;
    ULONG           FileSystemNameLength;
    WCHAR           FileSystemName[1];
} FILE_FS_ATTRIBUTE_INFORMATION, *PFILE_FS_ATTRIBUTE_INFORMATION;
```

The file system attributes can be one or more of the following (note that additions to these values are likely with different versions of the operating system that add additional functionality):

```
#define FILE_CASE_SENSITIVE_SEARCH   0x00000001
#define FILE_CASE_PRESERVED_NAMES    0x00000002
#define FILE_UNICODE_ON_DISK         0x00000004
#define FILE_PERSISTENT_ACLS         0x00000008
#define FILE_FILE_COMPRESSION        0x00000010
#define FILE_VOLUME_IS_COMPRESSED    0x00008000
```

NTFS, for example, sets all of these attribute values except for the FILE_VOLUME_IS_COMPRESSED.

The MaximumComponentNameLength field is typically set to 255 characters by most native FSD implementations. Your FSD can set this field to any appropriate value. The FileSystemName field simply identifies the current FSD processing the request. NTFS, for example, will set the contents of the buffer to NTFS.

If the buffer supplied by the caller is too small to contain all of the information your FSD wishes to return, your driver should return the STATUS_

BUFFER_OVERFLOW return code and copy in as many bytes of information as it possibly can.

There are other volume information request types that have not yet been fully implemented by the I/O Manager, and they are not yet completely supported, even by the native FSD implementations. For example, there are query volume information types such as `FileFsQuotaQueryInformation` (enumerated type value = 6 in Version 3.51 and value = 7 in Version 4.0) and a corresponding `FileFsQuotaSetInformation` (enumerated type value = 7 in Version 3.51 and value = 8 in Version 4.0), which will become part of the set volume information request. Your FSD should currently return **STATUS_INVALID_PARAMETER** for all query volume information request types other those previously defined.

The sequence of steps followed in processing a query volume information request is extremely simple:

1. Obtain a pointer to the volume control block for which the request operation has been dispatched.

2. Acquire the VCB shared.

3. Find out the type of information requested and get a pointer to the caller-supplied buffer from the current stack location.

   The following fields give you this information:

   — The **Parameters.QueryVolume.FsInformationClass** field from the current stack location will tell you the type of information requested.

   — The I/O Manager always supplies a system virtual address for a buffer allocated by the I/O Manager.

     A pointer to this buffer can be obtained from the **AssociatedIrp.SystemBuffer** field in the IRP. The length of this buffer is given by the **Parameters.QueryVolume.Length** field in the current stack location.

4. Ensure that the length of the buffer supplied is at least equal to the size of the associated structure (appropriate for the type of volume information request).

   If the amount of information your FSD returns exceeds the length of the supplied buffer, then return **STATUS_BUFFER_OVERFLOW** *after* filling in as much information as the supplied buffer can contain.

5. Complete the IRP after releasing any resources that were acquired.

IRP_MJ_SET_VOLUME_INFORMATION

A user can also request that volume attributes should be modified. Currently, the only set volume information type request that your FSD should consider supporting is a request to set the label for the logical volume. This label is a string identifier, supplied by the user so as to be able to identify the volume more easily. Although other set volume information request types have been defined (e.g., `FileFsQuotasetInformation`), they have not been well-defined yet, and they are not supported by the native FSD implementations.

The sequence of steps executed in response to a set volume information request closely mirrors those followed by the query volume information described previously.

1. The FSD obtains a pointer to the VCB from the file object supplied with the request.

2. The VCB should be acquired exclusively.

3. The type of request and a pointer to the caller supplied buffer can be obtained from the IRP.

   The request type for a set volume information request can be determined from the `Parameters.SetVolume.FsInformationClass` field in the current I/O stack location. Currently, the only legitimate request type is `FileFsLabelInformation` (enumerated type value = 2). The type of structure passed in by the caller for this request type is defined as follows:

   ```
   typedef struct _FILE_FS_LABEL_INFORMATION {
       ULONG       VolumeLabelLength;
       WCHAR       VolumeLabel[1];
   } FILE_FS_LABEL_INFORMATION, *PFILE_FS_LABEL_INFORMATION;
   ```

   A pointer to the system buffer allocated by the I/O Manager can be obtained from the `AssociatedIrp.SystemBuffer` field in the IRP. The length of the system-allocated buffer can be obtained from the `Parameters.Set-Volume.Length` field.

4. After validating that the length of the caller-supplied buffer is correct, the FSD should perform appropriate operations to update the label (string) associated with the logical volume.

5. If the request type is anything other than what is supported by the FSD, an error code of `STATUS_INVALID_PARAMETER` should be returned to the caller.

6. The IRP can now be completed after releasing the VCB resource.

The actual code implementing a query/set volume information request is very similar to that shown in Chapter 10, *Writing A File System Driver II*, for handling query/set file information requests. Study that code example for details on how the FSD should structure the query/set volume information dispatch entry routine to execute the logical steps previously detailed.

Dispatch Routine: Byte-Range Locks

Windows NT supports mandatory byte-range file locks. The term *mandatory* implies that it is the responsibility of the FSD to ensure that access to a byte range by a thread during I/O operations is validated against any byte-range locks that have been granted for the file stream. Therefore, two or more threads do not have to actively cooperate in order to synchronize access to the file stream; as long as one of the threads is careful about obtaining the appropriate byte-range locks on the file, it can be ensured that data access (read or write) by any other thread belonging to other processes will be closely monitored. If such access is not allowed by the nature of the lock granted (and depending on the type of access requested), the FSD will deny the I/O operation with an error code of STATUS_ FILE_LOCK_CONFLICT.

The native NT FSD implementations do not appear to check for byte-range lock conflicts encountered during paging I/O operations. However, if your FSD is even stricter about checking for locked byte ranges and returns the STATUS_FILE_ LOCK_CONFLICT error code to the VMM, the VMM, in turn, will either raise an exception, informing the caller about the error, if this happened to be synchronous paging I/O request; or will pop up an error message box, indicating loss of write-behind data in the case of an asynchronous I/O write operation.

Byte-range locks in general are associated with processes and *not* with individual threads within a process. Therefore, if a single thread in the process acquires a specific byte-range lock, this will not prevent other threads within the same process from continuing to access the locked byte range even if the type of access performed conflicts with the nature of the granted byte-range lock. The byte lock obtained will prevent conflicting accesses by threads belonging to processes other than the one that obtained the lock.

NOTE   It is possible for threads within a process to obtain thread-specific byte-range locks by specifying a Key value when performing the lock operation. The Key argument is described later in this section. However, you should note that this method is often employed by a thread to ensure that the byte-range can be accessed only in a very selective manner by other threads.

The Windows NT I/O subsystem defines the following kinds of byte-range locks:

Read locks obtained for a specific byte range

> Multiple processes can potentially obtain a read lock concurrently for the same byte range or for an overlapping byte range on the same file stream. The read lock simply guarantees the caller that no write/modify operations

are allowed on the file stream as long as the read lock is maintained by the process.

Write (exclusive) lock obtained for a byte range

Write locks are exclusive locks (i.e., once a process acquires a write lock for a specific byte range, no other process is allowed either to read or write in that byte range). By definition, granted write locks are non-overlapping.

Different processes can concurrently lock different byte ranges in the same file stream. It is also quite possible (and not at all unusual) for a thread to obtain a byte-range lock starting and/or extending well beyond the current end-of-file. This is simply a means whereby the process can ensure that appending the file stream can be performed in some sort of synchronized fashion.

Note that byte-range locking can possibly allow a process to synchronize access to the byte stream even across multiple nodes, as long as the network protocol providing remote file system access supports the byte-range locking protocol. For example, the LAN Manager redirector client and server support the byte-range locking protocol. The NFS (Network File System) protocol supports only advisory byte-range locks, whereas the DFS (Distributed File System) protocol can be used to obtain mandatory file locks.

It may be obvious to you by now that supporting byte-range file locks is not really an FSD-specific operation. In fact, it can be implemented in a fairly generic fashion, allowing multiple, installable file systems to take advantage of common code. The Windows NT I/O subsystem designers recognized this and have actually implemented file-lock-supporting code in the FSRTL. These routines are used by the native NT FSD implementations. Unfortunately, for reasons that seem incomprehensible, the developers do not want to encourage third-party FSD designers to take advantage of such support provided in the FSRTL. This may (I hope) change in the future.

In this section, we saw how to provide support for file lock operations if you have to implement such support yourself. Obviously, if any FSD-independent code is provided by Microsoft for the support of byte-range lock requests, you should utilize that code instead.

Type of File Lock Requests Received by an FSD

Broadly speaking, the FSD will receive two types of requests related to byte-range lock operations:

Requests to obtain a byte-range lock for a file stream

The request could specify either a read or a write lock. Furthermore, the caller could specify either a blocking or nonblocking lock request. If the caller agrees to block, the IRP describing this request is not completed until the lock is granted or the IRP is canceled (which could be due to the caller closing the file handle). If the caller does not wish to wait for the lock to be granted and if some other thread has already acquired a conflicting lock that would prevent the current request for a byte-range lock from being completed successfully, an error code of `STATUS_LOCK_NOT_GRANTED` is returned to the caller.

Requests to unlock one or all byte-range locks acquired by the process for a specific file object

The caller can request that a specific, uniquely identifiable locked byte range be unlocked, or the caller can request that all byte-range locks on the file stream acquired using a specific file object and owned by the calling process be unlocked.

When a process closes all open handles associated with a file object for a file stream, if the process had ever acquired any byte range locks using that file object on the file stream, the I/O Manager will issue an unlock-all type of byte-range unlock request on the file stream, on behalf of the process closing the handle to the file stream. Similarly, whenever an FSD receives a cleanup request on a file stream for a specific file object, the FSD is expected to automatically unlock all byte-range locks that may have been acquired by the calling process using the file object for which the cleanup is being received.*

Lock requests

The lock request is dispatched to the FSD dispatch routine serving as the `IRP_MJ_LOCK_CONTROL` major function entry point. The lock request is distinguished by a minor function code of `IRP_MN_LOCK`. The arguments supplied to the FSD as part of the lock request are as follows:

Pointer to the file object

The FSD can easily obtain the file object pointer from the IRP for the open file stream on which the lock operation has been requested. Note that most FSD implementations will reject a byte-range file lock request if the object on which the lock has been requested is not an open, ordinary file. Therefore, directories, open logical volumes, and other such open objects typically cannot be locked with byte-range locks.

---

* There is a subtle point here that you must be aware of: the FSD must not unlock all byte-range locks owned by the process on the file stream associated with the file object on which the cleanup request has been received. Rather, only those byte-range locks must be unlocked for which the file object and the process ID both match.

ByteOffset

The starting offset for the lock request. This is contained in the `Parame-ters.LockControl.Length` field in the current stack location for the I/O request packet. As noted earlier, this offset could be well beyond the current end-of-file.

Length

The number of bytes that should be locked for the file stream. Once again, note that the `ByteOffset` value plus the `Length` value could extend well beyond the current end-of-file. This is a legitimate situation for lock requests.

Key

This is an unsigned long value that the requesting thread can associate with the lock to be granted. If the lock is granted, subsequent accesses to the byte range will only be allowed if the process ID and the key value match. You may recall from the discussion on read/write requests, presented in Chapter 9, *Writing a File System Driver I*, that the requesting thread can supply a `Key` argument with the I/O request. That argument is subsequently used when checking whether or not the I/O request will be allowed to proceed.

This is a method where a thread in a process can potentially exclude even other threads in the same process from accessing the locked byte range.

Process ID

Although not explicitly supplied as part of the IRP sent to the FSD, the FSD can easily determine the current process ID for the process requesting the lock operation, by using the `IoGetRequestorProcess()` I/O Manager service routine. This routine accepts a pointer to the IRP as an argument and returns a pointer to the process structure (of type **PEPROCESS**).

FailImmediately

This **BOOLEAN** value can be obtained by checking for the presence of the `SL_FAIL_IMMEDIATELY` flag in the `Flags` field of the current stack location in the IRP. The presence of the flag indicates that `FailImmediately` should be set to TRUE, which in turn means that the caller would not like to wait if the lock cannot be immediately granted.

The absence of the flag indicates that the caller does not mind waiting for the lock request to be granted at some later time. In this case, set the value of `FailImmediately` to FALSE.

WriteLockRequested

The presence of the `SL_EXCLUSIVE_LOCK` flag in the `Flags` field of the current I/O stack location indicates that the caller wishes an exclusive (write) lock for the byte range specified. In this case, set the value of `WriteLockRe-quested` to TRUE.

The absence of the SL_EXCLUSIVE_LOCK flag indicates that the caller wishes to obtain a read (shared) byte-range lock only, and therefore the value of WriteLockRequested should be set to FALSE.

Unlock requests

The unlock request is distinguished by any one of the following minor function code values:

IRP_MN_UNLOCK_SINGLE

The FSD must unlock only one byte-range lock. The lock that would be unlocked (if found) is the single matching lock for which all of the following passed-in parameters match:

— Process ID associated with the lock, identifying the owner of the byte-range lock

— File object

— Starting offset

— Length in bytes of the locked range

— Key value

If any of the parameters listed here do not match, then no unlock operation will be performed.

IRP_MN_UNLOCK_ALL

This is the brute-force approach employed by a process to unlock all of the byte-range locks acquired by any thread associated with the process using the target file object. In response to this request, the FSD will unlock all byte-range locks for which the following match:

— Process ID associated with the lock, identifying the owner of the byte-range lock

— File object

This request is typically sent by the I/O Manager to an FSD when a process closes all open handles associated with a file object, but there are other open handles associated with the same file object belonging to other processes. If all handles for a file object have been closed, the I/O Manager skips sending the unlock-all request, since the expectation is that the FSD will generate this request internally in response to a cleanup request received by the file system driver.

IRP_MN_UNLOCK_ALL_BY_KEY

A thread or a process can unlock all byte-range locks for a file object owned by all threads belonging to the process, as long as the supplied key value and the key stored with the byte-range lock match. Typically, this method is slightly less brute-force than the previous one, since this can also be used by a thread to close a specific set of byte-range locks all identified by the same key value.

In response to this request, the FSD will unlock byte-range locks for which all of the following match:

— Process ID associated with the lock, identifying the owner of the byte-range lock

— File object

— Key value

In order to determine the parameters supplied with the unlock IRP, use exactly the same fields (and methods) as described earlier for the lock request operations.

Structures Required for File Lock Support

To implement byte-range lock support in your FSD, you will typically require some variation of the following structures:

```
typedef struct SFsdFileLockAnchor {
    LIST_ENTRY            GrantedFileLockList;
    LIST_ENTRY            PendingFileLockList;
} SFsdFileLockAnchor, *PtrSFsdFileLockAnchor;

typedef struct SFsdFileLockInfo {
    SFsdIdentifier                NodeIdentifier;
    uint32                        FileLockFlags;
    PVOID                         OwningProcess;
    LARGE_INTEGER                 StartingOffset;
    LARGE_INTEGER                 Length;
    LARGE_INTEGER                 EndingOffset;
    ULONG                         Key;
    BOOLEAN                       ExclusiveLock;
    PIRP                          PendingIRP;
    LIST_ENTRY                    NextFileLockEntry;
} SFsdFileLockInfo, *PtrSFsdFileLockInfo;

#define      SFSD_BYTE_LOCK_NOT_FROM_ZONE        (0x80000000)
#define      SFSD_BYTE_LOCK_IS_PENDING           (0x00000001)
```

Typically, you should embed an **SFsdFileLockAnchor** structure into the FCB for the file stream. This structure serves as a list anchor for the following two linked lists:

- A list containing **SFsdFileLockInfo** structures, each of which represents a granted lock for the file stream

- A list containing **SFsdFileLockInfo** structures, each of which represents a pending lock for the file stream

The SFsdFileLockInfo structure represents an instance of a granted or pending byte-range lock request. An instance of this request is allocated whenever a byte-range lock request is received. The structure is freed only when the lock is failed immediately, the IRP is canceled (or the file handle closed) while the lock request is still queued, or an unlock operation is eventually received for a granted file lock. The OwningProcess, StartingOffset, Length, Key, and ExclusiveLock fields are initialized based upon information supplied in the byte-range lock request as described earlier.

The PendingIRP field is only valid when the request has been queued, awaiting an unlock operation. This field then points to the IRP received containing the byte-range lock request for which STATUS_PENDING was returned. The Ending-Offset field contains a value that is computed and stored for convenience.

The NextFileLockEntry field is used to queue the SFsdFileLockInfo structure to either the GrantedFileLockList or the PendingFileLockList in the SFsdFileLockAnchor structure contained in the FCB for the file stream on which the lock operation has been requested.

The FileLockFlags field is used internally to determine where the structure has been allocated from and also to mark a pending lock request for easy identification.

Logical Steps Involved

The I/O stack location contains the following structure relevant to processing the lock control request issued to an FSD:

```
typedef struct _IO_STACK_LOCATION {

    // ...

    union {

        //...

        // System service parameters for:  NtLockFile/NtUnlockFile
        struct {
            PLARGE_INTEGER Length;
            ULONG Key;
            LARGE_INTEGER ByteOffset;
        } LockControl;

        // ...
    } Parameters;

    // ...

} IO_STACK_LOCATION, *PIO_STACK_LOCATION;
```

Processing a file lock or unlock request is quite a simple operation to implement. The following steps outline the processing required for file lock operations:

1. Obtain the parameters described earlier that are supplied with a typical byte-range lock request.

2. Obtain FSD-specific pointers to the FCB and CCB structures for the file stream.

3. Acquire the FCB `MainResource` exclusively.

4. Allocate and initialize a new `SFsdFileLockInfo` structure to contain the caller-supplied parameters.

5. Check if any conflicting locks have been previously granted.

   For an exclusive lock request, the FSD must check if any portion of the requested byte range overlaps with a byte range on which a file lock had been previously granted. To check this, the FSD can simply scan through all of the granted file locks identified by the `SFsdFileLockInfo` structures linked to the `GrantedFileLockList` in the FCB.

   For a shared lock request, the FCB should ensure that no portion of the requested byte range overlaps with a previously granted exclusively locked range. Overlaps with previously granted shared byte-range locks are acceptable if the current request also wants to obtain a lock for shared (read) access.

6. If no conflict has been found, queue the `SFsdFileLockInfo` structure to the `GrantedFileLockList` to indicate that a new file lock has been granted and complete the IRP with `STATUS_SUCCESS` returned to the caller.

7. If a conflict is detected, check whether the caller is prepared to wait to obtain the file lock.

   If the caller is not prepared to wait (i.e., if `FailImmediately` is set to TRUE), then complete the IRP with a status code of `STATUS_LOCK_NOT_GRANTED`. Otherwise, queue the IRP to the `PendingFileLockList` list anchor, contained within the `SFsdFileLockAnchor` structure in the FCB.

   To properly queue the request, initialize the `PendingIRP` field in the `SFsdFileLockInfo` structure to point to the IRP sent to the FSD by the I/O Manager for the file lock request. Also set the `SFSD_BYTE_LOCK_IS_PENDING` flag value in the `FileLockFlags` field. Mark the IRP itself as pending, set a cancellation routine for the IRP, and return a status code of `STATUS_PENDING` to the I/O Manager.

   The expectation is that for queued lock requests, the FSD will complete the request whenever the lock is granted (i.e., whenever the conflicting conditions have been removed).

8. If any file locks have been granted, be sure to update the `IsFastIoPossible` field value to `FastIoIsNotPossible` in the `CommonFCBHeader` for the file stream.

9. Release the FCB `MainResource` and return control back to the I/O Manager.

To process a byte-range unlock request, the FSD typically performs the following logical steps:

1. Obtain required parameters, depending upon the type of unlock request.

   For example, for a `IRP_MN_UNLOCK_SINGLE` request, the FSD must get all of the information, described earlier, that is required to uniquely identify the single byte-range lock for which the unlock request has been received. However, for the case of `IRP_MN_UNLOCK_ALL`, the FSD simply needs to identify the process requesting the unlock operation and the file object for which the unlock operation has been requested.

2. Obtain FSD-specific pointers to the FCB and CCB structures for the file stream.

3. Acquire the FCB `MainResource` exclusively.

4. Scan through all of the `SFsdFileLockInfo` structures linked to the `GrantedFileLockList` list head in the FCB.

   The intent here is simple. If any matching file-lock structures are encountered, the unlock operation is processed for the structure. Processing the unlock operation is simple since it only involves unlinking the structure from the `GrantedFileLockList` and freeing up the allocated structure.

WARNING   Whenever the unlock-all request is issued to the FSD, your driver must perform one additional step. It must scan through the `PendingFileLockList`, searching for any pending, matching file-lock requests. If such requests are found, your driver must complete the pending IRP (waiting for the byte-range lock) after removing any cancellation routine that may have been set, and then the FSD should unlink the `SFsdFileLockInfo` structure from the `PendingFileLockList` linked list and free it.

---

5. Go through all of the entries in the `PendingFileLockList` to see if any locks can now be granted.

   Since some unlock operations may have been performed in the preceding step, the FSD should now scan through the list of pending lock requests to see if any of them can be granted. If any such request can be granted, the pending IRP associated with the request should be completed with `STATUS_SUCCESS` after any cancellation routine that may have been specified is unset. The `SFsdFileLockInfo` structure for the pending request (that has now been granted) should also be moved from the `PendingFileLockList` to the `GrantedFileLockList` (and the `SFSD_BYTE_LOCK_IS_PENDING` flag should be cleared).

6. If all granted file locks have been removed, be sure to update the `IsFastIo-Possible` field value to `FastIoIsPossible` or `FastIoIsquestion-able` in the `CommonFCBHeader` for the file stream.

   Note that the actual value will depend on the state of the opportunistic locks associated with the FCB.

7. Release the FCB `MainResource` and return control back to the I/O Manager.

If your FSD follows this simple sequence of steps for lock control operations, you should be able to successfully implement byte-range lock support in your file system driver implementation.

Opportunistic Locking

Opportunistic locks (oplocks, for short), simply stated, are guarantees made by a network LAN Manager server node to one or more LAN Manager client nodes about the types of file stream accesses that will be allowed on a specific file stream. They are currently valid only within the LAN Manager network environment and allow a client to perform some type of local node caching, knowing that it will be protected from returning stale data to the user because of the presence of these guarantees.

For example, consider a situation where a server on node *server_node1* shares a local drive letter *X:*. Furthermore, imagine that a user on node *client_node1* connects to this shared drive letter using the LAN Manager network and opens a regular file *foo* for both read and write access. In the absence of any server guarantees on the file stream *foo*, every read operation made by the user thread on the client node would result in the LAN Manager redirector having to issue a network read request to obtain the latest data from the server node. The LAN Manager server software, in turn, would have to request the file data from the local file system driver managing the shared logical volume corresponding to the drive letter *X:*. As you could imagine, this would lead to extremely slow access (and therefore a small throughput value) for the user on the client node.

Similarly, every write operation performed by the user on the client node would result in the LAN Manager redirector having to send the updated data to the server node across the network. The LAN Manager server software, in turn, would have to issue the write to the local file system managing the shared logical volume corresponding to the drive letter *X:* on which the file stream *foo* resides.

You can also imagine what this kind of data transfer would do in terms of saturating your network.

Needless to say, the LAN Manager redirector code on the client node could not hope to use the services of the NT Cache Manager at all, since data could never be cached locally.

To avoid this sort of constant data transfer to and from the client and server nodes participating in a LAN Manager network, the network protocol designers invented a crude form of cache support built into the protocol called opportunistic locking. This caching protocol allows the LAN Manager server to make one of three kinds of guarantees to the network redirector software on one or more client nodes:

- If an exclusive oplock is granted to a client node for a file stream, the client node is assured that no other thread, either executing locally on the server or on any other client node, will be allowed to access (or even open) the file stream for which the exclusive oplock has been obtained.

  Consider a client node that requests an open operation of file *foo* on shared drive letter *X:* served (say) by the sample FSD on the server. In response to the client node's open request made by the LAN Manager server locally on the server node (issued on behalf of the thread of the client that has actually requested the open), the sample FSD will create FCB and CCB structures, and also initialize the file object structure passed in by the I/O Manager. Note that this is no different from any other regular open operation except that the request originates on the server node in the LAN Manager server software (which executes in kernel mode) on behalf of a network client.

  Now, also imagine that after the open operation completes, the LAN Manager server asks the sample FSD to issue an exclusive oplock for the file stream *foo*. Imagine also that the sample FSD participates in the oplock protocol implementation, and therefore agrees to the request. Now, it is the responsibility of the sample FSD to notify the LAN Manager server whenever any thread requests an open for the file stream *foo* for either read or write access.* The reason for this is as follows: when the local FSD (in our case, the sample FSD) grants an oplock to the LAN Manager server on the server node, the server software, in turn, grants the oplock to the network redirector client. For the exclusive oplock, this assures the client that no other thread is actively reading or writing the same file stream. Now, the client software on the remote client node can cache file stream data on the remote node without having to worry about data consistency issues.

---

* For an exclusive oplock, the FSD is allowed to let threads open the file stream without breaking the oplock if they only open the file for read attributes and/or write attribute access.

Read caching

> The network redirector client obtains file stream data from the server node and then satisfies all read requests from the user thread locally. Data could even be returned directly from the system cache in this situation.

Write caching

> The user thread could modify the data for the file stream and the network redirector client would simply cache the modified data in the system cache on the remote node, from which it would be asynchronously written out every once in awhile.

As you can see, having an exclusive oplock on a file stream can improve network throughput tremendously.

What happens when another thread, either from the same client node, from some other client node, or locally from the server node also tries to open file *foo* for read and/or write access? The local FSD that granted the oplock (in our case, the sample FSD) will have to break the oplock (i.e., inform the LAN Manager server that it should, in turn, inform the client that the client can no longer run amuck with the file data). Since this is an exclusive oplock, where the client may actually have modified data cached remotely, the local FSD must then wait for the client node to flush (and purge) all cached information to the server. The flush results in write requests being issued to the local FSD from the server software on behalf of the remote client. Eventually, all of the data is updated on the server node, and the local FSD on the server can allow the new open to proceed. The client is also now aware that it no longer has exclusive access to the file stream and will therefore not try to modify the data remotely and keep it cached.

Note that the local FSD on the server node makes the new open request wait until all of the data has been updated by the client to the server node. The exclusive oplock is considered completely broken only after the data transfer has been completed.

- There are also shared oplocks that can be granted by a local FSD to the server software, which will grant the oplock to one or more network redirector clients.

Consider the situation where multiple threads, residing on one or more client nodes, including local threads on the server node itself, have file *foo* open for read and write access. Although the local FSD will no longer grant an exclusive oplock to the file stream *foo*, it will allow client nodes to request shared oplocks. Shared oplocks are the next best thing to exclusive oplocks because they assure the network redirector software on the client node that as long as the oplock is granted, the client node can cache data remotely for read operations.

Whenever the local FSD on the server node receives a write request, it is expected to break all of the read oplocks that were granted to all of the client nodes concurrently accessing the file stream *foo*. The oplock breaks inform the network redirector software on the client nodes that the data they have cached may no longer be valid. The network redirector software on all the client nodes will, in response to the oplock break, purge the system cache of all cached data. The next read request issued by a thread on one of the remote nodes will cause the network redirector software on that remote node to request fresh data from the server.

- Finally, due to its DOS heritage, the LAN Manager protocol also provides for batch oplocks to be granted to client nodes.

Consider the batch files (with extension *.bat*) that are simple scripts, which can be executed by the DOS shell on any Windows NT machine. The method used by the shell to execute the different statements in a batch file follows:

— The shell opens the batch file.

— It reads the next line to be executed.

— It closes the batch file.

This sequence is repeated in a loop until the entire batch file has been executed. Now consider the situation where the file opened by a remote client on the shared drive *X:* is called *foo.bat*. Furthermore, imagine that the shell on the remote client is busily going through the loop where it opens the file stream, reads a line, and closes the file stream. This would typically result in a whole lot of open/close requests flying across the network.

Instead, the network redirector client typically requests a batch oplock from the server software, which in turn requests this oplock from the FSD on the server node. Once a batch oplock has been granted, the network redirector software on the client node will no longer close the file handle in response to a close performed by the user thread (the shell) on that remote node. Instead, the network redirector will continue to keep the file open, fully expecting the user thread to come back and rerequest an open operation, once the current line read from the file stream has been executed. Furthermore, the grant of a batch oplock has the same characteristics as an exclusive oplock, where the remote client is assured that it has full and exclusive access to the file stream.

NOTE	Maintaining cache coherency across multiple nodes for shared file objects is a difficult problem to solve. A lot of research has been done on the subject, and you can consult some of the references provided at the end of the book for more information.
	There are also commercially available file system implementations that do a much more sophisticated job of maintaining cache coherence across nodes. An example of this is the Andrew File System (AFS) implementation originally designed at Carnegie Mellon University and the OSF DFS (Distributed File System) implementation.
	Although I believe that the method devised by the LAN Manager Network protocol is crude at best, it does work and supporting this feature could make remote accesses to shared logical volumes managed by your FSD much faster.

Some Points to Remember About Oplocks

When (and if) you decide to support the oplock protocol, keep the following points in mind:

- Oplocks are typically only requested by the LAN Manager server software on behalf of a remote client.

  There is nothing, however, to prevent some other component from requesting an oplock from the FSD.

- Oplocks are requested from the FSD on the server node that manages a shared logical volume.

  Although this may seem obvious, keep sight of the fact that as the FSD managing the shared logical volume on the server node, you have full control over whether or not to support the opportunistic locking protocol. Furthermore, under normal situations, oplock requests will only be issued to your FSD if the logical volume that your FSD is managing has been shared across the LAN Manager Network.

- Oplocks have funky semantics that, unfortunately, need to be maintained.

  As an example, consider the case when an exclusive oplock is being broken by the local FSD because another thread wishes to open file *foo* on the server for read and/or write access. Your FSD would typically expect to block the new open request until the client node that has the exclusive oplock completes the break by flushing all modified data back to the server.

  Typically, that is exactly what your FSD should do. However, the engineers who designed this messy protocol found that, because the LAN Manager server software on the server node has a fixed number of worker threads that it uses to service remote requests, it is theoretically possible that all of these threads get blocked on servicing open requests for file streams that have opportunistic locks acquired by some remote clients. In such situations, neither the FSD nor the server software can truly determine when the open request would complete (with either a success or failure code), since this would depend on how quickly the client nodes could flush the data back to the server. It may even be possible for the server to encounter a deadlock if all threads are blocked because of the presence of exclusive oplocks and there are no threads available to service the client flush request required to complete the oplock break sequence.

In typical DOS-style Microsoft fashion, the designers decided to work around this problem by allowing the LAN Manager server to specify a special flag in the open request. The flag value of `FILE_COMPLETE_IF_OPLOCKED` is specified in the `Parameters.Create.Options` field in the create IRP. If such an option has been specified, the FSD is not supposed to block the current open, even though the oplock break has not yet been completed. Instead, the FSD must execute the open, returning the `STATUS_OPLOCK_BREAK_IN_PROGRESS` return code in the `Status` field (provided all other conditions would allow the open request to succeed). This code value is equivalent to `STATUS_SUCCESS` (i.e., the macro `NT_SUCCESS(STATUS_OPLOCK_BREAK_IN_PROGRESS)` will return TRUE).

The strange thing about the `FILE_COMPLETE_IF_OPLOCKED` flag is the semantics associated with this flag value. The FSD allows the open to succeed, knowing full well that there is now nothing to prevent the caller from violating the trust and performing read/write operations even before the oplock break has been completed. However, the expectation is that, since the caller could only be the LAN Manager server, it will do the right thing and not issue any I/O requests until the client that has the exclusive/batch lock on the file stream has flushed all its data, and the oplock break has been completed.

WARNING   As an FSD designer, you can never trust any other component to do the right thing. Therefore, do not buy into this philosophy in general and always, always, validate before allowing a caller to proceed with a file system operation.

Unfortunately, when providing support for opportunistic locks, the FSD may have to conform to the model determined by the I/O subsystem designers, which requires some trust to be maintained. The only recourse available to you in this case is not to support oplocks (which could lead to degraded performance for users of your FSD).

- Your FSD does not have to support oplock requests.

  If you have begun to think that oplocks are too strange for your tastes, I would agree with you. Therefore, note that you do not have to support opportunistic locking in your FSD. However, if your FSD manages logical volumes that could potentially be shared, supporting oplocks (oddities and all) would be a nice feature to have.

- Even if your FSD does provide oplock support, a remote client that tries to map the file stream in memory will not be able to enjoy any data coherency guarantees.

  As described in Chapter 5 in the discussion on the NT VMM, it is currently not possible for an FSD (including a network redirector) to purge user-mapped pages from the system cache. Therefore, processes on remote clients that decide to map a file stream in memory are effectively shut out from any synchronization/cache coherency guarantees provided by the LAN Manager network protocol.

How Is an Oplock Granted and Broken?

The LAN Manager server issues an oplock request by utilizing the File System Control (FSCTL) interface (described later in this chapter). Basically, your FSD will receive FSCTL requests that indicate the server wishes to obtain an exclusive/shared/batch oplock on a particular file stream identified by the file object used in the file system control IRP.

If your FSD grants the oplock request, it must mark the IRP as pending and queue the IRP internally. A return code of STATUS_PENDING to the caller of the file system control request indicates that the oplock has been granted.*

So, once again, the rules are simple:

- When you receive an oplock request, either return a status code immediately of STATUS_OPLOCK_NOT_GRANTED, indicating that the request was denied, or return STATUS_PENDING, which the caller treats as success in obtaining the oplock.

- An oplock is broken by simply completing the IRP that was queued (and STATUS_PENDING returned) when the oplock had been previously granted.

  Typically, the LAN Manager server software specifies an IRP completion routine that is invoked whenever the oplock is broken (i.e., the IRP is simply completed by the FSD, and this is sufficient to indicate that the break has occurred). This completion routine initiates the break processing across the

---

* In the wonderfully twisted world that some designers at Microsoft live in, all of this makes perfect sense.

network, which could result in I/O flush operations from the remote client node to the FSD. Remember that the LAN Manager server software executes in kernel mode, is very tightly integrated with the rest of the I/O subsystem, creates and manages its own IRP structures (just as the I/O Manager does), and is therefore capable of using all sorts of methods directly without having to go through the NT I/O Manager.

There are a couple of other return values you should be aware of:

- The special return code status of **STATUS_OPLOCK_BREAK_IN_PROGRESS** returned in response to a create/open request, indicating that a break is underway, and the caller should wait until the break has been completed

- A value of **FILE_OPBATCH_BREAK_UNDERWAY**, returned sometimes in the **Information** field of the **IoStatus** structure when a create/open request is received

    This value is only returned in the **Information** field if the create/open request is being denied due to a sharing violation, but your FSD wishes to inform the caller that a break operation is underway for the file stream. The intent here is to allow the caller to possibly modify the share access requested and resubmit the create/open request.

- A value of **FILE_OPLOCK_BROKEN_TO_LEVEL_2** (with value = 0x00000007) returned in the **Information** field when an IRP is being completed to indicate an oplock break

    This is another one of the optimizations added by the oplock protocol designers. If an exclusive or a batch file oplock is being broken, the FSD has the option of offering a shared oplock to the thread whose exclusive/batch lock is being broken. The idea here is that even if the original requesting network redirector code on the remote node can no longer have the absolute power that an exclusive/batch oplock could provide, it can at least take advantage of the functionality (and guarantees) that come with owning a shared oplock.

    Therefore, when breaking an exclusive/shared oplock, the FSD could (but is not required to) return the **FILE_OPLOCK_BROKEN_TO_LEVEL_2** value in the **Information** field. In turn, the network redirector software on the client node also has the option of either accepting this newly offered shared oplock, or not.

- A value of **FILE_OPLOCK_BROKEN_TO_NONE** (with value = 0x00000008) returned in the **Information** field when an IRP is being completed, to indicate an oplock break.

    This is the alternative **Information** field value returned by the FSD whenever an oplock is being broken, and it does not offer even a shared oplock in return.

Oplock Processing Sequence

The following sequence of operations is performed in granting an oplock request from the perspective of an FSD supporting the oplock functionality:

1. The LAN Manager server requests an opportunistic lock on an open file stream uniquely identified by a file object structure on behalf of a remote LAN Manager redirector client.

   The request is issued to the FSD in the form of a file system control (FSCTL) IRP. FSCTL requests are discussed in more detail later in this chapter. Note for now, however, that the major function code in the IRP is `IRP_MJ_FILE_SYSTEM_CONTROL`. The minor function is `IRP_MN_USER_FS_REQUEST`. The possible FSCTL code values to request an opportunistic lock are:

   — `FSCTL_REQUEST_OPLOCK_LEVEL_1`

   This is a request for a Level 1, or an exclusive oplock, on the file stream. Here is the code value:

   ```
   CTL_CODE(FILE_DEVICE_FILE_SYSTEM, 0,
            METHOD_BUFFERED, FILE_ANY_ACCESS)
   ```

   — `FSCTL_REQUEST_OPLOCK_LEVEL_2`

   This is a request for a Level 2, or a shared oplock, on the file stream. Here is the code value:

   ```
   CTL_CODE(FILE_DEVICE_FILE_SYSTEM, 1,
            METHOD_BUFFERED, FILE_ANY_ACCESS)
   ```

   — `FSCTL_REQUEST_BATCH_OPLOCK`

   This is a request for a batch oplock on the file stream. Here is the code value:

   ```
   CTL_CODE(FILE_DEVICE_FILE_SYSTEM, 2,
            METHOD_BUFFERED, FILE_ANY_ACCESS)
   ```

2. The FSD decides either to grant or deny the request for an oplock.

   The rules defined to grant/deny the oplock request are as follows:

   — For an exclusive lock or a batch lock:

   If there is more than one open handle for the file stream (indicated by the `OpenHandleCount` field in the FCB in the case of the sample FSD), the oplock request is denied. All synchronous oplock requests are always denied since, by the method employed to grant the oplock (i.e., return `STATUS_PENDING`), it would be foolish to grant the oplock request.*

---

* The I/O Manager always blocks on behalf of the requesting thread for file objects opened for synchronous processing. Granting an oplock in such a situation would result in the invoking thread being blocked forever in the I/O Manager code.

If there is only one open handle for the file stream (representing the open operation performed by the thread requesting the exclusive/batch oplock), and if no exclusive/batch oplocks have currently been granted on the file stream, the request will succeed.

If there is only one Level 2 oplock previously granted to the same thread now requesting an exclusive oplock, the Level 2 oplock will be broken and the new exclusive/batch oplock granted.

In any other situation, the oplock request will be denied.

— For a shared oplock:

Just as in the case of the exclusive oplock request, all synchronous oplock requests are immediately denied. Otherwise, if there are no oplocks currently outstanding on the file stream or if the only type of oplocks that have been granted are shared oplocks, the request is allowed to succeed.

Note that even if an exclusive/batch oplock is currently being broken (break is underway), the request will be denied.

3. If a decision is made to grant the oplock, the IRP will be marked pending, a cancellation routine will typically be set for the IRP, the IRP will be queued by the FSD on some internal list associated with the FCB, and `STATUS_PENDING` will be returned to the caller.

4. If a decision is made to deny the oplock request, the IRP will be completed with a return code value of `STATUS_OPLOCK_NOT_GRANTED`.

Consider the situation when an oplock (shared/exclusive/batch) has been granted. The following events will lead to the oplock being broken:

• An exclusive/batch oplock had been granted, and another thread decides to open the file.

The FSD knows that it must break the exclusive/batch oplock to continue processing the open request. The only determination to be made by the FSD at this time is whether to offer a shared oplock in return or to simply break the oplock completely. If the file stream is being superseded or overwritten, the FSD will break the oplock completely, and no shared oplock will be offered.

However, if the file stream is not being overwritten or superseded, a shared oplock will be offered in lieu of the exclusive/batch oplock that is now being broken.

• A write request is received by the FSD, and shared oplocks had previously been granted.

The FSD must break the shared oplocks completely.

- A lock/unlock request is received by the FSD, and shared oplocks had previously been granted.

  The FSD must break the shared oplocks completely.

- A read request is received by the FSD, and exclusive/batch oplocks had previously been granted.

  The FSD must break the exclusive/batch oplock and offer a shared oplock instead.

- A flush buffers request is received, and oplocks had previously been granted.

  The FSD must break the oplock and offer a shared oplock instead.

- The end-of-file mark or allocation size value is decreased.

  The FSD must break any oplocks granted completely.

- A cleanup request is received for the file object, indicating that all user handles have been closed for the file object.

  Any oplocks granted using the particular file object must be completely broken and outstanding IRPs completed.

- The remote client that requested the oplock no longer needs it.

  The remote network redirector client that requested the oplock can request a break of the oplock. This break notification is issued to the FSD via the LAN Manager server in the form of a FSCTL request. The code value of the FSCTL code is **FSCTL_OPLOCK_BREAK_ACKNOWLEDGE** which is defined as follows:

  `CTL_CODE(FILE_DEVICE_FILE_SYSTEM, 3, METHOD_BUFFERED, FILE_ANY_ACCESS)`

  Note that this FSCTL is also used by a client to acknowledge an oplock break initiated by the FSD (described later). However, an asynchronous (spontaneous) FSCTL from a client node with this value indicates that the caller, itself, wants to break the oplock. When this request is received by the FSD, all it has to do is complete the IRP that was queued when the oplock was originally granted, clean up any oplock state maintained, and complete any pending IRPs that may have been received and blocked awaiting a break.

If the LAN Manager server has requested oplocks on a file stream using a particular file object on behalf of a remote network redirector client, and the client decided to perform I/O operations conforming with the state of the oplock that had been granted, the oplock cannot be broken by the FSD.

Whenever the FSD decides to break an oplock before allowing the current request to proceed, the current IRP is simply made to block until the oplock break has been completed.

Once the FSD has determined either to break or downgrade the oplock (from an exclusive/batch oplock to a shared oplock), the following sequence of events must be executed by the FSD (in each case, the thread that requested the oplock broken must acknowledge the break as described later).

Oplocks that are completely broken

> The FSD will complete the original IRP that was queued when granting the oplock. The `Information` field value in the `IoStatus` structure will be set to `FILE_OPLOCK_BROKEN_TO_NONE`.

Oplocks that are downgraded to shared oplocks

> The FSD will complete the original IRP that was queued when granting the oplock. The `Information` field value in the `IoStatus` structure will be set to `FILE_OPLOCK_BROKEN_TO_LEVEL_2`.

As previously mentioned, the FSD makes the current IRP (causing the oplock break to occur) block, awaiting acknowledgment of the oplock break notification.

To acknowledge an oplock break, the LAN Manager server issues a new FSCTL request to the FSD. The possible FSCTL code values are as follows:

`FSCTL_OPLOCK_BREAK_ACKNOWLEDGE`

> This FSCTL code value is used by the LAN Manager server on behalf of a remote network redirector client to acknowledge (or initiate) an oplock break notification.
>
> If this FSCTL code is received by the FSD after it broke or downgraded a Level 1 (exclusive) or batch oplock, the FSD is assured that the remote client has completed flushing all of the dirty data that may have been cached remotely back to the server node.
>
> If the FSD offered a shared oplock to the client in lieu of an exclusive or batch oplock that was being broken, receipt of this FSCTL code in the IRP indicates to the FSD that the client node has accepted the new shared oplock that was offered. The FSD would then perform the following steps:
>
> a. Update internal structures to reflect the fact that the original exclusive/ batch oplock has been broken completely.
>
> b. Process the current FSCTL IRP as if it were a request to obtain a new shared oplock, mark the IRP pending, set a cancellation routine, and return `STATUS_PENDING` to the caller, indicating that a new Level 2 (shared) oplock has been granted.
>
> If the oplock being broken was originally a shared oplock, or if the FSD did not offer a shared oplock in lieu of the exclusive/batch oplock being broken, the FSD can simply update internal data structures to indicate that oplock break processing has been completed. The FSCTL IRP should be completed

with a STATUS_SUCCESS return code, and the Information field in the IoStatus structure of the FSCTL IRP should be set to FILE_OPLOCK_BROKEN_TO_NONE.

Any IRPs that were queued by the FSD awaiting the oplock break can be allowed to continue processing at this time.

NOTE   If the FSCTL request containing the FSCTL_OPLOCK_BREAK_AC-KNOWLEDGE FSCTL code value is issued as a synchronous I/O request, the FSD cannot grant any shared oplock and will always complete the FSCTL IRP with status code set to STATUS_SUCCESS and the Information field value set to FILE_OPLOCK_BROKEN_TO_NONE.

FSCTL_OPBATCH_ACK_CLOSE_PENDING

An FSCTL IRP with this FSCTL code value is issued to the FSD by the LAN Manager server on behalf of a remote network redirector client in response to an oplock break notification request for either an exclusive or a batch oplock request.

This FSCTL is issued instead of the FSCTL_OPLOCK_BREAK_ACKNOWLEDGE FSCTL to indicate that the network redirector client does not want the shared oplock, offered by the FSD in lieu of the exclusive/batch oplock, being broken.

The FSD can simply clean up internal data structures to indicate that the oplock break has been completed and complete the FSCTL IRP with status code set to STATUS_SUCCESS.

Any IRPs that were awaiting the oplock break notification can be allowed to proceed once this FSCTL has been processed.

There is one additional FSCTL code that your driver should expect to receive: FSCTL_OPLOCK_BREAK_NOTIFY. The caller wants to be notified when a Level 1 oplock break operation has been completed. If no Level 1 oplock break operation is in progress when the request is received, even if there are oplocks (exclusive/shared/batch) currently granted for the file stream, the IRP should be immediately completed with STATUS_SUCCESS. However, if a Level 1 oplock break operation is underway when this request is received, the IRP should be queued and only completed when the oplock break operation has been completed.

FSRTL Support for Oplock Processing

The native Windows NT FSD implementations use common routines provided by the FSRTL to provide oplock support. Unfortunately, Microsoft has chosen not to encourage third-party developers to use the routines exported by the FSRTL package. However, the description of the functionality expected from your FSD should help you in designing and developing your own opportunistic locking support package.

Dispatch Routine: File System and Device Control

File system drivers receive file system control requests to perform processing that cannot otherwise be requested via the standard dispatch entry points. Device control requests are also directed by the I/O Manager to the file system driver that performs a mount operation on a target physical or virtual device.

Types of FSCTL Requests

Most file system driver implementations respond to one or more file system control requests. The I/O Manager dispatches a file system control request (FSCTL request) to the FSD via an IRP with a major function code value of `IRP_MJ_FILE_SYSTEM_CONTROL`. There are four types of distinguishing minor function codes that the FSD must check for whenever it receives a FSCTL request from the Windows NT I/O Manager:

`IRP_MN_USER_FS_REQUEST`

>   This minor function code is used in the most common case, when a thread opens a file system object (file/directory/volume/device) and issues a FSCTL to the file system driver. There is a set of standard system-defined FSCTL codes (defined by Microsoft) that can be used by user threads; these will be discussed later in this section.

>   In addition to the Microsoft-defined FSCTL codes, it is always possible for FSD designers to develop their own private FSCTL codes, used internally between helper applications/user threads and the FSD itself. These can be issued to the FSD either to request some required functionality or to transfer data to and from the driver and the user-space application processes.

>   For example, your FSD may provide some special information in response to specific FSCTL requests issued by a helper application from user space. Or, your helper application may issue a special FSCTL request to request the FSD to format a specific disk. To accomplish such functionality, you would typi-

cally define some private FSCTL codes, to be used only by your helper applications and the FSD.

Issuing FSCTL requests is the easiest, most private, and most convenient method of information transfer between a kernel-mode driver and a user space thread. To use this method of data transfer, simply define a new FSCTL code, using the guidelines extensively documented in the DDK, implement support for the specific FSCTL in the kernel-mode FSD, and have a user-space thread issue the FSCTL whenever required. That is all you have to do to accomplish the data transfer, or to have the FSD perform some specific operation requested by the user thread.

IRP_MN_MOUNT_VOLUME

This special request is issued only by the I/O Manager to request a mount operation, in response to a change in media reported by a lower-level driver (for removable media only), or more likely, when the first user open is received for a file/directory residing on a physical disk that has not had a mount operation performed on it.

Later in this chapter, you can read a detailed discussion on the mount process and the functionality provided by the FSD in response to a mount request identified by the `IRP_MN_MOUNT_VOLUME` minor function code.

IRP_MN_LOAD_FILE_SYSTEM

This request originates in the I/O Manager. It is only issued by the I/O Manager to special mini-FSD implementations, requesting them to perform a load of the full file system driver image. Later in this chapter is a discussion on how you can design and develop a file system recognizer for your FSD. This FSCTL code is discussed in detail at that time.

IRP_MN_VERIFY_VOLUME

This is also a special type of FSCTL issued by the I/O Manager to an FSD managing a mounted logical volume on removable media. This request is issued by the I/O Manager when a lower-level disk driver indicates that the media in the removable driver appears to have been removed or changed. We will discuss how an FSD can develop an appropriate response to be executed in response to this type of FSCTL request.

Methods of Data Transfer for FSCTL Requests

Each FSCTL code value (used with the `IRP_MN_USER_FS_REQUEST` minor function) uniquely determines the method used for data transfer for that particular FSCTL operation, if such data transfer is requested. The two least significant bits in the FSCTL code value are used to identify the method of data transfer for the particular FSCTL request.

WARNING   When a file system driver creates a device object to represent the file system itself or to represent an instance of a mounted logical volume, it can specify whether it wishes to receive buffered I/O requests (DO_BUFFERED_IO flag set in the Flags field for the device object), direct I/O requests (DO_DIRECT_IO flag set), or the user-supplied buffer pointer (neither of the two flags should be set).

You must note, however, that those flags are not used to determine the method of data transfer for file system control or device control requests. The method used in such cases is specific to each FSCTL or IOCTL sent to the driver and is determined by the FSCTL or IOCTL *code value* as described below.

The following are the available options:

- If the FSCTL code is defined with **METHOD_BUFFERED**, the I/O Manager allocates a system buffer on behalf of the caller.

  This method of data transfer can be defined by setting a value of 0 in the two least significant bits of the FSCTL code.

  The caller can supply either an input buffer only (used to transfer information to the FSD), an output buffer only (used to receive information back from the FSD), or both (data transfer occurs in both directions). However, the I/O Manager only allocates a single system buffer for the data transfer.

  The FSD can obtain the address of this single system buffer allocated by the I/O Manager from the **AssociatedIrp->SystemBuffer** field in the IRP. The Flags field in the IRP is set with the IRP_BUFFERED_IO and the IRP_ DEALLOCATE_BUFFER flag values (used internally by the I/O Manager).

  If an input buffer is supplied by the caller, the I/O Manager will copy data from the input buffer to the I/O Manager-allocated system buffer, before passing the request to the FSD. If an output buffer is supplied by the caller, the I/O Manager will set the **IRP_INPUT_OPERATION** flag value in the Flags field in the IRP. The I/O Manager will check for the existence of this flag upon IRP completion and will copy data from the system buffer to the user-supplied output buffer if this flag is set.

  Note that, since the I/O Manager supplies a single buffer for the use of the FSD, even in the case when a caller may have provided both an input and an output buffer, the size of the system buffer allocated by the I/O Manager will be the greater of the size of the input and output buffers provided by the requesting thread. The initial contents of the I/O Manager-allocated system buffer will be overwritten by the FSD when it returns information back to the I/O Manager.

- If the FSCTL code is defined with **METHOD_NEITHER**, the I/O Manager simply sends the user-supplied buffer pointers directly to the FSD.

  This method of data transfer can be defined by setting a value of 3 in the two least-significant bits of the FSCTL code.

  If the caller provides an input buffer (i.e., a buffer in which the caller has provided data for the FSD), the I/O Manager initializes the **Parameters.DeviceIoControl.Type3InputBuffer** field in the current stack location with the pointer to the caller-supplied buffer. Your FSD can obtain data provided by the caller directly from this buffer.

  If the caller also wants to receive data back from the FSD, it would provide an output buffer pointer when invoking the NT system service routine.[*] In this case, the I/O Manager initializes the **UserBuffer** field in the IRP with the address of the caller-supplied output buffer. The FSD can return data to the caller by using the address provided in this field to write to the caller-supplied buffer.

  Note that the user-supplied buffer pointer addresses are supplied as-is to the FSD by the I/O Manager. No checks are performed by the I/O Manager on the user-supplied virtual addresses for either the input or the output buffers provided by the caller. Therefore, it is FSD's responsibility to ensure that the virtual addresses are still valid when it tries to perform data transfer for such requests. If the request is posted for asynchronous processing, the FSD must lock the input and/or the output buffers itself and also obtain valid system virtual addresses for each buffer.

- If the FSCTL code is defined with either the **METHOD_IN_DIRECT** or the **METHOD_OUT_DIRECT** FSCTL codes, the I/O Manager allocates a system buffer for the caller-supplied input buffer and creates an MDL for the caller-supplied output buffer.

  The **METHOD_IN_DIRECT** method of data transfer can be defined by setting a value of 1 in the least two significant bits of the FSCTL code. The **METHOD_OUT_DIRECT** method of data transfer can be defined by setting a value of 2 in the least two significant bits of the FSCTL code.

  The caller can supply an input buffer and an output buffer for both types of data transfer methods. The I/O Manager allocates a system buffer corresponding to the input buffer provided by the caller and copies the caller-supplied data from the input buffer into the I/O Manager-allocated system buffer. The

---

[*] The system service routine provided by the Windows NT I/O Manager for FSCTL requests is called Nt-FsControlFile(). For more information on this system service, consult *Appendix A*. The Win32 subsystem also provides a method of issuing device IOCTL requests to kernel-mode drivers.

address of this I/O Manager-allocated system buffer can be obtained by the FSD from the `AssociatedIrp.SystemBuffer` field in the IRP.

If the caller supplies an output buffer when invoking the `NtFsControl-File()` system service routine, the I/O Manager creates an MDL for the output buffer and also locks the pages for the MDL. The only difference between the `METHOD_IN_DIRECT` and the `METHOD_OUT_DIRECT` methods is that the pages locked by the I/O Manager are locked with read access specified in the former case (for `METHOD_IN_DIRECT`) and write access specified in the latter (for `METHOD_OUT_DIRECT`).

Note that the I/O Manager does not copy any data back into the caller-supplied output buffer upon IRP completion; since the output buffer is directly accessible to the FSD (via the MDL created by the I/O Manager), no such copy operation is required.

Standard User File System Control Requests

The I/O stack location contains the following structure relevant to processing file system control requests issued to an FSD:

```
typedef struct _IO_STACK_LOCATION {

    // ...

    union {

        //...

        // System service parameters for:  NtFsControlFile
        // Note that the user's output buffer is stored in the UserBuffer field
        // and the user's input buffer is stored in the SystemBuffer field.
        struct {
            ULONG OutputBufferLength;
            ULONG InputBufferLength;
            ULONG FsControlCode;
            PVOID Type3InputBuffer;
        } FileSystemControl;

        // ...
    } Parameters;

// ...

} IO_STACK_LOCATION, *PIO_STACK_LOCATION;
```

The following FSCTL code values are defined by the system and should be supported by a disk-based FSD. For each FSCTL code mentioned below, there is a brief description of the type of processing performed by the native FSD implementations. This should provide you with a fairly good idea of the functionality expected from your FSD.

Note that each of these standard FSCTL requests is dispatched to the FSD in an IRP containing a major function code of `IRP_MJ_FILE_SYSTEM_CONTROL` and a minor function code of `IRP_MN_USER_FS_REQUEST`.

FSCTL_LOCK_VOLUME

Most NT FSD implementations typically execute the following steps:

a. If the file object supplied with the request does not refer to an open instance of the logical volume object, deny the request with an error code of `STATUS_INVALID_PARAMETER`.

b. Acquire the resource associated with your volume control block exclusively.

c. If the VCB state indicates that it is already locked, or if there are any open/referenced file objects for the logical volume represented by the VCB, deny the request (complete the IRP after releasing the VCB resource) with a `STATUS_ACCESS_DENIED` error code.

d. Mark the VCB as locked, preventing any new file create/open operations.

e. Flush any cached, modified metadata information about the logical volume (e.g., bitmaps).

f. Release the VCB resource and complete the IRP with a return code of `STATUS_SUCCESS`.

For the native FSD implementations, utilities such as *chkdsk* always lock a logical volume before beginning processing for the volume. Some FSD implementations may actually interpret this request as the beginning of a dismount sequence for a logical volume and prepare themselves accordingly.

FSCTL_UNLOCK_VOLUME

This simply undoes the lock operation performed with the `FSCTL_LOCK_VOLUME` request and clears any flags set in the VCB indicating that the volume has been locked.

Just as in the case of the lock volume request described, the FSD will reject the request if the file object supplied does not refer to an open instance of the previously locked logical volume.

FSCTL_DISMOUNT_VOLUME

The FSD will perform checks to ensure that the VCB indicates the logical volume was previously locked after acquiring the VCB resource exclusively. The FSD should then tear down all structures allocated to support the mounted logical volume, including the VCB structure itself. This would also include uninitializing any cache map for the stream file object created to cache logical volume metadata information (see the description later in this chapter about the volume mount sequence). Of course, your FSD should ensure that all modified information (including log files, bitmaps, etc.) for the logical volume have been flushed to secondary storage before discarding this information from memory.

Also, the FSD should somehow indicate in the volume parameter block structure for the physical/virtual device object on which the volume had been mounted that the volume is no longer mounted.

There are a variety of ways in which your FSD could accomplish this. One way is to set the DO_VERIFY_VOLUME flag in the `Flags` field of VPB structure for the device object representing the physical/virtual disk. Another method could be to simply clear the VPB_MOUNTED flag in the VPB structure for the physical/virtual device object. Finally, your FSD could take drastic measures and free up the VPB structure allocated for the physical/virtual device object and replace it with a newly allocated "clean" VPB structure (remember to allocate it from nonpaged pool).

If you wish to modify flags in the VPB structure for the real device object on which your FSD mounted the logical volume (e.g., you decide to clear the VPB_MOUNTED flag), you should consider acquiring a global I/O Manager spin lock to ensure synchronized access to the structure. Here is the routine you can invoke to acquire this global spin lock:

```
VOID
IoAcquireVpbSpinLock(
    OUT PKIRQL Irql
);
```

This routine will simply acquire the same global spin lock that the I/O Manager acquires internally before examining any VPB (e.g., to check whether the VPB is mounted during a create/open operation). Remember to pass in a pointer to a KIRQL structure so that the I/O Manager can return the IRQL at which your code was executing before it acquired the Executive spin lock. You will need this value when you are finished modifying the VPB structure, and you invoke this corresponding release spin lock routine:

```
VOID
IoReleaseVpbSpinLock(
    IN KIRQL Irql
);
```

Your FSD should check that this routine was invoked by a caller with appropriate privileges before allowing the request to be processed. Furthermore, if the logical volume was mounted on removable media that you had locked into the drive, do not forget to issue an IOCTL to the removable media disk driver unlocking the medium from the drive.

FSCTL_MARK_VOLUME_DIRTY

Your FSD should confirm that the file object passed in reflects a valid instance of an open operation on the logical volume itself. This is simply a request to ensure that your in-memory and on-disk data structures reflect that the system memory may contain information that needs to be flushed out to disk. If the system crashes before your FSD has a chance to perform a flush operation and clear the on-disk flag reflecting the fact that the volume is dirty, you may decide to perform the equivalent of a *chkdsk* operation during the next boot cycle before allowing a logical volume mount request to complete.

Remember to acquire the VCB exclusively before modifying any in-memory or on-disk structures indicating that the volume is dirty and needs to be flushed to disk.

FSCTL_IS_VOLUME_MOUNTED

Ensure as before that a valid file object has been sent to you for this request. Typically, your FSD would support this FSCTL if you support removable media. If your FSD supports removable media and has a volume mounted on some such removable medium, you should perform the equivalent of a *verify volume operation* (described later) to ensure that everything is all right with the volume. An appropriate status code containing the results of the verify operation should be returned as part of completing the IRP.

FSCTL_IS_PATHNAME_VALID

The `AssociatedIrp->SystemBuffer` field in the FSCTL IRP will contain a pointer to this structure:

```
typedef struct _PATHNAME_BUFFER {
    ULONG       PathNameLength;
    WCHAR       Name[1];
} PATHNAME_BUFFER, *PPATHNAME_BUFFER;
```

Your mission is to examine the characters contained in the pathname to see if they are supported by your FSD. Return a status code of either STATUS_OBJECT_NAME_INVALID or STATUS_SUCCESS.

FSCTL_QUERY_RETRIEVAL_POINTERS

This request will only be directed to your FSD if it manages a boot partition on which a paging file resides. Providing a bootable FSD requires support from Microsoft. Therefore, we will ignore this FSCTL-type request and return STATUS_INVALID_PARAMETER to the caller.

In addition to the FSCTL codes listed, your FSD may support many privately defined file system control codes. Furthermore, if you design a network redirector driver, you may wish to provide functionality such as:

- Starting the redirector on demand

- Binding to transports used by your redirector

- Returning statistics pertinent to your driver

- Enumerating all open connections

- Deleting specific connections to remote shared objects

- Stopping redirector activities

- Unbinding from specific transports

You must determine the sort of functionality your driver will provide and implement appropriate FSCTL support.

Verify Volume Support

If your FSD supports removable media, there may be occasions when a verify volume request is issued to your driver. Typically, this happens whenever a user injects media into the removable drive.

Disk driver's actions

Whenever the media status in the removable drive appears to have changed, the disk driver performs the following actions for I/O requests targeted to the device.

1. Check if the VPB indicates whether a logical volume had been previously mounted on the media in the removable drive.

   This can be easily determined by the disk driver by the presence/absence of the VPB_MOUNTED flag in the Flags field in the VPB structure. If the flag is not set, no logical mount operation has been performed, and the driver simply returns STATUS_VERIFY_REQUIRED for IRPs sent to the device.

2. If a logical volume had been mounted, indicate that the media needs to be verified.

   The disk driver will OR in the DO_VERIFY_VOLUME flag in the VPB structure. It will set the return code value for the IRP to STATUS_VERIFY_REQUIRED. It will then invoke the IoSetHardErrorOrVeriFyDevice() function, which will store the pointer to the supplied device object (one of the arguments to this well-documented function) in the Tail.Overlay.Thread->DeviceToVerify field of the IRP.

3. The disk driver will then complete the IRP.

FSD response

Note that most I/O operations to a disk drive with a mounted logical volume associated with the media in the drive originate in the FSD. Whenever an FSD gets a `STATUS_VERIFY_REQUIRED` error from an I/O request sent to the target device object for a logical volume, it performs the following actions:

1. Obtain a pointer to the target device object for the verify operation to be performed.

   The FSD should use the `IoGetDeviceToVerify()` function call to get a pointer to this device object. It should then reset the `DeviceToVerify` field in the TLS to NULL by invoking `IoSetDeviceToVerify()` function with the arguments: (`PsGetCurrentThread()`, NULL).

2. Initiate a verify operation.

   The FSD can simply invoke the `IoVerifyVolume()` function to initiate a verify operation:

```
NTSTATUS
IoVerifyVolume (
    IN PDEVICE_OBJECT        DeviceObject,
    IN BOOLEAN               AllowRawMount
);
```

   The FSD can pass in the pointer to the device object for the device to be verified (obtained earlier from the `IoGetDeviceToVerify()` function call). The `AllowRawMount` is typically set to FALSE, unless the user was trying to perform a create/open operation on the physical device itself, and the FSD encountered the verify status code when processing this request.

   Note that the invocation to `IoVerifyVolume()` will return either **STATUS_SUCCESS** or **STATUS_WRONG_VOLUME**.

I/O manager's response

When an FSD invokes the `IoVerifyVolume()` function call as described, the I/O Manager will do the following:

1. If the logical volume had not been previously mounted (FALSE in the scenario described here), simply invoke a mount sequence.

   The mount sequence consists of going through the linked list of all registered, loaded instances of file system drivers and invoking each one of them, requesting a mount operation. Later in this chapter, you will read a detailed discussion on how a mount request is processed by the FSD.

   Note that a mount request is issued to the FSD via an FSCTL that has a minor function value of **IRP_MN_MOUNT_VOLUME**.

2. Since the logical volume had been previously mounted, issue a verify volume FSCTL request to the FSD.

The I/O Manager will create a new IRP for the FSCTL request. The minor function code in the current I/O stack location will be set to `IRP_MN_VERIFY_VOLUME`. The I/O Manager will then issue the IRP to the FSD, since it manages the logical volume device object identified by the `DeviceObject` field in the VPB structure for the device object representing the removable drive to be verified.*

The `Parameters.VerifyVolume.Vpb` field in the current stack location of the verify volume IRP dispatched to the FSD contains a pointer to the VPB, associated with the device object representing the removable drive containing the media to be verified. The `Parameters.VerifyVolume.DeviceObject` field contains a pointer to the logical volume device object created by the FSD.

3. If the verify volume FSCTL returns `STATUS_SUCCESS`, there is nothing more the I/O Manager needs to do.

4. If the verify volume FSCTL returns `STATUS_WRONG_VOLUME`, the I/O Manager will initiate a fresh mount sequence for the device.

To initiate a new mount sequence, the I/O Manager will free the original VPB structure associated with the device object on which the mount operation will be attempted. It will allocate a new VPB structure and associate it with the device object. It will then begin the typical mount sequence.

FSD's response to the verify volume FSCTL request

The IRP issued by the I/O Manager to verify the volume can be easily identified by the FSD by the `IRP_MN_VERIFY_VOLUME` minor function code value in the current I/O stack location.

The I/O stack location contains the following structure relevant to processing the verify volume request issued to an FSD:

```
typedef struct _IO_STACK_LOCATION {

    // ...

    union {

        //...

        // Parameters for VerifyVolume
        struct {
```

---

* Sorry if that sounds cryptic but it is true, I promise.

```
            PVPB Vpb;
            PDEVICE_OBJECT DeviceObject;
        } VerifyVolume;

        // ...
} Parameters;

// ...

} IO_STACK_LOCATION, *PIO_STACK_LOCATION;
```

The FSD performs the following sequence of actions in response to the request:

1. Post the request if required.

   Note that a verify request is inherently synchronous, and the I/O Manager will wait in the context of the thread performing the verify operation if STATUS_ PENDING is returned. Your FSD would typically post the request if the IoIs-OperationSynchronous() function call returns FALSE.

2. Get a pointer to the VCB structure for the logical volume device object.

3. Acquire the VCB resource exclusively to ensure synchronized access.

4. Check if the RealDevice->Flags field is no longer marked with DO_ VERIFY_VOLUME.

   Since multiple IRP requests to the disk driver could fail with a verify volume status code, one of those requests could have already resulted in a volume verify operation being completed. There is nothing the FSD needs to do in this situation but return STATUS_SUCCESS.

5. Issue requests to the disk driver to obtain information from the physical media.

   The steps performed here are similar to those executed during a logical mount operation described below. Basically, the FSD must obtain whatever information is required from the physical media, including getting the drive geometry by issuing IOCTL requests to the disk driver and issuing read requests to obtain volume metadata information from disk.

   In order to ensure that the disk driver does not fail the I/O requests with a STATUS_VERIFY_VOLUME error code, the FSD must set the SL_OVERRIDE_ VERIFY_VOLUME flag in the Flags field of the stack location it sets up for the next lower driver in the chain.

   If any of the I/O operations sent to the lower-level driver fail, the FSD typically decides to return STATUS_WRONG_VOLUME. Skip directly to the step described below detailing the preprocessing required from the FSD before returning this error code to the I/O Manager.

6. Check the information obtained from disk.

   Your FSD may perform any appropriate checks to decide if the on-disk structures indicate the same volume as the one you had previously mounted.

7. If it determines that the volume is the same, flush and purge all cached metadata structures for the logical volume and reinitialize all cached information.

   This is similar to performing a remount operation on the logical volume. Once it has reinitialized cached data, your FSD should clear the DO_VERIFY_ VOLUME flag in the VPB. Then it should complete the IRP with STATUS_ SUCCESS as the return code.

8. If it decides that the volume is not the same as the one previously mounted, throw away all cached metadata information for the volume.

   Effectively, you will perform a forced dismount of the volume at this time. You should also clear the DO_VERIFY_VOLUME flag in the VPB. Then your FSD should complete the IRP with STATUS_WRONG_VOLUME as the return code. Since you will return the STATUS_WRONG_VOLUME error code, the I/O Manager will attempt a remount operation for the media.

9. Complete the FSCTL IRP with the appropriate return code value.

Handling Device IOCTL Requests

The I/O stack location contains the following structure relevant to processing the device IOCTL request issued to an FSD:

```
typedef struct _IO_STACK_LOCATION {

    // ...

    union {

        //...

        // System service parameters for:  NtDeviceIoControlFile
        // Note that the user's output buffer is stored in the UserBuffer
        // field and the user's input buffer is stored in the SystemBuffer
        // field.
        struct {
            ULONG OutputBufferLength;
            ULONG InputBufferLength;
            ULONG IoControlCode;
            PVOID Type3InputBuffer;
        } DeviceIoControl;

        // ...
    } Parameters;

    // ...
```

```
} IO_STACK_LOCATION, *PIO_STACK_LOCATION;
```

Typically, the FSD should simply forward a device IOCTL request to the target device object for the mounted logical volume. Study the following code fragment to see how this can be done.

```
NTSTATUS      SFsdCommonDeviceControl(
PtrSFsdIrpContext           PtrIrpContext,
PIRP                        PtrIrp)
{
    NTSTATUS                RC = STATUS_SUCCESS;
    PIO_STACK_LOCATION      PtrIoStackLocation = NULL;
    PIO_STACK_LOCATION      PtrNextIoStackLocation = NULL;
    PFILE_OBJECT            PtrFileObject = NULL;
    PtrSFsdFCB              PtrFCB = NULL;
    PtrSFsdCCB              PtrCCB = NULL;
    PtrSFsdVCB              PtrVCB = NULL;
    BOOLEAN                 CompleteIrp = FALSE;
    ULONG                   IoControlCode = 0;
    void                    *BufferPointer = NULL;

    try {
        // First, get a pointer to the current I/O stack location
        PtrIoStackLocation = IoGetCurrentIrpStackLocation(PtrIrp);
        ASSERT(PtrIoStackLocation);

        PtrFileObject = PtrIoStackLocation->FileObject;
        ASSERT(PtrFileObject);

        PtrCCB = (PtrSFsdCCB)(PtrFileObject->FsContext2);
        ASSERT(PtrCCB);
        PtrFCB = PtrCCB->PtrFCB;
        ASSERT(PtrFCB);

        if (PtrFCB->NodeIdentifier.NodeType == SFSD_NODE_TYPE_VCB) {
            PtrVCB = (PtrSFsdVCB)(PtrFCB);
        } else {
            PtrVCB = PtrFCB->PtrVCB;
        }

        // Get the IoControlCode value
        IoControlCode =
            PtrIoStackLocation->Parameters.DeviceIoControl.IoControlCode;

        // You may wish to allow only volume open operations.

        switch (IoControlCode) {
#ifdef    __THIS_IS_A_NETWORK_REDIR_
        case IOCTL_REDIR_QUERY_PATH:
            // Only for network redirectors.
            BufferPointer = (void *)
                (PtrIoStackLocation->
                    Parameters.DeviceIoControl.Type3InputBuffer);
            // Invoke the handler for this IOCTL.
```

```
                RC = SFsdHandleQueryPath(BufferPointer);
                CompleteIrp = TRUE;
                try_return(RC);
                break;
#endif      // _THIS_IS_A_NETWORK_REDIR_
        default:
                // Invoke the lower-level driver in the chain.
                PtrNextIoStackLocation = IoGetNextIrpStackLocation(PtrIrp);
                *PtrNextIoStackLocation = *PtrIoStackLocation;
                // Set a completion routine.
                IoSetCompletionRoutine(PtrIrp, SFsdDevIoctlCompletion,
                        NULL, TRUE, TRUE, TRUE);
                // Send the request.
                RC = IoCallDriver(PtrVCB->TargetDeviceObject, PtrIrp);
                break;
        }

        try_exit:    NOTHING;

    } finally {

        // Release the IRP context
        if (!(PtrIrpContext->IrpContextFlags
                                & SFSD_IRP_CONTEXT_EXCEPTION)) {
            // Free-up the Irp Context
            SFsdReleaseIrpContext(PtrIrpContext);

            if (CompleteIrp) {
                PtrIrp->IoStatus.Status = RC;
                PtrIrp->IoStatus.Information = 0;

                // complete the IRP
                IoCompleteRequest(PtrIrp, IO_DISK_INCREMENT);
            }
        }
    }

    return(RC);
}


NTSTATUS SFsdDevIoctlCompletion(
PDEVICE_OBJECT          PtrDeviceObject,
PIRP                    PtrIrp,
void                    *Context)
{
    if (PtrIrp->PendingReturned) {
        IoMarkIrpPending(PtrIrp);
    }

    return(STATUS_SUCCESS);
}
```

This code also illustrates how a network redirector can provide support for the
IOCTL_REDIR_QUERY_PATH IOCTL issued by the MUP component (discussed

earlier in Chapter 2, *File System Driver Development*). See the following code fragment for a skeletal **SFsdHandleQueryPath()** routine example.

```
NTSTATUS SFsdHandleQueryPath(
void            *BufferPointer)
{
    NTSTATUS                RC = STATUS_SUCCESS;
    PQUERY_PATH_REQUEST     RequestBuffer = (PQUERY_PATH_
REQUEST)BufferPointer;
    PQUERY_PATH_RESPONSE    ReplyBuffer = (PQUERY_PATH_
RESPONSE)BufferPointer;
    ULONG                   LengthOfNameToBeMatched =
                            RequestBuffer->PathNameLength;
    ULONG                   LengthOfMatchedName = 0;
    WCHAR                   *NameToBeMatched = RequestBuffer->FilePathName;

    // So here we are. Simply check the name supplied.
    // You can use whatever algorithm you like to determine whether the
    // sent-in name is acceptable.
    // The first character in the name is always a "\"
    // If you like the name sent-in (probably, you will like a subset
    // of the name), set the matching length value in LengthOfMatchedName.

    // if (FoundMatch) {
    //         ReplyBuffer->LengthAccepted = LengthOfMatchedName;
    // } else {
    //         RC = STATUS_OBJECT_NAME_NOT_FOUND;
    // }

    return(RC);
}
```

The following definitions are required by the code fragment:

```
#define IOCTL_REDIR_QUERY_PATH      \
CTL_CODE(FILE_DEVICE_NETWORK_FILE_SYSTEM, 99,
         METHOD_NEITHER, FILE_ANY_ACCESS)

typedef struct _QUERY_PATH_REQUEST {
    ULONG                       PathNameLength;
    PIO_SECURITY_CONTEXT        SecurityContext;
    WCHAR                       FilePathName[1];
} QUERY_PATH_REQUEST, *PQUERY_PATH_REQUEST;

typedef struct _QUERY_PATH_RESPONSE {
    ULONG                       LengthAccepted;
} QUERY_PATH_RESPONSE, *PQUERY_PATH_RESPONSE;
```

File System Recognizers

Simply stated, a file system recognizer is a mini-FSD implementation that loads initially instead of the full FSD.

Functionality Provided by a File System Recognizer

The function of the file system recognizer driver is as follows:

- Help conserve system resources by loading the recognizer instead of the complete FSD.

  The mini-FSD is, by definition, a small driver providing almost no functionality (except what is discussed below) and so consuming very few system resources.

- If a valid logical volume needs to be mounted, load the full (original) FSD so that it can proceed with mounting the volume and servicing user requests.

  Once the full FSD has been successfully loaded into memory, the file system recognizer essentially becomes dormant and stays out of the way. Because of the low resource requirements for the mini-FSD, keeping it loaded in memory even after the full FSD has been loaded is a small price to pay compared to the benefits of using the mini-FSD in the first place.

Basically, the file system recognizer helps the Windows NT operating system conserve system resources by obviating the necessity of always loading the entire FSD even if no logical volumes belonging to the FSD are ever mounted (or used) by users of the system. For example, consider the CD-ROM drive that exists on your system. It is possible that you may not use the CD-ROM at all during the current boot cycle. Or, it is quite possible that you have formatted all of your hard disk partitions with the NTFS file system format and therefore, you never need to use the FASTFAT file system driver on your machine until you decide to use a diskette formatted with the FAT file system format.

In such situations, loading the entire FASTFAT and/or CDFS file system drivers into memory is an unnecessary operation that is costly in terms of the time required to boot-up the system as well as the memory consumption associated with the FSD that is inevitable even for a dormant, loaded FSD.

A mini-FSD is a cost-effective method of always being prepared for the possibility that a user may require the services of the associated FSD, while not incurring the performance and resource penalties of actually having a fully functional FSD loaded in memory until it becomes necessary to do so.

Steps Executed by the File System Recognizer

The mini-FSD (or the file system recognizer, as it is commonly known), executes the following logical steps once it is loaded into memory:

1. Create a device object representing the mini-FSD in lieu of the file-system-type device object that the full fledged FSD would create, had it been loaded.

   The file system recognizer creates a device object of type `FILE_DEVICE_CD_ROM_FILE_SYSTEM` (for a CD-ROM file system recognizer) or `FILE_DEVICE_DISK_FILE_SYSTEM` (for the more common, disk-based file system recognizer). As you may have noted from the initialization code presented in Chapter 9, this is similar to the operation generally executed by the full FSD implementation.

2. Register with the I/O Manager as a file system driver so that the mini-FSD gets invoked whenever an I/O request is received targeted to a physical device on which no mount operation has been performed.

   Just as in the case of any other fully functional disk-based FSD (as illustrated in Chapter 9), the mini-FSD also invokes `IoRegisterFileSystem()` to inform the I/O Manager that a fully functional FSD has been loaded into memory.

3. Upon receiving a mount request for a physical/virtual device, check the on-disk information on the device by performing I/O operations to determine whether the device contains a valid (recognizable) logical volume.

   Recall from earlier chapters the sequence of operations undertaken by the I/O Manager whenever it receives a create/open request for an object on a physical/virtual device. For example, consider the situation when a user decides to open file *X:\directory1\foo*. The NT Object Manager receives the request and translates *X:* (which is simply a symbolic link) to the linked object name, e.g., *\Device\PhysicalDrive0.**

   So the complete name of the request as determined by the NT Object Manager is now *\Device\PhysicalDrive0\directory1\foo*. Since the *\Device\PhysicalDrive0* name typically corresponds to the device object for the first partition on hard disk 0 (an object belonging to the I/O subsystem), the Object Manager recognizes that the request should be forwarded to the device object managed by the I/O Manager and therefore sends the request on to the I/O Manager for further processing. The portion of the name sent to the I/O Manager is *\directory1\foo*, with the target device object for the request being clearly identified by the NT Object Manager.

   The I/O Manager, in turn, examines the volume parameter block structure associated with the physical device object to see if any logical volume has been mounted on the device object. The presence of a mounted logical

---

* The \??\... names in Windows NT Version 4.0 are simply symbolic links themselves to the corresponding \Device\... entries.

volume associated with a physical/virtual device object can be detected by checking for the VPB_MOUNTED flag value in the **Flags** field of the VPB structure. If a logical mount operation had been successfully performed, the I/O Manager will send the create/open request to the FSD that manages the logical volume (represented by a logical volume device object associated with the physical device object) to actually process the request.

However, if the VPB indicates that no logical mount operation had been performed for the target physical/virtual device object, the I/O Manager sends an IRP with the IRP_MJ_FILE_SYSTEM_CONTROL major function code and the IRP_MN_MOUNT_VOLUME minor function code to each of the registered disk/CD-ROM file system drivers loaded in the system. The first FSD to successfully perform the mount operation causes the I/O Manager to stop issuing any further mount requests to the remaining FSDs.

Since the mini-FSD has registered itself as a fully functional, loaded FSD, it, too, receives such mount requests from the I/O Manager. Upon receiving such a mount request for the physical/virtual device (in our example, the device object identified by *Device**PhysicalDrive0*), the mini-FSD obtains the disk geometry and device type by issuing IOCTL requests to the device driver managing the device, and it also reads in the metadata information from appropriate physical sectors on the media.

The mini-FSD then checks to see whether the information obtained from the disk matches the expected information that would indicate that a valid, supported logical volume resides on the physical media (or on the virtual device).

4. If no valid structures are found on the target physical/virtual device, return an error code of STATUS_UNRECOGNIZED_VOLUME to the I/O Manager, which will cause the I/O Manager to pass on the request to the next registered file system (or mini-FSD).

   Any file system recognizer supplied along with your FSD must be capable of detecting the presence/absence of valid metadata information on the storage medium, to determine whether or not the disk actually contains a valid logical volume. These checks need not be conclusive; i.e., as long as the mini-FSD believes that a valid logical volume exists/does not exist on the disk, it can choose a reasonable course of action to pursue.

5. If structures (metadata) on the target physical device indicate that a valid logical volume exists on the device, then return STATUS_FS_DRIVER_ REQUIRED to the I/O Manager.

   Returning STATUS_FS_DRIVER_REQUIRED to the I/O Manager results in the I/O Manager issuing another IRP_MJ_FILE_SYSTEM_CONTROL request to the file system recognizer; this time though, the minor function code will be `IRP_MN_LOAD_FILE_SYSTEM` indicating that the mini-FSD should proceed with attempting to load the full FSD implementation into memory.

6. Upon receiving the FSCTL request with a minor function of IRP_MN_LOAD_ FILE_SYSTEM, attempt to load the full FSD into memory.

   This can be accomplished by using the `ZwLoadDriver()` support routine. See the sample code fragment provided for an example of the usage of this routine.

7. Remember the result of the load operation and take appropriate steps.

   Typically, if the load request succeeds, the mini-FSD can render itself dormant by simply unregistering itself from the list of registered file system implementations maintained by the I/O Manager. This ensures that the I/O Manager will no longer send mount requests to the mini-FSD.

   If the load request fails, it is recommended by the NT I/O subsystem designers that the mini-FSD remember this failure in a device extension field and never again (during the current boot cycle) attempt to reload the FSD. Instead, upon receiving further mount requests, the mini-FSD should simply reject them immediately with the return code `STATUS_UNRECOGNIZED_ VOLUME`. This will allow the I/O Manager to try some other loaded FSD instead.

   Note that it is not mandatory for your mini-FSD to remember a previous failure if it believes that the next time around there is a better chance of the load request succeeding.

You should note that file system recognizers typically exist only for disk-based (including CD-ROM-based) file system implementations. Network redirectors typically do not use a VCB structure, and they also do not typically have mini-FSD implementations.

The sample code fragment illustrates how you could develop your own file system recognizer:

Code Sample

```
NTSTATUS DriverEntry(
PDRIVER_OBJECT      DriverObject,
PUNICODE_STRING     RegistryPath)
{
    NTSTATUS                RC = STATUS_SUCCESS;
    UNICODE_STRING          DriverDeviceName;
    UNICODE_STRING          FileSystemName;
    OBJECT_ATTRIBUTES       ObjectAttributes;
    HANDLE                  FileSystemHandle = NULL;
```

```
    IO_STATUS_BLOCK              IoStatus;
    PtrSFsRecDeviceExtension     PtrExtension = NULL;

    try {
        try {
            // Initialize the IRP major function table
            DriverObject->MajorFunction[IRP_MJ_FILE_SYSTEM_CONTROL] =
                                                    SFsRecFsControl;
            DriverObject->DriverUnload = SFsRecUnload;

            // Before creating a device object, check whether the FSD has
            // been loaded already. You should know the name of the FSD
            // that this recognizer has been created for.
            RtlInitUnicodeString(&FileSystemName, L"\\SampleFSD");
            InitializeObjectAttributes(&ObjectAttributes, &FileSystemName,
                    OBJ_CASE_INSENSITIVE, NULL, NULL);
            // Try to open the file system now.
            RC = ZwCreateFile(&FileSystemHandle, SYNCHRONIZE,
                                    &ObjectAttributes,
                                    &IoStatus, NULL, 0,
                                    FILE_SHARE_READ | FILE_SHARE_WRITE,
                                    FILE_OPEN, 0, NULL, 0);
            if (RC != STATUS_OBJECT_NAME_NOT_FOUND) {
                // The FSD must have been already loaded.
                if (NT_SUCCESS(RC)) {
                    ZwClose(FileSystemHandle);
                }
                RC = STATUS_IMAGE_ALREADY_LOADED;
                try_return(RC);
            }

            // Create a device object representing the file system
            // recognizer. Mount requests are sent to this device object.
            RtlInitUnicodeString(&DriverDeviceName,
                                L"\\SampleFSDRecognizer");

            if (!NT_SUCCESS(RC = IoCreateDevice(
                    DriverObject,               // Driver object for the file
                                                // system rec.
                    sizeof(SFsRecDeviceExtension), // Did a load fail?
                    &DriverDeviceName,      // Name used above
                    FILE_DEVICE_DISK_FILE_SYSTEM,
                    0,                          // No special characteristics
                    FALSE,
                    &(PtrFSRecDeviceObject)))) {
                try_return(RC);
            }

            PtrExtension =
                (PtrSFsRecDeviceExtension)(PtrFSRecDeviceObject->
                                                    DeviceExtension);

            PtrExtension->DidLoadFail = FALSE;
```

```
                // Register the device object with the I/O Manager.
            IoRegisterFileSystem(PtrFSRecDeviceObject);

        } except (EXCEPTION_EXECUTE_HANDLER) {
            /* we encountered an exception somewhere, eat it up */
            RC = GetExceptionCode();
        }

        try_exit:    NOTHING;
    } finally {
        /* start unwinding if we were unsuccessful */
        if (!NT_SUCCESS(RC) && PtrFSRecDeviceObject) {
            IoDeleteDevice(PtrFSRecDeviceObject);
            PtrFSRecDeviceObject = NULL;
        }
    }

    return(RC);
}

void SFsRecUnload(
PDRIVER_OBJECT          PtrFsRecDriverObject)
{
    // Simple. Unregister the device object, and delete it.
    if (PtrFSRecDeviceObject) {
        IoUnregisterFileSystem(PtrFSRecDeviceObject);
        IoDeleteDevice(PtrFSRecDeviceObject);

        PtrFSRecDeviceObject = NULL;
    }

    return;
}

NTSTATUS SFsRecFsControl(
PDEVICE_OBJECT          DeviceObject,
PIRP                    Irp)
{
    NTSTATUS                    RC = STATUS_UNRECOGNIZED_VOLUME;
    PIO_STACK_LOCATION          PtrIoStackLocation = NULL;
    PtrSFsRecDeviceExtension    PtrExtension = NULL;
    PDEVICE_OBJECT              PtrTargetDeviceObject = NULL;
    UNICODE_STRING              DriverName;

    FsRtlEnterFileSystem();

    try {
        try {
            PtrIoStackLocation = IoGetCurrentIrpStackLocation(Irp);
            ASSERT(PtrIoStackLocation);

            // Get a pointer to the device object extension.
            PtrExtension =
                (PtrSFsRecDeviceExtension)(PtrFSRecDeviceObject->
                                                    DeviceExtension);
```

```
switch (PtrIoStackLocation->MinorFunction) {
case IRP_MN_MOUNT_VOLUME:
    // Fail the request immediately if a previous load has
    // failed. You are not required to do this, however, in
    // your driver.
    if (PtrExtension->DidLoadFail) {
        try_return(RC);
    }

    // Get a pointer to the target physical/virtual device
    // object.
    PtrTargetDeviceObject =
        PtrIoStackLocation->
                Parameters.MountVolume.DeviceObject;

    // The operations that you perform here are highly FSD
    // specific. Typically, you would invoke an internal
    // function that would
    // (a) Get the disk geometry by issuing an IOCTL
    // (b) Read the first few sectors (or appropriate sectors)
    //     to verify the on-disk metadata information.
    // To get the drive geometry, use the documented I/O
    // Manager routine called IoBuildDeviceIoControlRequest()
    // to create an IRP. Supply an event with this request
    // that you will wait for in case the lower-level driver
    // returns STATUS_PENDING. Similarly, to actually read on-
    // disk sectors, create an IRP using the
    // IoBuildSynchronousFsdRequest() function call with a
    // major function of IRP_MJ_READ.

    // After you have obtained on-disk information, verify the
    // metadata. RC =
    // SFsRecGetDiskInfoAndVerify(PtrTargetDeviceObject);

    if (NT_SUCCESS(RC)) {
        // Everything looks good. Prepare to load the driver.
        try_return(RC = STATUS_FS_DRIVER_REQUIRED);
    }
    break;
case IRP_MN_LOAD_FILE_SYSTEM:
    // OK. So we processed a mount request and returned
    // STATUS_FS_DRIVER_REQUIRED to the I/O Manager.
    // This is the result. Talk about an ungrateful I/O
    // Manager making us do more work!
    RtlInitUnicodeString(&DriverName,
L"\\Registry\\Machine\\System\\CurrentControlSet\\Services\\SFsd");
    RC = ZwLoadDriver(&DriverName);
    if ((!NT_SUCCESS(RC)) && (RC !=
                                STATUS_IMAGE_ALREADY_LOADED)) {
        PtrExtension->DidLoadFail = TRUE;
    } else {
        // Load succeeded. Mission accomplished.
        IoUnregisterFileSystem(PtrFSRecDeviceObject);
    }
```

```
                break;
            default:
                RC = STATUS_INVALID_DEVICE_REQUEST;
                break;
            }

        } except (EXCEPTION_EXECUTE_HANDLER) {
            RC = GetExceptionCode();
        }

        try_exit:    NOTHING;

    } finally {
        // Complete the IRP.
        Irp->IoStatus.Status = RC;
        IoCompleteRequest(Irp, IO_NO_INCREMENT);
    }

    FsRtlExitFileSystem();

    return(RC);
}
```

The following structure definitions are used by the code fragment:

```
typedef struct SFsRecDeviceExtension {
  BOOLEAN         DidLoadFail;
} SFsRecDeviceExtension, *PtrSFsRecDeviceExtension;

PDEVICE_OBJECT  PtrFSRecDeviceObject = NULL;
unsigned int    SFsRecDidLoadFail = 0;

extern NTSTATUS ZwLoadDriver(
IN PUNICODE_STRING         DriverName);
```

Notes

As you can see, developing a file system recognizer (mini-FSD) is not difficult at all. One point to note, in the event that you do provide a file system recognizer module with your FSD implementation, is how you should configure the Registry in order to load the recognizer automatically.

Chapter 9 lists the entries required in the Windows NT Registry to install a full FSD. You should make the following modifications:

- Modify *HKEY_LOCAL_MACHINE\SYSTEM\CurrentControlSet\Services\Sample-FSD\Start* to have a value of 4.

- You should also add a new entry for the file system recognizer, e.g., *HKEY_LOCAL_MACHINE\SYSTEM\CurrentControlSet\Services\SFsRec.*

This key should at least include the following value entries:

— `ErrorControl : REG_DWORD : 0`

— `Group : REG_SZ : Boot File System`

— `Start : REG_DWORD : 0x1`

— `Type : REG_DWORD : 0x8`

This indicates that the type of kernel service is `SERVICE_RECOGNIZER_ DRIVER` (a file system recognizer).

What Happens After the FSD Is Loaded?

Once a file system has been successfully loaded, the mini-FSD returns `STATUS_ SUCCESS` to the Windows NT I/O Manager. The I/O Manager then queries all the loaded FSD instances once again, asking each one to mount the logical volume on the target physical/virtual device object.

This mount request will eventually reach the newly loaded (our sample) file system driver. The request is dispatched to the driver as a FSCTL request. The IRP contains a major function code of `IRP_MJ_FILE_SYSTEM_CONTROL` and a minor function code of `IRP_MN_MOUNT_VOLUME`. The `Flags` field in the current I/O stack location is a value of (`IRP_MOUNT_COMPLETION`|`IRP_ SYNCHRONOUS_PAGING_IO`).

The I/O stack location contains the following structure relevant to processing the mount request issued to an FSD:

```
typedef struct _IO_STACK_LOCATION {

    // ...

    union {

        //...

        // Parameters for MountVolume
        struct {
            PVPB Vpb;
            PDEVICE_OBJECT DeviceObject;
        } MountVolume;

        // ...
    } Parameters;

    // ...

} IO_STACK_LOCATION, *PIO_STACK_LOCATION;
```

The FSD must perform a logical mount operation upon receiving the mount request. The following sequence of logical steps are typically executed by the FSD when it receives the mount request:

1. The FSD will obtain the partition information, i.e., the driver geometry, by building a device IOCTL IRP and issuing it to the driver managing the target device object.

   The `IoBuildDeviceIoControlRequest()` support routine, provided by the I/O Manager, can be used to create an IRP that is then sent to the lower-level driver. Typically, the IOCTL code used is `IOCTL_DISK_GET_PARTITION_INFO` for read/write media.

   Note that CDFS issues two separate IOCTL requests to the disk driver with IOCTL codes specified as `IOCTL_CDROM_CHECK_VERIFY` and `IOCTL_CDROM_GET_DRIVE_GEOMETRY`, respectively.

2. Once partition information has been successfully obtained, the FSD will typically create a device object representing the instance of the mounted volume.

   The device object created would have a specified type of either `FILE_DEVICE_DISK_FILE_SYSTEM` or `FILE_DEVICE_CD_ROM_FILE_SYSTEM`.

   Note that the sample FSD defines a volume control block structure representing an instance of a mounted logical volume. The sample FSD implementation allocates this VCB structure as the device extension for the device object created to represent the mounted logical volume. Your driver does not have to use the same methodology. However, this would be a good place for your driver to allocate a VCB structure (from nonpaged pool) and initialize it appropriately.

   To see the kind of initialization performed by the sample FSD, consult this code fragment:

```
void SFsdInitializeVCB(
PDEVICE_OBJECT                PtrVolumeDeviceObject,
PDEVICE_OBJECT                PtrTargetDeviceObject,
PVPB                          PtrVPB)
{
    NTSTATUS                  RC = STATUS_SUCCESS;
    PtrSFsdVCB                PtrVCB = NULL;
    BOOLEAN                   VCBResourceInitialized = FALSE;

    PtrVCB = (PtrSFsdVCB)(PtrVolumeDeviceObject->DeviceExtension);

    // Zero it out (typically this has already been done by the I/O
    // Manager but it does not hurt to do it again).
    RtlZeroMemory(PtrVCB, sizeof(SFsdVCB));

    // Initialize the signature fields
    PtrVCB->NodeIdentifier.NodeType = SFSD_NODE_TYPE_VCB;
    PtrVCB->NodeIdentifier.NodeSize = sizeof(SFsdVCB);
```

```
// Initialize the ERESOURCE object.
RC = ExInitializeResourceLite(&(PtrVCB->VCBResource));
ASSERT(NT_SUCCESS(RC));
VCBResourceInitialized = TRUE;

// We know the target device object.
// Note that this is not necessarily a pointer to the actual
// physical/virtual device on which the logical volume should
// be mounted. This is a pointer to either the actual
// device or any device object that may have been
// attached to it. Any IRPs that we send should be sent to this
// device object. However, the "real" physical/virtual device
// object on which we perform our mount operation can be
// determined from the RealDevice field in the VPB sent to us.
PtrVCB->TargetDeviceObject = PtrTargetDeviceObject;

// We also have a pointer to the newly created device object
// representing this logical volume (remember that this VCB
// structure is simply an extension of the created device object).
PtrVCB->VCBDeviceObject = PtrVolumeDeviceObject;

// We also have the VPB pointer. This was obtained from the
// Parameters.MountVolume.Vpb field in the current I/O stack
// location for the mount IRP.
PtrVCB->PtrVPB = PtrVPB;

// Initialize the list-anchor (head) for some lists in this VCB.
InitializeListHead(&(PtrVCB->NextFCB));
InitializeListHead(&(PtrVCB->NextNotifyIRP));
InitializeListHead(&(PtrVCB->VolumeOpenListHead));

// Initialize the notify IRP list mutex
KeInitializeMutex(&(PtrVCB->NotifyIRPMutex), 0);


// Set the initial file size values appropriately. Note that your
// FSD may guess at the initial amount of information you would
// like to read from the disk until you have really determined
// that this a valid logical volume (on disk) that you wish to
// mount. PtrVCB->FileSize = PtrVCB->AllocationSize = ??

// You typically do not want to bother with valid data length
// callbacks from the Cache Manager for the file stream opened for
// volume metadata information
PtrVCB->ValidDataLength.LowPart = 0xFFFFFFFF;
PtrVCB->ValidDataLength.HighPart = 0x7FFFFFFF;

// Create a stream file object for this volume.
PtrVCB->PtrStreamFileObject = IoCreateStreamFileObject(NULL,
                                    PtrVCB->PtrVPB->RealDevice);
ASSERT(PtrVCB->PtrStreamFileObject);

// Initialize some important fields in the newly created file
// object.
```

```
    PtrVCB->PtrStreamFileObject->FsContext = (void *)PtrVCB;
    PtrVCB->PtrStreamFileObject->FsContext2 = NULL;
    PtrVCB->PtrStreamFileObject->SectionObjectPointer =
                    &(PtrVCB->SectionObject);

    PtrVCB->PtrStreamFileObject->Vpb = PtrVPB;

    // Link this chap onto the global linked list of all VCB
structures.

ExAcquireResourceExclusiveLite(&(SFsdGlobalData.GlobalDataResource),
                                                TRUE);
    InsertTailList(&(SFsdGlobalData.NextVCB), &(PtrVCB->NextVCB));

    // Initialize caching for the stream file object.
    CcInitializeCacheMap(PtrVCB->PtrStreamFileObject,
                    (PCC_FILE_SIZES)(&(PtrVCB->AllocationSize)),
                        TRUE,          // We will use pinned
                                       // access.
                        &(SFsdGlobalData.CacheMgrCallBacks),
                        PtrVCB);


    SFsdReleaseResource(&(SFsdGlobalData.GlobalDataResource));

    // Mark the fact that this VCB structure is initialized.
    SFsdSetFlag(PtrVCB->VCBFlags, SFSD_VCB_FLAGS_VCB_INITIALIZED);
    return;
}
```

Remember to perform the following modifications to the device object created to represent the mounted logical volume instance:

— Check the alignment restriction enforced by the target physical/virtual device object.

If the alignment requirement mandated by the target device object is greater than that specified by your FSD, modify the **AlignmentRequirement** field in the newly created device object to reflect that of the target device.

— Remember to clear the **DO_DEVICE_INITIALIZING** flag from the **Flags** field in the newly created device object.

For device objects created during driver load time, the I/O Manager automatically performs this task for you. If, however, you forget to clear this flag value for device objects created by your FSD after the driver initialization has been completed, your FSD will not receive any IRPs, because the I/O Manager will fail any requests sent to the device immediately.

— Set the **StackSize** value in the newly created device object to be equal to (**TargetDeviceObject->StackSize + 1**).

3. Set the `DeviceObject` field in the `PtrVPB` structure, sent to the FSD as part of the mount request to point to the new device object.

   This is how a logical association is created between the VPB structure and the logical volume device object created by your FSD. This pointer value is used by the I/O Manager to determine the target device object whenever a create/open request is received for a mounted logical volume.

4. Clear the `DO_VERIFY_VOLUME` flag (if set) in the device object for the real (physical/virtual) device.

   If you do not clear this bit, any read operations issued by your FSD to the device will fail. Remember, though, if you clear this bit, you must reset it on your way out of the mount routine.

5. Read in some of the information required to verify that the logical volume can be mounted by your FSD.

   You can simply use `CcMapData()` to map the sectors described by the on-disk volume structures. Remember that this routine returns a pointer to a buffer control block structure and also a buffer pointer to the mapped-in information, which is valid as long as the range is not unpinned.

6. Verify that the structures on disk are legitimate, performing additional read operations if required.

7. Create and initialize an FCB structure to represent the root directory.

   Typically, the FSD always maintains an internal reference on the root directory FCB, to keep it around in memory as long as the volume stays mounted. The `PtrRootDirectoryFCB` field in the VCB structure is initialized by the sample FSD to point to the newly created and opened root directory for the logical volume.

   Note that opening the root directory will involve reading the root directory contents from disk. Your FSD may use stream file objects created for internal directory I/O operations.

   By this time you should have a fairly good idea of the range that you need to perform map operations for and you should update the file size values in the VCB structure appropriately.

8. The native Windows NT FSD implementations appear to read the volume label off the disk to ensure that the volume was not previously mounted.

   If this happens to be a remount request for a previously mounted volume,[*] the FSD must remove the newly created VCB and stream file object structures

---

[*] Any user/kernel thread with the appropriate privileges may have issued a mount request. The I/O Manager will also issue a mount request if a previously issued verify volume operation (for removable media) to the FSD had a return code of other than `STATUS_SUCCESS`.

(ensuring that any pinned ranges have been unpinned) and reinitialize the old VCB structures appropriately. Reinitialization involves setting the following fields:

— The `OldVCB->PtrVPB->RealDevice` must be updated to point to the `PtrVPB->RealDevice` field contents.

— The `OldVCB->TargetDeviceObject` field must be initialized to refer to the new `TargetDeviceObject`, obtained from the current I/O stack location for the mount IRP.

— The `PtrVPB->RealDevice->Vpb` field must be reinitialized to `OldVCB->PtrVPB`.

— The cache map for the stream file object associated with the `OldVCB` must be reinitialized.

— Any other FSD-specific operations should be performed here to ensure that any cached information from the previous mount has been discarded.

9. Now that the mount/remount operation is nearly finished, you should re-enable volume verification if you have cleared the DO_VERIFY_VOLUME flag from the real target device object.

10. Typically, native NT FSD implementations will issue an IOCTL request to the target device object to lock removable media in the drive (at least, NTFS appears to do this).

11. Set the appropriate flag value in your VCB structure to indicate that the mount/remount operation was successful.

    For example, the sample FSD will set the **SFSD_VCB_FLAGS_VOLUME_MOUNTED** flag in the **VCBFlags** field.

12. Unpin any byte ranges that were pinned due to an invocation of **CcMapData()** and release any resources that may have been acquired.

13. Return **STATUS_SUCCESS** if the mount logical volume operation succeeded.

    If your FSD encounters an error during the mount process (e.g., I/O errors encountered when attempting to read on-disk information), it should return the appropriate error value after cleaning up any structures that may have been allocated in processing the mount request.*

    If your FSD returns **STATUS_SUCCESS** to the I/O Manager for the mount request, the I/O Manager will set the **VPB_MOUNTED** flag in the VPB structure.

---

* If a mount request issued by the I/O Manager fails for the physical device object representing the system boot partition, the NT I/O Manager will bugcheck the system with the INACCESSIBLE_BOOT_DEVICE bugcheck code.

Once the logical volume has been mounted by a loaded FSD, the I/O Manager will send the original create/open request that resulted in all of this processing being performed. The create/open request will be sent to the newly created device object representing the mounted instance of the logical volume and referred to by the `DeviceObject` field in the VPB structure.

NOTE   Mount operations performed on a logical volume are often very complex, especially for more sophisticated FSD implementations such as NTFS, which is a log-based file system driver. Therefore, you should use the steps listed previously as a general guideline to follow when designing the volume mount operation specific to your file system driver.

In the next chapter, we'll see how to design and develop filter drivers that could help provide unique value-added functionality for the Windows NT operating system.

12

Filter Drivers

The Windows NT I/O subsystem was designed to be extensible. One of the ways in which the capabilities of the I/O subsystem can be extended is by developing filter drivers. Chapter 2, *File System Driver Development*, provided an introduction to filter drivers in Windows NT. This chapter takes a detailed look at designing and implementing filter drivers for the Windows NT operating system.

First, we'll discuss why you may want to use filter drivers to achieve some of your objectives. This is followed by a discussion of some fundamental steps involved in developing filter drivers, including how to attach to a target device object, how to create your own IRP structures, how to use completion routines to perform postprocessing upon IRP completion, and how to stop filtering by detaching from a target device object.

We'll conclude with a discussion of some issues you should be familiar with when attempting filter driver design and development. The diskette accompanying this book provides a complete sample filter driver implementation that can be used as a template in designing your own kernel-mode filter driver.

Why Use Filter Drivers?

The fundamental reason for any of us to design and develop kernel-mode software for Windows NT is to provide added value beyond what is provided with the core operating system environment. This is also the motivating factor behind the design and development of filter drivers.

Two design principles adopted by the NT I/O Manager make developing value-added software easier than with other operating systems.

First, the I/O Manager design implements a client-server model for the I/O subsystem. Any user- or kernel-mode component can request the services of practically any other loaded kernel-mode driver. The requesting module is then the client of the target driver that will satisfy the request. There are few restrictions mandated by the I/O Manager on when a client component can invoke a driver (the server for the request) and what kind of services can be requested.

One example of the usage of this client-server model is when file system drivers request services from lower-level device drivers. What is more unusual, though certainly possible, is for file systems to request services from other file system drivers installed on the machine, or even for lower-level intermediate drivers to request services from higher-level file system drivers.

You should give careful consideration to the following whenever you design a driver that requests services from either other higher-level kernel-mode drivers or kernel-mode drivers at the same level in the calling hierarchy:

- The different scenarios under which your driver can be invoked
- The different scenarios under which your driver would request services from other kernel-mode modules
- Restrictions on when you can incur page faults within your driver module
- Assumptions made by higher-level drivers, such as file systems; the file systems adapt their behavior depending on what the top-level component is for an I/O request
- Resource acquisition hierarchies that must be defined and strictly implemented for resource acquisition across kernel-mode modules

Second, the NT I/O Manager supports a layered driver model. As each IRP is processed, it passes through various layers of the driver hierarchy until it is finally resolved by some driver via a call to `IoCompleteRequest()`. Therefore, it's easy for a third-party driver to insert itself into the existing calling hierarchy and get the opportunity to process the I/O Request Packets.

In order to cooperate with the I/O Manager in supporting such a layered driver module, your design must conform to the following basic requirements:

- Always invoke the services of other kernel-mode drivers in the standard manner by using the `IoCallDriver()` function.
- Once an IRP has been sent on to another driver, do not touch it.
- You can, however, register a completion routine to be invoked when the IRP has been completed.
- Unless you develop tightly coupled drivers that use privately defined IOCTLs to communicate with each other, you must never depend on whether the

request you have forwarded goes directly to your target driver or is intercepted by another filter driver module.

- The filter driver module must present the same interfaces as those presented by the original target of the request.

- Treat other driver modules as black boxes.

- Your driver must not be dependent upon how the target driver implements processing for your I/O request.

What Is a Filter Driver?

A filter driver is a kernel-mode driver. It is developed primarily to intercept requests targeted to an existing kernel-mode driver, to allow the addition of new functionality beyond what is currently available.

Figure 12-1 illustrates this concept.

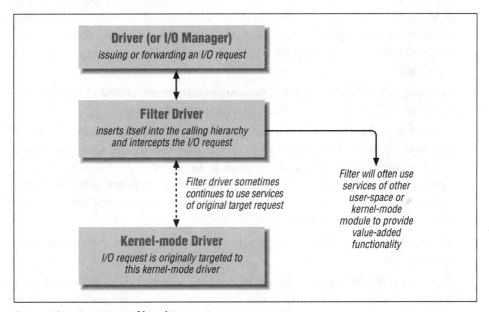

Figure 12-1. Inserting a filter driver to intercept requests

As shown in Figure 12-1, I/O requests targeted to a specific driver are intercepted by the filter driver module. The filter driver may either use the services of the original target of the I/O request, or use the services of other user-mode or kernel-mode software to provide value-added functionality.

When Can I Use a Filter Driver?

You should consider designing a filter driver whenever you wish to affect the current flow of processing for certain I/O requests. Therefore, if you want to provide some software that will extend, modify, or completely supplant an existing module and if you wish to maintain complete transparency to the user when providing your specialized functionality, consider designing a filter driver.

For example, suppose you decide to design and implement on-line encryption/decryption functionality for the data stored on existing Windows NT file systems. Currently, the operating system does not provide any such functionality. However, hypothesize that you possess the technology to implement a secure encryption algorithm. What you would really like to do is the following:

- Use the services of the Windows NT native file systems to store and retrieve user data

  It would not be cost-effective to design your own file system implementation to store encrypted data on disk. Besides, users would typically wish to continue to use native Windows NT file system services for storing their data and would like to use your software only to encrypt sensitive data stored on such file systems.

- Intercept all user write requests and encrypt data being stored to disk for targeted files, directories, or complete mounted logical volumes

  Given that you will not design a new file system driver, you will want to intercept existing file system requests so that the user can specify files, directories, or even entire mounted logical volumes to be encrypted on-the-fly. When a write request issued by the user is received, your software module should somehow be able to intercept such write requests and encrypt the user-supplied data before it is stored to disk.

- Intercept all user read requests and decrypt data (if required) before returning it to the user

  Now that you have successfully encrypted user-supplied data and stored it on disk using the services of the native file systems, you must also provide the services of decrypting the data whenever an authorized user tries to read it.

It seems obvious that a filter driver would serve your purposes admirably in the preceding example problem. The filter driver would allow you to intercept user I/O requests and perform your encryption/decryption processing on the data, transparently to the user. Furthermore, it is not necessary to design your own file system or special device driver to manage and transfer data on secondary storage devices, and therefore your filter driver would continue to use the services provided by existing drivers on the system.

More Examples of Filter Drivers

Other examples of situations where a filter driver could be used include:

To provide virus detection functionality

Imagine for a minute that you want to provide a new virus-detection module for the Windows NT operating system. This virus-detecting module performs its tasks in real-time; therefore, it will attempt to detect any viruses in files being copied to a mounted logical volume and refuse the data transfer if such a virus is found. How would you go about doing this?

Figure 12-2 illustrates how a filter driver that layers itself above a mounted logical volume device object managed by a file system driver can perform the virus detection functionality.

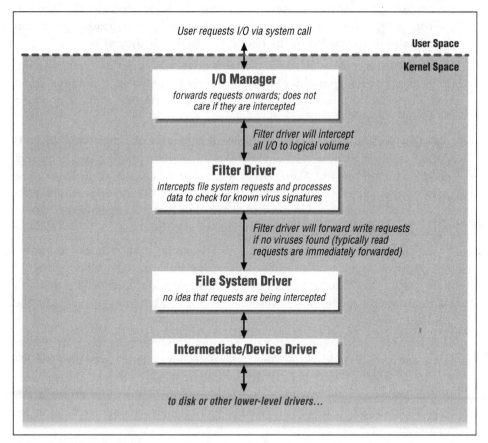

Figure 12-2. Filter driver used in virus detection

The virus detection software module can be implemented as a filter driver that intercepts I/O targeted to one or more mounted logical volumes. Whenever any user's I/O request is received by the Windows NT I/O Manager for a file residing on a mounted logical volume, the I/O Manager normally forwards the request to the file system driver managing the mounted logical volume.

Before forwarding the request, however, the I/O Manager also checks to see if any other device object has layered itself over the device object representing the mounted logical volume and redirects the request to that device object, which is at the top of the layered list of device objects. In order to intercept I/O requests, the virus-detecting filter driver module has to create a device object that layers (or attaches) itself to the device object representing the mounted logical volume.

Therefore, the filter driver module intercepts the I/O before it reaches the file system. Now, the virus-detection module can check for any virus signatures in the data being written out to disk. Note that in most cases, read requests can be immediately forwarded by the filter driver to the file system.

If any virus signature is detected, the filter driver can reject the write request, protecting the user's physical disks from possible corruption. If no virus signature is detected, the filter driver can safely forward the IRP to the file system for further processing.

Note that the file system driver has no idea that some other filter driver is layered above it. It behaves (as always) as if the user request has been sent directly to it by the I/O Manager. By the same token, the filter driver must always be cognizant of the fact that the file system does not know about its existence and must therefore ensure that it does not do anything that would violate any fundamental assumptions made by the FSD.

Virus-detection software must also be able to automatically check for viruses that might be present on existing media (especially on removable media). In most cases, virus-detection software will also provide functionality that will scan removable media whenever they are reinserted into a drive on the machine.

This functionality requires that your virus-detection software layer itself over the lower-level disk driver (for the removable drive) itself, layer over the file system (in order to accurately detect media changes), or require the software to understand and utilize information presented in Chapter 11, *Writing a File System Driver III*, on how file system drivers handle volume verification for removable media.

Implement HSM functionality.

Hierarchical storage management (HSM) means different things to different people. However, it often involves automatic transfer of infrequently used data to slower but cheaper secondary storage media and an automatic transfer back to regular storage if the migrated data files are accessed. Figure 12-3 illustrates how a filter driver could be part of such an HSM solution.

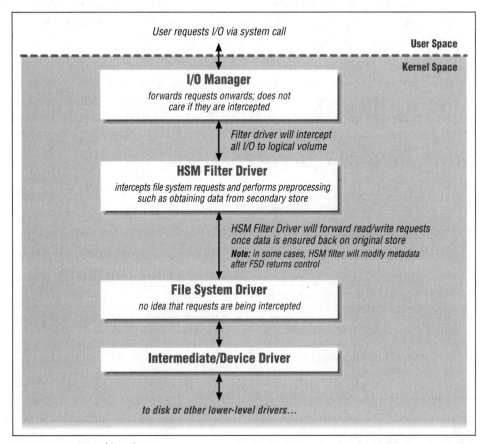

Figure 12-3. HSM filter driver

Consider an HSM filter driver that migrates older, infrequently accessed files to a slower device. If a user now wishes to access or modify the migrated file, the HSM driver will typically transfer data back to the local file system before forwarding the request to the FSD. In this way, the FSD can be completely ignorant about the migration/retrieval of data performed by the HSM driver.

Often, HSM drivers leave a little *stub file* on the original file system as a placeholder, once data has been migrated. The actual size of this stub file is generally 0 bytes, although it may contain some metadata stored by the HSM driver for administrative convenience. If a user tries to list the directory entries for a directory whose files have been migrated, the HSM module may have to massage the information returned by the FSD (e.g., file size) in response to a file information request in order to maintain complete transparency about the migration operation that was performed. Therefore, the HSM module may choose to register a completion routine before forwarding directory control or file information requests to the FSD, allowing it to perform appropriate modification of the information returned by the FSD before it is finally returned to the caller.

You could undoubtedly come up with many additional ways in which the functionality provided by the I/O subsystem could be extended. The preceding examples are simply a sample of the number of ways in which filter drivers can help you implement your ideas for providing added value to the system.

Basic Steps in Filtering

There are a few operations that you should become familiar with when you design and implement a new filter driver:

- Attaching to a target device object, to intercept calls directed to that object

- Building IRPs that can be dispatched to drivers managing target device objects

  Note that your driver may either build associated IRPs for a master IRP sent to you or create new master IRP structures.

- Specifying a completion routine to be invoked when an attached driver finishes processing an IRP

- Detaching from the target device object when appropriate

Attaching to a Target Device Object

Before proceeding with the discussion on how to attach to a target device object, it is useful to understand the following terms:

- The *filter driver* is the kernel-mode driver that you design and implement.

- The *source device object* (also known as the *filter-driver device object*) is the device object that you create in order to perform a logical attachment between your driver and the original target of the I/O requests.

- The *target device object* is the device object, representing a physical, virtual, or logical device, to which I/O request packets are currently directed.

  Your goal is to intercept the I/O request packets sent to the target device object.

- The *target driver* is the kernel-mode driver that manages (and provides the dispatch functions for) the target device object.

The process of associating a source device object created by your filter driver with the target device object, such that the I/O Manager will automatically redirect requests to your driver is called an *attach* operation.

As mentioned earlier, filter drivers provide their value-added functionality by intercepting requests targeted to an existing driver. Once a filter driver has begun intercepting all of the requests targeted to the existing driver module, it can either augment the functionality provided by the existing driver or supplant it altogether.

There are a few simple steps your driver must perform to successfully attach to a target device object:

1. Get a pointer to the target device object.

2. Create your own device object that will be used in the attach operation.

3. Ensure that your driver is set up to process the I/O requests, originally directed to the target device object, that will now be redirected to it instead.

4. Ensure that the fields in your device object are set correctly to maintain complete transparency to the modules that normally invoke the target driver.

5. Request the I/O Manager to create an attachment between the two device objects.

Once the attach operation has been completed, the I/O Manager will begin redirecting I/O requests to your device object instead of forwarding them to the driver managing the target device object.

Code Fragment

The following code fragment illustrates how the attach operation can be implemented by your filter driver.

```
NTSTATUS SFilterAttachTarget(
PUNICODE_STRING                    TargetDeviceName,
ACCESS_MASK                        DesiredAccess,
BOOLEAN                            InvokedFromDriverEntry)
{
    // Declarations ...

    try {

        // Get a pointer to the target device object. Read the discussion
        // provided later in this chapter for information on how to
        // ensure that a file system is always mounted
        // before you attach to the underlying device object.
        if (!NT_SUCCESS(RC = IoGetDeviceObjectPointer(TargetDeviceName,
                            DesiredAccess,
                            &PtrTargetFileObject,
                            &PtrTargetDeviceObject))) {
```

```
            try_return(RC);
    }


    // File Object has been referenced. No need to reference the
    // device object, since a successful attach operation will ensure
    // that the device object is not deleted without our being
    // notified. Further, if you do reference the underlying device
    // object, you will effectively exclude all new open operations,
    // just in case the device object can be opened exclusively only
    // (since the reference will count as an open operation).

    // Now, create a new device object for the attach operation.
    if (!NT_SUCCESS(RC = IoCreateDevice(
                            SFilterGlobalData.SFilterDriverObject,
                            sizeof(SFilterDeviceExtension),
                            NULL,           // unnamed device object
                            PtrTargetDeviceObject->DeviceType,
                            PtrTargetDeviceObject->Characteristics,
                            FALSE,
                            &(PtrNewDeviceObject))))) {
        // failed to create a device object, leave.
        try_return(RC);
    }

    // Initialize the extension for the device object. The extension
    // stores any device-object-specific (global) data (e.g., a
    // pointer to the device object to which you performed the attach
    // operation).
    PtrDeviceExtension = (PtrSFilterDeviceExtension)
                            PtrNewDeviceObject->DeviceExtension;
    SFilterInitDevExtension(PtrDeviceExtension,
                        SFILTER_NODE_TYPE_ATTACHED_DEVICE);
    InitializedDeviceObject = TRUE;

    // If we were not invoked from the DriverEntry() function, mark the
    // fact that this device object is no longer being initialized.
    // If the device object is created during driver initialization,
    // the I/O Manager will do this for us.
    if (!InvokedFromDriverEntry) {
        PtrNewDeviceObject->Flags &= ~DO_DEVICE_INITIALIZING;
    }

    // Acquire the resource exclusively for our newly created device
    // object to ensure that dispatch routines requests are not
    // processed until we are really ready.
    ExAcquireResourceExclusiveLite(
            &(PtrDeviceExtension->DeviceExtensionResource), TRUE);
    AcquiredDeviceObject = TRUE;

    // The new device object has been created. Perform the attachment.
    RC = IoAttachDeviceByPointer(PtrNewDeviceObject,
                                    PtrTargetDeviceObject);
    // The only reason we would fail (and possibly get STATUS_NO_SUCH_
    // DEVICE)
```

```
        // is if the target was being initialized or unloaded and neither
        // should be happening at this time.
        ASSERT(NT_SUCCESS(RC));

        // Note that the AlignmentRequirement, the StackSize, and the
        // SectorSize values will have been automatically initialized for
        // us in the source device object (the I/O Manager does this as
        // part of processing the IoAttachDeviceByPointer() request).

        // We should set the Flags values correctly to indicate whether
        // direct I/O, buffered I/O, or neither is required. Typically,
        // FSDs (especially native FSD implementations) do not want the I/O
        // Manager to touch the user buffer at all.
        PtrNewDeviceObject->Flags |= (PtrTargetDeviceObject->Flags &
                        (DO_BUFFERED_IO | DO_DIRECT_IO));

        // Initialize the TargetDeviceObject field in the extension.
        // This is used by us when (if) we wish to forward I/O requests
        // to the target device object.
        PtrDeviceExtension->TargetDeviceObject = PtrTargetDeviceObject;
        PtrDeviceExtension->TargetDriverObject =
                                PtrTargetDeviceObject->DriverObject;
        // Some bookkeeping.
        SFilterSetFlag(PtrDeviceExtension->DeviceExtensionFlags,
                        SFILTER_DEV_EXT_ATTACHED);

        // We are there now. All I/O requests will start being redirected
        // to us until we detach ourselves.

    try_exit:   NOTHING;

    } finally {
        // Cleanup stuff goes here.
        if (AcquiredDeviceObject) {
            SFilterReleaseResource(&(PtrDeviceExtension->
                                        DeviceExtensionResource));
        }

        if (!NT_SUCCESS(RC) && PtrNewDeviceObject) {
            if (InitializedDeviceObject) {
                // The detach routine will take care of everything.
                // A code fragment for the detach routine is provided
                // later in this chapter.
                SFilterDetachTarget(PtrNewDeviceObject,
                                        PtrTargetDeviceObject,
                                        PtrDeviceExtension);
            }
        }

        // Dereference the file object. Once you have done so, you can
        // forget all about the target file object. But please remember to
        // always do this! Failure to dereference the file object will
        // result in a dangling file object structure that in turn will
        // prevent unloading/dismounting of the target device object.
```

```
        if (PtrTargetFileObject) {
            ObDereferenceObject(PtrTargetFileObject);
            PtrTargetFileObject = NULL;
        }
    }

    return(RC);
}
```

The following definition of a device extension structure, as defined by the sample
filter driver code, will be useful in understanding the previous code fragment:

```
typedef struct _SFilterDeviceExtension {
    // A signature (including device size).
    SFilterIdentifier              NodeIdentifier;
    // This is used to synchronize access to the device extension
    // structure.
    ERESOURCE                      DeviceExtensionResource;
    // The sample filter driver keeps a private doubly linked list of all
    // device objects created by the driver.
    LIST_ENTRY                     NextDeviceObject;
    // See Flag definitions below.
    uint32                         DeviceExtensionFlags;
    // The device object we are attached to.
    PDEVICE_OBJECT                 TargetDeviceObject;
    // Stored for convenience. A pointer to the driver object for the
    // target device object (you can always obtain this information from
    // the target device object).
    PDRIVER_OBJECT                 TargetDriverObject;
    // You can associate other information here.
} SFilterDeviceExtension, *PtrSFilterDeviceExtension;

#define    SFILTER_DEV_EXT_RESOURCE_INITIALIZED        (0x00000001)
#define    SFILTER_DEV_EXT_INSERTED_GLOBAL_LIST        (0x00000002)
#define    SFILTER_DEV_EXT_ATTACHED                    (0x00000004)
```

Notes

The code fragment for the **SFilterAttachTarget()** function illustrates how
simple it is to perform an attachment between a device object created by your
driver and another named device object. The code fragment follows closely the
sequence of steps listed earlier for performing the attach operation.

You should note that the attachment can be performed as easily if the target
device object is not a named device object. However, you cannot open an
unnamed device object; therefore, in order to be able to attach to an unnamed
device object, your driver must have some other (driver-specific) method devised
to obtain a pointer to the target device object.

The following sections describe some of the support functions provided by the
I/O Manager that will prove useful to you in developing your filter driver (to
perform an attachment between your device object and the target device object).

IoGetDeviceObjectPointer()

The arguments for this function are well-described in the DDK:

```
NTSTATUS
IoGetDeviceObjectPointer(
    IN PUNICODE_STRING      ObjectName,
    IN ACCESS_MASK          DesiredAccess,
    OUT PFILE_OBJECT        *FileObject,
    OUT PDEVICE_OBJECT      *DeviceObject
);
```

The `IoGetDeviceObjectPointer()` function is often used by filter drivers to obtain a pointer to a target physical/virtual device object or to the highest-layered device object attached to the target device object. Here are the steps executed by the I/O Manager to implement this function:

1. The I/O Manager performs an open operation on the target object, identified by the `ObjectName` argument (e.g., `\Device\C:`).

   Note that the open request will typically recurse back into the NT I/O Manager. The `DesiredAccess` value determines whether or not a mount sequence is initiated by the I/O Manager in processing the open operation; the I/O Manager may choose to initiate a mount sequence if no logical volume has yet been mounted on the target physical/virtual device when the open request is being processed.

2. The I/O Manager then obtains a pointer to the file object that is created as a result of processing the open request.

   The open request (if successful) returns a file handle. The I/O Manager uses the `ObReferenceObjectByHandle()` function to obtain a pointer to the associated (referenced) file object.

3. The I/O Manager uses the `IoGetRelatedDeviceObject()` function to get a pointer to the highest-layered device object that may be attached to the target device.

   The argument to the `IoGetRelatedDeviceObject()` function is the file object pointer obtained in Step 2.

4. Finally, the I/O Manager closes the file handle obtained in Step 1 before returning control to the caller.

The I/O Manager can safely return pointers to the file object representing the successful open operations, as well as to the associated device object, even though the handle obtained from the open operation has been closed, because the file object structure is referenced in Step 2.

What Happens After the Attach Operation?

In order to appreciate the value of attempting an attach operation, you should understand what happens once you have performed the attach. You know that the I/O Manager will now reroute the IRPs destined for the target device object to your driver (and your source device object) instead. But how does the I/O Manager do this? To answer this question, let's look at the attach operation in greater detail.

The attach operation

Recall from Chapter 4, *The NT I/O Manager*, that each device object structure has a field called `AttachedDevice`. This field is used by the I/O Manager to keep track of the linked list of attached devices for a particular target device object. Note that I mentioned a *linked list* of attached device objects and not just a single attached device object; the clear implication is that multiple filter device objects could potentially exist that are attached to a specific target device object. Therefore, you can conceive of a chain (or a layer) of attached filter device objects; each of these attached device objects will have an opportunity to process IRPs sent to the target device object.

There are three ways in which your driver can request an attach operation:

`IoAttachDeviceByPointer()`

When your driver invokes the I/O Manager to perform an attach between the target device object and your source device object using `IoAttachDevice-ByPointer()`, the I/O Manager performs the following sequence of operations: `IoAttachDeviceByPointer()`, `IoAttachDeviceToDe-viceStack()`, and `IoAttachDevice()`.

a. The I/O Manager will get a pointer to the topmost device object that had been previously attached to the target device object.

The code used to do this is encapsulated within an I/O Manager routine called `IoGetAttachedDevice()`, which is available to third-party developers as well:

```
PDEVICE_OBJECT
IoGetAttachedDevice(
    IN PDEVICE_OBJECT DeviceObject
);
```

The implementation of this function appears to be pretty trivial and is demonstrated in this code fragment:*

---

* Note that the actual code implemented by the I/O Manager is probably slightly different than the fragment presented here; however, the logic presented here is accurate.

```
PDEVICE_OBJECT
IoGetAttachedDevice(PDEVICE_OBJECT TargetDeviceObject) {
    PDEVICE_OBJECT    ReturnedDeviceObject = TargetDeviceObject;

    while (ReturnedDeviceObject->AttachedDevice) {
        ReturnedDeviceObject = TargetDeviceObject->AttachedDevice;
    }

    return(ReturnedDeviceObject);
}
```

Think of the attached list of device objects as a stack-based list. The last object inserted into the list will be at the head of the list. Extend this analogy a bit further, and you can see that the last device object to perform the attach operation will be the first object to get a crack at the IRPs sent to the target device object.

In order to maintain this last-in-first-chance-at-IRP ordering, the I/O Manager gets a pointer to the topmost device object in the linked list of device objects in order to continue processing the attach request. If, however, yours happens to be the first attach request for the target device object, the I/O Manager will directly use the pointer to the target device object (supplied by you) in the following steps.

Now, the I/O Manager will ensure that the device object you are attempting to attach to is not being deleted.

If the device object is being deleted or if the corresponding driver has an unload pending against it, the I/O Manager will immediately reject your attach request. You can expect to get an error such as **STATUS_NO_SUCH_DEVICE** from the I/O Manager. If everything seems to be in order, the I/O Manager proceeds to the next step.

b. The I/O Manager will physically complete the attach operation.

The following steps are executed by the I/O Manager to complete the attach operation:

i. The **ReturnedDeviceObject->AttachedDevice** field is set to point to the source device object.

ii. The **StackSize** field in the source device object is set to (**ReturnedDeviceObject->StackSize + 1**).

Note that once the attach has been completed, the I/O Manager will redirect all IRPs sent to the target device object to your driver. The I/O Manager does not know what you will do with the IRPs; it can assume the worst case, however, (in terms of I/O stack location usage) where you may simply perform some preprocessing or register a completion routine and forward the IRP to the next driver in the list of layered drivers. Since the attaching of your device object could require the IRP to be routed through one more layered driver, the I/O Manager ensures that the number of stack locations that will be allocated for all subsequent IRPs directed to the target device object will be enough to last through all the drivers that may process the IRP. The I/O Manager will set the `AlignmentRequirement` field and the `SectorSize` field in the source device object created by your driver to be the same as those in the target device object.

IoAttachDeviceToDeviceStack()

This function call was first made available in Windows NT Version 4.0. It is functionally similar to the preceding `IoAttachDeviceByPointer()` routine and is invoked in the same manner (i.e., your driver must supply both the source and target device object pointer values). However, this function performs one additional task: if the attach operation completes successfully, `IoAttachDeviceToDeviceStack()` will return a pointer to the previous highest-layered device object to which your source device object was attached.

The returned device object pointer value can prove to be useful if your filter driver forwards any intercepted IRPs to the next driver in the calling hierarchy.

Note that if your driver happened to be the first to perform an attach operation to the target device object, the returned device object pointer will be the same as the target device object pointer supplied by your driver when invoking the `IoAttachDeviceToDeviceStack()` function.

NOTE   Prior to Version 4.0, your driver could first invoke `IoGetAttachedDevice()` followed by `IoAttachedDeviceByPointer()` to achieve practically the same functionality as is now provided by the `IoAttachDeviceToDeviceStack()` function. Also, the `IoGetDeviceObjectByPointer()` function returns a pointer to the highest-layered device object attached to the target device object.

IoAttachDevice()

This function is defined as follows:

```
NTSTATUS
IoAttachDevice(
    IN PDEVICE_OBJECT        SourceDevice,
    IN PUNICODE_STRING       TargetDevice,
    OUT PDEVICE_OBJECT       *AttachedDevice
);
```

The `IoAttachDevice()` function also performs an attachment between two device objects. However, this function accepts the target device name instead of a pointer to the target device object. It will open the target device object on behalf of your driver and use the target device object pointer to perform the actual attach operation.

The steps executed by this function are as follows:

a. The `IoAttachDevice()` function invokes `IoGetDeviceObject-Pointer()` internally, to obtain a pointer to the target device object.

The `DesiredAccess` value is set to `FILE_READ_ATTRIBUTES`.

b. The `IoAttachDevice()` function executes the same sequence of steps as those described earlier, in performing an attach operation between the source device object and the target device object.

Just as in the case of the `IoAttachDeviceByPointer()` function, the I/O Manager initializes the `StackSize`, `AlignmentRequirement`, and `SectorSize` fields in the `SourceDevice` object structure.

c. The I/O Manager dereferences the file object pointer returned from the internal call to `IoGetDeviceObjectPointer()`.

d. A pointer to the previous highest-layered device object (for the target device) is returned to the caller in the `AttachedDevice` argument.

Note that your driver must have created the source device object before you can invoke the `IoAttachDevice()` function.

You may be wondering whether it would be preferable to invoke `IoAttachDevice()` directly, instead of invoking `IoGetDeviceObjectPointer()` in your driver followed by a call to `IoAttachDeviceByPointer()` or `IoAttachDeviceToDeviceStack()`.

There is one subtle difference between the two methods of performing an attach operation. This difference is only important if your driver wishes to layer over an FSD logical volume device object (as opposed to layering over a lower-level device driver disk device object).

The `IoAttachDevice()` function will always open the target device (identified by the device name that you supply to the function) with the `DesiredAccess` value set to `FILE_READ_ATTRIBUTES`. This type of open request will not result in a mount operation being initiated by the I/O Manager on the target physical/virtual/logical device if such a mount operation has not yet taken place. Therefore, if your driver wishes to attach to the device object representing the mounted logical volume on drive `C:` and if the name supplied by your driver is `\Device\C:`, you cannot really be sure that `IoAttachDevice()` will do what you expect, since you may actually end up with your source device object having been attached to the physical device object identified by `\Device\C:`.

However, if your driver wishes to ensure that it is always attached to an FSD device object representing a logical volume mounted on the target drive, then you can invoke `IoGetDeviceObjectPointer()` function directly from your driver by specifying the `DesiredAccess` to some value like `FILE_READ_ACCESS`. This type of `DesiredAccess` value will result in the I/O Manager initiating a mount process (if no logical volume has yet been mounted on the target device), and the returned device object pointer will refer to the device object representing the mounted logical volume.* Your FSD can then request the attach by invoking `IoAttachDeviceByPointer()` or `IoAttachDeviceToDeviceStack()`.

Once you invoke one of preceding three functions, `IoAttachDevice-ByPointer()`, `IoAttachDeviceToDeviceStack()`, and `IoAttach-Device()` successfully, you can be assured that the attach operation has been completed by the NT I/O Manager.

You must be careful whenever you request an attach operation, since all new IRPs targeted to the target device object will immediately begin getting rerouted to you, instead of being sent to the original target of the I/O request. Therefore, be prepared to handle such requests immediately or block them until you complete all your initialization.

IRP routing after the attach

Now that you have performed the attach, you should start getting first access to all the IRPs sent to the target device object, right? Well, not quite. You may get first chance at IRPs, or you may get called after some other driver has had its way with the IRP, or your driver may never be called for an IRP sent to the target device object.

Why? To understand when your filter driver is invoked (and when it is not), you need to understand the I/O Manager-supplied utility function called `IoGetRe-latedDeviceObject()`. This function is also available to you when you develop a kernel-mode driver and is defined as:

```
PDEVICE_OBJECT
IoGetRelatedDeviceObject(
    IN PFILE_OBJECT FileObject
);
```

---

* Another method that you could use to ensure that a mount is always initiated (if required) by the I/O Manager is to specify a name such as `\Device\C:\` instead of `\Device\C:` only. The trailing `\` indicates that you wish to open the root directory (as opposed to performing a *direct device open* of the target device) and will force the I/O Manager to initiate a mount sequence.

The function `IoGetRelatedDeviceObject()` is always invoked internally by the NT I/O Manager whenever it needs to determine where it should send an IRP for a user-initiated I/O operation (e.g., the `NtReadFile()` function invoked by a thread).[*] The following steps are executed in this function:

1. The I/O Manager checks whether the supplied `FileObject` has a mounted Volume Parameter Block (VPB) associated with it.

   VPB structures were discussed in detail earlier in this book. You may recall that when a file system successfully mounts a logical volume, a pointer to the device object (created by the FSD) representing the mounted logical volume is stored in the `VPB->DeviceObject` field.

   If the `FileObject->Vpb` field is nonnull and if the `FileObject->Vpb->DeviceObject` field is nonnull, the I/O Manager will invoke the `IoGetAttachedDevice()` function for the `FileObject->Vpb->DeviceObject` structure and use the returned device object pointer when invoking `IoCallDriver()`.

   The implication here is that if a logical volume has been mounted on a physical/virtual/logical device object, the I/O Manager will redirect I/O requests to the highest-layered driver that has performed an attach operation on the device object created by the FSD to represent the mounted logical volume.

   When will the `Vpb` pointer for a file object not be set to NULL? Well, recall that the `Vpb` pointer for a file object is set by the FSD whenever a successful create/open operation has been performed on the file object (as was described in Chapter 11, *Writing a File System Driver III*). Therefore, you should infer that if a file stream residing on a logical volume has been successfully opened, and subsequently an I/O operation is received for the file stream, this particular check made by the I/O Manager will succeed and the IRP will be appropriately dispatched.

2. If the preceding check fails because the `Vpb` pointer is set to NULL, then the I/O Manager tries harder to determine where to send the IRP.

   In the previous case, the `Vpb` pointer was nonnull because the file stream had been opened. However, for certain file objects, the `Vpb` pointer may still be NULL. In this case, the I/O Manager checks whether the file object has an associated device object that was mounted by some file system. This can be done by checking the `FileObject->DeviceObject` field. If nonnull (indicating that the file object is associated with some "real" device object), and if

---

[*] Note that the I/O Manager also uses the `IoGetRelatedDeviceObject()` function internally when processing a synchronous/asynchronous page write or a synchronous page read request. Therefore, filter drivers layered over a FSD will get the opportunity to process page faults and/or paging I/O writes (including those initiated due to memory-mapped files).

the `FileObject->DeviceObject->Vpb->DeviceObject` is nonnull (indicating that a file system has mounted this device object), then the I/O Manager will invoke the `IoGetAttachedDevice()` function on the `File-Object->DeviceObject->Vpb->DeviceObject` structure and use the returned device object pointer when invoking `IoCallDriver()`.

3. If both of these checks fail to yield a device object structure pointer, the I/O Manager uses the device object associated with the file object.

When both the preceding checks fail, more than likely the I/O request is being issued to an open physical/virtual/logical device that has not yet been mounted. If an I/O operation is being issued directly to this device object (e.g., for raw access to the device), the I/O Manager will invoke the `IoGetAttachedDevice()` function on the `FileObject->DeviceObject` structure and use the returned device object pointer when invoking `IoCallDriver()`.

Given this information, you can see that even after you attach to a target device object, it is not guaranteed that you will receive the IRP before any other driver in the calling hierarchy. If some other driver has attached itself to your device object, that driver is ahead of yours in the call chain. Then, it is no longer certain that you will ever see the IRP, since it is left completely to the discretion of each driver whether or not it will forward the IRP to the next driver or complete the IRP itself.

You should also note one important point: what happens if you attach to a device object representing a physical disk partition after a file system has mounted itself onto the device object? Well, as you can easily infer, you will not get to process most IRPs because the I/O Manager will always send the IRP to the file system driver first (or rather, to the highest-layered device object attached to the file system volume device object). The FSD, in turn, will forward the IRP (for actual, physical I/O operations) directly to the target physical/virtual device object (to which you have attached yourself) via an invocation to `IoCallDriver()`. Your device object will not even be considered to receive the IRP.

NOTE   Most FSD implementations store a pointer to the target physical/virtual device object when they mount a logical volume on the device object in their VCB structure. They use this device object pointer when invoking `IoCallDriver()`. They do not, however, invoke `IoGetAttachedDevice()` on the target device object pointer before invoking `IoCallDriver()`.

Create/open requests

The I/O Manager performs the following actions to determine the target driver to which the create/open request should be sent, before actually forwarding the request to a target FSD or filter driver:

- For relative create/open requests, the I/O Manager determines the target driver from the related file object specified in the create/open request.

  Recall from earlier chapters that create/open requests can be specified with a filename relative to the name contained in the (supplied) previously open directory file object. For relative file create/open requests, the I/O Manager obtains a pointer to the target device object by invoking the `IoGetRelated-DeviceObject()` function on the related file object.

- For all other create/open requests, the I/O Manager sends the request either to the highest-layered driver attached to the device object representing the mounted logical volume or directly to the device object representing the target physical/virtual/logical device.

  A create/open request can specify either a device open (e.g., `\Device\C:`) or a file/directory on a logical volume mounted on the physical/virtual/logical device object.

  When a request is received by the I/O Manager for a direct device open operation, the I/O Manager uses the target device object supplied by the Object Manager and forwards the create/open request to the device driver managing this device object. Note that any filter driver attached to this target device object will not get to intercept this create/open request.

  For all other create/open requests, the I/O Manager always tries to ensure that an FSD mounts a logical volume on the target physical/virtual/logical device. Once an FSD has claimed the device and mounted a logical volume on the target device object, the I/O Manager uses the `IoGetAttachedDe-vice()` function to get a pointer to the highest-layered device object attached to the volume device object created by the FSD. If no filter driver has attached itself to the volume device object, the create/open request is forwarded directly to the responsible FSD.

If your driver wishes to intercept all create/open requests that may be sent to a particular logical volume, ensure that your filter driver creates a device object that attaches itself to the target device object representing the mounted logical volume before the IRP for the mount operation is completed but after the FSD has completed mount-related processing.

The obvious way to accomplish this is to intercept mount requests issued to the target FSD, register a completion routine to be invoked once the mount request

(IRP) has been completed, and initiate (and complete) the attach sequence from within your completion routine before returning control to the I/O Manager.

Building IRPs

Whether you develop a file system driver or a filter driver, you will undoubtedly find it necessary to create IRPs that your driver will subsequently use in dispatching I/O requests. You can either decide to allocate and initialize such IRPs yourself, or you could decide to use one of the I/O Manager-supplied utility functions to help you in these tasks.

The following routines can prove useful when you start creating your own I/O request packets. Note that the Windows NT DDK also provides a description of the functions presented here.

IoAllocateIrp()

The `IoAllocateIrp()` function is used internally by the I/O Manager to allocate IRPs. It is also available to third-party driver developers. This function is defined as follows:

```
PIRP
IoAllocateIrp(
    IN CCHAR        StackSize,
    IN BOOLEAN      ChargeQuota
);
```

Parameters:

`StackSize`

> The I/O Manager uses the value contained in this argument to determine the number of I/O stack locations that could possibly be used in processing this IRP. The I/O Manager must allocate sufficient memory to contain the specified number of I/O stack locations. Your driver can use the `TargetDeviceObject->StackSize` value to pass to the `IoAllocateIrp()` function.

`ChargeQuota`

> This determines whether the memory allocated for the IRP should be charged to the quota allocated to the requesting process. Typically, filter drivers will set this argument to FALSE (the I/O Manager generally sets it to TRUE when invoking the function internally to forward user I/O requests to a target FSD).

Functionality Provided:

The I/O Manager will allocate an IRP either from a zone containing preallocated IRPs[*] or by directly invoking `ExAllocatePoolWithQuotaTag()`/`ExAllocatePoolWithTag()`. Once this function returns a success code back to your driver, you can check the value of the `Zoned` field in the IRP to determine whether or not the IRP was allocated from a zone (if you are curious enough to do so). All IRP structures are always allocated from nonpaged pool.

For reasons of efficiency and to avoid kernel memory fragmentation, the I/O Manager preallocates two separate zones for IRP structures that require only a single I/O stack location and for those that require four (or fewer) I/O stack locations. If, in an invocation to `IoAllocateIrp()`, a thread requests more than four I/O stack locations, the I/O Manager cannot use either of the two preallocated zones. In this situation, the I/O Manager requests memory via a call to the NT Executive `ExAllocatePool()` function.

Of course, in high-stress situations, it is always possible that the IRP zones may be exhausted and the I/O Manager will resort to requesting memory from the NT Executive pool management support package.

The `IoAllocateIrp()` function also initializes certain fields in the IRP before returning the IRP to your driver. Note that the entire structure is zeroed by the I/O Manager before any fields are initialized. The initialized fields include the `Type`, `Size`, `StackCount`, `CurrentLocation`, `ApcEnvironment`, and `Tail.Overlay.CurrentStackLocation` fields.

The I/O Manager tries to ensure that a valid IRP pointer is returned to the thread that invokes this function. If the IRP can be allocated from a zone, the I/O Manager tries to get a free IRP structure from the appropriate zone. If the number of I/O stack locations requested precludes allocation from a zone (i.e., it is greater than 4)[†] or if the appropriate zone is exhausted, the I/O Manager allocates the IRP by invoking the appropriate NT Executive function (listed previously). If no memory is available for the IRP structure and if the previous mode of the caller is kernel mode, the I/O Manager will request memory from the `NonPagedPool-MustSucceed` memory pool. Therefore, although it is possible that the `IoAllocateIrp()` function will return NULL if the previous mode happened to

---

[*] Beginning with Windows NT Version 4.0, the I/O Manager may decide to use lookaside lists instead of zones. The `Zoned` field in the IRP has been renamed to `AllocationFlags`. The flag value in this field determines whether the IRP has been allocated from a fixed-size block of memory (e.g., a zone or lookaside list), from the nonpaged-must-succeed pool, or from the system nonpaged pool. This change, however, does not fundamentally affect the discussion presented in the chapter.

[†] The number of I/O stack locations associated with preallocated IRPs is subject to change. Therefore, your driver must never depend on the fact that the I/O Manager will allocate IRPs with a certain number of stack locations from a zone.

be user mode and if system memory was seriously depleted, failure to obtain memory for an IRP when the caller executes in the context of the system process will result in a bugcheck.

WARNING   Contrary to the documentation in the Windows NT DDK, you should not invoke the `IoInitializeIrp()` function (described below) for the new IRP structure obtained by calling `IoAllocateIrp()`.

As a matter of fact, the `IoInitializeIrp()` function performs exactly the same initialization as will have already been performed by `IoAllocateIrp()` for you. Also, part of the initialization performed by `IoInitializeIrp()` involves zeroing the entire IRP structure. This is unfortunate for those unwary developers that do call `IoInitializeIrp()` on IRPs obtained via `IoAllocateIrp()`, since zeroing the IRP structure will erroneously clear the `Zoned` flag in the IRP and will subsequently often lead to a system crash at very unexpected times.*

IoInitializeIrp()

This function is provided to support drivers that allocate IRP structures themselves (instead of requesting an IRP from the I/O Manager) and is defined as follows:

```
VOID
IoInitializeIrp(
    IN OUT PIRP     Irp,
    IN USHORT       PacketSize,
    IN CCHAR        StackSize
);
```

Parameters:

`Irp`

This is the IRP structure to be initialized.

`PacketSize`

This is the size of the IRP to be initialized. Typically, this will be the value computed by the `IoSizeOfIrp()` macro supplied in the DDK.

`StackSize`

This is the number of I/O stack locations for which memory has been allocated by your driver.

---

* When the I/O Manager tries to release memory allocated for the IRP, it will check the `Zoned` flag value to determine whether memory should be returned back to the zone or should be released back to the system nonpaged pool. Even if the IRP had been allocated from a zone, the `Zoned` flag will have been cleared by `IoInitializeIrp()`, and the I/O Manager will erroneously return the memory back to the system nonpaged pool leading to a subsequent system crash.

Functionality Provided:

Typically, your driver will invoke the `IoInitializeIrp()` after it has allocated an IRP by directly invoking `ExAllocatePool()` (or from some zone/lookaside list maintained by your driver), instead of requesting that the I/O Manager allocate the IRP structure on your behalf.

The `IoInitializeIrp()` function initializes the `Type`, `Size`, `StackCount`, `CurrentLocation`, `ApcEnvironment`, and `Tail.Overlay.Current-StackLocation` fields. These are exactly the same fields as those initialized by invoking `IoAllocateIrp()` (described previously). The IRP is zeroed before any fields are initialized.

Note that the IRP initialization performed by both the `IoAllocateIrp()` and the `IoInitializeIrp()` functions is rudimentary. Therefore, your driver is responsible for performing all of the additional initialization for the IRP. The actual fields that your filter driver will initialize depends heavily upon the type of I/O request that you are issuing and the target device object (kernel-mode driver) to which you will be issuing the request. Read Chapter 4 to understand the nature of the various fields in the IRP. You should also review the sample filter driver code provided in the accompanying diskette to see how some of the fields are initialized.

IoBuildAsynchronousFsdRequest()

```
PIRP
IoBuildAsynchronousFsdRequest(
    IN ULONG                MajorFunction,
    IN PDEVICE_OBJECT       DeviceObject,
    IN OUT PVOID            Buffer OPTIONAL,
    IN ULONG                Length OPTIONAL,
    IN PLARGE_INTEGER       StartingOffset OPTIONAL,
    IN PIO_STATUS_BLOCK     IoStatusBlock OPTIONAL
);
```

Parameters:

`MajorFunction`

> The I/O Manager initializes the first I/O stack location with the `MajorFunction` code value.

`DeviceObject`

> This is a pointer to the device object that will be the immediate target for the I/O request. The I/O Manager obtains the number of stack locations to be allocated from the `StackSize` field in the `DeviceObject` structure. Furthermore, for read/write I/O requests (for which the IRP is being created), the I/O Manager determines the type of buffering required for the target driver (`DO_DIRECT_IO`, `DO_BUFFERED_IO`, or neither of the two).

Buffer

Your driver can supply the buffer pointer, which is only required for requests of type `IRP_MJ_READ` and `IRP_MJ_WRITE`. Note that for these two `Major-Function` types, the `Buffer` argument is not optional.

Length

This is the length of any `Buffer` that may have been supplied.

StartingOffset

This is the starting offset for a read/write operation.

IoStatusBlock

This contains the results of the operation are returned in this structure (if supplied).

Functionality Provided:

`IoBuildAsynchronousFsdRequest()` will create and initialize a new IRP that can be used by your driver to issue an `IRP_MJ_READ`, `IRP_MJ_WRITE`, `IRP_MJ_SHUTDOWN`, or `IRP_MJ_FLUSH_BUFFERS` request to another kernel-mode driver. This function executes the following sequence of steps:

1. It allocates a new IRP using `IoAllocateIrp()`.

2. The `MajorFunction` field in the first I/O stack location is initialized to the value supplied by your driver.

3. The `UserIosb` field in the IRP is initialized to the value contained in the `IoStatusBlock` argument.

   Note that upon IRP completion, the I/O Manager uses the field (pointer) value to return the status of the I/O operation.

4. For read/write requests, the I/O Manager performs some additional initialization of the IRP.

   The I/O Manager initializes the appropriate values in the first I/O stack location for read/write requests. For write requests, the `Parameters.Write.Length` and `Parameters.Write.ByteOffset` fields in the first I/O stack location are initialized to the `Length` and `StartingOffset` arguments (respectively) supplied by your driver, and for read requests, the `Parameters.Read.Length` and `Parameters.Read.ByteOffset` fields are initialized.

   If the `Flags` field in the `DeviceObject` structure for the target device object specifies `DO_BUFFERED_IO`, the I/O Manager allocates a system buffer (of the supplied `Length`) and initializes the `AssociatedIrp->SystemBuffer` field to refer to the newly allocated buffer. This buffer will be automatically deallocated by the I/O Manager when the IRP has been completed (and any data obtained has been copied into the supplied `Buffer` for `IRP_MJ_READ` I/O requests). Furthermore, the I/O Manager will copy data from the supplied `Buffer` to the allocated system buffer for `IRP_MJ_WRITE` requests before returning the newly allocated IRP to your driver.

If the `Flags` field in the target `DeviceObject` structure specifies `DO_DIRECT_IO` instead, the I/O Manager allocates an MDL describing the supplied `Buffer`. The I/O Manager also probes and locks the pages for the MDL (for write access in the case of `IRP_MJ_READ` requests and for read access otherwise). The `MdlAddress` field in the IRP is initialized to point to this allocated MDL. You should note that the I/O Manager always frees all MDLs associated with an IRP as part of the postprocessing performed in the `IoCompleteRequest()` function.

If neither direct I/O nor buffered I/O has been specified, the I/O Manager will simply set the `UserBuffer` field in the IRP to point to the supplied buffer.

5. The I/O Manager will initialize the `Tail.Overlay.Thread` field with the value obtained from `KeGetCurrentThread()`.

   This is required for subsequent, asynchronous processing of media-verify requsts that may be initiated by lower-level disk drivers (in the case of removable media), or for reporting a hard error to the user.

It is important that your driver be aware of those fields in the IRP that the `IoBuildAsynchronousFsdRequest()` function does not initialize. The I/O Manager expects that your driver will initialize the following fields (if appropriate):

`RequestorMode`
> Your driver should typically set this value to `KernelMode` if you are executing in the context of a system worker thread. Otherwise, your driver can use the `ExGetPreviousMode()` function to determine the value to be set in this field.

`Tail.Overlay.OriginalFileObject`
> Set this field to point to the file object structure associated with the I/O request. You will need to do this for all requests except the `IRP_MJ_SHUTDOWN` IRP.

`FileObject`
> Set the field to point to the same value as `Tail.Overlay.OriginalFileObject`.

Your driver can invoke the `IoBuildAsynchronousFsdRequest()` routine at a high IRQL (e.g., IRQL `DISPATCH_LEVEL`). Furthermore, your driver will set a completion routine to be invoked when the IRP completes, allowing you to trigger any postprocessing that may be required. You can also free the IRP using the `IoFreeIrp()` function after you have completed postprocessing for the request.

WARNING   Remember to set a completion routine that will free the IRP allocated via a call to `IoBuildAsynchronousFsdRequest()`. Failure to do so will result in the I/O Manager performing normal completion-related postprocessing on the IRP (see Chapter 4 for details on the postprocessing performed by the I/O Manager). This will lead to unexpected system crashes, since the IRP is not typically set up correctly for such postprocessing.

IoBuildSynchronousFsdRequest()

```
PIRP
IoBuildSynchronousFsdRequest(
    IN  ULONG                 MajorFunction,
    IN  PDEVICE_OBJECT        DeviceObject,
    IN  OUT PVOID             Buffer OPTIONAL,
    IN  ULONG                 Length OPTIONAL,
    IN  PLARGE_INTEGER        StartingOffset OPTIONAL,
    IN  PKEVENT               Event,
    OUT PIO_STATUS_BLOCK      IoStatusBlock
);
```

Parameters:

As you can observe in the preceding function definition, this routine takes virtually the same arguments as those expected by the `IoBuildAsynchronousFsdRequest()`. The only caveats that you must be aware of are as follows:

- The `IoStatusBlock` argument is no longer optional.

    The I/O Manager expects to complete any IRP allocated using `IoBuildSynchronousFsdRequest()`. Therefore, you should provide a valid pointer to an `IO_STATUS_BLOCK` structure when invoking this function. The results of the I/O operation will be returned to you in this structure.

- Your driver must provide a pointer to an initialized `Event` object.

    Note that by definition, the IRP created by the I/O Manager is expected to be used for a synchronous call to a some kernel-mode driver. Therefore, the I/O Manager expects that the caller (your driver) will wish to wait for completion of the IRP. When the IRP is completed, the I/O Manager will signal the event object supplied by your driver. Remember to initialize the event object before invoking the `IoBuildSynchronousFsdRequest()` function (and to set the event object to the not-signaled state).

Your driver may choose not to wait for the completion of the request. However, you must have some means of deallocating the event structure (and the I/O status block) in this case.

Functionality Provided:

`IoBuildSynchronousFsdRequest()` will create and initialize a new IRP that can be used by your driver to issue a synchronous I/O request to another kernel-mode driver. Internally, this routine invokes `IoBuildAsynchronousFsd-Request()` to do most of the work of allocating and initializing the IRP structure.

After obtaining an IRP structure from the call to `IoBuildAsynchronousFsd-Request()`, this function initializes the `UserEvent` field in the IRP with the supplied **Event** pointer value. Finally, the `IoBuildSynchronousFsd-Request()` function inserts the allocated IRP into the list of pending IRPs for the current thread using the `ThreadListEntry` field in the IRP. The IRP is automatically dequeued by the I/O Manager from the list of pending IRPs as part of the postprocessing performed on the IRP during `IoCompleteRequest()`.*

Your driver can associate a completion routine for synchronous I/O requests created using the `IoBuildSynchronousFsdRequest()` function. However, you must be careful if you wish to prevent the I/O Manager from completing the IRP by returning STATUS_MORE_PROCESSING_REQUIRED from your completion routine. This is because the IRP is inserted into the list of pending IRPs for the thread that invoked `IoBuildSynchronousFsdRequest()` and failure to remove the IRP from this list could cause a system crash at some later time.

TIP	If you need to ensure that the IRP is safely removed from the list of pending IRPs associated with a thread, you should execute the following steps:

— Ensure that you perform the next step in the context of the thread identified by the `Tail.Overlay.Thread` field in the IRP. You can do this by issuing a kernel-mode APC to the target thread (if required).

— At IRQL APC_LEVEL or higher, invoke the `RemoveEntryList()` macro on the `Irp->ThreadListEntry` field.

IoBuildDeviceIoControlRequest()

This function is defined as follows (consult the DDK also for information on this function).

---

* Actually, the dequeue operation takes place in the context of the thread that requested the I/O operation (when performing final postprocessing as part of the APC executed in the context of the requesting thread). Chapter 4 describes the postprocessing performed by the I/O Manager in greater detail.

```
PIRP
IoBuildDeviceIoControlRequest(
    IN ULONG                    IoControlCode,
    IN PDEVICE_OBJECT           DeviceObject,
    IN PVOID                    InputBuffer OPTIONAL,
    IN ULONG                    InputBufferLength,
    OUT PVOID                   OutputBuffer OPTIONAL,
    IN ULONG                    OutputBufferLength,
    IN BOOLEAN                  InternalDeviceIoControl,
    IN PKEVENT                  Event,
    OUT PIO_STATUS_BLOCK        IoStatusBlock
);
```

Parameters:

IoControlCode

This is the IOCTL code value that will be placed in the `Parameters.Devi-ceIoControl.IoControlCode` field is the first I/O stack location of the newly allocated IRP. The I/O Manager also uses this code to determine the manner in which data should be transferred between the calling module (your driver) and the target for the request.

DeviceObject

This is a pointer to the target device object for the request.

InputBuffer

This is used by your driver to send data to the target driver. Supplying an input buffer is optional, unless the `InputBufferLength` contains a nonzero value.

InputBufferLength

This is the length of any `InputBuffer` supplied by you.

OutputBuffer

Your driver can supply such a buffer to receive data from the target driver. You can also use this buffer to send information to the target driver if the method of data transfer is `METHOD_IN_DIRECT` or `METHOD_OUT_DIRECT`.* You must supply a valid buffer pointer if `OutputBufferLength` contains a nonzero value.

OutputBufferLength

If this field contains a nonzero value, you must supply a valid `Output-Buffer` pointer. This field contains the length of the supplied `OutputBuffer` (if any).

---

* The contents of this buffer (used to send data to the target driver) will naturally be overwritten if the target driver returns information back to you.

InternalDeviceIoControl

If set to TRUE, the `MajorFunction` code value in the first I/O stack location is set to `IRP_MJ_INTERNAL_DEVICE_CONTROL`, otherwise it is set to `IRP_MJ_DEVICE_CONTROL`.

Event

IOCTL requests are considered inherently synchronous; therefore, the I/O Manager expects you to supply a valid, initialized event object pointer. This event will be signaled by the I/O Manager when the IRP is completed.

IoStatusBlock

Upon IRP completion, the I/O Manager will return the results of the operation in this argument, supplied by your driver.

Functionality Provided:

The `IoBuildDeviceIoControlRequest()` function allocates and initializes an IRP that can subsequently be used to issue an IOCTL to another kernel-mode driver. Internally, this function uses the services of `IoAllocateIrp()` to allocate a new IRP structure. This function initializes the following fields in the allocated IRP (in addition to those initialized by `IoAllocateIrp()`):

UserEvent

This field is initialized to the pointer value supplied in the `Event` argument. The I/O Manager will set this event to the signaled state upon completion of the I/O request packet.

UserIosb

This field is initialized to the passed-in `IoStatusBlock` value.

Parameters.DeviceIoControl.OutputBufferLength

This field is initialized to the value supplied in the `OutputBufferLength` argument.

Parameters.DeviceIoControl.InputBufferLength

This field is initialized to the value supplied in the `InputBufferLength` argument.

Parameters.DeviceIoControl.IoControlCode

This field is initialized to the passed-in `IoControlCode` value.

Furthermore, the `IoBuildDeviceIoControlRequest()` function also determines the method of data transfer, based upon the `IoControlCode` value:*

- If the `IoControlCode` indicates that the data transfer method is 0 (`METHOD_NEITHER`), the I/O Manager allocates a system buffer if either `InputBufferLength` or `OutputBufferLength` are nonzero.

  The system buffer allocated has a length that is the greater of the `InputBufferLength` and `OutputBufferlength` values. The `IoBuildDeviceIoControlRequest()` function initializes the `AssociatedIrp.SystemBuffer` field in the IRP to point to the allocated system buffer.

  If `InputBufferLength` is nonzero, the `IoBuildDeviceIoControlRequest()` function will copy the contents of the `InputBuffer` into the allocated system buffer. If the `OutputBufferLength` is nonzero, the I/O Manager will set the `IRP_INPUT_OPERATION` flag in the IRP, indicating that the `IoCompleteRequest()` function must copy the contents of the allocated system buffer into the caller supplied output buffer.

  Note that the I/O Manager keeps track of the caller-supplied output buffer by setting the `UserBuffer` field in the IRP to point to the `OutputBuffer`.† The system buffer allocated by the I/O Manager is automatically deallocated upon IRP completion.

- If the `IoControlCode` indicates `METHOD_IN_DIRECT` (value = 1) or `METHOD_OUT_DIRECT` (value = 2), the I/O Manager allocates a system buffer for the `InputBuffer` and/or creates an MDL to describe the `OutputBuffer`.

  If the `InputBuffer` pointer is nonnull, the `IoBuildDeviceIoControlRequest()` function allocates a system buffer of length `InputBufferLength`. The `AssociatedIrp.SystemBuffer` field in the IRP is set to point to this allocated buffer. The I/O Manager copies the contents of the caller-supplied `InputBuffer` into the allocated system buffer. Note that the system buffer will be automatically deallocated upon IRP completion.

  If the `OutputBuffer` pointer is nonnull, the `IoBuildDeviceIoControlRequest()` function will create an MDL to describe the supplied `Output-`

---

* Recall from Chapter 11, *Writing a File System Driver III*, that the IOCTL code value determines the method used in data transfer. The possible methods are `METHOD_BUFFERED`, `METHOD_IN_DIRECT`, `METHOD_OUT_DIRECT`, or `METHOD_NEITHER`. The two least-significant bits in the IOCTL code determine the data transfer method.

† The target driver must not use this buffer pointer directly unless it is completely sure that it has been invoked in the context of the original user thread. Trying to access this buffer in the context of any other thread will lead to system memory/data corruption and also probably a system crash. Moreover, there is no real reason to use the pointer, since the target driver can access the caller-supplied output buffer directly via the I/O-Manager-provided MDL.

`Buffer`. Furthermore, the I/O Manager will lock the pages described by the MDL. The MDL will be automatically destroyed by the I/O Manager (and pages unlocked) upon IRP completion.

- If the `IoControlCode` indicates `METHOD_NEITHER` (value = 3), the I/O Manager will initialize the IRP with the caller-supplied buffer pointer values.

  The `Parameters.DeviceIoControl.Type3InputBuffer` field is set to the pointer value supplied in the `OutputBuffer` argument. The `User-Buffer` field is set to the `InputBuffer` value.

IoMakeAssociatedIrp()

Filter drivers and file system drivers can use this function to create one or more associated IRPs for a given master IRP. An associated IRP is just like any other IRP, except for the fact that it is logically associated with a single master IRP. An associated IRP can be easily identified by checking for the presence of the `IRP_ASSOCIATED_IRP` flag in the IRP.

A master IRP can potentially have several IRPs associated with it, but each associated IRP must be uniquely associated with a single master IRP (that is, there exists a one-to-many relationship between a master IRP and its associated IRPs). Associated IRPs cannot become master IRPs themselves, so an associated IRP cannot have other IRPs associated with it. The number of associated IRPs outstanding for a given master IRP can be ascertained by checking the `IrpCount` field in the master IRP structure.

The `IoMakeAssociatedIrp()` function is defined as follows:

```
PIRP
IoMakeAssociatedIrp(
    IN PIRP    Irp,
    IN CCHAR   StackSize
);
```

Parameters:

`Irp`
 This is a pointer to the master IRP for this associated IRP (to be created).

`StackSize`
 This is the number of stack locations to be allocated for the associated IRP.

Functionality Provided:

The `IoMakeAssociatedIrp()` function returns a newly allocated associated IRP to your driver. The following steps are executed by the I/O Manager when you invoke this function.

1. The I/O Manager allocates an IRP either from a zone/lookaside list or by requesting nonpaged memory from the NT Executive pool management package.

2. This IRP is initialized in exactly the same manner as described for `IoInitializeIrp()`.

3. The I/O Manager sets the `IRP_ASSOCIATED_IRP` flag value in the newly created IRP.

4. The `AssociatedIrp.MasterIrp` field is initialized to the `Irp` argument supplied by your driver.

5. The `Tail.Overlay.Thread` field is initialized to the `Irp->Tail.Overlay.Thread` field value (obtained from the master IRP structure).

If, however, the I/O Manager fails to obtain memory for an IRP structure, it will return NULL to your driver.

Uses of associated IRP structures

Imagine that you have designed an FSD that breaks up a rather large I/O request into fixed-sized pieces and issues the I/O requests in parallel to underlying disk device drivers. You could then decide to simply create multiple associated IRP structures, each describing a subset of the total I/O request, and then dispatch them concurrently (for asynchronous I/O) to the underlying device drivers.

Another use for these structures could be an intermediate driver that provides disk-striping functionality below the FSD. Now, whenever you receive an I/O request from an FSD to a striped device, you will need to break up this request into little stripes, and you would probably like to issue each of these I/O requests concurrently (since typically, each request will be issued to a different physical disk). Associated IRP structures are a natural choice at this time.

Note that you do not have to create associated IRP structures only when executing multiple I/O requests concurrently. You could just as well create associated IRPs that are used in sequential processing. However, associated IRPs lend themselves well to issuing multiple I/O requests in parallel to satisfy a specific user request.

Restrictions on the use of associated IRP structures

If you examine the IRP structure defined in the DDK/IFS kit closely, you will notice that information about associated IRPs is maintained in the following structure:

```
union {
    struct _IRP      *MasterIrp;
    LONG             IrpCount;
```

```
    PVOID               SystemBuffer;
} AssociatedIrp;
```

For the master IRP, the count of associated IRPs is maintained in the `IrpCount` field. For an associated IRP, a pointer leading back to the master IRP is maintained in the `MasterIrp` field. If neither of these fields are used, the `SystemBuffer` field can potentially contain a pointer to any system buffer allocated by the I/O Manager for buffered I/O requests.

From the structure definition, certain restrictions can immediately be ascertained:

- If your driver supports buffered I/O and receives a system buffer allocated by the I/O Manager, you will lose the pointer to this buffer in trying to maintain the associated IRP count in your master IRP.

- An associated IRP cannot be dispatched to a driver that expects to receive buffered I/O requests.

- An associated IRP cannot become a master IRP.

  If you develop a filter/intermediate driver that resides below an FSD, it is quite possible that the FSD will create an associated IRP and dispatch it to your driver. If your code tries to create an associated IRP itself (for the IRP received by you), you will run into all sorts of problems.

Completion of associated IRPs

The I/O Manager invokes completion routines for each of the stack locations contained in the associated IRP structure. However, once the completion routines have been invoked (and assuming that none of the completion routines returns `STATUS_MORE_PROCESSING_REQUIRED`), the `IoCompleteRequest()` function performs the following steps for an associated IRP structure:

- The I/O Manager obtains a pointer to the master IRP for the associated IRP being completed.

- The `AssociatedIrp.Count` field in the master IRP is decremented by 1.

- The memory for the associated IRP structure is freed and so are any MDLs referred to by the associated IRP.

- If the `AssociatedIrp.Count` field in the master IRP is equal to 0, the I/O Manager internally invokes `IoCompleteRequest()` on the master IRP.

As is obvious from this list, many of the steps that would normally be performed when completing a regular IRP structure are skipped by the I/O Manager when processing the completion for an associated IRP.

NOTE   As described earlier, associated IRP structures cannot be used in con-
                junction with buffered I/O data transfers. Therefore, the I/O Manag-
                er does not have to worry about copying over any data from a
                system buffer to a driver/user-supplied buffer. Associated IRPs are
                typically only used with the direct I/O method of data transfer, in
                which case an MDL describing the user buffer would probably have
                been utilized for the data transfer operation (if any).

There are two things your driver can do to prevent this automatic completion of
the master IRP by the I/O Manager (in case you wish to control when the master
IRP is actually freed):

- Your driver can specify a completion routine for the associated IRP.

  Your driver should return `STATUS_MORE_PROCESSING_REQUIRED` from
  this completion routine, which will cause the I/O Manager to immediately terminate further processing of the associated IRP. This will prevent manipulation of the associated IRP count by the I/O Manager and thereby also prevent
  completion of the master IRP. Completion routines are described in greater
  detail in the next section.

- Your driver can increase the `AssociatedIrp.Count` field in the master IRP
  before dispatching the associated IRP to a lower-level driver.

  Although this may sound repugnant (and like bad software engineering), it
  does work. Your driver can simply increase the `AssociatedIrp.Count`
  field in the master IRP by 1 before dispatching any associated IRPs that may
  have been created. This will result in the count not being equal to 0, even
  after IRP-completion processing of all associated IRPs has been performed by
  the I/O Manager. Since the count does not equal 0, the I/O Manager will not
  complete the master IRP.

Completion Routines

The I/O Manager allows kernel-mode drivers to register completion routines associated with I/O stack locations in an IRP. This allows the kernel-mode driver the
opportunity to perform any required postprocessing on the IRP after `IoComple-
teRequest()` has been invoked either by the driver itself or by some other
kernel-mode driver.[*]

---

[*] Completion routines are used by many types of kernel-mode drivers, including file system drivers, filter
drivers, and other intermediate drivers.

There can be multiple completion routines associated with each IRP, because completion routines are associated with stack locations in the IRP (and most IRPs have multiple stack locations). However, only one kernel-mode driver can process any particular stack location and therefore, only one completion routine can be associated with each such stack location.

The I/O Manager invokes completion routines in sequence in the `IoCompleteRequest()` function, starting with invoking the completion routine associated with the last stack location to be processed (before `IoCompleteRequest()` was invoked) and proceeding in reverse sequence until the completion routine associated with the first I/O stack location in the IRP has been invoked. This allows for a natural unraveling of I/O stack locations with the last-in-first-out order being preserved.

Figure 12-4 illustrates the sequence in which completion routines are invoked for an IRP with four stack locations.

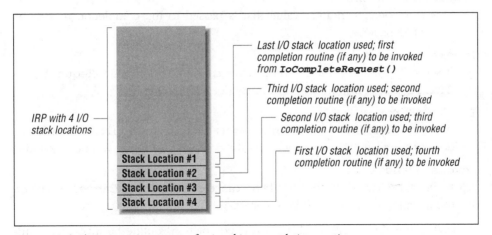

Figure 12-4. I/O manager sequence for invoking completion routines

Specifying a completion routine for IRPs

Your driver should use the `IoSetCompletionRoutine()` macro, which is made available by the NT I/O Manager. Currently, this macro is defined as follows:

```
#define IoSetCompletionRoutine( Irp, Routine, CompletionContext,       \
                                Success,  Error, Cancel )              \
{                                                                      \
    PIO_STACK_LOCATION irpSp;                                          \
    ASSERT( (Success) | (Error) | (Cancel) ? (Routine) != NULL : TRUE ); \
    irpSp = IoGetNextIrpStackLocation( (Irp) );                       \
    irpSp->CompletionRoutine = (Routine);                             \
    irpSp->Context = (CompletionContext);                            \
    irpSp->Control = 0;                                              \
    if ((Success)) { irpSp->Control = SL_INVOKE_ON_SUCCESS; }        \
```

```
        if ((Error)) { irpSp->Control |= SL_INVOKE_ON_ERROR;}                    \
        if ((Cancel)) { irpSp->Control |= SL_INVOKE_ON_CANCEL; } }
```

Parameters:

`Irp`

> This is a pointer to the IRP structure.

`CompletionRoutine`

> This is a pointer to the completion routine, supplied by your driver, of type
> `PIO_COMPLETION_ROUTINE`. This completion function must be defined as
> follows:

```
typedef
NTSTATUS (*PIO_COMPLETION_ROUTINE) (
    IN PDEVICE_OBJECT    DeviceObject,
    IN PIRP              Irp,
    IN PVOID             Context
);
```

`CompletionContext`

> This is an opaque pointer value that is passed to the completion routine by
> the I/O Manager.

`InvokeOnSuccess`

> If set to TRUE and if the returned status code to `IoCompleteRequest()` is
> `STATUS_SUCCESS`, the completion routine will be invoked.

`InvokeOnError`

> If set to TRUE and if the returned status code to `IoCompleteRequest()`
> does not evaluate to a success value, the completion routine will be invoked.

`InvokeOnCancel`

> If set to TRUE and the IRP has been canceled (i.e., `Irp->Cancel` is TRUE),
> the completion routine will be invoked.

Typically, your driver will request that the completion routine be invoked regardless of why the `IoCompleteRequest()` function was called. Therefore, you should set `InvokeOnSuccess`, `InvokeOnError`, and `InvokeOnCancel` to TRUE.

Notice that the completion routine information is placed in the next I/O stack location. This is logical, since that is the I/O stack location to be initialized for the next driver in the calling hierarchy.

Many kernel-mode drivers (especially filter drivers) execute the following steps:

- Allocate a new IRP structure using any one of the I/O Manager-supplied functions described earlier in this chapter.

- Initialize the first I/O stack location (obtained by using the `IoGetNextIrp-StackLocation()` function) with appropriate values and set a completion routine using the `IoSetCompletionRoutine()` function.

The problem with this approach is that when the filter driver completion routine does get invoked, you will find that the device object pointer supplied to your completion routine is NULL. The reason for this will become obvious as you read the following discussion on how the I/O Manager invokes completion routines. Basically, the problem is that your driver neglected to create a stack location for itself in the newly allocated IRP structure, and hence the I/O Manager has no way of determining the device object pointer it should pass on to your completion routine.

To avoid this potential problem (especially if your driver plans to use the passed-in device object pointer in the completion routine), ensure that your driver always creates and initializes a stack location for itself. To do this, you must execute the following steps after obtaining a new IRP structure:

- Use `IoSetCurrentStackLocation()` to set the IRP pointers to the first stack location in the IRP.

- Initialize the first stack location (use `IoGetCurrentStackLocation()` to obtain a pointer to this stack location) with appropriate values. Note that the I/O Manager will update this stack location with a pointer to your device object when you invoke `IoCallDriver()`.

- Use `IoGetNextIrpStackLocation()` to get a pointer to the next stack location (to be used by the driver you will invoke with the newly allocated IRP).

- Initialize the next IRP stack location with appropriate values and use `IoSet-CompletionRoutine()` to set your completion routine for the next I/O stack location.

Invoking completion routines

Completion routines are invoked by the `IoCompleteRequest()` function, implemented by the I/O Manager. The `IoCompleteRequest()` function, in turn, is invoked by the kernel-mode driver that will complete processing for the current IRP. The following pseudocode extract illustrates how the I/O Manager invokes completion routines associated with the IRP being completed.

```
while (PtrIrp->CurrentLocation < (PtrIrp->StackCount + 1)) {
    currentStackLocation = IoGetCurrentIrpStackLocation(PtrIrp);

    ...

    // Prepare to process beginning at the next I/O stack location.
    // If any completion routine returns
```

```
// STATUS_MORE_PROCESSING_REQUIRED and later reissues the
// IoCompleteRequest() call, the I/O Manager will begin processing
// at the next stack location (which is the correct thing to do).
(PtrIrp->Tail.Overlay.CurrentStackLocation)++;
(PtrIrp->CurrentLocation)++;

if (PtrIrp->CurrentLocation == (PtrIrp->StackCount + 1)) {
    // Some driver has set up a completion routine for the
    // last valid I/O stack location itself (probably using an
    // associated IRP).
    PtrDeviceObject = NULL;
} else {
    // Device Object of the driver that set the completion routine.
    // Notice that PtrIrp->Tail.Overlay.CurrentStackLocation was
    // incremented before we use IoGetCurrentIrpStackLocation()
    // here.
    PtrDeviceObject =
                IoGetCurrentIrpStackLocation(PtrIrp)->DeviceObject;
}
PtrContext = currentStackLocation->Context;

if ((NT_SUCCESS(PtrIrp->IoStatus.Status) &&
        currentStackLocation->Control & SL_INVOKE_ON_SUCCESS)
        ||
    (!NT_SUCCESS(PtrIrp->IoStatus.Status) &&
        currentStackLocation->Control & SL_INVOKE_ON_FAILURE)
        ||
    (PtrIrp->Cancel && currentStackLocation->Control
                        & SL_INVOKE_ON_CANCEL)) {
        // Invoke the completion routine.
        RC = currentStackLocation->
CompletionRoutine(PtrDeviceObject,PtrIrp, PtrContext);
        if (RC == STATUS_MORE_PROCESSING_REQUIRED) {
            return;
        }
    }
}

...
} // end of while more stack locations to process.
```

Notice that the flag values in the `Control` field for the current stack location, when combined with state information about why the IRP was completed and the status code saved in the IRP, determine whether or not the I/O Manager will invoke a completion routine for that particular stack location. Also note that the I/O Manager simply starts processing the IRP beginning at the current stack location (i.e., the stack location for the driver that invoked `IoCompleteRequest()`) and continues on until all stack locations have been processed.

WARNING   The I/O Manager is meticulous about supplying the correct device
object pointer to the driver that sets a completion routine. If your
driver (that must have some device object created to even receive
the IRP in the first place) sets a completion routine, then your completion routine will be invoked with a pointer to your own device
object. It is possible, however, for your driver to create a new IRP
and immediately set a completion routine in the first I/O stack location (to set up for the next driver in the calling hierarchy). In this
case, your completion routine will be invoked with the device object pointer set to NULL (since there was no stack location set up for
your driver, there is no device object pointer that the I/O Manager
can supply to you).

Finally, you may have noticed something strange about the preceding
pseudocode fragment. If the completion routine invoked returns a special status
code (STATUS_MORE_PROCESSING_REQUIRED), the I/O Manager simply stops
postprocessing for the particular IRP and returns control immediately to the caller.
This should give you some ideas on how IRPs can be reused by a higher-level
driver even after they have been completed by a lower-level kernel-mode driver.
This issue is discussed in greater detail later in this chapter.

Be careful about a particular bug that manifests itself when your filter driver specifies a completion routine in an IRP and then forwards the IRP to the next driver
in the calling hierarchy. The following code fragment illustrates a methodology
used sometimes by higher-level Windows NT drivers that can result in incorrect
execution:

```
PtrCurrentIoStackLocation = IoGetCurrentIrpStackLocation(PtrIrp);
PtrNextIoStackLocation = IoGetNextIrpStackLocation(PtrIrp);
// The following code can cause problems for the driver above
// in the calling hierarchy!!!
*PtrNextIoStackLocation = *PtrCurrentIoStackLocation;
RC = IoCallDriver(...);
```

If you examine this code fragment carefully, you will notice that the driver
executing this code has literally copied the entire contents of the current I/O stack
location into the stack location passed on to the next driver in the calling hierarchy. The copied data includes information contained in the Control field (the
SL_INVOKE_XXX flag values), as well as the function pointer and context
contained in the CompletionRoutine and Context fields respectively.

The net result is that the completion routine associated with the current I/O stack
location is now also associated with the next I/O stack location and will therefore

be invoked twice for the same IRP. Both NTFS and FASTFAT implementations in Windows NT (up until Version 4.0 SP2) contain this bug.*

To protect yourself against such badly behaved drivers, execute the following code sequence in your completion routine:

```
NTSTATUS      SFilterSampleCompletionRoutine(
PDEVICE_OBJECT              PtrSentDeviceObject;
PIRP                        PtrIrp;
PVOID                       SFilterContext)
{
    // Some declarations above.
    PDEVICE_OBJECT          SFilterDeviceObject = NULL;
    ...

    // The following line must exist in all completion routines. Read
    // Chapter 4 for more information.
    if (PtrIrp->PendingReturned) {
        IoMarkIrpPending(PtrIrp);
    }

    // To protect myself from bugs in other drivers ... !!!
    // Ensure that you have some way to get a pointer to your device
    // object.
    SFilterDeviceObject = ...; // assume that we get the value from
                               // the context.
    if (PtrSentDeviceObject != SFilterDeviceObject) {
        // We were called erroneously. Return control back to the I/O
        // Manager.
        return;
    }

    // Other processing goes here.
    ...
}
```

Some points to consider regarding completion routines

Completion routines are directly invoked in the context of the thread that calls `IoCompleteRequest()`. Since your driver cannot be sure about the thread execution context in which the completion routine is invoked, it must be especially careful with regard to the memory accessed by the driver or other resources (e.g., pointers, object handles) that may be accessed. Ensure that the processing performed by the completion routine can be executed in any arbitrary thread context.

Also note that completion routines are often invoked at a high IRQL. It is not unusual to have your completion routine invoked at IRQL **DISPATCH_LEVEL**.

---

* It appears as though this behavior is exhibited only in the dispatch routine for `IRP_MJ_DEVICE_CON-TROL` as implemented by FASTFAT and NTFS.

Therefore, your completion routine code cannot be made pageable, nor can it access paged memory.

Although you may sometimes be able to get away with invoking `IoCall-Driver()` from within your completion routine, many kernel-mode driver dispatch entry points are not equipped to handle being invoked at a high IRQL. Therefore, try to avoid invoking driver dispatch entry points directly from your completion routine. You could, instead, initiate such processing asynchronously using a worker thread.

WARNING   In Chapter 4, we saw how your driver must always propagate the pending returned information from your completion routine. Failure to do this will result in unexpected system behavior, including system hangs and crashes. Review the information provided in Chapter 4 to ensure that your completion routine does behave correctly about propagating such information.

Using completion routines

Filter drivers often use completion routines to perform postprocessing of data returned by the target driver. For example, an encryption module that you may develop could decrypt data on-the-fly in a completion routine after the compressed data has been retrieved by the file system from secondary storage.

There are less esoteric things, as well, that are done using completion routines. For example, an intermediate driver or a file system driver could break up a relatively large I/O request into more manageable pieces and issue multiple I/O requests to lower-level disk drivers. The data returned from the disk drivers can then be collated in a completion routine associated with each IRP sent to the lower-level drivers.

Sometimes FSDs, filter drivers, or fault-tolerant drivers will use completion routines to determine whether a specific I/O request must be reissued to the lower-level driver, in case the I/O failed. This type of retry operation might make sense under certain circumstances.

Subject to the restrictions discussed previously, the kind of processing that you can perform in your completion routine is only limited by your imagination.

About this STATUS_MORE_PROCESSING_REQUIRED business ...

As you must have observed from the pseudocode fragment presented earlier, when IRP completion postprocessing is being performed by the I/O Manager, the postprocessing is abruptly terminated if any completion routine invoked returns a special return status of type `STATUS_MORE_PROCESSING_REQUIRED`.

This is a method provided by the I/O Manager to allow any kernel-mode driver in the calling hierarchy to interrupt the IRP completion. It is possible for the same IRP to be completed, via `IoCompleteRequest()`, once again at some later time, and the I/O Manager will begin processing (once again) starting at the current I/O stack location.

By returning `STATUS_MORE_PROCESSING_REQUIRED`, your kernel-mode driver essentially informs the I/O Manager that it needs to hold on to and use the IRP for some additional time. Managing the IRP from that point onward is the responsibility of your driver. This is no different from how your driver would manage an IRP received in a dispatch routine for the very first time. The only point to note is that the kind of processing you can perform directly in your completion routine is limited, since the completion routine is invoked in the context of an arbitrary thread (possibly) at a high IRQL. However, you can certainly dispatch the same IRP to some worker thread for further asynchronous processing.

You should note that the only action performed by the I/O Manager, before it stops the postprocessing of the IRP, is to invoke any completion routines for stack locations lower in the calling hierarchy. Therefore, the IRP state is completely maintained when your completion routine gains control of the IRP. The reason that the I/O Manager terminates processing of the IRP so completely once your driver returns `STATUS_MORE_PROCESSING_REQUIRED` is because the I/O Manager has no idea what your driver intends to do to the IRP (or has already done to the IRP). Your driver may have just freed the memory allocated for the IRP (by invoking `IoFreeIrp()`) before returning `STATUS_MORE_PROCESSING_` `REQUIRED` to the I/O Manager and hence any attempt by the I/O Manager to even read any field in the IRP structure could lead to a system crash.

Synchronous I/O requests and STATUS_MORE_PROCESSING_REQUIRED

There is one potential problem that you must understand if you expect to return `STATUS_MORE_PROCESSING_REQUIRED` from a completion routine provided by your driver. Recall from Chapter 4 that the NT I/O Manager tries to optimize processing of user I/O requests that are considered *inherently synchronous*. In the case of these types of I/O requests, the I/O Manager always blocks the invoking thread until the request has been completed via `IoCompleteRequest()`. Because of this, the I/O Manager avoids issuing an APC to perform the final postprocessing in the context of the thread issuing the I/O request. Instead, the `IoCompleteRequest()` code simply returns control to the caller (after performing some basic postprocessing), and the invoking thread that is blocked, awaiting completion of the request, performs the final postprocessing by invoking `IopCompleteRequest()` directly.

For inherently synchronous I/O requests, the I/O Manager code that initially creates an IRP and forwards it onward to the first kernel-mode driver (typically, a filter driver that intercepts FSD requests or the FSD itself) executes the following code sequence:

```
// Invoke the first driver in the calling hierarchy to process the IRP.
RC = IoCallDriver(...);
if (RC == STATUS_PENDING) {
        // Wait until the request is completed. The IoCompleteRequest()
        // code will now be forced to use a kernel-mode APC to complete
        // the request.
        KeWaitForSingleObject(...);
} else {
        // This request completed synchronously. Therefore, I can safely
        // assume that the IRP is no longer required. Furthermore, the
        // IoCompleteRequest() has not issued an APC to perform the final
        // postprocessing. Therefore, let me perform such postprocessing
        // by invoking the appropriate (internal) routine directly.
        IopCompleteRequest(...);
        // Note that the call to IopCompleteRequest() above will result in
        // memory for the IRP being freed.
        }
```

Sometimes, filter drivers that layer themselves above an FSD write code as follows:

```
NTSTATUS SFilterBadFSDInterceptRoutine(
...)
{
    // Assume appropriate declarations, etc.
    ...


    // The filter driver sets a completion routine called
    // SFilterCompletion().
    IoSetCompletionRoutine(PtrIrp, SFilterCompletion,
                           SFilterCompletionContext,
                           TRUE, TRUE, TRUE);


    // Now, simply dispatch the call and return whatever the FSD returns.
    // The problem with this (described below) is that the FSD may not
    // return STATUS_PENDING. This may cause us headaches later.
    return(IoCallDriver(...));
}

NTSTATUS SFilterCompletion(
...)
{
    // Assume appropriate declarations, etc.


    ...
```

```
    // Hardcoded return of STATUS_MORE_PROCESSING_REQUIRED.
    return(STATUS_MORE_PROCESSING_REQUIRED);
}
```

Consider the following situation. The FSD synchronously processes the IRP and returns an appropriate status, either STATUS_SUCCESS or an error (except STATUS_PENDING because, from the FSD's perspective, IRP processing has been completed synchronously). Your filter driver passes the returned status code to the I/O Manager, believing that the completion routine will be able to intercept IRP postprocessing by returning STATUS_MORE_PROCESSING_REQUIRED.

Unfortunately, although your filter driver believes that it has stopped IRP completion postprocessing by returning STATUS_MORE_PROCESSING_REQUIRED from the completion routine, the previous I/O Manager code fragment will not care about the abrupt stoppage of the IRP completion and will invoke IopComple-teRequest() directly, which, in turn, will free the memory for the IRP. This will lead to a system crash (or corruption) when your filter driver continues processing the IRP.

To avoid this problem, you may consider the following guiding principles:*

- If you complete an IRP in your driver synchronously, do not invoke IoMark-IrpPending() and do not return STATUS_PENDING from your dispatch routine.

- If you pass the IRP to a lower layer, protect yourself from the preceding problem by always marking the IRP pending and always returning STATUS_PENDING.

  The other way of protecting yourself is to ensure that if you inadvertently forwarded to the I/O Manager a return code of STATUS_PENDING, you cannot return STATUS_MORE_PROCESSING_REQUIRED from your completion routine (unless you are really sure that this is not an inherently synchronous I/O operation from the I/O Manager's perspective). The next rule formalizes this behavior.

- If you ever return STATUS_PENDING (regardless of whether it is because you decide to return this status code yourself or because some lower-level driver does so and you simply pass-on the return code), you must have marked the IRP pending.

- If you ever mark the IRP pending, you must return STATUS_PENDING.

---

* These ideas/guidelines came out of a discussion on a Usenet newsgroup where this topic was hotly debated. Appendix F, *Additional Sources for Help*, lists some sources for help during FSD or filter driver development, including a Usenet newsgroup.

Here's a simplistic method that can be followed by any filter driver that layers itself on top of an FSD:

```
NTSTATUS SFilterBetterFSDInterceptRoutine(
...)
{
    // Assume appropriate declarations, etc.
    ...

    // The filter driver sets a completion routine called
    // SFilterCompletion().
    IoSetCompletionRoutine(PtrIrp, SFilterCompletion,
                           SFilterCompletionContext,
                           TRUE, TRUE, TRUE);

    // Now, invoke the lower-level driver but force synchronous requests to
    // always be completed via an APC.
    IoMarkIrpPending(PtrIrp);
    IoCallDriver(…)
    return(STATUS_PENDING);
}
```

This code will degrade performance somewhat (though whether such degradation will be noticeable is debatable), but will always lead to correct handling of the IRP, even if your completion routine returns STATUS_MORE_PROCESSING_ REQUIRED. As soon as you return STATUS_PENDING (after having marked the IRP pending), the I/O Manager code invoking your driver will wait for the completion of the IRP using the KeWaitForXXX() function, and IRP completion (via IopCompleteRequest()) will only be finished when the IRP is finally completed and no completion routine returns STATUS_MORE_PROCESSING_ REQUIRED. The downside is that the I/O Manager will be forced to issue an APC to complete the IRP, which incurs a performance penalty even for synchronous I/O requests.

Detaching from a Target Device Object

There will be occasions when your driver may wish to stop filtering and would like to detach itself from the target device object. This may also happen because the target device object could be in the process of being deleted by the driver that created it. An example of this is when file system drivers managing removable media delete a device object representing a mounted instance of a logical volume because the user has replaced the media in the drive. If a user decides to format a disk device, the FSD will dismount the logical volume mounted on the device (if any) at the request of the user application. This will also result in deletion of the logical volume device object and your driver must be prepared to delete the attached device object in this case.

To request that your device object be detached from a target device object, use the `IoDetachDevice()` function (described in the DDK) supplied by the I/O Manager. This function expects a single argument, the target device object you wish to detach from. You must supply the target device object pointer that you obtained when first attaching to the target.[*]

Note that your driver must not ever try to detach from a target device object if another driver has layered itself on top of your device object. You can always check for this case by examining the **AttachedDevice** field in your own device object and declining to detach from the target if the field contents are nonnull. Failure to do this will not only result in memory leaks, but will break the drivers that are layered above yours, since their device objects will also get detached abruptly (without their knowledge or consent). Detaching (when it is not initiated by the I/O Manager) can only be performed safely in a last-in-first-out fashion, starting with the highest-layered device object attached to a specific target device object. The only exception to this rule is when the I/O Manager asks your driver to perform the following detach.

Starting with Version 4.0 of the operating system, the I/O Manager will request that you detach from a target device object if the driver managing the target device object decides to delete the object for some reason. For example, as mentioned earlier, an FSD may dismount a volume if requested to do so by a user application and will therefore delete the device object representing the particular instance of the mounted logical volume.[†] In this case, the FSD will invoke `IoDeleteDevice()` to perform the delete operation. In turn, the I/O Manager will ask the first driver that has attached a device object to the one being deleted to detach its own device object. This call will be sent to your driver in the form of a fast I/O function call.[‡]

Your driver must detach its device object at this time and probably also delete it as well. If you do choose to delete your device object using `IoDeleteDevice()`, the I/O Manager will now call any driver that has a device object attached to your device object (being deleted) to detach itself from your device object. Note that the fast I/O detach call does not accept failure (there is no return

---

[*] This is one reason why your driver should always store the target device address in some device object extension field. Also note that the address you supply is the address of the highest-layered device object that you received when (for example) your driver invoked the `IoAttachDeviceToDeviceStack()` function.

[†] In Windows NT Version 3.51 and earlier, if the I/O Manager detected a nonnull **AttachedDevice** field for a device object on which `IoDeleteDevice()` was invoked, it would bugcheck the system. This was not very conducive to supporting filter drivers cleanly.

[‡] Note that I said the first driver will be asked to perform the detach and not the top-layered driver. This is because the I/O Manager expects each driver (starting with the first one) that had attached to the target device object to first detach itself and then invoke `IoDeleteDevice()` on itself, resulting in a recursive detach for the next (higher-layered) attached device and so on.

value for the function definition), so your driver has no choice but to do the I/O Manager's bidding. If you fail to perform the detach operation, the I/O Manager will bugcheck the system.

TIP	Even if multiple drivers have attached themselves to a particular target device object, the method described previously allows each such driver to cleanly detach and delete its own (attached) device object when the target device object is being deleted. To make this happen, however, each driver that has its fast I/O detach function invoked must first perform the detach operation and then immediately perform a delete operation for its device object.

Some Dos and Don'ts in Filtering

Designing filter drivers is often an iterative process. Your filter driver is likely to encounter unique problems and issues that are specific to the type of driver you are trying to design and the type of target driver that your filter will attach itself to. However, there are certain fundamental principles that you should keep in mind when you begin the process of designing and implementing a filter driver. Many of these principles were mentioned earlier in this chapter. Here then, is a recap of some of the basic principles that you should always keep in mind when designing your filter driver:

Always understand the nature of the driver you wish to filter

This may seem obvious to some of you but it cannot be stressed often enough. There are some who believe that using a canned approach to designing filter drivers may be adequate. This may well be the case—sometimes. However, in most cases, if you fail to understand the characteristics of your target driver, you will end up with problems late in the cycle that could be difficult to rectify easily.

As an example, consider the situation where you decide to filter all requests targeted to a specific logical volume managed by a native FSD (e.g., NTFS). You will layer your own device object over the target device object representing the mounted logical volume. So far, so good. However, you should now understand the various ways in which the FSD gets invoked, since those are exactly the situations in which your dispatch entry points will be invoked.

For example, in Chapter 10, *Writing A File System Driver II*, you read that the FSD read/write entry points can be invoked in many different ways: via a system call from a user application, due to a page fault on a mapped file, from the Cache Manager due to asynchronous read/write requests, recursively via the FSD and the Cache Manager due to cached I/O being performed by the user application, and so on. The important point to note here is that in some situations, it may be acceptable for your filter driver to post an I/O request to be handled asynchronously, but in other situations (e.g., when servicing a page fault), your filter driver should never try to post the request for asynchronous handling, since this could lead to a deadlock or hang. (Remember that the VMM or the Cache Manager may have preacquired FSD resources.)

Similarly, you must be extremely careful about how your filter driver performs synchronization, especially when it filters file system I/O requests. As you read in earlier chapters, the NT VMM and the Cache Manager often preacquire FSD resources via fast I/O calls. This is necessary in order to maintain the system locking hierarchy and avoid deadlock. However, if your filter driver layers itself on top of an FSD, then by definition your filter driver becomes part of the intertwined set of kernel modules that are affected by the locking sequence implemented in processing I/O requests, and therefore, you must somehow ensure that your filter driver does not violate the locking hierarchy in any way. You could do this by ensuring that any resources acquired when processing read/write/create/cleanup/close requests are end-resources (i.e., you would acquire such a resource and not acquire any other until the resource was released; furthermore, for filter drivers, you would not pass-on an IRP unless the acquired resource was released), or you could preacquire resources yourself in the context of the invoking Cache Manager or VMM thread when the fast I/O call is intercepted.*

Note that in the event that your filter driver decides to filter lower-level device objects (e.g., one representing a physical disk device), you might be able to ignore many complicated issues that you would otherwise face when intercepting file system I/O. There are other issues that a filter driver layering itself over a disk driver must be careful of; for example, IRPs sent to a lower-level disk driver may often be associated IRPs created by an FSD, and therefore a filter driver layering itself over the disk driver must not try to create associated IRPs itself. Similarly, lower-level disk drivers are often expected to complete their processing asynchronously by queuing the request and returning control immediately to the higher-level kernel-mode drivers. Your filter driver must conform to such expectations or you could risk destabilizing the entire system.

In all situations, more knowledge and experience about the target driver will prove to be better than less.

---

* The problem with the second approach is that replacing the lazy-write/read-ahead callbacks obtained from the file object could turn out to be very difficult.

Know what your driver attaches itself to

As described earlier in this chapter, your driver may try to attach to a file system (mounted) logical volume device object but may actually end up attaching to the physical disk device object if the volume is not mounted. Therefore, be careful about how you open the target device as a prerequisite to performing the attach operation.

Beware of maintaining unnecessary references

If you inadvertently maintain an extra reference on a target device object (or file object obtained when performing the attach), you may prevent all further open requests to the target and defeat your original goal of intercepting I/O requests (there will be none to intercept). Furthermore, in the case of FSD-created device/file objects, you may end up preventing a volume dismount/ lock operation because of such unnecessary references maintained by you and prevent a user from doing useful things like reformatting a drive or ejecting a removable piece of media.

Be careful about the thread context in which your dispatch entry point executes

This is a problem that many of us encounter when beginning to design and implement filter drivers. You may have implemented a kernel-mode filter driver function that executes as follows:

```
NTSTATUS SFilterBadFilterRead(
...)
{
    // Declarations, etc. go here.
    IO_STATUS_BLOCK        LocalIoStatus;
    void                   *LocalBufferPointer;
    ...

    // Here, I will make the caller wait until I read some data
    // from another logical volume. This data will somehow help me in
    // processing the caller's request. ZwReadFile() is easy to use
    // and therefore I will try to use it.
    ZwReadFile(GlobalFileHandle, ...,
                    &LocalIoStatus, LocalBufferPointer, ...);

    ...
}
```

This code fragment seems reasonable, but there are two problems (at least) with it that will result in the `ZwReadFile()` routine returning an error status back to you. First, the fragment attempts to use a `GlobalFileHandle` that was presumably obtained when the target of the read operation was first opened (probably during driver initialization). Unfortunately, file handles are process-specific, and therefore, it is highly likely that the previously described file handle will be invalid in the context of most user threads that invoke the system service to request I/O. Instead of using the global file handle directly,

you could create a new file handle in the context of the caller thread (use
`ObOpenObjectByPointer()` described in Chapter 5, *The NT Virtual
Memory Manager*, if you had previously stored a pointer to the underlying
file object), or you may open a new handle to the target object in the context
of the calling thread, or you could post the request to be handled in the
context of a thread that can use the handle, or finally, you could avoid using
`ZwReadFile()` and instead create IRPs that you dispatch directly to the
target of the request.

Similarly, you will notice that the code attempts to use pointers to memory
that is either off the kernel-mode stack or allocated in kernel-mode. When
you try to use `ZwReadFile()`, the recipient of the request will check the
previous mode of the caller (which in all likelihood is user mode) and will
reject the request if passed-in addresses are kernel-mode virtual addresses
(virtual address with a value > 0x7FFFFFFF).

The point to note, once again, is that the context of the thread in which your
filter driver dispatch routine executes must always be kept in mind as you
design and implement your driver.

Be creative

Imagine that you wish to prevent the Windows NT I/O Manager from automatically assigning drive letters during system boot-up to certain drives
connected to the system.* How would you go about doing that?

If you go back and read the system boot-up sequence overview described in
Chapter 4, you will note that the I/O Manager opens the device object (representing the physical device) created by the disk device driver in order to
obtain the characteristics of the device before assigning a drive letter to it.
You can then deduce that, perhaps by designing and implementing a filter
driver that layers itself, early in the boot sequence, over the target disk device
objects, you could somehow prevent this drive letter assignment. How?
Maybe, if your driver recognized the I/O Manager open request and failed
this open operation for each target disk device object, the I/O Manager may
conclude that the disks were unusable and (hopefully) decide not to assign
drive letters to these disk drives.†

---

* This may be necessary if you have a large disk farm connected to the system. You know that there are
a finite number of drive letters available, and you may decide that one method to allow a user to utilize
all of the disks in this large disk farm would be to present logical groupings of disks under a single drive
letter. There are other alternatives, as well, that you may decide to implement that are beyond the scope
of this book.

† Unfortunately, it is not as easy to prevent drive letter assignment as is described here. But the description provided here is definitely a good starting point.

There are many ways in which filter drivers can be used. Not all of these ways have as yet been exploited. Therein lies an opportunity for you to be creative and design stable, safe software modules that extend the capabilities of the Windows NT I/O subsystem and provide substantial added value to your customers.

In this chapter, we discussed filter driver design and development. In order to understand how to design filter drivers that are reliable and useful, you should understand the kernel-mode environment in which your filter driver will execute. The contents of this book and the sample filter driver implementation provided on the accompanying diskette should help you in creatively designing and implementing your own value-added software for the Windows NT operating system.

IV

The Appendixes

Loose ends, important but peripheral issues, are all covered in the appendixes.

- Appendix A, *Windows NT System Services*
- Appendix B, *MPR Support*
- Appendix C, *Building Kernel-Mode Drivers*
- Appendix D, *Debugging Support*
- Appendix E, *Recommended Readings and References*
- Appendix F, *Additional Sources for Help*

Windows NT
System Services

For various reasons, Microsoft has not documented the native Windows NT I/O services provided by the Windows NT I/O Manager. Application developers are instead expected to use either the Win32 subsystem APIs, or the APIs provided by one of the other supported subsystems, e.g., the POSIX subsystem.

This appendix contains a list of most of the exported, native Windows NT I/O-Manager-provided system services. As was mentioned earlier in the book, the Windows NT system services are quite powerful and comprehensive, and allow the caller to more easily request certain operations that would often otherwise require multiple Win32 API calls. The majority of the structure types and flag definitions required to use the various system services described in this appendix are provided in the Windows NT DDK. Those definitions that are not provided in the DDK can be obtained from the header files supplied with the Windows NT IFS kit. Many such undefined types are described here as well.

NT System Services

The Windows NT system services allow the caller to request normal file stream manipulation operations. These include requests to create a new file or open an existing file stream, requests to perform I/O on the file, get and set file attributes, map a file into a process virtual address space, and requests to close a file handle. Nearly all of the services provided by the native system services can also be requested using Win32 API calls or any one of the various APIs provided by the supported subsystems. However, system and application software developers may sometimes require functionality that may not be easily (or efficiently) provided by any one subsystem. As an example, creating a link to an existing file cannot be easily accomplished (if at all) using the Win32 subsystem. This functionality, however, is more easily requested if an application were to use the POSIX subsystem instead.* In such situations where you may need otherwise hard-to-request functionality, requesting file system services by using the native system service calls provided by the I/O Manager can be quite useful.

Kernel-mode file system and filter driver developers may also wish to scan through the system services documented here to get a good sense of how the I/O Manager translates user requests into corresponding file system dispatch routine invocations, and also how user-specified arguments are eventually passed on to the file system implementation. Descriptions of certain system services also include comments on the responsibilities of an FSD processing such a request.

NtCreateFile()

Parameters

`FileHandle`

> Returned handle (created by the I/O Manager) if call succeeds.

`DesiredAccess`

> Desired access flags can be one or more of the following:

> `DELETE`

>> Required if `FILE_DELETE_ON_CLOSE` is set in `CreateOptions` below. File can be deleted by caller.

> `FILE_READ_DATA`

>> Caller can request to read data.

> `FILE_WRITE_DATA`

>> Caller may write file data. The caller is also allowed to append to the file.

> `FILE_READ_ATTRIBUTES`

>> File attributes flags can be read.

> `FILE_WRITE_ATTRIBUTES`

>> The caller can change file attribute flag values.

> `FILE_APPEND_DATA`

>> The caller can only append data to the file.† This access value is not allowed in conjunction with the `FILE_NO_INTERMEDIATE_BUFFERING` `CreateOptions` flag.

> `READ_CONTROL`

>> ACL and ownership information for the file stream can be read.

---

* Multiple (hard) links to a file stream are currently supported only by the NTFS driver, out of all of the native file system implementations provided by Microsoft for the Windows NT platform.

† Any byte offset specified in a write operation will be ignored.

WRITE_DAC

Discretionary ACL associated with the file can be written.

WRITE_OWNER

Ownership information can be written.

FILE_LIST_DIRECTORY

Caller can list files contained within the directory. Not valid for data files.

FILE_TRAVERSE

The opened directory can be in the pathname of a file. Not valid for data files.

FILE_READ_EA

Caller can read extended attributes associated with the file.

FILE_WRITE_EA

Required if `EaBuffer` is not null. Caller may write extended attributes to the file.

SYNCHRONIZE

Caller can wait for the returned file handle for completion of asynchronous I/O requests. Required if either `FILE_SYNCHRONOUS_IO_ALERT` or `FILE_SYNCHRONOUS_IO_NONALERT` flags in `CreateOptions` have been set. If this flag is not specified, I/O completion for asynchronous I/O requests must be synchronized by either using an event or an APC routine.

FILE_EXECUTE

File stream is an executable image. If `FILE_EXECUTE` is set but neither `FILE_READ_DATA` nor `FILE_WRITE_DATA` are set, then I/O can only be performed by mapping the file into the process virtual address space.

ObjectAttributes

The caller must allocate memory for this structure of type `OBJECT_ATTRIBUTES`. Fields in the structure are initialized as follows:

Length

Size, in bytes, of the structure.

ObjectName

A unicode string specifying the name of file. The name can be either a relative name (`RootDirectory` is nonnull) or an absolute name (`Root-Directory` is NULL).

RootDirectory (optional)

The previously opened handle for a directory; `ObjectName` will be considered relative to this directory (if specified).

SecurityDescriptor (optional)
> If nonnull, the specified ACLs will be applied only if the file is created. If the SecurityDescriptor is NULL and if the file is created, the FSD determines which (if any) ACLs will be associated with the file (typically, a default ACL associated with the parent directory is propagated to the created file).

SecurityQualityOfService (optional)
> Specifies the access a server should be given to a client's security context. Only nonnull when a connection is being established to a protected server.

Attributes
> Combination of OBJ_INHERIT (child processes inherit open handle) and OBJ_CASE_INSENSITIVE (lookups should be processed in a case-insensitive fashion).

IoStatusBlock
Caller-supplied structure to receive results of create/open request.

AllocationSize (optional)
The initial allocation size of file. Only used when the file is initially created, overwritten, or superseded. If the FSD cannot allocate the requested disk space for the file, the create/open request will fail.

FileAttributes
Attributes are only applied if file is newly created, superseded, or overwritten. Any combination is allowed but all flag values override the FILE_ATTRIBUTE_NORMAL flag. Attributes can be one or more of the following:

FILE_ATTRIBUTE_NORMAL
> A normal file should be created.

FILE_ATTRIBUTE_READONLY
> A read-only file should be created.

FILE_ATTRIBUTE_HIDDEN
> A hidden file should be created.

FILE_ATTRIBUTE_SYSTEM
> The created file should be marked as a system file.

FILE_ATTRIBUTE_ARCHIVE
> Mark the file to-be-archived.

FILE_ATTRIBUTE_TEMPORARY
> The file to-be-created is marked as a temporary file. Note that modified cached data for the file is often not flushed to secondary storage for temporary files by the Cache Manager.

FILE_ATTRIBUTE_COMPRESSED
The file to be created is a compressed file.

ShareAccess
The type of share access requested by the caller. The share access can be a combination of the following:

FILE_SHARE_READ
The file can be concurrently opened for read access by other threads.

FILE_SHARE_WRITE
Other file open operations requesting write access should be allowed.

FILE_SHARE_DELETE
Other file open operations requesting delete access should be allowed.

Note that the share access flags allow the requester to control how the file can be shared by separate threads and processes. If none of the share values are specified, no other subsequent open operation will be allowed to proceed until the file handle is closed (and an **IRP_MJ_CLEANUP** issued to the FSD).

CreateDisposition
The disposition specified by the caller determines the actions performed by an FSD if a file does or does not exist. Any one of the following values can be specified:

FILE_SUPERSEDE
It the file exists, it should be superseded; if the file does not exist, it should be created.

FILE_CREATE
If the file does not exist, it should be created; if the file exists, an error should be returned (typically **STATUS_OBJECT_NAME_COLLISION** is returned).

FILE_OPEN
If the file exists, it should be opened; if the file does not exist, an error should be returned (often **STATUS_OBJECT_NAME_NOT_FOUND** is returned).

FILE_OPEN_IF
Open the file if it exists, create the file if it does not already exist.

FILE_OVERWRITE
If the file exists, it should be opened and overwritten. If it does not exist, the create operation should fail (often **STATUS_OBJECT_NAME_NOT_FOUND** is returned).

FILE_OVERWRITE_IF

If the file exists, it should be opened and overwritten. If it does not exist, the file should be created.

Superseding a file requires the caller to have **DELETE** access to the existing file (other threads that may have concurrently opened the file should allow **FILE_SHARE_DELETE** share access). Overwriting a file requires **FILE_WRITE_DATA** access instead (other threads that may have concurrently opened the file should allow **FILE_SHARE_WRITE** share access).[*] For overwrite operations, new file attributes are logically ORed with existing attributes whereas for supersede operations, the new attributes replace the existing file attributes.

CreateOptions

Options used when the file is created or opened. One or more of the following should be specified:

FILE_DIRECTORY_FILE

File being created or opened must be a directory file. If this option is not specified, it does not mean that the file being opened cannot be a directory file (unless **FILE_NON_DIRECTORY_FILE** below is specified).

FILE_NON_DIRECTORY_FILE

File being created or opened cannot be a directory file. This flag is mutually exclusive with the **FILE_DIRECTORY_FILE** flag value.[†] If this option is not specified, it does not mean that the file being opened cannot be a nondirectory file (unless **FILE_DIRECTORY_FILE** above is specified).

FILE_WRITE_THROUGH

A write operation cannot complete until data has been written to nonvolatile storage.

FILE_SEQUENTIAL_ONLY

A hint provided by the caller indicating that access to the file data will be sequential (this is not binding however; therefore, the caller may specify this flag and yet access the file in a random fashion).

FILE_RANDOM_ACCESS

A hint provided by the caller indicating that the file data will not typically be accessed sequentially (this flag is mutually exclusive with the **FILE_**

---

[*] Logically speaking, a supersede operation is equivalent to the directory entry for the file being deleted and recreated whereas the overwrite operation simply means that the contents of the file are overwritten (the directory entry is unaffected).

[†] The I/O Manager checks to ensure that **CreateOptions** are specified correctly; the I/O Manager also verifies that incompatible **CreateOptions** and **DesiredAccess** have not been specified.

SEQUENTIAL_ONLY flag). Note that the semantics associated with this flag are not binding upon the caller; therefore, the caller may specify this flag and yet access the file sequentially.

FILE_NO_INTERMEDIATE_BUFFERING

The file data cannot be cached in memory. This option is incompatible with the FILE_APPEND_DATA DesiredAccess flag. If this flag is specified, the byte offset and length supplied by the user in all subsequent I/O requests must be an integral multiple of the device sector size; otherwise, the incorrect I/O requests will be rejected. The file position supplied in any subsequent call to NtSetInformationFile() (described later in this appendix) using the returned file handle, with the FileInformationClass parameter set to FilePositionInformation, must also be a multiple of the device sector size. All buffers supplied by the caller must be aligned appropriately based upon the alignment requirements of the underlying device.

FILE_SYNCHRONOUS_IO_ALERT / FILE_SYNCHRONOUS_IO_NONALERT

The two flags are mutually exclusive with respect to each other. Both flags indicate that all I/O operations on the file stream using the created file object will be performed synchronously. This means that while any I/O operation is outstanding, all other I/O requests (including those from any thread that already has a pending, in-progress I/O request) will be blocked.

The I/O Manager maintains a current file pointer position whenever either of these two flags is specified.

The only difference between the two flags is that when the FILE_SYNCHRONOUS_IO_ALERT flag is specified, any wait performed on behalf of the caller is subject to premature termination from alerts.

Whenever either flag is specified, the SYNCHRONIZE DesiredAccess flag must also be set.

FILE_CREATE_TREE_CONNECTION

Only used by the LAN manager redirector. The LAN manager redirector creates a new connection to a remote (shared) object upon receiving this open request.

FILE_COMPLETE_IF_OPLOCKED

The open request should be completed immediately (with an alternate success code), even if the target file has an oplock associated with it, instead of blocking the requesting thread until the oplock has been broken (see Chapter 11, *Writing a File System Driver III*).

FILE_NO_EA_KNOWLEDGE

The caller does not understand how to handle extended attributes. If extended attributes are associated with the file being opened, the FSD must fail the open operation.

FILE_DELETE_ON_CLOSE

The directory entry for the file being opened should be deleted when the last handle to the file stream has been closed.

FILE_OPEN_BY_FILE_ID

The file name is actually a **LARGE_INTEGER**-type identifier that should be used to locate and open the target file (see Chapter 9, *Writing a File System Driver I,* for details).

FILE_OPEN_FOR_BACKUP_INTENT

The file is being opened for backup purposes, and the FSD should initiate a check for the appropriate privileges and determine whether the open should be allowed to proceed or be denied.

FILE_NO_COMPRESSION

The file cannot be compressed.

EaBuffer (optional)

A caller-allocated buffer containing a list of extended attributes to be set on the file only if the file is being created. Must be set to NULL if the file is only being opened. The **FILE_FULL_EA_INFORMATION** structure defines the format of the extended attributes in **EaBuffer**. Each extended attribute entry must be **longword** aligned. The **NextEntryOffset** field in the structures specifies the number of bytes between the current entry and the next. For the last entry, the **NextEntryOffset** field is zero.

If extended attributes are specified and if the extended attributes for the newly created file cannot be successfully created, the create/open request will fail. Therefore, creation of extended attributes is an atomic operation with respect to creation of the file.

EaLength

Value should be 0 if **EaBuffer** is set to NULL. Otherwise, it contains the length (in bytes) of the EAs listed in **EaBuffer**.

Return code

STATUS_SUCCESS indicates that the operation succeeded and a valid handle is being returned; **STATUS_PENDING** indicates that the operation will be performed asynchronously by the FSD, while **STATUS_REPARSE** indicates that the name should be parsed again by the object manager (e.g., a new volume has been mounted).

In the case of an error, an appropriate error code is returned. This includes (but is not limited to) the following return code values:

- STATUS_OBJECT_TYPE_MISMATCH

- STATUS_NO_SUCH_DEVICE

- STATUS_ACCESS_DENIED (a commonly used error code value)

- STATUS_FILE_IS_A_DIRECTORY

- STATUS_NOT_A_DIRECTORY

- STATUS_INSUFFICIENT_RESOURCES

- STATUS_OBJECT_NAME_INVALID

- STATUS_DELETE_PENDING

- STATUS_SHARING_VIOLATION

- STATUS_INVALID_PARAMETER

IRP

Overlay.AllocationSize
    Set to the caller-supplied AllocationSize value (if any).

AssociatedIrp.SystemBuffer
    The EaBuffer supplied by the caller (if any).

Flags
    The IRP_CREATE_OPERATION, IRP_SYNCHRONOUS_API, and IRP_
    DEFER_IO_COMPLETION flag values are set.

I/O stack location

MajorFunction
    IRP_MJ_CREATE

MinorFunction
    None.

Flags
    One or more of SL_CASE_SENSITIVE, SL_FORCE_ACCESS_CHECK, SL_
    OPEN_PAGING_FILE, and SL_OPEN_TARGET_DIRECTORY.

Control
    Irrelevant from the FSD's perspective.

Parameters.Create.SecurityContext
    Points to an IO_SECURITY_CONTEXT structure (allocated by the I/O
    Manager) containing the AccessState and DesiredAccess (specified by

the caller). The FSD can validate the access requested by the caller using the help of the security subsystem (if the FSD supports access checking).

Parameters.Create.Options

Bits 0 to 15 contain the caller-specified `CreateOptions`; bits 16 through 23 are reserved by the I/O Manager; and bits 24 through 31 specify the `CreateDisposition`.

Parameters.Create.FileAttributes

`FileAttributes` specified by the caller.

Parameters.Create.ShareAccess

`ShareAccess` specified by the caller.

Parameters.Create.EaLength

`EaLength` specified by the caller (the buffer supplied—if any—is pointed to by the `AssociatedIrp.SystemBuffer` field in the IRP).

DeviceObject

Points to the FSD-created device object representing either the FSD itself or the mounted logical volume.

FileObject

A file object structure allocated by the I/O Manager for this particular create/open request.

Notes

Create or open requests are inherently synchronous requests. Therefore, the I/O Manager will block the calling thread until the request has been processed by the FSD (even if `STATUS_PENDING` is returned by the FSD) and the `IRP_DEFER_IO_COMPLETION` flag will be set in the `Irp->Flags` field.

The following flags are set in the `FileObject->Flags` field:

FO_SYNCHRONOUS_IO

Set by the I/O Manager if either `FILE_SYNCHRONOUS_IO_ALERT` or `FILE_SYNCHRONOUS_IO_NONALERT` have been specified by the caller.

FO_ALERTABLE_IO

Set by the I/O Manager if `FILE_SYNCHRONOUS_IO_ALERT` is specified by the caller.

FO_NO_INTERMEDIATE_BUFFERING

Set by the I/O Manager and by FSDs if `FILE_NO_INTERMEDIATE_BUFFERING` is specified by the caller.

FO_WRITE_THROUGH

Set by the I/O Manager and by FSDs if `FILE_WRITE_THROUGH` is specified by the caller.

FO_SEQUENTIAL_ONLY

Set by the I/O Manager if FILE_SEQUENTIAL_ONLY is specified by the caller.

FO_TEMPORARY_FILE

Set by the FSD if FILE_ATTRIBUTE_TEMPORARY is specified by the caller.

FO_FILE_FAST_IO_READ

Set by the FSD if the file is successfully opened for EXECUTE access; also set by the FSD and by the FSRTL package whenever a cached read operation completes, indicating that time stamps for the file (directory entry) should be updated when all handles have been closed.*

NtOpenFile()

```
NTSTATUS NtOpenFile(
    OUT PHANDLE             FileHandle,
    IN ACCESS_MASK          DesiredAccess,
    IN POBJECT_ATTRIBUTES   ObjectAttributes,
    OUT PIO_STATUS_BLOCK    IoStatusBlock,
    IN ULONG                ShareAccess,
    IN ULONG                OpenOptions,
);
```

Parameters

FileHandle

Returned handle (created by the I/O Manager) if the call succeeds.

DesiredAccess

See the description of this argument for the NtCreateFile() system call described above.

ObjectAttributes

The caller must allocate memory for this structure of type OBJECT_ATTRIBUTES. Fields in the structure are initialized as follows:

Length

The size, in bytes, of the structure.

ObjectName

A unicode string specifying name of file. The name can be a either a relative name (RootDirectory is nonnull) or an absolute name (RootDirectory is NULL).

---

* The FO_FILE_MODIFIED flag is set by the FSRTL package to indicate that time stamps should be updated due to a fast I/O write request.

`RootDirectory` (optional)

The previously opened handle for a directory; `ObjectName` will be considered relative to this directory (if specified).

`SecurityDescriptor` (optional)

NULL pointer.

`SecurityQualityOfService` (optional)

NULL pointer.

`Attributes`

A combination of `OBJ_INHERIT` (child processes inherit open handle) and `OBJ_CASE_INSENSITIVE` (lookups should be processed in a case-insensitive fashion).

`IoStatusBlock`

A caller-supplied structure to receive results of create/open request.

`ShareAccess`

The type of share access requested by the caller. The share access can be a combination of the following:

`FILE_SHARE_READ`

The file can be concurrently opened for read access by other threads.

`FILE_SHARE_WRITE`

Other file open operations requesting write access should be allowed.

`FILE_SHARE_DELETE`

Other file open operations requesting delete access should be allowed.

Note that the share access flags allow the requester to control how the file can be shared by separate threads and processes. If none of the share values are specified, no other subsequent open operation will be allowed to proceed until the file handle is closed (and an `IRP_MJ_CLEANUP` is issued to the FSD).

`OpenOptions`

Options used when the file is opened. See the description for `NtCreateFile()` for more details.

Return code

`STATUS_SUCCESS` indicates that the operation succeeded and a valid handle is being returned, `STATUS_PENDING` indicates that the operation will be performed asynchronously by the FSD, while `STATUS_REPARSE` indicates that the name should be parsed again by the object manager (e.g., a new volume has been mounted).

In the case of an error, an appropriate error code is returned. See the description for NtCreateFile() for more details.

IRP/ I/O stack location

The IRP and I/O stack location for an open request are set up in essentially the same manner as that for a NtCreateFile() system call.

Notes

Time stamps for the file are not affected when an open request is received by the FSD.

NtReadFile()

```
NTSTATUS NtReadFile(
     IN HANDLE            FileHandle,
     IN HANDLE            Event OPTIONAL,
     IN PIO_APC_ROUTINE   ApcRoutine OPTIONAL,
     IN PVOID             ApcContext OPTIONAL,
     OUT PIO_STATUS_BLOCK IoStatusBlock,
     OUT PVOID            Buffer,
     IN ULONG             Length,
     IN PLARGE_INTEGER    ByteOffset OPTIONAL,
     IN PULONG            Key OPTIONAL
);
```

Parameters

FileHandle

   Returned to the caller from a previous successful NtCreateFile() or NtOpenFile() invocation.

Event (optional)

   The caller can wait for the supplied event object (created by the caller) for completion of the asynchronous read request. The event will be signaled by the I/O Manager when the read operation is completed.

ApcRoutine (optional)

   An optional, caller-supplied APC routine invoked by the I/O Manager when the read operation completes.

ApcContext (optional)

   The caller-determined context to be passed in to the ApcRoutine. This argument should be NULL if ApcRoutine is NULL.

IoStatusBlock

   The caller must supply this argument to receive the results of the read operation. The Information field in the IoStatusBlock is set to the number of bytes actually read by the FSD.

Buffer

   A caller-allocated buffer to receive data read from secondary storage.

Length

   The size, in bytes, of the `Buffer` supplied by the caller.

ByteOffset

   The starting byte offset where the read begins. Caller can specify `FILE_USE_FILE_POINTER_POSITION` rather than an explicit byte offset or pass NULL; in either case the FSD will perform the read from the current file pointer position. The I/O Manager maintains the file pointer position whenever the file stream is opened for synchronous I/O, and therefore, specifying a byte offset effectively results in an atomic seek-and-read service for the caller.

Key (optional)

   If the byte range is locked, a matching `Key` value (if supplied by the caller) will result in the FSD allowing the read to proceed. This can be used to selectively share data between threads belonging to the same process.

Return code

`STATUS_SUCCESS` indicates that the operation succeeded and some subset of the range requested by the caller is being returned by the FSD; `STATUS_PENDING` indicates that the operation will be performed asynchronously by the FSD.

In the case of an error, an appropriate error code is returned. This includes (but is not limited to) the following return code values:

- `STATUS_ACCESS_DENIED`
- `STATUS_INSUFFICIENT_RESOURCES`
- `STATUS_INVALID_PARAMETER`
- `STATUS_INVALID_DEVICE_REQUEST`
- `STATUS_END_OF_FILE`
- `STATUS_FILE_LOCK_CONFLICT`

IRP

MdlAddress

   Any MDL created by the I/O Manager (or by some other kernel-mode component) describing the buffer in which data should be returned by the FSD.

UserBuffer

A pointer to the user-supplied buffer. This field is effectively overridden by the presence of any MDL pointer in the `MdlAddress` field.*

Flags

One or both of `IRP_PAGING_IO` and `IRP_NOCACHE` may be set. `IRP_PAGING_IO` is only set by the I/O Manager if the I/O request is a result of a synchronous or an asynchronous paging I/O operation requested by the Virtual Memory Manager.

I/O stack location

MajorFunction

`IRP_MJ_READ`

MinorFunction

One or more of the following:

IRP_MN_DPC

The IRP was dispatched at a high IRQL.

IRP_MN_MDL

The caller wants an MDL returned containing the requested data.

IRP_MN_COMPLETE

The caller has finished with the MDL returned from a previous call (with `IRP_MN_MDL` specified).

IRP_MN_COMPRESSED

The caller does not want any compressed data decompressed.

Flags

One or more of **SL_KEY_SPECIFIED** and **SL_OVERRIDE_VERIFY_VOLUME**.

Parameters.Read.Length

The read **Length** specified by the caller.

Parameters.Read.Key

The **Key** specified by the caller.

Parameters.Read.ByteOffset

The **ByteOffset** specified by the caller.

DeviceObject

Points to the FSD-created device object representing the mounted logical volume.

---

* See Chapter 9 for details. The FSD will check for the presence of an MDL first and will use any MDL pointed to by the `MdlAddress` field. If `MdlAddress` is set to NULL, the FSD will use the `UserBuffer` pointer directly (since typically, FSDs prefer to neither specify `DO_DIRECT_IO` nor `DO_BUFFERED_IO` for handling user buffers).

FileObject

> The file object representing the open instance of the file to be read.

Notes

The `LastAccessTime` for the file stream being read is typically updated by the FSD upon completion of the read request.

NtWriteFile()

```
NTSTATUS NtWriteFile(
    IN HANDLE              FileHandle,
    IN HANDLE              Event OPTIONAL,
    IN PIO_APC_ROUTINE     ApcRoutine OPTIONAL,
    IN PVOID               ApcContext OPTIONAL,
    OUT PIO_STATUS_BLOCK   IoStatusBlock,
    OUT PVOID              Buffer,
    IN ULONG               Length,
    IN PLARGE_INTEGER      ByteOffset OPTIONAL,
    IN PULONG              Key OPTIONAL
);
```

Parameters

FileHandle

> Returned to the caller from a previous successful `NtCreateFile()` or `NtOpenFile()` invocation.

Event (optional)

> The caller can wait for the supplied event object (created by the caller) for completion of the asynchronous write request. The event will be signaled by the I/O Manager when the write operation is completed.

ApcRoutine (optional)

> The optional, caller-supplied APC routine invoked by the I/O Manager when the write operation completes.

ApcContext (optional)

> The caller-determined context to be passed in to the `ApcRoutine`. This argument should be NULL if `ApcRoutine` is NULL.

IoStatusBlock

> The caller must supply this argument to receive the results of the write operation. The `Information` field in the `IoStatusBlock` is set to the number of bytes actually written by the FSD.

Buffer

> A caller-allocated buffer containing data to be written to secondary storage.

Length

The size, in bytes, of the `Buffer` supplied by the caller.

ByteOffset

The starting byte offset where the write begins. Caller can specify `FILE_USE_FILE_POINTER_POSITION` rather than an explicit byte offset or pass in NULL; in either case the FSD will perform the write from the current file pointer position. The I/O Manager maintains the file pointer position whenever the file stream is opened for synchronous I/O and therefore specifying a byte offset effectively results in an atomic seek-and-write service for the caller (the file pointer is updated appropriately according to the starting offset from where the write begins and the number of bytes written).

In order to simply write to the current end-of-file, the caller can specify `FILE_WRITE_TO_END_OF_FILE` in the `ByteOffset` argument.

If the file was opened for `FILE_APPEND_DATA`, any caller-supplied byte offset is ignored.

Key (optional)

If the byte range is locked, a matching `Key` value (if supplied by the caller) will result in the FSD allowing the write to proceed. This can be used to selectively allow file modification between threads belonging to the same process.

Return code

`STATUS_SUCCESS` indicates that the operation succeeded and some subset of the range requested by the caller was written by the FSD; `STATUS_PENDING` indicates that the operation will be performed asynchronously by the FSD.

In the case of an error, an appropriate error code is returned. This includes (but is not limited to) the following return code values:

- `STATUS_ACCESS_DENIED`
- `STATUS_INSUFFICIENT_RESOURCES`
- `STATUS_INVALID_PARAMETER`
- `STATUS_INVALID_DEVICE_REQUEST`
- `STATUS_FILE_LOCK_CONFLICT`

IRP

MdlAddress

Any MDL created by the I/O Manager (or by some other kernel-mode component) describing the buffer containing data to be written. This could also be a MDL returned from a previous write request with `MinorFunction` set to

IRP_MN_MDL, in which case the MDL will eventually be freed by the Cache Manager.

UserBuffer

Pointer to the user-supplied buffer. This field is effectively overridden by the presence of any MDL pointer in the **MdlAddress** field.

Flags

One or both of **IRP_PAGING_IO** and **IRP_NOCACHE** may be set.

I/O stack location

MajorFunction

IRP_MJ_WRITE

MinorFunction

One or more of the following:

IRP_MN_DPC

The IRP was dispatched at a high IRQL.

IRP_MN_MDL

The caller wants an MDL returned, which will eventually be filled with modified data (by the caller).

IRP_MN_COMPLETE

The caller has finished with the MDL returned from a previous call (with **IRP_MN_MDL** specified).

IRP_MN_COMPRESSED

The caller is sending compressed data to the FSD.

Flags

One or more of **SL_KEY_SPECIFIED** and **SL_WRITE_THROUGH**.

Parameters.Write.Length

The number of bytes to be written specified by the caller.

Parameters.Write.Key

The **Key** specified by the caller.

Parameters.Write.ByteOffset

The starting **ByteOffset** specified by the caller.

DeviceObject

Points to the FSD-created device object representing the mounted logical volume.

FileObject

The file object representing the open instance of the file to be written.

Notes

The `LastWriteTime` for the file stream being written is typically updated by the FSD upon completion of the write request. The FSD should set the `SL_FT_SEQUENTIAL_WRITE` flag before forwarding a write-through write request to the next driver in the calling hierarchy.

NtQueryDirectoryFile()

```
NTSTATUS NtQueryDirectoryFile(
    IN HANDLE                   FileHandle,
    IN HANDLE                   Event OPTIONAL,
    IN PIO_APC_ROUTINE          ApcRoutine OPTIONAL,
    IN PVOID                    ApcContext OPTIONAL,
    OUT PIO_STATUS_BLOCK        IoStatusBlock,
    OUT PVOID                   FileInformation,
    IN ULONG                    Length,
    IN FILE_INFORMATION_CLASS   FileInformationClass,
    IN BOOLEAN                  ReturnSingleEntry,
    IN PUNICODE_STRING          FileName OPTIONAL,
    IN BOOLEAN                  RestartScan
);
```

Parameters

`FileHandle`

Returned to the caller from a previous, successful `NtCreateFile()` or `NtOpenFile()` invocation.

`Event` (optional)

The caller can wait for the supplied event object (created by the caller) for completion of the asynchronous query directory request. The event will be signaled by the I/O Manager when the query directory IRP is completed by the FSD.

`ApcRoutine` (optional)

The optional, caller-supplied APC routine invoked by the I/O Manager when the query directory operation completes.

`ApcContext` (optional)

The caller-determined context to be passed-in to the `ApcRoutine`. This argument should be NULL if `ApcRoutine` is NULL.

`IoStatusBlock`

The caller must supply this argument to receive the results of the query directory operation. The `Information` field in the `IoStatusBlock` is set to the number of bytes returned by the FSD (in the buffer pointed to by the `FileInformation` argument).

FileInformation

A caller-allocated buffer to receive information about files contained in the directory. Alignment requirements for the buffer and the contents of the buffer (returned by the FSD) are determined by the `FileInformation-Class` of the argument.

Note that the buffer passed to the FSD in the query directory IRP is an I/O Manager-allocated system buffer. Copying data from the system buffer to the actual caller-allocated buffer (pointed to by the `FileInformation` argument) is performed by the I/O Manager upon completion of the IRP.

Length

The size, in bytes, of the buffer supplied by the caller in `FileInformation`.

FileInformationClass

Specifies the kind of information requested by the caller. This can be one of the following:

FileNameInformation

The supplied buffer must be `longword`-aligned, as is the returned information. The size of the buffer must at least be equal to `sizeof(FILE_NAMES_INFORMATION)`. The caller expects to receive the long names of file entries contained in the directory in the caller-supplied buffer.

The `FILE_NAMES_INFORMATION` structure is defined as follows:

```
typedef struct _FILE_NAMES_INFORMATION {
    ULONG NextEntryOffset;
    ULONG FileIndex;
    ULONG FileNameLength;
    WCHAR FileName[1];
} FILE_NAMES_INFORMATION, *PFILE_NAMES_INFORMATION;
```

FileDirectoryInformation

The supplied buffer must be `quadword`-aligned, as is the returned information. The size of the buffer must at least be equal to `sizeof(FILE_DIRECTORY_INFORMATION)`. The caller expects to get basic information (such as the filename, file attributes, various time stamps associated with the file, and so on) for the matching directory entries.

Here is the `FILE_DIRECTORY_INFORMATION` structure:

```
typedef struct _FILE_DIRECTORY_INFORMATION {
    ULONG                   NextEntryOffset;
    ULONG           FileIndex;
    LARGE_INTEGER   CreationTime;
    LARGE_INTEGER   LastAccessTime;
    LARGE_INTEGER   LastWriteTime;
    LARGE_INTEGER   ChangeTime;
    LARGE_INTEGER   EndOfFile;
    LARGE_INTEGER   AllocationSize;
```

```
    ULONG            FileAttributes;
    ULONG            FileNameLength;
    WCHAR            FileName[1];
    } FILE_DIRECTORY_INFORMATION, *PFILE_DIRECTORY_INFORMATION;
```

FileFullDirectoryInformation

The supplied buffer must be **quadword**-aligned, as is the returned information. The size of the buffer must at least be equal to sizeof(**FILE_ FULL_DIR_INFORMATION**). The caller expects to get all of the information that could be obtained via the **FileDirectoryInformation** information class and in addition, expects to get back information about extended attributes associated with the matching directory entries.

This is the **FILE_FULL_DIR_INFORMATION** structure:

```
typedef struct _FILE_FULL_DIR_INFORMATION {
ULONG NextEntryOffset;
ULONG FileIndex;
LARGE_INTEGER CreationTime;
LARGE_INTEGER LastAccessTime;
LARGE_INTEGER LastWriteTime;
LARGE_INTEGER ChangeTime;
LARGE_INTEGER EndOfFile;
LARGE_INTEGER AllocationSize;
ULONG FileAttributes;
ULONG FileNameLength;
ULONG EaSize;
WCHAR FileName[1];
} FILE_FULL_DIR_INFORMATION, *PFILE_FULL_DIR_INFORMATION;
```

FileBothDirectoryInformation

The supplied buffer must be **quadword**-aligned, as is the returned information. The size of the buffer must at least be equal to sizeof(**FILE_ BOTH_DIR_INFORMATION**). The caller expects to get all of the information that could be obtained via the **FileFullDirectoryInformation** information class and in addition, expects to get back 8.3 versions of file names (if such alternate names are supported by the FSD) for matching directory entries.[*]

Here is the **FILE_BOTH_DIR_INFORMATION** structure:

```
typedef struct _FILE_BOTH_DIR_INFORMATION {
ULONG NextEntryOffset;
ULONG FileIndex;
LARGE_INTEGER CreationTime;
```

---

[*] Note that if your FSD does not support alternate/short (8.3) versions of filenames, the information returned by your driver in the FILE_BOTH_DIR_INFORMATION structure for each matching directory entry will essentially be the same as would be returned by your FSD in the FILE_FULL_DIR_ INFORMATION structure; the ShortNameLength field must be initialized to 0 for each entry, and the ShortName pointer field must be initialized to NULL.

```
    LARGE_INTEGER LastAccessTime;
    LARGE_INTEGER LastWriteTime;
    LARGE_INTEGER ChangeTime;
    LARGE_INTEGER EndOfFile;
    LARGE_INTEGER AllocationSize;
    ULONG FileAttributes;
    ULONG FileNameLength;
    ULONG EaSize;
    CCHAR ShortNameLength;
    WCHAR ShortName[12];
    WCHAR FileName[1];
    } FILE_BOTH_DIR_INFORMATION, *PFILE_BOTH_DIR_INFORMATION;
```

Once a query directory request for a particular `FileInformationClass`
type is submitted by a thread using a specific file handle, the `FileInforma-`
`tionClass` type must not change when any subsequent query directory
requests are submitted using the same file handle.

ReturnSingleEntry

If TRUE, the caller only wants information on a single matching directory
entry returned.

FileName (optional)

The search pattern, specified by the user, for the first query directory request,
issued using the particular file object (or file handle); the FSD attempts to find
matching directory entries based upon this pattern. If no name is supplied,
the FSD uses "*", a wildcard that matches any directory entry.

RestartScan

Normally, the FSD begins the search for a matching directory entry from the
last file pointer position (based upon the previous query directory request);
however, this flag allows the caller to indicate whether the search should
begin from the starting byte offset in the directory.

Return code

STATUS_SUCCESS indicates that the operation succeeded and information on at
least one directory entry is being returned by the FSD; STATUS_PENDING indicates that the operation will be performed asynchronously by the FSD.

In the case of an error, an appropriate error code is returned. This includes (but is
not limited to) the following return code values:

- STATUS_ACCESS_DENIED

- STATUS_INSUFFICIENT_RESOURCES

- STATUS_INVALID_PARAMETER

- STATUS_INVALID_DEVICE_REQUEST

- STATUS_BUFFER_OVERFLOW

- STATUS_INVALID_INFO_CLASS

- STATUS_NO_SUCH_FILE

- STATUS_NO_MORE_FILES

IRP

MdlAddress

Any MDL created by the FSD, if the request is dispatched to a worker thread for asynchronous processing.

UserBuffer

The pointer to the user-supplied buffer. This field is effectively overridden by the presence of any MDL pointer in the **MdlAddress** field.

I/O stack location

MajorFunction

IRP_MJ_DIRECTORY_CONTROL

MinorFunction

IRP_MN_QUERY_DIRECTORY

Flags

One or more of SL_RESTART_SCAN, SL_RETURN_SINGLE_ENTRY, and SL_ INDEX_SPECIFIED.

Parameters.QueryDirectory.Length

The **Length** specified by the caller for the buffer in which information is received.

Parameters.QueryDirectory.FileName

The search pattern specified by the caller. The FSD must search for matching entries in the target directory using this specified pattern. The user-specified pattern is typically stored by the FSD in the CCB for the target directory for the particular open operation (of the target directory), when the first such query directory request is received. The caller can temporarily override this search pattern in subsequent query directory requests by specifying a different pattern than the one stored by the FSD; however, the behavior of the FSD in response to such query directory requests containing a new search pattern is highly FSD-specific and not well-defined by the I/O subsystem. Some FSDs may honor the new search pattern while others may choose to ignore it.

Parameters.QueryDirectory.FileInformationClass

The type of information requested by the caller.

`Parameters.QueryDirectory.FileIndex`
> Any starting index, to begin the scan from, specified by the caller.

`DeviceObject`
> Points to the FSD-created device object representing the mounted logical volume.

`FileObject`
> File object representing the open instance of the target directory.

Notes

The query directory request is an inherently synchronous request. Therefore, the I/O Manager will block the requesting thread until the operation has been completed by the FSD.

The FSD returns information on the following directory entries:

- Information about a single matching directory entry is returned if either `ReturnSingleEntry` is TRUE or if the specified search pattern does not contain any wildcards.

- The number of matching files for which information can be returned in the caller-supplied buffer, constrained by the length of the buffer.

- The total number of directory entries (files or directories) in the target directory being queried.

Information on matching directory entries can be returned in any order. Most returned entries are either **quadword**-aligned or **longword**-aligned. See Chapter 10, *Writing A File System Driver II*, for information on how directory control requests are processed by the FSD. The maximum length of a file name is constrained (on Windows NT platforms) to be less than or equal to `FILE_MAXIMUM_FILENAME_LENGTH`.

If no matching entry was found for the very first query directory request received by the FSD using the particular file object, an error code of `STATUS_NO_SUCH_FILE` is returned to the caller; if no match is found for any subsequent query directory request, the `STATUS_NO_MORE_FILES` error code is returned.

The FSD maintains context about the returned information in the CCB structure associated with the specified file object. Therefore, requests to obtain directory information from different threads sharing the same file handle (and sharing the same file object and correspondingly the same CCB structure) will share (and affect) the same context maintained by the FSD.

NtNotifyChangeDirectoryFile()

```
NTSTATUS NtNotifyChangeDirectoryFile(
    IN HANDLE              FileHandle,
    IN HANDLE              Event OPTIONAL,
    IN PIO_APC_ROUTINE     ApcRoutine OPTIONAL,
    IN PVOID               ApcContext OPTIONAL,
    OUT PIO_STATUS_BLOCK   IoStatusBlock,
    OUT PVOID              Buffer,
    IN ULONG               Length,
    IN ULONG               CompletionFilter,
    IN BOOLEAN             WatchTree
);
```

Parameters

FileHandle

Returned to the caller from a previous successful `NtCreateFile()` or `NtOpenFile()` invocation.

Event (optional)

The caller can wait for the supplied event object (created by the caller) for completion of the asynchronous notify change directory request. The event will be signaled by the I/O Manager when the notify change directory IRP is completed by the FSD.

ApcRoutine (optional)

An optional, caller-supplied APC routine invoked by the I/O Manager when the notify change directory operation completes.

ApcContext (optional)

Caller-determined context to be passed-in to the `ApcRoutine`. This argument should be NULL if `ApcRoutine` is NULL.

IoStatusBlock

The caller must supply this argument to receive the results of the notify change directory operation. The `Information` field in the `IoStatusBlock` is set to the number of bytes returned by the FSD (in the buffer pointed to by the `FileInformation` argument).

If too many changes have occurred and information about such changes cannot be returned by the FSD in the supplied buffer, the FSD will set the `Information` field to 0 and the `STATUS_NOTIFY_ENUM_DIR` return code will be returned in the `Status` field of the `IoStatusBlock` argument.

Buffer

A caller-allocated buffer to receive information about the names of files contained in the target directory that have been affected. The format of returned information is defined by the `FILE_NOTIFY_INFORMATION` structure, which is defined as follows:

```
typedef struct _FILE_NOTIFY_INFORMATION {
    ULONG NextEntryOffset;
    ULONG Action;*
    ULONG FileNameLength;
    WCHAR FileName[1];
} FILE_NOTIFY_INFORMATION, *PFILE_NOTIFY_INFORMATION;
```

Length

The size, in bytes, of the buffer supplied by the caller.

CompletionFilter

Specifies a combination of flags that indicate the changes the caller is interested in monitoring on the target directory.

These flags can be one or more of the following (see Chapter 10 for details on how the FSD processes the notify change directory request):

FILE_NOTIFY_CHANGE_FILE_NAME

Some file has been added, deleted, or renamed.

FILE_NOTIFY_CHANGE_DIR_NAME

Some subdirectory has been added, deleted, or renamed.

FILE_NOTIFY_CHANGE_NAME

A combination of `FILE_NOTIFY_CHANGE_FILE_NAME` and `FILE_NOTIFY_CHANGE_DIR_NAME`.

FILE_NOTIFY_CHANGE_ATTRIBUTES

Attributes of any directory entry (representing either a file or a directory) have been changed.

FILE_NOTIFY_CHANGE_SIZE

Allocation size or end-of-file position have been changed for any directory entry.

FILE_NOTIFY_CHANGE_LAST_WRITE

The last write time stamp value for a directory entry has been changed.

FILE_NOTIFY_CHANGE_LAST_ACCESS

The last access time stamp value for a directory entry has been changed.

FILE_NOTIFY_CHANGE_CREATION

The creation time stamp value for a directory entry has been changed.

---

* The possible values (bit-flags) that can be returned in this field are given in Chapter 10.

FILE_NOTIFY_CHANGE_EA

Extended attributes associated with a directory entry (file or directory) have been changed.

FILE_NOTIFY_CHANGE_SECURITY

Security attributes associated with a directory entry have been changed.

FILE_NOTIFY_CHANGE_STREAM_NAME

Applies to FSDs that support multiple byte streams associated with files. A new file stream may have been added, deleted, or renamed, in which case the caller should be notified.

FILE_NOTIFY_CHANGE_STREAM_SIZE

The size of a file stream may have changed.

FILE_NOTIFY_CHANGE_STREAM_WRITE

The contents of an alternate stream have been changed (i.e., the stream data was modified).

WatchTree

If TRUE, the caller wants to recursively monitor changes to all subdirectories contained within the target directory.

Return code

STATUS_PENDING indicates that the IRP has been successfully queued by the FSD and will be completed once one or more of the specified changes (being monitored by the caller) have occurred; STATUS_SUCCESS indicates that at least one monitored change had already occurred before the latest notify change directory IRP was even received by the FSD, and the caller is being notified of the fact.

Once STATUS_PENDING is returned by the FSD, the caller must examine the contents of the Status field in the IoStatusBlock argument to determine the results of the notify change directory request, once the request has been completed.

In the case of an error (or a buffer overflow condition), an appropriate error code is returned. This includes (but is not limited to) the following return code values:

- STATUS_ACCESS_DENIED
- STATUS_INSUFFICIENT_RESOURCES
- STATUS_INVALID_PARAMETER
- STATUS_INVALID_DEVICE_REQUEST
- STATUS_NOTIFY_ENUM_DIR

IRP

UserBuffer

A pointer to the user-supplied buffer. This field is effectively overridden by the presence of any MDL pointer in the **MdlAddress** field. If your FSD supports buffered I/O, then the I/O Manager will have allocated a system buffer for your FSD, and this buffer can be accessed via the **Associate-dIrp.SystemBuffer** field in the IRP.

I/O stack location

MajorFunction

IRP_MJ_DIRECTORY_CONTROL

MinorFunction

IRP_MN_NOTIFY_CHANGE_DIRECTORY

Flags

Can be set with **SL_WATCH_TREE**.

Parameters.NotifyDirectory.Length

The **Length**, specified by the caller, for the buffer in which information is received.

Parameters.NotifyDirectory.CompletionFilter

The type of changes being monitored by the caller.

DeviceObject

Points to the FSD-created device object representing the mounted logical volume.

FileObject

The file object representing the open instance of the target directory being monitored.

Notes

The notify change directory request interprets a return code of **STATUS_PENDING** to indicate that the IRP has been successfully queued.

NtQueryInformationFile()

```
NTSTATUS NtQueryInformationFile(
    IN HANDLE                   FileHandle,
    OUT PIO_STATUS_BLOCK        IoStatusBlock,
    OUT PVOID                   FileInformation,
    IN ULONG                    Length,
    IN FILE_INFORMATION_CLASS   FileInformationClass
);
```

Parameters

FileHandle
Returned to the caller from a previous, successful NtCreateFile() or NtOpenFile() invocation.

IoStatusBlock
The caller must supply this argument to receive the results of the query file information request. The Information field in the IoStatusBlock is set to the number of bytes returned by the FSD (in the buffer pointed to by the FileInformation argument).

FileInformation
A caller-allocated buffer to receive information about the specified file. The format of returned information is defined by the FileInformationClass argument.

Length
The size, in bytes, of the buffer supplied by the caller.

FileInformationClass
Used by the caller to specify the type of information requested for the target file. See Chapter 10 for a detailed discussion on the types of information provided by file system drivers and for corresponding structure definitions.

Return code

STATUS_SUCCESS indicates that the operation succeeded; STATUS_PENDING indicates that the operation will be performed asynchronously by the FSD.

In the case of an error (or a buffer overflow condition), an appropriate error code is returned. This includes (but is not limited to) the following return code values:

- STATUS_ACCESS_DENIED
- STATUS_INSUFFICIENT_RESOURCES
- STATUS_INVALID_PARAMETER
- STATUS_INVALID_DEVICE_REQUEST
- STATUS_BUFFER_OVERFLOW

IRP

AssociatedIrp.SystemBuffer
A pointer to an I/O Manager-allocated buffer. The I/O Manager always allocates a system buffer to contain information returned by the FSD. Contents of this buffer are copied to the user-supplied buffer by the I/O Manager (before the system buffer is deallocated by the I/O Manager).

Flags

The `IRP_BUFFERED_IO`, `IRP_DEALLOCATE_BUFFER`, `IRP_INPUT_OPER-ATION`, and `IRP_DEFER_IO_COMPLETION` flags are set. However, these are only used internally by the I/O Manager.*

I/O stack location

MajorFunction

`IRP_MJ_QUERY_INFORMATION`

MinorFunction

None.

Flags

None.

Parameters.QueryFile.Length

The `Length`, specified by the caller, for the buffer in which information is received.

Parameters.QueryFile.FileInformationClass

The type of information requested by the user.

DeviceObject

Points to the FSD-created device object representing the mounted logical volume.

FileObject

The file object representing the open instance of the file for which information has been requested.

Notes

The I/O Manager is responsible for filling in information for some of the `FileIn-formationClass` values. See Chapter 10 for further details.

NtSetInformationFile()

```
NTSTATUS NtSetInformationFile(
    IN HANDLE                 FileHandle,
    OUT PIO_STATUS_BLOCK      IoStatusBlock,
    OUT PVOID                 FileInformation,
    IN ULONG                  Length,
    IN FILE_INFORMATION_CLASS FileInformationClass
);
```

---

* See Chapter 4, *The NT I/O Manager*, for a discussion on the `IRP_DEFER_IO_COMPLETION` flag.

Parameters

`FileHandle`

Returned to the caller from a previous, successful `NtCreateFile()` or `NtOpenFile()` invocation.

`IoStatusBlock`

The caller must supply this argument to receive the results of the set file information request. The `Information` field in the `IoStatusBlock` is initialized to the number of bytes actually set by the FSD (from the buffer pointed to by the `FileInformation` argument).

`FileInformation`

A caller-allocated buffer, containing information about the modified attributes of the target file. The format of the supplied information is defined by the `FileInformationClass` argument.

`Length`

The size, in bytes, of the buffer supplied by the caller.

`FileInformationClass`

Used by the caller to specify the type of attributes being modified for the target file. See Chapter 10 for a detailed discussion on the types of attributes that can be modified by the caller and for corresponding structure definitions.

Return code

`STATUS_SUCCESS` indicates that the operation succeeded; `STATUS_PENDING` indicates that the operation will be performed asynchronously by the FSD.

In the case of an error, an appropriate error code is returned. This includes (but is not limited to) the following return code values:

- `STATUS_ACCESS_DENIED`
- `STATUS_INSUFFICIENT_RESOURCES`
- `STATUS_INVALID_PARAMETER`
- `STATUS_INVALID_DEVICE_REQUEST`
- `STATUS_CANNOT_DELETE`
- `STATUS_DIRECTORY_NOT_EMPTY`

IRP

`AssociatedIrp.SystemBuffer`

Pointer to an I/O Manager-allocated buffer. The I/O Manager always allocates a system buffer to contain a copy of the user-supplied modified attributes for the file stream. This system buffer is deallocated by the I/O Manager after the IRP has been completed.

Flags

The `IRP_BUFFERED_IO`, `IRP_DEALLOCATE_BUFFER`, and `IRP_DEFER_IO_` `COMPLETION` flags are set. However, these are only used internally by the I/O Manager.[*]

I/O stack location

MajorFunction

`IRP_MJ_SET_INFORMATION`

MinorFunction

None.

Flags

None.

Parameters.SetFile.Length

The `Length`, specified by the caller, for the buffer in which information about modified attributes is supplied.

Parameters.SetFile.FileInformationClass

The type of attributes for which modified information has been provided by the user.

Parameters.SetFile.FileObject

The file object representing an open instance of the target directory for a rename/link operation.

Parameters.SetFile.ReplaceIfExists

Used during rename operations to reflect the value of the `ReplaceIfEx-ists` field in the `FILE_RENAME_INFORMATION` structure.

Parameters.SetFile.AdvanceOnly

This flag is set to TRUE for a special request initiated by the Windows NT Cache Manager to indicate that the `ValidDataLength` for the file stream has been changed.

DeviceObject

Points to the FSD-created device object representing the mounted logical volume.

FileObject

The file object representing the open instance of the file whose attributes are being modified.

---

[*] See Chapter 4 for a discussion on the `IRP_DEFER_IO_COMPLETION` flag.

Notes

Some `FileInformationClass` types are handled directly by the I/O Manager
(e.g., `FilePositionInformation`). See Chapter 10 for further details on how
other `FileInformationClass` types are supported by file system drivers.

NtQueryEaFile()

```
NTSTATUS NtQueryEaFile(
     IN HANDLE             FileHandle,
     OUT PIO_STATUS_BLOCK  IoStatusBlock,
     OUT PVOID             Buffer,
     IN ULONG              Length,
     IN BOOLEAN            ReturnSingleEntry,
     IN PVOID              EaList OPTIONAL,
     IN ULONG              EaListLength,
     IN PULONG             EaIndex OPTIONAL,
     IN BOOLEAN            RestartScan
);
```

Parameters

`FileHandle`

Returned to the caller from a previous, successful `NtCreateFile()` or
`NtOpenFile()` invocation.

`IoStatusBlock`

The caller must supply this argument to receive the results of the query
extended attributes operation. The `Information` field in the `IoStatus-`
`Block` is set to the number of bytes returned by the FSD (in the buffer
pointed to by the `Buffer` argument).

`Buffer`

A caller-allocated buffer to receive information about extended attributes associated with the target file. Information for each matching extended attribute
(returned by the FSD) is `longword`-aligned and is contained within a `FILE_`
`FULL_EA_INFORMATION` structure.

Only complete `FILE_FULL_EA_INFORMATION` structures are returned by
the FSD. The `NextEntryOffset` value in the structure (if nonzero) indicates the relative offset of the next entry in the buffer. Note that the FSD
maintains context to determine the next extended attribute for which information must be returned.

Also note that the value of each named extended attribute begins after the
end of the `EaName` (null-terminated) field in the `FILE_FULL_EA_INFORMA-`
`TION` structure. The `EaNameLength` field in the structure does not include
the null-terminator for the extended attribute; therefore, the value for each of

the named extended attributes can be located by adding (`EaNameLength +
1`) to the address of `EaName`.

Length

The size, in bytes, of the buffer supplied by the caller.

ReturnSingleEntry

If TRUE, the caller only wants information on a single, matching extended
attribute returned.

EaList

This optional buffer can contain a list of named extended attributes for which
information must be returned by the FSD. The structure of each entry in this
buffer is of type `FILE_GET_EA_INFORMATION` and is follows:

```
typedef struct _FILE_GET_EA_INFORMATION {
    ULONG NextEntryOffset;
    UCHAR EaNameLength;
    CHAR  EaName[1];
} FILE_GET_EA_INFORMATION, *PFILE_GET_EA_INFORMATION;
```

The I/O Manager checks to ensure that the contents of the EA list are consistent; each of the entries contained in the list must be `longword`-aligned and
each entry must either point to a complete, valid next entry in the list or the
`NextEntryOffset` value must be set to 0. If errors are encountered, the
I/O Manager may return a warning code of `STATUS_EA_LIST_
INCONSISTENT`.

EaListLength

The length of the `EaList` buffer if such a buffer is present; this argument
should be set to 0 if `EaList` is set to NULL.

EaIndex

An optional, zero-based index value specified by the caller. The FSD will
return information about extended attributes, beginning with the EA identified
by this index. If, however, `EaList` is nonnull, this argument will be ignored.

RestartScan

Normally, the FSD begins the scan for extended attributes from the last
extended attribute returned (based upon the immediately preceding query
extended attributes request); however, this flag allows the caller to indicate
whether the scan should begin with the first EA associated with the file
stream. This flag is ignored if either `EaList` or `EaIndex` are nonnull.

Return code

`STATUS_SUCCESS` indicates that the operation succeeded and information on at
least one extended attribute is being returned by the FSD; `STATUS_PENDING`
indicates that the operation will be performed asynchronously by the FSD.

In the case of an error, an appropriate error code or a warning is returned. This includes (but is not limited to) the following return code values:

- STATUS_ACCESS_DENIED

- STATUS_INSUFFICIENT_RESOURCES

- STATUS_INVALID_PARAMETER

- STATUS_INVALID_DEVICE_REQUEST

- STATUS_NO_MORE_EAS

- STATUS_INVALID_EA_NAME

- STATUS_INVALID_EA_FLAG

IRP

AssociatedIrp.SystemBuffer

Any system buffer allocated by the I/O Manager to receive information about EAs from the FSD, if the FSD has specified DO_BUFFERED_IO in the device object flags.

MdlAddress

Any MDL created by the I/O Manager if the FSD has specified DO_DIRECT_IO in the device object flags.

UserBuffer

Pointer to the user-supplied buffer if neither DO_DIRECT_IO nor DO_BUFFERED_IO have been specified by the FSD. This field is effectively overridden by the presence of any MDL pointer in the **MdlAddress** field.

I/O stack location

MajorFunction

IRP_MJ_QUERY_EA

MinorFunction

None.

Flags

One or more of SL_RESTART_SCAN, SL_RETURN_SINGLE_ENTRY, and SL_INDEX_SPECIFIED.

Parameters.QueryEa.Length

The Length specified by the caller for the buffer in which information is received.

Parameters.QueryEa.EaList

A list of named EAs supplied by the caller. Note that the actual buffer passed-in to the FSD is a system buffer that was allocated by the Windows NT I/O

Manager. The I/O Manager copies the user-supplied EA list from the caller's buffer to the system buffer before sending the IRP to the FSD.

`Parameters.QueryEa.EaListLength`

The `EaListLength` specified by the caller to `NtQueryEaFile()`.

`Parameters.QueryEa.EaIndex`

The starting index, to begin the scan from, specified by the caller.

`DeviceObject`

Points to the FSD-created device object representing the mounted logical volume.

`FileObject`

File object representing the open instance of the target file stream.

Notes

The `NtQueryEaFile()` is an inherently synchronous I/O operation. The I/O Manager will block the requesting thread if **STATUS_PENDING** is received by the FSD.

The FSD returns information on the following number of extended attributes:

- A single extended attribute if either **ReturnSingleEntry** is TRUE, or if the supplied **EaList** describes only a single named extended attribute.

- The number of matching extended attributes for which full information can be returned in the caller-supplied buffer, constrained by the length of the buffer.

- The total number of associated extended attributes associated with the target file stream, or the total number of matching extended attributes as described by the caller in the **EaList** buffer.

If an error was encountered by the FSD (e.g., an invalid character in an **EaName**), the **Information** field in the **IoStatusBlock** argument contains the byte offset to the EA entry that caused the failure, otherwise, it contains the number of bytes of extended attributes information returned by the FSD.

NtSetEaFile()

```
NTSTATUS NtSetEaFile(
    IN HANDLE              FileHandle,
    OUT PIO_STATUS_BLOCK   IoStatusBlock,
    OUT PVOID              Buffer,
    IN ULONG               Length,
);
```

Parameters

FileHandle

> Returned to the caller from a previous, successful NtCreateFile() or NtOpenFile() invocation.

IoStatusBlock

> The caller must supply this argument to receive the results of the set extended attributes operation. The Information field in the IoStatus-Block is set to the number of bytes written by the FSD from the buffer pointed to by the Buffer argument.

Buffer

> A caller-allocated buffer containing the extended attributes to be associated with the target file. Information about each matching extended attribute must be longword-aligned and must be contained within a FILE_FULL_EA_ INFORMATION structure. The NextEntryOffset value in the structure (if nonzero) must indicate the relative offset of the next entry in the buffer.

> As in the case of the NtQueryEaFile() function described earlier, the value of each named extended attribute must begin immediately after the end of the EaName (null-terminated) field in the FILE_FULL_EA_INFORMATION structure. The EaNameLength field in the structure should not include the null-terminator for the extended attribute; therefore, the value for each of the named extended attributes can be located by the FSD by adding (EaName-Length + 1) to the address of EaName.

Length

> The size, in bytes, of the buffer supplied by the caller.

Return code

STATUS_SUCCESS indicates that the operation succeeded; STATUS_PENDING indicates that the operation will be performed asynchronously by the FSD.

In the case of an error, an appropriate error code or a warning is returned. This includes (but is not limited to) the following return code values:

- STATUS_ACCESS_DENIED
- STATUS_INSUFFICIENT_RESOURCES
- STATUS_INVALID_PARAMETER
- STATUS_INVALID_DEVICE_REQUEST
- STATUS_INVALID_EA_NAME
- STATUS_INVALID_EA_FLAG

IRP

`AssociatedIrp.SystemBuffer`
> Any system buffer, allocated by the I/O Manager, containing a copy of the information about modified/new EAs provided by the caller if the FSD has specified `DO_BUFFERED_IO` in the device object flags.

`MdlAddress`
> Any MDL created by the I/O Manager if the FSD has specified `DO_DIRECT_IO` in the device object flags.

`UserBuffer`
> The pointer to the user-supplied buffer if neither `DO_DIRECT_IO` nor `DO_BUFFERED_IO` have been specified by the FSD. This field is effectively overridden by the presence of any MDL pointer in the `MdlAddress` field.

I/O stack location

`MajorFunction`
> `IRP_MJ_SET_EA`

`MinorFunction`
> None.

`Parameters.SetEa.Length`
> The `Length` specified by the caller for the buffer in which information is supplied.

`DeviceObject`
> Points to the FSD-created device object representing the mounted logical volume.

`FileObject`
> The file object representing the open instance of the target file stream.

Notes

The `NtSetEaFile()` is an inherently synchronous I/O operation. The I/O Manager will block the requesting thread if `STATUS_PENDING` is received by the FSD.

The FSD uses the following rules in applying caller-specified EAs to the target file stream:

- If a supplied EA has a unique `EaName` among the existing EAs associated with the file stream, the FSD adds the new user-supplied EA to the list of EAs associated with the file.

- If the supplied EA has an **EaName** that matches an existing EA associated with the file stream and if the supplied **EaValueLength** is nonzero, the FSD will replace the existing EA with the user-supplied extended attribute.

- If the supplied EA has an **EaName** that matches an existing EA associated with the file stream and if the supplied **EaValueLength** is zero length, the FSD will delete the existing EA.

If an error was encountered by the FSD (e.g., an invalid character in an **EaName**), the **Information** field in the **IoStatusBlock** argument contains the byte offset to the EA entry that caused the failure; otherwise, it contains the number of bytes of extended attributes information applied by the FSD to the file stream.

NtLockFile()

```
NTSTATUS NtLockFile(
    IN HANDLE                FileHandle,
    IN HANDLE                Event OPTIONAL,
    IN PIO_APC_ROUTINE       ApcRoutine OPTIONAL,
    IN PVOID                 ApcContext OPTIONAL,
    OUT PIO_STATUS_BLOCK     IoStatusBlock,
    IN PLARGE_INTEGER        ByteOffset,
    IN PLARGE_INTEGER        Length,
    IN PULONG                Key,
    IN BOOLEAN               FailImmediately,
    IN BOOLEAN               ExclusiveLock
);
```

Parameters

FileHandle

Returned to the caller from a previous, successful **NtCreateFile()** or **NtOpenFile()** invocation.

Event (optional)

Caller can wait for the supplied event object (created by the caller) for completion of the lock request. The event will be signaled by the I/O Manager when the lock-file operation is completed.

ApcRoutine (optional)

An optional, caller-supplied APC routine invoked by the I/O Manager when the lock-file operation completes.

ApcContext (optional)

A caller-determined context to be passed-in to the **ApcRoutine**. This argument should be NULL if **ApcRoutine** is NULL.

IoStatusBlock

> The caller must supply this argument to receive the results of the lock-file operation. The `Information` field in the `IoStatusBlock` is set to the number of bytes locked by the FSD.

ByteOffset

> The starting byte offset for the byte-range to be locked on behalf of the caller.

Length

> The number of bytes to be locked.

Key

> The `Key` is a caller-defined (opaque) value associated with the locked byte range. This value can be used to selectively share data between threads belonging to the same process (if a unique value is chosen by the requesting thread).

FailImmediately

> If set to TRUE and if the lock cannot be obtained immediately by the FSD for the caller (e.g., some other thread was previously granted a conflicting lock on an overlapping byte range), the lock request is completed with an appropriate error code. If, however, `FailImmediately` is set to FALSE, the request will block indefinitely until the lock can be obtained (all conflicting locks held by other threads on overlapping byte ranges have been released).

ExclusiveLock

> Specifies whether an exclusive (write) lock should be acquired or whether a shared (read) lock is sufficient.

Return code

STATUS_SUCCESS indicates that the operation succeeded, and the lock was granted; STATUS_PENDING is returned if the requesting thread wishes to wait for the byte-range lock and the lock cannot be immediately obtained (the IRP is queued by the FSD/FSRTL package).

In the case of an error, an appropriate error code is returned. This includes (but is not limited to) the following return code values:

- STATUS_ACCESS_DENIED

- STATUS_INSUFFICIENT_RESOURCES

- STATUS_INVALID_PARAMETER

- STATUS_INVALID_DEVICE_REQUEST

- STATUS_LOCK_NOT_GRANTED

I/O stack location

MajorFunction
    IRP_MJ_LOCK_CONTROL

MinorFunction
    IRP_MN_LOCK

Flags
    One or more of SL_FAIL_IMMEDIATELY and SL_EXCLUSIVE_LOCK.

Parameters.LockControl.Length
    The byte-range Length specified by the caller.

Parameters.LockControl.Key
    The Key specified by the caller.

Parameters.LockControl.ByteOffset
    The starting ByteOffset specified by the caller.

DeviceObject
    Points to the FSD-created device object representing the mounted logical
    volume.

FileObject
    The file object representing the open instance of the file for which a byte-
    range lock has been requested.

Notes

Byte-range locks obtained by a thread on Windows NT platforms are mandatory
locks. Therefore, the FSD is responsible for enforcing the semantics associated
with the lock when subsequent I/O requests are received for the target file
stream. To check whether an I/O operation should be allowed to proceed for a
locked byte range, the FSD uses the following attributes associated with the
locked range:

- The starting byte offset for the locked range
- The number of bytes that have been locked
- The process that owns the locked range
- The Key value associated with the locked range

Byte-range locks are owned by processes and are not associated with individual
threads within a process. Therefore, to control access to locked byte-ranges by
multiple threads within the same process, a unique Key value should be associated with the locked byte range.

Exclusive locks prohibit any read or write access by any other process other than
the owning process for the locked byte range. Shared locks allow other processes

to continue to read the data contained within the locked range but do not allow other processes to modify such data. Byte-range exclusive locks requested by a process cannot overlap with any other locked range within the file.

Note that callers can request byte-range locks that start or extend beyond the current end-of-file. This allows the requester to control who can extend the file stream.

NtUnlockFile()

```
NTSTATUS NtUnlockFile(
    IN HANDLE              FileHandle,
    OUT PIO_STATUS_BLOCK   IoStatusBlock,
    IN PLARGE_INTEGER      ByteOffset,
    IN PLARGE_INTEGER      Length,
    IN PULONG              Key
);
```

Parameters

FileHandle

> Returned to the caller from a previous, successful `NtCreateFile()` or `NtOpenFile()` invocation.

IoStatusBlock

> The caller must supply this argument to receive the results of the unlock-file operation. The `Information` field in the `IoStatusBlock` is set to the number of bytes unlocked by the FSD.

ByteOffset

> The starting byte offset for the byte range to be unlocked on behalf of the caller. This value must match exactly the starting `ByteOffset` supplied in a previous `NtLockFile()` request.

Length

> The number of bytes to be unlocked. This value must match exactly the `Length` supplied in a previous `NtLockFile()` request.

Key

> The `Key` is a caller-defined (opaque) value associated with the locked byte range. This value must match exactly the `Key` value supplied in a previous `NtLockFile()` request.

Return code

`STATUS_SUCCESS` indicates that the operation succeeded and the lock was released; `STATUS_PENDING` is returned if the FSD processes the request asynchronously.

In the case of an error, an appropriate error code is returned. This includes (but is not limited to) the following return code values:

- STATUS_ACCESS_DENIED

- STATUS_INSUFFICIENT_RESOURCES

- STATUS_INVALID_PARAMETER

- STATUS_INVALID_DEVICE_REQUEST

- STATUS_RANGE_NOT_LOCKED

I/O stack location

MajorFunction
> IRP_MJ_LOCK_CONTROL

MinorFunction
> One of the following:

> IRP_MN_UNLOCK_SINGLE
>> The single, locked byte range described in the IRP should be unlocked.

> IRP_MN_UNLOCK_ALL
>> All previously locked byte ranges owned by the requesting process should be unlocked.

> IRP_MN_UNLOCK_ALL_BY_KEY
>> All previously locked byte-ranges, owned by the requesting process that match the supplied **Key** value, should be unlocked.

Flags
> None.

Parameters.LockControl.Length
> The byte-range **Length** specified by the caller. This should be exactly equal to the **Length** value supplied in a previous request to **NtLockFile()**.

Parameters.LockControl.Key
> The **Key** specified by the caller.

Parameters.LockControl.ByteOffset
> The starting **ByteOffset** specified by the caller. This should be exactly equal to the **ByteOffset** value supplied in a previous request to **NtLockFile()**.

DeviceObject
> Points to the FSD-created device object representing the mounted logical volume.

`FileObject`

The file object representing the open instance of the file for which an unlock operation has been requested.

Notes

Only the process that owns a particular byte-range lock can successfully request that the lock be released. Whenever a process closes all open handles for a particular file stream, all outstanding byte-range locks owned by the process for the file stream will be released.

NtQueryVolumeInformationFile()

```
NTSTATUS NtQueryVolumeInformationFile(
    IN HANDLE               FileHandle,
    OUT PIO_STATUS_BLOCK    IoStatusBlock,
    OUT PVOID               FsInformation,
    IN ULONG                Length,
    IN FS_INFORMATION_CLASS FsInformationClass
);
```

Parameters

`FileHandle`

Returned to the caller from a previous, successful `NtCreateFile()` or `NtOpenFile()` invocation for any file or directory contained in the target logical volume, or from a successful open request on either the target volume or the underlying device object.

`IoStatusBlock`

The caller must supply this argument to receive the results of the query volume information operation. The `Information` field in the `IoStatus-Block` is set to the number of information bytes returned by the FSD.

`FsInformation`

A caller-allocated buffer in which volume information is returned. The structure of returned information depends upon the value of the `FsInformationClass` argument.

`Length`

The size of the `FsInformation` buffer.

`FsInformationClass`

The type of information requested by the user. This can be one of the following:

`FileFsVolumeInformation`

The following structure defines the format of the information returned by the FSD:

```
typedef struct _FILE_FS_VOLUME_INFORMATION {
LARGE_INTEGER      VolumeCreationTime;
ULONG              VolumeSerialNumber;
ULONG              VolumeLabelLength;
BOOLEAN            SupportsObjects;
WCHAR              VolumeLabel[1];
} FILE_FS_VOLUME_INFORMATION, *PFILE_FS_VOLUME_INFORMATION;
```

FileFsSizeInformation

The following structure defines the format of the information returned by the FSD:

```
typedef struct _FILE_FS_SIZE_INFORMATION {
LARGE_INTEGER      TotalAllocationUnits;
LARGE_INTEGER      AvailableAllocationUnits;
ULONG              SectorsPerAllocationUnit;
ULONG              BytesPerSector;
} FILE_FS_SIZE_INFORMATION, *PFILE_FS_SIZE_INFORMATION;
```

FileFsDeviceInformation

The following structure defines the format of the information returned by the FSD:

```
typedef struct _FILE_FS_DEVICE_INFORMATION {
DEVICE_TYPE        DeviceType;
ULONG              Characteristics;
} FILE_FS_DEVICE_INFORMATION, *PFILE_FS_DEVICE_INFORMATION;
```

FileFsAttributeInformation

The following structure defines the format of the information returned by the FSD:

```
typedef struct _FILE_FS_ATTRIBUTE_INFORMATION {
ULONG              FileSystemAttributes;
LONG               MaximumComponentNameLength;
ULONG              FileSystemNameLength;
WCHAR              FileSystemName[1];
} FILE_FS_ATTRIBUTE_INFORMATION, *PFILE_FS_ATTRIBUTE_INFORMATION;
```

Return code

STATUS_SUCCESS indicates that the operation succeeded and the volume information has been returned by the FSD; STATUS_PENDING is returned if the FSD decides to process the request asynchronously.

In the case of an error, an appropriate error code is returned. This includes (but is not limited to) the following return code values:

- STATUS_INSUFFICIENT_RESOURCES

- STATUS_INVALID_PARAMETER

- STATUS_INVALID_DEVICE_REQUEST

- STATUS_BUFFER_OVERFLOW

IRP

`AssociatedIrp.SystemBuffer`

The I/O Manager allocates a system buffer in which the FSD can return the requested volume information. The I/O Manager copies the returned information into the caller's buffer once the IRP is completed by the FSD.

I/O stack location

`MajorFunction`

`IRP_MJ_QUERY_VOLUME_INFORMATION`

`MinorFunction`

None.

`Flags`

None.

`Parameters.QueryVolume.Length`

The `Length` of the buffer provided by the caller.

`Parameters.QueryVolume.FsInformationClass`

The `FsInformationClass` value specified by the caller. This determines the type of information returned by the FSD.

`DeviceObject`

Points to the FSD-created device object representing the mounted logical volume.

`FileObject`

The file object representing the open instance of a file, directory, volume, or device using which a query volume information operation has been requested.

Notes

Regardless of the type of access requested in the open request for a file, directory, device, or volume, the user can always request volume information using the file handle received from the successful open operation.

NtSetVolumeInformationFile()

```
NTSTATUS NtSetVolumeInformationFile(
    IN HANDLE             FileHandle,
    OUT PIO_STATUS_BLOCK  IoStatusBlock,
    IN PVOID              FsInformation,
    IN ULONG              Length,
    IN FS_INFORMATION_CLASSFsInformationClass
);
```

Parameters

FileHandle

Returned to the caller from a previous successful **NtCreateFile()** or **NtOpenFile()** invocation on the target volume.

IoStatusBlock

The caller must supply this argument to receive the results of the set volume information operation. The **Information** field in the **IoStatusBlock** is set to the number of information bytes written by the FSD.

FsInformation

A caller-allocated buffer in which volume information is supplied. The structure of supplied information depends upon the value of the **FsInformationClass** argument.

Length

The size of the **FsInformation** buffer.

FsInformationClass

The type of information provided by the user. Currently, this can be the following:

FileFsLabelInformation

The following structure defines the format of the information supplied by the user:

```
typedef struct _FILE_FS_LABEL_INFORMATION {
    ULONG VolumeLabelLength;
    WCHAR VolumeLabel[1];
} FILE_FS_LABEL_INFORMATION, *PFILE_FS_LABEL_INFORMATION;
```

Return code

STATUS_SUCCESS indicates that the operation succeeded; **STATUS_PENDING** is returned if the FSD decides to process the request asynchronously.

In the case of an error, an appropriate error code is returned. This includes (but is not limited to) the following return code values:

- STATUS_ACCESS_DENIED
- STATUS_INSUFFICIENT_RESOURCES
- STATUS_INVALID_PARAMETER
- STATUS_INVALID_DEVICE_REQUEST

IRP

`AssociatedIrp.SystemBuffer`

The I/O Manager allocates a system buffer into which the caller-provided volume information is copied before the IRP is dispatched to the FSD.

I/O stack location

`MajorFunction`

`IRP_MJ_SET_VOLUME_INFORMATION`

`MinorFunction`

None.

`Flags`

None.

`Parameters.SetVolume.Length`

The `Length` of the buffer provided by the caller.

`Parameters.SetVolume.FsInformationClass`

The `FsInformationClass` value specified by the caller. This determines the type of attribute to be modified for the logical volume.

`DeviceObject`

Points to the FSD-created device object representing the mounted logical volume.

`FileObject`

The file object representing the open instance of the logical volume on which a set volume information operation has been requested.

Notes

For the `FileFsLabelInformation FsInformation` class value, a value of 0 in the `VolumeLabelLength` field indicates that the current volume label (if any) should be removed. The FSD expects that any new volume label supplied by the caller should be a wide character string.

NtFsControlFile()

```
NTSTATUS NtFsControlFile(
    IN HANDLE               FileHandle,
    IN HANDLE               Event OPTIONAL,
    IN PIO_APC_ROUTINE      ApcRoutine OPTIONAL,
    IN PVOID                ApcContext OPTIONAL,
    OUT PIO_STATUS_BLOCK    IoStatusBlock,
    IN ULONG                FsControlCode,
    IN PVOID                InputBuffer OPTIONAL,
    IN ULONG                InputBufferLength,
```

```
    OUT PVOID              OutputBuffer OPTIONAL,
    IN ULONG               OutputBufferLength
);
```

Parameters

FileHandle

Returned to the caller from a previous, successful `NtCreateFile()` or `NtOpenFile()` invocation.

Event (optional)

The caller can wait for the supplied event object (created by the caller) for completion of the asynchronous FSCTL request. The event will be signaled by the I/O Manager when the FSCTL operation is completed.

ApcRoutine (optional)

An optional, caller-supplied APC routine invoked by the I/O Manager when the FSCTL operation completes.

ApcContext (optional)

The caller-determined context to be passed-in to the `ApcRoutine`. This argument should be NULL if `ApcRoutine` is NULL.

IoStatusBlock

The caller must supply this argument to receive the results of the FSCTL operation. The `Information` field in the `IoStatusBlock` is set to the number of bytes returned by the FSD in the `OutputBuffer` (if any).

FsControlCode

The FSCTL code value specifying the type of file system control function requested.

InputBuffer

A caller-allocated buffer in which information to be sent to the FSD is supplied.

InputBufferLength

The size of the input buffer.

OutputBuffer

A caller-allocated buffer in which the FSD returns information to the caller.

OutputBufferLength

The size of the output buffer.

Return code

`STATUS_SUCCESS` indicates that the operation succeeded; `STATUS_PENDING` is returned if the FSD processes the request asynchronously.

In the case of an error, an appropriate error code is returned. This includes (but is not limited to) the following return code values:

- `STATUS_ACCESS_DENIED`

- `STATUS_INSUFFICIENT_RESOURCES`

- `STATUS_INVALID_PARAMETER`

- `STATUS_INVALID_DEVICE_REQUEST`

IRP

`AssociatedIrp.SystemBuffer`

If the FSCTL code value specifies `METHOD_BUFFERED` or `METHOD_IN_DIRECT`/`METHOD_OUT_DIRECT`, the I/O Manager initializes this field with a pointer to a system buffer allocated by the I/O Manager. For `METHOD_BUFFERED`, the size of the allocated system buffer is equal to the size of the larger of the two buffers supplied by the caller (the `InputBuffer` and the `OutputBuffer`).* For `METHOD_IN_DIRECT`/`METHOD_OUT_DIRECT`, the I/O Manager allocates a system buffer to correspond to any `InputBuffer` supplied by the caller.

`MdlAddress`

If the FSCTL code value specifies `METHOD_IN_DIRECT`/`METHOD_OUT_DIRECT` and the `OutputBuffer` argument supplied by the requesting thread is nonnull, the I/O Manager allocates an MDL describing the caller's `OutputBuffer` and initializes the `MdlAddress` field with the MDL pointer value. Note that the physical pages backing this MDL are locked into memory by the I/O Manager.

`UserBuffer`

If the FSCTL code value specifies `METHOD_NEITHER`, the I/O Manager initializes this field with the `OutputBuffer` pointer provided by the caller.

`Flags`

Set to `IRP_MOUNT_COMPLETION` and `IRP_SYNCHRONOUS_PAGING_IO` for mount volume and verify volume FSCTL requests.

I/O stack location

`MajorFunction`

`IRP_MJ_FILE_SYSTEM_CONTROL`

---

* The I/O Manager copies the contents of the `InputBuffer` into the system buffer before dispatching the IRP to the FSD. When the IRP is completed and if the caller had provided an `OutputBuffer`, the I/O Manager copies any information returned by the FSD back into the caller's `OutputBuffer`.

MinorFunction

One of the following:

IRP_MN_MOUNT_VOLUME

A mount request is being issued to the FSD.

IRP_MN_LOAD_FILE_SYSTEM

The FSD is being loaded by a mini file system recognizer.

IRP_MN_VERIFY_VOLUME

A verify volume request is issued to the FSD.

IRP_MN_USER_FS_REQUEST

Set when a user FSCTL request is received by the I/O Manager, via an invocation to NtFsControlFile(), for either a private FSCTL request or for one of the set of public FSCTL requests supported by most FSDs and/or network redirectors.

Flags

Set to SL_ALLOW_RAW_MOUNT if a target volume is opened for direct access when MinorFunction is initialized to IRP_MN_VERIFY_VOLUME.

Mount requests

Parameters.MountVolume.Vpb

The VPB associated with the physical, virtual, or logical "real" device object representing the media on which the logical volume should be mounted.

Parameters.MountVolume.DeviceObject

Pointer to the device object representing the partition on the device object on which the logical volume should be mounted. Note that the pointer may refer to some intermediate (filter driver) device object structure that has been attached to the target device object.

DeviceObject

Points to the FSD-created device object representing the file system driver (or to the highest-layered filter device object attached to the FSD device object).

FileObject

Initialized to NULL.

Load FSD request

DeviceObject

Points to the file system recognizer driver-created device object representing the file system recognizer driver.

FileObject

Initialized to NULL.

Verify volume requests

`Parameters.VerifyVolume.Vpb`
   The VPB associated with the physical, virtual, or logical "real" device object representing the media on which the mounted logical volume should be verified.

`Parameters.VerifyVolume.DeviceObject`
   Pointer to the device object representing the media containing the mounted logical volume to be verified.

`DeviceObject`
   Points to the FSD-created device object representing the mounted volume to be verified.

`FileObject`
   Initialized to NULL.

User FSCTL requests

`Parameters.FileSystemControl.OutputBufferLength`
   The `OutputBufferLength` specified by the caller.

`Parameters.FileSystemControl.InputBufferLength`
   The `InputBufferLength` specified by the caller.

`Parameters.FileSystemControl.FsControlCode`
   The `FsControlCode` specified by the caller.

`Parameters.FileSystemControl.Type3InputBuffer`
   Used when the FSCTL code value specifies `METHOD_NEITHER` for handling user buffers, this field contains a pointer to the user-supplied `InputBuffer`.

`DeviceObject`
   Points to the FSD-created device object representing the mounted volume.

`FileObject`
   Initialized to the file object instance representing an open file/directory or volume.

Notes

When dispatching any I/O read request to a lower-level driver while processing a verify volume request itself, the FSD must set the `SL_OVERRIDE_VERIFY_VOLUME` flag in the next I/O stack location before forwarding the IRP. See Chapter 11 for a detailed discussion on how FSDs process FSCTL requests.

NtDeviceIoControlFile()

```
NTSTATUS NtDeviceIoControlFile(
      IN HANDLE             FileHandle,
      IN HANDLE             Event OPTIONAL,
      IN PIO_APC_ROUTINE    ApcRoutine OPTIONAL,
      IN PVOID              ApcContext OPTIONAL,
      OUT PIO_STATUS_BLOCK  IoStatusBlock,
      IN ULONG              IoControlCode,
      IN PVOID              InputBuffer OPTIONAL,
      IN ULONG              InputBufferLength,
      OUT PVOID             OutputBuffer OPTIONAL,
      IN ULONG              OutputBufferLength
);
```

Parameters

FileHandle

Returned to the caller from a previous, successful **NtCreateFile()** or **NtOpenFile()** invocation. The target file or device must have been opened for Direct Access Storage Device (DASD) access.

Event (optional)

The caller can wait for the supplied event object (created by the caller), for completion of the asynchronous IOCTL request. The event will be signaled by the I/O Manager when the IOCTL operation is completed.

ApcRoutine (optional)

An optional, caller-supplied APC routine invoked by the I/O Manager when the IOCTL operation completes.

ApcContext (optional)

A caller-determined context to be passed-in to the **ApcRoutine**. This argument should be NULL if **ApcRoutine** is NULL.

IoStatusBlock

The caller must supply this argument to receive the results of the IOCTL operation. The **Information** field in the **IoStatusBlock** is set to the number of bytes returned by the FSD in the **OutputBuffer** (if any).

FsControlCode

The IOCTL code value specifying the type of device I/O control function requested.

InputBuffer

A caller-allocated buffer in which information to be sent to the FSD is supplied.

InputBufferLength

The size of the input buffer.

OutputBuffer

   A caller-allocated buffer in which the FSD returns information to the caller.

OutputBufferLength

   The size of the output buffer.

Return code

STATUS_SUCCESS indicates that the operation succeeded; STATUS_PENDING is returned if the FSD processes the request asynchronously.

In the case of an error, an appropriate error code is returned. This includes (but is not limited to) the following return code values:

- STATUS_ACCESS_DENIED

- STATUS_INSUFFICIENT_RESOURCES

- STATUS_INVALID_PARAMETER

- STATUS_INVALID_DEVICE_REQUEST

IRP

AssociatedIrp.SystemBuffer

   If the IOCTL code value specifies METHOD_BUFFERED or METHOD_IN_
   DIRECT/METHOD_OUT_DIRECT, the I/O Manager initializes this field with a
   pointer to a system buffer allocated by the I/O Manager. For METHOD_BUFF-
   ERED, the size of the allocated system buffer is equal to the size of the larger
   of the two buffers supplied by the caller (the InputBuffer and the
   OutputBuffer).* For METHOD_IN_DIRECT/METHOD_OUT_DIRECT, the
   I/O Manager allocates a system buffer to correspond to any InputBuffer
   supplied by the caller.

MdlAddress

   If the IOCTL code value specifies METHOD_IN_DIRECT/METHOD_OUT_
   DIRECT and the OutputBuffer argument supplied by the requesting
   thread is nonnull, the I/O Manager allocates an MDL describing the caller's
   OutputBuffer and initializes the MdlAddress field with the MDL pointer
   value. Note that the physical pages backing this MDL are locked into memory
   by the I/O Manager.

UserBuffer

   If the IOCTL code value specifies METHOD_NEITHER, the I/O Manager initializes this field with the OutputBuffer pointer provided by the caller.

---

* The I/O Manager copies the contents of the InputBuffer into the system buffer before dispatching
the IRP to the FSD. When the IRP is completed and if the caller had provided an OutputBuffer, the
I/O Manager copies any information returned by the FSD back into the caller's OutputBuffer.

I/O stack location

MajorFunction
> IRP_MJ_DEVICE_CONTROL or IRP_MJ_INTERNAL_DEVICE_CONTROL

MinorFunction
> None.

Flags
> Can be set to SL_OVERRIDE_VERIFY_VOLUME by the FSD when requesting I/O operations from the lower-level driver while processing verify-volume requests.

Parameters.DeviceIoControl.OutputBufferLength
> The OutputBufferLength specified by the caller.

Parameters.DeviceIoControl.InputBufferLength
> The InputBufferLength specified by the caller.

Parameters.DeviceIoControl.FsControlCode
> The FsControlCode specified by the caller.

Parameters.DeviceIoControl.Type3InputBuffer
> Used when the IOCTL code value specifies METHOD_NEITHER for handling user buffers, this field contains a pointer to the user-supplied InputBuffer.

DeviceObject
> Points to the FSD-created device object representing the mounted logical volume or target device.

FileObject
> Initialized to the file object instance representing an open file or device.

Notes

Most device IOCTL requests are forwarded by the FSD to lower-level device drivers managing the physical/virtual/logical device on which the volume has been mounted. See Chapter 11 for a detailed discussion on how FSDs process IOCTL requests.

Note that the IRP_MJ_SCSI IOCTL code has been defined to be the same as IRP_MJ_INTERNAL_DEVICE_CONTROL control code value.

NtDeleteFile()

```
NTSTATUS NtDeleteFile(
    IN POBJECT_ATTRIBUTES ObjectAttributes
);
```

This system call is functionally equivalent to invoking NtSetInformationFile() with FileInformationClass set to FileDispositionInformation.

NtFlushBuffersFile()

```
NTSTATUS NtFlushBuffersFile(
    IN HANDLE               FileHandle,
    OUT PIO_STATUS_BLOCK    IoStatusBlock,
);
```

Parameters

FileHandle

Returned to the caller from a previous, successful `NtCreateFile()` or `NtOpenFile()` invocation.

If the supplied handle represents an open instance of either the mounted logical volume or the root directory on the mounted logical volume, all cached data for open files belonging to the mounted logical volume will be flushed by the FSD. If, however, the handle refers to an instance of any other open directory on the volume, no data will be flushed to disk.

If the handle represents an open instance of a specific file, the FSD will write the cached data for the file to secondary storage by the FSD.

IoStatusBlock

The caller must supply this argument to receive the results of the flush buffers operation. The `Information` field in the `IoStatusBlock` is set to the number of bytes flushed to secondary storage by the FSD.

Return code

`STATUS_SUCCESS` indicates that the operation succeeded.

In the case of an error, an appropriate error code is returned. This includes (but is not limited to) the following return code values:

- `STATUS_ACCESS_DENIED`
- `STATUS_INSUFFICIENT_RESOURCES`
- `STATUS_INVALID_PARAMETER`
- `STATUS_INVALID_DEVICE_REQUEST`

I/O stack location

MajorFunction

`IRP_MJ_FLUSH_BUFFERS`

MinorFunction

None.

DeviceObject

Points to the FSD-created device object representing the mounted logical volume.

FileObject

Initialized to the file object instance representing an open file, directory, or volume.

Notes

Chapter 11 discusses how the flush file buffers IRP is handled by the FSD.

NtCancelIoFile()

```
NTSTATUS NtCancelIoFile(
    IN HANDLE              FileHandle,
    OUT PIO_STATUS_BLOCK   IoStatusBlock,
);
```

Parameters

FileHandle

Returned to the caller from a previous, successful **NtCreateFile()** or **NtOpenFile()** invocation.

IoStatusBlock

The caller must supply this argument to receive the results of the flush buffers operation.

Return code

STATUS_SUCCESS indicates that the operation succeeded.

In the case of an error, an appropriate error code is returned. This includes (but is not limited to) the following return code values:

* **STATUS_ACCESS_DENIED**

* **STATUS_INVALID_PARAMETER**

* **STATUS_INVALID_DEVICE_REQUEST**

Notes

This system call will not return control back to the caller until all pending I/O requests initiated by the requesting thread using the particular file handle, have been either canceled or completed.

Requests initiated by other threads belonging to the same process or by the same thread but using different file handles will not be affected.

This appendix has listed some of the Windows NT I/O-Manager-provided system services that you can use either from a user-space application or from within a kernel-mode driver. There is a cost, however, associated with using such routines directly. This cost (especially for user-space applications) is the potential loss of portability that your software will suffer if and when these system services are changed and/or made obsolete by Microsoft. The benefit is that certain functionality becomes easier to request by using such Windows NT system services directly.

B

MPR Support

The Multiple Provider Router (MPR) exports general networking APIs in Win32 and interacts with underlying network providers to provide the exported networking services. Applications do not interact with the network provider DLLs directly; rather, they invoke the common networking APIs and are thereby protected from the vagaries of specific network providers. Also, a common look and feel is presented by the MPR to applications that request such networking services.

If you design and implement a network redirector, you may choose to implement a network provider dynamic link library (DLL); this will allow you to leverage existing commands and interfaces (e.g., the net command) that users can utilize to request services from your network redirector. Such services can include determining the capabilities of your network, establishing a connection to a remote resource, getting information about connected resources, closing connections, and so on.

The MPR will dynamically load your DLL and call the appropriate entry points whenever your network is active.

Registry Modifications

The MPR examines the contents of the following key in the Registry to determine the various network provider DLLs that are present and also to determine the order in which these network providers should be invoked:

HKEY_LOCAL_MACHINE\System\CurrentControlSet\Control\NetworkProvider\order

The order key has a value-entry called ProviderOrder, which is a string-type value. The string value is a comma-separated list of key names. Each key name identifies a network provider by referring to the Registry key associated with that provider. Each key name is actually a relative path from `HKEY_LOCAL_MACHINE\System\CurrentControlSet\Services\`, defining a node that the network vendor would have created during its installation.

As an example, consider the following entry in the Registry:

```
HKEY_LOCAL_MACHINE\System\CurrentControlSet\Control\NetworkProvider\
    order\ProviderOrder = "LanmanWorkStation,YourNetworkServiceKeyName"
```

This informs the MPR that it should expect to find two specific Registry key entries:

```
HKEY_LOCAL_MACHINE\System\CurrentControlSet\Services\LanmanWorkStation
```

and

```
HKEY_LOCAL_MACHINE\System\CurrentControlSet\Services\
    YourNetworkServiceKeyName
```

It also informs the MPR that the order in which requests should be directed to the network providers present on the system is first, to the LAN Manager Work Station network provider and then your network provider.

You are expected to have the following entries in the Registry associated with the `YourNetworkServiceKeyName` key:

- `Group:REG_SZ:NetworkProvider`
- `NetworkProvider` (subkey)

    The `NetworkProvider` subkey should have the following values:

    Name (`REG_SZ`)
        The name of the network provider. This name is displayed to the user as the name of the network in the browse dialogs.

    `ProviderPath` (`REG_EXPAND_SZ`)
        The full path of the DLL that implements the network provider. MPR will perform a `LoadLibrary()` on this path.

Network Provider DLL Implementation

On Windows NT platforms, your network provider can implement one or more of the following functions:

Function Name	Ordinal Value
`NPGetConnection()`	12
`NPGetCaps()`[1]	13
`NPDeviceMode()`	14

Function Name	Ordinal Value
NPGetUser()	16
NPAddConnection()	17
NPCancelConnection()	18
NPPropertyDialog()	29
NPGetDirectoryType()	30
NPDirectoryNotify()	31
NPGetPropertyText()	32
NPOpenEnum()	33
NPEnumResource()	34
NPCloseEnum()	35
NPSearchDialog()	38

[1] This is the only function that is mandatory for your network provider to implement since it is the method by which the user (and the MPR DLL) can determine the capabilities of your network.

Note that your DLL does not need to contain stubs for those functions that are not supported and/or implemented by your network provider.

When implementing the network provider DLL, you should keep the following points in mind:

Speed

When your network provider DLL gets invoked, you should quickly try to determine whether the target resource is one that belongs to you or not. If your DLL does not own the resource, return **WN_BAD_NETNAME** (the list of error code definitions is given later in this appendix) so that the MPR can continue cycling through the list of available providers.

Validation

Your network provider DLL must validate calls using the following ordering sequence:

a. First, check if your network has been started (or if your network redirector is loaded and active).

b. Next, check if you support the requested operation.

c. If any network resources are specified, check whether you own such resources.

d. Validate the supplied parameters to your function call (if any).

Routing

The MPR cycles through all of the network providers listed in the Registry, until one of them accepts the request and processes it or until all of the available network providers have been invoked and none of them accepts the request. If your network provider is invoked and you do not wish to process the request, return an appropriate error code (e.g., ERROR_BAD_NETPATH, ERROR_BAD_NET_NAME, ERROR_INVALID_PARAMETER, ERROR_INVALID_ LEVEL). If, however, your network provider returns an error code that is a significant error code (e.g., ERROR_INVALID_PASSWORD) that indicates that the operation was processed unsuccessfully or if your network provider DLL returns a success code, the MPR DLL conveys the results back to the requesting application (and stops routing the request to any other network providers).

Return Values/Errors

Functions implemented in your network provider DLL can return either WN_ SUCCESS or an appropriate error code. If returning an error, the function should also invoke the WNetSetLastError() or SetLastError() function calls to report the error. If you are returning a general error (such as insufficient memory), simply invoke the SetLastError() function; otherwise, use the WNetSetLastError() function:

```
VOID WNetSetLastError (
    DWORDerror,
    LPTSTRlpError,
    LPTSTRlpProvider)
```

where the arguments are as follows:

error

The error code value. If this is a Windows-defined error code, lpError is ignored. Otherwise, you could set this to ERROR_EXTENDED_ERROR to indicate that a network-specific error is being reported.

lpError

A string describing the network-specific error.

lpProvider

A string naming the network provider that raised the error.

To report general errors, execute the following steps:

```
// error condition occurs that should be reported.
// error code is contained in providerError.
SetLastError(providerError);
return(providerError);
```

To report network-specific errors, do the following:

```
// lpErrorString contains the error to be reported.
WNetSetLastError(ERROR_EXTENDED_ERROR, lpErrorString, lpProviderName);
return(ERROR_EXTENDED_ERROR);
```

Note that the `NtGetCaps()` function does not return any error code value; rather, it returns a capabilities mask value.

Here are the possible status code values that can be returned (your provider, however, is free to return any Windows-defined error code):

```
#define WN_SUCCESS          00h // success
#define WN_NOT_SUPPORTED    01h // function not supported
#define WN_NET_ERROR        02h // miscellaneous network error
#define WN_MORE_DATA        03h // warning: buffer too small
#define WN_BAD_POINTER      04h // invalid pointer specified
#define WN_BAD_VALUE        05h // invalid numeric value specified
#define WN_BAD_PASSWORD     06h // incorrect password specified
#define WN_ACCESS_DENIED    07h // security violation
#define WN_FUNCTION_BUSY    08h // this function cannot be reentered and
                                // is currently being used, OR
                                // the provider is still initializing and
                                // is not ready to be called yet.
#define WN_WINDOWS_ERROR    09h // a required Windows function failed
#define WN_BAD_USER         0Ah // invalid user name specified
#define WN_OUT_OF_MEMORY    0Bh // out of memory
#define WN_NOT_CONNECTED    30h // device is not redirected
#define WN_OPEN_FILES       31h // connection could not be canceled
                                // because files are still open
#define WN_BAD_NETNAME      32h // network name is invalid
```

Note that the `WN_FUNCTION_BUSY` code value is also used to indicate that the network provider DLL is currently initializing itself. When this error code is returned to the application, it is possible that the application may decide to retry the operation.

NPGetCaps()

This function allows your network provider DLL to specify which functions are supported by your network from the set of functions specified by the caller. This function is defined as follows:

```
DWORD NPGetCaps(
    IN DWORD nIndex)
```

Parameters

`nIndex`
   Capability set that the caller is interested in.

The return value is typically a bit mask, indicating which of the specified services are supported by your network provider DLL. If you return 0, the caller will take that to mean that none of the specified services are supported by your network. For certain `nIndex` values, however, you must return a constant value instead of a bit mask.

Possible nIndex values

Version information

The `nIndex` value will be set to `WNNC_SPEC_VERSION` (= 0x01).

Set the high word of the return code to 4 (indicating the major version number) and the low word to 0 (for the minor version number).

Network provider type

The `nIndex` value will be set to `WNNC_NET_TYPE` (= 0x02).

The high word of the returned value should contain the provider type and the low word should contain the subtype (if any). The following types have been defined by Microsoft:[*]

```
#define WNNC_NET_NONE      0x00000
#define WNNC_NET_MSNET     0x10000
#define WNNC_NET_LANMAN    0x20000
#define WNNC_NET_NETWARE   0x30000
#define WNNC_NET_VINES     0x40000
```

Network provider version

The `nIndex` value will be set to `WNNC_DRIVER_VERSION` (= 0x03).

Returns your driver version number.

User information

The `nIndex` value will be set to `WNNC_USER` (= 0x04).

If you support this capability, return the `WNNC_USR_GETUSER` (= 0x01) constant value.

Connection manipulation

The `nIndex` value will be set to `WNNC_CONNECTION` (= 0x06).

Set any of the following bit fields:

```
#define WNNC_CON_ADDCONNECTION      0x01
#define WNNC_CON_CANCELCONNECTION   0x02
#define WNNC_CON_GETCONNECTIONS     0x04
#define WNNC_CON_ADDCONNECTION3     0x08
```

Provider-specific dialogs

The `nIndex` value will be set to `WNNC_DIALOG` (= 0x08).

Set any of the following bit fields:

```
#define WNNC_DLG_DEVICEMODE      0x01
#define WNNC_DLG_PROPERTYDIALOG  0x20 // PropertyText is also
                                      //           implied.
```

---

[*] You can request Microsoft to assign a provider type value for your use.

```
#define WNNC_DLG_SEARCHDIALOG       0x40
#define WNNC_DLG_FORMATNETWORKNAME  0x80
#define WNNC_DLG_PERMISSIONEDITOR   0x100
```

Administrative functionality

The **nIndex** value will be set to **WNNC_ADMIN** (= 0x09).

Set any of the following bit fields:

```
#define WNNC_ADM_GETDIRECTORYTYPE   0x01
#define WNNC_ADM_DIRECTORYNOTIFY    0x02
```

Enumeration

The **nIndex** value will be set to **WNNC_ENUMERATION** (= 0x0B).

Set any of the following bit fields:

```
#define WNNC_ENUM_GLOBAL   0x01
#define WNNC_ENUM_LOCAL    0x02
```

Startup

The **nIndex** value will be set to **WNNC_START** (= 0x0C).

The MPR issues this request to determine how long it should wait (*timeout value*) for network providers to start. Therefore, if your network provider is not responding (or returns busy), the MPR may decide to retry an operation, depending upon the current timeout value and the elapsed time interval. The default value is set to 60 seconds for each network provider. The administrator could, however, change this default value by specifying the **HKEY_ LOCAL_MACHINE\SYSTEM\CurrentControlSet\Control\NetworProvider\RestoreTimeout** value (type **REG_DWORD**), which determines the timeout in milliseconds for all network providers.

If you return 0, the MPR will assume that your network provider is disabled. If you return 0xFFFFFFFF, the MPR interprets this to mean that you do not know how long it will take you to start and will wait for the current default timeout value (60 seconds or whatever is specified by the administrator).

NOTE   There is a single timeout value used by the MPR for all network providers. If your network provider DLL returns a timeout value that is greater than the current MPR default timeout (whether specified by the administrator or not), the MPR will use your specified timeout value. Therefore, be judicious in determining the appropriate timeout value you decide to return.

Consult the SDK documentation, and the documentation supplied on the Microsoft Developers Library CD-ROM for more information on how to implement the other network provider APIs for the Windows NT operating system.I

C

Building Kernel-Mode Drivers

The *BUILD.EXE* utility supplied with the Windows NT DDK is the Microsoft-provided (and supported) program to assist developers in compiling and linking Windows NT kernel-mode drivers.* *BUILD* automatically establishes file dependencies, isolates target-dependent (e.g., header file and library include path information, compiler names and switches, linker switches) and platform-dependent information (x86, PowerPC, MIPS, Alpha platforms), and, thereby, provides a simple method for creating kernel-mode drivers and libraries and also user-mode applications (if you so desire).

BUILD expects you to tell it which files need to be compiled, the name and type information for the target driver or library to be generated, information identifying the target platform, and any special compilation and/or link options that you would like to specify. Once you provide this information, *BUILD* determines the appropriate file dependencies and uses the services of *NMAKE* and the installed compiler to generate your target driver, library, or application.

Inputs

As input, *BUILD* expects you to supply a text file named *SOURCES*, in the same directory as that containing the files to be compiled. The *SOURCES* file contains information that identifies your source files, the target to be built and other relevant information. *BUILD* also uses any environment variables that you may have specified, and any command-line options that you provide when you invoke *BUILD*. Finally, *BUILD* uses the platform-specific rules and other options specified

---

* Note once again that the Microsoft DDK does not include a compiler. You must purchase a compiler separately.

in the following files that are supplied with the DDK (in the *$BASEDIR\INC* directory*):

MAKEFILE.DEF

> This is the primary control file used by *BUILD*. You should study the contents of this file to better understand how options specified by you can affect the manner in which your target driver or library is created.

WARNING   The *MAKEFILE.DEF* file is poorly documented and extremely convoluted. It is a prime example of how not to implement a makefile. Unfortunately for us, it is also the only source available if we wish to understand some of what happens when *BUILD* is invoked.

MAKEFILE.PLT

> This file contains target-platform-specific information. The target platform is either specified by you as a command-line option to *BUILD* or determined via an environment variable.† This file is included by *MAKEFILE.DEF*.

I386MK.INC / ALPHAMK.INC / MIPSMK.INC / PPCMK.INC

> This file contains target-platform-specific build controls and is also included by *MAKEFILE.DEF*.

Output

BUILD generates the target driver, library, or application you specified in the *SOURCES* file. The *BUILD.LOG* (containing the list of commands invoked by *BUILD* and any compiler- or linker-generated statements), *BUILD.WRN* (containing warnings generated during the build process), and *BUILD.ERR* (containing errors that prevent the successful completion of the build process) files are generated as by-products of the build process.

Two types of Windows NT drivers can be built:

Free build

> This is the nondebug version of your driver. This is also the version you will typically ship to your customers. This version is normally compiled with full optimization enabled, and I would advise that you strip the free version of all symbolic information before shipping it.

---

* The *BASEDIR* environment variable is automatically set up for you by the installation utility during the DDK installation process and its value is set to the base directory path specification where you installed the DDK.

† The *BUILD_DEFAULT_TARGETS* environment variable is typically initialized to the target platform type value (e.g., -386).

The free build environment does not define the DBG environment variable; therefore, any conditional debug code that you include in your driver can be automatically filtered out during the compilation process as shown here:

```
#if DBG
    // Include the debug code here. This code is automatically
    // filtered out for the free/retail build.
#endif // DBG
```

Contrary to what you might expect, the free version of your driver does contain symbolic information. To remove this symbolic information from the free build, execute the following sequence of steps:

— Execute the command *DUMPBIN   /HEADERS   your-driver-name.sys | MORE* on the binary.

— Note the value associated with the "*image base*" in the OPTIONAL HEADER VALUES section. This value should typically be 10000 (hex).

— Execute the command *REBASE -b InitialBaseValue -x Symbol-Dir-Name your-driver-name.sys*.

— A file by the name of *your-driver-name.dbg* will be created in the specified symbol directory, and the free binary will no longer contain any symbolic information.

Checked build

This is the debug version of your driver that you will typically build and use during development. Assertions in the driver code, debug print statements, debug breakpoints, and symbolic information are all compiled into the checked binary, and optimization is disabled for the debug build.

You should never ship the checked build to your customers or attempt to execute the checked build without having a debugger attached to the system. Otherwise, you may experience hangs and/or system crashes when assertions or breakpoints are hit.

To build the free, or retail, version of your driver, use the free build environment, which is set up automatically when you invoke the Free Build Command Window. Similarly, you should use the Checked Build Command Window to build the checked version of your target driver.

Building Your Driver

1. In your driver source directory, create a file called *MAKEFILE* containing the following:

```
# DO NOT EDIT THIS FILE!!!  Edit .\sources. if you want to add a new
# source file to this component.  This file merely indirects to the
```

```
# real make filethat is shared by all the driver components of the
# Windows NT DDK
```

```
!INCLUDE $(NTMAKEENV)\makefile.def
```

2. Also in your driver source directory, create a *SOURCES* file, specifying the source files to be built, the target type and name, and any other additional command-line switch values you wish to have passed-on to the compiler and linker. The *\DDK\DOC\SOURCES.TPL* file is a template that you should study and use when attempting to create your own *SOURCES* file. Below is the *SOURCES* file I used in compiling the sample file system driver:

```
# - Execute the "build" command to make the sample FSD driver

# The TARGETNAME variable is defined by the developer.  It is the name
# of the target (component) that is being built by this makefile.  It
# should NOT include any path or file extension information.

TARGETNAME=sfsd

# The TARGETPATH and TARGETTYPE variables are defined by the developer.
# The first specifies where the target is to be built.  The second
# specifies the type of target (either PROGRAM, DYNLINK, LIBRARY,
# UMAPPL_NOLIB, or BOOTPGM).  UMAPPL_NOLIB is used when you're only
# building user-mode apps and don't need to build a library.

TARGETPATH=obj

TARGETTYPE=DRIVER

# The INCLUDES variable specifies any include paths that are specific
# to this source directory.  Separate multiple directory paths with
# singlesemicolons.  Relative path specifications are okay.  The
# INCLUDES variable is not required.  Specifying an empty INCLUDES
# variable(i.e., INCLUDES= ) indicates no include paths are to be
# searched.
#
# NOTE: The "fsdk\inc" refers to the Microsoft-supplied File Systems
#       Developers Kit.

INCLUDES=..\inc;\ddk-40\inc;\fsdk\inc-40;

# The SOURCES variable is defined by the developer.  It is a list of
# all the source files for this component.  Each source file should be
# on a separate line, using the line continuation character.  This
# will minimize merge conflicts if two developers are adding source
# files to the same component.  The SOURCES variable is required.  If
# there are no platform common sourcefiles, an empty SOURCES variable
# should be used. (i.e., SOURCES= )

# Source files common to multiple platforms

SOURCES=sfsdinit.c      \
        registry.c      \
```

```
        create.c        \
        misc.c          \
        cleanup.c       \
        close.c         \
        read.c          \
        write.c         \
        fileinfo.c      \
        flush.c         \
        volinfo.c       \
        dircntrl.c      \
        fscntrl.c       \
        devcntrl.c      \
        shutdown.c      \
        lckcntrl.c      \
        security.c      \
        extattr.c       \
        fastio.c


    # Next specify any additional options for the compiler.
    # Define the appropriate CPU type (and insert defines
    # in the appropriate header file) to get the right
    # values for "uint8," "uint16," etc. typedefs.

    C_DEFINES=   -DUNICODE -D_CPU_X86_

    # The type of product being built - NT = kernel mode
    UMTYPE=nt
```

3. Since I specified that the *obj* subdirectory should contain the target driver, I have created the *obj*, *obj\i386*, *obj\i386\checked*, and *obj\i386\free* directories on my computer, for creating the x86 version of the driver. Similarly, you should create the appropriate directories depending upon the target directory you specify and the target platform that you are compiling for.[*]

4. Execute *BUILD* to create your target driver, library, or application.

For More Information

The DDK documentation provides a guide to compiling and linking your kernel-mode drivers. Consult this documentation, the *SOURCES* files provided on the diskette accompanying this book and the *SOURCES* files that are supplied with sample source code provided with the DDK for more information.

---

[*] If you fail to do so, *BUILD* will automatically create all of the subdirectories mentioned here, except the *checked* and *free* sub-directories, which you will have to create yourself (manually).

D

Debugging Support

The *WINDBG.EXE* debugger can be used for source-level debugging of Windows NT kernel-mode drivers. You can use this debugger in one of two ways:

- To interactively debug a live Windows NT system
- To perform analysis of a previously obtained crash dump (also known as post-mortem analysis)

Unfortunately, *WINDBG* has more than a few reliability problems (unexplained application crashes) and also behaves in an eccentric fashion occasionally. However, more often than not, *WINDBG* will work reasonably well and should be a valuable tool in helping you debug your kernel-mode code.

Interactive Debugging of a Live System

You will need two machines, each running Windows NT, in order to use *WINDBG* to debug a live system.* The machine that executes the driver(s) to be debugged is called the *target machine*. The machine on which *WINDBG* will execute is called the *host machine*. The two machines communicate using a null-modem serial cable which you will need to purchase. One end of this null-modem serial cable must be connected to the serial (COM) ports on each of the two systems (the host and target). If the machines that you use have multiple available COM ports, you can choose any one that you prefer; by default on x86 systems, *WINDBG* expects to use COM2 but this default can easily be overridden using an appropriate option (/DEBUGPORT=*PortName*) on the target machine boot command line.†

---

* It is possible to do things such as debugging an Alpha target using an x86 machine as the host (or vice versa). However, I have tried to avoid this whenever possible.

† You need not use the same COM port on both the host and target machines.

Use the sequence of steps given below to quickly get started with debugging your file system or filter driver:

1. Install either a checked or a free version of the Windows NT operating system on the target machine.

   If you install a checked build, the target machine will execute a lot slower than it will with a free build. However, you may benefit from the assertions and/or any debug print statements that the operating system contains.

TIP   If you have sufficient space available on the boot partition of the target system, you could install both the free and the checked builds in separate boot directories and thereby retain the flexibility to boot using either type of operating system build.

---

2. Install a free version of the Windows NT operating system on the host machine.

   You should note that the version of the operating system on both the target and host systems do not need to be the same. However, you will require the particular version of *WINDBG* executing on the host supplied with the SDK associated with the version of the operating system executing on the target.

   Therefore, if you wish to debug a target machine executing Version 3.51 of the Windows NT operating system, you must use the *WINDBG* application that was supplied with the SDK for Version 3.51 of Windows NT. If, however, you wish to debug a target machine executing Version 4.0 of the operating system, you cannot use the same *WINDBG* application that you use to debug Version 3.51; you must use the debugger supplied with the SDK for Version 4.0 of the operating system instead.

3. Install the appropriate SDKs on the host system.

   If you intend to debug multiple operating system releases, install each of the appropriate SDKs on the host system. For example, you could install the SDK for both Version 3.51 of the operating system and Version 4.0 of the operating system on a single host system running Version 4.0. This would give you the capability of debugging drivers on both operating system releases using the single host system.

   At the time of writing this book, I worked with both the 3.51 and 4.0 versions of the Windows NT operating system. Therefore, on most of the host systems that I used for debugging purposes, I created a . . . *MSTOOLS-40* directory to contain the SDK for the 4.0 version of the operating system and a

...*MSTOOLS-351* directory to contain the SDK for the 3.51 version of the operating system.*

4. Copy the target system's debug symbol files to the host machine.

   This symbolic information is required to get meaningful stack traces on the host system. The checked and free versions of the operating system have different symbol files associated with them. These symbol files are supplied with the Windows NT operating system distribution CD. They can typically be found in the *SUPPORT\DEBUG\<platform-type>\SYMBOLS* directory on the distribution CD. I would advise that you retain the subdirectory layout used on the distribution CD when you copy the symbol files to the host system (use the `XCOPY /S source-path target-path` command to achieve this).

   In order to successfully debug both types (retail/free and checked) of operating system binaries, you can create separate `CHECKED` and `FREE` subdirectories on the host system that can contain the appropriate symbol files. For example, you can create the following layout:

   — Create the ...*DEBUG-40\CHECKED\SYMBOLS*† path to contain the debug symbol files for the checked build of the 4.0 release of the Windows NT operating system.

   — Create the ...*DEBUG-40\FREE\SYMBOLS* path to contain the debug symbol files for the free build of the 4.0 release of the Windows NT operating system.

   — Create the ...*DEBUG-351\CHECKED\SYMBOLS* path to contain the debug symbol files for the checked build of the 3.51 release of the Windows NT operating system.

   — Create the ...*DEBUG-351\FREE\SYMBOLS* path to contain the debug symbol files for the free build of the 3.51 release of the Windows NT operating system.

   Debug symbol files change with every new service pack of the operating system. Be aware of this fact and copy over the appropriate new debug symbol files whenever you install a new Windows NT service pack.

5. On the target symbol, modify the [`operating systems`] section of the *boot.ini* file‡ to enable debugging of the target. Add the following options to

---

* You can similarly install the appropriate versions of the DDK. Since I often use the host system as a compile-link-debug machine, installing the SDK and the DDK is a requirement for me.

† You can create this subtree anywhere you like on the host system; you can specify this search path to *WINDBG* using the Options→ User DLLs→ Symbol Search Path textbox.

‡ This file has the hidden and system attributes set. You will need to remove the hidden and system attributes before you modify the file and then reset them after modifications have been completed.

the appropriate boot command for either or both of the free and checked versions you may have installed:

/DEBUG

> This option enables kernel-mode debugging of the target. The /NODEBUG option disables such debugging (and any of the options given below such as /DEBUGPORT, /BAUDRATE, etc. are ignored).

/DEBUGPORT=*PortName*

> You can use this option to specify an alternate COM port to which you have connected the null-modem serial cable on the target system.*

/BAUDRATE=*BaudRate*

> Specify the highest available baud rate at which both the target and host systems can communicate.

There are other options such as /SOS, /MAXMEM, and /CRASHDEBUG, which are documented in the DDK that you can also specify. These options are not critical, however, to enabling kernel-mode debugging of the target system.

As an example of how to set up boot commands correctly on the target system, study the contents of the *boot.ini* file given below. This is a file that I have set up on one of the target x86 systems I use to debug newly developed kernel-mode drivers:

```
[boot loader]
timeout=30
default=C:\

[Operating Systems]
multi(0)disk(0)rdisk(1)partition(1)\WINNT40="Windows NT Workstation
Version 4.00"
multi(0)disk(0)rdisk(1)partition(1)\WINNT351="Windows NT Workstation
Version 3.51"
multi(0)disk(0)rdisk(2)partition(2)\WINNT40.CKD="Windows NT
Workstation Version
    4.0 (Checked)" /DEBUG /DEBUGPORT=COM1 /BAUDRATE=57600
multi(0)disk(0)rdisk(2)partition(2)\WINNT351.CKD="Windows NT
Workstation
    Version 3.51 (Checked)" /DEBUG /DEBUGPORT=COM1 /BAUDRATE=57600
multi(0)disk(0)rdisk(2)partition(2)\WINNT40.CKD="Windows NT Workstation
    Version 4.00 - Checked"
multi(0)disk(0)rdisk(2)partition(2)\WINNT351.CKD="Windows NT
Workstation
    Version 3.51 - Checked"
C:\="Microsoft Windows 95"
```

6. Configure the *WINDBG* application on the host machine.

---

* To specify an alternate COM port for the host system, you will need to configure the *WINDBG* application settings on the host system as shown in Figure D-1.

You should configure *WINDBG* kernel debugger options to accurately reflect the COM port you are using on the host machine, the baud rate at which you want the host to communicate with the target, and whether you want the initial breakpoint (during target machine startup) to be activated or not. Figure D-1 depicts a screen shot of a configuration I've set up.

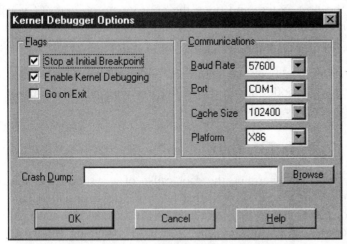

Figure D-1. Configuring the WINDBG kernel debugger options

You may also need to specify the path where you have copied symbols on the host system. Use the `User DLLs` menu option (from the `Options` main-menu option list) to specify the path leading to the symbol files.

TIP	Once you have configured *WINDBG* correctly, save the program with an appropriate name, to allow you to simply open the same program for subsequent debugging sessions (and avoid having to re-configure each time).

---

7. Copy symbolic information (*your-driver-name.dbg* file or the binary itself) for your driver to the symbol file directory on the host system.

8. Ensure that you have the source files located on the host system for use in source-level debugging sessions.

   If you use your host system as the compile machine as well, then your source files will be easily located by *WINDBG*. If, however, you use some other system to compile and link your binary, ensure that source files are copied onto the host system at the same location where they exist on the compile machine.

TIP   If possible, share the source directory tree on the compile machine
and access it directly from the host system (using the same drive letter as the one on which they are located on the compile machine).

---

9. Start *WINDBG* on the host system and open the appropriate program (if you
   had saved your configuration earlier).

10. Boot the target system using the appropriate boot command option.

The source and target systems will connect with each other and you can proceed
with debugging your kernel-mode driver. Read the documentation on using
WINDBG that is provided with the Windows NT DDK.

Analyzing a Crash Dump

Occasionally, you may need to determine the root cause of a system crash that
may have occurred on a Windows NT system that has your driver installed (and
executing), but was not connected to any debugger at the time of the crash. As
long as you have access to the crash-dump file, you have a fighting chance of
determining the cause of the crash.

NOTE   The crash dump is a file that contains the saved system state—including the contents of physical memory—for the machine that experienced a crash.

To analyze a crash dump, configure a Windows NT system exactly as you would
otherwise configure a host system for interactive debugging (except that you do
not need to physically connect the system via a serial cable to any target
machine). Invoke *WINDBG* as follows:

```
WINDBG -y path-to-symbol-files-directory -z path-to-crash-dump-file
```

Once you invoke *WINDBG* as shown above, you can pretty much execute the
same sequence of steps that you would otherwise execute in debugging a live
target system during interactive debugging. The *DUMPCHK* utility shipped with
the DDK can be useful in checking the validity of a crash dump file before you
use it with *WINDBG*.

Recommended Readings and References

This appendix lists some books and papers that should assist you in finding additional information on the topics covered in the book.

Books on Operating Systems

Bach, Maurice. *The Design of the UNIX Operating System*. Englewood Cliffs, NJ: Prentice Hall Inc., 1986.

Custer, Helen. *Inside Windows NT*. Redmond, WA: Microsoft Press, 1993.

Custer, Helen. *Inside the Windows NT File System*. Redmond, WA: Microsoft Press, 1994.

Deitel, Harvey. *An Introduction to Operating Systems*. Reading, MA: Addison-Wesley Publishing Co., 1984.

Goodheart, Berny, and James Cox. *The Magic Garden Explained: The Internals of UNIX System V Release 4, An Open-Systems Design*. Englewood Cliffs, NJ: Prentice Hall Inc., 1994.

Hwang, Kai, and Fayé Briggs. *Computer Architecture and Parallel Processing*. Singapore: McGraw-Hill Book Co., 1985.

Mitchell, Stan. *Inside the Windows 95 File System*. Sebastopol, CA: O'Reilly & Associates, Inc., 1997.

Tannenbaum, Andrew. *Operating Systems: Design and Implementation*. Englewood Cliffs, NJ: Prentice Hall Inc., 1987.

Vahalia, Uresh. *UNIX Internals: The New Frontiers*. Upper Saddle River, NJ: Prentice Hall Inc., 1996.

Books on CPU Architectures

Heinrich, Joe. *MIPS R4000 User's Manual*. Englewood Cliffs, NJ: Prentice Hall Inc., 1993.

Intel Corporation. *80386 Programmer's Reference Manual*. Beaverton, OR: Intel Corporation, 1986.

Intel Corporation. *Intel486 Processor Family Programmer's Reference*. Beaverton, OR: Intel Corporation, 1992.

Sites, Richard, and Richard Witek. *Alpha AXP Architecture Reference Manual, Second Edition*. Newton, MA: Digital Press, 1995.

Books on Driver Development

Baker, Art. *The Windows NT Device Driver Book: A Guide For Programmers*. Upper Saddle River, NJ: Prentice Hall, PTR, 1997.

Egan, Janet, and Thomas Teixeira. *Writing a UNIX Device Driver, Second Edition*. John Wiley & Sons, Inc., 1992.

Selected Papers

Bach, M. J., et al. "A Remote-File Cache for RFS." *USENIX 1987 Summer Conference Proceedings*, June 1987.

Bershad, B. N., J. B. Chen, D. Lee, and T. H. Romer. "Avoiding Cache Misses Dynamically in Large Direct-Mapped Caches." *Proceedings of the Sixth International Conference on Architectural Support for Programming Languages and Operating Systems*, ACM, 1994.

Bershad, B. N., J. B. Chen, D. Lee, and T. H. Romer. "Dynamic Page Mapping Policies for Cache Conflict Resolution on Standard Hardware." *Proceedings of the First Symposium on Operating Systems Design and Implementation*, USENIX Association, November 1994.

Gingell, R., J. Moran, and W. Shannon. "Virtual Memory Architecture in SunOS." *USENIX Conference Proceedings*, USENIX Association, Summer 1997.

Howard, J. H., M. L. Kazar, S. G. Nichols, D. A. Nichols, M. Satyanarayanan, R. N. Sidebotham, and M. J. West. "Scale and Performance in a Distributed File System." *ACM Transactions on Computer Systems*, vol. 6, no. 1, February 1988.

Kazar, M. L., Leverett et al. "Decorum File System Architectural Overview." *USENIX Conference Proceedings*, June 1990.

Kleiman, S. R. "Vnodes: an Architecture for Multiple File System Types in Sun UNIX." *USENIX Conference Proceedings*, Summer 1986.

McKusick, M. K., W. N. Joy, S. J. Leffler, and R. S. Fabry. "A Fast File System For UNIX." *Transactions on Computer Systems*, vol. 2, no. 3, August, 1984.

Morris, J. H., M. Satyanarayanan, M. H. Conner, J. H. Howard, D. Rosenthal, and F. D. Smith. "Andrew: A Distributed Personal Computing Environment." *Communications of the ACM*, March 1986.

Patterson, D. A., G. Gibson, R. H. Katz. "A Case for Redundant Arrays of Inexpensive Disks (RAID)." *Proceedings of ACM SIGMOD Conference,* June 1988.

Rosenthal, David. "Evolving the Vnode Interface." *USENIX Conference Proceedings*, Summer 1990.

Sandberg, R., D. Goldberg, S. Kleiman, D. Walsh, and B. Lyon. "Design and Implementation of the Sun Network File System." *USENIX Conference Proceedings*, Summer 1985.

Satyanarayanan, M., J. J. Kistler, P. Kumar, M. E. Okasaki, E. H. Siegel, and D. C. Steere. "Coda: A Highly Available File System for a Distributed Workstation Environment." *IEEE Transactions on Computers*, vol. 39, no. 4, April, 1990.

Satyanarayanan, M., J. H. Howard, D. A. Nichols, R. N. Sidebotham, and A. Z. Spector. "The ITC Distributed File System: Principles and Design." *Proceedings of the Tenth ACM Symposium on Operating Systems Principles*, 1985.

Seltzer, M., K. Bostic, M. MsKusick, and C. Staelin. "An Implementation of a Log-Structured File System for UNIX." *USENIX Association Conference Proceedings*, January 1993.

Walker, B., G. Popek, R. English, C. Kline, and G. Thiel. "The LOCUS Distributed Operating System." *Proceedings of the 9th ACM Symposium on Operating System Principles*, October 1983.

F

Additional Sources for Help

There are a limited number of online resources and consulting services available for designing and developing Windows NT kernel-mode drivers. Consulting services have begun mushrooming at a relatively rapid rate, however, in the past few months and therefore it is becoming a little easier to get professional assistance these days as compared to a few years ago.[*] Here is a short list of the resources that were available at the time this book went to press.

WARNING   Please note that I do not endorse any of the companies or products mentioned here. Furthermore, I cannot accept responsibility for any of the comments, opinions, or services that you may receive and/or adopt as a result of using the resources listed in this appendix.

Usenet Newsgroup

comp.os.ms-windows.programmer.nt.kernel-mode
    As the name suggests, this newsgroup contains postings on issues related to kernel-mode design and implementation for the Windows NT operating system. It is sometimes monitored by Microsoft support engineers, and a fair number of experienced consultants in Windows NT driver development post responses to the group.

---

[*] Note that this can also be a problem, since many lay claim to understanding the Windows NT operating system, but not all such claims are necessarily true.

Mailing Lists

ntfsd@atria.com

ntfsd-digest@atria.com

> These are peer-to-peer discussion groups, established in 1994, focused on Windows NT file systems development. To subscribe to either of these lists, send email to *majordomo@atria.com* with a blank `Subject` line, and with a message body consisting either of `subscribe ntfsd` or `subscribe ntfsd-digest`.
>
> To read back issues of the mailing list, see *ftp://ftp.atria.com/archives/ntfsd*.
>
> To unsubscribe, send email to the above majordomo address with a message body consisting either of `unsubscribe ntfsd` or `unsubscribe ntfsd-digest`.

DDK-L Mailing List

> Information about this mailing list can be obtained from *http://www.albany.net/~danorton/ddk/ddk-l/faq.shtml*.

Firms Providing Training and/or Consulting Services

- NT Core Services, Inc., *http://www.ntcoresvcs.com*
- Kernel Mode Systems, *http://www.cmkrnl.com*
- Open Systems Resources, Inc., *http://www.osr.com*
- INTEC, *http://www.intec.es*
- Tetradyne Software, Inc., *http://www.tetradyne.com*
- Cherry Hill Software, *http://www.albany.net/~danorton*

In addition to the sources of information listed in this appendix, there are many online sites that maintain information about Windows NT kernel-mode driver development, including FAQs, DDK documentation errata, and other NT internals information. You should be able to easily locate such sites via a simple search using any of the available search engines.

Index

About the Author

Rajeev Nagar has been working on operating systems (specifically storage management systems) for the past six years. He has designed and implemented kernel software for the Windows NT, AIX, HPUX, and SunOS platforms. His file system development work has included local, disk-based file systems, networked file systems, and distributed file systems. His undergraduate degree is in computer engineering, and he has a master's degree in computer science. Rajeev has implemented an OSF distributed file system client on the Windows NT platform, as well as other filter drivers for storage management products.

Colophon

A vulture is featured on the cover of *Windows NT File System Internals*. Vultures are divided into two famlies—New World vultures, a family that includes the majestic but near-extinct California condor, and Old World vultures. Both families are closely related to eagles and hawks, but, unlike their relatives, vultures are carrion eaters, not hunters. A vulture will rarely kill for food. Instead, they sit by and wait for another animal to die before starting to dine. Vultures often live in open country where herds of large mammals, such as cattle, can be found. They fly in slow circles, searching the ground for dead, sick, or injured animals. They also watch for running packs of jackals or hyenas, who often lead them to food. When food has been spotted, the vulture swoops down to the ground, and other circling vultures follow.

Both Old World and New World vultures have heads and necks that are almost bare, covered only by a thin layer of down. Many vultures have a thick ruff of feathers around their neck. These adaptations allow the vulture to place its head deep inside carcasses without soiling its plumage. The digestive enzymes of the vulture allow it to survive on decaying meat that would be toxic to other animals.

Although the modern view of vultures is often one of disgust and comtempt, some ancient cultures revered them as embodiments of immortality.

Edie Freedman designed the cover of this book, using a 19th-century engraving from the Dover Pictorial Archive. The cover layout was produced with Quark XPress 3.3 using the ITC Garamond font. Whenever possible, our books use Rep-Kover™, a durable and flexible lay-flat binding. If the page count exceeds Rep-Kover's limit, perfect binding is used.

The inside layout was designed by Nancy Priest and implemented in FrameMaker 5.0 by Mike Sierra. The text and heading fonts are ITC Garamond Light and Garamond Book. The illustrations that appear in the book were created in Macromedia Freehand 7.0 by Robert Romano. This colophon was written by Clairemarie Fisher O'Leary.

More Titles from O'Reilly

Windows

Developing Windows Error Messages

By Ben Ezzell
1st Edition January 1998 (est.)
300 pages (est.), Includes diskette
ISBN 1-56592-356-1

Although the computer industry has made enormous advances in the last 25 years, the development of error messages has somehow been left behind. Error messages have only progressed from reporting errors as numerical codes to popping up rather simple text messages. And the vast majority of these messages are aimed more at the programmer, rather than the user.

Windows Error Messages focuses on the three important elements of an effective error message: notification, explanation, and solution. This book teaches C, C++, and Visual Basic programmers how to write effective error messages that notify the user of an error, clearly explain the error, and most important, offer a solution to the error. Throughout the book the author uses examples that illustrate incomplete error messages and then describes how to make them more effective. The book also discusses methods for preventing and trapping errors before they occur and tells how to create flexible input and response routines to keep unnecessary errors from happening.

The enclosed disk contains a public domain dynamic link library—ErrorMessage.DLL. This DLL contains mechanisms and dialogs that present all error messages in a standard format as well as responses for different levels of errors.

Inside the Windows 95 File System

By Stan Mitchell
1st Edition May 1997
378 pages, Includes diskette
ISBN 1-56592-200-X

In this book, Stan Mitchell describes the Windows 95 File System, as well as the new opportunities and challenges it brings for developers. Its "hands-on" approach will help developers become better equipped to make design decisions using the new Win95 File System features. Includes a diskette containing MULTIMON, a general-purpose monitor for examining Windows internals.

Win32 Multithreaded Programming

By Aaron Cohen & Mike Woodring
1st Edition December 1997 (est.)
720 pages (est.), Includes CD-ROM
ISBN 1-56592-296-4

This book clearly explains the concepts of multithreaded programs and shows developers how to skillfully construct efficient and complex applications. While basic objects, like mutexes and semaphores, used in multithreaded programming are sufficiently documented, it's often unclear when to use one object instead of another. It's also unclear how to handle a possible corruption of data. This book systematically illustrates all aspects of Win32 multithreaded programming, including what has previously been undocumented or poorly explained.

Contents include:

- How the Windows operating systems handle threads
- Multithreading primitives in the Win32 API
- Techniques for generating thread-safe dynamic link libraries
- Advanced techniques for thread synchronization
- Basic scenarios for building multithreaded user interfaces
- Debugging multithreaded applications

The CD-ROM features Mcl, the authors' C++ class library for multithreaded programming, which both wraps multithreaded API functions and easily supports more complex multithreaded scenarios. For programmers using MFC, and additional library, Mcl4Mfc, is included for MFC compatibility.

Dictionary of PC Hardware and Data Communications Terms

By Mitchell Shnier
1st Edition April 1996
532 pages, ISBN 1-56592-158-5

This comprehensive dictionary provides complete descriptions of complex terms in two of the most volatile and interesting areas of computer development: personal computers and networks. It contains up-to-date information about everything from a common item like "batteries" to an obscure font technology called "Speedo." Also available online. See *http://www.ora.com/reference/dictionary/* for details.

O'REILLY™

TO ORDER: **800-998-9938** • *order@oreilly.com* • *http://www.oreilly.com/*
OUR PRODUCTS ARE AVAILABLE AT A BOOKSTORE OR SOFTWARE STORE NEAR YOU.
FOR INFORMATION: **800-998-9938** • **707-829-0515** • *info@oreilly.com*

Access Database Design & Programming

By Steven Roman
1st Edition June 1997
270 pages, ISBN 1-56592-297-2

This book serves as a "second course" in Access, providing experienced Access users who are novice programmers with frequently overlooked concepts and techniques necessary to create effective database applications. Unlike other Access books, it takes the reader behind the details and focuses on core concepts in three major areas:

- Database design. The easy-to-use Access interface, as well as most books and published documentation, have promoted the "create before you design" school of database creation. This book examines the principles of sound relational database design and provides an informative overview that carefully shows how to normalize tables to eliminate data redundancy without losing data.
- Queries. The Access interface can be used for some kinds of queries, but not for others. This book examines multi-table queries (i.e., various types of joins) and shows how to implement them indirectly by using the Access interface or directly by using Access SQL.
- Programming. This section features an introduction to the Data Access Object (DAO) and Microsoft Access object models, which allow a developer to place a database under program control. It serves as a handy introduction and primer for basic database operations, like modifying a table under program control, dynamically adding and deleting records, or repositioning a record pointer.

Windows NT File System Internals

By Rajeev Nagar
1st Edition September 1997
794 pages, Includes diskette
ISBN 1-56592-249-2

Windows NT File System Internals presents the details of the NT I/O Manager, the Cache Manager, and the Memory Manager from the perspective of a software developer writing a file system driver or implementing a kernel-mode filter driver. The book provides numerous code examples included on diskette, as well as the source for a complete, usable filter driver.

Topics covered in the book include:

- An introduction to NT system components
- The NT I/O Manager
- The NT Virtual Memory Manager
- The NT Cache Manager
- Structured driver development under Windows NT
- Writing a file system driver
- Writing a filter driver

Inside the Windows 95 Registry

By Ron Petrusha
1st Edition August 1996
594 pages, Includes diskette
ISBN 1-56592-170-4

What Windows 95 developers have been looking for! An in-depth examination of the Windows 95 registry, the new central "storage facility" for settings that replaces most of the old SYSTEM.INI and WIN.INI settings found in Windows 3.x.

This book covers remote registry access, differences between the Win95 and NT registries, and registry backup. You'll also find a thorough examination of the role that the registry plays in OLE, coverage of undocumented registry services, and more. Petrusha shows programmers how to access the Win95 registry from Win32, Win16, and DOS programs in C and Visual Basic. VxD sample code is also included.

The book includes a diskette with registry tools such as REGSPY, a program that shows exactly how Windows applications, libraries, and drivers use settings in the registry.

O'REILLY™

TO ORDER: **800-998-9938** • *order@oreilly.com* • *http://www.oreilly.com/*
OUR PRODUCTS ARE AVAILABLE AT A BOOKSTORE OR SOFTWARE STORE NEAR YOU.
FOR INFORMATION: **800-998-9938** • **707-829-0515** • *info@oreilly.com*

Perl

Perl Resource Kit—UNIX Edition

By Larry Wall, Nate Patwardhan, Ellen Siever,
David Futato & Brian Jepson
1st Edition November 1997
1812 pages, ISBN 1-56592-370-7

The *Perl Resource Kit—UNIX Edition*
gives you the most comprehensive collection of Perl documentation and commercially enhanced software tools available
today. Developed in association with Larry
Wall, the creator of Perl, it's the definitive Perl distribution for
webmasters, programmers, and system administrators.

The *Perl Resource Kit* provides:

*   Over 1800 pages of tutorial and in-depth reference
    documentation for Perl utilities and extensions, in 4 volumes.

*   A CD-ROM containing the complete Perl distribution, plus
    hundreds of freeware Perl extensions and utilities—a
    complete snapshot of the Comprehensive Perl Archive
    Network (CPAN)—as well as new software written by Larry
    Wall just for the Kit.

Essential Perl Software Tools All on One Convenient CD-ROM

Experienced Perl hackers know when to create their own, and
when they can find what they need on CPAN. Now all the power
of CPAN—and more—is at your fingertips. The *Perl Resource
Kit* includes:

*   A complete snapshot of CPAN, with an install program for
    Solaris and Linux that ensures that all necessary modules are
    installed together. Also includes an easy-to-use search tool
    and a web-aware interface that allows you to get the latest
    version of each module.

*   A new Java/Perl interface that allows programmers to write
    Java classes with Perl implementations. This new tool was
    written specially for the Kit by Larry Wall.

Experience the power of Perl modules in areas such as CGI, web
spidering, database interfaces, managing mail and USENET news,
user interfaces, security, graphics, math and statistics, and much
more.

Programming Perl, 2nd Edition

By Larry Wall, Tom Christiansen &
Randal L. Schwartz
2nd Edition September 1996
670 pages, ISBN 1-56592-149-6

Programming Perl, second edition, is the
authoritative guide to Perl version 5, the
scripting utility that has established itself
as the programming tool of choice for the
World Wide Web, UNIX system administra-
tion, and a vast range of other applications. Version 5 of Perl
includes object-oriented programming facilities. The book is
coauthored by Larry Wall, the creator of Perl.

Perl is a language for easily manipulating text, files, and processes. It provides a more concise and readable way to do many jobs
that were formerly accomplished (with difficulty) by programming with C or one of the shells. Perl is likely to be available
wherever you choose to work.And if it isn't, you can get it and
install it easily and free of charge.

This heavily revised second edition of *Programming Perl* contains a full explanation of the features in Perl version 5.003.
Contents include:

*   An introduction to Perl

*   Explanations of the language and its syntax

*   Perl functions

*   Perl library modules

*   The use of references in Perl

*   How to use Perl's object-oriented features

*   Invocation options for Perl itself, and also for the utilities that
    come with Perl

Perl 5 Desktop Reference

By Johan Vromans
1st Edition February 1996
46 pages, ISBN 1-56592-187-9

This is the standard quick-reference guide for
the Perl programming language. It provides a
complete overview of the language, from variables to input and output, from flow control to
regular expressions, from functions to document formats—all packed into a convenient,
carry-around booklet. Updated to cover Perl version 5.003.

Learning Perl, 2nd Edition

*By Randal L. Schwartz & Tom Christiansen,
Foreword by Larry Wall
2nd Edition July 1997
302 pages, ISBN 1-56592-284-0*

In this update of a bestseller, two leading
Perl trainers teach you to use the most
universal scripting language in the age of
the World Wide Web. With a foreword by
Larry Wall, the creator of Perl, this
smooth, carefully paced book is the "official" guide for both formal (classroom) and informal learning. It is now current for
Perl version 5.004.

Learning Perl is a hands-on tutorial designed to get you writing
useful Perl scripts as quickly as possible. Exercises (with complete solutions) accompany each chapter. A lengthy, new chapter
in this edition introduces you to CGI programming, while touching also on the use of library modules, references, and Perl's
object-oriented constructs.

Perl is a language for easily manipulating text, files, and processes. It comes standard on most UNIX platforms and is available
free of charge on all other important operating systems. Perl
technical support is informally available—often within minutes—from a pool of experts who monitor a USENET newsgroup
(*comp.lang.perl.misc*) with tens

of thousands of readers.

Contents include:

- A quick tutorial stroll through Perl basics
- Systematic, topic-by-topic coverage of Perl's broad capabilities
- Lots of brief code examples
- Programming exercises for each topic, with fully worked-out
answers
- How to execute system commands from your Perl program
- How to manage DBM databases using Perl
- An introduction to CGI programming for the Web

Advanced Perl Programming

*By Sriram Srinivasan
1st Edition August 1997
434 pages, ISBN 1-56592-220-4*

This book covers complex techniques for
managing production-ready Perl programs
and explains methods for manipulating
data and objects that may have looked like
magic before. It gives you necessary background for dealing with networks, databases, and GUIs, and includes a discussion of internals to help
you program more efficiently and embed Perl within C or C within Perl.

Learning Perl on Win32 Systems

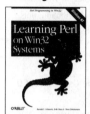

*By Randal L. Schwartz, Erik Olson &
Tom Christiansen
1st Edition August 1997
306 pages, ISBN 1-56592-324-3*

In this carefully paced course, leading
Perl trainers and a Windows NT practitioner teach you to program in the language that promises to emerge as the
scripting language of choice on NT. Based
on the "llama" book, this book features tips for PC users and
new, NT-specific examples, along with a foreword by Larry Wall,
the creator of Perl, and Dick Hardt, the creator of Perl for
Win32.

Mastering Regular Expressions

*By Jeffrey E. F. Friedl
1st Edition January 1997
368 pages, ISBN 1-56592-257-3*

Regular expressions, a powerful tool for
manipulating text and data, are found in
scripting languages, editors, programming
environments, and specialized tools. In
this book, author Jeffrey Friedl leads you
through the steps of crafting a regular
expression that gets the job done. He examines a variety of tools
and uses them in an extensive array of examples, with a major
focus on Perl.

O'REILLY™

TO ORDER: **800-998-9938** • *order@oreilly.com* • *http://www.oreilly.com/*
OUR PRODUCTS ARE AVAILABLE AT A BOOKSTORE OR SOFTWARE STORE NEAR YOU.
FOR INFORMATION: **800-998-9938** • **707-829-0515** • *info@oreilly.com*

How to stay in touch with O'Reilly

1. Visit Our Award-Winning Web Site

http://www.oreilly.com/

★ "Top 100 Sites on the Web" —*PC Magazine*
★ "Top 5% Web sites" —*Point Communications*
★ "3-Star site" —*The McKinley Group*

Our web site contains a library of comprehensiveproduct information (including book excerpts and tables of contents), downloadable software, background articles, interviews with technology leaders, links to relevant sites, book cover art, and more. File us in your Bookmarks or Hotlist!

2. Join Our Email Mailing Lists

New Product Releases

To receive automatic email with brief descriptions of all new O'Reilly products as they are released, send email to:
listmanager@list.ora.com
Put the following information in the first line of your message (*not* in the Subject field):
subscribe oreilly-news

O'Reilly Events

If you'd also like us to send information about trade show events, special promotions, and other O'Reilly events, send email to:
listmanager@list.ora.com
Put the following information in the first line of your message (*not* in the Subject field):
subscribe oreilly-events

3. Get Examples from Our Books via FTP

There are two ways to access an archive of example files from our books:

Regular FTP

- ftp to:
  ftp.oreilly.com
  (login: anonymous
  password: your email address)
- Point your web browser to:
  ftp://ftp.oreilly.com/

FTPMAIL

- Send an email message to:
  ftpmail@online.oreilly.com
  (Write "help" in the message body)

4. Contact Us via Email

order@oreilly.com
To place a book or software order online. Good for North American and international customers.

subscriptions@oreilly.com
To place an order for any of our newsletters or periodicals.

books@oreilly.com
General questions about any of our books.

software@oreilly.com
For general questions and product information about our software. Check out O'Reilly Software Online at **http://software.oreilly.com/** for software and technical support information. Registered O'Reilly software users send your questions to: **website-support@oreilly.com**

cs@oreilly.com
For answers to problems regarding your order or our products.

booktech@oreilly.com
For book content technical questions or corrections.

proposals@oreilly.com
To submit new book or software proposals to our editors and product managers.

international@oreilly.com
For information about our international distributors or translation queries. For a list of our distributors outside of North America check out:
http://www.oreilly.com/www/order/country.html

O'Reilly & Associates, Inc.
101 Morris Street, Sebastopol, CA 95472 USA
TEL   707-829-0515 or 800-998-9938
           (6am to 5pm PST)
FAX   707-829-0104

Titles from O'Reilly

Please note that upcoming titles are displayed in italic.

WEBPROGRAMMING

Apache: The Definitive Guide
Building Your Own Web Conferences
Building Your Own Website
CGI Programming for the World Wide Web
Designing for the Web
HTML: The Definitive Guide, 2nd Ed.
JavaScript: The Definitive Guide, 2nd Ed.
Learning Perl
Programming Perl, 2nd Ed.
Mastering Regular Expressions
WebMaster in a Nutshell
Web Security & Commerce
Web Client Programming with Perl
World Wide Web Journal

USING THE INTERNET

Smileys
The Future Does Not Compute
The Whole Internet User's Guide & Catalog
The Whole Internet for Win 95
Using Email Effectively
Bandits on the Information Superhighway

JAVA SERIES

Exploring Java
Java AWT Reference
Java Fundamental Classes Reference
Java in a Nutshell
Java Language Reference, 2nd Edition
Java Network Programming
Java Threads
Java Virtual Machine

SOFTWARE

WebSite™ 1.1
WebSite Professional™
Building Your Own Web Conferences
WebBoard™
PolyForm™
Statisphere™

SONGLINE GUIDES

NetActivism   NetResearch
Net Law   NetSuccess
NetLearning   NetTravel
Net Lessons

SYSTEM ADMINISTRATION

Building Internet Firewalls
Computer Crime: A Crimefighter's Handbook
Computer Security Basics
DNS and BIND, 2nd Ed.
Essential System Administration, 2nd Ed.
Getting Connected: The Internet at 56K and Up
Linux Network Administrator's Guide
Managing Internet Information Services
Managing NFS and NIS
Networking Personal Computers with TCP/IP
Practical UNIX & Internet Security, 2nd Ed.
PGP: Pretty Good Privacy
sendmail, 2nd Ed.
sendmail Desktop Reference
System Performance Tuning
TCP/IP Network Administration
termcap & terminfo
Using & Managing UUCP
Volume 8: X Window System Administrator's Guide
Web Security & Commerce

UNIX

Exploring Expect
Learning VBScript
Learning GNU Emacs, 2nd Ed.
Learning the bash Shell
Learning the Korn Shell
Learning the UNIX Operating System
Learning the vi Editor
Linux in a Nutshell
Making TeX Work
Linux Multimedia Guide
Running Linux, 2nd Ed.
SCO UNIX in a Nutshell
sed & awk, 2nd Edition
Tcl/Tk Tools
UNIX in a Nutshell: System V Edition
UNIX Power Tools
Using csh & tsch
When You Can't Find Your UNIX System Administrator
Writing GNU Emacs Extensions

WEB REVIEW STUDIO SERIES

Gif Animation Studio
Shockwave Studio

WINDOWS

Dictionary of PC Hardware and Data Communications Terms
Inside the Windows 95 Registry
Inside the Windows 95 File System
Windows Annoyances
Windows NT File System Internals
Windows NT in a Nutshell

PROGRAMMING

Advanced Oracle PL/SQL Programming
Applying RCS and SCCS
C++: The Core Language
Checking C Programs with lint
DCE Security Programming
Distributing Applications Across DCE & Windows NT
Encyclopedia of Graphics File Formats, 2nd Ed.
Guide to Writing DCE Applications
lex & yacc
Managing Projects with make
Mastering Oracle Power Objects
Oracle Design: The Definitive Guide
Oracle Performance Tuning, 2nd Ed.
Oracle PL/SQL Programming
Porting UNIX Software
POSIX Programmer's Guide
POSIX.4: Programming for the Real World
Power Programming with RPC
Practical C Programming
Practical C++ Programming
Programming Python
Programming with curses
Programming with GNU Software
Pthreads Programming
Software Portability with imake, 2nd Ed.
Understanding DCE
Understanding Japanese Information Processing
UNIX Systems Programming for SVR4

BERKELEY 4.4 SOFTWARE DISTRIBUTION

4.4BSD System Manager's Manual
4.4BSD User's Reference Manual
4.4BSD User's Supplementary Documents
4.4BSD Programmer's Reference Manual
4.4BSD Programmer's Supplementary Documents
X Programming
Vol. 0: X Protocol Reference Manual
Vol. 1: Xlib Programming Manual
Vol. 2: Xlib Reference Manual
Vol. 3M: X Window System User's Guide, Motif Edition
Vol. 4M: X Toolkit Intrinsics Programming Manual, Motif Edition
Vol. 5: X Toolkit Intrinsics Reference Manual
Vol. 6A: Motif Programming Manual
Vol. 6B: Motif Reference Manual
Vol. 6C: Motif Tools
Vol. 8 : X Window System Administrator's Guide
Programmer's Supplement for Release 6
X User Tools
The X Window System in a Nutshell

CAREER & BUSINESS

Building a Successful Software Business
The Computer User's Survival Guide
Love Your Job!
Electronic Publishing on CD-ROM

TRAVEL

Travelers' Tales: Brazil
Travelers' Tales: Food
Travelers' Tales: France
Travelers' Tales: Gutsy Women
Travelers' Tales: India
Travelers' Tales: Mexico
Travelers' Tales: Paris
Travelers' Tales: San Francisco
Travelers' Tales: Spain
Travelers' Tales: Thailand
Travelers' Tales: A Woman's World

O'REILLY™

TO ORDER: **800-998-9938** • **order@oreilly.com** • **http://www.oreilly.com/**

OUR PRODUCTS ARE AVAILABLE AT A BOOKSTORE OR SOFTWARE STORE NEAR YOU.

FOR INFORMATION: **800-998-9938** • **707-829-0515** • **info@oreilly.com**

O'Reilly & Associates, Inc.
101 Morris Street
Sebastopol, CA 95472-9902
1-800-998-9938

Visit us online at:
http://www.ora.com/
orders@ora.com

O'REILLY WOULD LIKE TO HEAR FROM YOU

Which book did this card come from?

_____

Where did you buy this book?
- ❏ Bookstore
- ❏ Direct from O'Reilly
- ❏ Bundled with hardware/software
- ❏ Other _____

- ❏ Computer Store
- ❏ Class/seminar

What operating system do you use?
- ❏ UNIX
- ❏ Windows NT
- ❏ Other _____

- ❏ Macintosh
- ❏ PC(Windows/DOS)

What is your job description?
- ❏ System Administrator
- ❏ Network Administrator
- ❏ Web Developer
- ❏ Other _____

- ❏ Programmer
- ❏ Educator/Teacher

❏ Please send me O'Reilly's catalog, containing a complete listing of O'Reilly books and software.

Name _____ Company/Organization _____

Address _____

City _____ State _____ Zip/Postal Code _____ Country _____

Telephone _____ Internet or other email address (specify network) _____

Nineteenth century wood engraving
of a bear from the O'Reilly &
Associates Nutshell Handbook®
Using & Managing UUCP.

POST CARD

PLACE
STAMP
HERE

NO POSTAGE
NECESSARY IF
MAILED IN THE
UNITED STATES

BUSINESS REPLY MAIL
FIRST CLASS MAIL   PERMIT NO. 80   SEBASTOPOL, CA

Postage will be paid by addressee

O'Reilly & Associates, Inc.
101 Morris Street
Sebastopol, CA 95472-9902